Photograph by Alistair Whyte

Voltaire and his world

Studies presented to W. H. Barber

edited by

R. J. Howells, A. Mason,

H. T. Mason and D. Williams

VOLTAIRE FOUNDATION
TAYLOR INSTITUTION
OXFORD

1985

© 1985 UNIVERSITY OF OXFORD

ISBN 0 7294 0332 7

PRINTED IN ENGLAND
AT THE ALDEN PRESS, OXFORD

Contents

W. H. Barber: an appreciation

A FESTSCHRIFT is generally a tribute not only to distinction in scholarship and academic life, but to the more elusive human qualities that make a valued colleague, mentor and friend. William Barber is richly deserving of this volume on all these counts.

As a scholar he is known pre-eminently for his great contribution to Voltaire studies. But his net has been cast much more widely. Apart from literature and history of ideas, notably in the two centuries of French classicism, he is well versed in the history of science. His expertise on Pierre Bayle is no more than hinted at in his published work. For volume vi of the New Cambridge Modern History he undertook the section on 'Cultural change in Western Europe, 1688-1725', covering several countries and a vast range of subjects. To his present editorship of Voltaire's complete works he brings considerable editorial experience with the MHRA. His committee and public service activity has been broad, including the presidency of the Society for French Studies, and membership of the Whitford committee on copyright law.

Born in 1918, he attended the Merchant Taylors' School in London. He went up to Oxford in 1937, taking a degree in French and German in 1940. He then began War service, which was to continue until 1946 when he taught at the College of the Rhine Army in Germany. Returning to Oxford to undertake research, after two years he was appointed to the University College of North Wales at Bangor. His *Leibniz in France*, drawn from his D.Phil. thesis, was published by OUP in 1955, and in the same year he was appointed to a Readership in French at Birkbeck College in the University of London. The qualities of his study of *Candide*, appearing in the Arnold series in 1960, were such that it has since been reprinted several times. They also marked clearly his affinity with Voltaire. It was he, with the late Professor Owen Taylor, who persuaded Theodore Besterman in 1967 to launch the enormous undertaking of a critical edition of Voltaire's complete works. He was Joint Secretary to the enterprise from the beginning, and in 1977 he succeeded Besterman as General Editor. Professor of French by conferred title since 1968, he became sole Head of Department at Birkbeck College in 1978. Two signal honours from France were to follow. In the next year he was elected Membre d'Honneur of the Société d'Histoire Littéraire de la France. Shortly after his retirement in 1983 he was named to the Légion d'Honneur. Retirement however is hardly the right term for the direction of a programme of 150 Voltaire volumes – some sixty have now appeared – edited by 120 scholars from 12 countries.

If one had to choose a single word to characterise William, that word might be 'humane'. Humane firstly in the sense of *litterae humaniores*. He is a man of wide knowledge, familiar with classical culture and at home in several European cultures and languages. He is also thoroughly competent in the technical skills of the scholar such as bibliographical description or identification of different states of a text. He has the rigour of a scholar in demanding exactness, and distinguishing probability from proof. But he also writes well, not a very common accomplishment. He can wear learning lightly, as in his article on Voltaire's astronauts (*FS*, 1976). His nice sense of the occasion is evident in his contribution to the Festschrift for Will Moore, his own former tutor at Oxford, which he opens and closes with a theatrical conceit around 'la maison de Molière'. Yet he does not go in for flourishes. A witty title will also be informative ('Penny plain, twopence coloured' on the doctoring of an early memoir on Voltaire); a conclusion will usually be a careful summary. He is ready to draw on modern parallels, but alert for anachronism. He is always conscious of those for whom he is writing.

His wife Madeline has had her own career as secondary school teacher, headmistress, and as a scholar. Each has aided the other in this way, but also through constant support and affection. This brings me to the second sense of the term I chose. Both are consistently civilised in their dealings with others. Even under pressure William remains calm. His is courteous even under provocation. Two generations of young scholars have had cause to be grateful for his support and patience as well as his knowledge. This applies to the many research students whose work he has brought to successful presentation (and often beyond it, to publication), but also to other researchers and colleagues who have come to him for advice. As Head of Department he maintained by his owm example a high standard of behaviour, mutual respect and responsibility. The trust and affection of his colleagues throughout Birkbeck was manifested by his election as Vice-Master of the College in 1979. Relieved of some of these burdens upon retirement, he has actively taken on others, as well as devoting himself to Voltaire. He continues to demonstrate the combination of modesty, remarkable efficiency, wide activity and humanity.

R.J.H.

The untimely death of Professor Owen Taylor, longtime close collaborator and friend of William Barber, has deprived this volume of a contributor. The Editors wish to express their deep regret at his passing.

Guides, philosophers and friends: the background of Voltaire's *Discours en vers sur l'homme*

DENNIS FLETCHER

WRITTEN in emulation, if not imitation, of Alexander Pope's *Essay on Man* (1733-1734), Voltaire's *Discours sur l'homme* provide an intriguing subject for the study of some of the ways in which ideas were transmitted in the climate of literary cosmopolitanism which characterised the Enlightenment. One way in particular, that of personal contact and oral communication, will perforce receive more attention here than it is normally accorded in the world of scholarship, since it is considered to be the key factor in the filiation of ideas under discussion. One figure likewise will be at the centre of this discussion: Henry St John, Viscount Bolingbroke, the frustrated statesman who, forced to abandon affairs of state, took up philosophical pursuits and with all the proselytising ardour of the convert did all he could at different times to direct the steps of both Voltaire and Pope along the same philosophical path which he had himself chosen. Ira O. Wade presents the period from 1734 to 1739 in Voltaire's intellectual development as the final stage in that gradual transformation of poet into philosopher which had been initiated by Bolingbroke in the early 1720s.[1] The *Discours sur l'homme*, in which Voltaire is out to show his mettle as a *poète-philosophe*, were composed almost entirely between 1737 and 1738. It is possible then that some of the ideas in this work are coloured to a certain extent by his early contacts with Bolingbroke. Others which show an affinity with the *milord's* may well owe their presence in the *Discours* to Voltaire's reading of the *Essay on Man* and to the intellectual sustenance which was supplied to the author of that poem by his noble 'guide, philosopher, and friend'.[2] The very idea of Bolingbroke feeding ideas to Pope may well appear laughable if judged by the respective ratings of these two writers in the charts of fame established by posterity. Pope, however, would have found equally

1. *The Intellectual development of Voltaire* (Princeton, New Jersey 1969), pp.128-35, 240-41.
2. *Essay on Man* [*EM*], IV.390. For illuminating coverage of this aspect of the subject, see Brean S. Hammond, *Pope and Bolingbroke: a study of friendship and influence* (Columbia 1984).

5

laughable the suggestion that Bolingbroke might become regarded as a mere fly in the amber of his verse. There is no reason to suppose that he did not genuinely believe that it would be his friend's name which would speed along 'the stream of Time' leaving his own to follow in its wake. That being so, it would seem sensible to take the master-pupil relationship which Pope explicitly states in the final section of his *Essay* to have existed between himself and Bolingbroke as a legitimate context within which to consider the question of sources and influences.

Bolingbroke's contribution to Pope's poem is impossible to assess exactly on the basis of the available evidence. One of the most important (and elusive) ways in which Pope was influenced was through discussions between Bolingbroke and himself. In these long conversations which took place during their walks at Dawley or Twickenham, they doubtless exchanged views, but one has the distinct impression, from the tone and tenor of their correspondence, that Bolingbroke must have dominated these exchanges much of the time. 'Come then, my Friend, my Genius, come along, / Oh master of the poet, and the song!' exclaims Pope, the captivated audience (*EM*.IV.373-74) grateful to acknowledge ('Form'd by thy converse' *EM*.IV.379) the debt he owed to his voluble mentor. Some idea of the sheer volume of talk of philosophical import which made up Bolingbroke's 'converse' can be gained from the repeated references in his philosophical essays to previous conversations with Pope which had covered a great deal of the same ground.[3] In the 'Introduction' to his 'Letters, or Essays, addressed to Alexander Pope, Esq.', it is made clear that his friend, after having successfully tried his hand at philosophical poetry with the first of his Ethic Epistles, has pressed his 'Genius' not only to discourse as he had done often before but also to write upon 'the noblest subjects of philosophical meditation'. The request met with a predictable response: 'I shall throw upon paper

---

3. Cf. 'Introduction' to 'Letters, or Essays, addressed to Alexander Pope, Esq.', v.80 in Bolingbroke, *Works* (London 1809) (all subsequent references to volumes and page numbers are to this edition): 'All I dare promise you is, that my thoughts, in what order soever they flow, shall be communicated to you just as they use to be when we converse together on these, or any other subjects; when we saunter alone; or, as we often have done with good Arbuthnot, and the jocose Dean of St Patrick's, among the multiplied scenes of your little garden [...] These Epistolary Essays, therefore, will be writ with as little regard to form, and with as little reserve, as I used to show in the conversations which have given occasion to them, when I maintained the same opinions, and insisted on the same reasons in defence of them.'

for your satisfaction and for my own, some part at least of what I have thought and said formerly on the last of these subjects, as well as the reflections that they may suggest to me further in writing on them' (v.77). The possibility of material other than the contents of these Epistolary Essays having been thrown upon paper for Pope's use is certainly not too far-fetched. Indeed, the testimony of Lord Bathurst, as retailed by Hugh Blair, who dined with him in 1763, was that: '"The Essay on Man" was originally composed by Lord Bolingbroke in prose, and that Mr Pope did no more than put it into verse: that he had read Lord Bolingbroke's manuscript in his own handwriting; and remembered well, that he was at loss whether most to admire the elegance of Lord Bolingbroke's prose, or the beauty of Mr Pope's verse.'[4] Bathurst told the Rev. Joshua Parry in a letter of 1769 that Bolingbroke had shown him a 'dissertation in prose' which he had written for Pope.[5] Presumably, this was the same manuscript as that referred to by Joseph Warton in 1780: 'Lord Bathurst repeatedly assured me, that he had read the whole scheme of the Essay on Man, in the handwriting of Bolingbroke, and drawn up in a series of propositions, which POPE was to versify and illustrate.'[6] Pope himself in conversation with Joseph Spence made no secret of his indebtedness to Bolingbroke for the help he had received in the composition of the *Essay on Man*, and tends to corroborate Bathurst's evidence:

He [Pope] mentioned then, and at several other times, how much (or rather how wholly) he himself was obliged to him [Bolingbroke] for the thoughts and reasonings in his moral work, and once in particular said that beside their frequent talking over that subject together, he had received (I think) seven or eight sheets from Lord Bolingbroke in relation to it, as I apprehended, by way of letters, both to direct the plan in general and to supply the matter for the particular epistles.[7]

In the advertisement to Bolingbroke's 'Fragments or minutes of essays', we read: 'The foregoing Essays, if they may deserve even that name, and the Fragments, or Minutes, that follow them were thrown upon paper

4. See James Boswell, *Life of Johnson*, ed. G. B. Hall, revised by L. F. Powell (Oxford 1971), iii.402.

5. See George Sherburn, 'Two notes on the *Essay on Man*', *Philological quarterly* 12 (1933), pp.402-403; p.402.

6. Joseph Warton, *An essay on the genius and writings of Pope*, fourth edition (London 1782), ii.62.

7. Joseph Spence, *Observations, anecdotes, and characters of books and men*, ed. James M. Osborne (Oxford 1966), 311 (Osborne's entry number).

in Mr Pope's life-time, and at his desire. They were all communicated to him in scraps, as they were occasionally writ [...] They are nothing more than repetitions of conversations often interrupted, often renewed, and often carried on a little confusedly.'[8] There can be little doubt that Pope was always eager to have in writing what he had previously heard expounded to him by Bolingbroke. If one of the 'scraps' conveyed to him was indeed the material referred to by Bathurst, Spence and others (which might have been incorporated into the *Fragments* or even into the *Essays*), such substantial reassurance would surely have been welcomed as he prepared to venture into the new field of philosophical meditation in verse. Without underestimating Pope's capacity to think for himself or his awareness of contemporary philosophical debates, one should keep in mind that he regarded Bolingbroke, from the moment of his return from exile in 1725, as a philosopher and an oracle. 'Lord B. is above triffling, he is grown a great Divine', he repeats to Swift at this time.[9] Ten years later the author of the *Essay on Man* is amused by the quaint idea that he, a mere tyro in philosophy, could be treated in the same way as he had treated his learned friend: 'I was thought a divine, a philosopher, and what not?' 'Do not laugh at my gravity, but permit me to wear the beard of a philosopher' he writes to Swift, 'till I pull it off, and make a jest of it myself' (*Correspondence*, iii.433).

The exaggerated esteem in which Pope held Bolingbroke's authority as a philosopher would have resulted in a predisposition towards his friend as a source of ideas for his poem, even if all these ideas were available to him from other sources. Maynard Mack in the Introduction to his influential Twickenham edition of the poem[10] minimises Bolingbroke's influence, and emphasises the other sources Pope could have drawn upon: 'his reading; the talk of the town; above all, the traditional patterns of theodicy and ethics on which Bolingbroke, Shaftesbury, King and Leibniz alike drew' (p.xxxi). In the notes to his edition, Mack admits that he has been 'liberal of analogues', presented not as sources but as aids to explication. These analogues he says testify to 'the wide acceptance of the ideas Pope manipulates' (Preface, pp.v-vi). The final five lines which sum up Pope's poem, although they have a strong resemblance,

8. Bolingbroke, *Works*, vii.278.

9. Letter of Pope and Bolingbroke to Swift, 14 December 1725; *Correspondence of Alexander Pope*, ed. G. Sherburn (Oxford 1956), ii.350.

10. All references are to this edition (London 1950).

phrasal and ideational, to various statements in Bolingbroke's works, are treated as commonplaces. They are not, however, felt to deserve being presented as analogues, since they do not come under the heading of 'writings Pope could have known while writing the *Essay on Man*'. The close correspondence between the ideas in Pope's own poem and those of Bolingbroke's *Essays* and *Fragments* deserve more attention however than it receives in Mack's edition, especially if we interpret more positively his dismissive reference to Pope's 'snapping up of trifles from the table of his philosopher and friend' so as to include those vital *written* scraps which are avowedly based on table-talk or its peripatetic equivalent.

Among the many admirers of the *Essay on Man* may be counted Voltaire, who in a 1756 addition[11] to the 22nd *Lettre philosophique* delivered himself of the judgement that it was 'le plus beau Poème didactique, le plus utile, le plus sublime qu'on ait jamais fait dans aucune langue'. Ringing the changes on the Platonic Republic of philosophers from which poets were banished, Voltaire notes: 'Platon parlait en Poète dans sa prose peu intelligible; et Pope parle en Philosophe dans ses admirables vers.' As for the philosophic content of Pope's poem, he remarks that 'le fond s'en trouve tout entier dans les *Caractéristiques* du Lord Shaftesbury; et je ne sais pourquoi M. Pope en fait uniquement honneur à Monsieur de Bolingbroke, sans dire un mot du célèbre Shaftesbury, élève de Locke'. In another addition to the vulgate in 1756 – the preface of the *Poème sur le désastre de Lisbonne*[12] – we are told that Pope, in the *Essay on Man*, 'développa dans ses vers immortels les systèmes de Leibnitz, du lord Shaftesbury, et du lord Bolingbroke' and Voltaire devotes a lengthy footnote to quoting and commenting upon several passages for which the poet was indebted to Shaftesbury's *Characteristics*. In a later note (M.ix.472) referring to the *Essay on Man*, however, he seems to have forgotten Shaftesbury and curiously yokes together Pope and Bolingbroke as if they were joint authors of the poem, rather than just two friends whom he had more often seen together than apart. He tends to exaggerate the intimacy of his friendship with Pope and, to a lesser extent, with Bolingbroke;[13] it is certain he would not have enjoyed the

11. *Lettres philosophiques*, ed. R. Naves (Paris 1964), pp.256-57.
12. Voltaire, *Œuvres complètes*, ed. L. Moland (Paris 1877-1885) [hereafter M.], ix.465-69.
13. Voltaire could be touchy about the closeness of his relations with the Bolingbrokes. Witness his sharp reaction to Du Bourg's remark in the preface to his translation of

confidence of either enough to know of any closer collaboration between them than that which is directly referred to by Pope in the *Essay*. The immediate prehistory of the composition of this work dates from the philosophical novitiate of Pope which began with Bolingbroke's return from exile in 1725 and is recorded thenceforth in the correspondence between the epistolary duo and their friend Swift. During his stay in England, Voltaire never really penetrated the magic circle of Bolingbroke's close friends, and though he had probably corresponded with Pope before his arrival, he saw comparatively little of him. By the time the *Essay on Man* was on the stocks, he was back in France. Relations between Bolingbroke and himself had cooled considerably by that time, but the warm friendship which had existed between them before Voltaire's visit to England had already established the basis of an enduring intellectual influence.

Before we consider the early development of this friendship from its inception in 1722, it is worth recalling that Bolingbroke who was to assume the role of mentor to Voltaire, and later to Pope, had himself undergone a form of philosophical initiation. In 1716, the first year of his exile, taking up the stance of a philosopher in the classical Stoic mould, he had bravely but not altogether successfully attempted to suppress his resentment at being banished. Though some of his *Reflections upon exile* have a hollow ring, the overall impression one receives is nevertheless of a moral and intellectual stock-taking meant as a prelude to working out a personal philosophy based on a realistic view of 'the established course of things', 'this beautiful disposition of things, whereof even our sufferings make a necessary part' (*Works*, i.172). Pope's 'whatever is, is right' (*EM*.1.294) is anticipated in the final pages of this early essay of Bolingbroke's (*Works*, i.172-73):

Let us submit to this order, let us be persuaded that whatever does happen ought to happen, and never be so foolish as to expostulate with nature. The best resolution we can take is to suffer what we cannot alter, and to pursue, without repining, the road which Providence, which directs everything, has marked out to us [...] Resignation to the will of God is true magnanimity. But the sure mark of a pusillanimous and base spirit is to struggle against, to censure the order of Providence, and, instead of mending our own conduct, to set up for correcting that of our Maker.

Bolingbroke's *Letters on the study and use of history* that Voltaire had had occasion to see Lady Bolingbroke: 'Occasion de voir! j'ai passé trois ans avec eux.'

If such passivity characterises his deistic philosophy from the outset, it is counterbalanced by a spirited attack on all those who ignore the principle of religious toleration. In his *Letter to Sir William Windham* dated 1717, he remarks that 'it will be hard to find an example, where one sect of Christians has tolerated another which it was in their power to extirpate [...] Persecution has been reduced into system, and the disciples of the meek and humble Jesus have avowed a tyranny, which the most barbarous conquerors never claimed' (*Works*, i.124-25). This platform of rational deism and secular humanitarianism determined the fundamental orientation of Bolingbroke's thinking: what he needed was a more patently 'philosophical' framework for his opinions. This was provided by Lévesque de Pouilly, and duly acknowledged by Bolingbroke: 'You led me first, in my retreat, to abstract philosophical reasonings' (*Works*, iv.395). *The Substance of some letters to Mr. de Pouilly*, and another essay, which was a pendant to it, *A letter occasioned by one of archbishop Tillotson's sermons*, were written by Bolingbroke about two years after accepting Pouilly's guidance in 1718. In the interim, his 'apprentissage philosophique', as he called it,[14] had extended over a wide range of intellectual activity, most of it reflecting interests shared by Pouilly including Newtonian science and ancient history, as well as theodicy. As far as the latter is concerned, both of Bolingbroke's essays confirm the basic position of the earlier *Reflections upon exile*: 'The theist is modest. He is content to know what God has done, and he acknowledges it, for that very reason, wise and good, right and fit to be done.'[15] Irreverent conceptions of the Deity are castigated, particularly the blasphemous practice of attaching the moral attributes of an imperfect humanity to an all-perfect God.[16] In a letter of 1719, Bolingbroke refers approvingly to Charron's view that an insufficiently elevated conception of divinity inhibits the pure worship of God.[17] The cruel and capricious God of the Old Testament is rejected in the *Letter occasioned by one of archbishop Tillotson's sermons* (*c.*1720) as a reflection of the unworthy notions of the Supreme Being entertained by a legislator having to deal with a despicable people characterised by 'ignorance, superstition, pride, injustice and

14. Letter to Mme de Ferriol of 26 June 1719 (Bodleian Library, Ms. French D.18).

15. *A letter occasioned by one of archbishop Tillotson's sermons, Works*, v.17.

16. Cf. *Works*, iv.400, v.56, 58, 59.

17. *Lettres historiques, politiques, philosophiques de Bolingbroke*, ed. P. H. Grimoard (Paris 1808): iii.32; Bolingbroke to Alary, 7 July 1719.

barbarity' and Bolingbroke concludes: 'if we believe in Moses and his God, we cannot believe in that God whom our reason shows us' (*Works*, v.67). In much the same vein, Voltaire in his *Epître à Uranie* of 1722 presents the God of the Garden of Eden and the Flood in the same light as Bolingbroke had done but extends his purview to include the New Testament and Jansenist theology. After painting his picture of the unloving and unloveable God of the Christians, he concludes:

> Je ne reconnais point à cette indigne image
> Le Dieu que je dois adorer:
> Je croirais le déshonorer,
> Par une telle insulte et par un tel hommage.

When, towards the end of 1722, Bolingbroke and Voltaire met for the first time, they evidently saw eye to eye on the question of religious belief. For Voltaire the meeting in the château of La Source, where Bolingbroke and his wife had taken up residence in 1720, was a revelation; Bolingbroke's physical presence and particularly his voice made an impression which remained stamped upon his mind until his dying day. The talk on this occasion was, it appears from Voltaire's report, mainly of literary matters, including, of course, his epic poem *La Ligue* from which he gave readings. Bolingbroke's reaction was genuinely favourable, witness his letter to Mme de Ferriol of 4 December 1722: 'Mons de Voltaire a passé quelques jours ici. J'ay été charmé et de luy et de son ouvrage. Je me suis attendu à trouver beaucoup d'imagination dans l'un et dans l'autre, mais je ne me suis pas attendu à trouver l'auteur si sage, ni le poème si bien conduit.'[18] The friendliness on both sides, thus guaranteed, quickly burgeoned into firm friendship. In 1723 Bolingbroke's solicitude ('le tendre intérêt que tu prends à ma vie') when Voltaire was laid low with small-pox elicited a grateful response from his friend, whose warmth of feeling can still be felt through the fulsome verse:

> Et toi, cher Bolingbroke, héros qui d'Apollon
> As reçu plus d'une couronne,
> Qui réunis en ta personne
> L'éloquence de Cicéron,
> L'intrépidité de Caton,

18. Bodleian Library, Ms. French D.18.

L'esprit de Mécénas, l'agrément de Pétrone,
Et la science de Varron.[19]

This friendship provided a basis for closer intellectual converse between the poet with aspirations towards the realms of philosophy and the self-acknowledged philosopher who, by this time, considered that he had completed his basic training in the discipline and was not averse to having an acolyte appreciative of his oracular utterances.

In a letter to Pope 18 February 1724, Bolingbroke writes:

I am at a little house on the banks of the Seine where I intend to see no body these seven or Eight days, except the company I have carry'd with me, which are my Judgment, and my Imagination. My Judgment resides in the head of an excellent young Man [Lévesque de Pouilly, 30 years old] whom I hope some time or other to bring you acquainted with, & my Imagination in that of Voltaire, who says that he will introduce himself to you, and that the Muses shall answer for him.[20]

In the intensive discussions which took place at this rural retreat, as well as in the more salon-like atmosphere of La Source, Voltaire had as much to learn from the younger of his two companions as from the elder. His correspondence reveals his great respect for Pouilly's character, intellect and knowledge. When Bolingbroke took Pouilly with him on his return to England in 1725 and was his host for some eighteen months, did these triangular discussions continue? Did Pope take the place of Voltaire in them? No evidence is available which would permit an answer to these questions. In his reply to the letter quoted above, Pope praises Voltaire's *La Ligue*, a copy of which had been sent to him by Bolingbroke, and remarks on its author:

I esteem him for that honest-principled Spirit of true Religion which shines thro' the whole; and from whence (unknown as I am to Mr de Voltaire) I conclude him at once a Free thinker and a Lover of Quiet; no Bigot, but yet no heretick: one who honours Authority and National Sanctions without prejudice to Truth or Charity; One who has Study'd Controversy less than Reason, and the Fathers less than Mankind; in a word, one worthy from his rational temper of that share of Friendship and Intimacy with which you honour him.[21]

The idea of Bolingbroke, Voltaire and Pope as kindred spirits, fellow rationalists with common ideals is, on the whole, acceptable enough. The degree to which either the Bolingbroke-Voltaire relationship or the

19. *Epître à monsieur de Gervasi* (M.x.258).
20. Pope, *Correspondence*, ii.221-22.
21. *Correspondence*, letter of 9 April 1724; ii.229.

Bolingbroke-Pope one can be characterised as a master-pupil relationship is more difficult to judge. In this connection, Bolingbroke's opinion of his putative tutees is worth quoting. Pouilly's brother, Lévesque de Burigny, a staunch supporter of Natural Religion, and a friend of both Bolingbroke and Voltaire, has this to say:

J'avais vu aussi plusieurs fois M. de Voltaire chez Milord Bolingbroke, qui l'aimait; je me souviens qu'un jour on parlait chez ce Seigneur de Pope & de Voltaire; il les connaissait tous deux également; on lui demanda auquel des deux il donnait la préférence; il nous répondit que c'étaient les deux plus beaux génies de France & d'Angleterre; mais qu'il y avait bien plus de philosophie dans la tête du Poëte Anglais que chez Voltaire.[22]

In a letter he wrote to Voltaire in 1724, Bolingbroke can be seen assuming the role of an avuncular director of studies, anxious to guide the steps of his young friend, whose imagination he respected but whose intellectual baggage he regarded as somewhat light, towards the solid ground of Lockean epistemology and Newtonian physics. The great progress which his protégé was to make thereafter is attested by his *Lettres philosophiques*, the popularising works on Newtonianism, the *Traité de métaphysique* and the *Discours en vers sur l'homme*.

Voltaire's enhanced stature did nothing to displace Pope in Bolingbroke's estimate of their respective talents in the philosophical field, however; writing to his former mentor just before the latter's death in 1750, Bolingbroke rather ponderously rejects false modesty and opines: 'Enfin, mon cher Pouilly, dans cette foule d'hommes que j'ai pu connaître et dont j'ai cherché à étudier l'esprit et le caractère, je n'en ai encore vu que trois qui m'aient paru dignes qu'on leur confiât le soin de gouverner des nations [...]. Je vous dirai [donc] hardiment que ces trois hommes sont vous, Pope et moi.'[23] Bolingbroke's high regard for Pope's intellectual acumen and his competence as a philosopher may be based on his friend's contribution to discussions or merely on his capacity for understanding and assimilation. His less favourable opinion of Voltaire may well be due to the fact that he lost touch with him after his visit to England yet continued to keep fresh in his mind the memory of the young beginner avid for instruction. The effect of the instruction Bolingbroke

---

22. *Lettre de M. de Burigny à M. l'abbé Mercier sur les démêlés de M. de Voltaire avec M. de Saint-Hyacinthe* (Londres 1780), p.27.

23. 'Avertissement' to the fifth edition (Paris 1774) of Pouilly's *Théorie des sentiments agréables*.

provided was doubtless largely catalytic, reinforcing and quickening Voltaire's progress in a direction which he had already chosen. That Pope, the Roman Catholic, with a taste for a more liberal theology, could regard himself as heading in the same direction as Voltaire, 'the free thinker', ensured a substantial amount of common ground between the *Essay on Man* and the *Discours en vers sur l'homme*. That both authors paid homage to the same philosophical mentor justifies a comparison of these poems with Bolingbroke's philosophical writings. A convenient, if not comprehensive, framework for such a comparative study is provided by Pope's peroration to his *Essay*, in which, he claims, he

> Shew'd erring Pride, WHATEVER IS, IS RIGHT;
> That REASON, PASSION, answer one great aim;
> That true SELF-LOVE and SOCIAL are the same;
> That VIRTUE only makes our Bliss below;
> And all our Knowledge is, OURSELVES TO KNOW.

Bolingbroke, the humble theist of the *Reflections upon exile*, had already castigated the presumption of those who dared 'to censure the Order of Providence'. In his later, more diffuse, philosophical essays he expands his earlier remarks, relating man's impious pride to a more ample theodicean context. The Great Chain of Being is introduced: 'the whole world, nay the whole universe, is filled with beings, which are all connected in one immense design'.[24] This chain stretches 'almost from nonentity up to man' and probably 'continues up to natures infinitely below the divine, but vastly superior to human' (*F*.xlix; viii.219). In this 'gradation of sense and intellect' man has his due place, one with which he frequently feels discontented since his pride leads him to regard himself as the measure of all things and to disregard the fact that 'the world was made for the universe, not for man' (*F*.xliv; viii.191). In this cosmic perspective Bolingbroke argues (*F*.xlvi; viii.364-65):

Since Infinite Wisdom designed that there should be various orders of intellectual beings in the plan of the universe, differently placed, differently constituted and some superior to others, it will follow that nothing can be more absurd than the complaints of creatures who are in one of these orders, that they are not in another, if in truth there are any creatures except men, unreasonable enough to make such complaints.

Pope expatiates upon the 'vast chain of being' (*EM*.i.237), and the

---

24. *Fragments, or minutes of essays* (hereafter: *F*): *F*.l; viii.232.

prideful discontent of humans (*EM*.I.173-74):

> What would this Man? Now upward will he soar,
> And little less than Angel, would be more;

Like Bolingbroke, he finds it (*EM*.I.263-66):

> Just as absurd for any part to claim
> To be another, in this gen'ral frame:
> Just as absurd, to mourn the tasks or pains
> The great directing MIND of ALL ordains.

The effect upon the Scale of Being of such misplaced aspirations being realised would in Pope's eyes be truly cataclysmic (*EM*.I.241-44):

> On superior powr's
> Were we to press, inferior might on ours:
> Or in the full creation leave a void,
> Where, one step broken, the great scale's destroy'd;[25]

The prospect elicits indignation reminiscent of the irascible Bolingbroke's (*EM*.I.257-58):

> All this dread ORDER break – for whom? for thee?
> Vile worm! – Oh Madness, Pride, Impiety.

Voltaire's attitude to the Great Chain of Being is not nearly as clear-cut as Pope's and Bolingbroke's. He is in fact decidedly sceptical (*Discours*, VI.27-30):

> Montre-moi si tu peux cette chaîne invisible
> Du monde des esprits et du monde sensible;
> Cet ordre si caché de tant d'êtres divers,
> Que Pope après Platon crut voir dans l'univers.

The Chain of Being and particularly the notion of plenitude is vigorously rebutted by him later in a long note to the *Poème sur le désastre de Lisbonne* (1756) which rejects the rigid approach of the systematisers, seen as a threat to the idea of God's total freedom of action and of the flexibility of the albeit general dispensation of Providence. The note concludes: '*Tout est enchaîné* ne veut dire autre chose sinon que tout est arrangé. Dieu est la cause et le maître de cet arrangement. Le Jupiter d'Homère était l'esclave des destins; mais dans une philosophie plus épurée Dieu

---

25. Bolingbroke similarly raises the spectre of a situation where man was 'so superior to his actual rank in the scale of intelligent beings, that this rank must have been void, and the scale imperfect' (*F*.lxvi; viii.363).

est le maître des destins' (M.ix.473). God had already in *Discours VI* presented himself in this light to all denizens of the universe ('Des destins et des temps connaissez le seul maître') before making it clear to them that they would have to get used to a state of affairs which was not going to change (96-98):

> Rien n'est grand ni petit; tout est ce qu'il doit être.
> D'un parfait assemblage instruments imparfaits,
> Dans votre rang placés demeurez satisfaits.

Man, however, remained as dissatisfied and stubbornly self-important as he had always been (79-80):

> Mais enfin, de ce monde et l'oracle et le maître,
> Je ne suis point encor ce que je devrais être.

The authorial comment ('Cette indocile espèce / Sera-t-elle occupée à murmurer sans cesse?' ll.99-100) shows an exasperation with such misplaced pride which will be echoed by the impatient Jesrad in the face of Zadig's searching questions about the bewildering operations of Providence. 'Zadig, à genoux, adora la Providence et se soumit' we are told. Voltaire, the exemplary deist, will likewise, for all his anguish, knuckle down and accept the horror of the Lisbon disaster as inevitable:

> Humble dans mes soupirs, soumis dans ma souffrance,
> Je ne m'élève point contre la Providence.
> [...] Je ne sais que souffrir, et non pas murmurer.

In his preface to this poem, Voltaire maintains that Pope's axiomatic 'Whatever is, is right' is quite acceptable. He himself had earlier summed up the argument of the first epistle of Pope's *Essay*: 'tout ce qui est est bien, parce qu'un Etre infiniment sage en est l'auteur'.[26] In his 'anti-Pascal' of 1734 he had voiced similar sentiments: 'l'homme [...] est ce qu'il doit être' (*Remarque* I), 'Penser que la terre, les hommes et les animaux sont ce qu'ils doivent être dans l'ordre de la Providence est, je crois, d'un homme sage' (*Remarque* VI). This placid rationalism consolidated by the intellectual converse with Mme Du Châtelet at Cirey, was so severely shaken by the Lisbon earthquake (besides other ills which flesh is heir to) that 'Tout est bien' came to be used by him as the

26. Letter to Mme Du Deffand, 18 March 1736 (Best.D1039). For a lengthier quotation from this letter and a more detailed examination of the Voltaire-Pope relationship, see George R. Havens 'Voltaire and Alexander Pope', in *Essays on Diderot and the Enlightenment: in honor of Otis Fellows*, ed. J. Pappas (Geneva 1974), pp.124-50.

supremely ironic description of the human condition, a tag with which
to damn the creed of philosophical Optimism. Pope and Bolingbroke
could not but fall foul eventually of that 'outraged humanitarianism' of
Voltaire's which the editor of the Twickenham edition of the *Essay on Man*
rightly categorises as 'religiously immature'.[27] It is worth remembering
however that Voltaire's deism matured early and survived the onslaughts
of outrageous fortune to flourish in his later years when he turned to
England for an exemplar of Natural Religion. Dr Freind of his *Histoire
de Jenni* stands for what he had seen in Pope's *Essay* (at the time of the
Lisbon earthquake), and for what he had already proclaimed in the
Discours en vers sur l'homme to be the fundamental basis of his creed: 'le
respect pour la Divinité, la résignation qu'on doit à ses ordres suprêmes,
la saine morale, la tolérance'.

'Know then thyself, presume not God to scan'. Pope intended the
opening line of the second epistle of his *Essay on Man*, as Mark Pattison
noted in his edition of the poem, to underline the contrast between 'the
futility of metaphysical speculation on the attributes of the Deity and
the more profitable employment of the study of man'.[28] The final lines
of this same epistle ('See! and confess one comfort still must rise, / 'Tis
this, Tho' Man's a fool, yet GOD IS WISE') bear a close resemblance to
Bolingbroke's formulation of a similar intention in his *Fragment* LII
(viii.264): 'to show that God is wise and man a fool, and that of all fools,
the most presumptuous, and at the same time, the most trifling are
metaphysical philosophers and divines'. It is blasphemous folly on their
part, Bolingbroke remarks, 'to reason about what Infinite Wisdom and
Power might, or should have done, instead of contenting themselves to
know what they have done, and pronouncing it, for that reason, fittest
to be done' (*F.*vi; vii.382): 'since Infinite Wisdom not only established
the end, but directed the means, the system of the universe must
necessarily be the best of all possible systems' (*F.*xliii; viii.176). One
form of presumption which he found especially infuriating is exemplified
in Samuel Clarke, who is repeatedly berated for maintaining that 'the
divine moral attributes [...] are the same in God as they are in our ideas'
and that 'God, out of a tender and hearty concern for the happiness of
man, (strange words to be applied to the Supreme Being!) desires to be
imitated by him in those perfections which are the foundation of his own

27. Introduction, p.xlv, note 4.
28. Cited by Maynard Mack, p.53.

unchangeable happiness' (*F*.iv; vii.354-55). Attempts to deduce our moral obligations from the moral attributes of the Deity amount, in Bolingbroke's eyes, to the monstrous irreverence of fashioning God in man's image (*F*.vii; vii.385), limiting his perfection and tainting him with man's imperfection. The repugnance he feels for the idea of making God the object of human imitation is expressed in one of the *Fragments* he addressed to Pope, who shared his distaste for those neo-platonists who 'quitting sense call imitating God' (*EM*.ii.26). The doctrine is dangerous, he feels, since it encourages a taste for those abstractions which have led so many 'to imagine an uninterrupted scale of intelligence from man up to God, to flatter themselves with notions not only of imitating him but of being united to him' (*F*.iv; vii.360). Totally inimical to mystical experience of any sort, Bolingbroke is equally impatient with those who, spurning his own down-to-earth, empirical approach, based on Locke's sensationalism and aimed at inferring God's will *a posteriori* from his works, prefer airy speculation dependent upon the abstractions of *a priori* reasoning. Among God's works, as Pope proclaims, Man is 'the proper study of Mankind' (*EM*.ii.2). 'Let us', suggests Bolingbroke (*F*.vi; vii.369), 'take things as we find them, more anxious to know what is, than to imagine what may be. Let us turn our eyes on ourselves and consider how we are made'.

Voltaire echoes these sentiments in the introduction to his *Poème sur la loi naturelle* (1752): 'Ecartons ces romans qu'on appelle systèmes, / Et pour nous élever descendons dans nous-mêmes,' and acknowledges Pope's primacy in the field of philosophical verse: 'Il porta la flamme dans l'abîme de l'être; / Et l'homme avec lui seul apprit à se connaître.' In his sixth *Discours en vers sur l'homme* ('Sur la nature de l'homme'), he describes human nature in terms reminiscent of Pope's ('énigme obscure', 'labyrinthe') but emphasises too the rich rewards in terms of self-knowledge which may be earned from 'scanning' one's self rather than the Deity. His conception of God showed up the contrast between divine perfection and human imperfection particularly strongly during the period when he was composing the *Discours*. W. H. Barber notes the way in which he insists in a letter of 1738 upon 'la volonté infiniment libre de l'Etre infiniment puissant' and points out the similarity between this view and the stance taken up by Samuel Clarke in his debate with Leibniz some twenty years before.[29] Clarke continues to influence Voltaire in his *Traité de métaphysique* (1739) and in *La Métaphysique de Newton* (1740) where the possibility of a liberty of indifference (i.e. of unmotivated free choice) is suggested. In the second of Voltaire's *Discours en vers sur l'homme*, 'De la liberté', we are told (31-34):

> Qui conçoit, veut, agit, est libre en agissant,
> C'est l'attribut divin de l'Etre tout-puissant;
> Il en fait un partage à ses enfants qu'il aime;
> Nous sommes ses enfants, des ombres de lui-même.

The serenity of the Cirey period of Voltaire's life is reflected here in the easy accommodation of God's power and his goodness, as it is throughout all the *Discours*. The tension between these attributes of the Deity will make itself felt acutely later as Voltaire's disillusion with philosophical optimism grows. Bolingbroke's staunch defence of free-will throughout all his writings underlines the affinity between Voltaire and himself in the late 1730s. It is his dislike of the *constraints* put upon divine freedom and power by Clarke which animates the prolonged attacks which he makes upon his compatriot in his philosophical *Essays* and *Fragments*. He objects vehemently to Clarke's notion of 'an eternal reason of things, [...] the true criterion of moral good and evil, the rule by which the Creator and the creature are alike obliged to act' (*F*.ii; vii.339). Voltaire is moved by the Lisbon disaster to question these 'eternal truths', presented by Clarke and others as independent of God's will and 'in themselves of eternal necessity' (*F*.lviii; viii.308-309): 'Direz-vous: "C'est l'effet des eternelles lois / Qui d'un Dieu libre et bon nécessitent le choix?"' Unlike Bolingbroke, who took the view that the moral attributes of God are absorbed in his wisdom and was therefore reluctant to refer to his goodness, Voltaire is from the outset of his career attracted by the consoling idea of the loving-kindness of a fatherly God. In the last few years of his life he resolves the tension between God's omnipotence and his goodness by remaining attached to the latter, acknowledging, what would once have been unthinkable to him, that God's power was inevitably limited. The imperfection of God's creatures compared with their Creator – a constant theme of Voltaire's deistic writings – finally enables him to renew his worship of the more loveable God of an earlier period of his life.

29. W. H. Barber, *Leibniz in France from Arnauld to Voltaire* (Oxford 1955), p.202.

The benign God of the fifth *Discours sur l'homme* leads mankind to happiness through pleasure and, as surely as Pope's (or Bolingbroke's), identifies self-love with social love:

> Partout d'un Dieu clément la bonté salutaire
> Attache à vos besoins un plaisir nécessaire
> Les mortels, en un mot, n'ont point d'autre moteur.   [29-31]

> O moitié de notre être, amour-propre enchanteur
> Sans nous tyranniser règne dans notre coeur
> Pour aimer un autre homme, il faut s'aimer soi-même
> Que Dieu soit notre exemple, il nous cherit, il s'aime.   [Variant, 47-50]

> Nous nous aimons dans nous, dans nos biens, dans nos fils,
> Dans nos citoyens, surtout dans nos amis,
> Cet amour nécessaire est l'âme de notre âme   [51-53]

Bolingbroke articulates the same doctrine in prose aimed to show that 'the business of the philosopher is to dilate, to press, to prove, to convince' (v.79; *F*.vi; vii.378):

Men are led, by a chain of necessary consequences, from the instinctive to the rational law of nature, if I may speak so. Self-love operates in all these stages. We love ourselves, we love our families, we love the particular societies to which we belong, and our benevolence extends at last to the whole race of mankind. Like so many different vortices, the centre of them all is self-love, and that which is the most distant from it is the weakest.

The 'short and spirited strokes', which in Bolingbroke's opinion should distinguish poetic discourse, are evident in a passage of the *Essay on Man* wherein Pope's verse corresponds quite closely with Bolingbroke's prose (*EM*.IV.363-68):

> Self-love but serves the virtuous mind to wake,
> As the small pebble stirs the peaceful lake;
> The centre mov'd, a circle strait succeeds,
> Another still, and still another spreads,
> Friend, parent, neighbour, first it will embrace,
> His country next, and next all human race.

The rational deism of Bolingbroke, Pope and Voltaire in the works under consideration is notable for its recognition of the secondary role which reason plays in human affairs. 'Self-love, [...] the original spring of human actions, is under the direction of instinct first, and of reason afterward' (*F*.vi; vii.369), notes Bolingbroke, who is well aware that the second phase of this process in which 'a due use of our reason makes social and self-love coincide, or even become in effect the same' (*F*.li; viii.241) is never reached by many. The pessimistic seventeenth-century view of the passions as destructive forces in the human psyche having been severely eroded, if not abandoned, self-love is seen as man's driving force, 'that active principle, inflaming and inflamed by his passions', and reason as 'a less active principle which instead of impelling, requires to be impelled', 'a gift [...] not given to destroy, but to direct and govern the passions' (*F*.li; viii.245, 244). Pope's account of the workings of human psychology echoes Bolingbroke's (*EM*.ii.53-54, 59-60, 67-70):

> Two principles in human nature reign;
> Self-love, to urge, and Reason to restrain;
>
> Self-love, the Spring of motion, acts the soul
> Reason's comparing balance rules the whole
>
> Most strength the moving principle requires;
> Active its task, it prompts, impels, inspires.
> Sedate and quiet the comparing lies
> Form'd but to check, delib'rate, and advise.

It is not unlikely that he had discussed with his 'guide' what the latter, in his early *Reflections concerning innate moral principles*, called 'the main Spring and first Mover of all human actions' and Man's 'Love of that which gives him pleasure and Aversion for that which gives him pain'.[30] Certainly Bolingbroke and Voltaire would have endorsed Pope's lines (*EM*.ii.87-88): 'Self-love and Reason to one end aspire, / Pain their aversion, Pleasure their desire'. All three acknowledge the essential part played by rational judgement in the pursuit of happiness, attainable to all in different ways but in equal measure. In each case, however, what distinguishes man from the beasts is given less prominence than what he has in common with them. The Cartesian theory of 'l'automatisme des bêtes', rejected by Voltaire, is also given the quietus by Bolingbroke who suggests to Pope the possibility 'that intellectual faculties and corporeal senses, of the same and of different kinds, are communicated in some proportion or other to the whole race of animals', (*F*.l; viii.231), and is not above bringing in Pope's dog, Bounce, to strengthen the suggestion, (*F*.lxiii; viii.345). The poet's feeling of kinship with the animal world is conveyed in his nostalgic evocation of a state of nature wherein 'Man walk'd with beast, joint tenant of the shade' (*EM*.iii.152);

---

30. *Reflections* (London 1752), pp.5, 7.

his elevation of animals to equal status with mankind in the Creator's design for the world (*EM*.III.27-48); and his account of the model which the animal kingdom provided Man in his ascent to civilisation (*EM*.III.169-98). Pope's *Essay* often tends to favour 'honest Instinct', 'quick Nature' vis-à-vis 'heavier Reason' (III.88, 91, 92); its moral dynamic encompasses passions as 'the elements of Life' (*EM*.I.170) and proclaims: 'The surest virtues (thus) from Passion shoot, / Wild Nature's vigor working at the root' (*EM*.II.183-84). Man's pride arouses in him pretensions to a place higher in the Scale of Being than that allotted to him: 'Men would be angels, angels would be gods' (*EM*.I.126) in Pope's words. Voltaire, who (like Pope, but unlike Bolingbroke) is not averse to enlisting members of the heavenly host to act as spokesmen for the Almighty, calls upon an ethereal spirit in his second *Discours* to rebuke such misplaced ambition: 'Tes destins sont d'un homme, et tes vœux sont d'un Dieu' (l.83). He takes the hint offered by Pope in the lines 'While Man exclaims, 'See all things for my use' / 'See man for mine!' replies a pamper'd goose' (*EM*.III.45-46) and proceeds to 'dire d'une manière gaie, et sous l'enveloppe d'*une fable*, ce qu'un Anglais a dit tristement et sèchement dans des vers métaphysiques traduits lâchement' (letter to D'Argental, 6 January 1739; Best.D1746). Pope's taut couplet contrasts with Voltaire's veritable carnival of the animals (*Discours* VI, 43ff.) reminiscent of La Fontaine but also prefiguring the technique of the mature *conteur*.

The condemnation of 'pride', as A. O. Lovejoy pointed out,[31] is 'frequently, in the eighteenth century, one of the ways of expressing a primitivistic anti-intellectualism'. This strain is evident in numerous other forms in our three authors. All of them profess disdain for the refinements of civilisation as compared with the superior attractions of the simple life. In the first of Voltaire's *Discours sur l'homme* happiness is deemed to be more accessible to 'le simple, l'ignorant, pourvu d'un instinct sage' than to 'le triste savant qui croit le définir' (53, 56). The peasants' lot, idealised at some length (61-100), is presented as a happy one since 'La paix, le doux sommeil, la force, la santé, / Sont le fruit de leur peine et de leur pauvreté' (79-80). For Bolingbroke and Pope, happiness appears to be based on much the same rudimentary requirements. According to Bolingbroke, 'Agreeable sensations, the series whereof constitutes happiness, must arise from health of body, tranquillity of mind and a compete-

31. '"Pride" in eighteenth-century thought', *Modern language notes* 36 (1921), p.35.

DENNIS FLETCHER

ncy of wealth' (F.lii; viii.259). Pope agrees: 'Reason's whole pleasure, all the joys of Sense, / Lie in three words, Health, Peace, and Competence' (*EM*.IV.79-80). These somewhat terre-à-terre views of what constitutes happiness do not seem to harmonise very well with the more elevated conception derived from Shaftesbury and adopted by Pope: 'Virtue alone is Happiness below' (*EM*.IV.310) until we remember that virtue is synonymous with benevolence, the prime attribute of the eighteenth-century Man of Feeling. Feeling indeed suffuses Pope's view of God's Creation; it is noticeable that the Chain of Love, a concept absent from his friend Bolingbroke's scheme of things, gives a more vitalist tinge to his own description of cosmic unity. The energy of nature is reflected in a more dynamic conception of virtue, which rejects the moral stasis of Stoicism (*EM*.II.101-104):

> In lazy Apathy let Stoics boast
> Their Virtue fix'd; tis fix'd as in a frost,
> Contracted all, retiring to the breast;
> But strength of mind is Exercise not Rest.

Voltaire condemns the Stoics for equating virtue with 'insensibilité' (*Discours* VII.14-15) and identifies it rather with its polar opposite – not the self-indulgent vaporous variety of 'sensibilité', but the powerful emotion which drives man to positive good. He shares with Pope the view that 'Reason, however able, cool at best / Cares not for service, or but serves when prest' (*EM*.III.85-86) and that an emotional commitment to one's fellow man – 'LOVE of GOD, and LOVE of MAN' (*EM*.IV.340) – is an essential prerequisite of virtuous action. In the last of his *Discours*, 'Sur la vraie vertu', l'Homme-Dieu's pronouncement ('Aimez Dieu [...] mais aimez les mortels', 44) echoes the earlier 'anti-Pascal''s passionate rebuttal of over-exclusive devotion to God: 'Il faut aimer, et très tendrement, les créatures' (*Remarque* X). The 'honnête homme indolent' is for Voltaire a contradiction in terms, the virtuous man is at once 'une âme sensible', and a man of action 'au cœur tendre et sublime / Qui soutient hardiment son ami qu'on opprime' (99, 101-102). The warm approval of the abbé de Saint-Pierre's coinage, 'bienfaisance', which is the note on which the seventh *Discours* ends, anticipates the crusading beneficence of Voltaire's campaigns against particular instances of injustice in the 1760s. The good works which Voltaire seems to have in mind in the late 1730s, however, belong to a more restricted, personal sphere of action. Consisting mainly of strenuous attempts to combat libels and slanders, they show up the

24

self-styled 'implacable ennemi du calomniateur' (*Discours* VI.189) as only somewhat less disinterested when defending his friends (Mme Du Châtelet, for example, in the *Epître sur la calomnie*) than when he is conducting his own defence.

This activity, nothing if not purposeful, does at least reflect the importance which Voltaire attached to both friendship and self-improvement. His progress towards a personal philosophy – mirrored during the Cirey period in the significantly unpublished *Traité de métaphysique* – was furthered by a formidable female philosopher in the person of the 'divine Emilie' who believed as strongly as her friend and work-mate in the value of intensive study. Voltaire speaks for them both in the fourth of his *Discours* (115-18):

> Le travail est souvent le père du plaisir:
> Je plains l'homme accablé du plaisir.
> Le bonheur est un bien que nous vend la nature.
> Il n'est point ici-bas de moisson sans culture.

Earlier in his career, he had received this same message in much the same terms from his friend, Bolingbroke.[32] Later, it will be transmitted, more memorably, by Candide.

32. See Bolingbroke's letter of 27 June 1724 to Voltaire (Best.D190) and, for our final sentence, note 1 of Theodore Besterman's commentary.

The allegorical engravings in the Ledet-Desbordes edition of the *Eléments de la philosophie de Newton*[*]

ROBERT L. WALTERS

> Iconology is the doctrine of representation, which
> signifies speaking pictures or the discourse of images.
>
> George Richardson 1779

WHEN Voltaire arrived in Holland at the end of 1736, he was hard at work on his manuscript of the *Eléments de la philosophie de Newton*. He seems simultaneously without delay to have begun publishing and revising the work. He sought the help of Willem Jacob 's-Gravesande, professor of mathematics, astronomy and philosophy at Leiden University, an important Newtonian. Herman Boerhaave, whom Voltaire was consulting at Leiden about his health, was also a Newtonian, and between them 's-Gravesande and Boerhaave attracted hundreds of foreigners to Leiden each year. They showed remarkable patience with their French poet-student-patient turned scientist. Voltaire and 's-Gravesande became friends and kept up a friendly correspondence until the latter's death. A. Rupert Hall remarks that 'although 's-Gravesande was by no means the first semipopular exponent of Newtonian science and the experimental method [...] his *Mathematical elements of physics* was easily the most influential book of its kind, at least before 1750.'[1] Voltaire put the final touches to what became the first edition of the *Eléments* under the guidance of Europe's most influential spokesman for Newtonianism.

During the months of January and February 1727 Voltaire travelled back and forth between Leiden and Amsterdam.[2] He was revising his

---

[*] I wish to thank Madeline Lennon and Bernard Bonario, Department of Visual Arts, Roger Emerson, Department of History, and Dean William Cameron of the School of Library and Information Science, all of The University of Western Ontario, for valuable advice during the preparation of this article.

1. *Dictionary of scientific biography* (New York 1970-1980), v.510. The article ''s-Gravesande' is by A. Rupert Hall.

2. See Best.D1270, textual notes by Theodore Besterman. Besterman finds no evidence 'that Voltaire left Leyden for Amsterdam in January 1737'. Voltaire's dealings with Ledet and with the printers and engravers working on the Eléments seem evidence that he is in

popularisation of Newtonian science in Leiden as the type was being set and the sheets were coming from the press in Amsterdam. Voltaire enjoyed an ideal arrangement with his publishers Etienne Ledet et Compagnie and Jacques Desbordes,[3] especially with Etienne Ledet with whom he was on excellent terms. Ledet had already brought out a two-volume *Œuvres* (Amsterdam 1732) and was preparing a new four-volume *Œuvres*, the supervision of which was Voltaire's official excuse for being in Holland, when he fled there as the storm erupted over *Le Mondain* and *La Pucelle* at the end of 1736. Ledet was making a profit as Voltaire's publisher and showed his gratitude to the author. He lodged him as a guest in his own home, when Voltaire was in Amsterdam, as Voltaire wrote to Thieriot: 'Le libraire Ledet qui a gagné quelque chose à débuter mes faibles ouvrages et qui en fait actuellement une magnifique édition a plus de reconnaissance que les libraires de Paris n'ont d'ingratitude. Il m'a forcé de loger chez lui quand je viens à Amsterdam voir comment va la philosophie Neutonienne' (Best.D1262).

The correspondence during the winter of 1737 gives us some idea how the volume on Newton was going and Voltaire's own part in the work. On 16 January he wrote to madame Du Châtelet that the first sheet of the *Eléments* had been printed (Best.D1258 and D1273) and that the printing would take two months. Voltaire went into the print-shop himself to supervise the work of printers and engravers (Best.D1271). He even had the work on the *Œuvres* suspended in favour of the *Eléments* (Best.D1273). About 25 January Voltaire sent madame Du Châtelet some proofs of the *Eléments* (Best.D1269 and D1274).

Toward the middle of January madame Du Châtelet began urging Voltaire to stop the publication of the *Eléments de la philosophie de Newton* in Holland. Rather he should submit his work to the censor in France and bring out a French edition, thus rehabilitating himself with the

Amsterdam part of the time. It seems unlikely that each time a letter is dated Amsterdam Voltaire is concealing his whereabouts or making a slip. See Jeroom Vercruysse, 'Voltaire et la Hollande', *Studies on Voltaire* 46 (1966), p.36.

3. Two title pages were printed with different engraved *vignettes*, one listing Ledet et Compagnie as publishers, the other Jacques Desbordes. There was a firm called Ledet et Desbordes, as we learn in a letter from Ledet to Voltaire (Best.D2667) in 1742. Desbordes's one-third interest was taken over by three people. Ledet tells Voltaire these new partners need know nothing about what solely concerns Ledet et Compagnie, that is Voltaire's works. When I mention the Ledet edition of the *Eléments*, I mean the edition that appeared in Amsterdam in March 1738.

French authorities. She was quite certain Voltaire would follow her suggestion (Best.D1273):

mon courier arriuera p̄r̄ suspendre tous ses projets. Il fera suspendre l'édition, il en est d'autant plus le maitre que come c'est le même libraire qui imprime ses oëuures, il les a fait discontinuer, et le libraire en reprendra l'impression et suspendra celle de la philosophie [...] j'empêcheray que la philosophie soit imprimée en Holande auant de l'être à Paris, qu'il y foure rien sur la métaphisique.

Eventually Voltaire followed this plan. However, another three weeks or a month went by devoted frantically to the *Eléments*, Voltaire postponing again and again his departure for France. When he finally did leave in the second half of February the publishers were to go ahead with the printing of the *Eléments*. The sheets as they came from the press would be given to the chevalier de Jaucourt,[4] who would send them to a M. Du Faÿ, who would communicate them to Voltaire. Finally when Ledet ran out of text for the *Eléments de Newton*, the printing of the *Œuvres* would be resumed. The work would continue until Voltaire's projected return to Holland in June, having in the meantime, he hoped, obtained the *privilège* for the publication of the *Eléments* in France. To make sure Ledet did not bring out the Dutch edition Voltaire withheld the last five chapters, including the final chapter on God.[5]

Voltaire's postponement of his departure for Cirey in February can be explained by the two activities that had preoccupied him continually during his stay in Holland, his Newtonian studies with 's-Gravesande, 'mon amy et mon maitre' (Best.D1287), and the supervision of the printing of the *Eléments*, still being written and revised. 'Je ne pourrai partir que vers le 16 ou le 17 [février]. J'en suis au désespoir. Mais figurez vous que j'avais commencé une besogne où j'employais sept ou huit

4. Voltaire wrote to Jaucourt 'ce 1er mars': 'J'aÿ emporté monsieur le regret d'avoir si peu profité de l'honneur de vous connaitre, et l'espèrance que vous voudrez bien avoir quelque bonté pour cet enfant assez déguenillé que j'ai laissé chez Ledet. Le père vous en aura obligation toute sa vie. Je compte que le Det vous envoye les feuilles, et que vous voulez bien les faire tenir à mr du Faÿ qui vous les rendra' (Best.D1292). Du Faÿ left for London, and Voltaire had to make other arrangements (Best.D1305). There is no evidence that Ledet ever sent the proof sheets of the *Eléments*.

5. See Best.D1487. Madame Du Châtelet writes to the comte d'Argental after the Amsterdam *Eléments* appeared, 'Votre ami en est très fâché parce qu'il y manque les 5 derniers chapitres. Il auoit cru que cela les contiendroit, mais rien ne peut arrêter l'auidité des libraires.' She goes on to mention the last chapter, 'où mr de V. rendoit compte des sentimens de mr Neuton sur la métaphysique'. Voltaire in Best.D1489 writes to Thieriot: 'Le dernier chapitre surtout qui regarde les sentiments téologiques de mr Neuton n'est pas sorty de mes mains.'

personnes par jour; que j'étais seul à les conduire; qu'il faut leur laisser des instructions aisées & apaiser une famille qui s'imagine perdre sa fortune par mon absence' (Best.D1282).

In his commentary on this letter Voltaire wrote to madame de Champbonin Theodore Besterman identifies quite rightly the *besogne* as the *Eléments de la philosophie de Newton*:

No doubt Voltaire is referring to the *Eléments*, and as this is a book of only 400 pages his words may seem surprising; but in fact even as late as this it was common practice in printing-houses to divide a manuscript for simultaneous setting by several compositors; this secured speed, and protected the publisher or author against surreptitious copying; the author was often present, and Voltaire certainly was, no doubt correcting as fast as the proofs were run off.

Since the last eighty pages of the Ledet edition of the *Eléments* are not by Voltaire and could only have been put together by the anonymous mathematician after Voltaire tried to stop the publication of the *Eléments*,[6] since the setting of Voltaire's material was to go on actively after Voltaire's departure, as the correspondence with Jaucourt shows, one wonders how much of the work had been set and printed by mid-February. Half would perhaps be a generous estimate. In that case 200, rather than 400 pages would make Voltaire's words even more surprising, if it were not for one fact that Besterman did not mention. The 1738 Amsterdam edition of the *Eléments de la philosophie de Newton* contains signed copper engravings of an allegorical nature, most of them dated as well, which relate directly to Voltaire's work, and geometrical illustrations relating directly to the scientific aspects of the text, all unsigned and undated.

These engravings consist of an allegorical frontispiece, a portrait of Voltaire, four allegorical headpieces or *vignettes*, three allegorical tailpieces or *culs-de-lampe*, plus two decorative engravings used when very little space is left at the end of a chapter.[7] The frontispiece and portrait were printed separately, the *vignettes* and *culs-de-lampe* all appear on the same sheets, in the same gatherings as the text. Although the four *vignettes* are

6. The part by the 'mathématicien à gages' (Best.D1519) presumably begins on page 318. See Best.D1505 where Voltaire writes to Thieriot of a change in style and an increase in confusion at that point: 'Je vous en diray ensuitte pourquoy.'

7. In the days of hand-made books no two copies of the same edition were exactly the same. The author is basing the following description of the 1738 Amsterdam *Eléments* on his own copy of that edition.

repeated, always in the same order, up to the point where Voltaire is no longer the author, and the *culs-de-lampe* repeated as needed, when at least a half-page remains after the last line of text of a chapter, they all (but one) appear in the first three gatherings of the octavo volume: A, B, and C. The remaining one appears for the first time on leaf 6, recto, of gathering D. In addition there are 54 geometrical figures, all engraved on copper as well, which appear on the same sheets as text, seven scientific plates printed separately, one folding plate, plus four simpler wood-cut illustrations.

The first sheet, forming gathering A, has five allegorical engravings; the second, gathering B, has two; the third, gathering C, has seven. Each *vignette* and *cul-de-lampe* was used many times, so several plates of each design were cut, as examination shows. There are obvious changes in design, and the quality of the engraving deteriorates towards the end of the volume. Even if the same engravers worked on the signed allegorical pieces and the unsigned scientific plates, which seems unlikely, there would be five artists among the 'sept ou huit personnes' Voltaire kept busy.

Each sheet of paper that had printing on both sides had to go through the printing press twice, then twice through the roller press with which the engravings were printed. In the eighteenth century engravings were sometimes printed before the text, rather than the other way, but it was usual to complete both sides including engravings while the paper was damp. The printing of the *Eléments*, it is clear, was a considerable undertaking, the typesetting, the engraving, the printing on two presses, the handling and drying of the finished sheets. If we consider Voltaire's habit of revising, correcting as the printing progressed, it is not astonishing that he was supervising seven or eight persons.

In his correspondence for January 1737 Voltaire mentions the designing and engraving necessary for the *Eléments* to two correspondents. To Frederick he writes, 'Je suis venu à Leide travailler à rendre l'ouvrage moins indigne de [madame Du Châtelet] et de vous. Je suis venu à Amsterdam le faire imprimer et faire dessiner les planches. Cela durera tout l'hiver' (Best.D1255). In his letter to the marquis d'Argens of 28 January 1737 Voltaire mentions both engravers and printers. 'Je n'attends que le moment d'être débarassé de mes graveurs, de mes imprimeurs pour venir vous embrasser' (Best.D1271). The order even suggests that the former are more important than the latter.

Unfortunately in Voltaire's published works these engravers remain anonymous workmen. Nowhere does he mention them by name, as far as I can discover. But then in general Voltaire does not show a particularly great interest in painting or painters. No great sensibility to the visual arts is reflected in his works, even though his *mondain*'s house is decorated by the paintings of the *doux* Corrège and the *savant* Poussin and by the sculpture of Bouchardon. Voltaire himself collected the paintings which still hang in the château at Ferney. Still, J. Vercruysse found references to only three Dutch painters, one being Rembrandt, in all of Voltaire's works.[8] The engravers who worked for him in Amsterdam were no doubt considered workmen rather than artists. Also Voltaire, once on the spot, had no need to correspond about these engravings, and the fact that all the allegorical ones appear by page 59 in a 400 page book and that the date 1737 is on all the dated engravings suggests that they were completed in his presence. There was no need for them to be discussed in his continuing correspondence with Ledet. There is one rather indirect reference to his portrait,[9] although not to the engraver, Jacob Folkema. Clearly Voltaire did not approve of his likeness.

We cannot be sure of Voltaire's precise role in the designing and engraving of the allegorical plates for the *Eléments de la philosophie de Newton*. It seems unlikely that he had nothing whatever to do with their design or iconology, or that he would not have discussed and approved the conception of the different engravings and their positions in his work. Years earlier, in 1722, Voltaire had given rather precise instructions for the engraved plates he wished prepared for an edition of *La Ligue*; he showed a familiarity with allegorical art and with the leading artists and engravers working in Paris at that time. On his way to Holland in September 1722 Voltaire wrote to ask Thieriot to approach Coypel, Troy and Galoches (Best.D121) and commission drawings according to his own descriptions. For example Troy was to present for the fifth canto Henri IV in armour asleep in a military camp. St Louis on a cloud places his crown on Henri's head, while pointing to a castle with open doors.

8. See Vercruysse, pp.115-17.
9. See Best.D1448, commentary. Besterman identifies 'cette mauvaise estampe' as the Folkema engraving based on the La Tour portrait. Ledet used similar portraits engraved by J. Folkema in the *Eléments* and the *Œuvres*. However, they were not printed from the same plate. The portrait in the *Œuvres* (BN Z Beuchot 4, vol. 1) has the caption 'François Devoltaire, né en 1695' and is signed 'Jacob Folkema sculpcit 1738'.

Time with his scythe in his hand stands at the castle gate; a crowd of heroes waits in the entrance way.

There was also to be an allegorical frontispiece: 'A la tête du poème; Henri quatre au naturel sur un trône de nuages tenant Louis quinze entre ses bras et luy montrant une renommée qui tient une trompette où sont attachées les armes de France.'

Voltaire in the same letter (Best.D121) reports he is on his way to see Bernard Picart in The Hague about doing other illustrations for his edition. Picart, considered one of the best book illustrators of the early eighteenth century,[10] was, however, too busy to undertake Voltaire's commissions (Best.D125). This letter to Thieriot and the descriptions, the names of the engravers show that Voltaire was knowledgeable about book art. It seems likely he would be as interested in the illustrations for the *Eléments de la philosophie de Newton*, as involved as he was in the composition and publishing of a work which set out to present the new scientific truth to an ignorant world.

Bernard Picart, the leading engraver active in Amsterdam between 1710 and his death in 1733, was the teacher of a whole generation of engravers including four of those involved with the *Eléments*. They are Jacob Folkema (1692-1767), who engraved the allegorical frontispiece, the portrait of 'Mr. de Voltairre' (*sic*) and two of the four vignettes, one of which he drew and engraved; Louis-Fabricius Dubourg (1693-1775), who drew the frontispiece and one of the *vignettes*, François-Morellon La Cave, whose dates are given neither by Bénézit nor by Thieme-Becker, but who was active in Amsterdam in the 1730s and did illustrations for *La Henriade* and Voltaire's tragedies. He drew and engraved the three allegorical *culs-de-lampe* with scientific significance. The final pupil of Picard is Jakob van (or van der) Schley (1715-1779).[11] According to Bénézit (ix.386) he finished several plates that Picart left unfinished at his death and illustrated an edition of *La Vie de Marianne* (The Hague 1735). Both Folkema and Dubourg were successful artists of their age, and their names appear in histories of prints and engravings. Of the two

10. See E. Bénézit, *Dictionnaire critique et documentaire des peintres, sculpteurs, dessinateurs et graveurs*. Nouvelle édition (Paris 1976), vii.296.

11. Bénézit is the source for the information on these artists. They also appear in *Allgemeines Lexikon der bildenden Künstler*, éd. Ulrich Thieme, Felix Becker, Hans Vollmer (Leipzig 1907-1950). For Picart see also 'Eloge historique de Bernard Picart' in his *Impostures innocentes, ou recueil d'estampes* (Amsterdam 1734). The *éloge* is preceded by an engraved portrait of Picart signed J. van der Schley with a text explaining the allegorical elements.

smaller *culs-de-lampe*, one was engraved in 1737 by G. Kendet,[12] whose name has not found its way into the lists of painters and engravers. The remaining one is signed 'B. Picart *del* 1729'. It was probably something small and decorative on hand by a famous artist then dead for three of four years. It may have been used to honour the master of the other artists. Bernard Picart was an artist Voltaire had met in 1722, as we have seen.

Anyone who handles this first edition of the *Eléments de la philosophie de Newton* is struck by the beauty of the engravings, the quality of the paper, the care with which Ledet and Voltaire must have supervised their workmen. Yet the excellence of this edition has received almost no attention. The reason is not difficult to find. Voltaire disowned the edition, denounced the publishers who, at the end of their patience, had the work finished by a Dutch mathematician, and brought it out without Voltaire's permission a year after his departure for Cirey. Voltaire, without delay, had a more 'correct', expanded edition brought out by Prault in Paris. (The title page says Londres). The Amsterdam edition appeared in March 1738; the Prault version was on sale by July.[13]

In the second edition the engraving of the geometrical plates is less clear than in the first. There are no frontispiece; one of the allegorical *vignettes* has become an ornament or *fleuron*, engraved by Duflos,[14] on the title page. There is a portrait of Newton engraved by Dupin. The other allegorical pieces have disappeared. We know that this edition was brought out with great haste, and began as a copy of the Amsterdam edition. The pages by the Dutch mathematician were not removed. Voltaire added *éclaircissements*, a *table des chapitres*, a chapter on tides, and a *table des matières*. All changes to the main body of the text are on cancels. This was the edition Voltaire praised and sent to his friends.[15] Yet a

12. Georges Bengesco mentions all the engravers in his bibliographical description of the first edition of the *Eléments* (*Voltaire, Bibliographie de ses œuvres*, ii.27). We do not find the name of Dubourg, who designed the frontispiece and one of the *vignettes*, but did no engraving.

13. See Best.D1539. About 3 July Voltaire arranged the distribution of copies of the Prault edition to his friends.

14. Bénézit lists several engravers named Duflos who were working in Paris at this time. It could be Claude-Augustin-Pierrre (1700-1786) or Philothée-François (1710-1746) who engraved this *fleuron*. The engraving has been reversed in being copied, and the heavenly body top centre has become a six-pointed star. The portrait of 'Marie François Aroüet de Voltaire, né à Paris en 1694' is unsigned (BN Z Beuchot 240).

15. Voltaire wanted them distributed quite generously. He wrote to Thieriot (Best.D1545): 'L'Abbé Moussinot, ou m^r Cousin (mon phisicien) viendra chez vous avec beaucoup de

large part of the Amsterdam edition had been prepared 'sous les yeux de l'auteur', not the case for the Prault edition, prepared in haste in Paris, while Voltaire was in Cirey. Prault printed a note by Voltaire condemning the Amsterdam edition and claiming the new edition was 'purgée d'une infinité de fautes d'impression, qui rendaient le sens de l'Auteur absolument inintelligible; l'Editeur de Hollande n'avait pas même eu le soin de placer comme il faut les lettres des figures, et les éditions qu'on pourrait faire sur celle de Hollande, seraient encore plus fautives. Nous les avons toutes corrigées selon les mémoires envoyés par l'auteur au journaliste anglais.'[16] Ledet replied justifying his edition: 'Rien n'est plus imaginé de la part du Sieur de Voltaire, que ce qui est marqué dans cet avertissement; l'Ouvrage a été fait réellement sous ses yeux à Amsterdam, et [il] a vendu sa copie fort cher [...] il se trouve de plus en cette édition un titre-planche magnifique, qui n'est point dans la prétendue édition de Londres, avec la beauté du papier, de l'impression et l'ornement des vignettes et culs de lampe en taille-douce.' Although Ledet does not answer all of Voltaire's complaints, he is right to point out the beauty of his edition. In discussing these allegorical engravings, we shall go from the simple to the more complex, beginning with the *vignettes* and *culs-de-lampe* and then discussing the full page frontispiece.

The first two *vignettes* are first used to head the two dedications to 'Madame la marquise du Ch**'. The poem without title, usually known as the *Epître à madame Du Châtelet sur la philosophie de Newton* and which begins,

> Tu m'appelles à toi vaste et puissant génie,
> Minerve de la France, divine Emilie[17]

is headed by a *vignette* (fig. 1) signed, 'L. F. Dubourg *inv*; J. Folkema *sculp*.' In the background beyond a pair of baroque curtains, drawn as if framing a stage, we see a bookcase on the left, on the right through an opening (it is difficult to call it a window) a tree and a colonnade. In front of the curtains there is a seated female figure in classical dress holding an open book. Her left breast is bare. To her right we see a mirror standing on a table. She looks to her left towards a *putto* with

Neutons dont vous disposera pour vos amis et pour les miens.'
16. These quotations are taken from a leaf inserted in my copy of the Amsterdam *Eléments* after the title page. Ledet reprinted the 'Avertissement des libraires de Londres' and added his 'Avertissement des libraires d'Amsterdam'.
17. *Eléments de la philosophie de Newton* (Amsterdam 1738) p.3.

wings. In his right hand he holds a pair of straight ordinary compasses, the points of which are raised. With his left hand he is removing a blindfold from his eyes. Between the woman and the *putto* stands a celestial sphere. On the floor we see books, a rule, a caliper compass,[18] and a square.

The *cul-de-lampe* (fig. 5), signed R. M. La Cave *inv. et sculp.* 1737', filling the bottom half of page 8 on which the *Epître* ends, shows within a baroque frame a female figure seated at a table holding a pen in her hand and writing. On her head is a helmet; she holds beside her with her left hand a spear and shield. Her breasts are both covered. A winged *putto*, hovering behind her, places a laurel wreath on her helmet. Behind her, between two pilasters, is a large window. The attributes of helmet, shield and spear identify her as Minerva, goddess of wisdom.

The *vignette* (fig. 2), placed before the prose dedication, also 'à madame la marquise du Ch**', is signed 'J. v. Schley *invenit et fecit* 1737'. Again we see a female figure in classical dress, similar to the one in the first *vignette*. She is seated out of doors under a tree with an open book on her lap. With her left hand she holds a pair of straight compasses, the points raised. Her right hand is held over her heart; her left breast is uncovered. At her right we see a *putto* without wings, kneeling and holding an armillary sphere. To her left there are two *putti*; the one farthest from her is seated and holds his left hand over his eyes. To his right a winged *putto*, standing, holds a lighted torch in his right hand; he looks toward the seated *putto* and points with his left hand to the central figure. On the ground at the bottom of the engraving lie books, an ink-well, a piece of paper and a pen.

In the third *vignette* (fig.3), first appearing on page 14, just before the first chapter, signed 'J. Folkema *inv. et sculp.* 1737', within an elaborate but essentially rectangular frame we find sixteen *putti* on an open terrace engaged in various activities, holding different attributes. One on the far left pulls back a baroque curtain in front of the base of a column. Below in the corner three *putti* examine a celestial sphere; one measures it with a compass, points down. To the right at the very bottom, two *putti* examine an open book, a rule to their right, a quantity of scientific instruments occupying the rest of the foreground: armillary sphere,

18. John Harris, *Lexicon technicum: or, an universal English dictionary of arts and sciences*, fourth edition (London 1725). These compasses with half circles near the point where the two sides join were also called gunner's calipers.

protractor, compass, books. Above them, slightly to the left of the centre of the engraving, are a group of three more *putti*; one carries three large books, two examine a globe. The remaining *putti* hover in the air; one holds a book and the caduceus of Mercury. At top centre a *putto* holds an astronomical instrument, a small globe within a circle. A group of three, right centre, have an artist's palette, a tablet or picture, and a chisel (?). Above them, in the upper right corner, the remaining two *putti* hold a musical instrument like a guitar and a pair of compasses.

The second *cul-de-lampe* (fig. 6), signed 'F. M. La Cave *inv. et sculp.* 1737', shows a man in a long dressing-gown and wig, seated at a table in a corner of a room. He too holds an open book. Behind him on one wall is a large window; the other wall is lined with books from the floor up to a heavy baroque curtain filling the corner. To the man's right stands a winged *putto* holding out a pair of compasses with his right hand. In his left he holds a lighted torch. The scene is framed by a baroque frame similar in all the *culs-de-lampe*.

The final *vignette* (fig. 4), signed 'J. v. Schley *invenit et fecit* 1737', shows a group of four *putti* on clouds. The upper one holds a set of pipes of Pan, the lower one a quadrant. Both have wings. Of the other two, without wings, the one on our right holds a glass or telescope to his eye, as he looks at a heavenly body at the top centre of the engraving. The remaining *putto* holds a pair of compasses, points raised, in his left hand, a lighted torch in his right.

The final *cul-de-lampe* (fig. 7), signed 'F. M. La Cave *inv. et sculp.* 1737', also has an irregularly shaped baroque frame similar to the other two. It presents an exterior scene at the centre of which sits a cupid (rather than a *putto*). He has a quiver which he is emptying onto the ground. Instead of arrows the quiver is full of compasses and pens. Behind him is the suggestion of a tree and an expanse of sky. When this *cul-de-lampe* was re-engraved, a sun at the horizon with expanding rays was added to the background.[19]

These decorative engravings all have a great deal of charm and add to the beauty of the book. They all contain these little boys, which the art historians prefer to call *putti* although they can be, and often are,

19. In the author's copy this design appears on p.59, on p.160, and on p.187 without the sun. The second version with the sun appears on p.271 and p.354. In BN Z Beuchot 258 the *cul-de-lampe* on p.59 has the sun.

cherubs or cupids, depending on their religious or erotic significance.[20] The subject matter of Watteau's 'Embarkation for Cythera' requires that the *putti* that fill the air be cupids; the religious paintings by Rubens, that great master of baroque painting, are frequently full of a heavenly host of cherubs. At other times these little boys, sometimes with wings, often without, serve a purely decorative purpose, or their presence in a scene which otherwise would seem a portrayal of everyday life serves as a sign that there is another meaning, that the scene is allegorical. If the *putto* holds an attribute of some sort, such as a trumpet or a pair of compasses, the attribute is probably a key to the meaning.

The presence of compasses, squares and rules, of Minerva or Mercury has caused some scholars to look for masonic meaning in such allegorical engravings as Cochin's frontispiece for the *Encyclopédie* and Bernard Picart's many allegorical engravings.[21] Anyone who has read Margaret Jacob's *The Radical enlightenment* and Voltaire's works, especially his correspondence from 1736 to 1741, the period of greatest scientific activity, will be struck by the similarities between her description of the Newtonian enlightenment with its Whigs, Masons, and deists, and Voltaire's interests. We even encounter the same people: Prosper Marchand, Jean Rousset de Missy, 's-Gravesande, the professor at Leiden, Desaguliers, the Huguenot refugee who became a guiding force in British Freemasonry and helped in the establishment of the movement in The Hague (Jacob, pp.122-25). Bernard Picart, the artist and engraver, was active in Dutch masonic and artistic circles, as Mrs Jacob has shown. Both Jacob Folkema and L. F. Dubourg, who worked on the engravings for the *Eléments de Newton*, appear in her study (Jacob, p.155). There can be no doubt that during his stay in Holland Voltaire associated with booksellers, publishers, intellectuals and artists with a Newtonian outlook, and that many of them were Masons, as well as members of the Knights of Jubilation, a sort of private masonic lodge.[22]

As professor Georges May points out, many scholars have not been convinced of the masonic propaganda in the frontispiece of the

20. The *putti* were also called *génies* as in the text to the van der Schley portrait of Picart, see n.11.

21. Margaret C. Jacob, *The Radical enlightenment: pantheists, Freemasons, and republicans* (London 1981), frontispiece. Engraving 'Minerva Duce' by Bernard Picart, 1722.

22. Mrs Jacob publishes extracts from the records of the Knights of Jubilation. One record lists Picart as 'Dauber and engraver of the order' (p.296).

Encyclopédie.[23] I would suggest that in the case of the allegorical engravings in the *Eléments de la philosophie de Newton*, there are two more fruitful approaches to their meaning than through Freemasonry, tempting as that approach may be. Voltaire's text could offer us keys to their meaning, or we could find it in the iconologies and emblem books of the period.

The tradition of allegorical art was still very much alive throughout the eighteenth century. The iconologies set out to give artists and readers a clear visual vocabulary for portraying and interpreting abstract ideas, as the complete title to the 1709 English edition of Cesare Ripa's *Iconologia* makes clear:

Iconologia: or moral emblems, by Caesar Ripa, wherein are express'd various images of virtues, vices, passions, arts, humours, elements and celestial bodies; as design'd by the ancient Egyptians, Greeks, Romans, and modern Italians: useful for orators, poets, painters, sculptors, and all lovers of ingenuity: illustrated with three hundred twenty-six humane figures, with their explanations.

Ripa's *Iconologia* first appeared in Rome without illustrations in 1593. An illustrated version followed in 1602. The work went through numerous editions during the seventeenth and eighteenth centuries, and was translated into many languages. The illustrations were redesigned many times by different artists. A French translation appeared in Paris in 1636, reprinted in 1637 and 1644. Another French edition appeared in Amsterdam in 1698.[24] An edition in Dutch followed the next year. We have quoted the title of the English edition of 1709. The Hertel edition in German (1756-1760) offers illustrations in a baroque or rococo style similar to the engravings in the *Eléments*. Another edition in French by J. B. Boudard was published in Parma in 1759, reprinted in Vienna in 1766. A final eighteenth-century version appeared in London in 1779, prepared by the architect George Richardson, expanded to 'four hundred and twenty-four remarkable subjects, moral and instructive'.[25] This list is far from complete.

23. See *Diderot studies* 16 (1973), pp.159-74. Georges May in his article 'Observations on an allegory; the frontispiece of the *Encyclopédie*' discusses the problems of interpreting allegorical art as well as the arguments for Louis-Philippe May's masonic interpretation.

24. *Iconologie ou explication nouvelle de plusieurs images, emblèmes, et autres figures [...] tirée des recherches et des figures de César Ripa, moralisées par J. Baudoin* (Paris 1644; reprint New York, London 1976).

25. George Richardson, *Iconology or a collection of emblematical figures containing four hundred and twenty-four remarkable subjects* (London 1779; reprint New York, London 1979). His introduction offers a history of Ripa's work. See also the printed catalogue of the Bibliothèque

39

These iconologies had been widely known for more than a century before the publication of the *Eléments de la philosophie de Newton* and flourished for another fifty years after that date. Artists for 200 years would have been familiar with Ripa's *Iconologia*, probably in more than one version. They also knew the many emblem books, also published all over Europe and translated into many languages.[26] Emblem books usually contained illustrations for mottos or short poems. They often were extremely obscure so that only the very erudite or initiated could understand them. One can easily imagine that there were masonic emblem books that only Masons could understand, but such obscurity seems quite foreign to the spirit of Ripa.

The illustrations in the seventeenth-century versions of Ripa show human figures within a small oval. They have the attributes given them in the prose descriptions which have been often shortened to a mere half-dozen lines from the half page or more of the original. Landscape is reduced to a minimum; nothing extraneous is included. This is not the case in the eighteenth-century baroque or rococo versions, where landscape and background are filled in. A second scene in the background may serve as comment on the principal virtue or vice, and *putti* appear performing tasks or holding the attributes associated with the central figure. For example, in the 1756 Hertel version[27] Truth is represented by a female figure with bare breasts and legs. She holds a sun, an open book and a palm branch, and stands with one foot on a globe of the world. Beside her is a *putto* with a mirror and a set of scales. In the background we see Christ preaching to his disciples. The whole volume constantly reveals its South German Catholic origin. Although the illustrations in Voltaire's *Eléments* are certainly not Christian, they are artistically close in conception to the more elaborate baroque illustrations. The draperies and elaborate frames correspond to their frames, floral and architectural detail. Only some of the German illustrations contain *putti*; all the allegorical illustrations in the *Eléments* have them. Geometrical compasses are extremely frequent in Ripa. In the Paris 1643 version Horographie, Iconographie, Considération, Symmétrie, Mesure, Mathé-

nationale under Ripa.

26. See Mario Praz, *Studies in seventeenth-century imagery* (Rome 1964). This volume contains 'A bibliography of emblem books', pp.234-576.

27. Cesare Ripa, *Baroque and rococo pictorial imagery: the 1758-60 Hertel edition of Ripa's 'Iconologia' with 200 engraved illustrations*, edited by Edward A. Maser (New York 1971).

matique, Corographie, Uranie (Astronomie), Théorie, Pratique, Géographie all have compasses, which signify measurement, perfection (the circle drawn with a compass is the perfect form), abstract measurement if the points of the compass point upwards, concrete practicality, the measurement of the material world, if they point downwards. The mirror is an attribute of Abstraction, of Truth and of Science (*Scienza*) 'The Glass [mirror] denotes abstraction, that is to say, by accidents, which the sense comprehends; the understanding comes to know their nature, as we by seeing the accidental forms of things in a glass consider their essence.'[28] Truth has an open book that tells us 'the truth of things may be found in good authors', or as the French version puts it, 'Le livre qu'elle tient ouvert signifie que dans les écrits des bons auteurs qui nous apprennent les sciences, se trouve la vérité des choses' (Ripa, Paris 1644, p.192).

In the twentieth century, iconology as a science may seem rather naive, even simplistic. The fashion for allegories has passed in painting; our poets and artists feel less need to invent physical human shapes for abstractions. The *Encyclopédie* in its short article 'Iconologie' suggests that the 'science' corresponded to a continuing human need: 'Comme les paiens avaient multiplié leurs divinités à l'infini, les poètes et les peintres après eux se sont exercés à revêtir d'une figure apparente des êtres purement chimériques ou à donner une espèce de corps aux attributs divins, aux saints, aux fleuves, aux provinces, aux sciences, aux arts, aux vertus, aux vices, aux passions, aux maladies, etc.' (viii.488).

These allegorical engravings in the *Eléments de la philosophie de Newton* all convey a specific message for which they were designed. They all have to do with study and science, the search for truth. The study is carried out with books and with certain instruments, which belong primarily to geometry: square and compass (in the iconologies the square measures the finite, the concrete, the compass the abstract, the perfect), rule and plumb line. The three sorts of spheres, armillary,[29] terrestrial, and celestial appear frequently in these images, three ways of representing the earth and its relation to the heavens, to the zodiac, the stars, to the solar

---

28. The English edition (London 1709) was prepared by P. Tempest. See p.78.

29. Armillary spheres were of two types. The metal bands that formed them could represent the equator and important meridians on the earth's surface or else these bands represented the orbits of the moon and planets around the earth according to a pre-Copernican view of the universe.

system. They are traditional symbols, not always corresponding to the new Newtonian view. On page 125 a new plate was used for the *vignette* with the 16 *putti*.[30] The one top centre holding a compass and a sort of armillary sphere has a clear circle of stars around his head, not visible the first two times this engraving appeared. He has the three principal attributes of astronomy in the iconologies. The wreath of stars characterises the corresponding female figure representing astronomy in the frontispiece to the *Encyclopédie*.

Voltaire's book is about astronomy and the system of the world, but it is also about light, quite literally about the light from the sun, and how it behaves, how the prism turns white light into spectra of coloured light, how raindrops turn white sunlight into rainbows, how mirrors reflect light, and how our eyes permit us to see, and how eyeglasses can correct our vision. The themes of light, vision and enlightenment are present in the engravings. Large windows admit light to the interior scenes, torches emit light, which, even though held by the cupid-like *putto* are not there to inflame the unsuspecting heart, but rather to reveal the open books or the female personification of science with her raised compass. The *putto*, removing the blindfold that cupid often wears, looks through his compass to the celestial sphere, to the personification of science with her open book, and on to the mirror. The cupid who empties his quiver of compasses and pens onto the ground is more a symbol of mathematics than of love.[31]

Voltaire's book is dedicated to 'madame la marquise du Ch**'. Is not this female figure with compass and open book really Voltaire's celebrated mistress and scientific friend? The reader is invited to think so, by the arrangement of the *vignettes* and *culs-de-lampe* when they appear for the first time. We will probably never know for sure if Voltaire furnished the ideas for the artist and engraver, if he arranged the engravings in the places where they occur, especially for the first time. The two *vignettes* before the two dedications to madame Du Châtelet show essentially the

30. See Harcourt Brown, *Science and the human comedy* (Toronto 1976), p.138. Professor Brown reproduces this *vignette* with the 16 *putti*, pointing out that 'none of the instruments shown are Newtonian, nor do any of the sixteen cherubs appear to be engaged in post-Newtonian scientific exercises'. The attributes identify them rather with the muses and liberal arts as represented in the iconologies.

31. A *putto* with a blindfold or quiver is, of course, cupid. In these engravings cupid is abandoning his erotic activities for other pursuits. In one case he is no longer blind, in the other he keeps compasses and pens in his quiver, not the arrows of love.

Fig. 1: Vignette

Fig. 2: Vignette

Fig. 3: Vignette

Fig. 4: Vignette

Fig. 5: Cul-de-lampe

Fig. 6: Cul-de-lampe

Fig. 7: Cul-de-lampe

Fig. 8: Frontispice

same woman, whom we are invited to identify with her. The first four lines of the *Epître* which are on the same page as the first *vignette* encourage this identification:

> Tu m'appelles à toi vaste et puissant Génie,
> Minerve de la France, immortelle Emilie,
> Disciple de Newton, et de la Vérité,
> Tu pénètres mes sens des feux de ta clarté.[32]

The *cul-de-lampe* at the end of the poem shows us Minerva writing at her desk. A *putto* places the laurel wreath of fame and immortality around her helmet. Is madame Du Châtelet not the 'Minerve de la France' of the poem? Is she not the personification of genius, truth and learning (p.8)?

> Puissai-je auprès de vous, dans ce Temple écarté,
> Aux regards des Français montrer la Vérité [...].
> Le Compas à la main j'en tracerai les traits,
> De mes crayons grossiers je peindrai l'Immortelle.

In the *cul-de-lampe* that immediately follows these lines La Cave portrays her, divine Minerva.

The second *vignette*, with the same female figure with open book on her lap and raised compass, is followed by two sentences which again invite an identification with madame Du Châtelet, in addition to the more obvious identification with Science and Truth (pp.9-10):

Madame,
Ce n'est point ici une marquise, ni une philosophie imaginaire. L'étude solide que vous avez faite de plusieurs nouvelles vérités et le fruit d'un travail respectable, sont ce que j'offre au public pour votre gloire, pour celle de votre sexe, et pour l'utilité de quiconque voudra cultiver sa raison et jouir sans peine de vos recherches.

There is considerable hyperbole on Voltaire's part in these claims, as there is in his statement to Frederick in January 1737, at the very time the copper plates for the *Eléments* were being engraved under Voltaire's supervision: 'J'avois esquissé les principes assez faciles de la philosophie de Neuton et madame du Chastelet avoit sa part à l'ouvrage. Minerve dictoit et j'écrivois' (Best.D1255). In the next sentence Voltaire mentions the designing of the plates in the passage already quoted from this letter. The very fact that he is working so hard with 's-Gravesande's help to

32. The *vignette*, 'à Madame la marquise du Ch**', and these four lines occupy all of page 7.

make his work less unworthy of madame Du Châtelet is proof, however, that she cannot be considered its author and Voltaire only her scribe. The *Eléments de la philosophie de Newton* is Voltaire's tribute to his Lady Newton, a hymn of glory to her, to her sex. The engravings echo the paean of praise to the French Minerva, the divine Emilie of the dedicatory *Epître*. The fact that they are repeated in order through the edition does not change the significance they acquire from their position the first time they are used.

The *cul-de-lampe* (fig. 6), which shows a man in his library reading, could either represent Voltaire, the author, studying science in books prior to writing about Newton, or else the reader enlightening himself by reading the *Eléments de la philosophie de Newton*. As for the attributes held by the *putto*, the lowered compasses suggest practice, rather than theory, or that Newtonianism is based on the measurement of the physical universe, on experiments; the torch is a symbol of learning or enlightenment.

The larger frontispiece (fig. 8), the 'Titre-Planche magnifique' that Ledet calls to our attention is a far more complex work of art, and its impact on the reader is greater coming as it does opposite the title page. In the lower half of the frontispiece a writer, pen in hand, crowned with a laurel wreath, robed in a Roman toga, sandals on his feet, sits at a table in a library, shelves of books beside him. The floor is strewn with books, a piece of paper and geometrical instruments: a square, a parallel rule, a pair of gunner's compasses. To the right we see a terrestrial globe, a sort of quadrant or instrument for measuring angles, and an open book. On a stand to the right of the table top is a geometrical quadrant with plumb line and bob. The same sort of baroque curtains we have observed in the *vignettes* give a theatrical quality to the scene. The upper half of the engraving presents a world of sky and clouds which extends downwards and invades the writer's study. To the left on a throne of clouds sits a man in classical garb, in his right hand a compass resting on a celestial globe. With the index finger of his left hand he points to a band encircling the globe with the signs of the zodiac. To our right, slightly lower than the man, we see a female figure with the same hair style, the same flowing draperies, the same bare left breast as in the *vignettes* throughout the edition. She holds a mirror. She is supported in mid-air by six winged *putti*. Her eyes are fixed in admiration on the man on his cloud throne.

At the top of the engraving there is a ceiling of dark clouds, pierced above the male figure by rays of light which pass behind his head and fall on the lady's mirror. The light in turn is reflected down, not very realistically, into the writer's world, and this light is the element in the design which visually unifies the engraving as a whole with its lower and upper worlds. It falls onto the writer and the table in front of him, particularly onto the sheet of paper on which he is writing. Finally the light extends to the books and objects on the floor, especially to a quarter of the terrestrial globe, where we make out the traditional four parts of the world, so often personified in the iconologies: Europe, Asia, Africa, America.

The *putti*, the cloud throne, the path of the light, which does not obey the laws of reflection of light, the placing of Europe, Asia, Africa, and America all in the same half of the northern hemisphere, the engraving as a whole in fact, all announce its allegorical nature, which demands explanation.

The title page opposite the frontispiece invites us to identify the two males with Newton and Voltaire, Newton above on his cloud, Voltaire at this desk.

ELEMENS
DE LA
PHILOSOPHIE
DE NEUTON
Mis à la portée de tout le monde.
Par M^r. DE VOLTAIRE

Lines in the dedicatory *Epître* give further clues: 'le compas de Newton mesurant l'univers' for example, or the poet's salutation to the moon: 'Newton de ta carrière a marqué les limites', or the reference to the heavens: 'au haut des cieux que Newton s'est soumis'. The poem continually associates Newton with the heavens, the immensity of space. His index finger touches the celestial globe just above the moon in the engraving.

The writer with his crown of laurel leaves is the famous poet-dramatist, who has abandoned his poetic fame for the study of geometry, science, and truth. Again the poem helps us with the explanation. The author has given up the laurels won in the theatre for natural philosophy (p.4):

Je renonce aux lauriers, que longtemps au théâtre
Chercha d'un vain plaisir mon esprit idolâtre [...]

Le charme tout puissant de la philosophie
Elève un esprit sage au-dessus de l'envie.

In the correspondence for this period Voltaire seems obsessed by science and the need to complete the book on Newton. He has no time for the theatre.

It seems unlikely that the faces of the writer and the celestial astronomer were intended as portraits of Voltaire or Newton, or that the reader would recognise them by their features. It is rather their attributes that identify them. The female figure too is first of all identified as truth, or philosophy, or science because of the mirror. She also suggests education, who in the iconologies has bare breasts to suggest her rôle as nourisher, and is illuminated by rays of light from above. But after reading the two dedications we see her also as madame Du Châtelet, the author's muse, the greater-than-human disciple of the superhuman Newton: 'immortelle Emilie, disciple de Newton et de la Vérité, l'auguste Vérité', intermediary between Newton and Voltaire, bearer of light. She is placed in Newton's world, rather than in Voltaire's. She is the means by which the Newtonian truth – rather it is the divine truth, since the light does not originate with Newton but comes from an even higher, but invisible realm above the dark clouds – reaches Voltaire. The *putti* by their presence around her serve to glorify and exalt her, as a host of cherubs would glorify the Virgin in a baroque painting. They hold none of the traditional attributes.

This allegorical frontispiece communicates also the divine nature of Newtonian science. The light of science comes from God. Newton's head is in the pure white light, which is less pure and white by the time it strikes the mirror, and more diffused yet when it reaches Voltaire, who passes it on to the world.

As we have seen, Voltaire had written a final chapter for the *Eléments* on Newton's theological views, which he never let out of his hands. Without it his study of Newtonian science is at least by implication anti-Christian, while preaching a unified universe operating according to intelligible laws dependent on a creator, whose great prophet is Newton. The miracle of the rainbow has been explained by Newton. The irregular motions of the planets have been explained by Newton. His law of universal attraction, the soul of nature, depends, Voltaire argues, directly on the author of nature (*Eléments*, Amsterdam 1738, p.371). In another passage Voltaire argues that the denial of empty space leads to materialism and therefore to atheism, while Newton's view, where empty space exists and matter is finite, leads logically to a belief in God (pp.214-15). In keeping with these arguments the frontispiece reveals the light coming from a divine, although hidden, source. There are parallels in the iconologies, where light breaking through dark clouds and descending to humans is divine. In the 1758-1760 Hertel edition of Ripa Wisdom, Grace, Hope, and Conversion all receive a stream of light from heaven, as the text explains.

In the *Epître* there are echoes of Newton's view of absolute space and the immensity of God, that is, of the theological views Newton developed in the general *scholium* at the end of the *Principia* (p.5) in the lines:

> L'espace qui de Dieu contient l'immensité,
> Voit rouler dans son sein l'Univers limité.

Also Voltaire gives a Newtonian view of God creating the world and of Newton bringing the secrets of the creator into the light (p.5):

> Dieu parle, & le Chaos se dissipe à sa voix;
> Vers un centre commun tout gravite à la fois,
> Ce ressort si puissant l'ame de la Nature,
> Etoit enséveli dans une nuit obscure,
> Le compas de Neuton mesurant l'Univers,
> Leve enfin ce grand voile & les Lieux sont ouverts.

The frontispiece also shows Voltaire the poet illuminating the world by his pen. The torches and large windows in the smaller engravings convey this image of light and enlightenment. The text of the *Eléments* as well often uses poetic images of light to describe understanding, teaching and learning: 'mais l'obscurité des Grecs venait de ce qu'en effet ils n'avaient point de lumière; et les ténèbres de Newton viennent de ce que sa lumière était trop loin de nos yeux. Il a trouvé des vérités: mais il les a cherchées et placées dans un abîme, il faut y descendre et les apporter au grand jour' (p.13).

In addition to portraying the mission of Voltaire in spreading the light to the world, and the role of the Truth-Science-madame Du Châtelet figure as inspirer of the author and bringer of light, the frontispiece is finally and primarily a tribute to Newton himself. The engraving glorifies and praises him. He has the highest place. His head is in the divine light near its source, he is enthroned on his heavenly clouds. Truth stares at him in admiration, as he measures the universe. He seems lost in thought, or else his eyes penetrate beyond the physical universe to the divine truth. Throughout the *Eléments* Voltaire presents us a Newton of heroic proportions, a superhuman, nearly divine figure. Voltaire's admiration is expressed again and again in prose and in verse. After describing one of Newton's experiments on light, Voltaire exclaims, 'J'avoue que je ne peux assez admirer ici cette profondeur de recherche, cette sagacité plus qu'humaine, avec laquelle Newton a poursuivi ces vérités si imperceptibles; il a reconnu par les mesures et par le calcul ces étranges proportions-ci' (p.171). At another point, in introducing attraction as an explanation for the refraction of light Voltaire says, 'Enfin Newton seul a trouvé la véritable raison qu'on cherchait. Sa découverte mérite assurément l'attention de tous les siècles. Car il ne s'agit pas ici seulement d'une propriété particulière à la lumière, quoique ce fût déjà beaucoup; nous verrons que cette propriété appartient à tous les corps de la nature' (p.97). This admiration for Newton reaches its summit after a discussion of the irregularities of the moon's orbit (p.263):

On ne peut s'empêcher d'admirer avec quelle sagacité Newton a démêlé toutes ces inégalités, réglé la marche de cette planète, qui s'était dérobée à toutes les recherches des astronomes; c'est là surtout qu'on peut dire:
Nec propius fas est mortali attingere Divos.[33]

In the dedicatory *Epître* to madame Du Châtelet, Voltaire even asks the heavenly hosts if they are not jealous of the great man (p.6):

Confidens du Très-Haut, Substances éternelles
Qui brûlés de ses feux, qui couvrez de vos aîles
Le Trône où votre Maître est assis parmi vous,
Parlez, du grand Neuton n'étiez-vous point jaloux?

Allegories are open to interpretation. A masonic analysis of these *vignettes, culs-de-lampe* and of the frontispiece might uncover secret significance. I suspect, however, that other meanings for squares, compasses, rules, architectural details, light, would take nothing away from those meanings found in the iconologies and available to the general reading public. Voltaire set out to reach the widest public possible. The volume on its title page claimed that he had put these elements within the understanding of everyone. Even if Ledet rather than Voltaire was responsible for the phrase, 'mis à la portée de tout le monde', masonic secrecy seems inconsistent with Voltaire's purpose.

33. *Eléments*, p.263. This is the final line of Edmund Halley's prefatory ode to Newton's *Principia*.

The *Eléments de la philosophie de Newton* is far more than a sober, mathematical account of Newtonian optics, attraction, and the system of the world. It reflects the fervour of the enthusiast or convert who has found the truth and must spread it to the public. Voltaire is intellectually and emotionally involved in this task. In those months when in Leiden and Amsterdam he was revising his book and supervising its publication, he seemed under a spell, under 'le charme tout puissant de la philosophie' (p.4).

The illustrations to the Ledet edition speak to this enchantment, that extends far beyond the geometrical diagrams and charts, beyond the text itself. The frontispiece and other allegorical engravings are visual renderings of Voltaire's experience. No critic would place the *Eléments de la philosophie de Newton* among Voltaire's greatest works, nor would they rank the art of Folkema, Dubourg, van Schley and La Cave along side that of Dürer and Rembrandt. Nevertheless, these engravings convey a message to anyone who has learned the pictorial language of the iconologies and make of the volume an offering of love and praise to madame Du Châtelet, and a glorification of the great Sir Isaac Newton. The enthusiasm that makes Voltaire abandon the theatre and history for science, keeps him at the feet of 's-Gravesande and in the printing shop with its engravers and printers in early 1737 may not have survived to the following year, when his truncated work appeared without his permission. The earlier commitment to Newton is evident throughout the volume. The engravings, especially the frontispiece, capture Voltaire's mood. His exact rôle in their design and execution may never be known. However, he was there as these pages came from the press. In them we sense the same obsession that caused him to write to Jeanne Françoise Quinault as he began the composition of the Eléments: 'il y a dans le monde un diable de Newton, qui a trouvé précisément combien le soleil pèse, et de quelle couleur sont les rayons qui composent la lumière. Cet étrange homme me tourne la tête. Daignez m'écrire pour me rendre aux muses' (Best.D1133).

Tragedy and didacticism: the case of Voltaire

EVA JACOBS

THAT Voltaire ultimately failed as a tragedian is beyond doubt. In spite of brave attempts by a very small band of devoted scholars to rescue from oblivion a part or the whole of his immense output of dramatic tragedies, the general reader, the theatre-going public, the academic establishment itself, have remained obstinately persuaded that Voltairian tragedy is a corpse beyond resuscitation, and unworthy even of a serious post-mortem. The few who are inclined to contest the justice of the final burial can point to the almost incredible vigour and success of Voltaire's plays during his lifetime, in France and throughout Europe, and question whether the admiration and popularity these achieved can have been wholly misdirected. It is tempting to assert, in view of the incontrovertible historical fact of Voltaire's recognised eminence as a tragedian in his own times, that if we were to explore his tragedies with the sympathy and attention they must deserve, their dramatic and poetic qualities, so clear to his contemporaries, would somehow be revealed. But it is perhaps more realistic, and probably more valuable, to try to discover what it is that to the modern sensibility makes Voltaire's tragedies so irremediably flawed.

The opening lines of Jacques Truchet's illuminating study *La Tragédie classique en France* (Paris 1975) suggest possible approaches to an investigation of this kind: 'Pour l'historien, la tragédie classique est un genre littéraire; pour l'homme de théâtre et pour le grand public, un répertoire; pour le philosophe, une essence ou une catégorie' (p.7). The second of these three descriptions of classical tragedy has long ceased to be relevant to any discussion of Voltaire's lasting contribution to the genre. His decline as an acted playwright by the beginning of the twentieth century was as absolute as had been his reign at the Comédie-Française during the eighteenth. Occasional attempts at revivals, the last of which was an expensive and doomed production of *L'Orphelin de la Chine* at the Comédie-Française in 1965, have served only to confirm the theatre-going public in its neglect of this aspect of an otherwise revered author. The empirical fact of theatrical failure is probably not worth investigating here, since the more significant failure is clearly that of Voltairian tragedy as belonging to 'un genre littéraire' or 'une essence'. Drama which is no longer alive in the theatre may yet be recognised as being of literary merit, though in fact surprisingly few examples of this dichotomy spring to mind. I shall therefore leave aside the question of Voltairian tragedy on the stage, and concentrate on the literary and 'philosophical' aspects of Voltaire's ultimate failure.

The 'nature' of tragedy as an essence or a category, to use Jacques Truchet's terms, has long been, and continues to be, explored, but Voltaire is virtually ignored in books that address themselves to questions relating to the principles of tragedy. T. R. Henn's *The Harvest of tragedy* (London 1976) and D. D. Raphael's 1959 Mahlon Powell Lectures, printed as *The Paradox of tragedy* (London 1960), fail to mention him; Oscar Mandel's *A definition of tragedy* (New York 1961) cites only Voltaire's opinion of Hamlet's character; George Steiner's well-known contribution to the discussion, *The Death of tragedy* (London 1961), pays due attention to Corneille and Racine, but Voltaire as a dramatist gets a couple of derogatory remarks. Geoffrey Brereton's coherent and closely argued study, *Principles of tragedy* (London 1968), devotes several pages to Voltaire, as might be anticipated from the writer's special concern with French literature, but although the title of his book would lead one to expect the material on Voltaire to centre on his tragedies, it is in fact the relation of the *Poème sur le désastre de Lisbonne* and *Candide* to the 'principles of tragedy' which receives all the attention. This is the more curious in that Dr Brereton's book is primarily, though not exclusively, about dramatic tragedy, and where there is a long development on a non-dramatic writer, Pascal, for instance, there is at least the excuse that Pascal wrote no plays. As for Voltaire's tragedies, they are dismissed in a few words: 'His plays, at least in intention, were exemplary, and the fact that they assumed certain fixed moral standards is enough to disqualify them as tragedies according to the evidence we have so far assembled' (p.128). Dr Brereton's 'evidence' leads him to conclude that tragedy is by definition exploratory and empirical, asking questions and not offering answers, and thus without the possibility of didactic value. A related point had already been made by Steiner, though in a discussion of Ibsen and not Voltaire: 'In tragedy, there are no temporal remedies. The point cannot be stressed too often. Tragedy speaks not of secular dilemmas which may be resolved by rational innovation, but of the unalterable bias towards inhumanity and destruction in the drift of the world' (p.291). Indeed, although the 'essence of tragedy' remains a subject of lively debate, on this point, at least, there seems to be unanimity among critics. Agreed to be essential in this strict sense of the word are the notion of inexorable fate (however defined), and the concept of tragedy as irreparable, to use Steiner's phrase (p.8). If either the author or the action of the play offer possible or actual remedies, 'true' tragedy is deemed not to have been attained, nor to be attainable. Didacticism rules out tragedy by definition, therefore, in that it supposes, even if it does not always propose, remedies: and remedies deny the notion of inexorable fate. The disqualification of Voltaire as a tragedian is thus confirmed, explicitly by Brereton, implicitly by Steiner and other theoreticians of tragedy, whose silence on the subject of the writer considered by his contemporaries to be the equal of Corneille and Racine, is thus explained.

The view that the playwright who has a message is incapable of tragedy is offered in a more narrowly defined version by some historians of literature, who claim that it is in particular the philosophy of the Enlightenment, characterised by optimism about man's potential for happiness on this earth, that is in fundamental contradiction to any coherent tragic vision of the universe. This is a simpler, sharper, and in many ways more attractive general theory for explaining Voltaire's failure as a tragedian than the looser didactic theory. It concludes the developed analysis of philosophical propaganda in Voltairian tragedy offered by Ronald S. Ridgway:

Voltaire n'avait pas tort d'exprimer une philosophie sur la scène. Mais cette philosophie est aussi éloignée que possible de l'univers tragique qu'il voulait évoquer. Il y a là une contradiction fondamentale entre le génie de Voltaire et son moyen d'expression. Sa tentative de prolonger un genre qui ne pouvait survivre dans le climat intellectuel du siècle des lumières était condamnée inéluctablement à l'insuccès.[1]

This analysis implies, of course, a basic acceptance of an 'essentialist' view of tragedy, similar to, if narrower than, that suggested by Brereton, Steiner and so many others.

The common acceptance of the opinion that tragedy and didacticism cannot co-exist obliges those who believe that Voltaire's tragedies should be added to the list of that writer's permanent and living contribution to

1. Ronald S. Ridgway, *La Propagande philosophique dans les tragédies de Voltaire*, Studies on Voltaire 15 (Genève 1961), pp.239-40.

world literature, to meet this impediment head on. Jacques Truchet quotes in part Ridgway's conclusion given above, points, perhaps rather irrelevantly for the purposes of his argument, to Voltaire's enormous success with his contemporaries, and claims that 'l'idée qu'une tragédie ne peut être philosophique (au sens, encore une fois, du XVIIIe siècle) parce qu'elle doit être métaphysique, repose sur un *a priori* qui résisterait à peine à une étude objective du théâtre grec, duquel elle semble tirer son origine' (p.158). Later in his book, in a fascinating chapter entitled 'Aujourd'hui', when talking more generally about the modern selectivity regarding 'great' French tragedians, which in effect excludes all writers who practised that genre in the seventeenth and eighteenth centuries except for Corneille and Racine, Truchet claims again that it is due to 'la prise en charge de la tragédie par la métaphysique, surtout vers le moment de la seconde guerre mondiale'.[2] English critics are praised by Truchet for an ironical reaction to abstract and metaphysical views of French tragedy, although in fact Geoffrey Brereton, quoted with approval by Truchet, does reach conclusions as to those principles, as I have shown, and these conclusions explicitly exclude Voltairian tragedy (p.184). Truchet's preference, even if he does not state the point so baldly, would seem to be for an empirical definition of French tragedy as a genre, opening the door for the rehabilitation of Voltaire, who undoubtedly practised the genre. But this approach merely begs the question, offering a tautology (Voltaire was a tragedian because he wrote tragedy), while leaving the equally empirical fact of his long-term failure untouched. Thus the first of Jacques Truchet's descriptions of tragedy, 'pour l'historien, la tragédie classique est un genre littéraire', turns out not to be very fruitful in an attempt to discover why Voltaire failed as a tragedian, and I do not propose to investigate the matter further along those lines. But the question of tragedy as an essence or a category remains a tantalising one, in spite of Truchet's desire to reduce its importance.

A different approach to Voltaire as a tragedian is taken by Jack Vrooman.[3] After a detailed description of central elements in five of

2. p.173. Truchet also blames the emergence, towards 1955, of the 'nouvelle critique', but since its effect on the consideration of Voltaire as a tragedian has been negligible, I do not intend to pursue this suggestion.

3. Jack Rochford Vrooman, *Voltaire's theatre: the cycle from 'Œdipe' to 'Mérope'*, Studies on Voltaire 75 (Genève 1970).

Voltaire's most important tragedies, Vrooman appears to conclude that 'the reasons for Voltaire's immense success as a dramatist among his contemporaries are the very reasons that later critics cite as the cause of his ultimate failure [...] Voltaire simply did not satisfy the tastes of a later day' (pp.190, 192). But a further and final chapter consists of an eloquent attempt to persuade us as modern readers that we are wrong. This chapter offers conviction and passion, but little analysis, and is, in fact, conducted in entirely abstract terms, with hardly a mention of specific tragedies. It is curiously unpragmatic – as sermons perhaps tend to be – and concentrates either on ignoring the facts or on claiming that they ought to be otherwise. Pronouncements such as 'the plays are still capable of producing aesthetic pleasure' (p.206) can obviously not be proved to be inexact, but equally obviously mean something quite different in practical reality from such statements applied to Racine or Shakespeare. Faced with the following assertion: 'It seems impossible that one could react indifferently or experience boredom when confronted by plays that continue to reflect life and also contain the power to affect it' (p.206) one is ineluctably drawn to Vrooman's epigraph to his concluding chapter, itself a quotation from Voltaire: 'il est impossible que toute une nation se trompe en fait de sentiment, et ait tort d'avoir du plaisir' (p.195) and tempted to turn it against his own hopeful argument. The virtual unanimity of negative opinion regarding Voltaire's tragedies in fact makes some of Vrooman's final remarks seem slightly comical in their optimism: 'As drama they are still capable of stirring the emotions and stimulating the intelligence [...] As art they remain dynamic' (p.207). But Voltaire's tragedies are not undiscovered masterpieces: they are a rejected part of the corpus of a great writer. As such they will always be appealing to specialists, but that appeal is very different from the appeal of universally recognised artistic excellence. His plays can be dissected, explained, or placed in a biographical, historical or theatrical context with pleasure and profit. But no amount of such effort will alter the public's perception that Voltaire failed as a tragedian.

Neither Truchet nor Vrooman appear to offer a convincing reply to the generally held opinion that this failure is due in large part to the intrinsic incompatibility of tragedy and didacticism. Truchet's dismissal of this view as unjustifiably *a priori*, and Vrooman's implicit denial of its relevance to a serious appraisal of Voltaire's achievement as a tragic playwright, do not remove it from its central place as the most plausible of the explanations given for the undoubted fact of Voltaire's eclipse as a tragedian. I intend to examine in greater detail the proposition that tragedy and didacticism are incompatible, and to try to establish whether it is indeed precisely Voltaire's attempt to ally the two that offends modern sensibility. I shall, of course, bear in mind the two major 'essentialist' formulations of the objection to the marriage of tragedy and didacticism that I indicated: the general one that tragedy must be irreparable, and the narrower one that enlightenment optimism precludes 'true' tragedy. But I propose to use Voltaire's own tragedies as a basis for this examination, rather than to extrapolate from the example of other tragedians. It is obviously impossible to discuss all, or even a significant proportion, of Voltaire's twenty-seven tragedies in an article, and rather than choose those that might most straightforwardly bear out my argument, but which might not be entirely typical of Voltaire's output, I have decided to examine the three that are generally thought to be at the pinnacle of his artistic achievement in that genre. These are *Zaïre* (1732), *Mahomet* (1741) and *Mérope* (1743), and they have the added advantage of being easily available in the Pléiade *Théâtre du XVIIIe siècle* (vol. i), edited by Jacques Truchet (Paris 1972).

Zaïre tells the touching story of a young slave in the harem of the sultan of Jerusalem, loved by her master and about to become his (only!) wife, when she rediscovers her Christian family and is persuaded to put off the wedding until she has been baptised. A series of misunderstandings leads to her murder at the hands of her jealous lover, who then learns that the 'other man' is in fact her brother. Structurally, the play neither directly asks questions nor offers answers, to recall Dr Brereton's analysis (see above, p.52). This is because chance plays the key role in the structure of the tragedy. Zaïre's rediscovery of her family happens at precisely the 'right' moment, just in time to prevent the happy wedding of the deserving couple; the misunderstanding between them is contrived by unnecessary withholding of information all round; a letter is intercepted which, fortunately for the 'tragedy', if unfortunately for the characters, omits the only word which would enlighten the hero and avert the catastrophe. It is, of course, impossible to ask meaningful questions about chance, which is why French classical tragedy had developed the sophisticated aesthetic doctrine of *vraisemblance*. *Vraisemblance* excludes chance completely, theoretically at least, from tragic drama. Nor can answers be given about how to deal with human problems caused by chance, since its definition is precisely that it is unpredictable. The result is that the reader of *Zaïre*,[4] who may indeed be moved by this sad story, in the way that any reader may be moved by a newspaper account of an unexpected disaster to individuals, is not able to absorb the play and its meaning, and to convert it to his own use. Is the play then not didactic? I would maintain that strictly speaking, as a play, it is not. This will explain one of the more curious historical facts about it, which is that ever since its appearance the meaning of *Zaïre* has been interpreted in widely differing ways.[5] These interpretations range from the view that it is a 'Christian sermon', to the view that it is aggressively anti-religious, or even specifically anti-Catholic. In order to explain the difficulty of interpretation, it has been suggested that Voltaire simply failed in his didactic intentions, and even that, in this tragedy, he had none. I would argue rather that there is a great deal of didacticism connected with *Zaïre*, but that it is not intrinsic to the action of the play. Looked at in terms of what might be learned from the play by an unprejudiced notional reader, because didacticism cannot cope with the variety of prior beliefs among real readers, it is clear that in *Zaïre* Voltaire does offer much food for thought. Two attractive, blameless individuals are caught up in a conflict that is rooted in the history of the group to which each belongs. Christian Zaïre and Moslem Orosmane are separated from each other by the carnage wreaked by two religions which both believe that they possess knowledge of absolute truth concerning God and his demands from mankind. If man's desire for happiness in this life is legitimate – which for Voltaire as for all the *philosophes* it certainly was – religious dogma, which is the ultimate cause of the tragedy, is an obstacle which could be removed from the affairs of men if they would learn intellectual modesty, reasonableness and tolerance.

There is no doubt that an unprejudiced reader is tempted by the presentation of the material of the play towards generalisations regarding religion, the futility of war, the individual as the prisoner of history and so on. The murder of Zaïre by Orosmane is more significant as an example of the continuing carnage between Christian and Moslem than as the result of Orosmane's unreasoning jealousy, although structurally,

4. I use the word 'reader' advisedly, since the acid test of French classical tragedy, a test that Voltaire himself wished to be applied to his own works, is how it stands up to careful and repeated reading.

5. See Voltaire, *Zaïre*, ed. Eva Jacobs (London 1975), pp.30ff.

within the play, it is Orosmane's jealousy (poorly modelled on Othello's) that is the cause. Voltaire is totally unsuccessful in making the reader believe in this jealousy, so much so that he has to add a more immediate cause, the intercepted letter, as a provocation to murder. The reader's attention is thus focused on chance in the structure of the play, with a resultant absence of any sense of significance in the action as such. The effect is one of curious dislocation. We gain a great awareness of the importance of the events for mankind in general, for our understanding of the world in which we live, for our hopes of a better life. But this has very little to do with our emotional response to the action and the characters. For Voltaire himself the real significance (perhaps the real 'tragedy') of his play lies in history, in the known and documented propensity of men to irrationality and bloody conflict. But underlying propositions or analyses about man and his history do not make for tragedy which, being a sub-set of drama, must be about individuals. I do not mean simply that the writer should have the gift of psychological portrayal, though that is obviously useful, but that what he has to say should concern itself primarily with the individual, his relation to the world and his personal fate. The structure of *Zaïre*, based as it is on chance, allows for little in the way of meaningful interpretation of an individual's existential situation, but offers interesting general considerations. The lessons of history fail to become tragedy, precisely because the focus is on generalisation. The Enlightenment was, of course, given to generalisation on a grand scale; the sociological view of man it created depends on the belief that generalisations are valid. It does not matter here whether the conclusions of those generalisations were optimistic or pessimistic. In spite of some disagreement among historians, it is still usually said, and I would agree, that broadly speaking, the enlightenment view of man and his potential was optimistic. It is not, however, the optimism itself that makes philosophical tragedy impossible, but, as we see in *Zaïre*, the shift in the main focus from the portrayal of individuals to general propositions about mankind.

In any case, whatever else it is, *Zaïre* is not optimistic. It certainly does not offer answers, or even the hope that men will cease to slaughter one another for unprovable ideas. To point to folly is not to show belief in remedies. Enlightenment optimism as such, then, cannot be blamed for the long-term failure of *Zaïre*. What about the other 'essential' point identified by theoreticians of tragedy, that is the need in tragedy for a sense of inexorable fate leading to catastrophe? I have shown how chance plays the vital role in the working out of the plot, and it is tempting to point simply to this glaring defect to explain the dissatisfaction felt with *Zaïre* as tragic drama. But in many of Corneille's tragedies, even if chance as such is not the basis of the structure, there is no sense of inexorable fate leading to catastrophe, so that it is difficult to put too much weight on this point. I prefer to suggest as a working hypothesis the idea that a tragedy cannot function when the focus of interest and ultimate significance of the play is outside the action and its effect on the individuals portrayed, and when, as I have shown in the case of *Zaïre*, structure and meaning are divorced.

Whose tragedy is *Mahomet*? Certainly not Mahomet's own. His villainous machinations meet with complete success. The loss of Palmire by her suicide leads him to a rather unconvincing cry of sorrow, brief and uncharacteristic as it is, followed by a determination to benefit from the fruits of wickedness. Evil triumphs dramatically, much as it had done in Crébillon's *Atrée et Thyeste*, though the revenge motive in fact makes Atrée, for all his abominable deeds, a more human character than Mahomet. The chain of crime and vengeance gives a more authentic tragic resonance to Crébillon's play than does the cold ambition of Mahomet, with his manipulation of men and ideas for his own purposes. Are Séide and Palmire candidates for heroes of tragic stature? I would argue that they are not, being merely pawns in Mahomet's game. Terrible things happen to them: they kill their own father, and both die, the one by poison and the other by her own hand. But they are never more than puppets worked by Mahomet, lacking in both choice and responsibility. As victims of a deception of which the audience is made aware early on in the play, a deception perpetrated by a character of far more commanding stature, they hardly exist in their own right. The manipulation of Othello by Iago, of which the audience is equally aware, focuses attention on Othello, but that of Séide and Palmire by Mahomet focuses it back on Mahomet. In this play, Voltaire has succeeded in structuring the plot without having recourse to chance (coincidence being a lesser sin), but once again the real tragedy lies outside the play. Whether one believes that the play is a veiled attack on Christianity as a whole, or on Jansenism, or on fanaticism and intolerance in general, the fact remains that both the tragedy and the centre of interest lie beyond our perception of the fate of the individuals concerned, and that the true significance of it all is in history and abstraction, rather than in the drama itself. For Mahomet, the outcome is a triumph; for his victims, it is a tragedy only in the loosest sense of a sad event, but we are awakened once again to an understanding of men's propensity to act irrationally, to believe what they are told, to hate those with different beliefs to the point of murder. *Mahomet* is one instance of these general propositions, which history bears out with appalling frequency. This is why it has been possible for critics to say with conviction that Voltaire is *really* talking about Christianity or, anachronistically, about Hitlerism or Stalinism or anything else. He is, of course, in a sense talking about all of these, with his usual analytical intelligence. But the sense of the tragic fate of individuals is again absent, or at least totally subordinate to the reader's awareness of historical analysis and abstraction. Voltaire openly avows his central purpose in the main title he himself gave the play: *Le Fanatisme*. One can hardly imagine Corneille entitling *Horace* 'Le Patriotisme', or Racine entitling *Britannicus*, say, 'L'Ambition'. Not just because such speculation applied to seventeenth-century tragedy would be absurd, but because such titles would give very little idea of the plays themselves. *Le Fanatisme*, on the other hand, does give a precise account of the focus of *Mahomet*. Mahomet himself is not a fanatic at all, but the play offers a penetrating account of how fanaticism is created, fostered and used by unscrupulous leaders for their own ends, and of how weak individuals become the most violent fanatics. The historical lesson is there, the warning for the present and the future, even the tragedy of human kind, but not the tragedy of the characters presented. Once again, it is not enlightenment optimism that prevents the modern reader from having any sense of the tragic. There is no optimism at all in the play. If any is discernible, it is in connection with the play, in Voltaire's presumable belief that there is some point in using drama to try to influence the public to an awareness of such questions. Nor is it the suggestion of remedies that prevents the sense of the tragic, for *Mahomet*, in showing the triumph of evil, offers no remedies. But the play is an excuse for ideas, and more straightforwardly so than *Zaïre*. They are given quite successful dramatic form, in that the plot is skilfully handled, but the characters and what happens to them fade into insignificance when compared to the weight of the ideas.

Although *Mérope* was not staged until 1743, Voltaire completed the first draft of the play in 1736 or 1737, before writing *Mahomet*. For a few years he was really thinking about both plays at the same time, which is curious, since *Mahomet* is Voltaire's most patently 'philosophic' play, while *Mérope* is generally considered to be his 'purest' tragedy. In the light of the modern 'essentialist' view of tragedy, which announces the absolute incompatibility of didacticism and 'true' tragedy, *Mérope* could be expected to represent the writer's lasting claim to a place among the great tragedians of world literature. It is a claim that eighteenth-century audiences would gladly have supported, for *Mérope* was a huge success with Voltaire's contemporaries. Nevertheless, in spite of the apparent advantage of a play without didacticism for the rehabilitation of Voltairian tragedy, Jack Vrooman, who has undertaken that rehabilitation, does present *Mérope* as carrying an underlying didactic message, but one much more in line with modern expectations for tragedy: 'Having cried out against man's injustice to man in his polemical play [*Mahomet*], one which mirrored the playwright's personal hatred of fanaticism and was designed to evoke anger on the part of the audience, Voltaire now attempts to reconcile the human predicament with divine justice' (pp.157-58). The chronology of the two plays does not allow for this compensatory interpretation of *Mérope*, but the notion that *Mérope* is primarily about divine justice is an interesting one, developed further by Vrooman (p.166):

The progression from *Zaïre* to *Mahomet* showed with increasing clarity the degree of human responsibility for man's misfortunes, and sought by a rational approach to attribute suffering to natural [*sic*] causes. *Mérope* marks a decided change in both interpretation and focus. Voltaire now shows supernatural forces to be responsible for shaping human destiny [...] The role of chance, which in varying degrees contributed to the outcome of his earlier plays, is now greatly reduced. It is replaced by a concept of fate that approaches that of the Greeks.

Vrooman goes on to make large claims for the play (pp.170, 171):

In *Mérope* one finds a reconciliation between human moral codes and divine justice [...] The gods may allow injustice to triumph momentarily; but in the ultimate scheme of things, man gains through suffering the knowledge that only through submission to the will of the gods and the acceptance of a universe that lies beyond his control can he overcome misery and achieve true happiness [...] Voltaire, who as the champion of reason had shown religion to be the creation of an impostor in *Mahomet*, turns in *Mérope* to the revelation of a religious feeling that combines admiration and resignation before a universe that does not admit to explanation through reason alone [...] A calm reigns at the end of *Mérope*. There is an extraordinary feeling of awe before the religious aspect of the universe and a transformation of pity and fear into joy through the medium of art.

Posterity, with the notable exception of the writer of these eulogies, continues to remain blind to such beauty. It is perhaps arguable that Voltaire did have some intention of the kind that Vrooman describes so eloquently, but in art, as in life, good intentions are not enough. *Mérope* shows the downfall of a wicked usurper, Polyphonte, who is put to death at the wedding altar by a strong young man, the legitimate heir to the throne, whose mother he is about to marry against her will. The gods are said to have reserved this fifteen-year long vengeance for this moment of the final triumph of good over evil, and the play ends with the young man's expression of his gratitude to them: 'Elle [la gloire] n'est point à moi: cette gloire est aux dieux: / Ainsi que le bonheur, la vertu nous vient d'eux.'[6] It is possible that Voltaire's deism, still generally optimistic in the late 1730s and early 1740s, finds expression here, but that is a long way from saying that the tragedy itself in any meaningful way exemplifies these lines. In drama, the action of the gods is perceived only when symbolic of the inexorable fate of men. Polyphonte does not suffer death as the inevitable result of his own wicked actions (weakness arising through remorse, for instance, or the climax of hatred built up through the years), but merely as the outcome of Mérope's son turning up just at the very moment when he has finally decided to force her to marry him. Oreste commits a very similar murder at the wedding altar of Pyrrhus and Andromaque, but Pyrrhus's fate, stemming from the rejection of Hermione and his abandoned passion for Andromaque, along with his carelessness for the political and personal consequences of his desires, is in a very different sense from that of Polyphonte the result of his actions. The whole structure of Racine's play leads to Pyrrhus's inevitable death, whereas the series of *coups de théâtre* offered by Voltaire in *Mérope* allows for any outcome the author chooses to present. To speak of fate in the case of *Andromaque* is entirely plausible. But the gods, in the case of *Mérope*, are abstractions, an idea only, and not a very convincing one, divorced from the whole structure of the play. To that degree, *Mérope* is a less satisfactory play than *Zaïre* or *Mahomet*, where the ideas are at least more interesting and much more fully worked out in their own right.

It does not seem entirely fair, in any case, to examine so solemnly the

6. *Théâtre du XVIIIe siècle*, ed. Jacques Truchet, i.869.

superficial notion of divine justice in *Mérope*. Voltaire's contemporaries did not venture into such exalted realms in their praise of the play. What impressed them was the way in which the author had met the self-imposed challenge of writing a tragedy which totally excluded the presentation of sexual love, his conduct of the plot, his fine versification, and, above all, his portrayal of a middle-aged mother as a heroine. He certainly seems to have structured his play deliberately so as to give his heroine the maximum opportunity to display her feelings as a mother. In Maffei's play, which was his immediate model, Mérope is twice on the point of killing her son, not knowing, of course, who he is. The first time, she is prevented from doing so by the young man's mention of his supposed father, Polydore, and by the entry of Polyphonte. The second time, she is ready to kill him with an axe as he lies sleeping, but Polydore is fortunately there, hiding, and he reveals the young man's identity. Voltaire eliminated the second of these scenes and invented instead an episode where it is Polyphonte who is about to kill the young man, ostensibly to please Mérope, who has previously sought his death; meanwhile, Mérope has learnt of his true identity and bursts out with one of Voltaire's most famous one-liners, 'Barbare! il est mon fils', in a moment considered by Voltaire's contemporaries to express the height of tragic emotion. To the psychological tension generated in the audience by the question already found in Maffei's play: 'Will the mother kill her own son?', Voltaire has added the new question: 'Will she watch silent while her son is being killed?' One is reminded rather of the endless permutations on the subject of love concocted by the *précieux*, postulating more and more extraordinary situations. The idea of *the* mother, looked at from all angles, overwhelms the portrayal of *a* mother. The same tendency towards abstraction as was discerned in *Zaïre* and *Mahomet* is present here. While *Mérope* is not didactic in the usual sense of offering explicit or implicit 'philosophical' propaganda, it suffers from the same fault as the other two plays in focusing the attention on abstraction rather than on individuals.

The object of my enquiry has been to try to establish why Voltairian tragedy fails to make any æsthetic appeal to the modern sensibility. In spite of the temptation to adopt the ready-made answer, the assumptions of 'essentialist' views of tragedy, so justly criticised by Jacques Truchet for their apriorism, do not in fact appear to offer 'rules' for tragedy that Voltaire very obviously contravened on every occasion. I have selected three of Voltaire's plays, chosen on the basis of their availability rather than in terms of any thesis, and examined them in relation to the two central 'essentialist' views that seem most immediately applicable to Voltairian tragedy, and that have indeed been adopted to explain its long-term failure (see above, pp.53 and 54). The broad theory states that tragedy must be irreparable, the narrower one that enlightenment optimism is fundamentally anti-tragic in its conception of man and the world. It has thus been easily concluded that the didacticism at the core of Voltairian tragedy prevents it from being 'true' tragedy. But the didacticism of *Zaïre* and *Mahomet* does not extend to remedies, and both tragedies may properly be thought of as irreparable. Such possibility of reparation as there is lies well outside the action of each play. *Mérope*, the least didactic of the plays, may be said to offer reparation in the shape of a happy ending, but very little existential meaning can be read into it, in spite of Vrooman's efforts to persuade us of its religious significance. If, more narrowly, it is the optimism of the Enlightenment that precludes the tragic spirit, then neither *Zaïre* nor *Mahomet* are at all optimistic, and *Mérope* is optimistic only in the most superficial sense of that happy ending. Neither 'essentialist' theory, then, excludes these three tragedies. I have tried to replace 'essentialist' arguments by more empirical ones, even though they may themselves lead to what I hope is a more refined 'essentialist' theory.

I would argue that it is not 'reparability' as such, nor enlightenment optimism, that prevent Voltaire's plays from arousing tragic emotion, but rather the fact that in his plays the ideas stand outside and finally overwhelm the action. We are less interested in what happens to the individuals, than in what the action signifies. The tragedies, although superficially about people, appeal ultimately to the intellect rather than the emotions. This is not just because Voltaire is deficient in an ability to 'peindre les âmes', as is so often and so justly, said, but primarily because his interests lie elsewhere: in pointing the lessons of history, above all, or, less obviously, as in the case of *Mérope*, in exploring a 'condition' in the sense that Diderot was to use that word. But Diderot rightly saw that tragedy has to be about individuals.[7] This, to him, made it an unsatisfactory genre, as he believed his didactic object needed generalised characters to exemplify his ideas. It seems that Diderot was

7. Diderot, *Entretiens sur Le Fils naturel*, in *Œuvres esthétiques*, ed. Paul Vernière (Paris 1965), p.140.

probably wrong in imagining that any kind of satisfactory serious drama can be achieved on the basis of generalised characters; his own failure as a dramatist, when he attempted to put his ideas into practice, certainly does not inspire confidence in his theories.

It is undeniably Voltaire's didactic intentions that made him conceive the characters and structure of his plays in the way he did. It remains, therefore, a distinct theoretical possibility that didacticism and tragedy are incompatible, though this question needs extensive exploration. It must be remembered, for instance, that didactic intentions are at the heart of the theory of seventeenth-century French classical tragedy. But since neither 'reparability' nor optimism give a precise description of the didacticism of the three plays I have discussed, I venture to offer a more refined 'essentialist' view of tragedy. Like the two 'essentialist' theories I have examined, it too is negative. It appears to be easier to say what tragedy must not be, than what it is. Excluded from tragedy are plays where the audience perceives that the focus of the writer's attention is on general ideas rather than on individual destiny, where the ideas do not immediately and necessarily arise from the dramatic structure of the play, where an effort towards abstraction on the part of the audience is needed in order to draw maximum significance from the events. *Zaïre* and *Mahomet* illustrate this quite clearly; *Mérope*, hardly a didactic play, still shows Voltaire's tendency towards generalisation.

I myself am far from believing that the conclusion I have reached offers a sufficient answer to the question I have asked as to why Voltairian tragedy fails to appeal to the modern sensibility. But it is a necessary answer. Grave also are Voltaire's purely literary defects: poetry which is at times sublime, but at others appallingly trite or careless; unconvincing or inconsistent characterisation; complex and sometimes incredible plots – the lists of his failings is endless. To speak of his qualities, and they, too, are many, is not to my purpose here. But I am inclined to think that any amount of polishing of the verse, of restructuring of the events, of taking advice from friends, all of which Voltaire did, would not have helped. Voltaire failed to achieve a true identity of message and character, of meaning and structure in his plays. The truth is that the ideas interest us, but the plays, as dramatic machines, do not engage us. Voltaire's contemporaries, perhaps because they were innocent of 'essentialist' theories of tragedy, were evidently easier to please; but who can deny that posterity has the absolute right to judge?

The burlesque as a philosophical principle in Voltaire's *contes*

R. J. HOWELLS

THE Enlightenment may be said to be, in various ways, 'reductionist'. Reductionist in its French classical concern for stripping away the inessentials in literary form and content. It inherits the social orientation of its writing. Classical brevity becomes Enlightenment wit. It still works with univerals such as 'le cœur humain' or 'le goût'. It cleaves to absolutes like nature and reason, despite altering their meanings, and seeks for new simplicities behind the varieties of practice. Here, however, we begin to move into a reductionism of the opposite kind. General theories are confronted by particular facts. Reductionism means experimentation and the scientific method. It is a suspicion of all abstract systems, an insistence on the concrete and the immediate, on the evidence of the senses. We perceive the authentic literary expression of the age not in the high genres of verse tragedy and epic but in their lower counterparts of prose comedy and narrative fiction. The burlesque in Voltaire corresponds to this second sense of reduction. But it is dependent on the first. Like all burlesque, it operates both within and against the received norms of elevated discourse.

The burlesque is a comic practice whose principal or immediate reference is to high literature. Genette, calling it a 'travestissement satirique', treats it as a subclass of literary works. His strict formalist definition requires that it be the textual transposition of a classical epic, conforming to the canonical model which is Scarron's verse burlesque of the *Aeneid*, the *Virgile travesti* (1648 etc.).[1] Antoine Adam, and Francis Bar, also centre their accounts of the burlesque on the literary production of the French mid-seventeenth century.[2] But they admit texts that do not derive from any other single work, and include lyric verse, narrative prose and the comic theatre (Saint-Amant, Sorel, Scarron, Cyrano,

1. *Palimpsestes* (Paris 1982), pp.64-73.
2. A. Adam, 'Note sur le burlesque', *XVIIe siècle* 4 (1949), pp.81-91; F. Bar, *Le Genre burlesque en France au XVIIe siècle* (Paris 1960).

Furetière and indeed Molière). Adam cites the contemporary Naudé describing the burlesque as 'l'explication des choses les plus sérieuses par les expressions tout à fait plaisantes et ridicules'. For Bar it is a mixture of high and low registers: a style, which can be found not necessarily in a whole work but within a phrase.[3] I shall work from this stylistic criterion, though stressing the primary or normative value of the 'high' level. My treatment of Voltaire's writing will focus on the phrase. But it will argue that the consistent double discourse which we find there is also that of the 'conte' as a whole.

Finally, can we relate the burlesque of the mid-seventeenth century to a particular philosophy? Bar treats it as an aesthetic phenomenon, suggesting parallels both with the 'grotesqueries' of the baroque and with 'popular' genre painting such as that of the Dutch. Adam too notes the 'familiar' element, but also the wit, the parodic treatment of myth and a link with freethought. Certainly some of its practitioners were 'libertins' of sceptical and even materialist inclination (the earlier Sorel, Cyrano, probably Molière). Others, notably Scarron, were not. What they share is an ambivalence towards poetic and elevated discourse (which any form of comic rewriting implies). Objectively, if not by authorial intention, burlesque writing functions as a form of demystification. The burlesque deconstructs. Naudé's remark is striking. 'Explication' is from 'ex-plicare', to 'un-fold'. The English 'explain', we may add, is from 'ex-planus', making flat. The burlesque is a heterogeneous discourse which disrupts in various ways the implicit norm within it, elevated discourse. It opens up and brings down. It confronts the high with the low. When the latter is given a positive weight it becomes a basis for new values.

The term 'burlesque' is rarely used in connection with Voltaire. This is true of studies which go beyond the *contes*.[4] Critics concerned with

3. It is to be noted that Adam and Bar (and even Genette, p.169) implicitly include mock-heroic forms under the burlesque. This inclusion becomes explicit in A. Kibédi Varga, 'Le Burlesque: le monde renversé selon la poétique classique', pp.153-60 of *L'Image du monde renversé et ses représentations littéraires et para-littéraires de la fin du XVIe siècle au milieu de XVIIe*, ed. Jean Lafond and Augustin Redondo (Paris 1979). Likewise in John D. Jump, *The Burlesque* (London 1972), which covers a wide variety of subgenres, and practitioners from Aristophanes onwards. The latter study begins with a useful general definition: 'Burlesque consists in the use or imitation of serious matter or manner, made amusing by the creation of an incongruity between style and subject.'

4. The excellent analysis of Voltaire's style in Lanson, *L'Art de la prose* (Paris 1908) does not use the term, and nor does Auerbach in his penetrating remarks in *Mimesis* (Berne 1946).

those *contes* predicated on true love generally recognise the parody of the heroic, and may employ our term to characterise this.[5] But it is not clearly defined or applied systematically.[6] Rarely does it appear in recent close analyses of devices in the prose fiction. Many, however, point to the kind of effects that I am concerned with. They are described in the kind of terms that I shall be using – reduction and dislocation – implying similar ideological functions.[7] The path that I am treading, then, is by no means a new one. I am, however, offering a principle of analysis

Equally classic in its field, R. Naves, *Le Goût de Voltaire* (Paris 1938; reprint, Geneva 1967) has no entry for 'burlesque' in its index. (This despite Voltaire's interesting observations in the *Lettres philosophiques*, xxii, 'Appendice', ed. G. Lanson (Paris 1909) and A. M. Rousseau (Paris 1964), ii, pp.147-48.) Closer to the 'contes', Diana Guiragossian in her study of *Voltaire's facéties* (Geneva 1963) uses the term only in passing, and J. Macary in his Introduction to the *Facéties* (Paris 1973) not at all (though both note such antecedents as Domenichi, *Facetie, motti e burle*, which were in Voltaire's library). Voltaire's nearest approach to the seventeenth-century verse genre is *La Pucelle*, ed. J. Vercruysse, *The Complete works of Voltaire* 7 (Geneva 1970). Virgil W. Topazio's early article, 'Voltaire's *Pucelle*: a study in burlesque', *Studies on Voltaire* 2 (1956), pp.207-23, lacks rigour.

5. For example, William F. Bottiglia, *Voltaire's 'Candide': analysis of a classic*, Studies on Voltaire 7 (1959), pp.228-33 on 'use of burlesque or parody'.

6. There are some valuable remarks, however, in the introductions to the *Romans et contes* ed. Frédéric Deloffre and Jacques Van den Heuvel (Paris 1979), pp.832-33, 919-20, 1018-20.

7. Rhetoric and syntax: 'Voltaire réduit au minimum [...] les conjonctions, relatifs, et tous autres termes de coordination et subordination' (Lanson, 1930 ed., p.155). 'L'écriture de Voltaire procède par coupures, ellipses, litotes – par toutes les formes de la *soustraction*' ([author's emphasis], J. Starobinski, 'Sur le style philosophique de *Candide*', *Comparative literature* 28 (1976), pp.193-200 (p.194)). See too Pierre Haffter, 'L'usage satirique des causales dans les contes de Voltaire', *Studies on Voltaire* 53 (1967), pp.7-28. Use of tenses: Edwin P. Grobe, 'Discontinuous aspect in Voltaire's *Candide*', *Modern language notes* 82 (1967), p.334-46. The concrete: 'l'expression particulière et matérielle [occulte] le rapport logique' (Lanson, p.174). 'Scientific' implications: 'an experimental set-up', 'among the conditions [...] none but the material and natural are given serious consideration' (Auerbach, pp.403, 410); see too Ulrich Leo, 'Phenomenological and experimental styles in the French Enlightenment', *Romanische Forschungen* 62 (1950), pp.201-207; or the links with 'the mechanical philosophy' suggested in Bottiglia, pp.74ff. The parodic writing results in an 'hétérogenéité du discours', which places the Voltairean text in a polemical relation with all previous texts (Starobinski, pp.193, 195). 'The reduction that his tales effectuate regarding the events that they narrate is counterbalanced by the skilful use of a language which points to its own devices, and therefore serves to indicate a mechanism for catching the less obvious manipulations in societal discourse' (Maureen F. O'Meara, '*Le Taureau Blanc* and the activity of language', *Studies on Voltaire* 148 (1976), pp.115-75 (p.153)). Almost explicit in this last quotation, as implicit in all that precedes, is the notion of a Voltaire *deconstructionist* in the modern critical sense. This reading is explored in O'Meara, as in Jacques Wagner's insistently modernist account of the *Lettres philosophiques*, 'Lisibilité et dénégation: propos sur un préambule voltairien', *Studies on Voltaire* 155 (1976), pp.2223-64. The answer, as in my first paragraph, is that Voltaire 'deconstructs' within a received framework.

which is both critically consistent and historically appropriate (that is, reflecting the recognised conventions of writing in the period, in which the heroic order remained the essential point of reference). The concept of the burlesque provides the necessary link between the literary, the comic and the ideological. I shall first establish the reductive pattern, in its negative and its positive aspects of derision and materialist truth. Then I shall consider images of mechanical imitation (reduction), and of dismembering (breakdown). Finally I shall indicate how the 'conte' itself, as tale and as telling, is the multiplication of these devices.

A rhetorical analysis works with textual specifics. The following is a selective list of comic devices, loosely classified.[8]

Enumeration, repetition, accumulation: 'J'ai eu le temps de passer de Surinam à Bordeaux, d'aller de Bordeaux à Paris, de Paris à Dieppe, de Dieppe à Portsmouth, de côtoyer le Portugal et l'Espagne, de traverser toute la Méditerranée, de passer quelques mois à Venise' (*Candide*, xxiv, pp.210-11).[9]

Antithesis for deflation: 'Zadig éprouva que le premier mois du mariage, comme il est écrit dans le livre du *Zend*, est la lune du miel, et que le second est la lune de l'absinthe' (*Zadig*, iii, p.62).

Zeugma: 'le bruit des chars qui entraient le soir chez Zadig l'importunait, le bruit de ses louanges l'irritait davantage' (*Zadig*, iv, p.66).

(Combined: 'Le prieur [...], aimé de ses voisins, après l'avoir été autrefois de ses voisines' (*L'Ingénu*, i, p.285)).

Cultural register: (of the beautiful Princess Formosante) 'Ce fut d'après ses portraits et ses statues que dans la suite des siècles Praxitèle sculpta son Aphrodite, et celle qu'on nomma la "Vénus aux belles fesses"' (*La Princesse de Babylone*, i. p.350).

Literalisation of cliché: (directly) 'je le suivrai jusqu'au bout du monde, si le monde a un bout' (*Jenni*, ii, p.602); (indirectly) 'l'univers avait les yeux sur ses deux pieds' (*Zadig*, vii, p.73).

Literalisation of allegory: 'nous nous en servons [des ciseaux de la

8. On comic style in the seventeenth-century burlesque, see Bar, especially ch.13, 'La rhétorique du burlesque'; a classification of devices also in Pierre Bornecque, 'Le comique et le burlesque dans le *Roman comique* de Scarron', *XVIIe siècle* 110-11 (1976), pp.25-43. For the 'contes' see the modest and useful article by M. H. Gertner, 'Five comic devices in *Zadig*', *Studies on Voltaire* 117 (1974), pp.133-52.

9. All page-references are to the *Romans et contes*, ed. Frédéric Deloffre and Jacques Van den Heuvel (Paris 1979), which provides my corpus. Chapter- or section-numbers within each work are included to facilitate reference to other editions.

70

Vérité] pour couper les griffes de l'Inquisition, que voyez étalées sur cette table' (*Eloge historique de la Raison*, p.571).

Literalisation by misinterpretation: 'On me demanda si j'étais pour le mouton noir ou pour le mouton blanc. Je répondis que cela m'était fort indifférent, pourvu qu'il fût tendre' (*Scarmentado*, p.139).

Inconsequence: 'J'ai été sur le point d'être étranglé parce que la reine avait des rubans jaunes' (*Zadig*, x, p.83).

Periphrasis or euphemism: 'On le mena dans le château que fit construire le roi Charles V, fils de Jean II, auprès de la rue Saint-Antoine, à la porte des Tournelles' [= la Bastille] (*L'Ingénu*, ix, p.311).

Gratuitous precision: 'Il avait huit lieues de haut: j'entends, par huit lieues, vingt-quatre mille pas géométriques de cinq pieds chacun' (*Micromégas*, i, p.19).

Anaculturalism: 'Il étudiait, selon la coutume, au collège des jésuites de sa planète' (*Micromégas* i, p.20).

Anachronism?: 'Le département de la haute Asie' (*Le Monde comme il va*, i, p.39).

Anachronism formally stated: 'Il écrivit une lettre au grand prêtre de Memphis [...], sur du papier d'Egypte qui n'était pas encore en usage' (*Le Taureau Blanc*, v, p.544).

Disruptive narratorial intervention direct: 'Mélinade (c'est le nom de la dame, que j'ai eu mes raisons pour ne pas dire jusqu'ici, parce qu'il n'était pas encore fait) [...]' (*Le Crocheteur borgne*, p.5).

Questioning the status of the narrator: 'C'est, je crois, pour cette raison [...]' (*Candide*, i, p.145).

Mock-authentication: '*L'Ingénu / Histoire véritable / Tirée des manuscrits du père Quesnel*'.

Naive chapter-headings (as in the romances): 'L'Ingénu court chez sa maîtresse et devient furieux'.

Undermining the fictive illusion: 'Alors tout disparut. Rustan se retrouva dans la maison de son père, dont il n'était pas sorti, et dans son lit, où il avait dormi une heure' (*Le Blanc et le noir*, p.265).

Reference to other fictions, and to the material production of the book: 'O Muses! [...] les continuateurs téméraires [...] ont osé falsifier *Candide*, *L'Ingénu*, et les chastes aventures de la chaste Jeanne [...] dans des éditions bataves. Qu'ils ne fassent pas ce tort à mon typographe, chargé d'une nombreuse famille, et qui possède à peine de quoi avoir des caractères, du papier et de l'encre' (*La Princesse de Babylone*, xi, p.413).

The forms of words. Doubtful forms: 'Son estafier [...] lui servait à boire du vin de Porto, ou d'Oporto' (*Candide*, v, p.157).

Invented forms: 'qu'un rossignol fasse un rossignolet à sa rossignole' (*Les Oreilles du comte de Chesterfield*, ii, p.579).

Sequences: 'La controverse des MAIS' (*Jenni*, iii).

As anagrams: 'Nabussan [...] fils de Nussanab, fils de Nabassun, fils de Sanbusna' (*Zadig*, Appendice, p.118).

Etymology: 'Leur dignité est "cardinal", comme qui dirait "gond de porte"'.

Onomastics; comic reference to heroic literature, or foreign language: 'l'un est le cardinal Sacripante, et l'autre le cardinal Faquinetti' (*Lettres d'Amabed*, xx, pp.524-5).

All received norms. Institutional and written authority: 'comme il est dit dans le livre du *Zend*'; tradition, custom: 'selon la coutume'.

What is consistent through all this range of examples is reductionism. They present a cultural antithesis, which characteristically proceeds from the elevated to the base. In the first examples, this mutation is marked by formal rhetorical opposition. Relations of the spirit become relations of the flesh ('voisins' › 'voisines', and following). Metaphorical becomes literal (the 'literalisation' group). The elevated is linked with the trivial ('rubans'). In the second section we have the same movement from high to low without the formally marked antithesis. The elaborate periphrasis ('château [...] Tournelles') implies the hidden low meaning. The fabulously huge is measured, segmented, quantified. The interplanetary is brought down to earth; the exotic is treated as an administrative unit. The final section is that in which the elevated element is revealed to be the mystique of fiction itself. It is not only reduced by the parody of the form and content of the romance. It is dismantled by the identification of its material constituents. Lexical and morphological gaming points to the forms of words and language. We are disturbingly reminded that the story is fashioned at the whim of its writer, and may be counterfeited by another. The book is made of print and paper. It is physically produced by someone who thereby earns money to keep his large family. All these reductive movements are within the province of the burlesque. They have led us to formulate already most of the propositions that were cited from critics, and which will be developed here.

From these examples, we may now characterise the two orders. First –

as the framework and norm of discourse – the 'high' order. We have the almost infinite 'disponibilité' of the protagonist in heroic fiction (vast travels, indifference to time, ideal beauty, mysterious names, mortal peril, overwhelming love, but immaculate chastity, and at last, the honeymoon). We have giants, and goddesses. We have sacred objects, books of wisdom and the priests of religions. We have kings (and courts, attendants and carriages). We have great names from the past, and the continuity of dynasties and of high art through the centuries. In a word, we have high culture, unaffected by time, space or materiality. Then the 'low' order which works within and against this. The disruptive elements can be grouped into a number of categories. Several of my early examples use the senses: (unpleasant) taste, hearing, sight. The body, notably its lower regions (buttocks, feet). Animals. Food. Sexuality in various aspects: women (in the great misogynist tradition); a dependent family with numerous offspring. Money and trade. Material objects (ink and paper; table, bed and door; ribbons). Repetition; quantification. The particular and the immediate. The here and now.

The low order, especially when juxtaposed continually with the high order, is by cultural convention comic. Implicitly it puts the high order into question. Depending on the degree of contrast in register, it may function as a derisive version of the high order. Derision is its negative significance. At the same time however it is – like the high order – consistent within itself. It is homogeneous philosophically. It consists of that which is tangible and verifiable. It has a positive potential. It may offer a more modest but surer truth.

The farthest down we can go is to the burlesque bedrock. Quantities: 'Je vous conseille de douter de tout, excepté que [...] deux et deux font quatre' (L'Homme aux quarante écus, p.447). Physiological functions: 'Le lendemain, les trois philosophes agitèrent la grande question: quel est le premier mobile de toutes les actions des hommes. Goudman [...] dit que le principe de tout était l'amour et l'ambition. Grou, qui avait vu plus de pays, dit que c'était l'argent; et le grand anatomiste Sidrac assura que c'était la chaise percée' (Les Oreilles du comte de Chesterfield, vii, p.592). (Note that the titles of these two tales themselves point respectively to the minima that I have just defined.) Here are the real basics. But, because quantity and physiology are certitudes, one can build on them. 'L'Homme aux quarante écus' pursues economic truth with a Geometer, and then increases his wealth to become 'L'Homme aux deux cents écus pour le moins' (p.443). The man who finds the source of all human conduct in bowel movements is an 'anatomiste'. Here is the basis of science, systematically observed facts. And here is the tool of science, mensuration. Physiology and arithmetic are the burlesque basics. But they are also the itinerary of the philosophical hero of the age. 'Notre grand Locke était médecin, il fut le seul métaphysicien de l'Europe, et il rétablit les monnaies d'Angleterre' (*Jenni*, iv, p.612).

The same two principles constitute the valid activity of the 'philosophes' in *Micromégas*. '"Puisque vous êtes du petit nombre des sages, dit-il à ces messieurs, [...], dites-moi, je vous en prie, à quoi vous vous occupez". "Nous disséquons des mouches, dit le philosophe, nous mesurons des lignes, nous assemblons des nombres; nous sommes d'accord sur deux ou trois points que nous entendons, et nous disputons sur deux ou trois mille que nous n'entendons pas"' (vii, pp.34-35). Equally they constitute the juvenile excellence of Micromégas himself. 'Il n'avait pas encore deux cent cinquante ans [...] lorsqu'il devina, par la force de son esprit, plus de cinquante propositions d'Euclide. [...] Vers les quatre cent cinquante ans, au sortir de l'enfance, il disséqua beaucoup de ces petits insectes qui n'ont pas cent pieds de diamètre' (i, p.20). These principles generally stand him in good stead. Voltaire consistently marks his adherence to our philosophical order, in contrast with his travelling companion. Confronted with a new phenomenon, the latter 's'imagina bien vite que [...]', whereas the former 'examina l'animal fort patiemment' (iv, p.28). Likewise among the earthmen who offer statements about the soul, forms of 'imagination' are prevalent, except in the 'petit partisan de M. Locke'. The latter begins by reducing his ambitions and declaring once more the 'high' order to be dependent on the 'low'. 'Je ne sais pas, dit-il, comment je pense, mais je sais que je n'ai jamais pensé qu'à l'occasion de mes sens.' Exclusively high accounts are disabled by the use of the same opposition for comic effect. The Cartesian affirms that the mind is an 'esprit pur' which has been endowed with metaphysical ideas 'dans le ventre de sa mère' (vii, p.35). It is evident that in this writing the comic and the philosophical systems are interlocked.[10]

10. Cartesianism itself, in a sense, is the common source of the philosophical and the burlesque. Cartesian dualism divides reality into thought and extension, deprecating the latter. These are our high and low orders. The gap is so great that their juxtaposition is philosophically problematical and culturally comical. Transsubstantiation may thus receive the same Voltairean treatment as innate ideas: the communicant has 'Dieu dans son estomac.' This last is one of many examples of Voltaire's burlesque polemic cited – but not correctly

We look now at some images of what might be called mechanical imitation. The low or burlesque order comprehends most animals. Our examples included sheep and birds. We might equally have cited dogs (spaniels in *Zadig*, iii, p.62; *Pot-pourri*, vii, p.245), moles (*Micromégas*, iv, p.26, *Pot-pourri*, x, p.249) or cows (*Aventure indienne*, p.282). Bears occur several times (*Candide*, xxii, p.209; *L'Ingénu*, i, p.290; *Jenni*, i, p.598). But Voltaire is particularly drawn to two species: parrots and monkeys. 'Je lui dis que je me tuerais; il répliqua, en riant, qu'on ne se tuait point, qu'il était fait à ces façons-là, et me quitta comme un homme qui vient de mettre un perroquet dans sa ménagerie' (*Zadig*, xvi, p.103). 'Les Fa tutto et les Fa molto [moines] sont des espèces de singes élevés avec soin pour faire des tours de passe-passe devant le peuple' (*Amabed*, xiii, p.515). As the latter example reminds us, the appeal of these particular analogies lies partly in the fact that they are already culturally moralised. One is said to 'parrot' elevated discourse (like the philosophers in *Micromégas*); one does 'monkey-tricks' imitating, in this case, religious ceremony. In the perspective of the philosophical burlesque, the effect may be put more precisely. 'Psittacisme' and 'singeries' reduce such discourses to their external and mechanical elements.

Animals which perform we associate notably with fairgrounds and popular culture. It is to such terms that Voltaire reduces past wisdom. 'Autrefois les oracles de la justice, ainsi que ceux de la morale, n'étaient que ridicules. Le docteur Balouard déclamait au barreau, et Arlequin dans la chaire' (*L'Homme aux quarante écus*, p.459). Two other analogies nicely combine these motifs. The assurance that in God's plan 'toutes les âmes honnêtes [...] seront heureuses un jour' is rebutted with the remark 'Quel conte de Peau d'Ane!' (*Jenni*, x, p.647). The dispute over the papal condemnation in *Unigenitus* of Quesnel's 101 propositions is assimilated to Mother Goose, and also perhaps to the Arabian Nights: 'On craignit un schisme, comme du temps des cent et un contes de ma mère l'oie' (*L'Homme aux quarante écus*, p.466).

There are in fact two works which function systematically through these particular reductions. *Le Taureau blanc* features a whole menagerie of animals, each the equivalent of an elevated person or event in the Old Testament. All are actually present in the source text; some as literal transformations already (Nebuchadnezzar › the Bull; Satan › the snake);

labelled – in William H. Trapnell, *Voltaire and the Eucharist*, Studies on Voltaire 198 (1981), pp.182-98.

others as associates, thrust by Voltaire into the foreground (Noah's dove; Jonah's fish). (The Old Testament is of course intrinsically burlesque for Voltaire, by its heterogeneity of cultural registers, just as Homer was for the Moderns in the 'Querelle'). The tone of *Le Taureau blanc* is almost affectionate. That of *Pot-pourri*, demonstrating the variety of burlesque possibilities, is brutal. Organised religion is reduced to the grosser aspects of the 'Foire'. The text begins with a mock-genealogy of Jesus. 'Brioché fut le père de Polichinelle, non pas son propre père, mais père de génie. Le père de Brioché était Guillot-Gorju, qui fut fils de Gilles, qui fut fils de Gros-René, qui tirait son origine du prince des sots et de la mère sotte' (p.239). Luther's revolt against the pope over the selling of indulgences, and his founding of a new Church with fewer ceremonies – the opium of the people – are quite rigorously transposed into the low register. 'Un jour, un de ses domestiques [=Luther], receveur des billets et ouvreur de loges, ayant été cassé aux gages, se souleva contre Bienfait [= le pape], et institua d'autres marionnettes qui décrièrent toutes les danses de madame Gigogne [= l'Eglise de Rome], et tous les tours de passe-passe de Bienfait. Il retrancha plus de cinquante ingrédients qui entraient dans l'orviétan, composa le sien de cinq ou six drogues' (p.249).

Marionettes, like monkeys and parrots, serve to demean culturally. They demean morally. They reduce the phenomenon with which they are associated to behaviourism, by derisory mechanical imitation. But, again, they also take us 'down' to the truth. They offer a philosophically legitimate model. The texts themselves spell out this latter significance. 'Pourquoi trouvez-vous si étrange que dans quelques pays il y ait des singes qui obtiennent les bonnes grâces des dames? Ils sont des quarts d'hommes,' says Cacambo. He then adds, 'comme je suis un quart d'Espagnol' (*Candide*, xvi, p.181). The last clause reinforces the point with a parallel but approving burlesque truth. Cacambo is a quarter Spaniard literally and philosophically. Just as the monkey is a *reductio* of European man, he himself – the 'bon sauvage' of so many philosophical fictions of the period – stands in this relation. More simply, from another story, 'il était nu comme un singe' (*Lettre d'un Turc*, p.132). Man stripped down is an ape.[11]

11. It is worth noting that Voltaire also burlesques the glimmerings of evolutionary theory ('Il était démontré que la race des hommes était bâtarde d'une race de babouins' (*L'Homme aux quarante écus*, p.439)). His norms are anti- or a-historical. Truth for him is not the daughter of Time but of Reason (*Eloge historique de la raison*).

Parrots are more satisfyingly Voltairean; no doubt in part because they can talk. If their discourse is metaphysical, they may be merely parrotting in the pejorative sense, without an experimental basis for their assertions. 'Le perroquet répondit: "Oui". Ce mot frappa Zadig; cependant, comme il était bon physicien et qu'il ne croyait pas que les perroquets fussent prophètes, il se rassura bientôt' (*Zadig*, vi, p.71). This parrot, however, assenting to the proposition that Zadig's happiness will not last, is right. 'Voilà de quoi dépendent les destins des hommes!' Having saved his life by the merest chance (ch.iv), the bird now confirms that destiny is a tale told by a parrot, signifying nothing. May not the various metaphysical discourses offered later by Jesrad, in 'L'Hermite', be read as 'psittacisme'? Narrators I shall come to later. The other image was that of the puppets at the 'Foire'. Just as we may be said to be determined by our bowel movements, so we may be called 'les marionnet-tes de la Providence' (*Les Oreilles du comte de Chesterfield*, iv, p.584).

Most of the philosophers in *Micromégas* – each parrotting his particular master's voice – are like automata. This effect is established initially by the burlesque conceit of literalising their moral tininess. From the point of view of Micromégas and his friend, established normatively in the narrative, they are minute. It seems, as a result, that they cannot be possessed of a 'soul' or principle of moral independence. For the protag-onist they are 'ces petites machines'. The narrator compares them to 'des atomes', and to 'la graine dont nous sommes formés' (v, p.30). Earlier they are characterised as tiny earthbound animals, living on 'notre petite fourmilière', or in 'la taupinière' (i, p.19; iv, p.26). This confluence of mechanistic, organic and animal images is philosophically very signifi-cant. In 1750 we are still in the era of Cartesian beast-machines. But we have also just seen the publication of La Mettrie's *L'Homme-machine*. Experimental attempts are being made to derive organic from inorganic matter. The old Lucretian tradition is about to be given its systematic modern form of scientific materialism. Quantity and physiology are indeed the bedrock. The continual flux of matter is affirmed in more than one 'conte'. In *La Princesse de Babylone* the proposition is attributed to a phoenix, who demystifies himself delightfully: 'La résurrection, madame, lui dit le phénix, est la chose du monde la plus simple. Il n'est pas plus surprenant de naître deux fois qu'une. Tout est résurrection dans ce monde; les chenilles ressuscitent en papillons; un noyau mis en terre ressuscite en arbre; tous les animaux ensevelis dans la terre ressuscitent en herbes, en plantes' (iv, p.373). A more solemn version, from *Micromégas*, is still proposed as a reductionist truth: 'Il faut rendre son corps aux éléments, et ranimer la nature sous une autre forme, ce qui s'appelle mourir; quand ce moment de métamorphose est venu, avoir vécu une éternité, ou avoir vécu un jour, c'est précisément la même chose' (ii, p.23).

This breaking-down brings us to images of dismemberment. Physical violence is in effect the burlesque *reductio* of all human relationships, as in the farce or the fairground Punch and Judy. Physical assaults are common in seventeenth-century burlesque writing. Implicitly or explicitly they parody the unreal perils of the romance, by literalising them; they point to the reality and the interaction of our physical selves; they may imply a reduction of the human to the mechanical. In the prose fiction of the eighteenth century the tradition is maintained, uniquely, by the violence in some of Voltaire's *contes*. In fact he outdoes all predecessors. Kicking, beating, whipping, raping, stabbing, burning, shooting, strangling, drowning, impaling, the loss of a limb or other physical feature ... It would be difficult to name any kind of assault that does not occur somewhere. Physical assault clearly belongs to our 'low' order. It partakes of the corporeal and the material, often too of repetition. It marks once more the bedrock of physiology and quantity.[12]

One notable injury is the loss of an eye. This is suffered by Memnon (p.127), and Pangloss (*Candide*, iv, p.154), the latter event recalled in *L'Homme aux quarante écus* (p.461). It almost happens to Zadig (ch.i). It is the permanent condition of the protagonist in *Le Crocheteur borgne*. Except perhaps in the case of Memnon, it is always associated with

12. An apparent difficulty: in my list of comic devices the only physical assault, Zadig 'sur le point d'être étranglé', was placed in the *high* order. That was indeed its function in the quotation, because it was juxtaposed with the trivia of yellow ribbons. In the fuller context of Zadig's position as first minister and royal favourite at the illustrious court of Babylon, however, it is of the low order, brutal reality intruding on his serene elevation. Meaning depends on structural opposition. Thus ethics are down-to-earth compared with astrology, monadology, etc. (*Zadig*, vi, p.72); but ethics are airy-fairy compared with crude fact: 'Cette excellente morale n'a jamais été démentie que par les faits' (*La Princesse de Babylone*, i, p.352). More generally, violence in the *contes* is usually perpetrated by the high order: ecclesiastical, civil or military force, romantic pirates or idealised savages, blow of fortune or act of God. But this 'décalage' is precisely the point. We are shown the opposition between the high idea of a world coherent and benevolent, on the one hand, and on the other the reality of human institutions quickly reduced to dealing in repetitious violence or a supposedly Divine plan which manages little better.

sexuality, which is a reductionist truth. In a discourse of two orders, the loss of a binocular vision seems likely to carry implications. In fact the philosophical significance of this condition – obviously relevant to the metaphysical order of Optimism – is formally stated in one tale. 'Nos deux yeux ne rendent pas notre condition meilleure; l'un nous sert à voir les biens, et l'autre les maux de la vie' (*Le Crocheteur borgne*, p.3). This burlesque literalisation of alternative world-views is complemented at the end of *Memnon*. The protagonist, a victim of the world's continual assaults, is assured that in the universal order all is well. 'Ah! je ne croirai cela, répliqua le pauvre Memnon, que quand je ne serai plus borgne' (p.130). From the one-eyed perspective of the burlesque this proposition is valid. (Myopic, or worm's-eye, are the analogous conceits implied by the 'taupinière' and the 'fourmilière' mentioned earlier.) Philosophically the proposition is valid in that it reminds us that sense-data are the only certain data. A theory cannot stand up against experience. As a wise teacher admits, 'Je leur dis quelquefois que tout est le mieux du monde; mais ceux qui ont la gravelle, ceux qui ont été ruinés et mutilés à la guerre n'en croient rien, ni moi non plus' (*Histoire d'un bon bramin*, p.236).

This time we have begun with the explicitly philosophical meaning. The loss of an eye is more tidily allegorical than most other forms of assault. One or two, however – like certain animals – may have each its particular significance too. Burning is common enough in the *contes*. But when it is the climax of an *Aventure indienne* featuring Pythagoras, we perceive that the phrase 'renaître sous une autre forme' (p.282) is not just ironic. The phoenix also required to be burned in order to be reborn, and it was he who explained the universal cycle of matter (p.373). The male nose has traditional sexual associations. For Zadig, as for Pangloss, peril to the nose is linked by the narrative metonymically as well as metaphorically with sexuality (*Zadig*, ii; *Candide*, ii, iii).

We have moved from the explicit to the implicit, and from kinds of violence to particular occurrences. We now take more subtle assaults in which literary structure and style are a major element. Two examples from *Zadig* show how cultural prestige can be broken down by a single strike or, figuratively, by lighter but repeated blows. The universe has been in dispute for fifteen hundred years as to whether one should enter the temple of Mithras with the left or the right foot. 'Zadig entra dans le temple en sautant à pieds joints, et il prouva ensuite [...]'. The great issue is reduced at a stroke. The forceful action prepares the forceful proof. The narrator adds that this proof was criticised for not employing 'le bon style oriental'; he duly contrasts this high rhetorical mode with the modesty of Zadig's discourse: 'Zadig se contenta d'avoir le style de la raison' (vii, p.73). In the episode of 'Le Bûcher' the literal violence is back with the high order, in the form of the widow's traditionalist and unexamined acceptance of the obligation to immolate herself. This heroic folly is contrasted with Zadig's patient anatomisation – the style of Reason – of all the various causes she has for living (xi, pp.86-87). We should note that these examples illustrate respectively the categories of mechanical imitation and dismemberment. The principle of contrastive rhythm is also vital to the effect of both, affirming once more that of antithesis.

The most satisfying examples, then, are those in which the violence is literal, philosophical and stylistic all at the same time. The mutilation is not only in the narrative but of the narrative. When Zadig studies the Great Book of Nature, he reflects on the verities one discovers. 'Il [= on] nourrit et il élève son âme; il vit tranquille; il ne craint rien des hommes, et sa tendre épouse ne vient point lui couper le nez' (iii, p.62). The elevated discourse is abruptly cut off. The fakir on his bed of nails interrogates his pupil Omri about his life. '"Je tâche, dit Omri, d'être bon citoyen, bon mari, bon père, bon ami; je prête de l'argent sans intérêt aux riches dans l'occasion; j'en donne aux pauvres; j'entretiens la paix parmi mes voisins" – "Vous mettez-vous quelquefois des clous dans le cul?" demanda le bramin' (*Lettre d'un Turc*, p.132). The elevated discourse is punctured.

The 'conte' itself consists to a greater or lesser extent of a multiplication of such effects. Violence is repeatedly done to the moral entity who is the hero, and the philosophical entity that is the abstraction, ideal or theory. Each, initially simple and whole, is progressively assaulted. The latter is broken down by the base realities of the hero's experience, which is both a burlesque and a testing of theory against facts. It is broken down equally by the dislocated – burlesque – account of reality which hero and narrator offer. Both are an imitation at once derisive and serious. The antithetical and rhythmic effect of puncturing is almost as important as the semantic. It too occurs on the macro-level of the story as on that of the phrase, and contributes greatly to the mechanical quality which is both parodic of the romance and expressive of the assault of low realities upon the ideal. The ending of the exercise is often arbitrary. It is usually nevertheless far more modest and multivalent than the beginning. This points to the continual decomposition of each higher entity into a lesser multiplicity, ultimately into the organic and unitary minima, the burlesque truth, the cycle of matter.

Much of this scheme is best illustrated, inevitably, by *Candide*. That tale undoubtedly features the greatest amount of physical violence. The 'grands coups de pied dans le cul' which boot Candide out of the pristine paradise are the avatar of the regular literal and moral assaults to come. The attempted dissection of Pangloss (xxviii, p.227) figures the dissection of his doctrine. I have, however, studied *Candide* elsewhere from a wider angle.[13] Assaults are not lacking in *Zadig*. The hero himself, as we have noted, risks losing his nose (ii, p.61) and being strangled. He is also wounded twice (i, pp.58-59; ix, p.81), and is threatened at various times with impalement, the knout and burning. He spends time as a slave. The pattern of violence is confirmed in the philosophical climax of the story, the chapter entitled 'L'Hermite'. The Hermit crowns his career by burning down a house, and drowning a young man. It occurs too on a grand scale with the civil war that breaks out in Zadig's absence: 'Babylone est un grand coupe-gorge, [...] tout l'empire est désolé' (xiv, p.95). The implications here are various. Literally bowing under the weight of the universe, *homo erectus* reduced to a beast of burden is funny. 'Un chameau mourut à deux journées d'Horeb; on répartit sa charge sur le dos de chacun des serviteurs; Zadig en eut sa part. Sétoc se mit à rire en voyant tous ses esclaves marcher courbés' (x, p.83). But it also serves to introduce a lesson on weights and measures, those burlesque realities now the solid basis of trade and the utilitarian (pp.83-84). Zadig emerges from this peril and all others ultimately unscathed, to live happily ever after. In the romances, as in the chapter 'Les Combats' which begins the romance climax here, the protagonist remains intact. However, his apotheosis is consequent upon a radical breakdown – that of the society of Babylon in the civil war. The principle of the Hermit's violence seems similar, its lesson that of a cycle. The house burns down to reveal hidden

13. My 'Cette boucherie héroïque: *Candide* as carnival', *Modern language review* 80 (1985), pp.293-303, applies to this tale the carnivalesque reading of Rabelais by Mikhail Bakhtin (English translation *Rabelais and his world*, Cambridge, Mass. 1968). In the context of the present volume I have tried to give primacy to 'the transmission of ideas', but my debt to Bakhtin is still evident.

treasure. The young man is drowned so that his aunt and Zadig may live.

Violence to the heroic text transforms its message. First and pleasingly, a literal case of the 'texte éclaté'. Zadig writes upon a stone tablet an impromptu quatrain in praise of the King of Babylon, then modestly breaks it in half. One fragment reads as a new verse critical of the King and Zadig is in danger of execution (iv, pp.67-68). Here is a paradigm of the dislocation operated by the universe upon its marionettes, or by the author and the protagonist upon the elevated order of discourse. And here we begin to look at figures of the burlesque narrator. The job of dislocation is often done by the protagonist retelling and reflecting. Parodying the *plaintes* of the romance hero, this also picks up an 'interior' burlesque from seventeenth-century comic writing. There a naive character might ineptly recount a heroic story. An example is Vollichon's account of *Cinna* in the *Roman comique*.[14] As Voltaire systematises the 'naïf', so he systematises this device.[15] He gives it a clearly philosophical function by having his protagonist offer an 'anatomie' of his own story. 'Les malheurs de ma destinée' Zadig reviews thus: 'J'ai été condamné à l'amende pour avoir vu passer une chienne; j'ai pensé être empalé pour un griffon; j'ai été envoyé au supplice parce que j'avais fait des vers à la louange du roi; j'ai été sur le point d'être étranglé parce que la reine avait des rubans jaunes' (x, p.83). This account dismembers the logical totality by removing parts of it. It is a parody of the scientific account of causation because it knocks out the essential causes in order to focus upon the trivia. And yet, if all is determined (and especially if only the material is real) these trivial links in the chain are as important as any others. The naive version is derisive but also true.

Reality is a tale told by a dislocator. In Voltaire's appalling burlesque literalisation, an Englishman observes 'C'était au bourreau qu'il appartenait d'écrire l'histoire de notre île' (*La Princesse de Babylone*, viii, p.391). But what more appropriate, since – in terms of another art – 'en effet, l'histoire n'est que le tableau des crimes et des malheurs' (*L'Ingénu*, x,

---

14. Ed. A. Adam in *Romanciers du XVIIe siècle* (Paris 1968), p.964. For obvious reasons, Voltaire will prefer to break down *Polyeucte*: *Pot-pourri*, viii, p.247.

15. Charles Perrault's 'Chevalier', already deploying much of Voltaire's burlesque arsenal against the high order of the Ancients, represents an important intermediate stage in this process: see my 'Dialogue and speakers in the *Parallèle des Anciens et des Modernes*', *Modern language review* 78 (1983), pp.793-803.

p.315). It is told by someone who apparently does not care. Pococurante surveys high culture indifferently. Thus too do the gods survey humanity: 'Epicure, en admettant des dieux dans les planètes, avait bien raison d'enseigner qu'ils ne se mêlaient nullement de nos sottises et de nos horreurs' (*Jenni*, x, p.647). It is told by an idiot. 'J'ai bien peur, dit Memnon, que notre petit globe terraqué ne soit précisément les petites-maisons de l'univers' (*Memnon*, p.129). It is told by a parrot.

But if these accounts are derisory, they are also accurate. The 'naïf' is like the scientist in not going beyond what can be verified. Each offers description while eschewing explanation. 'Hypotheses non fingo' was Newton's principle. High discourse puts a gloss on reality, but the unmediated account simply tells the facts. '"Allez vite chercher votre perroquet," dit Rustan; [...] "Je vais le chercher [dit Topaze], vous en serez content; sa mémoire est fidèle, il conte simplement, sans chercher à montrer de l'esprit à tout propos et sans faire des phrases"' (*Le Blanc et le noir*, p.266). Few human narrators are so reliable. 'Je vais raconter ingénument comme la chose se passa, sans y rien mettre du mien: ce qui n'est pas un petit effort pour un historien' (*Micromégas*, iv, p.28). Ultimately Voltaire and the parrot, Jesrad and the philosophers, are all at one as narrators, offering a truthfully dislocated account of reality. When one tries to go beyond, to 'le bout des choses', a traditionally burlesque undermining awaits. The parrot was to reveal the order of the universe, but alas his account has been lost. The same revelation was promised at the end of *Micromégas*, but the book containing it turned out to be blank. Such derisory endings to high ambition push us back once more to the facts.

Perhaps, as non-endings, they also suggest that the tale does not stop. The cycle of matter is permanent. 'Matter', as we have seen, is the low order which the burlesque and scientific process opposes to the high. It is that to which the high discourse is reduced, by a continual process of breaking down. The permanency of matter is argued by Sidrac, 'le grand anatomiste'. In *Les Oreilles du comte de Chesterfield* – whose beneficence disabled by deafness then by death is another figure of the mutilated high order – it is Sidrac who closes the discussions. His sceptical profession of faith is at once classical, burlesque and materialist. 'Buvez chaud quand il gèle, buvez frais dans la canicule; rien de trop ni de trop peu en tout genre; digérez, dormez, ayez du plaisir; et moquez-vous du reste.' He is prepared, however, to read just one kind of narrative, one account of

reality. 'Tant d'historiens prétendus' are no more truthful than 'romanciers'. 'Je ne lis plus, Dieu merci, que l'histoire naturelle' (vii, p.594).

Voltaire's portrait of Augustus

ADRIENNE MASON

In his essay *De l'inconstance de nos actions* Montaigne suggests that even good authors are inclined to interpret every action of a character to fit with a fixed image that they themselves have chosen. But, he says, one historical figure defies any such easy classification. The baffling transformation of the youthful butcher Octavian into the revered emperor and statesman Augustus remains an enigma and will not fit into an historian's neat pigeon-hole.[1] Voltaire, however, recognised no such enigma. The portrait of Augustus that emerges from Voltaire's pen shows precisely the 'constante et solide contexture' (*Essai*, p.8) against which Montaigne warns. There is little attempt at judicious appraisal of evidence. Voltaire's emperor conforms, as we shall show, to a preconceived image and Voltaire selects his historical material carefully to fit the pattern.

Voltaire's interest in the Roman emperor does not however become apparent in a sustained way before the 1760s.[2] He was not tempted in any event by Roman history, preferring to turn his attention to less well-trodden paths. J. H. Brumfitt ascribes this neglect, probably correctly, to the polemicist's search for the most persuasive material: 'Roman history did not offer the same challenge to the deist propandist as did more ancient history, and it was too well known (or so it seemed) to stimulate Voltaire's historical interest in the way mediaeval and modern history did' (p.316).

Even so, it would have been difficult for Voltaire to disregard an historical figure who represented at the very least a metaphor for an age of political stability and literary brilliance and, for some, the subject of lively political debate. References to him do occur throughout Voltaire's career but these are invariably unfavourable and there seems little

---

1. *Essais*, ed. J. Plattard (Paris 1947), II, i, p.8
2. Although Voltaire wrote many fragments relating to Roman history, he did not write a major work. See *La Philosophie de l'histoire*, ed. J. H. Brumfitt, *The Complete works of Voltaire* 59 (Genève 1969), p.316. Further references to this edition of the works will be designated Voltaire.

evidence for any chronological evolution in Voltaire's judgement of the emperor. As early as 1728, for example, he reminds us that the Augustus of Virgil and Horace is the Octavian of the proscriptions,[3] a point reiterated in a letter to Frederick in 1737,[4] while in the *Essai sur les mœurs* Augustus is 'un tyran soupçonneux qui conservait avec adresse un pouvoir usurpé par le crime' (M.xi.90). Before the 1760s, however, such remarks are little more than occasional *boutades*, and while they would seem to indicate that Voltaire's view of the emperor was consistently unfavourable, they do not constitute a reasoned or systematic attack in an age in which according to Voltaire 'les temps des Scipion, de Sylla, de César, d'Auguste sont beaucoup plus présents à notre mémoire que les premiers événements de nos propres monarchies'.[5] But in 1764, Voltaire was to focus much more sharply on the figure of Augustus, drawing a portrait of the emperor which, at first presented only in dramatic form, was eventually augmented by a series of notes to become a more serious historical analysis. *Le Triumvirat*, which was originally entitled *Octave et le jeune Pompée*, was first mentioned in the correspondence for 1763[6] and composed in 1764. As the title suggests, the play centres on the young Octavian, one of the three *coupe-jarrets*,[7] as Voltaire christens that infamous trio. To Voltaire's chagrin, the play, its authorship a closely guarded secret for fear of *cabale*, was badly received and not subsequently revived. Two years later, however, the text of the play was published, this time with the revised title and spiced with what Voltaire describes as a 'ragoût piquant'[8] to make the strong meat of the play more palatable. The ingredients of Voltaire's sauce were copious notes offering a full-blown historical analysis not only of the young Octavian but also of his later career as emperor. Voltaire himself, predictably, did not accept the judgement of the *parterre* and found the play 'très bonne' (Best. D13325), transforming it into a piece for the reading public only because the subject matter was too rigorous, too 'English', to appeal to the

3. *Essai sur la poésie épique*, in *Œuvres complètes*, ed. L. Moland (Paris 1877-1885), viii.320. Further references to this edition will be designated M.

4. Voltaire, *Correspondence and related documents*, ed. Th. Besterman [henceforth Best.D] (Genève, Banbury, Oxford 1968-1977), Best.D1235; cf.D1255.

5. *Le Triumvirat*, M.vi.177.

6. Voltaire to the d'Argentals (23 June [1763], Best.D11276). Professor D. J. Fletcher's forthcoming edition will trace in detail the genesis of the play.

7. Voltaire to the d'Argentals (23 July 1763, Best.D11314).

8. Voltaire to the d'Argentals (23 July 1763, Best.D13325).

frivolous French theatre audience.[9] The remarks within the play were then augmented further by two short opuscules entitled *Du gouvernment et de la divinité d'Auguste*[10] and *Des conspirations contre les peuples* (M.xxvi.1-15), both a series of reflexions inspired by the portrait of the emperor within the play, but relating to more general themes. The former was then used again, with minor variants, to form the first section of an article on Augustus for the *Questions sur l'Encyclopédie* in 1770. The remainder of the article was largely compiled from the material already to be found in the notes to the play, so that, clearly, Voltaire's view of Augustus had not changed in any significant way between the publication of the notes and the appearance of the article 'Auguste'. In 1772 similar opinions are again put forward in the *Epître à Horace*. Voltaire upbraids Horace for his sycophancy, using to describe Augustus some of the same derogatory language that one finds in the notes to the play,[11] and there is no reason to suppose that Voltaire deviated from this view during the remaining six years of his life.

Though the larger reasons for Voltaire's interest in Augustus when he wrote *Le Triumvirat* are complex and remain in some respects mysterious, the immediate cause probably relates to Voltaire's long-standing feud with Crébillon *père*.[12] In 1748 Crébillon's play *Catilina* was played before a large audience and was very favourably received. This was, however, less a reflexion of the play's quality than the result of a *cabale* against Voltaire and criticism soon began to focus on the unflattering portrait of Cicero that emerged from the play. Seizing this opportunity, Voltaire rapidly penned a reply to Crébillon with a play on the same subject, *Rome sauvée* (1749). A few years later Crébillon himself decided to answer his critics, and in 1754 his version of *Le Triumvirat* appeared, giving a more favourable account of the Roman orator. The play was not well received but by that time Voltaire was reluctant to resume

9. Voltaire's doubt may be detected in a letter to the d'Argentals, Best.D11314, 23 July 1763: 'Si vous croyez que votre peuple ait les mœurs assez fortes, assez anglaises pour soutenir ce spectacle digne en partie des Romains et de la Grève, vous vous donnerez le plaisir de le faire essayer sur le théâtre.' Cf. Voltaire's preface to the play, M.vi.179.

10. M.xxv.587-89; cf. M.xvii.484.

11. M.x.442. The words 'fourbe', 'tranquille assassin', 'adroit' and 'politique' in particular are used elesewhere, cf. M.vi.186, 189 and M.xvii.486, 488. References to the murder of Cicero and incest with Julia are also common to the notes to the play and the article for the *Questions sur l'Encyclopédie*.

12. For a full account of the Voltaire-Crébillon quarrel, see Paul O. LeClerc, 'Voltaire and Crébillon *père*: history of an enmity', *Studies on Voltaire* 115 (1973), pp.89-135.

hostilities and, despite some gleeful gibes about his old rival, kept silent. In fact, madame Denis states categorically in a letter to Lambert: 'Vous pouvez être sur que vous n'imprimerez jamais le triumvirat sorti de la plume de Mr de Voltaire et même qu'il ne mettra plus de Romains sur le théâtre. On en est exaide.'[13]

In fact a revival of *Rome sauvée*, which Voltaire hoped for, would have been an adequate answer to Crébillon's *Le Triumvirat* since both plays took Cicero as their central figure, but no revival took place. Voltaire's enmity did not abate even after Crébillon's death in 1762 and it is quite probable that he nursed the desire to prove his dramatic superiority as late as 1764 when his own version of *Le Triumvirat* appeared. This is confirmed, as H. C. Lancaster indicates, by resemblances of plot and structure,[14] and the opening of the play is strikingly reminiscent of its earlier rival. Thereafter the plays diverge sharply. Crébillon's centres on events leading to the death of Cicero, whereas Voltaire's play begins after the murder of the Roman orator and centres on the character of Octavian. If a comparison between Voltaire's *Le Triumvirat* and another working of a similar theme may be made, it is with Corneille's *Cinna*. Although Voltaire allows his dramatic Octavian an act of clemency, he painstakingly explains in the notes that this may not be interpreted as a movement of compassion or an act of self-mastery and he reiterates at length his reasons for doubting the veracity of the *Cinna* episode.[15]

In fact historical accuracy is the much-vaunted cornerstone of Voltaire's own play, even though in the plot itself history had to be 'presque entièrement falsifiée'[16] for the sake of dramatic *bienséance*. Voltaire stoutly maintains that the moral climate, if not the historical facts, in the ember days of the Roman Republic have been painted 'avec le pinceau le plus fidèle' (M.vi.177). The persona he adopts in the preface and notes to the play is that of a painstaking historian concerned with the accurate representation of Roman *mores* and the notes do ostensibly provide a gloss to the parts of the play which departed from known historical

13. Best.D5908, 18 August [1754].
14. *French tragedy in the time of Louis XV and Voltaire 1715-1774* (Baltimore 1950), ii.358-59. 'Both plays deal with the iniquity of the second Triumvirate at the time of the proscriptions. In both Octavius loves a Roman woman who prefers Sextus Pompey. Both mention Antony, Fulvia, Lepidus and Cicero, the first two appearing on the stage in Voltaire's tragedy, the last two in Crébillon's. In both the young hero is Sextus Pompey and in both he is disguised.'
15. *Commentaires sur Corneille*, ed. D. Williams, Voltaire 54 (1975), pp.110-11.
16. In the Preface to *Le Triumvirat*, M.vi.177.

events. However, they go much further than that by presenting a 'true' portrait of the historical Augustus to counteract the dramatic Augustus, who had been allowed an act of clemency in line with dramatic tradition.[17]

Given this emphasis on fact, therefore, one might assume that Voltaire subjected his evidence to the same rigorous screening as he advocated in his writings on historiography. Certainly, in terms of available documentation Voltaire was well equipped. Original Latin sources were easily accessible to him linguistically: he draws on Dio, Cicero, Tacitus, Suetonius and Pliny, all of whom are mentioned explicitly in the notes, and he discusses in some detail the plausibility of Seneca's account of the conspiracy of Cinna.[18] Plutarch's life of Antony also seems a likely source of some details, especially as Voltaire's portrait of Antony, albeit a very conventional one, follows roughly the same lines as Plutarch. Among later historians, only Eachard is mentioned by name in Voltaire's discussion of the Cinna episode, but his history is dismissed as 'aussi fautive que tronquée' (M.vi.199). It is likely that Bayle was the source of information for the character of Fulvie, since she is discussed in the article 'Ovide' which Voltaire knew well,[19] and when he was working on the article for the *Questions sur l'Encyclopédie* Voltaire asks for the appropriate volumes of Graevius's *Thesaurus antiquorum romanorum* to be sent to him, mentioning Dio at the same time.[20] In a letter to Fawkener in 1752 he specifically mentions Vertot's *Le Triumvirat*[21] but no further reference is made to that at the time of writing either the play or the notes.

Other sources cannot be discounted since we know from the catalogue of Voltaire's library that he possessed most of ths standard works on Roman history, many of which he mentions, few of which he praises.

17. The dramatic tradition of the 'art de régner' play has been outlined by M. Baudin in 'L'art de régner in seventeenth-century French tragedy', *Modern language notes* 50 (1935), pp.417-26.

18. M.vi.199. Voltaire repeats the arguments already rehearsed in the *Commentaires sur Corneille*, see n.15 above.

19. See H. T. Mason, *Pierre Bayle and Voltaire* (London 1963), pp.118-19, 52.

20. Voltaire to Cramer, Best.D16059, 26 December 1769.

21. Best.D4851, 27 March 1752. Besterman claims that Vertot wrote no work that can thus be described, but Voltaire was probably referring to a dissertation delivered to the Académie des inscriptions. See *The Characters of Augustus, Horace and Agrippa, with a comparison between his two ministers Agrippa and Maecenas*, in *Three dissertations*, trans. and ed. G. Turnbull (London 1740). In the same letter writings by Montesquieu, Saint-Evremond and Saint-Réal on Roman history are mentioned.

Indeed, in a letter to the *Gazette littéraire de l'Europe*, dated May 1764 by Besterman, Voltaire protests that 'l'histoire romaine est encore à faire parmi nous', claiming that Montesquieu was possibly the only Frenchman who could have written it (Best.D11871). In any event, Voltaire had as little use for pure erudition as many of his compatriots and his portrait of Augustus is not designed as a scholarly evaluation of evidence. It was essentially a moral judgement and Voltaire's material is carefully chosen to construct a composite figure, Octavian-Augustus, as it were, whose career from start to finish was a model of self-seeking poltroonery. The cornerstone of Voltaire's argument, in line with the Tacitean hypothesis, was that Octavian underwent no sea-change on his translation to emperor. Strictly speaking, the play itself deals, as the title suggests, only with the rise to power of Octavian, always an embarrassment to pro-Augustan commentators.

The notes, however, are heavily interlarded with passages dealing with the Principate and the chronological distinction is not always firm. Voltaire has to agree with received opinion of the day that the Augustan period was successful but scant attention is paid to the practical achievements of the emperor, since it is entirely with the moral portrait of Augustus that Voltaire is concerned, both in the notes to the play and in the subsequent article in the *Questions sur l'Encyclopédie* where a large section is entitled 'Des mœurs d'Auguste' (M.xvii.484-86). Voltaire dwells with relish on the sexual depravity of the Roman emperor, drawing freely on Suetonius as a source without a hint of the contempt he shows elsewhere for 'ce faiseur d'anecdotes'.[22] Voltaire begins his catalogue of the emperor's misdemeanours, following a suggestion in Bayle's *Dictionnaire*, with a justification for the character of Fulvie, whose animosity towards Octavian is an important element in the structure of the plot. Voltaire explains her hostility by claiming that Octavian had tired of his erstwhile mistress who was at once his own mother-in-law and Antony's wife. He quotes in support Martial's scurrilous epigram to that effect saying that it is 'un des plus forts témoignages de l'infamie des mœurs d'Auguste'.[23] Augustus is accused of having been Caesar's

22. *Le Pyrrhonisme de l'histoire* (1768), M.xxvii.258.

23. M.vi.182-83. Martial's epigram (Book XI.xxi) is fully discussed by Bayle in his *Dictionnaire historique et critique* (see articles 'Fulvie' and 'Glaphyra'). Most of the charges laid against Augustus here are reproduced in the section 'Des mœurs d'Auguste' of the article in the *Questions sur l'Encyclopédie*, M.xvii.484-86.

catamite, of prostituting himself to Hirtius and like Antony, Sulla and Caesar, of unrestrained homosexuality (M.vi.183). Voltaire combines charges of perversion and effeminacy with political and financial self-seeking, while hetrosexual promiscuity, which might have been regarded more indulgently, is laced with blasphemy and gross disregard for private and public decency. Voltaire lingeringly describes an orgiastic banquet with the guests in Olympian fancy-dress, adultery committed openly in the presence of a consular husband, and Augustus's marriage to Livia, who was heavily pregnant with another man's child (M.vi.183).

Not content with this impressively varied catalogue of outrages Voltaire adds what he claims to be a well-documented charge of incest (M.vi.183):

Presque tous les auteurs latins qui ont parlé d'Ovide prétendent qu'Auguste n'eut l'insolence d'exiler ce chevalier romain, qui était beaucoup plus honnête homme que lui, que parce qu'il avait été surpris par lui dans un inceste avec sa propre fille Julia [...] Cela est d'autant plus vraisemblable que Caligula publiait hautement que sa mère était née de l'inceste d'Auguste et de Julie [*sic*].

This is a complete distortion of evidence and in all probability a conscious one. The whole question is reviewed by Bayle at considerable length in his article 'Ovide' in the *Dictionnaire*. Whether Ovid's offence was witting or unwitting voyeurism or, as some allege, adultery with the elder Julia, Augustus would have been unlikely to wait ten years to exile the unfortunate poet when he dispatched his own daughter to Pandateria immediately. Moreover, Voltaire's airy claim to the authority of 'presque tous les auteurs latins qui ont parlé d'Ovide' is to say the least disingenuous. In a recent piece of literary detective work, J. C. Thibault traces the whole history of the debate over the mystery of Ovid's exile and points out that speculation began in earnest only in 1437.[24] Ironically he cites Voltaire himself as one of the prime movers of the incest theory and argues that the source of the theory is probably Caligula's assertion which Voltaire uses ostensibly as supporting evidence.[25]

Clearly Voltaire is here subordinating historical accuracy to his declared intention of supplying a true moral portrait of the period. This is not in itself surprising. Such an approach was broadly consistent with Voltaire's view that ancient history was useful only in so far as it was

24. *The Mystery of Ovid's exile* (Berkeley 1964), p.125.
25. p.125. Only three writers are quoted as having made this allegation before Voltaire, two in the sixteenth century, one in the seventeenth.

relevant to contemporary society and that in any case primary sources at that remove were unreliable.[26] Voltaire, it would seem, is at all costs out to prevent his readers from making the mistake of assuming that the felicity of Augustan rule corresponds with any moral conversion or implies a discontinuity between the Octavian of the proscriptions and the imperial defender of public morality. Similarly, political comment is conspicuously limited. Voltaire concentrates his fire on the rise to power of Octavian through the Triumvirate and the later disgrace of Antony. In the notes he rejects the received tradition of Octavian as a reluctant partner in the proscriptions (particularly as regards the death of Cicero) and argues instead that Octavian's initial usurpation of power had been transformed into a subtle tyranny.

The portrait of Antony confirms this thesis. Here Voltaire follows the traditional Plutarchan model predictably enough but even he cannot resist according Antony a doubtful moral superiority over Octavian. Antony, debauched and brutal, a 'soldat grossier' (M.vi.184), is nevertheless allowed to be a courageous butcher by contrast with his lily-livered confederate. In the notes to the play, it is true, the charge of political opportunism is levelled against both Octavian and Antony. They are political opportunists: 'Il est bien évident que la vengeance du meurtre de César ne fut jamais que le prétexte de leur ambition' (M.vi.186). Each hated and mistrusted the other, both are motivated by self-interest and both are dubbed 'scélérats, sons loi, sans probité, fourbes ingrats, sanguinaires'.[27] In the later article for the Questions sur l'Encyclopedie, however, Voltaire keeps almost the same verbal formulae but this time directed exclusively at Octavian. Moreover, not content with this cumulation of vices, he adds to his list 'tranquille dans le crime' (M.xvii.486), thereby departing from the traditional interpretation he had respected in the play which allowed Augustus a measure of hesitation in his crime. Even in the text of the original play Voltaire cannot resist allowing Antoine to anticipate the future Augustus when he says to Octave: 'Vous voulez devenir un tyran populaire' (M.vi.193). Only one chink in Augustus's armour of self-interest is allowed and it is in itself an indictment. Discussing Dio's account of Augustus's superstitious beliefs,

26. This premise underpins most of Voltaire's serious writing on history. See La Philosophie de l'histoire, pp.14-17.
27. M.vi.186; cf. M.xvii.486.

Voltaire says: 'Auguste feignit toujours d'être superstitieux; et peut-être le fut-il quelquefois' (M.xi.191).

Augustus was therefore not only manipulative and dishonest, contriving to exploit the forces of superstition but at the same time, however implausible the juxtaposition may seem, Augustus was also guilty of the equally heinous offence in Voltaire's eyes of gullible credulity.

There are, then, no grey areas in Voltaire's portrayal of Augustus. The transformation of the brutal Octavian to the skilful emperor is not the result of a mysterious change of heart: it is, Voltaire suggests, a conscious deception. In the brief essay *Du gouvernement d'Auguste* (1766) he writes, '[Octave/Auguste] accumula insensiblement sur sa tête les dignités de la republique' (M.xxv.587), stressing the insidious nature of Octavian's consolidation of power. The ruthless material 'dépouillement' which Octavian practised on his compatriots at the time of the proscriptions was, Voltaire claims, followed by a period in which Octavian contrived to forge quite deliberately a new persona for public consumption. The event which Voltaire chooses as the basis of his argument is the conspiracy of Cinna which, refracted through the glass of historical and literary tradition, had become the symbol *par excellence* of imperial clemency. Voltaire opens his attack on Augustus's reputation by citing three instances taken from Suetonius and quoted with few apparent doubts as to their reliability, of occasions when Octavian/Augustus showed an excessive desire for revenge (M.vi.298). Here, Voltaire is guilty not only of using unreliable source material but also of linguistic *supercherie* since he begins his sentence with a reference to Augustus, but of the three anecdotes he quotes only one relates to the period of the Principate.[28] As far as the conspiracy of Cinna is concerned, Voltaire suggests that Seneca, who is the direct source of the tradition, is creating a moral example for the purposes of his argument rather than quoting a historical truth. In support of this theory, Voltaire argues that neither Tacitus nor Suetonius mentions the conspiracy, though Suetonius does deal in some detail with other conspiracies against the emperor. Dio merely follows Seneca and Seneca's account 'ressemble plus à une déclamation qu'à une vérité historique' (M.vi.199), an accurate observation but one that might equally apply to Voltaire's own treatment of this subject. Secondly, and more tendentiously, Voltaire argues that 'un

28. The allegation is repeated in the article for the *Questions sur l'Encyclopedie*, M.xvii.487.

simple courtisan subalterne' (M.vi.199) would have been extremely unlikely to challenge a respected and well established ruler such as Augustus and had he done so, would have been even more unlikely to be made consul for his pains. If Augustus pardoned at all it was either in response to political pressure from his wife Livia 'qui avait pris sur lui un grand ascendant' (M.vi.199), in which case he was weak minded, or as a political manœuvre, in which case he was devious. In either event, Augustus emerged badly (M.vi.199):

> Je crois bien qu'Auguste a pu pardonner quelquefois par politique, et affecter de la grandeur d'âme: mais je suis persuadé qu'il n'en avait pas; et, que sous quelques traits héroïques qu'on puisse le représenter sur le théâtre, je ne puis avoir d'autre idée de lui que celle d'un homme uniquement occupé de son intérêt pendant toute sa vie. Heureux quand cet intérêt s'accordait avec la gloire!

For Augustus self-interest and 'gloire' did indeed coincide in Voltaire's eyes: the greatness of Rome in the Augustan age acted as a kind of moral *trompe-l'œil* persuading us by its imperial and cultural brilliance to 'respecter ce que nous haïssons dans le fond du cœur' (M.vi.186). Voltaire is at pains to eliminate this confusion in his discussion of the emperor. The undoubted achievements of Augustus's reign are ignored or undervalued. Action is consciously and consistently subordinated to intentionality so that political adroitness is the only positive quality that Voltaire will allow, keeping the paradox of 'un monstre adroit et heureux' (M.xvii.488) remorselessly before his readers. Far from the historically accurate portrait that Voltaire promises, his depiction of Augustus is closer to a caricature, sharing some of the characteristics of Voltaire's fictional creations and something of their didactic purpose. Setting aside his own frequently expressed sentiments on the need for historical pyrrhonism, he quarries his sources tirelessly for anecdotal snippets detrimental to the emperor, ignoring or belittling counter-evidence and omitting to point out the unreliability of his material.[29] The result is a one-dimensional portrait of a thoroughgoing tyrant whose sole redeeming feature is the doubtful virtue of being born a pagan.

To accuse Voltaire of character assassination is, however, to beg the question. Why should Voltaire choose to range himself so firmly in the

29. Voltaire's uncritical use of Suetonius is the best example of this. To give specious authority to his assertions he lards the notes to the play with false assertions such as 'Les historiens disent ...', M.vi.186, n.2; 'Rien n'est plus connu ...', M.vi.183, n.1) or 'Presque tous les auteurs latins ...' (M.vi.183, n.1).

Tacitean camp, antagonistic to the emperor? Why, when Voltaire so seldom chooses classical Rome as a subject for historical investigation, should he launch an attack of such virulence on the ruler of Rome in the Golden Age? True, as Howard Weinbrot points out in his account of anti-Augustan feeling, other historians and writers shared Voltaire's cynicism about the moral integrity of the emperor, and a more historically scientific picture was emerging.[30] But Voltaire's presentation of Augustus was not an objective piece of historical writing, even by the standards of his own historical works. Consonant with the belief that ancient history is useful only in so far as it allows comparison with contemporary laws and *mores*, Voltaire's analysis of the moral comportment of the emperor would seem to have direct, if limited, moral significance for his contemporaries. While, undoubtedly, the occasional cause of the play was the lingering desire to tilt at Crébillon even after the latter's death, the subsequent addition of notes and the later transformation of these articles argue a more far-reaching purpose.

In the first place, it is possible that Voltaire's image of the Golden Age of Rome is at least to some extent a response to the teleological assimilation of the period into Christian cosmology, as demonstrated by Bossuet in the *Histoire universelle*. Augustus, whatever his earlier sins, had been the instrument of God in providing a peaceful world into which Christ might be born. Bossuet conjures an image of divine order from pagan chaos: 'Rome tend les bras à Cesar, qui demeure, sous le nom d'Auguste et sous le titre d'Empereur, seul maistre de tout l'empire [...] Victorieux par mer et par terre, il ferme le Temple de Janus. Tout l'univers vit en paix sous sa puissance, et Jésus-Christ vient au monde.'[31]

With his use of the historic present, his personification of Rome, arms outstretched towards an absolute but wise ruler, Bossuet extends the divine sanction to Augustus, allowing him a paternalistic peace-giving role, prior to the advent of Christ. It is an interpretation that Voltaire could be relied upon to refute, but the refutation is implied rather than direct. Bossuet is not specifically mentioned in the notes and would not appear to be a specific target, though, as J. H. Brumfitt points out, the

---

30. *Augustus Caesar in 'Augustan' England: the decline of a classical norm* (Princeton 1978). Judgements of Augustus in historical and literary works are assessed in chapters 1 and 2 and Weinbrot demonstrates that hostility to Augustus was far from uncommon.

31. *Discours sur l'histoire universelle*, ed. A. Gaste (Paris 1885), i.101.

Christian historian cast a long shadow, and Voltaire's interpretation of history was antithetically opposed to his.[32]

A more likely source of inspiration for Voltaire's extreme *parti pris* might seem to be the lively Augustan debate across the Channel in England. Two recent studies, the one previously mentioned by H. Weinbrot, the second by H. Erskine-Hill,[33] have between them illuminated the history and impact of the identification of Augustan England and eighteenth-century Rome. No comparable phenomenon, however, existed in France at the time. As H. Gillot points out in *La Querelle des Anciens et des Modernes en France*, the discussion of contemporary society as a recreation or a *dépassement* of the Augustan Age had been exhausted under Louis XIV when the French monarch was extolled as a new Augustus and Colbert as his Maecenas (Genève 1968, p.319). By the eighteenth century, the comparison had become a cliché and aroused little interest. Voltaire briefly takes up the idea in *Le Siècle de Louis XIV*, throwing his lot firmly in with the *Modernes* by affirming the superiority of the reign of Louis XIV over the Roman model (M.xiv.156). But for the most part, the metaphor remains casual and had none of the political overtones of the English debate. None the less Voltaire had come into contact with Bolingbroke and his friends who adopted a broadly anti-Augustan stance; he may through them have known of the attacks on Walpole and George Augustus and sympathised with their point of view. He certainly, too, knew Middleton's *Life of Cicero*[34] and may have been acquainted with other English examples of anti-Augustan literature, though there is no evidence that the precise issues of the debate made any impact. Indeed, in letter VIII of the *Lettres philosophiques* he is derisive of the vogue for comparison between the English Parliament and the Roman Senate.

It is possibly to the wider intellectual and moral implications of the Augustan debate that we can look to supply motive for Voltaire's minor vendetta against the Roman emperor. Voltaire offers little comment on the character of Augustus before the period we have already discussed, namely 1764-1766 and 1770, but from the earliest points of his career we can find a conscious identification of his own career with that of the

32. *La Philosophie de l'histoire*, pp.32-35.

33. *The Augustan idea in English literature* (London 1983). See in particular chapter 9.

34. Voltaire describes the Englishman's work as 'histoire excellente' in the notes to *Le Triumvirat*, M.vi.210.

court poets Virgil and Horace. This was in many respects an unsurprising convention and a continuing metaphor of the kind so often applied to the court of Louis XIV, but it was a compliment clearly accepted and sustained by Voltaire and used by many of his correspondents. Most notable in this respect was Frederick, who in his letters to Voltaire gracefully makes the comparison, particularly with Virgil, on repeated occasions. His comments on the patronage are, however, characteristically shrewd: writing to Voltaire in 1738 he couples an assertion of the prince's duty to protect great men with a dry reminder that these same great men will ensure the survival of the prince's own reputation.[35] It is a sentiment that Voltaire would presumably have endorsed since he had made exactly the same point in the *Essai sur la poésie épique* some ten years earlier. Speaking of Augustus's relationship to Virgil and Horace, he writes: 'cet heureux tyran savait bien qu'un jour sa réputation dépendrait d'eux: aussi est-il arrivé que l'idée que ces deux écrivains nous ont donné d'Auguste a effacé l'horreur de ses proscriptions; ils nous font aimer sa mémoire; ils ont fait, si j'ose le dire, illusion à toute la terre' (M.viii.321).

What Voltaire sees as the abject flattery by Virgil and Horace of Augustus is something he clearly found it hard to forgive from a very early stage in his career onwards. He makes frequent if passing reference to their poor judgement, and seems to be unaware or unimpressed by the exceptions to it – Horace, in particular, was far from uniformly admiring and on occasion ventures outspoken criticism.[36] Certainly, Voltaire is deeply suspicious of the uneasy relationship between patron and *protégé*, prince and poet. The analogy between his own situation and that of the two Roman poets moved him sufficiently to provoke a self-justificatory comparison. In 1772, when differences between Voltaire and Frederick had been patched up, he apostrophises Horace, chiding him and Virgil for serving an unworthy master, and claiming that Frederick by contrast made less excessive demands (M.x.442):

> Je suis un peu fâché pour Virgile et pour toi
> Que, tous deux, nés Romains, vous flattiez tant un roi.
> Mon Frédéric du moins, né roi très légitime

35. Best.D1564. Among other examples one may quote the following: Best.D1397, D1459, D2017, D3511, D3814, D18163. Voltaire is most frequently compared with Virgil, but Horace, Quintilian and Homer are also invoked.

36. For a brief discussion of Horace's attitude to Augustus, see Kenneth J. Reckford, *Horace* (New York 1969), pp.70-84.

Ne doit point des grandeurs aux bassesses du crime.
Ton maître était un fourbe, un tranquille assassin;
Pour voler son tuteur, il lui perça le sein;
Il trahit Cicéron, père de la patrie;
Amant incestueux de sa fille Julie,
De son rival Ovide il proscrivit ses vers
Et fit transir sa muse au milieu des déserts.
Je sais que prudemment ce politique esclave
Payait l'heureux encens d'un plus adroit esclave
Frédéric exigeait des soins moins complaisants:
Nous soupions avec lui sans lui donner d'encens;
De son goût délicat la finesse agréable
Faisait, sans nous gêner, les honneurs de la table;
Nul roi ne fut jamais si fertile en bons mots
Contre les préjugés, les fripons, et les sots.
Maupertuis gâta tout …
Le Plaisir s'envole; je partis avec lui.

According to this analysis, though Frederick may emerge more creditably than Augustus, the relationship between monarch and writer is none the less precarious and unequal, dependent on the whim of the ruler or the manipulation of courtiers. It is to this relationship that Voltaire refers when he writes to the d'Argentals in 1766 about his reasons for wishing to discredit Augustus: 'Je veux couler à fond la réputation d'Auguste; j'ai une dent contre lui depuis longtemps, pour avoir eu l'insolence d'exiler Ovide qui valait mieux que lui.'[37]

The key-word here is 'valait': political power and moral integrity were unlikely bed-fellows. Voltaire makes a related statement in a further letter, this time about the notes to *Le Triumvirat*, to Lacombe (Best. D13812):

Mais pour oser dire que nous sommes meilleurs que nos ancêtres, il faudrait que, nous trouvant dans les mêmes circonstances qu'eux, nous nous abstinsions avec horreur des cruautés dont ils ont été coupables [...] La philosophie ne pénètre pas toujours chez les grands qui ordonnent, et encor moins chez les hordes des petits qui éxécutent. Elle n'est le partage que des hommes placez dans la médiocrité, également éloignez de l'ambition qui opprime, et de la basse férocité qui est à ses gages.

It is hardly surprising if Voltaire, always unsure of his position in the French court, equally distrustful of the blandishments of foreign princes, and poised for ready flight at any time, should have felt a particular

37. Best.D13325, 30 May 1766.

sympathy with the harsh, mysterious exile of Ovid. He too had experienced exile and the wrath of monarchs. Ovid's exile precisely symbolised the absurd paradox whereby the morally corrupt can exercise an arbitrary and absolute power over those whose superiority lies in their talent. Augustus may have been fortunate, but he was never virtuous. He may have brought peace and prosperity to Rome but at the cost of reducing her citizenry to effete enslavement. Voltaire is less tempted than many to equate republican Rome and the pre-lapsarian state,[38] but he would seem to imply that the exercise of political power made the possibility of moral progress sometimes ascribed to Augustus extremely unlikely.

Thus the corruption that was so often a concomitant of power can be seen to contrast sharply in Voltaire's mind with the innocence and integrity of right-minded intellectuals and writers, regardless of the political situation in which they find themselves. In the context of the Roman world, as well as in others, Voltaire's perception of the role of philosopher and *littérateur* was universal and synchronic. Virgil, Horace and Ovid belong firmly in the pantheon of secular saints alongside Socrates and Spinoza, regardless of spatial or temporal distinctions. This point of view is apparent in an exchange of correspondence with J.-J. Rousseau in 1755. Voltaire argues that Virgil, Horace, Lucretius and Cicero were blameless as regards the proscriptions which were the handiwork of 'ce débauché d'Antoine [...] cet imbécille Lépide [...] ce tiran sans courage Octave Cépias, surnommé si lâchement Auguste'.[39] In his reply Rousseau concedes that the writers had no direct responsibility but counters with a much subtler argument:

D'ailleurs, il y a dans le progrès des choses, des liaisons cachées que le vulgaire n'apperçoit pas, mais qui n'échapperont point à l'œil du Philosophe, quand il y voudra réfléchir. Ce n'est ni Cicéron, ni Virgile, ne Seneque, ni Tacite qui ont produit les crimes des Romains et les malheurs de Rome. Mais sans le poison lent et secret qui corrompoit insensiblement le plus vigoureux gouvernement dont l'histoire fasse mention, Ciceron, ni Lucrèce, ni Salluste, ni tous les autres n'eussent point existé ou n'eussent point écrit. Le siècle aimable de Lelius et de Terence

---

38. Voltaire denies that virtue is the principle of a republic (M.vi.209-10) but is willing, however, to admit a degree of resigned nostalgia: 'Il y eut toujours des cœurs romains qui détestèrent la tyrannie, non seulement sous [Auguste] mais sous ses successeurs: on regretta la république mais on ne put la rétablir' (M.vi.241).

39. Best.D13812 [c.5 January 1767]. Voltaire repeats this point in the notes to *Le Triumvirat* (M.vi.188-89), confirming his belief that *belles-lettres* do not contribute towards moral decadence.

amenoit de loin le siècle brillant d'Auguste et d'Horace, et enfin les siècles horribles de Seneque et de Neron, de Tacite et de Domitien. Le goût des sciences et des arts nait chez un Peuple d'un vice intérieur qu'il augmente bientôt à son tour, et s'il est vrai que tous les progrès humains sont pernicieux à l'espèce, ceux de l'esprit et des conoissances, qui augmentent nôtre orgueil et multiplient nos égaremens, accélèrent bientôt nos malheurs.[40]

Voltaire shares neither Rousseau's historical prevision nor his pessimism. He claims that the greatest atrocities are committed by the unenlightened (Best.D6451), allowing at least a faint hope of progress. But enlightenment and power are poor bedfellows, and in practice Voltaire's view of power is scarcely more sanguine than that of Rousseau. In *Des conspirations contre les peuples*, the brief pendant to the historical analysis of *Le Triumvirat*, Voltaire shows that Augustus is just one in a colourful procession of ambitious, autocratic and bloody rulers (M.xxvi.1-15). Voltaire's de-mythification of Augustus subverts hope of any but the most limited and fortuitous conjunction of moral enlightenment and political power. If the Golden Age of Rome, the supreme symbol of the peaceful and ordered state in which arts and philosophy flourish, is demonstrably the product of political expediency and ambition masquerading as virtue, then any neo-Augustan Age is liable to prove no less illusory and fragile.

40. Best.D6469, 7 September [1755].

Voltaire and Louis Racine

HAYDN MASON

WHATEVER the limitations that critical posterity has found in Voltaire's poetry, there is a general consensus that as a poet he reigned alone in his own time. This view has dealt harshly with at least one contemporary, Louis Racine, who was of Voltaire's generation and during their early years a good friend. Son of the great seventeenth-century tragedian, Louis Racine was slightly the elder of the two poets, born in 1692. Like Voltaire, he early nursed bold literary ambitions. Having gained access to the Académie des inscriptions in 1719, he was aiming even higher, at the Académie française, a mere two years later while still under thirty years of age. Already, Voltaire considered himself and Racine the leading poets of their day, comparing the two of them to Horace and Virgil (Best.D79: even if one allows that the link may have been made somewhat tongue-in-cheek, nothing suggests that Voltaire did not believe whole-heartedly in the compliment awarded to himself and his fellow-poet). For a while the friendship flowered between the pair. Five letters from Voltaire to Racine remain extant from the years 1718-1721, testifying to the close rapport, which included dining together before a joint excursion to the Comédie-Française (Best.D79). When Racine set his cap at the Académie française, Voltaire's praise seems unfeigned and quite free of envy: 'vous avez sans doute un party[1] contre vous, mais si vous voulez me croire, vous le ramenerez en un jour, et vous aurez touttes les voix sans en excepter une. C'est ainsi qu'il vous convient d'entrer dans l'académie. [...] Il ne tient certainement qu'à vous de réussir' (Best. D101).

This friendship was fated, perhaps inevitably, to cool. From 1722, in any case, their paths diverged. Financial reasons obliged Racine to accept a post as tax inspector in Provence; this was the beginning of a long stay in the provinces, and he was not to return to settle in Paris again until he retired in 1746. No further letters from Voltaire to Racine survive

---

1. Doubtless Voltaire was referring to the cardinal de Fleury, who blocked Racine's candidature in all probability because of the latter's overt espousal of Jansenist opinions; Racine was not in fact ever to succeed in entering the Académie française.

from before 1736. Already in 1722 there are signs of a cooling. Voltaire expresses surprise to Thieriot that Racine is angry with him, asserting that 'Je ne lui dois que de l'amitié et non pas de l'asservissement' (Best. D121). The probable occasion of the discord was Racine's poem *La Grâce*. The work was not published in circulated editions until 1722, but it had been printed in 1720[2] and Voltaire had attacked it in the *Mémoires historiques et critiques* appearing in January 1722. The twelve-verse *Epître à Monsieur Louis Racine* expresses a sharp disagreement of outlook:

> Cher Racine, j'ai lu dans tes vers dogmatiques
> De ton Jansénius les leçons fanatiques.
> Quelquefois je t'admire, et ne te crois en rien.
> Si ton style me plaît, ton Dieu n'est pas le mien.

As we can see, Voltaire's criticism is directed at the substance rather than the form of Racine's work, for which he continues to profess respect at this stage. But the hostility to the latter's Jansenism is explicit – indeed, over-explicit perhaps even in Voltaire's view, as he was to amend 'dogmatiques' to 'didactiques' in the first line by the time the poem was published in 1724.[3] Later in 1722 he is asking for *La Grâce* to be sent to him, while he is composing some unspecified work on which he will say no more at present (Best.D125). There is a strong likelihood that this latter was the *Epître à Julie*; as we shall see, the two poems present some important parallels.

But the difference of opinion did not lead to outright hostility as was the case between Voltaire and Jean-Baptiste Rousseau. In 1736 Voltaire sends Racine the Préface to *Alzire*, taking the opportunity to praise the passage from the latter's epic poem *La Religion* 'que vous me fîtes l'honneur de me lire, il y a quelques années'. Never, adds Voltaire, will he be found in the ranks of Racine's enemies: 'Je me mets depuis longtemps au rang de vos plus grands partisans sans quoyqu'assurément je ne pense pas comme vous sur les matières que vous traittez. Mais cette différence de sentiments ne sert qu'à m'affermir davantage dans l'estime' (Best.D1060). That same year he calls upon Racine to support him in his campaign for a relaxation of the rules regarding rhyme in French. Rhyme should surely be intended for the ear alone; it should not matter

---

2. G. B. Watts, 'Louis Racine's *De la Grâce*', *PMLA* 55 (1940), p.780; E. Guitton, 'Un poème hardi et singulier: *La Grâce* de Louis Racine', *La Régence* (Paris 1970), pp.165-73.

3. G. B. Watts, 'Voltaire's verses against Louis Racine's *De la Grâce*', *MLN* 40 (1925), p.190.

that *terre* and *père* are spelt differently (Best.D1074). Racine had criticised this liberal attitude, as another letter to him from Voltaire at this time makes clear (Best.D1106). But Voltaire takes a conciliatory approach, expressing the wish that he could find time to visit Racine in Soissons and hear 'votre beau poème de la relligion'.

However, from 1738 their relationship becomes distinctly less amicable. The trouble is caused by Racine's decision to seek licence to publish a satire by J.-B. Rousseau against Voltaire. In the virulent feud between these latter two, Racine had chosen to show open support for Rousseau. Voltaire's personal friendship with Racine now appears to be at an end. If any further letters passed between them, none now survives, and Voltaire's only remaining direct address to Racine is the *lettre ostensible* entitled *Conseils à M. Racine sur son poème de 'La Religion'* and published anonymously in 1742 when finally Racine's major poem had appeared. In the *Conseils*, having commented (for the most part unfavourably) on *La Religion*, Voltaire goes on to criticise Racine for publishing an *épître* by Rousseau after his own poem and begs him not to hurl so much invective at his fellow-authors (M.xxiii.182-84).

The relationship does not, however, degenerate into one of those dramatically violent quarrels that are so common in Voltaire's career. The latter is often disapproving of Racine's work, but there is no deep personal animus and he is able on occasion to express praise along with the criticism. In the *Connaissance des beautés* (1749)[4] Voltaire particularly singles out for compliments a passage of seventeen verses in Chant iv of *La Grâce* which gives, he says, 'une très-belle idée de la grandeur de Dieu' (M.xxiii.382-83). Similar generalised praise is expressed for some verses of *La Grâce* and *La Religion* in the entry for Louis Racine within the *Catalogue des écrivains* (1768) to Voltaire's *Siècle de Louis XIV*, and approving comments occur in the *Questions sur l'Encyclopédie* (1770) upon some of Racine's remarks in his *Réflexions sur la poésie*.

---

4. It must be admitted that the evidence for Voltaire's authorship of the *Connaissance* remains dubious (cf. Th. Besterman, 'Note on the authorship of the *Connaissance des beautés*', *Studies on Voltaire* 4 (1957), pp.291-94). In the present instance, one may rejoin that the opinion expressed fits perfectly well with Voltaire's other views and that it relates to a section of *La Grâce* upon which he evidently concentrated (cf. below, p.106). Though of only secondary importance, one should also point out the close parallel between the introductory reference to Racine here ('Un fils du grand Racine, qui a hérité d'une partie des talents de son père') and that in Voltaire's article 'Auguste Octave' ('Louis Racine, fils du grand Racine, et héritier d'une partie de ses talents').

But the compliments, it must be confessed, are sparse. After 1738, the only specific works by Racine to elicit observations from Voltaire in his correspondence are the critical commentaries made by the son upon his illustrious father in the *Remarques sur les tragédies de Racine* and the *Traité de la poésie dramatique ancienne et moderne*. *La Grâce* and *La Religion* are no more heard of. Louis Racine's poetry has apparently begun to pall on Voltaire. In a letter of 1766 to the abbé d'Olivet he concedes that 'Louis Racine a frappé souvent des vers sur l'enclume de Jean, son père', but the faint praise serves merely to damn him (Best.D13233):

Pourquoi donc a-t-il si peu de réputation? C'est qu'il manque d'imagination et de variété; il n'y a rien chez lui de piquant; il n'a pas sacrifié aux grâces [...] et quoi qu'il tourne bien ses vers,
> On lit peu ces auteurs nés pour nous ennuier,
> Qui toujours sur un ton semblent psalmodier.

Racine stands convicted of the great sin: he is boring. The accusation had been consistently made by Voltaire ever since *La Religion* appeared in 1742. The *Conseils à M. Racine* open with a similarly devastating judgement: 'En lisant le poème de *la Religion* du fils de notre illustre Racine, j'ai remarqué des beautés; mais j'ai senti un défaut qui règne dans tout l'ouvrage: c'est la monotonie.' What is lacking is *invention*: 'je demande à M. Racine [...] plus de chaleur, plus de figures, et des tableaux plus frappants'. There is too much versifying of the ideas of others: 'Cet asservissement de l'esprit le gêne trop dans sa marche. Trop d'imitation éteint le génie' (M.xxiii.173-74). A similar opinion is expressed in the canonical judgement of the *Catalogue des écrivains* (1768) where Racine, now dead, is accorded his due place in the history of literature: 'RACINE (Louis), fils de l'immortel Jean Racine, a marché sur les traces de son père, mais dans un sentier plus étroit et moins fait pour les muses. Il entendait la mécanique des vers aussi bien que son père, mais il n'en avait ni l'âme ni les grâces. Il manquait d'ailleurs d'invention et d'imagination.' There are some good lines in *La Grâce* and *La Religion*, but the latter poem as a whole is an 'ouvrage trop didactique et trop monotone, copié des *Pensées de Pascal*' (M.xiv.118-19). It is the definitive obituary. Form, however, is not entirely divorced from substance: 'Janséniste comme son père, il ne fit des vers que pour le jansénisme.' The implication seems clear: Louis Racine's mediocrity had also revealed itself in the limited range of his material, the 'sentier plus étroit' which he had followed. He had been betrayed by his own obsessions.

From the *Conseils* onwards, therefore, once the full face of Louis Racine has been revealed in *La Religion*, Voltaire's criticisms do not cease to link the wrongness of the latter's ideas with the paucity of their expression.[5] Racine is not only monotonous and imitative; he also preaches false doctrine. He had, for instance, claimed that God could not have forgotten His own glory to the point of wishing to deceive us. Voltaire's reply is simple and direct: God does allow men to be deceived by Islam, even with its severe precepts that Muslims disobey at risk of damnation. He has also allowed China, 'la plus belle partie de la terre', to be deceived for nearly three thousand years 'par l'admirable et austère morale de Confucius'. Why does Racine, furthermore, claim that there are more Christians than Muslims in the world? He cannot know; and besides, what would he prove even if he were right? Hence his view of the world has a false basis, and for this reason it lacks breadth and nobility (M.xxiii.175-76). Likewise, he disfigures *La Grâce* when, after a fine passage on the greatness of God (cf. M.xxiii.382-83), he goes on to a libellous comment upon England (Chant IV, p.71):[6]

> L'Angleterre, où jadis brilla tant de lumière,
> Recevant aujourd'hui toutes religions,
> N'est plus qu'un triste amas de folles visions

Racine is mistaken, rejoins Voltaire; England is a land of enlightenment and freedom. But there are wider implications: 'Il est ridicule de penser qu'une nation éclairée ne soit pas plus heureuse qu'une nation ignorante. Il est affreux d'insinuer que la tolérance est dangereuse, quand nous voyons à nos portes l'Angleterre et la Hollande peuplées et enrichies par cette tolérance' (M.xxiv.122). This objection to Racine's observation upon England, first raised by Voltaire in the *Réflexions pour les sots* (1760), is revived with brief causticity in the article 'Catéchisme du Japonnais' of the *Dictionnaire philosophique* (1764), where the first and last verses are quoted, followed by the notation that Racine is 'un grand visionnaire', ignorant and prejudiced (M.xviii.85-86). Voltaire returns to the same attack another four years later in *L'ABC*. This time he takes the same

5. A possible exception might be made for the article 'Auguste Octave' in the *Questions sur l'Encyclopédie* (1770), which gives Racine credit for two minor points of reference to Corneille and Massillon. But here too Voltaire criticises Racine as well; and the marginal allusion can hardly be said to affect the general pattern.

6. All references to *La Grâce* and *La Religion* will be taken from Louis Racine's *Œuvres complètes* (Paris 1808), vol.i.

verses within a longer passage by Racine that concludes with the self-congratulatory couplet:

Vérité toujours pure, ô doctrine éternelle!
La France est aujourd'hui ton royaume fidèle.[7]

By now the satiric tone has become, if anything, sharper still: 'Voilà un plaisant original…! Un Français croit toujours qu'il doit donner le ton aux autres nations.' When was it in France, asks Voltaire (borrowing Racine's own phrases), 'ce temps jadis où brilla tant de lumière'? When France, for example, swarmed with monks and miracles? The deduction to be drawn is evident. Racine's art and morality alike are in error: 'Ce plat poète est un bien mauvais citoyen' (M.xxvii.366). This is the man who fails to see the strength of his own arguments proving that animals can reason and who, against his own evidence, concludes that animals are pure machines (*Les Adorateurs* (1769): M.xxviii.318-19). This is the man who dares to treat Pierre Bayle as 'cœur cruel et […] homme affreux', comparing him to Marius seated on the ruins of Carthage. Once again bad philosophy and bad poetry coincide: 'Voilà une similitude bien peu ressemblante. […] Marius n'avait point détruit Carthage comme Bayle avait détruit de mauvais arguments.' Racine exaggerates wildly, failing to appreciate what real cruelty means (and Voltaire provides some examples). The *philosophe*'s conclusion is lapidary: 'O gens de parti! gens attaqués de la jaunisse! vous verrez toujours tout jaune' (M.xvii.553-55). The passage comes from Voltaire's article on Bayle in the *Questions sur l'Encyclopédie* (1770), where he is repeating his criticism, made in the *Conseils à Racine* nearly thirty years earlier, of the poet's same 'injures atroces' about Bayle (M.xxiii.183). Here it has taken on the broader measure of an onslaught upon *esprit de parti*. Racine has become a minor but exemplary target in Voltaire's crusade to *écraser l'infâme*.

Let us return to look more closely at the specific impact of *La Grâce* and *La Religion*. We have already noted how from the initial reading Voltaire had recognised a hateful dogma in the first of these poems. The doctrine of all-prevailing Grace, the call to the reader to abase himself, reason and passions alike (subjects treated in the first three Cantos), held little appeal for Voltaire and stimulated no specific reaction. It is the fourth and final Canto that particularly attracts Voltaire's attention. For

7. The punctuation is slightly different in Racine's *Œuvres complètes*. I have followed the version in the Moland edition.

it is here that Racine boldly faces the doctrine of eternal damnation for all who have not been redeemed by Grace. This doctrine is adumbrated with chilling clarity. Ever since Adam, 'Les feux toujours brûlants sont allumés pour nous' (Chant IV, p.68). Nor does any human being deserve anything better:

> Des humains en deux parts Dieu sépare la masse:
> Il choisit, il rejette, il fait justice et grâce.
> Qui se plaindra, quand tous méritent l'abandon?

No one is safe until the very last moment of his life, even if he has led a blameless life till then (Chant IV, p.73):

> Jusqu'au dernier instant il faut toujours courir.
> Près d'atteindre le terme on peut encor périr.
> L'austère pénitent, le pâle solitaire,
> Couché sur le cilice, et blanchi sous la haire,
> Par un souffle d'orgueil, un impur mouvement,
> Un désir avoué, perd tout en un moment.

This is indeed a terrifying divinity (Chant IV, p.77):

> Il est père, il est Dieu: je crains le Dieu terrible.

Such is not Voltaire's God. The *Epître à Racine* had already made it clear:

> Si ton style me plaît, ton Dieu n'est pas le mien:
> Tu m'en fais un tyran; je veux qu'il soit un père.[8]

The latter verse is found, in revised form, in the *Epître à Uranie*:

> On te fait un tyran, en toi je cherche un Père.[9]

As we have noted, Voltaire's explicit comments on *La Grâce* relate particularly to Chant IV. He admires with one or two reservations a passage describing the greatness of God that appears in this section (M.xxiii.382-83), and conversely, takes issue on three separate occasions, as we have seen, with the lines that follow a little later, on England and France.

So there is good reason to believe that Voltaire had firmly in mind Racine's compelling account of the doctrine of everlasting punishment when replying to the thesis of a hateful God in the *Epître à Uranie*. He

8. M.x.479. 'mon père' in the first version (*Mémoires historiques et critiques*, 1722): cf. Watts, 'Voltaire's verses', p.190.

9. V.95. All references to the *Epître à Uranie* will be taken from the edition by I. O. Wade, *PMLA* 47 (1932), pp.1105-12.

particularly adapts to his theme the Jansenist poet's observation that this terrible deity sometimes mysteriously cuts off his blessings to whole nations (Chant IV, pp.70-71):

> Dans cette obscure nuit l'astre si nécessaire,
> La foi, quand il le veut, s'éteint ou nous éclaire.
> [...] Que de peuples, hélas, que de vastes contrées
> A leur aveuglement sont encore livrées,
> Assises loin du jour dans l'ombre de la mort!

Voltaire borrows heavily on this phraseology to express a different opinion about the peoples who are ignorant of the Christian God (vv.73-82):

> Il en demande compte à cent Peuples divers,
> Assis dans la nuit du mensonge,
> Et dans l'obscurité où lui-même les plonge,
> Lui qui vient, dit-on, éclairer l'Univers.
> Amérique, vastes contrées [...]
> Vous serez donc un jour à sa fureur livrées

But the rejection of Racine's doctrine is elsewhere couched in less specifically similar terms as Voltaire outlines his reasons for hating this conception of the divinity. The Jansenist's God is one who created us, miserable and guilty beings, in order to punish us, who made us in His image but only 'Afin de nous mieux avilir'. It is the main purpose of the first half of the poem to deny Racine's vision: all the more so because, argues Voltaire, whereas the Old Testament God sought to destroy mankind, the New Testament God paradoxically seeks to save us (vv.45i-l):

> O prodige! ô tendresse! ô mystère!
> Il venait de noyer les pères,
> Il va mourir pour les enfants.

Even more incredibly, He has chosen the insignificant and morally worthless race of Israelites for this redemptive act (vv.46-49):

> Il est un Peuple obscur, imbécile, volage,
> Amateur insensé des superstitions.
> Vaincu par ses voisins, rampant dans l'esclavage,
> Et l'éternel mépris des autres Nations.

Voltaire's satirical portraits of the Jewish people will be numerous in the years to come. It is particularly interesting to note, therefore, that in this, the first of a long series of such attacks, he has received some textual help from *La Grâce*. A passage of Racine's poem on Israel contains the following couplet (Chant I, p.40):

> Ce peuple, dont un voile obscurcissait les yeux,
> Murmurateur, volage, amateur de faux Dieux

Only the concept 'murmurateur' has not been quarried by Voltaire for his own poem. The contextual verses, however, present no close parallels, and it seems likely that his attention was particularly caught by these lines alone as he saw how he could modify them to his purpose. This passage, unlike the earlier ones quoted from *La Grâce*, does not come from Chant IV, which renders more plausible the hypothesis of a specific influence relating to these verses in isolation rather than to the whole passage.

Voltaire continues to show his respect for the poetic qualities of *La Grâce* until around 1737. We cannot know the precise date of composition of his seventh and last *Discours en vers sur l'homme*, but in all probability it dates from 1738.[10] Originally entitled 'Ce que c'est que la vertu', it was in an early version addressed to Louis Racine, the poem beginning with the following lines (M.ix.425):

> J'ai lu les quatre points des sermons poétiques
> Qu'a débités ta muse, en ses vers didactiques;
> Peut-être il serait mieux de prêcher un peu moins
> [...] Mais j'aime mieux cent fois ta mâle austérité,
> Et de tes vers hardis la pénible beauté,
> Qu'un écrit bigarré de grave et de comique
> [...] Instruis-moi donc, poursuis, parle, et dans tes discours
> Définis la vertu, que tu chantas toujours.

Racine's austere definition of virtue was manifestly quite different from that of Voltaire, who equates it at the end of the *Discours* with *bienfaisance*. But Voltaire has still retained his admiration for what he calls 'la pénible beauté' of the Jansenist poet's verses. Moreover, his classical taste

---

10. The Avertissement to the *Discours* erroneously claims that the first three date from 1734 and the last four from 1737 (M.ix.378). Although the footnote by Beuchot corrects the error (originally made in the Kehl edition and renewed by Moland), it lives on to bedevil scholarship concerning the work. For a full account of the genesis of the poem, cf. the edition by G. R. Havens to appear eventually in the *Œuvres complètes* (ed. Th. Besterman, W. H. Barber and others). A manuscript copy may be consulted, in the interim period, at the Voltaire Foundation in Oxford.

responds warmly to the consistent gravity of tone of Racine's poem, which he far prefers to those who, like Marot and Rabelais (explicitly named), confound comic and serious in an unacceptable combination.

The *philosophe* will return to *La Grâce* and its fourth Canto for one specific reference in the *Poème sur le désastre de Lisbonne* (1756). Using a Biblical image, Louis Racine had decried any suggestion that man should question his Creator's design (Chant IV, p.70):

> Quoi, le vase pétri d'une matière vile
> Dira-t-il au potier: 'Pourquoi suis-je d'argile?'

Voltaire uses the same metaphor, couched in similar terminology (M.ix.473):

> Le vase, on le sait bien, ne dit point au potier:
> 'Pourquoi suis-je si vil, si faible et si grossier?'

In *La Grâce*, Racine had just evoked God's grandeur in the passage that was to elicit Voltaire's praise (cf. above, p.107), and he had gone on to link that vision with the concept of God's utter indifference towards man. This sombre tone accords well with the questioning bewilderment of the Lisbon poem as Voltaire attempts his own means of resolving the paradox: 'Enfants du Tout-Puissant, mais nés dans la misère'.

Racine's *La Religion* evokes somewhat different responses from Voltaire, beginning with the anonymous answer of the *Conseils à M. Racine* (1742). By now the two poets are estranged because of their contrasting relationships with J.-B. Rousseau; indeed, the most virulent criticism in the *Conseils* is directed at Rousseau rather than Racine. But Racine himself is criticised also. He is convicted of dullness and negligence of style; the hope is however expressed that the poet will be able to make the necessary modifications. Voltaire then proceeds to a series of parallel passages between himself and Racine, ostensibly to show the former's superiority. But what particularly catches the eye is that on numerous occasions in *La Religion* Racine has copied from Voltaire's works, most of all from *La Henriade*. Where Voltaire, for instance, has written 'Vers un centre commun tout gravite à la fois' (*Epître à Madame Du Châtelet*), Racine's verse ran 'Vers un centre commun tous pèsent à la fois' (Chant V, p.199). Sometimes the parallel continues over several lines, as in a passage on Rome ancient and modern in *La Henriade* which Racine follows in Chant III. In all Voltaire lists eleven such examples.

The question of plagiarism perhaps inevitably must arise with two such contemporary poets, both essaying the epic mode and both on occasion writing upon similar topics. An amusing story is attributed to the abbé de Voisenon in the Avertissement to *Alzire* (1736) of how Racine, present at a reading of the play by Voltaire, thought he recognised one of his own lines: 'il répétait constamment entre ses dents: "Ce vers-là est à moi." Impatienté, l'abbé s'approcha de Voltaire et lui dit à l'oreille: "Rendez-lui son vers, et qu'il s'en aille"' (M.iii.371). The abbé failed to indicate the line in question, but it matters little. We have already seen sufficient examples of Voltaire imitating Racine, and Voltaire has provided an abundance of material in the *Conseils à Racine* to show that it was a two-way process.

The same phenomenon will be observed once again in Voltaire's *Poème sur la loi naturelle* (1756 – but composed in all probability in 1752), which draws in considerable measure on Racine's *La Religion*. The latter, attacking deists who claim to invest all their pride in the use of reason, writes (Chant v, p.201):

> Oui, le tout doit répondre à la gloire du maître:
> L'univers est son temple, et l'homme en est le prêtre

Voltaire, developing the deist view rejected by Racine, opens the third Part of the *Loi naturelle* with similar lines (3e Partie, vv.1-2):[11]

> L'Univers est un Temple où siège l'Eternel.
> Là chaque homme à son gré veut bâtir un Autel.

Racine reminds his readers of human solidarity as God's children (Chant VI, p.217):

> Enfants du même Dieu, nés de la même mère

So does Voltaire (3e Partie, v.100):

> Enfants du même Dieu, vivons du moins en frères

But here we must ask ourselves a question of importance: why should some works show a greater incidence of parallel passages than others? The *Epître à Uranie* responded directly, as we saw, to *La Grâce* because the latter offered, at the time when Voltaire was preparing the *Epître*, an impressive portrayal of the cruel God that Voltaire wished to refute, on his own account and also to quell the fears of hellfire felt by 'Uranie',

---

11. References to the *Poème sur la loi naturelle* will be taken from the critical edition by F. J. Crowley (Berkeley 1938).

his mistresss and journey companion to Holland in 1722, Mme de Rupelmonde. Similarly, *La Religion* will prove of value when Voltaire comes to pen the *Loi naturelle*.

The immediate inspiration for the latter poem was La Mettrie's *Anti-Sénèque*, an atheist materialist thesis arguing that virtue and vice are merely relative, remorse is only an atavistic prejudice, and natural law does not exist. This work, published in 1750 and read by Voltaire soon after publication, stirred him immediately to write a refutation; for he regarded its amoral opinions as insidious to the social structure. In order to defend conventional morality, he needs to argue the firm basis of natural law, consecrated by a God whose designs are clearly apparent in nature and whose existence we can discover in our own hearts.

Louis Racine's purpose in writing *La Religion* is summed up by him in a *pensée* of Pascal: 'A ceux qui ont de la répugnance pour la religion, il faut commencer par leur montrer qu'elle n'est pas contraire à la raison, ensuite qu'elle est vénérable; après, la rendre aimable, faire souhaiter qu'elle soit vraie, montrer qu'elle est vraie, et enfin qu'elle est aimable' (Préface, p.115). The six Cantos demonstrate, respectively, the existence of God; the necessity of revelation, established through self-knowledge; the Christian proofs of God; the coming of Christ and the foundation of Christianity; the superiority of Christian faith over the deist cult of reason; and the essentiality of religion, based on love.

From this summary alone, one might guess that of the six Cantos, Voltaire would find the first the most useful, as we shall presently see was the case.[12] By contrast, in Chant II, which has strong Pascalian overtones in verses such as these (p.157):

> Qui me débrouillera ce chaos plein d'horreur?
> Mon cœur désespéré se livre à sa fureur.

Racine appends a note to the latter line, taking issue with Voltaire. The latter, in his *Remarques sur Pascal* (1734) had refuted Pascal's vision of despair by an appeal to the general happiness of people living in London or Paris. Racine disagrees: 'Quelques agréments que nous puissions

12. This does not however imply a total indifference to other sections of the poem. La Harpe reported that at Ferney, Voltaire was heard more than once to 'réciter des passages du poème de *La Religion*, entre autres celui où l'auteur fait parler Lucrèce' (*Cours de littérature ancienne et moderne*, vii.198-99): cited in E. Guitton, *Jacques Delille (1738-1813) et le poème de la nature en France de 1750 à 1820* (Paris 1974), p.94. The Lucretius passage, from Chant II, is quoted at length in the entry on Louis Racine in the *Catalogue des écrivains* (M.xiv.119).

trouver sur la terre, nous sentons bien qu'ils sont, comme dit saint Augustin, *solatia miserorum*' (p.257). Similarly in Chant IV, discussing the Christian martyrs, he dismisses Voltaire's claim, in another *Remarque sur Pascal*, that martyrdom does not guarantee truth, since fanatics too sacrifice themselves; there is a distinction, claims Racine, between fanatics madly obsessed with their opinions and martyrs who are witnesses to the truth that they have seen (p.294). If anything, one might be surprised that in a work so strongly Pascalian in its approach to the Christian faith, there are but these two occasions of dissent with the author of the notorious anti-Pascalian commentary that had caused such scandal only eight years before. In both the parallels cited earlier between *La Loi naturelle* and *La Religion*, the conclusions reached by the two authors are diametrically opposed. If the universe is God's temple in which man worships, it is in Racine's case a Christian world, negating the deist profession of reason on which Voltaire's version of the workings of God is subsequently based. Likewise, although we may be 'enfants du même Dieu', the observation leads Racine to summon unbelievers back to the fold before the Last Judgement makes it forever too late; whereas for Voltaire it is related rather to an appeal for mutual support and tolerance. Indeed, Racine develops the doctrine of eternal punishment to its logical conclusion. If only those who love Christ can be saved, then even virtuous pagans are doomed too (Chant VI, p.219):

> Dans ce séjour affreux quels seront vos tourments,
> Infidèles Chrétiens, cœurs, durs, âmes ingrates,
> Quand, malgré leurs vertus, les Titus, les Socrates,
> (Hélas, jamais du ciel ils n'ont connu les dons!)
> Y sont précipités ainsi que les Catons?

This dismaying doctrine is denounced in Voltaire's *Loi naturelle*. Voltaire apostrophises the 'gazetier clandestin' (probably of the Jansenist *Nouvelles ecclésiastiques*) thus (3e Partie, vv.75-80):

> Penses-tu que Socrate et le juste Aristide,
> Solon, qui fut des Grecs et l'exemple et le guide,
> Penses-tu que Trajan, Marc-Aurèle, Titus,
> Noms chéris, noms sacrés, que tu n'as jamais lus,
> Aux fureurs des Démons sont livrés en partage,
> Par le Dieu bienfaisant dont ils étaient l'image?

His own concluding Prière makes clear where he himself stands (Prière, vv.5-8):

> Je vois sans m'alarmer l'Eternité paraître;
> Et je ne puis penser qu'un Dieu qui m'a fait naître,
> Qu'un Dieu qui sur mes jours versa tant de bienfaits,
> Quand mes jours sont éteints, me tourmente à jamais.

But in the first Canto, by contrast, there are grounds for closer concordances. Voltaire is bent on demonstrating a teleological purpose in Nature (2e Partie, vv.99-100):

> Chaque être a son objet, et dans l'instant marqué
> Il marche vers le but par le Ciel indiqué.

Racine had already pointed the way (Chant I, p.128):

> Tant d'êtres différents l'un à l'autre enchaînés,
> Vers une même fin constamment entraînés,
> A l'ordre général conspirer tous ensemble

The instincts of birds are invoked by both. So too are the workings of the human body, seen as an instance of divine Providence:

> l'œil est fait pour voir, l'oreille pour entendre
> [*La Religion*, Chant I, p.133]

> Le son dans son oreille est par l'air apporté:
> Sans efforts et sans soins son œil voit la lumière.
> [*Loi naturelle*, 1ère Partie, vv.30-31]

Both insist that the law which dictates feelings of remorse in us is inexorable:

> Ainsi de la vertu les lois sont éternelles.
> Les peuples ni les rois ne peuvent rien contre elles.
> [*La Religion*, Chant I, p.139]

> S'il n'était une Loi terrible, universelle,
> Que respecte le crime en s'élevant contre elle.
> [*Loi naturelle*, 1ère Partie, vv.75-76]

But Racine's thesis, even here, tends in a completely different direction. He insists upon a hidden God, whereas Voltaire strongly maintains that God is discoverable. The *philosophe* has to admit, however, that 'Sur ce vaste Univers un grand voile est jeté' (2e Partie, v.111). But while Racine asserts joyously: 'Oui, c'est un Dieu caché, que le Dieu qu'il faut croire' (Chant I, p.126), Voltaire finds a firm basis in our rational faculty (2e Partie, vv.113-14):

> Si la raison nous luit, qu'avons-nous à nous plaindre?
> Nous n'avons qu'un flambeau; gardons-nous de l'éteindre.

This is the crucial difference. Voltaire trusts in reason, Racine insists on faith – although he uses arguments appealing to reason. Even so, Voltaire's *Poème sur la loi naturelle* is a *profession de foi*, not unlike certain aspects of Jean-Jacques Rousseau's Vicaire Savoyard some years later. In advance of Jean-Jacques, Voltaire finds the divine principle located not, first of all, as he does so generally elsewhere, in cosmic design, but in the human conscience, as is made clear from the outset, in the introductory Exorde (vv.35-36):

> Dans le fond de nos cœurs il faut chercher ses traits:
> Si Dieu n'est pas dans nous, il n'exista jamais.

It is possible that even here the reading of *La Religion* had some influence, for Racine too insists on the rôle of conscience, albeit in characteristically more rigorous tones. The impious, he argues, cannot hide from God (Chant i, p.138):

> Dans ses honteux plaisirs, s'il cherche à se cacher,
> Un éternel témoin les lui vient reprocher;
> Son juge est dans son cœur ...

After this deist apology Voltaire apparently severs any close links with Louis Racine. When he comes to compose the dark reflections of the *Poème sur le désastre de Lisbonne* in late 1755, his plangent tones often echo the final Canto of *La Grâce* and the equally dark picture in Chant ii of *La Religion*. But, with the one specific exception noted above, there appear to be no more than general parallels. Such inspiration as he had received from Racine seems at an end. The Jansenist poet, one must assume, had begun to bore him, as he suggests in his correspondence. Generally speaking, pessimism had been more trenchantly expressed by Pascal. Louis Racine is a minor figure among the fellow-travellers on Voltaire's intellectual way: mildly stimulating for a time because of his poetic style but always expressing repugnant ideas, and in the last twenty-five years of Voltaire's life interesting only for the marginal value of his commentaries upon his father.

Despite (or perhaps in part because of) this summary judgement, Louis Racine has not received from posterity the critical attention he deserves. Modest though his accomplishments may be when set alongside his father's, he is yet not without merits. The energetic insistence upon God's utter cruelty and indifference may be unattractive to modern tastes, not to say bordering upon the pathological in its call for total submission and adoration of this terrifying deity. But the forcefulness of the expression, and that 'pénible beauté' which Voltaire justly recognised, deserve retrieval from the oblivion to which, until recently, his writings had been condemned. Latterly, however, the work of recuperation has begun. Racine is beginning to be seen as worthy of being set alongside Voltaire as an epic poet of stature. *La Religion* reveals itself as not just a didactic apology for Christianity but also as a harrowing debate within a 'conscience divisée': 'le poème serait l'épopée moderne par excellence, l'épopée de la conscience critique'. *La Grâce* and *La Religion* speak of exile, doubt, anguish.[13] Far from being a simple throw-back to the golden age of Jansenism in the previous century, Louis Racine is coming to be recognised as a man very much of his own time, conscious of the threatened breakdown of religious values in a universe becoming ever more alien to makind. In the second Canto of *La Religion* he speaks of 'le terrible réveil' which he had experienced from the innocent confidence of his youth, when he first realised his true situation on earth (p.144):

> Je me regardai seul, sans appui, sans défense,
> Egaré dans un coin de cet espace immense.

Voltaire's own response to Louis Racine can scarcely ever be described as more than tepid. Even so, at its most attentive, one gains the impression that it is to this underlying sense of *Angst*, the intense need to prove God, and their most poignant expressions that Voltaire is responding when he turns to Racine for inspiration. It is but one more aspect of the relationship, still awaiting its full exploration by scholarship, between Jansenism and the Enlightenment.

13. S. Menant, *La Chute d'Icare: la crise de la poésie française (1700-1750)* (Geneva 1981), pp.338-49. Cf. also E. Guitton, *Jacques Delille*, esp. pp.84-95; 'Un poème'; R. Finch, *The Sixth sense: individualism in French poetry 1686-1760* (Toronto 1966), pp.248-94.

Voltaire's dialogue with the materialists

E. D. JAMES

VOLTAIRE's debate with the materialists was, or was to become, a fraternal dispute in which his opponents' views occasioned him more regret than resentment. The materialists, on the other hand, came to regard Voltaire's views as an expression of advancing senility.[1]

The battle lines were drawn in traditional fashion. The materialists saw nature as the source of its own order. Voltaire was unable to conceive of an intelligible order of nature which was not the creation of a presiding intelligence. In his early discussions in the *Traité de métaphysique* (c.1734), Voltaire puts *pro* and *contra* quite dispassionately, but appears to entertain no doubts about the inadequacies of materialist arguments, which he sees through the eyes of Samuel Clarke.[2] Yet here as elsewhere in Voltaire's philosophical discussions, arguments that are rejected early in his career become part of his own thinking at a later stage.

A fundamental principle of Voltaire's thinking, to which he clung resolutely throughout his life, was that the existence of contingent beings required the existence of an eternal necessary being. He differs with the materialists over the nature of that being. The argument is formulated early in ch. 2, 'S'il y a un Dieu', of the *Traité de métaphysique*: 'Je suis [...] réduit à avouer qu'il y a un être qui existe nécessairement par lui-même de toute éternité, et qui est l'origine de tous les autres êtres. De là il suit essentiellement que cet être est infini en durée, en immensité, en puissance; car qui peut le borner? Mais, me direz-vous, le monde matériel est précisément cet être que nous cherchons.' The claim that matter is the eternal being and source of all carries implications which Voltaire will always find unacceptable. If matter is the necessary being, then according to Voltaire every particle and every feature of it, including thought, must exist necessarily. Since, however, the various forms of matter have a contingent existence and not all forms of matter have the

---

1. See R. Pomeau, *La Religion de Voltaire* (Paris 1956, revised 1969), 3e partie, ch.5 and p.392 note 4.

2. See S. Clarke, *Traités de l'existence de Dieu, des devoirs de la Religion naturelle et de la vérité de la Religion chrétienne, traduits de l'Anglois* par M. Ricotier (Amsterdam 1727-1728).

power of thought and none the intrinsic power of motion, matter cannot be the necessary and eternal source of all there is. For Voltaire, then, there must be a creative intelligence at the origin of the universe.[3]

By the time of the *Métaphysique de Newton* (1740) Voltaire is already in retreat. He admits that the atheist may not be silenced by the affirmation, however magisterial, of the essential inertness of matter and of the consequent necessity of a Prime Mover:

Mais, si l'athée répond qu'il n'y a rien en repos, que le repos est une fiction, une idée incompatible avec la nature de l'univers; qu'une matière infiniment déliée circule éternellement dans tous les pores des corps; s'il soutient qu'il y a toujours également des forces motrices dans la nature, et que cette permanente égalité de forces semble prouver un mouvement nécessaire; alors il faut encore recourir contre lui à d'autres armes, et il peut encore prolonger le combat.

This amalgam of ancient materialism and modern mechanics is countered by Voltaire with the argument, equally old and new, from design. *Caeli enarrant gloria dei.*[4] The atheist and materialist onslaught on that argument was not to have its full impact on Voltaire until a later date.

What marks an interesting stage in Voltaire's thinking on the question of the eternity of matter is the *Dialogues entre Lucrèce et Posidonius* of 1756.[5] Voltaire's familiarity with the widely studied work of the famous Epicurean poet will not surprise.[6] More in need of explanation is the choice of the Stoic eclectic Posidonius, writing, like Lucretius, in the first century B.C. Nothing of Posidonius's work survives, but Cicero knew him and it is no doubt from Cicero's *De natura deorum* that Voltaire, who much admired Cicero's philosophical writings, learnt of Posidonius. That Voltaire chooses a Stoic for his mouthpiece is no accident, for his philosophical outlook has much in common with Stoicism, especially an eclectic or late Stoicism. What engaged his sympathy particularly was the Stoic belief that the universe is providentially ordered by a rational principle. And the paradoxically materialistic basis of Stoic rationalism was not uncongenial to one who was uncertain whether there was such a thing as soul and, if there was such a thing, what its relation was to matter. It is not of course that Voltaire actually derives his ideas from

---

3. *Traité de métaphysique*, ed. H. Temple Patterson, revised edition (Manchester 1957), p.9.

4. *Œuvres complètes*, ed. L. Moland (Paris 1877-1885) [hereafter M.], xxii.405.

5. In *Dialogues et anecdotes philosophiques*, ed. R. Naves (Paris 1939), pp.35-50.

6. See Adrienne M. Redshaw, 'Voltaire and Lucretius', *Studies on Voltaire* 189 (1980), pp.19-43.

Posidonius, whose doctrines have always been a matter for more or less scholarly conjecture, but Posidonius is a symbolic figure onto whom Voltaire projects his own brand of deism.

Lucretius, on the other hand, stands for the scientist anti-providentialist materialism of certain of Voltaire's contemporaries, notably Diderot, who were indeed influenced by Lucretian ideas. Although Voltaire is never able to relinquish his belief in the existence and necessity of a controlling universal intelligence, Lucretian materialism offered a genuine temptation to him, and his dialogues between Lucretius and Posidonius are genuine dialogues in which there is an honest exchange of ideas.

There are two dialogues, the first treats of cosmology, and the second of the nature of the soul. In the first, the issue is whether the order of the universe is self-engendered – either having been eternally as it is or having evolved into its present state – or whether it was created. Posidonius approaches the question *a priori* and asserts that: 'Nous autres mathématiciens [*sc.* Newtonians], nous ne pouvons convenir que des choses qui sont prouvées évidemment par des principes incontestables.' Lucretius does not demur but argues that his own principles are themselves of that kind. As an atomist he argues that the atoms arranged themselves so as to produce the present state of the universe. But Posidonius contends, as Voltaire invariably contends, that the present admirable order of the universe can only have been the work of an intelligent being. It is notable, even so, that Posidonius never clearly argues for the existence of a creator of the universe. To Lucretius's question: 'Qui donc aura fait le monde?' he does reply 'un être intelligent', but this is after he has accepted, at least for the sake of argument, Lucretius's atomistic principles (*Dialogues*, pp.35-36). One might think that Voltaire is here respecting the character of the historical Posidonius's beliefs, but Voltaire is not at all averse from attributing to his spokesmen ideas which historically they did not hold. It would seem, rather, that Voltaire is more clearly convinced of the need of the existence of an ordering intelligence in the universe than he is of the need of a creator. This, however, does not wholly explain the sympathetic exposition accorded to Lucretian materialism.

Lucretius takes it as common ground between Posidonius and himself that matter is eternal. Posidonius observes that this is not proven, but argues that in any case even if matter were eternal it could not construct works in which are evident such sublime purposes. A stone may be eternal, it will never produce the *Iliad*. The example of the *Iliad* had already been used by Fénelon, who was concerned to refute the claim that the design in things could have come about by chance.[7] Diderot, of whose work Voltaire was aware, was equally concerned – for or against that claim – in his *Pensées philosophiques* and his *Lettre sur les aveugles*. Voltaire's Lucretius, moreover, argues for a transformation of the inorganic into the organic, and it is hard to believe that Voltaire has not Diderot in mind in putting this argument into Lucretius's mouth. The difficulty, of course, was still, in the middle of the eighteenth century, to formulate any plausible account of such a transformation. Lucretius is made to say: 'Non, une pierre ne composera point l'*Iliade*, non plus qu'elle ne produira un cheval; mais la matière, organisée avec le temps et devenue un mélange d'os, de chair et de sang, produira un cheval, et, organisée plus finement, composera l'*Iliade*.' This sounds rather like wishful thinking. Posidonius replies quite plausibly: 'Il faudrait avoir vu naître des hommes et des animaux du sein de la terre, et des blés sans germe, etc., etc., pour oser affirmer que la matière toute seule se donne de telles formes; personne que je sache n'a vu cette opération: personne ne doit donc y croire.' 'Ce qu'un siècle n'a pas fait, pourquoi plusieurs siècles pourraient-ils le faire?' Lucretius falls back on the principle of the eternity of matter. 'Tous les philosophes conviennent que la matière est éternelle; ils conviendront que les générations le sont aussi' (*Dialogues*, pp.36-37). One is struck by the confidence with which Lucretius is allowed to press his case against Posidonius's use of well-tried Voltairian arguments.

Both Lucretius and Posidonius urge against one another's arguments the objection that each is asserting something without any proof or evidence. Lucretius argues that no-one has seen the beginning of things and hence that it is legitimate to believe them eternal. To Posidonius's retort that he must admit the existence of an intelligent being who formed the design visible in the universe, in the same way as he believes in the existence of the architect of the Capitol, Lucretius is made to reply that the analogy is invalid. Posidonius has seen architects, he has not seen the author of nature. Unlike the Capitol, matter exists of its own nature. And since it must have a form, why not admit that it is of its own nature that it has the form it has? Lucretius concludes by demanding which of

7. Fénelon, *Traité de l'existence et des attributs de Dieu*, I, iii.

their two views presents the most difficulties. 'Ne vous est-il pas beaucoup plus aisé de reconnaître la nature qui se modifie elle-même que de reconnaître un être invisible qui la modifie? Dans le premier cas vous n'avez qu'une difficulté, qui est de comprendre comment la nature agit; dans le second cas, vous avez deux difficultés, qui sont de comprendre et cette même nature, et un être inconnu qui agit sur elle' (*Dialogues*, p.38). Once again, the force and directness with which Lucretius is allowed to make his materialist case are remarkable. In particular, his claim that 'la matière existe par sa nature' passes without comment.

Lucretius, suggesting that matter itself possesses intelligence, is allowed to criticise very pertinently the Clarkean argument which Voltaire had used in earlier works to show the incoherence of the thesis of the inherence of intelligence in matter. That familiar argument runs: if matter possessed thought of itself, that would mean that it possessed it necessarily. And if that property were necessary to it, it would have it always and everywhere. Yet not all matter thinks. Lucretius replies that just as movement is only potential in matter until it is made actual when matter is propelled, so thought will be the attribute of a body only when that body is organised to think. To which Posidonius replies that to organise matter to make it think, a purposive intelligence is necessary. This is the argument from design in another aspect. Since the design or purpose precedes the structure, Lucretius, for whom there are no antecedent purposes, cannot account for the structures in things. Similarly with movement, which Posidonius sees as essentially extrinsic to matter, and therefore requiring, like intelligence, an originator. 'Les desseins de cette intelligence supérieure éclatent de toutes parts, et vous devez les apercevoir dans un brin d'herbe comme dans le cours des astres. On voit que tout est dirigé à une fin certaine.' But again Lucretius is allowed to formulate a radical challenge to the fundamental Voltairian doctrines put into the mouth of Posidonius. 'Ne prenez-vous point pour une fin ce qui n'est qu'un usage que nous faisons des choses qui existent?' He rejects Panglossian-style arguments of the kind: 'Les hommes portent des chaussures [donc] les jambes ont été faites par un Etre suprême pour être chaussées.' More fundamentally, the evolution of organic structures and of the cosmos is represented as having come about spontaneously and not as a result of the action of a formative mind (*Dialogues*, p.41).

The last word is nevertheless given to Posidonius – which is to say Voltaire, though, since Lucretius and Posidonius can plausibly be seen as incarnating two conflicting tendencies in Voltaire's thought, it might be better to say that Posidonius expresses the resultant or dominant doctrine of Voltaire. Legs are not made for the purpose of wearing footgear, which is not essential. They are made for walking and to support the body, which are normal and natural functions. This, of course, would still not meet the counter-argument that it is because we have legs that we support ourselves and walk on them. Even less would it meet Diderot's later claim (which Voltaire would never know) 'Les organes produisent les besoins et réciproquement les besoins produisent les organes.'[8] Inanimate nature, for its part, provides the example of the rays of the sun coming four or five million leagues to strike the eyes of every animal at exactly the same determinate angle, creating in them the sensation of light. In this, Posidonius, very evidently speaking for Voltaire, sees 'une mécanique, un dessein admirable'. While having genuine sympathy for the materialist position, Voltaire is unable to conceive of pattern and structure as existing otherwise than as the creation of a mind. Order implies an intelligent orderer.

The conclusion does seem to be based on considerations of logical possibility, conceivability or imaginability and not on any rigid preconception of the nature of God. When Lucretius goes on to ask about the nature of the supreme being, its mode of existence, its purposes, notably in forming beings sensitive and unhappy – all questions about matters which he finds incomprehensible – he is told that the incomprehensibility of the supreme being is inevitable. 'C'est précisément parce que cet Etre suprême existe que sa nature doit être incompréhensible: car s'il existe il doit y avoir l'infini entre lui et nous [...] Concevez donc qu'on doit admettre l'incompréhensible quand l'existence de cet incompréhensible est prouvée' (*Dialogues*, p.42). One is reminded of Pascal's 'Tout ce qui est incompréhensible ne laisse pas d'être.'[9] At the end of this first *entretien*, Lucretius is made to begin to yield to Posidonius's arguments, but he could very well have pursued his doubts about any claim to prove the existence of a being through his works when the nature and the modes of existence and activity of that being are incomprehensible. The most that Voltaire/Posidonius might be entitled to claim is that if the world

8. Diderot, *Œuvres philosophiques*, ed. P. Vernière (Paris 1956), p.308.
9. *Pensées*, La 230; Br 430 *bis*. R. Naves (*Dialogues*, pp.479-80, note 40) makes a comparison with Pascal, but it seems doubtful whether Voltaire can properly be described as saying *credo quia absurdum*, as Naves claims.

were the product of a supreme being, that being would be intelligent and purposive.

This first dialogue of Lucretius and Posidonius is of significance as showing the extent of Voltaire's sympathy with the materialist point of view. He will not lose that sympathy in the years to come when he will feel obliged to attack the materialists, but the principle on which his objections to materialism are based is now clearly formulated also.

The second *entretien*, on the soul, gives further evidence of the closeness of Voltaire's thinking to that of the materialists, despite his refusal to admit the materiality of the soul. Challenged by Posidonius to justify his claim that the soul resides in the heart, Lucretius replies: 'quand je placerai l'âme dans la tête, au lieu de la mettre dans la poitrine, mes principes subsisteront toujours: l'âme sera toujours une matière infiniment déliée, semblable au feu élémentaire qui anime toute la machine [du corps]'. When Posidonius then asks: 'Et comment concevez-vous qu'une matière déliée puisse avoir des pensées, des sentiments par elle-même?' his last phrase is significant. Behind the queried 'par elle-même' lies Voltaire's conviction that thought is not a merely natural phenomenon but is induced in man by God. And insofar as he has a functional conception of soul – as thinking, willing, desiring, etc. – his is not a materialist conception, since a function, even a function of matter, is not a (material) thing. But granted that Voltaire denies that there is a substantial soul, the readiness with which he seems to accept the association of the functions of the soul with certain forms of matter which for the materialists *are* the soul or do duty for a soul, shows the affinity of Voltaire's thinking with that of the materialists. Besides the 'feu élémentaire' Posidonius refers also to that favourite Voltairian image of subtle substance, the ray of sunlight. 'Nous sommes déjà convenus dans notre premier entretien qu'il n'y a pas d'apparence qu'un rocher puisse composer l'*Iliade*. Un rayon de soleil en sera-t-il plus capable? Imaginez ce rayon de soleil cent mille fois plus subtil et plus rapide; cette clarté, cette ténuité, feront-elles des sentiments et des pensées?' Lucretius's reply is that the 'clarté' and the 'ténuité' of the sun's rays will perhaps produce feelings and thoughts when they are in 'des organes préparés'. (The notion that thought is a function of matter organised in a certain way is another idea close to Voltaire's heart.)[10] To Posidonius's challenge:

10. See *Lettres philosophiques*, ed. G. Lanson and A. M. Rousseau (Paris 1964), i.197.

'Quand je supposerais que c'est du feu qui pense en vous, qui sent, qui a une volonté, vous seriez donc forcé d'avouer que ce n'est pas par lui-même qu'il a une volonté, du sentiment et des pensées,' Lucretius stoutly replies: 'Non, ce ne sera pas par lui-même: ce sera par l'assemblage de ce feu et de mes organes.'

Here Voltaire seems to be debating with himself, but Posidonius makes clear his view that 'La production d'un être doit avoir quelque chose de semblable à ce qui le produit: or une pensée, une volonté, un sentiment, n'ont rien de semblable à de la matière ignée' (*Dialogues*, p.45). Yet when Posidonius comments on some lines of Lucretius: 'Voilà de très beaux vers; m'apprenez-vous par là quelle est la nature de l'âme?', Lucretius's reply is a Lockean formula favoured by Voltaire: 'je vous fais son histoire'. Equally Voltairian are Lucretius's added words 'et je raisonne avec vraisemblance'. Posidonius challenges the plausibility of Lucretius's arguments but claims no more certainty for his own arguments than he attributes to those of Lucretius (*Dialogues*, p.47).

By 1765 Voltaire had been visited by Damilaville, intermediary between himself and the materialist coterie led by d'Holbach and Diderot (see Pomeau, p.393). In 1768 appeared Lagrange's translation of Lucretius, stimulated by, and giving a further fillip to materialist thought.[11] Soon we find Voltaire renewing his refutations of theories of the chance origin of human and animal organisms.[12] Several such arguments from chance are examined by Voltaire in his article 'Athéisme' in the *Questions sur l'Encyclopédie*. One argument, in the manner of Diderot, and entitled 'Nouvelle objection d'un athée moderne', but which appears to be a summary of an up-dated version in Maupertuis's *Essai de cosmologie* of a passage in Lucretius, concerns the development of the various organic structures that serve the continuation of species: 'Peut-on dire que les parties des animaux soient conformées selon leurs besoins? Quels sont ces besoins? la conservation et la propagation. Or faut-il s'étonner que, des combinaisons infinies que le hasard a produites, il n'ait pu subsister que celles qui avaient des organes propres à la nourriture et à la

11. *Lucrèce, traduction nouvelle, avec des notes, par M. L.* G.* (Paris 1768). The work was revised for publication by the materialist Naigeon. A note to a passage in Book III of the *De rerum natura* refers triumphantly to Needham's supposed demonstration of spontaneous generation. Voltaire comments on this note in the article 'Dieu, Dieux' of the *Questions sur l'Encyclopédie*. For Voltaire and Needham see below.

12. For a discussion of such theories, see J. Roger, *Les Sciences de la vie dans la pensée française du XVIIIe siècle: la génération des animaux de Descartes à l'Encyclopédie* (Paris 1962).

continuation de leur espèce? Toutes les autres n'ont-elles pas dû nécessairement périr?' Voltaire replies: 'Ce discours, rebattu d'après Lucrèce, est assez réfuté par la sensation donnée aux animaux, et par l'intelligence donnée à l'homme. Comment des combinaisons *que le hasard a produites* produiraient-elles cette sensation et cette intelligence? [...] Sans doute, les membres des animaux sont faits pour tous les besoins avec un art incompréhensible.'

Much more incisive are some direct objections (acknowledged as Maupertuis's) to the argument from design. The objections of Maupertuis, who is not in fact a materialist but a sophisticated deist and *cause-finalier*, are summarised as follows:

Les physiciens modernes n'ont fait qu'étendre ces prétendus arguments, ils les ont souvent poussés jusqu'à la minutie et à l'indécence. On a trouvé Dieu dans les plis de la peau du rhinocéros [which allow it to move]: on pouvait avec le même droit, nier son existence à cause de l'écaille de la tortue [which impedes its movements]. [...] A quoi sert la beauté et la convenance dans la construction du serpent? Il peut, dit-on, avoir des usages que nous ignorons. Taisons-nous donc, au moins, et n'admirons pas un animal que nous ne connaissons que par le mal qu'il fait.

Voltaire's only answer to these telling objections, which he presents with admirable impartiality, is to re-affirm the existence of a controlling divine intelligence and to express in pious rhetoric a reverent agnosticism before the problem of evil:

Taisez-vous donc aussi, puisque vous ne concevez pas [cette] utilité plus que moi; ou avouez que tout est admirablement proportionné dans les reptiles [...] Il faut donc absolument reconnaître une intelligence ineffable, que Spinosa même admettait. Il faut convenir qu'elle éclate dans le plus vil insecte comme dans les astres. Et à l'égard du mal moral et physique, que dire et que faire? se consoler par la jouissance du bien physique et moral, en adorant l'Etre éternel qui a fait l'un et permis l'autre.[13]

The atheist and materialist adversary to whom Voltaire devoted the greatest attention was d'Holbach, whose *Système de la nature* appeared in 1770. Voltaire's refutation appeared in that same year in the form of a pamphlet, *Dieu. Réponse de Mr. de Voltaire au Système de la nature*, which re-appears in a revised and less conciliatory version in the *Questions sur l'Encyclopédie* as the article 'Dieu, Dieux', also of the same year. In this

---

13. *Dictionnaire philosophique*, ed. J. Benda and R. Naves (Paris 1954), pp.461-63. See Maupertuis, *Essai de cosmologie*, première partie, in *Œuvres de M. de Maupertuis* (Dresden 1752). This edition of the *Œuvres* was reviewed probably by Voltaire in the year of publication. See M.xxiii.535-45.

latter article, Voltaire is obviously concerned to play down points of convergence between himself and the materialist d'Holbach, no doubt with a view to gaining the support of orthodox opinion against the pernicious moral consequences, as he sees them, of atheism.[14]

In a letter, dated 26 September 1770, addressed to Suzanne Necker, Voltaire writes of d'Holbach's work: 'Le comble de l'impertinence est d'avoir fondé un système tout entier sur une fausse expérience faite par un Jésuite irlandais qu'on a pris pour un philosophe [...] Il était réservé à notre siècle d'établir un ennuyeux système sur une méprise' (Best. D16666). The 'Irish Jesuit' (who was neither Irish nor a Jesuit) was John Turberville Needham, and the 'méprise' his belief that he had demonstrated the occurrence of spontaneous generation with his experiments in the late 1740s. As it happened, Needham unintentionally drew himself to the attention of Voltaire in 1765 by replying to the early letters of Voltaire's anonymously published *Questions sur les miracles* of the same year. He seems to have taken the *Questions* for the work of an atheist. Of the several accounts of the matter given by Voltaire, that in the *Questions* itself is the most succinct. An 'Avertissement' preceding the fifth letter contains the following passage (M.xxv.393-94):

Ce prêtre [...] était celui-là même qui, plusieurs années auparavant, se mêla de faire des expériences sur les insectes, et qui crut avoir découvert avec son microscope, que la farine de blé ergoté, délayée dans de l'eau, se changeait incontinent en de petits animaux ressemblant à des anguilles. Le fait était faux, comme un savant italien [Spallanzani[15]] l'a démontré, et il était faux par une autre raison bien supérieure, c'est que le fait est impossible. Si des animaux naissaient sans germe, il n'y aurait plus de cause de la génération: un homme pourrait naître d'une motte de terre tout aussi bien qu'une anguille d'un morceau de pâté. Ce système ridicule mènerait d'ailleurs visiblement à l'athéisme. Il arriva en effet que quelques philosophes, croyant à l'expérience de Needham sans l'avoir vue, prétendirent que la

14. For a discussion of this work and its relation to the article 'Dieu, Dieux' of the *Questions sur l'Encyclopédie* see K. M. A. B. Muller, 'Voltaire and the atheistic controversy in eighteenth-century France' (unpublished Ph.D. dissertation, University of London 1984). In the original *Réponse* Voltaire concedes to d'Holbach that there are uncertainties in Newton's and Clarke's conception of the nature of God (but not in their arguments for his existence), uncertainties in the argument for the creation as against the eternity of matter, and in the conception of the substantiality of the soul (which Voltaire in any case does not hold). None of these concessions goes beyond what is found elsewhere in Voltaire by this time, and the original *Réponse* is no less a refutation of d'Holbach than is the article 'Dieu, Dieux' which revises it.

15. L. Spallanzani, *Nouvelles recherches sur les découvertes microscopiques et la génération des corps organisés, ouvrage traduit de l'italien de M. l'abbé Spalanzani ... par M. l'abbé Régley* (London, Paris 1769). Spallanzani had given advance notice of the results of his researches to Voltaire.

matière pouvait s'organiser d'elle-même; et le microscope de Needham passa pour être le laboratoire des athées.

The article 'Dieu, Dieux' in the *Questions sur l'Encyclopédie* contains a section headed 'Histoire des anguilles sur lesquelles est fondé le système' in which Voltaire cites d'Holbach's account of Needham's experiments. D'Holbach concludes: 'C'est ainsi que la nature inanimée peut passer à la vie, qui n'est elle-même qu'un assemblage de mouvements.'[16] Voltaire abandons the claim made in the *Questions sur les miracles* that Needham's system obviously leads to atheism. As he now rightly points out, the assertion that animalcules may come into being without originating in a germ cannot show that there is no God, for God could perfectly well have arranged things so that animalcules originated otherwise than from a germ. D'Holbach's conception of the origins of things, moreover, unlike Needham's, is essentially mechanistic, and mechanism is exposed to Voltaire's teleologically based criticisms in a way that Needham's vitalism is not. In Voltaire, the teleological argument involves an argument from a mind/matter dualism similar in form to Descartes's:

La matière est étendue, solide, gravitante, divisible; j'ai [*sic*] tout cela aussi bien que cette pierre. Mais a-t-on jamais vu une pierre sentante et pensante? Si je suis étendu, solide, divisible: je le dois à la matière. Mais j'ai sensations et pensées: à qui le dois-je? ce n'est pas à de l'eau, à de la fange; il est vraisemblable que c'est à quelque chose de plus puissant que moi. C'est à la combinaison seule des éléments, me dites-vous. Prouvez-le-moi donc.

Voltaire justifiably requires d'Holbach to prove that a simple combination of elements can produce mind. Not so justifiably he demands that d'Holbach should prove the negative proposition that human mind could not have been produced by a higher mind: 'faites-moi donc voir nettement qu'une cause intelligente ne peut m'avoir donné l'intelligence. Voilà où vous êtes réduit.' D'Holbach is not reduced to this extremity. If he were able to show that the birth of mind could have a natural explanation, then the onus would be on Voltaire to show that a supernatural explanation fits the facts better.

But Voltaire's criticism rests essentially on the difficulty of seeing how the purposive can arise from the non-purposive. 'L'auteur prétend que la matière aveugle et sans choix produit des animaux intelligents. Produire

16. Benda-Naves, p.516. P. H. Th. d'Holbach, *Système de la nature*, ed. Y. Belaval (Hildesheim 1966), i.27-28.

E. D. JAMES

sans intelligence des êtres qui en ont! Cela est-il concevable?' (Benda-Naves, p.517). One can only observe that there is no obvious logical or natural obstacle to the spontaneous emergence of purpose in what had no purposes. It certainly seems conceivable. Whether it actually happens is an empirical question. What seems to require explanation is the need we experience to give teleological explanation of entities or phenomena which cannot have purposes of their own, a need which tempts us to posit the existence or workings of a purpose originating outside them. But in the article 'Causes finales' of the *Questions sur l'Encyclopédie* d'Holbach is quoted as saying: 'Que l'on ne nous dise point que nous ne pouvons avoir l'idée d'un ouvrage sans avoir celle d'un ouvrier distingué de son ouvrage. *La nature n'est point un ouvrage*: elle a toujours existé par elle-même' (*Système*, ii.118). On this Voltaire comments: 'Vous supposez ce qui est [*sic*] question, et cela n'est que trop ordinaire à ceux qui font des systèmes' (Benda-Naves, p.540n). Voltaire's position is of course somewhat equivocal since we have found him all but admitting the eternity of matter. But that is not quite the same as accepting that it exists of itself and not at all the same as accepting that its structure is self-generated. Even so, if d'Holbach is perhaps too dogmatic, he is justified in questioning the need to make a leap into the transcendental. And his own thesis is of course not advanced without argument. He holds that (*Système*, ii.118):

Des éléments éternels, incréés, indestructibles, toujours en mouvement, en se combinant diversement, font éclore tous les êtres et les phénomènes que nous voyons [...] Ces éléments n'ont besoin pour cela que de leurs propriétés, soit particulières, soit réunies, et du mouvement qui leur est essentiel, sans qu'il soit nécessaire de recourir à un ouvrier inconnu pour les arranger, les façonner, les combiner, les conserver et les dissoudre.

Voltaire denies *a priori* that movement is essential to matter, but even if d'Holbach is right and Voltaire is wrong on this point, more than mere movement is required to explain the processes and reactions by which complex structures are formed.

Nevertheless, d'Holbach is able to argue further that even if we admit for the moment that it is impossible to conceive of the universe without a craftsman who fashioned it and who looks after it, the question remains: where are we to locate that craftsman? Will he be within or outside the universe? Is he matter or movement? Or is he only space, nothingness, the void? In all these cases, either he is nothing or he is contained in nature and subject to its laws. If such an agent is outside nature, then d'Holbach himself no longer has any idea of the place that that agent occupies, nor of an immaterial being, nor of the way in which spatially unextended mind or spirit can act on the matter from which it is separated, and he must conclude that the agent which moves it is corporeal or material and consequently liable to dissolution (*Système*, ii.118-19). Voltaire's retort relies on an appeal to a sense of humility before the God whose existence d'Holbach denies or represents as problematic. Concerning the difficulty of the concept of God, Voltaire asks: 'Etes-vous fait pour avoir des idées de tout, et ne voyez-vous pas dans cette nature une intelligence admirable?' and of the location of God: 'Est-ce à nous à lui trouver sa place? C'est à lui de nous donner la nôtre' (Benda-Naves, p.541n). D'Holbach and the reader are referred to Voltaire's *Réponse* – here the article 'Dieu, Dieux' – where Voltaire writes: 'L'auteur demande où réside cet être; et de ce que personne sans être infini ne peut dire où il réside, il conclut qu'il n'existe pas. Cela n'est pas philosophique: car de ce que nous ne pouvons dire où est la cause d'un effet, nous ne devons pas conclure qu'il n'y a point de cause [...] Ne tient-il donc qu'à dire: Il n'y a point de Dieu, pour qu'on vous en croie sur votre parole?' (Benda-Naves, p.517). Voltaire's comment depends on our seeing nature as an 'effect' which therefore by the very meaning of the term must have a cause. And because of the feeling of reverence which the thought of God induces in him, Voltaire readily accepts the mystery which envelopes the nature of the God whose existence as a supreme cause is logically entailed by the existence of the effects of that cause. D'Holbach, in whom the concept of God excites no reverence and mystery no humility, and for whom nature is not an effect, is in no way prompted to Voltaire's theistic conclusions or convictions. His way of looking at the problem is quite different from Voltaire's.

D'Holbach replies incisively to the Voltairian-style argument from design. As Voltaire would have it:

Si l'on portait une statue ou une montre à un sauvage qui n'en aurait jamais vu, il ne pourrait s'empêcher de reconnaître que ces choses sont des ouvrages de quelque agent intelligent, plus habile et plus industrieux que lui-même: l'on conclura de là que nous sommes pareillement forcés de reconnaître que la machine de l'univers, que l'homme, que les phénomènes de la nature, sont des ouvrages d'un agent dont l'intelligence et le pouvoir surpassent de beaucoup les nôtres.

D'Holbach makes no difficulty about admitting that nature is 'très puissante et très industrieuse', and Voltaire characteristically interprets this as showing that d'Holbach admits the existence of God *malgré lui*: 'Celui qui est assez puissant pour former l'homme et le monde est Dieu.' Voltaire is obviously unable to conceive of the source of the order in things as other than personal. But as d'Holbach astutely points out, the power and ingenuity of nature are not attributes that are manifest only in particularly remarkable natural phenomena. They are universally present in nature. We call 'industrieux' a man who can do things that we cannot do ourselves. But nature can do everything. Hence it is only by analogy with ourselves that we judge nature to be ingenious. And since we possess a quality which we call 'intelligence' with the aid of which we produce work in which we display our ingenuity, we conclude that those works of nature which most fill us with wonder are not of nature's own contriving but are attributable to an intelligent workman resembling ourselves, whose intelligence we assess in proportion to the wonder which his works produce in us – that is to say, in proportion to our own weakness and ignorance. We claim to perceive design in nature because we assimilate the more obviously remarkable structures in it to the structures that have been contrived by human intelligence, but we fail to take account of other structures in nature which are unamenable to this kind of anthropomorphic interpretation, but which are nevertheless part of an order of nature which is beyond our comprehension. 'Nous ne comprenons pas plus comment [la nature] a pu produire une pierre ou un métal qu'une tête organisée comme celle de Newton.'[17] Voltaire could have made exactly the same remark – but with contrary intent. Whereas Voltaire concludes from our ignorance and incomprehension to a need for humility before God, whose ways are necessarily beyond our understanding since he is infinite, d'Holbach in effect asks: if, when talking about God, we do not know what we are talking about, what sense is there in talking of God? From the postulate that the genesis of the natural order is incomprehensible to us, d'Holbach concludes that we are in no position to make claims as to the existence of a divine orderer.

This whole series of discussions of atheist materialism reveals the limits that are set to any agreement between the two sides by certain fundamental principles of Voltaire's thinking. It also shows how much

17. *Système*, ii.120-21; Benda-Naves, pp.541-42.

the two sides have in common. It appears that by the 1750s Voltaire inclines to share the materialists' view of matter as existing from eternity and as governed by immutable laws. And despite his insistence on the design and purpose visible in nature, one can even claim that he shares the mechanistic conception of the laws of nature held by a materialist such as d'Holbach. For Voltaire's conception of the workings of nature is in effect a conception of matter in motion. Nature appears to have purposes but in fact it has not. All purpose is divine purpose. So that when Voltaire objects to the absence of all teleology from the materialists' universe it is of the absence of God that he is speaking, not of the absence of an attribute intrinsic to nature. Voltaire's theism purports to guarantee the fundamental rationality of the order of the universe, which in his view materialism cannot guarantee. But his theism does not enable him to give any more rational an explanation of the actual order of things than does materialism. Both Voltaire and the materialists are condemned to portray the same imperfectly intelligible world. To postulate the existence of a divine orderer of nature distinct from nature is, as Voltaire's Lucretius remarked, not to add to understanding but to pose a distinct set of new problems. The relation between God and nature in Voltaire is a relation between spirit and matter closely analogous to the relation between soul and body in Descartes. And as in Descartes the mode of interaction of the two distinct substances is utterly mysterious. Voltaire's theism which at first seemed to be grounded in the discoveries of the mathematical sciences increasingly takes on the character of a sheer act of faith.

Voltaire and the 'maudites éditions de Jean Nourse'

GILES BARBER

On 18 December 1755 Voltaire, then staying at Monriond near Lausanne, wrote to Gabriel Cramer, the director of his Genevan printers with whom he most regularly corresponded:

Cependant cette maudite édition de Jean Nourse m'obligera de mettre en ordre l'Histoire véritable. C'est une affaire qu'il faut réserver pour mon retour dans votre voisinage. Malheureusement toutes ces éditions multipliées dégoutent le public: je crains surtout beaucoup, comme je vous l'ai toujours dit, pour celles des œuvres mêlées. Quelque peine que je me donne pour la rendre plus complète que les autres, vous ne pourrez vous en défaire que très difficilement. Il faudra vous armer de courage et de patience.[1]

Voltaire's reference to 'toutes ces éditions multipliées' probably indicates that he is thinking of all the unauthorised reprints of his works then coming out and not just of those bearing the name of 'Jean Nourse', but Nourse being named in particular, and indeed being virtually the only English publisher to be so honoured, it is the aim of this article to record the relations of Nourse with both Voltaire and his printer/publishers, the Cramers, to survey editions of works by Voltaire published by Nourse, and finally to asses whether Voltaire was in fact right in considering that Nourse's activities were disadvantageous.

Who then was 'Jean Nourse'? John Nourse was born in Oxford in 1705, the second son of a well-known local medical family. He entered the London booktrade in the early 1730s and eventually specialised in mathematical books (being Bookseller to the Commissioners of Longitude), in foreign language dictionaries and grammars, and in the sale and translation of recent continental literature. He conducted an extensive exchange trade with the Low Countries, visited both Holland and Paris, and was clearly recognised at the time as one of the more important booktrade intermediaries between England and the Continent in the

---

1. *Correspondence and related documents*, ed. Th. Besterman, *Œuvres complètes de Voltaire*: cited as Best.D. This letter Best.D6636.

mid eighteenth century. His role in the dissemination of the works of Montesquieu, Rousseau and Helvétius has recently been the subject of articles and now that a number of papers relating to his firm have been located other studies have appeared and a full study of his trade is planned.[2] He died in 1780 but although the firm remained in business, under one name or another, until the 1820s, its role in the European booktrade was insignificant after the late 1770s.

As we have seen Voltaire refers directly to Nourse by name in his correspondence, and, we note, in critical vein. The earliest of such references goes back to 15 June 1747 when Voltaire was in Paris and writing to Georg Conrad Walther of Dresden about a new edition of his works (Best.D3528):

Gardez-vous de suivre l'édition débitée sous le nom de Nourse à Londres, celle qui est intitulée de Genève, celle de Rouen, et surtout celle de Ledet, et d'Arkstée et Merkus à Amsterdam. Ces dernières sont la honte de la librairie, il n'y a guère de page où le sens ne soit grossièrement altéré, presque tout ce que j'ai fait est defiguré, et ces ouvriers ont pour comble d'impertinence déshonoré leur édition par des pièces infames qui ne peuvent être écrites, debitées et lues que par les derniers des hommes.

The phrase 'débitée sous le nom de Nourse à Londres' evidently suggests that Voltaire was identifying an edition but believed, or knew, that the imprint was false. It is not clear, however, whether he then knew Nourse was a real London publisher or not. Voltaire's suspicions were of course quite correct for the edition in question is that of the 1742 *Œuvres diverses*, 'nouvelle édition', six volumes in duodecimo (Bengesco 2127), usually ascribed to the press at Trévoux. A year later (13 June 1748) Voltaire wrote to Nicolas-René Berryer to denounce pirated editions of his works and to ask in particular that action should be taken (via his informant, the bookseller and binder J. H. Fournier of Versailles, Derome *le jeune*'s brother-in-law) against the Rouen printer of the 'Amsterdam' edition (Best.D3669). Another book of which Berryer has heard, Voltaire says,

est probablement une édition en six volumes faite à Trévoux, et que j'ai trouvée si mauvaise, si infidèle, et si pleine de fautes que j'ai supplié instamment M. Pallu de

2. Articles concerning Nourse include W. Kirsop, 'Voltaire, Helvétius and an English pirate', *Australian journal of French studies* 4 (1967), pp.62-73; G. Barber, 'Aspects of the booktrade between England and the Low Countries in the eighteenth century', *Werkgroep 18e Eeuw, Documentatieblad* 34 (1977), pp.47-64; R. Shackleton, 'John Nourse and the London edition of *L'Esprit des lois*', *Studies in the French eighteenth century presented to John Lough* (Durham 1978), pp.248-59; J. Feather, 'John Nourse and his authors', *Studies in bibliography* (1981), pp.205-25.

la supprimer autant qu'il pourrait. Cette misérable édition court les provinces et les pays étrangers avec beaucoup d'autres, et en cela il n'y a que du papier perdu. Voilà l'édition qui n'a pas mon *approbation*. L'édition de Trévoux est intitulée à *Londres chez Nourse* 1746.

This letter is interesting, not only in giving Voltaire's view as to where the 'Nourse' edition really came from, but also for his distinction, possibly primed as special pleading to get Berryer to act against the Rouen printer, between the roles played by editions generally available abroad and those one could buy relatively openly in Paris and even at Versailles.

By 1755 Nourse editions feature more frequently in the correspondence of Voltaire and his circle. On 24 November 1755 the Paris bookseller Charles Saillant wrote to Malesherbes:

J'ai l'honneur de vous envoyer un éxemplaire de la guerre de 1741 qui a éte achepté à Paris par un de mes amis. Cette édition est faite à l'instar de la nôtre; j'y ai apperçû quelques différences: j'ai sousligné les endroits; le papier n'est pas de la même fabrique que le notre.

M. Thiriot vient de me remettre les 2 feuilles cy jointes d'une édition angloise du même ouvrage, dont on lui offre le nombre qu'il voudra; comme je ne sçai pas l'anglois, j'ignore s'il y a quelques différences de la nôtre.

M. Merkus d'Amsterdam nous a écrit ces jours cy que Gosse en faisoit une édition qu'il doit faire annoncer dans la Gazette.

Saillant continues this interesting letter by going on to say that several other editions have appeared and that Voltaire himself must have had a hand in them since only four copies reached Paris directly and these are all in the hands of respectable persons. Saillant's reliance on textual and paper differences suggests that at least one of the piracies was very close to the appearance of his edition, but his juxtaposition of the English edition (*The History of the war of seventeen hundred and forty one*, London, printed for J. Nourse, 1756, 8°), then evidently at an early stage in production, with one to be published by Pierre Gosse Junior of the Hague, is possibly very revealing since Nourse and Gosse had a regular exchange agreement dating back to 1742.[3] Three versions of the English translation are known, one with 251 pages, one with 260 pages, and a second edition also with 260 pages. More significant, perhaps, an edition of the French text, equally published in 1756, also bears the imprint 'Londres: chez Jean Nourse' and the possibility that this is a Dutch

3. Barber, 'Aspects of the booktrade', p.49.

edition, shared between Gosse and Nourse, and with variant title-pages, can not be discounted.

Three weeks later Voltaire referred to Nourse directly in the letter of 18 December 1755 quoted at the beginning of this article. The book referred to is probably the abridgement of the *Annales de l'Empire* published as *Abrégé de l'histoire universelle, depuis Charlemagne, jusques à Charlequint* (A Londres, Chez Jean Nourse, 1753, 2 volumes 12°). This edition is however also a shared edition since variant issues are known with a cancel title, printed in red and black, and giving the imprint as 'A La Haye, chez Jean Neaulme'.[4] The typographical practice suggests that the book was in fact printed in Holland. Nourse's English translation (*The General history and state of Europe*) appeared in early 1754 with later parts in 1755 and 1757.

We are, as will be argued, approaching a crucial period in the Nourse / Voltaire story and it is noticeable that the next time Nourse's name occurs under Voltaire's pen, in 1761, the tone is notably different and not just because the letter is in English. On 4 August of that year Voltaire wrote to the Earl of Chesterfield. He comments that they are both growing deaf as they grow older, that he has occupied himself by scribbling and that he has produced a commentary on the plays of Corneille: 'The work is prodigiously cheap, and no money is to be given but at the reception of the book. Nurse receives the names of the subscribers. Y^r name will be the most honourable and the dearest to me. I wish yr lordship long life, good eyes and good stomak' (Best.D9929). As André Rousseau has shown, this is the latest of the surviving letters to a number of distinguished Englishmen, William Pitt, the Prime Minister, Lord Bute, Lord Lyttleton, each sent with a special prospectus giving the price of the book as two guineas, and also deliberately linking the names of Corneille and Shakespeare at a difficult period in the middle of the Seven Years' War.[5] Both Nourse and the other leading French bookseller in London at that time, Paul Vaillant II, acted as agents and in the final list of subscribers some 103 English names appear in a total of 1185, not a high number perhaps but notable all the same in view of the current state of the war.

A final brief reference to Nourse comes in a letter of 19 April 1768

4. G. Barber, 'Some early English editions of Voltaire', *The British Library journal* 4 (1978), p.105.

5. A. M. Rousseau, *L'Angleterre et Voltaire* (1976), i.235-42; see also *Commentaires sur Corneille*, ed. D. Williams, *Complete works of Voltaire* 55 (Banbury 1975), App.4 and 5.

when Voltaire, writing to George Keate, asks for a copy of Samuel Bourne's *A series of discourses* (1760, second edition 1768) and says 'Ces discours sont imprimés chez Nurs' (Best.D14968). Here Voltaire in fact erred since neither edition was published by Nourse, but in any case he did succeed in acquiring a copy of the second edition of the work which features among his books.

Voltaire in fact owned a number of works bearing Nourse's name as can be seen from the catalogue of his library.[6] The nature of these books is not irrelevant: they were, in chronological order by date of publication (the date of acquisition by Voltaire being unknown):

Chaulieu, G. A. de, *Œuvres diverses*, nouvelle édition. Londres, chez J. Nourse, 1740. 2 vols [= Amsterdam?].

Estrades, G., comte d', *Lettres, mémoires et négociations de monsieur le comte d'Estrades, tant en qualité d'ambassadeur* ... Londres, chez J. Nourse, 1743. 9 vols. [= La Haye?].

Montaigne, M. E. de, *Essais*, nouvelle édition, augmentée de la vie de Montagne [*sic*] et de nouvelles notes qui ne se trouvent point dans les éditions précédentes. Londres, chez J. Nourse, 1745. 7 vols. [= Paris?].

Fielding, H., *Histoire de Tom Jones*, traduit de l'anglois par M.D.L.P. [P. A. de La Place]. Londre [*sic*], chez J. Nourse, 1750. 4 vols. [= Paris, Rollin?].

Richardson, S., *Lettres angloises, ou Histoire de Miss Clarisse Harlove*, [translated by A. F. Prevost]. Londres, chez Nourse, 1751. 6 vols. [= Paris?].

[La Beaumelle, L. A. de], *Mes pensées*, 6e édition. Londres, chez Nourse, 1752. [= Paris?].

[La Fare,   ], *Le Gouverneur, ou Essai sur l'éducation*. Londres, chez J. Nourse, 1760. [= Paris?].

La Beaumelle, L. A. de, *Lettres de monsieur de La Beaumelle à M. de Voltaire*. Londres, chez J. Nourse, 1763. [= Paris?].

Orme, R., *A history of the military transactions of the British nation in Indostan*, from the year MDCCXLV. To which is prefixed a Dissertation on the establishments made by Mahomedan conquerors in Indostan. London, printed for J. Nourse, 1763.

[Grosley, P. J.], *Nouveaux mémoires, ou Observations sur l'Italie et sur les Italiens*, par deux gentilshommes suédois. Traduits du suédois. Londres, chez J. Nourse, 1764. 3 vols. [= Paris].

Le Mercier de La Rivière, P. P. F. J. H., *L'Ordre naturel et essentiel des sociétés politiques*. Londres, chez J. Nourse, libraire, & se trouve à Paris, chez Desaint, libraire, 1767. 2 vols.

Frederick II of Prussia, *Examen de l'Essai sur les préjugés* [by d'Holbach]. Londres, Nourse, 1770. [= Berlin, Voss. Voltaire's copy annotated, in his own hand, 'par le Roy de Prusse'].

6. *Bibliothèque de Voltaire: catalogue des livres* (Moscou, Leningrad 1961).

Much could evidently be said about these twelve books and indeed a detailed physical examination of each would be necessary as well as a study of the circumstances of their publication before one could be sure how to interpret their evidence. For present purposes however three significant facts are clear: firstly, Orme's *History*, the only book in English, is equally the only book indisputably published by Nourse, who incidentally was a close friend of the author. Secondly, in the case of a few books, namely the Fielding, *Tom Jones*, Montaigne, *Essais*, and La Fare, *Le Gouverneur*, there is some evidence to suggest that the edition may be semi-genuine in that it may have been shared with a continental publisher, cancel titlepages being found in some cases. Thirdly, it is however clear that in the large majority of cases, some eight out of the twelve, the Nourse imprint is entirely false and that his name has been used by the clandestine continental publisher as a blind. Probably because Nourse became the best known English-born importer of foreign books in the mid eighteenth century and because he had an extensive exchange trade with both Pierre Gosse of the Hague and the Luchtmans brothers of Leiden, Nourse's name became highly popular with clandestine edition publishers. In this way one could almost say that he became the successor to the legendary Pierre Marteau of Cologne, and indeed one false imprint even reads, mockingly, 'Toujours à Londres, chez l'éternel Jean Nourse'. The point in the present context is evidently that Voltaire, as an informed bookman of his day all too well acquainted with the tricks of the trade, must have known, from these books in his library at the least, of Nourse's continental reputation.

The evidence from Voltaire's letters and from his own library links him directly with Nourse. Voltaire knew the name, he knew Nourse was a real London bookseller, and he probably knew that Nourse's name was widely used in false imprints. Further evidence links Nourse, less directly in one sense but more firmly in another, with Voltaire and the dissemination of his *œuvre*, a matter which, it will be argued, must also have been known to the *patriarche*.

One of Voltaire's aims in moving to Geneva in 1755 was to be near his latest authorised printers, the Cramer brothers. The acquisition (so to speak, for the brothers also became his servants to some extent) of the most famous writer in Europe revolutionised both the workings and the finances of the Cramer family firm. A new account book was opened for this period and only closed, in 1766, when the new trade was firmly established and certain family legal requirements altered the ownership of the company.[7] The Cramer *grand livre* is evidently a document of major importance in the study of the diffusion of the authorised editions of Voltaire's various works during this period and it is of course also backed up by the survival of so many letters from Voltaire to these printers. The account book shows that the Cramers sold books (not necessarily all by Voltaire) to only three English booksellers: John Nourse, Paul Vaillant II, and G. Seyffert. Vaillant, descended from French Huguenot stock, was with Nourse the major London importer of the mid-century period, while Seyffert, probably a German, did not apparently stay in business for long. Nourse's trade with the Cramers was notably the largest in value and turnover.

The Nourse account opens on 21 February 1758 with an entry for 'Marchandises generales et une Balle de Voltaire No. 1 à lui envoyée', valued at 544 livres. On 6 November 1758 further 'marchandises générales', together with '30 Ciceronis Opera', were sent in consignment number 2, value 830 livres. On 18 January 1759 more 'marchandises générales' and '3 balles de même', numbered 3, 4 and 5, were sent to Nourse for a total value of 2,172 livres, a considerable sum. On 13 July 1759 more 'marchandises' and one 'ballot de 300 [?] *Mort de Socrate*' numbered 6 and valued at 105 livres. April 1760 saw another consignment, numbered 7 but without further description beyond its value of 317 livres. Another load, number 8, this time described as 'un fardeau', was valued at 1,030 livres on 9 August. In 1761 three volumes of the *Bibliothèque de campagne* were sent to Nourse in September via a parcel addressed to Vaillant, while in October 1765 another general consignment, number 9, was sent for a total value of 252 livres.

The account book is clearly not as informative as one could wish and gives all too little detail of the consignments. Nevertheless it has considerable potential value. The opening date of all three English accounts is late 1757 or early 1758 and one is tempted to think that they were, in some way, a result of Gabriel Cramer's rapid trip to Holland in June 1757 when the English booksellers' Dutch contacts may have put the Londoners and the Genevans directly in touch. Only one particular work by Voltaire is mentioned in the Nourse account although it seems

7. G. Barber, 'The Cramers of Geneva and their trade in Europe between 1755 and 1766', *Studies on Voltaire* 30 (1964), pp.377-413.

reasonable to assume, from the form of the record, that other works by him were present in each shipment.

The most interesting consignments are of course numbers three, four and five, all sent, for a very high total value, on 18 January 1759, just three days after the first explicit mention in the *grand livre* of *Candide*. On 15 January 1759 the account book records the dispatch of a thousand copies of the novel to the Paris bookseller Robin and a further two hundred were sent on 16 January to Marc-Michel Rey at Amsterdam. Study of the account book and in particular of the pages devoted to the accounts of the transportation and forwarding agents used by the Cramers (the Duplain of Lyons and François Forel of Morges) suggest that only Nourse and Knock & Eslinguer of Frankfort received consignments of any note in the second half of that month. Unfortunately the size of Cramer's edition is unknown (though clearly over 1,200 copies) but it would have been typical of both Voltaire and the Cramers to endeavour to ensure a European diffusion for the book by not only sending copies to Paris and Amsterdam but also to English and German market centres.

The large number of clandestine reprints produced in 1759 shows the book's instant status as a classic. The bibliography of all these editions is complex but in general both bibliographical evidence and textual variations do little other than explain the filiation of these editions.[8] With regard to Voltaire and the early text of *Candide* there are three fixed points and one indeterminate one. The three fixed points are: the surviving circulation manuscript (probably written in mid-1758 and sent to the duc de La Vallière), the first edition produced, with cancels, by the Cramers, and the text corrected by Voltaire for the 1761 *Seconde suite des Mélanges de littérature, d'histoire et de philosophie*, the first public, if tacit, admission of Voltaire's authorship. When the work occurs later on in the complete works the format and general style of presentation change, the text is slightly revised, and the state of the text is clearly different from that of the 1759 editions.

The indeterminate element in establishing the early text is the existence of two editions which both contain an extra paragraph in chapter 25, this paragraph being missing from the circulation manuscript and the Geneva edition but, notably, present in the 1761 text and in later editions. The two editions to have this extra paragraph are an Italian one (with 190

8. For the latest bibliography of the 1759 editions of *Candide* see *Candide*, édition critique par R. Pomeau, Voltaire 48 (Oxford 1980), pp.86-110.

pages), of unknown origin, and a London one, the ornaments in which also occur in a number of books printed for John Nourse. The early history of *Candide* is therefore closely linked with the relations of Voltaire, the Cramers, and the London bookseller.[9]

Comparison of the differences between the Geneva and London editions is fruitful but must be based on a full comprehension of the production history of the Geneva one. The first edition of *Candide* is a duodecimo produced in the classic French style and printed on whole sheets, one third of which were cut off, folded, and then inserted into the middle of the gathering of eight leaves made up by folding the larger part of the sheet. In French terms this procedure (also common in England but with a different folding pattern) was called 'in-12 carton dedans', being different from the Dutch system in which the odd four leaves made up a separate section and followed the first one of eight leaves. The text of *Candide* therefore collates: $12°A-M^{12}N^6$. From the evidence of several surviving copies it is clear however that the other half of sheet N (N7-N12) originally contained a) a blank page, b) an 'Avis au relieur' concerning cancels, c) two bifolia being the conjugate cancels for B4.9 and D6.7. It is worth noting that these cancels are both of conjugate leaves, that is that they are not single leaves tipped in on the stubs left behind by the removal of the erroneous leaves, but double sections taking their place in the structure of the gathering and with a full fold in its spine. Once in place in fact their presence could not be detected in a normal copy but for the presence of the 'Avis'. They represent a thorough and careful job in altering the text and, as such, seem not untypical of the Cramers' work.

The textual differences between the Geneva and London editions suggest that they fall into three groups or sorts. First come those passages where London clearly reproduces the original Geneva text before this was cancelled. These changes all occur on the signatures B4.9 and D6.7. On page 31 Geneva quite properly corrects the evidently erroneous way in which London starts a separate paragraph for 'Mais il y a ...'; on pages 41 and 83 textual and stylistic changes are made by Geneva. An uncancelled copy of the Geneva text substantiates that London is following the earlier readings. A second type of difference is found on page

9. G. Barber, 'Modèle genevois, mode européenne: le cas de *Candide* et de ses contrefaçons', *Cinq siècles d'imprimerie genevoise* (Genève 1981), ii.49-67.

103 where London silently corrects an evident error in Geneva, reducing 'que ce ce fut' to 'que ce fut'.

The third class of difference concerns the readings on pages 125 and 242. On the first of these the circulation manuscript, London, the Italian edition and the 1761 edition all read 'précipitamment' whereas Geneva alone reads 'précisément'. It is worth giving the immediate context: 'mais ils se levèrent précipitamment [précisément] avec cette inquiétude & cette allarme que tout inspire dans un pays inconnu'. The second case, on page 242, is that London, the Italian edition (page 155) and the 1761 text all contain an additional paragraph, 'Candide était affligé ...', absent from both the circulation manuscript and from the Geneva text. This paragraph is critical of contemporary German poets and has been variously interpreted as an attack on either Frederick the Great or Albrecht von Haller which, it has been suggested, Voltaire may at the last moment have wished to withdraw.

The extra paragraph in question occupies the second half of page 242 (signature L1 verso) in the London edition so that the London compositor, who otherwise seems to have followed his Genevan colleague closely, is half a page out until the end of the chapter (xxv) on page 244 where he ends neatly at the foot of the page, the Genevan having had room for a woodcut of a shield, drum and flag to fill out what would otherwise have been a blank. Both start chapter twenty-six at the top of page 245 (L3 recto). This change has therefore affected pages 242, 243 and 244, signatures L1 and L2; that is, looking at the full sheet, both the outer forme (page 244) and the inner forme (pages 242, 243). If London was again following an uncancelled Geneva text, why does no copy of the Geneva edition show any sign of cancellation?

Should Voltaire and the Cramers have wished, late on, to make this major change on page 242 there were in fact three methods open to them: a) leaves L1 and L2 (pp.241-44) could be cut out and single leaf cancels, with closed-up text and an extra ornament, could be pasted on to the stubs; b) the two leaves could be cut out and a bifolium pasted in on one of the stubs. Both of these solutions were fiddly, not in the Cramer tradition, and left traces. A third solution, since both inner and outer forme were involved, was to reprint the whole of leaf L. This solution would leave no trace – and would not even have to be mentioned in the 'Avis au relieur': it was absolute and even if it necessitated extra cost and the loss of all the copies of the original sheet L it was probably worthwhile in view of the size, and possibly the importance, of the change to be made.

Short of finding one of the original sheets, the theory can probably not be proved. It needs however to be seen in the light of the evidence not only of the earlier, cancelled, passages but also of that of both page 125 (signature F4 verso) and of the Italian edition. André Morize, writing in the apparatus of his admirable critical edition, found 'précisément', the Genevan reading, 'absurde' and certainly the Cramer text (and editions clearly copied from it) are in a strange no-man's-land since the circulation manuscript, London, Italy and 1761 all give 'précipitamment'.[10] The difference here is limited to one word: one can see how a compositor might make the mistake quite easily, and it is equally difficult to see Voltaire suddenly wanting to make this change and then going back on it in 1761. The explanation could lie in a compositorial error, a misreading or mis-remembering of 'précisément' for 'précipitamment', printed in earlier sheets and only later spotted and corrected to the proper word while sheets were still being printed. Proof is clearly lacking although there seems to be some evidence that press corrections were in general not made by the Cramers, at least in this book.[11] However as only some sixteen copies of the genuine Geneva edition have been located it is clear that the statistical sample is, as yet, small and thus that such a possibility can not be totally ruled out. The practice of correction under press is of course well known and would fit the facts in this particular instance.

In this context what is interesting is that while the Italian edition follows the cancelled Geneva text in signatures B and D, it, like London, gives the variant text in signatures F (page 125) and L (pages 242-44). It should also be noted that a second London edition of 1759 similarly follows the cancelled text early on and the variant text later. Clearly the first London edition is copied from the uncorrected sheets B and D: both London editions and the Italian one *may* have a similar basis to sheet L and, if 'précipitamment' is a press correction, they might here have the corrected form. Again proof is lacking but such an explanation is based on our knowledge that mixed sheet copies did circulate and moreover it again fits the recorded facts.

It seems unlikely that Nourse was deliberately sent an 'interesting' state of the text. As we have seen the book was sent out in mid January

10. Voltaire, *Candide*, édition critique par A. Morize (Paris 1913).
11. I collated eight copies of the Geneva text in 1983/84 and found but one minor change.

1759. Official disapproval of the publication broke out simultaneously in both Paris and Geneva a month later. Nourse's consignments of books had to travel by boat along the Lake of Geneva, over to Basle, down the Rhine and finally over to England. When on 26 April Nourse first announced the availability of the French text in London (and the fact that he had a translation in hand) he must already have known that the book was a 'cause célèbre'. Had Nourse been sent a personal copy directly it seems more than likely that it would have reached him far earlier. We should conclude that his consignment of 18 January contained a copy or copies with mixed sheets representing, in different formes, both early and late states of the text.

So far we have seen that Voltaire knew of, and indeed criticised, the false editions published under Nourse's name but that later he used Nourse to take subscriptions for his Corneille. We have also seen that it was precisely in the intervening period of the later seventeen fifties that Nourse became a good, and possibly an important, customer of the Cramers. We should now look at the relationship from the other end and consider Nourse's sale and publication of Voltaire's works.

The *Gentleman's magazine* for February 1733 contains an advertisement for '*La Zayre*, de M. de Voltaire [...] augmentée de l'Epitre Dedicatoire', sold by John Nourse. Certainly Nourse, who had only just set up in business, was then very interested in the theatre but there is no trace of any such edition bearing his name and this seems to have been the announcement of an import. Nine years later, in 1742, Nourse enters into regular contractual relations with Pierre Gosse of the Hague; in that year too the Trévoux edition uses his name as their imprint cover. In 1746 Nourse starts trading with the Luchtmans of Leiden but no Voltaire is mentioned in these accounts. In 1753 Nourse seems to have shared an edition of the *Abrégé de l'histoire universelle* with Jean Neaulme of the Hague and he may also have shared one of the *Histoire de Charles XII* since a bill to him from the London printer William Strahan is known for fifty copies of a titlepage to this work. He also launched out into English translations with *A defence of the late Lord Bolingbroke's Letters* and the *Diatriba of Doctor Akakia*. Nourse also published an English translation of *The General history and state of Europe*, starting in 1754, and three editions of *The History of the war of seventeen hundred and forty one* in 1756 and 1757. He also had the French text reprinted in England in 1756 and may have produced editions of the *Orphelin de la Chine* and the *Poème sur la réligion naturelle*.

His account with the Cramers opens in 1758 and in the following year the two French text London editions of *Candide* clearly come from printers using ornaments frequently found in genuine Nourse publications. He certainly published three editions of the translation, *Candid: or, all for the best*, in 1759 (two) and 1771. In 1760 he imported the *Histoire de l'empire de Russie* and two other texts while the following year he took subscriptions for the Corneille and was one of the publishers of the *History of the Russian empire*. In 1762 he reprinted the *Histoire d'Elizabeth Canning et de Jean Calas* and thereafter little.

Nourse's main Voltairian activity seems therefore to have fallen in the period 1753 to 1761, to have taken the form early on of shared continental-printed editions, then to have branched out into some of his own, English-printed, French-text editions (even possibly going so far as to get his printers to get copies made of certain Cramer woodcut ornaments), and finally launching out into some English translations of solid historical works. He doubtless also sold imported foreign editions but information here is scant. He seems not to have been a party to Smollett's translation of Voltaire's works or to have dealt in straight philosophical items.

What then of Voltaire's 1755 condemnation of the 'maudites éditions de Jean Nourse'? Voltaire, as we have seen, probably knew that the edition in question was not actually published by John Nourse of London and in any case may have had a fairly tolerant attitude to straight reprints (as opposed to false collections) which did not compete immediately with his current publishers' interests. He may even have considered that such editions, together with Nourse's translations, did much to spread his message. Whatever Voltaire's final view may have been, the firm of Nourse was clearly known to Voltaire; Nourse is the English bookseller most frequently referred to in the correspondence; and, through his London edition or editions of the French text of *Candide* John Nourse played, in all probability, an important part in the history of the text of that masterpiece.

Voltaire par les livres 1789-1830

JEROOM VERCRUYSSE

L'ÉTUDE du 'mythe' voltairien retient de plus en plus l'attention de la recherche. Il est prématuré de vouloir saisir le phénomène dans son ampleur. Parmi toutes les approches, l'enquête quantitative n'a pas encore retenu souvent l'attention. Pourtant le calcul, tout relatif, des éditions de Voltaire et des pages qui lui ont été consacrées jette une lumière inattendue sur la 'fortune' du personnage. Nous avons donné une bibliographie des écrits français relatifs à Voltaire parus entre *Oedipe* (1719) et la chute de la royauté à l'ancienne en 1830. Les périodiques n'ont pas encore été dépouillés.[1] Pour la même période, une étude quantitative des éditions est très difficile: nombre de titres ont paru sous des marques d'emprunt, et la bibliographie matérielle devra d'abord déblayer ces quantités énormes. Et nous ne parlons que des ouvrages de langue française ou imprimés en France. Les ouvrages de La Porte, Hébrail, Morin d'Hérouville sont fautifs et incomplets. Bengesco n'a pas tout vu, peu s'en faut. Le *Catalogue hebdomadaire* de Bellepierre de Neuve-Eglise et de Philippe de Pierres, né en 1763 et devenu en 1782 le *Journal de la librairie*, expire en 1789 au bout de 37 volumes qui n'enregistrent certes pas la totalité des titres autorisés. En 1797 le *Journal typographique et bibliographique* de Pierre Roux prend la suite, devient le *Journal général de l'imprimerie et de la librairie* jusqu'en 1811 pour devenir par décret du 14 octobre la *Bibliographie de l'Empire*, ancêtre de l'actuelle *Bibliographie de la France*. Son premier directeur, Adrien Beuchot, reste en poste jusqu'en 1841. Sous sa direction, tout ce qui touche à Voltaire est traité en détail. Nous avons évoqué Bengesco qui a rendu des services certes, mais rapidement dépassé pour les spécialistes, il a définitivement rendu l'âme. Les deux superbes volumes du *Catalogue* de la Bibliothèque nationale publiés en 1978 remplacent largement les travaux du diplomate roumain pour ses collections qui sont riches certes, mais ne contiennent pas 'tout'. Pour les titres

---

1. Voir notre 'Bibliographie des écrits français relatifs à Voltaire, 1719-1830' publiée en tête (i.xi-c) de notre *Voltaire jugé par les siens 1719-1749*, collection de 122 brochures (New York 1984). Une première version donnant 629 titres avait paru en 1968 dans les *Studies on Voltaire*. Celle-ci en donne 987.

séparés parus jusqu'à 1800 on peut recourir au *Provisional handlist of separate eighteenth-century editions in the original languages* (Oxford 1981), fruit d'une vaste enquête portant sur 370 institutions de 17 pays; mais il est entendu que ce corpus est encore susceptible de nombreux enrichissements. Grâce à ces travaux, malgré les lacunes et les imperfections, nous croyons qu'il est possible d'entamer une enquête portant sur les publications de Voltaire et relatives à Voltaire en France, d'une révolution à l'autre, de 1789 à 1830. Quelques questions demeurent encore sans réponse, mais celles-ci ne pourraient pas modifier substantiellement nos conclusions.

Les éditions de Voltaire

L'œuvre complet de Voltaire est désormais mieux circonscrit que de son vivant. Nous avons pu montrer[2] que l'écrivain ne fut jamais satisfait d'aucune édition parue de son vivant. Confiant à Panckoucke le soin d'une nouvelle édition, Voltaire ne se doutait point qu'elle aboutirait au monument de Kehl, dont on ne dira pas assez les manipulations de textes et les supercheries et le caractère 'engagé'. Elle a servi de matrice à une foule d'éditions qui ne doivent plus intéresser que les bibliographes.

Nous comptons, très relativement, au moins 893.797 pages[3] imprimées à un nombre x d'exemplaires car les tirages ne sont pas mentionnés; imaginons un instant un tirage moyen de 500 exemplaires: nous ne sommes pas loin du *demi-milliard*. On croit rêver, et pourtant ...

Les éditions 'complètes' et 'choisies' dominent, représentant près de 61% de la production. En 40 ans, 40 éditions sont projetées, annoncées, commencées et achevées ou non, dont 39 entre 1817 et 1829, dont 4 pour 1817 (Desoer, Lefèvre & Déterville, Perronneau, Plancher), 6 pour 1825 (3 pour Baudoin frères, J. Didot aîné, Fortic & Verdière, Verdière), et 7 pour 1827 (2 pour Baudoin, Cosson & Garnery, Doyen & Delangle, Lefèvre, Werdet & Lequien, Lemoine & Baudoin, Mongie aîné), pour ne citer que des 'pointes'. Depuis 1817 il ne s'écoula pas une année qui

---

2. Voir notre 'Voltaire, Sisyphe en Jermanie: vers la meilleure des éditions possibles', *Studies on Voltaire* 179 (1979), pp.143-57. Voir également, U. Kölving, *Provisional table of contents for the Complete works of Voltaire* (Oxford 1983).

3. N'entrent pas en compte les 'notes' de Voltaire sur tel ou tel auteur, généralement publiées avec les écrits de l'un ou de l'autre.

ne vit une nouvelle annonce. Toutes ces éditions réunies comptent 767.450 pages.

Les anthologies ne sont pas encore à la mode mais notons cependant dès 1808 *Le Voltaire de la jeunesse* (Paris, J. Chaumerot) traduit en polonais l'année suivante (Wroclaw, W. B. Korn), puis en 1813 le *Cours élémentaire de littérature composé des articles répandus dans les divers ouvrages de Voltaire* de J. Savy-Laroque (Paris, Briand), en 1821 le *Voltaire en 1 vol.* de J. B. Gouriet (Paris, Baudoin frères), et autres qui offrent aux écoliers des 'choix', curieux quelquefois, du 'complet' proposé aux adultes.

Entre 1792 et 1829 on verra également surgir des recueils de lettres complétant l'édition de Kehl, révélant les échanges de missives avec Mme Du Deffand, P. M. Hennin, Panckoucke, Séguy, Vauvenargues, l'Académie de Dijon, Colini, Mme Du Châtelet, Raynal etc. Nous comptons pour ces recueils 10.865 pages.

Parallèlement aux éditions 'complètes' et 'choisies' apparaissent les éditions de titres séparés que nous groupons sous cinq rubriques.

1. Pour les récits en prose, nous relevons dix collections[4] de romans et de contes étalées de 1792 à 1830, qui atteignent 6.629 pages. *Candide* pointe l'oreille avec 5 éditions de 1793 à 1828, suivi par 4 éditions de *La Princesse de Babylone* entre 1812 et 1816, de 3 éditions de *L'Homme aux 40 écus* (ans III, V, 1826), tandis que *Micromégas* n'est publié qu'une seule fois, en 1826. Le tout additionné 'fait' pour les récits en prose 8.459 pages.

2. Les écrits philosophiques et polémiques acquièrent un meilleur résultat. En 1802 paraissent 3 éditions de *Pensées* rééditées en 1829. Il paraît autant d'éditions du *Dictionnaire philosophique* dans la forme salmigondis de Kehl: une masse à elles seules. L'édition de Didot en 1813 est tirée à 1.200 exemplaires; quinze ans plus tard surgissent les éditions Doyen et Ménard-Desenne. Les *Dialogues* sont édités deux fois (1822, 1830) de même que le *Discours aux Welches* en 1790. Ces écrits réunis comptent 15.418 pages.

3. Le succès des poèmes peut étonner. Vingt-deux éditions collectives des poèmes totalisent entre 1799 et 1830, 8.529 pages, 4 éditions en 1825 (Roux, Durfort & Froment pour deux, Debure) et 5 en 1823 (Debure pour quatre, P. Didot). Deux titres se partagent la faveur du public: nous

---

4. Une édition en 6 volumes in 12° de Lyon, attestée par Bengesco no 1529 n'a pas été retrouvée.

avons retrouvé 11 éditions de *La Pucelle d'Orléans* entre 1792 et 1825: nous savons que les éditions Nicolle-Belin et Gide-Nicolle (1813) ont été tirées à mille exemplaires. Mais ce n'est rien en comparaison des 48 éditions de *La Henriade* publiées de 1789 à 1823, comptant à elles seules quelque 13.170 pages, soit plus de la moitié des écrits en vers. Ici encore quelques tirages sont connus: 3.000 exemplaires pour l'édition Duponcet (1813), 2.000 pour celle de la Veuve Buynard (Lyon 1812). La production est ininterrompue de 1812 à 1830. Si Paris reste le centre de ce considérable succès, on notera 3 éditions à Avignon en 1813 et d'autres à Lyon (1812, 1818), à Toulouse (1791), Lille (1793), La Flèche (1813), Strasbourg (1822) et Reims (1826, année marquée par 4 éditions).

Cet éloge du bon roi selon le cœur de Voltaire traverse la Révolution (1789-1793, année de 3 éditions), reprend sous le Consulat (1801, 1802) et reparaît sous l'Empire (1812-1815) pour se renouveler chaque année sous la Restauration.

L'ensemble des poèmes atteint 25.491 pages.

4. Les œuvres historiques font mieux encore. Deux éditions de *Mélanges historiques* parues en 1827 (Bossange frères) et en 1830 (Lecointe, 6 volumes) s'effacent derrière le succès de l'*Histoire de Charles XII*. Dix-sept éditions sont publiées entre 1805 et 1830 dont quatre en province (Metz 1805, Lyon 1807, Strasbourg 1821, Alais 1821). Le *Siècle de Louis XIV* a connu 8 éditions entre 1803 et 1830, soit deux de plus que l'*Histoire de l'empire de Russie* de 1803 à 1829 dont une en ... 1812 (Paris, Nicolle & Bellin).

L'*Essai sur les mœurs* a été publié deux fois (1805, 1829) tout comme l'*Histoire du parlement* (1823, 1830) et le *Précis du siècle de Louis XV* (1808, 1819). Notons enfin une édition de *La Philosophie de l'histoire* (1825) sous le titre de *Résumé de l'histoire générale*.

Ce bel ensemble totalise 27.148 pages.[5]

5. Le grand triomphateur demeure le théâtre. Vingt-deux éditions collectives se succèdent entre 1800 et 1830 dont quatre pour la seule année 1822 (Menard & Desenne fils, Aillard, Saintin, Ladrange-Guibert-Lheureux et Verdière). Ces 22 éditions totalisent 33.528 pages.

Dans le domaine des titres séparés, la comédie est négligée: deux

---

5. Une édition de Paris 1802 attestée par le *Journal typographique* du 30 nivôse XI (p.124) et Bengesco no 1286, de même que des éditions de Metz en 1805 (Bengesco no 1285) et de Paris 1808 (no 1287) n'ont pas été retrouvées.

éditions de *Nanine* (1796, 1819) et du *Comte de Boursoufle* (1826, chez les concurrents Renouard et Touquet).

La tragédie passe avant tout. Notons 16 éditions de *Brutus* dont 12 de 1790 à 1795, et 4 autres de 1822 à 1826.[6] Le succès de l'époque révolutionnaire s'explique: mais sous la Restauration? *Mérope* affiche 11 éditions entre 1790 et 1829[7] et dépasse à peine les 10 éditions de *Mahomet* parues de 1791 à 1829. L'époque révolutionnaire voit également 6 éditions de *La Mort de César* entre 1789 et 1794, mais nous en trouvons 1 sous l'Empire (1811) et 3 sous la Restauration. De même *Zaïre* touche encore les cœurs: 10 éditions s'échelonnent plus régulièrement de 1791 à 1817.

L'écart se creuse profondément ensuite: *Oedipe* est publié 6 fois entre 1790 et 1828 tout comme *Tancrède* entre 1792 et 1825. *Sémiramis* connaît encore 5 éditions de 1789 à 1818 et on en note 4 entre 1789 et 1821, pour *Adélaïde Du Guesclin. Alzire* tombe à 3 éditions (1791, 1811, 1819) et *Olympie* (1789, 1792), *L'Orphelin de la Chine* (1793, 1811), *Hérode et Mariamne* (1789, 1817) sont réduites à 2 éditions. *Rome sauvée* (1791) et *Les Lois de Minos* (1793) ferment la marche avec 1 édition.

A cette impressionnante série qui souligne le succès constant du théâtre de Voltaire sous tous les régimes politiques, on peut joindre une édition de la *Lettre de M. de Voltaire à l'Académie française sur Shakespeare* qui en 1827 intervient dans le débat romantique.

L'ensemble de la rubrique 'théâtre' groupe 38.966 pages.

Quelques calculs:

– les œuvres complètes, choisies et les anthologies comptent: 767.450 p.

– les rubriques donnent:

= théâtre:	38.966 p.	
= histoire:	27.148 p.	
= poésie:	25.491 p.	126.347 p.
= philosophie/ polémique:	15.418 p.	
= lettres:	10.865 p.	
= romans & contes:	8.459 p.	

893.797 p.

Les écrits en vers, théâtre et poésie, représentent plus de la moitié des titres rubriqués (51,28%). C'est montrer assez que de 1789 à 1830 la

6. Un *Brutus* publié à Avignon par Mouriés et signalé à Carpentras n'a pas été retrouvé.

7. Dont une édition intégrée dans le *Théâtre classique* (Paris, Delalain, 1821) qui n'a pas été prise en compte.

librairie française propose un Voltaire essentiellement 'poète' et en second lieu, 'historien'. L'intérêt pour son œuvre 'philosophique' nous paraît moyen, et faible pour le 'conteur'. Autrement dit, ces quelques calculs nous montrent un Voltaire totalement différent de celui qui nous est présenté par la librairie depuis une cinquantaine d'années, et que le public, même érudit, reçoit et consomme tant bien que mal.

Autre constat. L'énorme succès des éditions 'complètes'. Toutes n'ont pas connu une fortune égale. Mais au départ une véritable rage concurrentielle semble stimuler l'édition française qui inondera le public de dizaines de millions de pages. N'oublions pas que les chiffres donnés sont à l'état unique et qu'il convient de les multiplier par un coëfficient dont la variabilité nous est malheureusement inconnue. On aura noté des tirages de 3.000 exemplaires pour *La Henriade*: un record sans doute. Mais avec l'hypothèse de 500 ... Quel autre écrivain a vu ses écrits multipliés aussi excessivement en un demi-siècle? Tout le monde est invité à s'acheter 'son' Voltaire et de préférence 'complet'. Il faut l'avoir chez soi, il fait partie du decorum intellectuel, qu'il soit présenté en éditions coûteuses, illustrées ou populaires, par fascicules, en souscription, voire au rabais. Le public a-t-il répondu à ces sollicitations? On l'ignore car nous ne disposons point de registres de ventes. Mais la concurrence souvent polarisée sur des titres semblables, semble montrer qu'il existe une appétence qui devrait être étudiée à part. L'examen des écrits consacrés à Voltaire au cours de la période 1789-1830 montre que l'attention ne se porte plus tellement sur les nouveautés, mais tend timidement vers une synthèse que nous croyons déceler également dans la faveur dont jouissent les éditions 'complètes'.

Les écrits relatifs à Voltaire

Dans ce domaine, toutes proportions gardées, les chiffres sont éloquents: 405 titres totalisent 38.765 pages, chiffre à multiplier par un coëfficient toujours inconnu.

Tous les genres sont représentés: prospectus, éloges, dithyrambes, décrets et lois, apologies, pamphlets, biographies, souvenirs et anecdotes, conversations, contes, dialogues, comédies et vaudevilles, essais littéraires et grammaticaux, littéraires et politiques, anthologies, parodies, dictionnaires, imitations, apocryphes, travestissements et suites, rien ne semble manquer à l'appel.

Rappelons quelques grandes étapes: le retour à Paris, le triomphe d'*Irène* et l'éloge mis au concours par l'Académie en 1778-1779, l'édition de Kehl avaient fourni la matière de nombreuses appréciations d'ensemble. Le remarquable *Examen des ouvrages de M. de Voltaire* de Linguet (Bruxelles 1788) offre une synthèse fondée sur le passé mais orientée vers le futur. La Révolution offre bientôt un nouveau sujet de discussions. La loi du 30 mai 1791 ordonnant le transfert au Panthéon suscite un second triomphe de Voltaire. Pour cette seule année nous notons 35 titres, deux de plus qu'en 1779. Un pluie de brochures, de motions, de commentaires quelquefois signés Beaumarchais ou Marie-Joseph Chénier s'abat sur la France. La ferveur nationale, légale, renchérit sur celle de 1778.

A ce temps fort succède une période de silence: tout est dit, ou semble avoir été dit. Mais l'œuvre est constamment republié. La génération qui a *vu* Voltaire disparaît lentement. Pour en fixer le souvenir, Charles Cousin dit d'Avalon lance son petit livre, un *Voltairiana* (Paris an IX) qui sera souvent réédité et augmenté, et nourrira bien des curiosités et des réflexions. Les *Soirées de Ferney* (Paris 1802) de Simien Despréaux de La Condamine vont dans la même ligne et rattrapent l'écho d'autres 'souvenirs' vrais ou faux, qui édifient petit à petit le mythe voltairien.

Mais lorsqu'en 1806 Marie-Joseph Chénier lance une remarquable *Ode à Voltaire* le combat change d'âme. Une nouvelle guerre de brochures révèle des forces plus équilibrées. Retour à l'ancien état des choses? Le Concordat a rendu à l'Eglise ses forces et l'Empire sait bien que 'Si Dieu n'existait pas …'. Personne ne sort vainqueur de cette guerre-éclair. Les dernières années du régime marquent un net arrêt, voire une léthargie dans le domaine critique. Ce sommeil engendre peut-être des forces nouvelles car autour de 1816-1818 la guerre reprend. Nous avons dit le succès des éditions d'œuvres complètes autour de ces années. Les Vicaires généraux de Paris signalent ce *danger* dans un *Mandement de carême* dans la meilleure tradition de l'ami Jean-Georges et autres. On republie Guenée, Linguet; Lepan attaque Condorcet dans une *Vie politique, littéraire et morale de Voltaire* souvent rééditée et contrefaite, notamment republiée en 1825 par la 'Société catholique des bons livres'. Défendu par les uns, le fameux mandement est sifflé, parodié par les voltairiens, Béranger en tête. Il est vrai que désormais le droit à la parole est mieux ménagé. Les éditeurs ripostent: Desoer plaide le droit à la différence; Clausel de Montals, Serieys, Azaïs ne dédaignent pas de prendre part à ce conflit qui prend très vite des allures symboliques. Le procès est relancé une fois de plus, plaidé par et pour une génération nouvelle, dans un langage nouveau.

Entretemps, les éditions se multiplient. Et quelquefois apparaissent d'étranges hybrides. Pierre Villiers publie en 1820 un *Voltaire chrétien. Preuves tirées de ses ouvrages* (Paris, Delaunay, 247 p.) dont le modèle sera imité en 1826 par l'abbé Athanase Mérault de Bizy avec un *Voltaire apologiste de la religion chrétienne* qui sera republié en 1827 à Liège, et en 1828.

Les initiatives curieuses, commerciales sans aucun doute, se multiplient. Le bouillant colonel Jean Baptiste Paul Touquet devenu éditeur-libraire lance ses 'Quatre Voltaire': 'des chaumières, de la petite propriété, du commerce, de la grande propriété', s'attire des procès en nombre, projette d'élever une statue à son auteur dont il distribue des médailles commémoratives (on dirait 'promotionnelles' de nos jours) et s'attaque à l'évêque de Troyes, Etienne Antoine de Boulogne, qui s'en est pris lui aussi aux 'mauvais livres' dans une *Instruction pastorale* (1821) qui sera souvent republiée et même traduite en italien et en espagnol.

De nouvelles orientations critiques se dessinent néanmoins. Paillet de Warcy publie une *Histoire de la vie et des ouvrages de Voltaire* (1824) en 959 pages. Sa volonté expresse de faire œuvre critique en publiant les avis et jugements portés sur Voltaire affermit les premiers efforts d'une critique historique, nourrie cette fois par la publication de témoignages fiables, notamment ceux des anciens secrétaires de Voltaire, Sébastien Longchamp et Jean-Louis Wagnière (1826), des éditions commentées, voire critiques comme les projets d'Adrien Beuchot dont l'entreprise voltairienne mériterait bien une étude particulière. Sa première tentative se soldera par un échec et une querelle bruyante avec la veuve Perronneau (1820-1821). Son éviction suscite une dizaine de pamphlets et c'est au bout de sept années de démarches qu'il occupera avec l'édition Lefèvre en 72 volumes achevée en 1834, la première place au rang de la critique voltairienne ou déjà voltairiste. Sous son emprise la critique historique, l'érudition se substitueront lentement à la polémique qui ne disparaîtra jamais entièrement. Le centenaire de la mort de Voltaire en 1878 en donnera encore une preuve éclatante.

A considérer aujourd'hui cette masse impressionnante de titres publiés en une cinquantaine d'années, nous ne pouvons trouver d'autre commun dénominateur que celui de 'Procès à Voltaire'. Commencé de son vivant, élargi au lendemain de sa mort, c'est sous la Restauration qu'il semble atteindre son sommet, débouchant sur une condamnation sans appel pour les uns, et un triomphe pour les autres. Jointes aux millions de pages de Voltaire qui ont été proposées aux Français et à leurs voisins au cours de cette période, les pièces du procès créent, des plus insignifiantes en apparence aux plus expressives, des plus adroites aux plus regrettables, un courant de pensée, nous dirions presqu'une composante du temps. La France a été soumise à cette époque à une authentique *voltairisation* et une grande part de ses citoyens s'est *voltairisée*. Intégré désormais dans la conscience collective, Voltaire ou mieux, un certain voltairianisme s'est dilué petit à petit dans le subconscient.[8]

C'est du moins ce que nous enseignent les livres de Voltaire et sur Voltaire publiés de 1789 à 1830.

8. Voir notre collection *Les Voltairiens 1778-1830* (New York 1978), en 8 vol. pour les pamphlets, et sous le même titre la collection de microfiches pour les ouvrages étendus (Paris 1978).

Leibniz à Rome en 1689: la question copernicienne

PAOLO CASINI

PENDANT son voyage en Italie, consacré officiellement aux recherches généalogiques sur la maison de Welf que lui avait confié son souverain Ernst August de Hanovre, Leibniz arriva à Rome le 14 avril 1689, juste à temps pour assister aux obsèques solennelles de Christine de Suède.[1] Pendant les six mois de son séjour, il allait assister à d'autres événements remarquables: la mort du pape Innocent XI, le conclave, les fêtes pour le nouveau pape Alexandre VIII. Tout protestant et philosophe qu'il était, il fut séduit par la pompe pontificale. Il était d'ailleurs très remuant: il fréquentait plusieurs bibliothèques – surtout la Bibliothèque Vaticane, dont on lui offrit la direction à condition qu'il se fît catholique – il pratiquait les savants, assistait aux expériences de physique, visitait les cabinets d'antiquités et les monuments, explorait les catacombes. Il donna même son expertise de chimiste à propos du prétendu sang des martyrs conservé dans des fioles dans les entrailles des catacombes.[2]

Le Freiherr von Leibniz, agé de 45 ans, avait surtout l'air d'un courtisan consommé, d'un diplomate initié à tous les secrets des chancelleries européennes. Quelques savants italiens le connaissaient déjà comme mathématicien; le philosophe Francesco Nazari et l'érudit Giovanni Ciampini avaient parlé de ses discussions avec Dodart sur le phosphore dans le *Giornale de' letterati*, en 1677;[3] le savant bibliothécaire du grand duc de Toscane, Antonio Magliabechi, avait reçu sa première lettre en

---

1. Sur le voyage de Leibniz en Italie cf. surtout: G. E. Gurhauer, *G. W. Freiherr von Leibniz* (Breslau 1846; Hildesheim 1966), ii.87ss.; *Leibniz: sein Leben, sein Wirken, seine Welt*, éd. W. Totok et C. Hase (Hannover 1966), pp.45ss.; l'introduction du t.1/5 de Leibniz, *Sämtliche Schriften und Briefe. Allgemeiner politischer und historischer Briefwechsel*, Deutsche Akademie der Wissenschaften zu Berlin (Berlin 1954) (ce volume présente la correspondance de Leibniz avec les 'politiciens' et 'historiens' – non pas celle avec les hommes de science – au temps du voyage); A. Maier, 'Leibnizbriefe in italienischen Bibliotheken und Archiven', in *Quellen und Forschungen aus italienischen Archiven und Bibliotheken*, Preussische Institut in Rom, xxvii.267-82.

2. *Vita del Sig. Barone G. G. di Leibniz data in luce dal Signor Lamprecht in lingua tedesca, e tradotta in lingua italiana ed arricchita di annotazioni da Giuseppe Barsotti lucchese* (Roma 1787); cf. la note ajoutée, pp.46-49.

3. J.-M. Gardair, *Le 'Giornale de letterati' de Rome (1668-1681)* (Firenze 1984), p.326.

1686; le mathématicien florentin Vincenzio Viviani, dernier disciple de Galilée, annota le nom de Leibniz dans un manuscrit de 1678 (Maier, p.270). Ce n'était que le début de relations très intenses: au cours des années suivantes, Leibniz écrira à peu près 350 lettres à ses correspondants italiens (dont 100 seulement nous sont parvenues), et en recevra 500. Cette correspondance, encore mal connue et éditée seulement en partie, rend 'le chapitre Lebniz et l'Italie l'un des plus obscurs de la Leibniz-Forschung' (Maier, p.267).

Ces ténèbres se dissipent au fur et à mesure qu'on apprend à mieux connaître le milieu des savants qui entretinrent des relations suivies avec Leibniz. Son image était alors celle d'un représentant typique de la 'polymathie' allemande, curieux de tout – histoire, diplômes, jurisprudence, chroniques ecclésiastiques, antiquités – plutôt que celle du philosophe qui nous est familière. A ce titre, il fut reçu à Rome dans les deux académies qu'animait monseigneur Giovanni Giusto Ciampini: la Conférence consacrée aux conciles ecclésiastiques, se réunissant au Collège de Propaganda Fide; et l'Accademia Fisico-Matematica, qui se transféra en 1689 de la maison de Ciampini à Piazza Navona, au palais de la Cancelleria Apostolica, auprès du cardinal Pietro Ottoboni, élu pape en octobre.[4] L'Accademia Fisico-Matematica avait survécu aux entreprises d'édition de Ciampini et Nazari, le *Giornale de' letterati*, qui dans ses différents avatars s'était efforcé de se tenir au pas des *Acta eruditorum* de Leipzig, des *Philosophical transactions*, du *Journal des savants*. L'échec final du *Giornale* (1668-1681) paraît être dû à des raisons complexes: défauts d'organisation, défaillance du patronage, autocensure, méfiances du milieu ecclésiastique. Quant à l'Accademia Fisico-Matematica, fondée en 1677, on y avait pratiqué toutes sortes d'expériences barométriques, sur la chaleur et la glace, sur l'optique, sur la phosphorescence. L'éclectisme de ses membres, médecins et 'virtuoses' de toutes disciplines, n'aboutit pas à des découvertes remarquables. Leibniz, selon une notice écrite beaucoup plus tard, 'fut très satisfait non seulement des vaillants hommes qui y participaient, mais aussi des expériences et des découvertes qu'ils y pratiquaient au jour le jour, et admira surtout les

4. Cf. *Dizionario biografico degli Italiani*, *sub voce* Ciampini, Giovanni Giusto, par S. Grassi Fiorentino; Gardair, pp.145ss.; W. E. Knowles Middleton, 'Science in Rome, 1675-1700, and the Accademia Fisicomatematica of G. G. Ciampini', in *British journal for the history of science* 8 (1975), pp.138-54.

beaux instruments acquis [...] par le docte prélat'.[5] La tolérance avec laquelle on traitait les thèmes scientifiques ne s'étendait guère aux problèmes théoriques de l'astronomie copernicienne, sujet tabou à Rome après les sentences prononcées par le Saint Office contre Copernic en 1616 et contre Galilée en 1633.

Leibniz – qui avait lu et commenté les *Discorsi* de Galilée dès le début de son séjour parisien[6] – se rendit compte aussitôt de l'insoutenable et paradoxale situation où se trouvaient les savants italiens, dont plusieurs étaient ecclésiastiques. Obligés de s'en tenir au système astronomique de Ptolomée – ou tout au plus à celui de Tycho Brahé – ils faisaient de l'astronomie d'observation étant intimement déchirés entre l'obéissance à l'Eglise et la conscience de la vérité. C'était sûrement le cas de l'astronome Francesco Bianchini, âgé alors de 27 ans, auquel Leibniz souhaitait de façon presque prophétique un brillant avenir.[7] D'origine véronaise, élève à Padoue du célèbre astronome galiléen Geminiano Montanari, Bianchini avait fait connaître à Rome la méthode de J. D. Cassini pour la mesure de la parallaxe des planètes d'une seule station; il avait donné lecture publique d'une dissertation *De methodo philosophandi in rebus physicis* où il louait les découvertes récentes; il laissa inédite l'ébauche d'un traité 'cartésien' sur la gravité des corps. Vers la fin du siècle, Bianchini sera le protagoniste du projet de la méridienne solaire de S. Maria degli Angeli – considérée à l'époque un prodige de technique et de théorie, et qui subsiste encore dans cette église romaine – et sera chargé de la réforme du calendrier.

Selon toute apparence, Leibniz s'adressa à Francesco Bianchini lorsqu'il se proposa d'aider les savants catholiques à se débarrasser de leurs entraves. On lit dans une lettre non datée, mais écrite sans aucun doute à Rome:

Il faut faire face aux calomnies de ceux qui proclament que la vérité est opprimée chez les catholiques et qui soustraient leurs esprits à la communion de l'Eglise. Il en va de l'honneur de l'Italie, dont les brillantes intelligences pourront ainsi jouir des lumières du siècle, non moins qu'ailleurs, et cultiver ces merveilleuses

5. *Vita* [...] *di Leibnitz*, p.47, note de G. Barsotti.
6. Cf. Leibniz, *Sämtliche Schriften und Briefe*, vi Reihe: *Philosophische Schriften*, vol.iii (Berlin 1980), pp.163ss. et 550ss.; W. H. Barber, *Leibniz in France from Arnauld to Voltaire* (Oxford 1955), pp.132ss.
7. Voir, sur F. Bianchini, *Dizionario biografico degli Italiani*, *sub voce* par S. Rotta; parmi ses biographes: Fontenelle, *Histoire de l'Académie des sciences* (1729), iv.x; A. Mazzoleni, *Vita di Monsignor Francesco Bianchini veronese* (Verona 1735).

découvertes que d'autres gens maintenant usurpent. Je crois que même les hommes éminents qui obéissent à la force de la censure [*summi viri … penes quos censura vis est*] ne peuvent considérer la chose autrement.[8]

Le plaidoyer de Leibniz s'insinue avec habileté dans la mauvaise conscience et l'hypocrisie des gardiens de l'orthodoxie. La force et l'évidence de l'astronomie héliocentrique sont désormais si grandes, ajoute-t-il, que 'l'astronome qui ne comprend pas ce système tâtonne dans les ténèbres; il ignore la beauté et la simplicité que les nouvelles découvertes célestes ont apporté au système du monde, et il obscurcit la gloire de Dieu lui-même, en négligeant l'occasion de reconnaître sa sagesse dans ses œuvres admirables'.

Avant de relire le noyau philosophique et scientifique de cette lettre, il vaut la peine de la replacer dans son contexte. La généreuse tentative du savant allemand se situe en effet dans une circonstance particulière et vise à persuader des personnes dont il faut préciser l'identité.

Le conclave s'ouvrit vers la moitié d'août. Pendant ses réunions, qui durèrent jusqu'au 6 octobre, Leibniz fréquentait la Bibliothèque Apostolique Vaticane pour ses recherches généalogiques. Il dut suivre de près les manœuvres internes et externes du conclave – comme le prouvent quelques notes manuscrites conservées à Hanovre – et il sut dès le début que le candidat favori de la majorité des cardinaux était le vénitien Pietro Ottoboni, protecteur de Ciampini et de son Accademia.[9] Quand Ottoboni résulta élu et prit le nom d'Alexandre VIII, Leibniz lui adressa un long *carmen gratulatorium* qui débute par ces couplets:

> Magne Pater, pro quo generalis publica voti
>   Omina, cum nondum vota darentur, erant;
> Cujus in adventu gaudens Europa, doloris
>   Inducias vulnus sentit habere suum…
> Surge laborantis spes optatissima mundi
>   Nomen Alexandri fataque magna vocant.

Tout au long des 170 vers de ce poème ampoulé, chargé d'images païennes et de réminiscences 'impériales', plein de flatteries qu'on ne saurait mettre décidément sur le compte de la courtisanerie ou d'une certaine naïveté, Leibniz donne libre essor à son idéal irénique: c'est le rêve d'une pacification universelle qui mît fin aux guerres de Louis XIV

8. Leibniz, *Mathematische Schriften*, éd. C. J. Gerhardt (Halle 1860), vi.147.
9. Cf. L. von Pastor, *Storia dei Papi*, trad. it. (Rome 1933), t.xiv, *passim*.

et ouvrît la perspective de la réunion des églises. Le rôle qu'il assigne à l'Eglise catholique est décisif:

> Gloria prima tua est, per te si poenitet orbem
>   Christicolam misere bella mover sibi.
> Tu dictis superans animos majore triumpho
>   Et virtute animi et numine victor eris.
> Ore tuo pendent populi, Tibi ridet Olympus
>   Et conjuratis viribus aether adest.
> Incipe divinae rivos effundere suadae
>   Incipe doctrinae spargere dulcis opes.[10]

Ce poème ne fait aucune allusion – et pour cause – à la réhabilitation de Copernic et de Galilée. Mais on va voir que le philosophe caressait discrètement son propos: comment persuader au nouveau pape, homme éclairé, de casser la scandaleuse sentence du Saint Office?

Revenons à Francesco Bianchini. Son biographe souligne les relations intimes subsistantes depuis des années entre le jeune astronome véronais et Pietro Ottoboni, patricien vénitien âgé de 81 ans en 1689. Lorsque le jeune clerc était arrivé à Rome, cinq ans plus tôt, il s'était installé dans le Palazzo Venezia 'pour mieux cultiver la personne de l'Eminentissime'. Et lorsqu'il fut admis à baiser le pied de l'élu du conclave, tout le monde assista à une scène pathétique de tendresse et de bienveillance. Alexandre VIII ne régna que dix-huit mois; mais, pape népotiste par excellence, pendant son bref pontificat il fut 'protecteur et partial de Francesco [...] Il le combla des marques de sa bienveillance. Il l'admettait familièrement dans ses chambres secrètes; il lui donnait quelque livre à lire: Francesco lisait, et le pape glissait doucement dans le sommeil.'[11]

Comment ne pas reconnaître le révérend père Francesco Bianchini sous l'adresse 'Ad RPB' qui se trouve en tête du post-scriptum accompagnant la lettre 'copernicienne' de Leibniz? Une première conclusion s'impose: Leibniz a écrit cette lettre en automne 1689, à une date proche de la fin du conclave et du *carmen gratulatorium*.

Passons maintenant à l'argument que Leibniz suggérait à Bianchini comme ballon d'essai, destiné au pape: c'est le principe de la relativité de tous les mouvements célestes, fondé sur un commentaire indirect d'un

---

10. *Sämtliche Schriften und Briefe*, 1/5, pp.478 et 483.
11. Mazzoleni, *Vita di* [...] *Bianchini*, pp.13 et 16.

fameux scolie des *Principia mathematica* de Newton.[12] Nous savons que Leibniz avait pris connaissance de la parution de ce livre grâce à un compte rendu, très objectif, inséré dans les *Acta eruditorum* de juin 1688. Il décida par conséquence de publier aussitôt sa propre hypothèse générale concernant la mécanique céleste. Les *Acta eruditorum* de février 1689 contiennent ce *Tentamen de motuum coelestium causis*, où Leibniz s'est efforcé de concilier la loi d'attraction selon l'inverse des carrés avec les tourbillons cartésiens, dans le cadre d'une cosmologie du *plenum*.[13] Les lois de Képler s'y résolvent en une 'circulation harmonique' des planètes assez fantaisiste.

Ce n'est qu'après la publication du *Tentamen* que Leibniz lut directement le texte des *Principia mathematica*: 'Après avoir bien considéré le livre de Newton', écrit-il à Huygens, 'que j'ai vu à Rome pour la première fois, j'ai admiré comme de raison quantité de belles choses qu'il y donne.'[14] Ce fut une lecture critique, faite la plume à la main. E. A. Fellmann a récemment retrouvé l'exemplaire annoté à Rome par Leibniz, et en a publié les intéressants *marginalia*.[15] On y reconnaît aisément les tout premiers germes d'une réaction personnelle de Leibniz face à la physique de Newton qui ira, on le sait, bien loin. Mais bornons-nous à remarquer que, même avant qu'on ne retrouvât l'exemplaire des *Principia* avec les notes marginales de Leibniz, on disposait, sans que personne s'en doutât, d'une longue 'note marginale' éditée depuis longtemps: il s'agit, justement, de la lettre 'copernicienne' écrite à Rome 'vers la fin de l'été 1689'[16] (comme les *marginalia*) et adressée à RPB. Cette longue note concerne le célèbre scolie du premier livre sur l'espace et le mouvement absolu. L'exemplaire étudié par Fellmann ne comporte pas de *marginalia* en cet endroit; mais tout se passe comme si Leibniz eût réservé son commentaire critique à la solution de la question copernicienne.

Elle est abordée avec beaucoup de diplomatie. Au début de sa lettre, Leibniz cite l'avis de quelques autorités catholiques, favorable au système copernicien; il fait allusion à la polémique entre G. B. Riccioli et Stefano

12. Voir Newton, *Philosophiae naturalis principia mathematica*, in *Opera quae extant omnia*, éd. S. Horsley (London 1779-1785), ii.6ss.

13. Le *Tentamen*, première et deuxième version, est maintenant dans *Mathematische Schriften*, vi.146ss. (précédé par la lettre à RPB, en note) et 161ss.

14. *Mathematische Schriften*, lettre à C. Huygens du 13 oct. 1690, vi.189.

15. G. W. Leibniz, *Marginalia in Newtoni Principia mathematica*, éd. critique par E. A. Fellmann (Paris 1973).

16. Datation des marginalia par Fellmann, p.21.

degli Angeli sur la chute des graves, polémique qui a vu la défaite de l'astronome jésuite; il touche avec beaucoup de prudence à la question de l'interprétation allégorique des Ecritures, cet écueil contre lequel Galilée avait fait naufrage. Enfin, il formule la théorie de la relativité de l'espace et du mouvement. Newton, après avoir affirmé dans son scolie une distinction nette entre l'espace absolu et l'espace relatif, le mouvement absolu et le mouvement relatif, admet que nous n'avons aucun moyen expérimental d'établir dans la pratique ces 'absolus'; mais, 'puisque on ne peut pas apercevoir les parties de l'espace, nous faisons usage de ses mesures sensibles [...] Au lieu des lieux ou places absolus, nous en employons de relatifs, sans aucun inconvénient dans la pratique.' Leibniz le prend au mot sur ce point et, sans le citer, lui fait écho: 'Il faut définir le mouvement de façon telle qu'il suppose un système de référence [*ut involvat aliquid respectivum*]; aussi, n'existe-t-il nul phénomène grâce auquel puisse-t-on déterminer de façon absolue [*absolute*] le mouvement et le repos, car le mouvement consiste dans le changement de site ou de lieu; et le lieu lui-même suppose quelque chose de relatif.'[17]

Est-ce un retour en arrière, à la théorie cartésienne du mouvement? Oui et non. Leibniz adopte la terminologie newtonienne. Il accepte l'écorce 'relativiste' du raisonnement de Newton, tout en rejetant son noyau 'absolutiste': le dogme de l'espace qui, 'sans relation avec quelque chose d'extérieur, reste éternellement semblable à soi même et immuable'. Leibniz objecte très clairement: 'On peut donc admettre n'importe quel système [astronomique], car pas même un ange ne saurait tirer de là une preuve métaphysique sûre de l'existence de quelque chose d'absolu. En effet, la condition des lois du mouvement est que tout se passe en la même manière dans les phénomènes; et il n'y a aucune possibilité de juger si et jusqu'à quel point un corps donné se meut ou reste en repos.'

Selon Leibniz, on ne peut supposer un point absolu dans l'espace que par pure convention. Il ajoute à sa critique de l'espace absolu newtonien, l'exemple d'une sphère roulant sur un bateau, en direction opposée à la marche du bateau, pour mieux fixer l'idée de la relativité de son mouvement par rapport à un point pris sur le rivage, qui reste en repos (relatif). Cette image s'inspire directement d'une image analogue de Newton, qui a toutefois chez Newton un sens contraire: l'exemple du marin marchant sur le pont du bateau, destiné à mieux fixer l'idée d'un système de

17. *Mathematische Schriften*, vi.146, d'où sont tirées aussi les citations suivantes.

référence en repos (absolu). Et Leibniz de conclure: comme tout mouvement est relatif:

on peut dire de même que la doctrine sphérique de Ptolomée n'est pas moins vraie que la doctrine théorique de Copernic; qu'il est également absurde d'embarrasser les mouvements de la terre avec les mouvements sphériques du premier mobile, et de vouloir appuyer la théorie planétaire sur d'innombrables épicycles et excentriques; tandis que l'hypothèse nouvelle – ou plutôt l'hypothèse ancienne renouvelée – présente à l'esprit cette même théorie [planétaire] accompagnée d'une simplicité admirable. Donc ceux qui affirment que l'hypothèse de Copernic est vraie doivent entendre par là qu'elle est la meilleure [*optima*] et la plus apte à expliquer les phénomènes, et qu'il n'y a pas d'autre vérité en ce domaine [...] Qui aura bien compris ceci, sauvegardés les droits de la censure [*salva censura*], suivra le système nouveau et sera un Copernicien convaincu.

Ce raisonnement, d'une logique impeccable, est très 'moderne', très en avance sur l'époque; même trop, car il dépasse le 'paradigme' newtonien et le cadre théorique de la dispute *de terra mota*. A ce titre, il pouvait être pris pour un adroit sophisme. Etait-il possible d'amener par ce moyen l'Eglise catholique à changer d'avis, comme le souhaitait Leibniz ('praeveniet censores revocandi aliquando decreti necessitatem'), à ne plus s'opposer au 'torrent du siècle et à la voix publique des savants'? Dans un post-scriptum, Leibniz engage le RPB à lui donner son avis par écrit en vue d'une publication prochaine: il s'agit, très probablement, du projet de réimprimer à Rome le *Tentamen*, qui aurait été ainsi le pivot de toute l'opération.

Nous ne savons rien de la réponse du père Bianchini. Fut-il convaincu par l'audacieux argument de Leibniz? Approuva-t-il la cosmologie fantaisiste du *Tentamen*? Ce texte curieux a donné bien de l'embarras à ses lecteurs, de Christian Huygens jusqu'aux critiques modernes, car – au contraire de l'argument copernicien que nous venons de voir – il est arriéré et fautif par rapport aux *Principia mathematica*.[18] Certes, si Leibniz s'attendait à une autorisation expresse d'en haut, il fut déçu. Néanmoins, il ne se résigna pas. Retourné à Hanovre, il insiste avec Bianchini: 'Habemus pontificem sapientissimum qui, si otium haberet audiendi, causam astronomiae melioris, haud dubie oppressam quorundam homi-

18. Cf. surtout E. J. Aiton, *The Vortex theory of planetary motions* (London, New York 1972), ch.6; A. Koyré, *Newtonian studies* (London 1966), pp.124ss.; A. R. Hall, *Philosophers at war: the quarrel between Leibniz and Newton* (Cambridge 1980), pp.148ss. Newton a écrit une réfutation vétilleuse du *Tentamen* en 1712: cf. *Correspondence of Sir Isaac Newton and Professor Cotes*, ed. J. Edleston (London 1850), pp.310ss.

num in his studiis minus versatorum praeposteris judiciis, in libertatem vindicaret. In quo negotio si quid a te aliisque amicis rerum intelligentibus praestari posset, profecto ipsam vobis ecclesiam romanam non mediocri beneficio obstringeretis.'[19]

Il revient à la charge treize ans après,[20] mais toujours en vain, car le décret anticopernicien ne perdra sa force à Rome que grâce à Benoît XIV dans la seconde moitié du dix-huitième siècle, et ne sera révoqué qu'au dix-neuvième. Quant à Bianchini, tout ami qu'il était de Leibniz, il devint bientôt l'un des premiers adeptes de son pire ennemi, Newton. Envoyé en Angleterre pour une mission semi-officielle en 1713, le prélat catholique rendit hommage au président de la Royal Society.[21] Grâce à Bianchini et à ses amis, le système copernicien fut reçu enfin sans difficulté en Italie; mais, cette fois, *sub specie newtoniana*.

19. Lettre de Leibniz à Bianchini datée de Hanovre, 18 mars 1690, dans J. G. H. Feder, *Commercii epistolici Leibnitiani selecta specimina* (Hannover 1805), p.296. Exprimant ses vues sur l'Eglise de Rome, Leibniz écrira à V. L. von Sechendorff le 27 décembre 1691: 'Diffundi lumen in Italiam et contagio quodam serpere studium purioris antiquitatis in nupero itinere didici'; *Sämtliche Werke*; *Briefwechsel*, I/7, p.497.

20. Dans une lettre à Bianchini, au sujet de la réforme du calendrier, datée de Hanovre, 13 octobre 1703: 'Saepe cogitavi mecum nihil magis obstare excellentibus italorum ingenii quam quod ea qua par est libertate philosophari non possunt [...] Eamque rem [la sentence contre Copernic] ego summi pontifici in animum revocandam putem, ut non veritati magis quam ingeniis italicis succurrat, eaque a vinculis liberet, quibus in scientia praesertim astronomica velut humi affiguntur'; dans E. Celani, 'L'epistolario di F. Bianchini', *Archivio veneto* 36 (1888), pp.183-84.

21. Cf. S. Rotta, dans *Dizionario biografico degli Italiani*; voir aussi: P. Casini, *Newton e la coscienza europea* (Bologna 1984), pp.181ss.; V. Ferrone, *Scienza natura religione: mondo newtoniano e cultura italiana nel primo settecento* (Napoli 1983), pp.62ss.

Fontenelle as a model for the transmission and vulgarisation of ideas in the Enlightenment

ROBERT NIKLAUS

FONTENELLE as a philosopher has been very differently assessed, his originality questioned and the accuracy of his scientific information challenged, but his status as a *philosophe* has remained unshaken. The broad lines of his thought are clear in spite of his equivocal silences, his guarded statements, and the fact that the attribution to him of some important works is still conjectural. But whether one believes with J. R. Carré[1] that Fontenelle's views remained broadly constant, or with M. Roelens[2] that we can trace an evolution in his thought (chiefly with regard to the idea of progress which increasingly qualifies his pessimism), whether one holds that his ideas played a seminal or merely a subordinate role in the shaping of eighteenth-century thought, it is obvious from the wide diffusion of his key works among the reading public of his times that he contributed significantly to the propagation of a new scientific and philosophical outlook on life. Although not a scientist in the true sense of the word his unrivalled knowledge of scientific developments coupled with his status as a *littérateur*, his eventual membership of the Académie des sciences of which he was appointed perpetual secretary in 1697, the Académie française (1691), the Académie des inscriptions et des belles-lettres (1701), the Royal Society and many other French and foreign academies whose standing was rising rapidly, his role in the leading salons of the seventeenth and eighteenth centuries enabled him to bridge what C. P. Snow was pleased to call the two cultures, and to add a dimension to the world of letters through the inclusion of popularised science. Yet it is curious to note that his most significant works: *Nouveaux dialogues des morts* (1683), *Entretiens sur la pluralité des mondes* (1686), *Histoire des oracles* (1686), were all written in the 1680s before honours were showered on him. Official recognition, however, when it came,

1. *La Philosophie de Fontenelle ou le sourire de la raison* (Paris 1932; Slatkine Reprints, Geneva 1970).
2. *Fontenelle; textes choisis* (Paris 1966).

undoubtedly helped to consolidate his reputation and to spread his influence, encouraging a younger generation to write in the same vein.

In general terms Fontenelle provides us with the first stereotype of 'le philosophe', who was to replace 'l'honnête homme' of the seventeenth century. Like his predecessor the 'philosophe' was an inveterate amateur, a dilettante, a man 'qui ne se pique de rien' as La Rochefoucauld aptly put it. He wished to cast off the folly of pride and all dogmatism. His preoccupations now extended far beyond the moral disquisitions and abstractions or generalities which were dear to the heart of the *précieux* society which nurtured Fontenelle; they included all fields of experience, but the true 'philosophe' is the 'philosophe ignorant' of Voltaire, humble when confronted by the great insoluble problems of mankind. Yet he sought encyclopedic knowledge in all matters ranging from the literary and philosophical to the scientific and technological, always bearing in mind the social utility of new theories and new discoveries. He used reason to determine the most probable answer to his questions and irony to undermine opposition. Thus he appealed to the intelligence of an élite which felt flattered, thereby rallying valuable support. He remained a member of the highly polished, essentially elitist society which included besides some aristocrats the intellectual and social leaders in all walks of life. The salons Fontenelle frequented were more strongly marked by preciosity than the later salons in which he felt rather less at home. His literary work reflects the gallantry and manners of his age, but his more significant publications testify to the growing interest in scientific speculation coupled with the recognition of the enhanced position of woman in society. In certain respects he may be considered as the first feminist of the Enlightenment. He saw woman as highly intelligent but unschooled and as yet unable to grasp the essential concepts of the new world which was unfolding. In the *Entretiens sur la pluralité des mondes* he ostensibly singled out a woman as his chief interlocutor whilst in practice he addressed himself to the common reader who may have had the benefit of a classical education but was singularly ill-informed about science. The Copernican system of astronomy was not widely understood. Although not a scientist nor indeed an original philosopher in the sense of Descartes, Locke, Leibniz or Spinoza, but an 'interprète de la nature' to use Diderot's memorable definition, Fontenelle was capable of relating new discoveries to the corpus of science, to synthesise data and draw meaningful conclusions. He placed emphasis on the new and the useful and, like the later Diderot, he did not hesitate to formulate hypotheses that might account for the recorded facts, provided they eschewed the irrational or supernatural. He promoted an empirical approach to knowledge subtended by an appeal to reason as the final arbiter even before he had read Locke's *Essay concerning human understanding*, but side by side with inductive reasoning he always made room for deductive reasoning as expounded by Descartes with an appeal to the common sense that is innate in us all. This did not prevent him or the later *philosophes* from questioning at times the very instrument on which they had to rely, a theoretical questioning which had little practical effect. In fact nothing that could not be subjected to reason was acceptable to them. Now the rationalist spirit and the critical spirit applied to the whole gamut of knowledge are the key to the *Encyclopédie*, the great collective enterprise begun in the middle of the eighteenth century. This being so, Fontenelle, as J. Proust has recently reminded us, is truly the first *encyclopédiste*, and d'Alembert who took over his mantle as perpetual secretary of the Académie des sciences merely continued his work. Whereas Fontenelle wrote annual summaries of scientific research and innovations in his *Histoire de l'Académie des sciences* between 1666 and 1679 and especially 1699 and 1740, d'Alembert, together with Diderot, embarked on a more comprehensive exercise which in theory was to suggest future lines of research as well as embody the results of current scientific investigations. D'Alembert's judicious *Eloge de Fontenelle* and tribute in the *Discours préliminaire* were fitting. He recognised that Fontenelle's science was outdated, that Newton's view of the system of the universe was correct, whilst Fontenelle held on to Descartes's *tourbillons* without ever troubling to put the issue between the two thinkers to any empirical test. D'Alembert said of Descartes: 'On ne pouvait alors imaginer rien de mieux.' He could hardly have said this of Fontenelle who clung far too long to the cartesian gospel that had guided his intellectual development in his formative years, this after reading the *Principia* of Newton, a man with whom he was in touch and who was elected a member of the Académie des sciences. Fontenelle wrote appreciatively of Newton in his *Eloge de Newton* (1727), yet he remained unconvinced by his arguments, and at the age of 95 he published a *Théorie des tourbillons*, admittedly drafted at an earlier date. Patriotism has been invoked as an explanation, but the reason may well lie in his deep misgivings over introducing any kind of mysticism into his general philosophy. The Cartesian, mechanistic framework suited him better. His deism is based on a God who has set the world in motion and may be likened to a rational watchmaker. This God is not unlike that of Voltaire who shared his dislike of metaphysics and was equally unmoved by the religious experience. The word God does not figure once in the *Entretiens sur la pluralité des mondes*, being conveniently left out of the unfolding of a rational universe. God is necessary to account for the creation of a world which is one and whose laws are constant, but he has no other function. This idea became commonplace and was endorsed by many *philosophes*. Fontenelle who, like Voltaire, knew the value of reiteration in popularising an idea, gained a wide recognition for that of the constancy of the laws of nature.

All the eighteenth-century thinkers read Fontenelle and wittingly or not owe him a debt. They recognised in him a precursor. Had he not extended the field of literature so as to include astronomy? In the same spirit Montesquieu brought law within the scope of literature, Voltaire philosophical theories, Rousseau social and political thought, Diderot scientific speculation, ethics and aesthetics. It might be argued that these writers would have acted as they did without benefit of example, but it may be doubted whether they would have written in precisely the same style. Whilst they criticised Fontenelle's literary affectations, his *galanterie*, his method of presentation and rhetoric, they followed him in practice in their several efforts at the vulgarisation and promotion of their ideas. Did not Montesquieu in the *Lettres persanes* indulge in indirect and oblique satire, in a style at once light and deft with some of the wit and preciosity that would be commended in the salons? The case of Diderot is even more peculiar for he often adopted a 'ton frivole' in works he did not publish in his lifetime and which were presumably intended for the enlightenment of posterity. Voltaire used logic and dramatic effect in his *contes philosophiques* which are also *contes* as Fontenelle had done, and the latter's retelling of the story of the alleged golden tooth validates the new critical method which Voltaire was to exploit in his historical works. Both writers knew how to make points by implication for the benefit of the perspicacious reader and both knew the positive effect of remaining silent on specific issues.

Fontenelle's philosophical position rests on a few constants which he shared with the *philosophes*: basic scepticism, objectivity coupled with real or affected detachment. Fontenelle's scepticism which owes something to Montaigne, so widely read throughout the eighteenth century, is colder, more incisive, more often reiterated. Diderot also frequently proclaimed the scepticism which underlies his thought: 'Le scepticisme est le premier pas vers la vérité', he proclaimed, sometimes substituting 'l'incrédulité' for 'le scepticisme', an alteration which Fontenelle would have deemed unnecessarily compromising; he was, however, more optimistic about the existence of an objective if unattainable truth than his predecessor. Fontenelle held firmly to the view that error was ineradicable in the human make-up and that as soon as one given prejudice was discarded another rushed in to take its place. The task of the *philosophe* can only be to lead people to cast aside those prejudices and superstitions that are most harmful, but war on superstition, the battle cry of the *philosophes*, was never far from Fontenelle's mind, although he viewed the outcome of the crusade with greater pessimism. D'Alembert seems to have shared his disillusion which falls short of despair when in the *Discours préliminaire* he refers to future 'siècles d'ignorance' and sees the triumph of reason as of a day. Both thinkers write from 'au-dessus de la mêlée', but their distrust of the future does not preclude a faith in nature and in reason itself. Negative thinking yields to positive thinking: condemnation of religion and metaphysics, mysticism, the supernatural and other forms of prejudice, side by side with the promotion of the critical method whether applied to history, the texts of the Bible and all the ideas which we take for granted, in particular the reality of ghosts, devils, oracles or miracles. Fontenelle was even more cautious that d'Alembert, whom Baruel called 'le renard de l'*Encyclopédie*', or Diderot who saw his *Pensées philosophiques* condemned to be burnt by the Parlement de Paris, and whose *Lettre sur les aveugles* landed him in the prison of Vincennes. Voltaire, too, found himself incarcerated in the Bastille and although he wrote: 'Tout le monde n'a pas le même goût que John Huss pour être brûlé', he took considerable risks, sacrificing caution to his temperament. Fontenelle's surprising omissions, silences and timidity irritated Voltaire, but they find some justification in the dangers of seventeenth-century life and form part of the tactics commonly used in the eighteenth century. The spurious or revealing cross-references and implied comments to be found everywhere in the *Encyclopédie* were rendered necessary by the censorship which prevailed and the *encyclopédistes*, like Fontenelle, had to leave it to the intelligent reader to draw his own inferences. Certainly Fontenelle set a pattern: to write from a secure base, to let people read between the lines, and at this game Voltaire was to prove a past master. Diderot was less able to dissemble, being too prone to fits of enthusiasm, and he was gauche when he tried to disarm criticism of his *Pensées philosophiques* by inserting just one *pensée* (LVIII) that professed Roman Catholic orthodoxy. Fontenelle was wise enough never to reply to criticism or engage in open controversy, but he was fortunate, according to Voltaire, in avoiding persecution for unorthodox views when Le Tellier's star was in the ascendant at the court of Louis XIV and the implications of the *Entretiens sur la pluralité des mondes* were being debated. It was d'Argenson who saved him, as Voltaire believed, but it was also surely his standing in society. Although no leader, nor one to assume the risks of leadership, he did express his disapproval of the Revocation of the Edict of Nantes which drove some of his friends into exile, and in an anonymous *Relation de l'île de Bornéo* (January 1686), which Pierre Bayle published in the *Nouvelles de la République des lettres*, poured ridicule on Mréo (an anagram for Rome), Eènugu (Geneva), Mliséo (Solime, a name sometimes given to Jerusalem). Astonishingly Bayle failed to decipher the anagrams which others were quick to spot. A work such as the *Entretiens* was read in different ways at different times and with each successive edition,[3] but it is not just that his emendations and additions attracted attention, it is rather that readers with new terms of reference and emboldened by unceasing propaganda saw in the work more than had been originally detected. This is even truer of the *Histoire des oracles*.[4] The public was not slow to see in Fontenelle's onslaught on pagan oracles a covert attack on Christian miracles, noting that the reasoning employed could be levelled at miracles. Fontenelle's careful exclusion of any reference to miracles and criticism of the Christian dogma served only to reinforce an 'enlightened' interpretation of the work.

Strictures on Fontenelle's method of vulgarisation are numerous and were made from the very first. Yet his principle that entertainment is an essential feature of successful popularisation which he demonstrated has never been abandoned, nor did his successors abandon the paradoxical

3. See Robert Shackleton's edition of the *Entretiens sur la pluralité des mondes* and *Digression sur les Anciens et les Modernes* (Oxford 1955), which lists all the collective and the separate editions of the *Entretiens* as well as providing a very full introduction to the author and his work.
4. M. Bouchard, *L'Histoire des oracles de Fontenelle* (Paris 1947).

idea that by appealing to the 'happy few', the intelligent and discerning reader, vulgarisation could be made more effective. The small *élite* for whom Fontenelle wrote soon grew in numbers as did the readers of Diderot's *Pensées philosophiques* which carried the epigraph: *Piscis hic non est omnium*. But in spite of the entertainment element it contained, Diderot's *Rêve de d'Alembert* was judged too dangerous for publication and was known only to the most privileged members of his intimate circle.

The choice of literary form became a matter of importance. Fontenelle chose the forms of dialogue, digression, apologue, discourse interspersed with anecdotes, maxims and observations. At first sight unpretentious and natural, these forms eschew traditional rhetoric, any systematic presentation of ideas, allowing the author the greatest possible licence as the form of *essais* had done for Montaigne. Fontenelle's choice was that of most of his successors who wrote *pensées, lettres, observations, dialogues, entretiens, essais*. Rousseau's *discours* avoided the formal *traité* and we have to await d'Holbach's *Système de la nature ou des lois du monde physique et moral* (1770) for a disliked word such as *système* to creep in. Polemical writing thrives on debate for which dialogue is a suitable form. In principle dialogue is a means of investigating a problem which allows the author to present both sides of a question without necessarily committing him to a formal conclusion but allowing the reader to decide where lies the greater weight of argument.[5] Of course the author, under the guise of objectivity, may urge his own views but Fontenelle, as later Diderot, by distancing himself from the reader succeeds in being at one with him in keeping an open mind and like him is groping for some ultimate truth, sometimes acknowledging in manifest derision that nothing has been or can be decided. The dialogue embodying real or apparent concessions on behalf of both interlocutors is realistic in that, when involving a friendly or intellectual as opposed to an emotional debate, speakers are led to modify their stance to preserve the niceties of social intercourse. Its basis lies in the spirit of contradiction which can take on a dramatic form that enlivens it. The technique of dialogue offers an ideal method of persuasion since it brings into play a number of characters, each with his own personality and standpoint, whilst leaving the author free to manipulate his characters and insert comments of his

5. John W. Cosentini has devoted a whole volume to *Fontenelle's art of dialogue* (New York 1952).

own on their statements, often ironical or satirical, but the reader is always left to act as judge or jury.

Fontenelle's first significant work was the *Nouveaux dialogues des morts* (1683), imitated from Lucian whose aim had been to criticise the gods and undermine religion. The variant of the dialogue form which he adopted was brought to perfection. Invariably lively, it deals in a light-hearted manner with new and important topics. Neither Fénelon nor Vauvenargues were to equal their predecessor in its use, Fénelon because he was too didactic, Vauvenargues because his temperament was at odds with the literary form adopted. The dialogue of the dead as a variant of the genre has certain advantages as well as drawbacks. J. W. Consentini has brought out the rich variety of dialogues used by Fontenelle, starting from an awareness of the effectiveness for philosophical debate of the platonic form. An obvious point, yet one commonly missed or ignored by critics, is that all Fontenelle's dialogues are in fact dialogues of the living. Ideas are considered outside time. Fontenelle's characters express truly representative ideas but with an emphasis which is his own. By so doing he presents through his dialogues between living or dead characters his own views on mankind, tipping the scales one way or the other by stress and language as well as comment. Rather more effectively than in the *Digression sur les Anciens et les Modernes* (1688) he demonstrates that ideas need to be considered *per se*, outside time, by sometimes giving preference to the venerable dead, sometimes to the more recent and less widely esteemed dead. All ideas have to be scrutinised afresh and objectively and exposed to the light of pure reason, the absolute reason as understood by Fontenelle and his contemporaries, which is to be found in the mind of even the most primitive man as Rousseau and other eighteenth-century thinkers would agree. In effect the *Nouveaux dialogues des morts*, 'des morts avec les vivants, des vivants avec les morts', eliminate time as a factor to sway our judgement.

In a letter to Mlle Volland, dated 11 September 1769, Diderot states that had he been willing to sacrifice the richness of his thought to nobility of style he would have called his characters in the *Rêve de d'Alembert* Democritus, Hippocrates and Leucippus, presumably instead of d'Alembert, Bordeu and Diderot. By opting for real, living persons he enlivened and also deepened his *entretiens*, enhancing the actuality of the discussion by mixing paradoxically the fictitious with the real and attributing to his characters ideas they would not or could not adopt. The element of humour introduced in this way in a contemporary dialogue finds its parallel in the humour involved in reporting an alleged conversation between persons of different centuries. The parallel between Diderot and Fontenelle can be pushed further, for Mlle de Lespinasse is no prude, yet she feels she must play the part of a lady naturally shocked by any statement that runs counter to the social convention governing her station in life, her sex and her age. Mlle de Lespinasse's preciosity differs somewhat from that of the marquise in the *sixième soir*, but we can note the sensibility of the marquise when faced with the beauty of the night, the undertones of romanticism and feminine emotion associated with the beauty of nature. Before Rousseau and Diderot and many others Fontenelle had pointed the way to the cult of nature, but his own view of nature was firmly based on reason and his *galanteries* are merely conventional. His flattery of the fair sex is an affectation that proved successful and was imitated.

Diderot refers to Fontenelle by name in the *Rêve de d'Alembert* when striving to demonstrate the relativity and consequent limitations of our thinking: 'Comme la rose de Fontenelle qui de mémoire de rose n'avait vu mourir un jardinier.' Peter France in *Rhetoric and truth in France from Descartes to Diderot* (1972) situates this statement in its context, rightly pointing out that after Mlle de Lespinasse had professed her admiration for Fontenelle, Bordeu had referred critically to the latter's 'ton frivole'. This is true and Diderot's homage is qualified, but in practice Diderot himself often adopted this 'ton frivole' and his feelings for Fontenelle are much the same as those for Boucher whom he called 'le Fontenelle de la peinture', in an effort to characterise a style that had its merits but which he finally condemned. In any case the rose of Fontenelle which may be found in the *cinquième soir* was sufficiently memorable to have stayed in Diderot's retentive memory and for him to assume that it had done so in that of his readers. He could appreciate a vivid image and a piece of reasoning by analogy, that great 'cheval de bataille' of the *philosophes*. Comparisons, metaphors, similes, anecdotes intersperse all their works. Diderot's rhetoric was more subtle, his technique for the dramatic presentation of ideas and for rendering conversations lively is more sophisticated, but they too amount to a rhetoric ultimately as artificial as that of Fontenelle. Efforts to get away from rhetoric prove abortive in all forms of discourse, for they merely lead to new forms which in turn become a *poncif*. When literature is used to convince, style necessarily becomes artificial, it is only the nature of the artifice that changes from one writer to another and one generation to the next. Any harsh judgement on Fontenelle's style needs to be softened by reference to prevailing taste and to the very long innings Fontenelle's specific manner was to enjoy.

The *Entretiens* which saw 28 editions in the author's lifetime was judged a masterpiece even after the science it presented was outdated and proved to be wrong. It still rewards study as a pedagogical masterpiece. The lessons in astronomy have been well planned. They proceed by steps well-adapted to the intellectual capacity of the marquise or any other uninformed reader of her class. It is astronomy without tears, taken in easy stages which are interesting and exciting and allow the pupil to ask questions and even anticipate on the conclusions, but also to make mistakes which can be graciously corrected without any dampening of enthusiasm. The lessons geared to the average ability of the adult pupil would be valid for a whole class. As in *Emile* the exposition is directed at one person but has a general validity. Fontenelle knows when he needs to make personal remarks, when to make apparently irrelevant observations, when to be circumstantial so as to surprise and hold the interest. The setting, seemingly arbitrary, is well-suited to the lesson: a seventeenth-century park with a shining moon that foreshadows a *fête galante*. In terms of the 1680s it is difficult to imagine improvements in the technique. Fontenelle's art is greater than that of Fénelon because he is less obviously didactic and also because his subject was new, topical and exciting. The passage of Halley's comet which had prompted Bayle to write his *Pensées sur la comète* (1682, 1683) had not allayed the absurd fears of the vast majority of the world population including the intellectual *élite*. For the notion, which lurks at the back of people's minds, of a God that might bring disaster upon the world according to a whim, Fontenelle substituted the God of Nature whose laws could be seen at work. Philosophical ideas based on the new science were inserted, expounded, interpolated and implied in a style that carried conviction with the literary-minded.

Diderot's *Rêve de d'Alembert* is superior in that his vision of a world in flux was more original and his powers of expression greater, so that the work exercises a more enduring seduction; but he shares with Fontenelle the ability to present in an apparently unsystematic yet perfectly logical way the key stages in the argument, and by clinging to the techniques of an apparently realistic yet bogus conversation with significant but contrived digressions, he finally achieves a broad synthesis which explains all the phenomena recorded. His speculations have greater resonance because they were more personal and original and were to find subsequent confirmation, but in essence we are always witnessing a kind of *leçon de choses* cleverly construed to lead one to the truth, or rather a conjectural truth. Rousseau's method is not very different. His problem like that of Fontenelle was to determine the necessary steps to be taken in line with the stage of development and understanding of the pupil. For both child and adult the teaching needs to be made interesting. Neither child nor adult welcomes the too logical and systematic exposition beloved by professional thinkers. By eschewing the rhetoric of the logically articulated in the classical manner and by adopting a new and more natural disorder the possibilities of which had not yet been fully exploited, the two interpreters of nature rendered their arguments more convincing.

In this connection Fontenelle's *Digression sur les Anciens et les Modernes* has first its title to commend it. Fontenelle has little to say on the famous quarrel itself. Only a careful reader can see through the cautious balance maintained and discern his personal sympathies. One needs to know of his concern for scientific progress and view of the nature of man to detect his bias, so anxious is he to win his reader over to his way of looking at the problem rather than to any given conclusion.

The *Histoire des oracles*, which had five editions in twenty years, marks an important landmark in the history and dissemination of ideas and fully warrants its inclusion in Malfère's well-known series: *Les Grands événements littéraires*, provided the term *littéraire* is interpreted in a very broad sense. It registered a stage in man's intellectual awareness and contributed to precipitate a change in man's outlook on the world. Its aim was to acquaint readers with the fruits of recent erudition on the subject of oracles and to confound those who obstinately clung to untenable theories. In a sense the work was unoriginal. It was based on that of the anabaptist A. Van Dale whose numerous examples were transcribed. Fontenelle did, however, reverse Van Dale's order of presentation and insidiously inserted his own views, those of a philosopher endowed with sweet reason. He did so with sufficient wit to establish the preeminence of reason and promoted the Cartesian notion that reason based on common sense is and always was the prerogative of the thinking man. Like Voltaire he was too much of a rationalist to reflect on the part of instinct in the creation of myths or indeed religions, and like Voltaire he saw priests throughout the world and at all times as impostors exploiting the credulity of simple folk. To achieve his ends he employed the oblique approach. By narrowing the problem to the consideration of pagan oracles and dismissing the notion that these had ceased with the advent of Christianity he placed himself on relatively safe ground and rendered it very difficult to challenge the new critical, historical method he was using. By providing a rational explanation of current misconceptions he sapped the position of his opponents. The manner of his treatment inevitably invited further investigations of kindred problems: magic, sorcery, supernatural interventions and miracles, including Christian miracles. The authority of the Fathers of the Church was restricted to theology but, after astronomy, theology too was to become a subject for consideration by the general reader. Fontenelle's flowery style, so much lighter than that of Van Dale and also of Malebranche and Bayle, proved to be entertaining without detracting from the serious content of the work.

The *Histoire des oracles* was read differently at different times. When it first appeared Louis XIV had grown sceptical of spells and similar supernatural nonsense, and had seen the futility of burning witches and poisoners alike on fairly dubious evidence. So he left Fontenelle in peace, particularly since his work reflected well on his reign. Soon, however, his confessor Le Tellier who secured a hold on him, perceiving the inherent danger to the Church of Fontenelle's ever popular work, launched an attack to which a reply was made, but not by Fontenelle himself who rode the storm precisely because he avoided any controversy. He held that a work could speak for itself. In fact Le Tellier's attack focussed attention on the work which was read with a fresh insight and promoted the publication of new editions. As the eighteenth century dawned readers became increasingly aware that the *Histoire des oracles* could be interpreted as a potentially powerful challenge to orthodoxy. It should be remembered that the abbé Bergier, not the worst of apologists of the Christian religion in the eighteenth century in spite of his mediocrity, was not alone in seeing in miracles the ultimate proof of the Christian religion. He based his many volumes of exegesis on one specific miracle, that of Saint Denis who carried his head under his arm. 'Je n'ai pas de peine à vous croire, Monseigneur. Il n'y a que le premier pas qui coûte,'

Mme Du Deffand is reputed to have said when told the story. In non-theological circles there could be no rejoinder to such a witticism. Much later Renan was to popularise the idea that the truth of a miracle is often in the mind of the believer and that miracles were frequently imposed on their performers to strengthen the faith of waverers and answer a psychological need. Whether or not by excluding miracles from his survey Fontenelle was wittingly inviting his readers to draw anti-Christian conclusions has been debated, but his work points in the direction of scepticism and agnosticism. In any case the critical and rational examination of Biblical as well as pagan texts was promoted and lent support to the work of Richard Simon and others. Later thinkers were highly critical of Fontenelle's guarded and oblique approach, but they had less to lose.

Many adopted his caution but without his consistency or success. Voltaire is a case in point. He was averse to taking risks. He had his hide-outs and advised Diderot to leave Paris at a critical moment in the publication of the *Encyclopédie*. He told his friends to lie if it was in a good cause. Yet all too often he was carried away by his temperament. Injustice worried him to the point that he was prepared to expose himself to real danger. Diderot also was not very successful in safeguarding his position, at least at the beginning of his career when he was worried by the police. This background explains in part his indulging in the *Encyclopédie*, in devious but fairly safe methods of propaganda. Fontenelle realised that he had a social position to uphold in the very interest of his ideas and that his enviable status provided him with protection only up to a point. The same is true of d'Alembert, whose standing was high through his work as a mathematician and his membership of several academies. Voltaire never denigrated the Académie française to which he was elected, and Diderot, who was never elected to that august body, nevertheless acquired some protection through the wide range of his friends and acquaintances and his position at the head of one of the great commercial ventures of the times in which the publishers had invested substantial capital. Moreover, the prestige of the *Encyclopédie* abroad as well as at home reflected well on France, and the relationships of Voltaire and Diderot respectively with Frederick II and Catherine II had not gone unnoticed by the authorities.

Fontenelle's practice of borrowing from other writers whose work he reshaped or re-interpreted set a pattern which many of the *philosophes* were to follow. Fontenelle translated Van Dale, much as Diderot translated and adapted Shaftesbury, and he used John Wilkins and Pierre Borel in a somewhat similar way to that of Diderot when borrowing or commentating on Haller and many other scientists, Hemsterhuys, Bemetzrieder and Helvétius. Neither in the case of Fontenelle nor in that of Diderot did borrowing preclude originality, but Diderot's re-interpretations were more significant because they proved to be more illuminating.

De l'origine des fables, a re-working of *Sur l'histoire*, inspired by Lucian, which J. R. Carré has dated 1678-1680, but which may be later since the abbé Trublet surmised it was written between 1691 and 1699, can be considered as a supplement to the *Histoire des oracles*. It purports to show how the gods were invented, how fables took root owing to the naiveté of the Greeks, except of course those belonging to the chosen people. This record of human folly marks a first step in the field of comparative religion. Fontenelle emphasises the role of imposture at the source of religions and challenges religious superstition and prejudice in the name of reason. The criteria of truth are implicit. Are the facts as recorded consonant with a rational explanation? Mankind, which was much the same in the past as it is today, was rationally motivated. But history is not only the record of the actions of self-interested kings, princes and priests, it is also the story of the customs of a given people, their religion and their fables, which are an attempt at explaining the world. They mark a necessary moment in the progress of reason. Man invented the gods. Like Voltaire, Fontenelle denied the religious experience as transcendental and all metaphysical concepts, and was wary of institutions and rites which were shamelessly exploited by charlatans. Voltaire's famous phrase: 'Ecrasez l'infâme' is implicit in Fontenelle's more guarded utterances.

Fontenelle dramatically and definitely put an end to any belief in oracles and to the suggestion that some of them forecast the advent of Christianity. Miracles too were indirectly dealt a blow from which they never recovered and the Church, recognising that the supernatural could no longer be readily invoked, changed its approach to the problem even if it did not change the creed.

In the *Nouvelles libertés de penser* Fontenelle criticised Pascal's argument, to win over freethinkers, based on *le pari*, as an irrational demonstration. Yet he accepted the role of passions and would have subscribed to the apology of passions so anti-Pascalian in spirit which Diderot expressed in the *Pensées philosophiques*. Diderot's attack on the 'Convulsionnaires de Saint-Médard', the aberrant Jansenists whose antics, based on religious fervour, he had observed with trepidation and derision, is in line with Fontenelle's position. In the *Pensées philosophiques* in which he refers to oracles and false miracles, quoting Montaigne, Plutarch and Cicero, he boldly proclaims: 'où donc est le miracle, peuple imbécile'. The god of the *philosophes* is Nature, a concept at once vague and particular, an all-embracing rational reality. There can be no spontaneous generation, nothing is fortuitous and monsters come within the laws of nature. For Fontenelle the existence of the world requires God as a first cause, a supreme architect, an intelligent geometrician not far removed from Voltaire's 'divin horloger', and Diderot's 'divin géomètre' in his early deistic phase as he makes clear in *De l'existence de Dieu*. For one and all the laws of nature are seen as constant and there is an absolute chain of cause and effect, at least in the inorganic world. Fontenelle already focussed attention on *animalcules* and the new biological data which would support his contention and saw no break in continuity between man and the animal, whose power to think should not be questioned since he had the same organs as man. Whilst not a materialist nor a forerunner of evolutionism he provided a stepping stone to the new science of life and fostered a brand of materialism based on cartesianism. He opposed the theories of Malebranche and like Diderot he believed in an autonomous world that had a beginning and would have an end, but unlike the later Diderot he believed that the marvels of nature and the anatomy of insects provided evidence of the existence of God. He opposed scholasticism and perceived some of the difficulties of a purely mechanistic conception of life, but remained essentially mechanistic in his biology. His *Doutes sur le système physique des causes occasionnelles* (1688) is most explicit on these matters and situates him in some half-way house between cartesianism and an early form of dialectical materialism. He accepts the idea of matter in motion but rejects that of a fortuitous assembly of atoms with which Diderot toyed before evolving his trans-formist hypothesis. In his later *Traité de la liberté* (probably written in the period 1690-1700), which was published anonymously in 1743 in the volume entitled *Nouvelles libertés de penser*, he takes a further step in the direction of the determinism Diderot expressed in his *Lettre à Landois* of 1756, which Fontenelle distinguishes from fatalism and where the question of moral responsibility is treated as one of politics and education.

The mechanism of determinism is seen as essentially physical and in line with English materialism. Paradoxically, Fontenelle's determinism did not prevent him from seeking to free man through social changes without reference to any religious considerations.

Another work, *Histoire des Ajaoiens* (1683), has been plausibly attributed to Fontenelle in spite of its professed atheism and denial of the immortality of the soul. It was certainly appreciated by Voltaire. It is based on the *Histoire des Sévarambes* by Veiras (1677-1679) and exploits a new genre: the real or fictitious journey so common in eighteenth-century novels and *contes*. The genre allowed Fontenelle to put forward his ideal society, one in which the nobility was to be abolished, magistrates elected and the monarchy replaced by a Council of three ministers. Religious practices were to be suppressed and a society based on nature and reason established. This programme is not without links with that of the abbé de Saint-Pierre. This work, together with the *Relation de l'île de Bornéo*, is evidence of a growing interest in foreign lands and manners as a means of criticising contemporary French society and foreshadows developments such as Montesquieu's use of Persians, Voltaire's use of England, Diderot's use of Tahiti to bring out the relativity of our *mores* which are then satirised before formulating on rational grounds a better organisation of society. Utopias became commonplace, but Fontenelle lacked the fire and the genius to exploit the potentialities of the genre to the full.

One example will suffice. In the *Relation de l'île de Bornéo*, possibly addressed to the Protestant Basnage, tolerance is vindicated. It is seen as a product of scepticism and incredulity, but there is nothing of Voltaire's missionary fervour. Fontenelle would never have worked for the rehabilitation of a Calas or a Sirven. He did not even see fit to defend openly his Protestant friends and trusted no one with his own personal convictions in the matter. There is no natural generosity in Fontenelle. He remains a rather cold, detached observer with an intelligent distrust of beliefs which cannot be subjected to scientific proof. Whilst he held prejudice to be folly he believed that it could never be wholly eradicated, for an old prejudice was merely replaced by a new one. He did not share the *philosophe*'s idealistic faith in progress, yet with growing confidence in reason as may be seen in his *Préface sur l'utilité des mathématiques* (1702) he discarded some of the pessimism of the *Nouveaux dialogues des morts*. But even so his chief concern was a plea for science and the need for state support to ensure its satisfactory development.

Those of Fontenelle's writings that were published anonymously were far less read than his main works and exercised less wide influence, but they are symptomatic of the times as well as contributing to a fuller understanding of his thought. He seems to have asked the right questions and often provided answers worthy of being followed up. His psycho-physiological determinism, so clearly at variance with Malebranche's insistence on the distinction between body and soul, is a case in point. Possibly Fontenelle's influence has been minimised owing to over-concentration on his adoption of Descartes's as opposed to Newton's physics. He was overshadowed by Voltaire's timely presentation of Newton. His style soon became dated although his use of the technique of conversation remained a model. Crébillon fils who adopted it in *Le Sopha* sounds hopelessly dated, yet the easy, clear, orderly flow of Fontenelle's discourse was admirably suited for the vulgarisation of scientific ideas according to the new scientific method, and his wit based on a use of logic which Voltaire has rendered familiar can be as cutting as that of Voltaire himself.

Fontenelle was no leader, but he was no outsider. In spite of recent and not very convincing efforts to show him as a warm and involved person, there surely was in his attitude to others a distance that masks a polite disdain. Voltaire never liked the man whom he satirised as the smaller of the two gigantic space travellers in *Micromégas* and whom he branded as the Secretary of the Academy of Saturn. He remains, however, as the embodiment of the intellectual who evolved the right critical methods without always reaching the right results. In spite of occasional lapses his was an unprejudiced mind bent on spreading the information gleaned from the scientific work of others, whilst safeguarding his position as an independent observer and refusing to be enrolled in any 'séquelle encyclopédique'. He strove to work out to his satisfaction a viable rational philosophy which he expressed with a disappointing reticence, although his caution is understandable. He stands out as a prototype rather than a true paradigm of the *philosophes* and his technique of vulgarisation, although it was subjected to many modifications in the course of the eighteenth century, is ultimately more significant than his ideas which have suffered from the inevitable march of time and attendant 'progress'. He fostered a listening public and a spirit from which the whole Enlightenment was to benefit.

Les jésuites selon Robert Challe, ou la mauvaise réputation

FRÉDÉRIC DELOFFRE

RAPPORTANT, avec un apparent scepticisme, ce que Robert Challe dit dans son *Journal de voyage* des jésuites qui foulent aux pieds le crucifix pour être autorisés à entrer au Japon, Prosper Marchand, dans les *Mémoires historiques et critiques touchant l'auteur des Illustres Françaises*,[1] ajoute (p.xxxiv):

> Quoi qu'il en soit, de Challes était si transporté de passion, ou, pour mieux dire, de fureur et de rage contre cette société, qu'on l'a plus d'une fois entendu s'écrier avec véhémence que, s'il tenait le dernier jésuite, il ne ferait aucune difficulté, pour en débarrasser une bonne fois le monde, de se jeter à corps perdu avec lui dans le plus affreux de tous les précipices. On ne saurait pousser plus loin l'amour du genre humain.

Prosper Marchand propose une explication de cette haine: 'Cet excessif acharnement contre les jésuites venait, dit-on, de ce que de Challes s'étant un jour oublié jusqu'à donner un soufflet au père Tachard, il s'était vu réduit à lui en faire amende honorable: anecdote flétrissante que, selon la maxime *Supprimit orator quae rusticus edit inepte*, il s'est bien gardé d'employer dans son *Journal*.'

On n'a pu jusqu'ici préciser les circonstances de cet événement, ni même en confirmer l'existence. La relation que le père Tachard a donnée du voyage aux Indes, et dont le manuscrit est conservé à la Bibliothèque nationale, ne le mentionne pas, et les archives de la Compagnie de Jésus pas davantage, à ce que nous a dit le conservateur du fonds de Chantilly. Il ne nous a pas été davantage possible de confirmer une autre indication de Prosper Marchand selon laquelle ce serait pour 'des saillies indiscrètes et imprudentes contre la Constitution et ses défenseurs' que Challe aurait été exilé vers 1717 ou 1718 à Chartres, ou effectivement il est mort en 1721. Du reste, il est clair que son hostilité à l'égard des jésuites a d'autres raisons qu'un ressentiment personnel. C'est précisément ce qui

---

1. Ces *Mémoires* figurent en tête de l'édition Marc-Michel Rey (Amsterdam 1748), des *Illustres Françaises*. Nous nous référons aux épreuves de cette notice, corrigées de la main de Prosper Marchand en vue d'un réemploi dans son *Dictionnaire historique*, et conservées à la Bibliothèque de Leyde.

en fait l'intérêt lorsqu'on veut les replacer dans le mouvement d'opinion qui, de Pascal à d'Alembert – pour ne parler que de la France – aboutit à l'expulsion de la Compagnie en 1764.

Depuis que Henri IV eut permis le retour en France de la Compagnie de Jésus, les discussions à son sujet portèrent, successivement ou à la fois, sur différents domaines: politique, bien sûr, théologique, moral, culturel (si on nous passe ce néologisme commode), domaine enfin de la propagation de la foi, en entendant par là à la fois le problème des succès de l'évangélisation par les jésuites sur le plan quantitatif et qualitatif, ainsi que celui des mobiles réels et des moyens employés à l'appui de leur prédication, notamment leurs pratiques commerciales. D'un adversaire de la Compagnie à l'autre, les jugements portés sur ces différents points peuvent être différents et même contradictoires.

Elève du collège de la Marche dans sa jeunesse, Challe n'a pas, comme Voltaire, bénéficié de l'éducation des collèges jésuites. S'il a joué la comédie 'avec des jeunes gens de son âge', c'est chez des particuliers, comme la maréchale de Castelnau, et il y a représenté des tragédies de Racine,[2] et non comme Voltaire, celles du père Porée. S'il lui arrive d'évoquer une pièce composée par les jésuites et jouée par leurs élèves, comme la comédie des *Moines*,[3] ce n'est ni pour louer ni pour blâmer le goût des jésuites pour le théâtre, mais pour souligner, avec eux, les défauts des moines mendiants. En un mot, le rôle culturel et éducatif des jésuites lui échappe, ou il le néglige.

Non pas totalement pourtant. Robert Challe est tout disposé à reconnaître les talents littéraires des jésuites. Leurs relations, dit-il, 'sont écrites d'un style brillant, amusant et même persuasif tant il est insinuant'. Mais ce serait mal le connaître que de voir dans ces mots un compliment. Ce qu'il préfère, c'est le style 'simple et naturel', qui a 'renoncé aux embellissements de la rhétorique' des missionnaires (*Journal de voyage*, ii.117). Car c'est la marque de la vérité que le naturel. De même, pour conter 'des vérités qui ont leurs règles toutes contraires à celles des romans', l'auteur des *Illustres Françaises* adopte 'un style purement naturel

2. Renseignement fourni par les *Mémoires*, f.76 du manuscrit conservé à la Bibliothèque nationale, n.a. 13799.

3. Voir les *Difficultés sur la religion proposées au père Malebranche*, éd. F. Deloffre et M. Menemencioglu (Paris, Oxford 1983), p.123 et n.II.207, III.376; et le *Journal de voyage aux Indes*, éd. par F. Deloffre et M. Menemencioglu (Paris 1983), ii.194.

et familier', parce que tout, 'en étant vrai, ne peut être que naturel'.[4] L'art même dont se servent les jésuites est un signe de fausseté.

Si on applique à Challe ce qu'il fait dire à François Martin, gouverneur de Pondichéry, son porte-parole, il a 'lu et relu vingt fois les *Lettres au Provincial*' (*Journal de voyage*, ii.166). Ce n'est pourtant pas le point de vue théologique qui a retenu son attention. Certes, il est très intéressé par le problème de la grâce, et, lorsqu'il en traite longuement dans un passage du *Journal de voyage aux Indes* composé apparemment dans une rédaction ancienne de ce journal, lorsqu'il avait une trentaine d'années, il se réfère avec révérence à saint Augustin. Mais il n'en conclut pas moins d'une façon très orthodoxe et nullement janséniste. Evoquant les deux cas retenus par les théologiens comme exemples indiscutés d'intervention de la grâce efficace, celui des deux larrons et celui de la conversion de saint Paul, il dit à propos du premier (*Journal de voyage*, i.107):

Voilà mon système établi sur la grâce: le bon larron s'y soumet et jouit de son fruit; l'autre la méprise, nonobstant la voix du Saint-Esprit qui s'expliquait par la bouche de son camarade, et est privé de la vie éternelle. N'est-ce pas là un exemple vif et pénétrant que la grâce descend sur tous les hommes, mais qu'elle ne les contraint point, puisque des deux larrons, un s'y soumit et l'autre la rejeta? Je fonde là-dessus le bon ou le mauvais usage que nous faisons, ou que nous pouvons faire, de la grâce. Elle devint efficace pour l'un, parce qu'il s'y soumit et qu'il ne lui put résister, ou ne lui résista pas; et devint infructueuse à l'autre, qui la méprisa.

Cette grâce efficace, en dehors de ces cas exceptionnels, 'serait-il même de sa justice [la justice de Dieu] de la verser?' (*Journal de voyage*, i.108). Mais si l'on admet que la grâce de Dieu ne manque jamais totalement aux hommes, et que sa justice l'empêche de se servir de la grâce totalement efficace, on est loin du jansénisme! A considérer la pensée de Challe sur la grâce telle qu'elle apparaît dans les *Difficultés sur la religion*,[5] on s'aperçoit qu'elle évolue vers un pélagianisme intégral, très comparable à celui de Voltaire dans l'*Epître à Uranie*. Non seulement la notion d'une grâce accordée arbitrairement par Dieu lui paraît contraire à la justice divine, qui, comme la justice humaine, ne doit punir que les fautes conscientes et volontaires, mais il l'estime absolument pernicieuse à la morale, comme

4. *Les Illustres Françaises, histoires véritables*, éd. F. Deloffre (Paris 1959), i.LXII, LXI.
5. Voir les références au mot *grâce* à l'index des *Difficultés sur la religion*, et notamment pp.397-400.

une doctrine de la fatalité. Aussi n'a-t-il rien à reprocher sur ce point à la théologie jésuite.

S'il est un point sur lequel il est en revanche en désaccord avec eux, c'est le dogme de l'infaillibilité. Comme beaucoup de ses contemporains, il rejette la 'ridicule et impertinente infaillibilité',[6] qu'il comprend d'ailleurs mal. Les jésuites la soutiennent.[7] Mais, de l'aveu même de Challe, ils ne la soutiennent que par politique. Nous ne sommes plus ici qu'à peine dans le domaine de la foi.

Sur le plan de la morale, l'opposition est bien plus fondamentale. Challe condamne très vivement la 'morale relâchée'[8] qu'il attribue, sinon à la conduite des jésuites, du moins à l'enseignement qu'ils dispensent, par le biais notamment de leurs casuistes et de leurs directeurs de conscience. Cette condamnation n'a rien pour surprendre de la part du moraliste sévère qu'est l'auteur des *Difficultés sur la religion*, mais on observera qu'il l'exprime différemment suivant les circonstances. Tantôt il vise spécifiquement les jésuites, mais il se contente alors de mentionner 'leurs équivoques, leur restriction mentale et leur direction d'intention' (*Journal de voyage*, ii.159). Tantôt il approfondit son propos, mais il l'élargit alors à toute la chrétienté, coupable en quelque sorte de 'crime contre l'humanité'. La démarche est presque la même dans le *Journal de voyage* et les *Difficultés sur la religion*.

Dans le premier cas, le point de départ des réflexions de l'auteur est le passage du navire devant le pic des Canaries, où le pape avait fixé le méridien partageant le monde entre Espagnols et Portugais. Il passe de là aux cruautés exercées par les Espagnols, 'jusqu'à faire étrangler et brûler les souverains du Nouveau Monde'. Ses réflexions s'achèvent sur une comparaison entre le christianisme et le paganisme. Celui-ci 'n'a point produit un scélérat de Machiavel. La direction d'intention, la

6. Lettre au *Journal littéraire*, 6 juillet 1718, dans F. Deloffre, 'Une correspondance littéraire au début du XVIIIème siècle: Robert Challe et le *Journal littéraire* de La Haye (1713-1718)', *Annales Universitatis Saravienses*, Philosophie-Lettres (1954), p.176.

7. Cf. 'quoiqu'ils disent et soutiennent à Rome que le pape est infaillible, ils ne feront ici aucun état de sa décision, et diront à leur ordinaire que le pape a été mal informé, ou que c'est un fou qui ne fait que radoter' (*Journal de voyage*, ii.160). Il est ici question de la condamnation recherchée à Rome par les franciscains à propos de l'affaire des 'rites chinois'; mais voir aussi ii.114-15.

8. *Journal de voyage*, ii.159; le porte-parole de Challe, François Martin, va même dans ce passage jusqu'à déclarer les casuistes jésuites 'gens brûlables en bonne justice'.

restriction mentale et autres inventions diaboliques lui étaient absolument inconnues' (*Journal de voyage*, i.101-102).

Dans les *Difficultés*, la discussion porte sur les 'merveilleux effets' du christianisme. Après avoir posé en fait que 'les sauvages vivaient dans l'innocence et dans la tranquillité', Challe reproche aux chrétiens d'avoir 'traversé les mers pour les chasser de leur patrie, dont on s'est emparé après les avoir dépouillés de leurs biens et exercé sur leurs corps les cruautés les plus barbares pour récompense de leur hospitalité et de la bonté avec laquelle on avait été reçu': 'Pour comble d'impudence et d'outrage, laissant voir à visage découvert qu'on se moque de Dieu et des hommes, le chef de cette religion a partagé à deux rois qui s'en disent les héros les terres de ces peuples infortunés.'

Suit une comparaison entre les actes cruels des païens, tels que les combats de gladiateurs, et ceux des chrétiens, comme les autodafés de l'Inquisition. Le raisonnement s'achève par une allusion à la restriction mentale, qui n'est pourtant pas nommément citée: 'Mais où trouvera-t-on dans aucune religion un dogme aussi affreux que celui qu'on nous débite: il y a des gens à qui on n'est pas contraint de garder la foi promise solennellement et sans avoir été contraint?' Ce qui permet à l'auteur de conclure par un amalgame où il oppose 'l'Evangile, les Pères, les casuistes, les théologiens et les gloses' à 'cette morale que la nature met dans le cœur de l'honnête homme' (*Difficultés sur la religion*, pp.245-46).

Si, dans les deux cas, Challe évite de citer nommément les jésuites, c'est encore pour élargir la condamnation de la morale qu'ils enseignent, selon lui, et l'étendre à toute la morale chrétienne dont la leur serait en quelque sorte la quintessence.

Il arrive encore assez souvent à Robert Challe, surtout dans les *Difficultés sur la religion* et dans la même intention générale d'anticléricalisme, de pratiquer, en matière de politique, le même amalgame concernant les jésuites, ou plutôt même d'éviter de les citer nommément pour reporter sur l'ensemble du corps ecclésiastique l'odieux d'une remarque critique. C'est pourquoi, des leçons fournies par les deux principaux manuscrits de ce texte, M et S, nous préférons celle de S, la mention des jésuites dans M nous paraissant interpolée:

Il y a longtemps qu'on a dit avec raison qu'il y avait plus de vanité sous un froc que sous un casque: rien n'est si insolent qu'un moine, qu'un cagot, qu'un jésuite,	Il y a longtemps qu'on a dit qu'il y a plus de vanité sous un froc que sous un casque. Il est certain que rien n'est si audacieux que le moindre valet de pied

lorsqu'il croit le pouvoir impunément; rien n'est si lâche, si flatteur, si rampant, lorsqu'il croit avoir besoin de quelqu'un qui ose n'en pas faire grand cas.

de couvent, que le moindre cagot, quand il croit le pouvoir être impunément, comme aussi rien n'est si lâche et si rampant devant ceux qui peuvent et qui osent les mépriser. Quels exemples n'ai-je pas vus là-dessus![9]

Il est du reste d'autres exemples indiscutables de l'omission volontaire de la référence aux jésuites dans des cas où il devrait normalement être question d'eux. Ainsi, lorsque, dès le début des *Difficultés sur la religion*, Challe rappelle 'l'indignation' qui le saisissait lorsque, tout jeune encore, il entendait parler de la 'puissance du pape' et de ces 'différends ordinaires entre la cour de Rome et les Etats catholiques' (p.45), thème qu'il reprend dans ses *Tablettes chronologiques* en citant cette fois les jésuites.[10] Ce gallicanisme, sans doute d'origine familiale, ne se conçoit pas en effet sans une hostilité particulière à l'égard de la Compagnie de Jésus, tout comme le rejet de l'infaillibilité dont il a été question plus haut.

Un exemple plus frappant encore de discrétion à l'égard des jésuites apparaît, toujours dans le début des *Difficultés*, peu après le passage qui vient d'être cité. Lorsque l'auteur déclare qu'il 'voudrai[t] qu'on instruisît l'empereur de la Chine de ce qu'il fait en souffrant nos missionnaires' (p.45), le terme de missionnaires est impropre: c'est celui de jésuites qu'il devrait employer, comme il le fait lorsqu'il oppose longuement les uns et les autres dans un passage du *Journal de voyage aux Indes* sur lequel nous reviendrons.[11] C'est en effet à la considération des pères jésuites qui lui avaient rendu de 'signalés services [...] dans les guerres civiles et étrangères' que l'empereur K'ang-hi avait signé en 1692 l'édit de tolérance auquel il est fait ici allusion.

Lorsqu'il ne se soucie pas de mettre en cause toute l'Eglise, Challe précise volontiers, complaisamment même, les reproches qu'il fait aux jésuites sur le plan politique. Ils se résument en une double image. A en croire les relations des Indes ou du Canada, ce sont 'de pauvres brebis du Seigneur, toujours prêts à répandre leur sang pour la gloire de son nom, gens détachés de toute ambition, et qui ne respirent que le martyre'.

---

9. *Difficultés sur la religion*, p.192.

10. 'J'y fais voir d'où viennent les richesses de l'Eglise [...] je développe toute la cour de Rome et ses maximes [...] Les jésuites, société formidable même aux têtes couronnées, n'y sont pas épargnés, mais je ne juge pas à propos de me les attirer sur les bras' (lettre du 22 janvier 1714, dans 'Une correspondance littéraire', p.160).

11. Il figure dans la 'Conférence avec M. Martin', ii.146-72; voir ci-après, pp.192, 198.

Cependant, le public est convaincu que ces relations sont 'de pures fables' et que 'leur esprit de domination, de supériorité, de commerce et de mauvaise foi, qui est la moëlle de leur compagnie, leur forme partout des scélérats que le prince ou le public s'immole' (*Mémoires*, f.121*v*).

Cet 'esprit de domination et de supériorité' se manifeste, au jugement de Challe, tant dans la vie courante que dans le maniement des grands intérêts du monde.

Couramment, on l'observe à propos de préséances. Lors du voyage aux Indes, Challe remarque qu'à Saint-Yago le père Tachard se fait donner comme monture par le gouverneur un splendide genêt d'Espagne; le fameux jésuite a d'autres prétentions sur lesquelles on ne nous en dit pas davantage – auxquelles l'évêque refuse de donner satisfaction (*Journal de voyage*, i.134). A Pondichéry, son débarquement est salué par cinq coups de canon: 'Je veux pieusement croire que son humilité ne s'attendait point à cet honneur,' commente le mémorialiste; 'que, même, il aurait empêché qu'on le lui rendît s'il avait prévu qu'on le lui rendrait; car, dès son baptême, il a renoncé aux pompes du monde. Hélas! sa modestie a été trompée' (ii.114).

S'il ne peut contester la réelle supériorité des jésuites dans plusieurs branches des sciences, il se demande si elle convient à leur état: 'Par parenthèse, est-ce là leur métier, ou devrait-ce l'être?'; il critique aussi l'usage qu'ils en font: 'Ce n'est qu'à l'abri de ces sciences profanes qu'ils se sont introduits [...] dans tous les royaumes d'Asie; qu'ils s'y sont élevés aux dignités; et qu'ils ont causé des révoltes des sujets contre les souverains, et des rebellions d'enfants contre leurs pères' (*Journal de voyage*, i.214). Il illustre surtout les fâcheuses conséquences de la présomption et de l'opiniâtreté des jésuites à propos d'un incident dont il a eu connaissance lors de son voyage aux Indes. Deux ans plus tôt, en 1688, deux frégates de la Compagnie des Indes passant au large du Cap, les pères qui se trouvent à leur bord exigent du commandant qu'il y fasse escale pour qu'ils puissent s'y livrer à des observations astronomiques. Comme il hésite à leur donner satisfaction, ne sachant pas si la guerre n'est pas déclarée avec la Hollande, ils le menacent 'de l'indignation de la société, et par conséquent de celle du Roi et de Mme de Maintenon', si bien qu'il cède enfin: ses deux vaisseaux chargés de deux à trois millions de marchandises sont alors saisis par les Hollandais, et lui-même est tué par un matelot qui n'a pas voulu qu'il mît le feu aux poudres du navire (i.215).

C'est l'intolérance des jésuites qui apparaît à propos d'un autre épisode. A l'escale de Moali, Challe et d'autres officiers de l'escadre assistent dans un oratoire des indigènes à une scène d'adorations et de prières d'une idole, sorte de tête de bœuf ou de vache. Le recueillement des assistants fait 'sérieusement réfléchir' l'écrivain, qui leur trouve plus de vénération pour leur dieu que les chrétiens n'en ont pour le Saint-Sacrement. Mais, loin d'être impressionné, un jésuite, le père de Châteauneuf, casse à coups de pierre un pot de terre qui se trouve dans une niche au-dessus de la porte de l'oratoire. Ce qui inspire à Challe les réflexions suivantes (*Journal de voyage*, i.249-50):

Les idolâtres n'ont point du tout trouvé cette action de leur goût [...] et le jésuite s'en serait assurément mal trouvé si les Français n'avaient pas été en état de le défendre.

> Aux zélés indiscrets tout paraît légitime
> Et la fausse vertu se fait honneur du crime.[12]

C'est, je crois, s'y prendre mal pour convertir les idolâtres que de les brusquer d'abord. Il faut commencer par leur faire connaître peu à peu le ridicule de leur religion, et comme insensiblement leur inspirer la bonne. Je crois que voilà le chemin qu'on doit suivre; du moins c'est celui que la Société a suivi dans la Chine; supposé qu'elle n'y porte pas trop loin sa complaisance. Ce n'est point ici le lieu de la mission du père de Châteauneuf; il ne fait qu'y passer: qu'a donc opéré son zèle indiscret? Il a scandalisé les spectateurs et inspiré de l'indignation aux gentils, qui se seraient vengés dans l'instant s'ils l'avaient osé. Voilà à quoi peut aboutir un zèle mal conduit. Il faut le dire. L'esprit de violence a toujours été celui de la Société, lorsqu'elle a eu la force en main.

L'esprit de 'supériorité' des jésuites prend des formes particulièrement agressives à l'endroit des autres ecclésiastiques. On a déjà dit que Challe se référait plusieurs fois à une comédie satirique composée par les jésuites et jouée par leurs élèves afin de tourner en ridicule les vices des capucins. A propos de l'escale qu'il fait à Pondichéry avec l'escadre de la Compagnie des Indes, il fait conter à François Martin comment les jésuites ont cherché à s'emparer de l'église et du jardin du prêtre desservant la paroisse (*Journal de voyage*, ii.152-54). Le même Martin expose longuement quel tort fait courir à la religion et au 'nom français' la rivalité malveillante qui oppose sans cesse les jésuites aux missionnaires.[13] On a sans doute là un des griefs les plus sensibles que Challe nourrit à l'égard de la

---

12. Il n'a pas été possible d'identifier la source de ces vers, qui sont peut-être de Challe lui-même.

13. Voir notamment *Journal de voyage*, ii.160.

Société. Sans doute prend-il plus facilement son parti des mauvaises plaisanteries que les jésuites font en France même à leurs adversaires jansénistes, comme lorsque les pères du collège d'Anchin à Douai incitent, par le moyen de prétendues lettres du grand Arnault, un professeur janséniste de l'université à vendre ses meubles et ses livres pour aller desservir une cure qui n'existe que dans l'imagination de ses persécuteurs.[14]

C'est, bien sûr, au niveau de l'Etat que l'esprit de domination des jésuites présente, selon Robert Challe, les inconvénients les plus graves. Il ne lui suffit pas de rappeler – comme le fera par exemple Mayeul-Chaudon dans son *Dictionnaire historique* – que le jésuite anglais Peters aurait, par ses conseils, précipité la chute de Jacques II et, indirectement, été cause de la guerre qui ruina la fortune de Challe;[15] il reporte la faute première des événements sur le père La Chaise, confesseur de Louis XIV, qui voulut 'que le père Priters [*sic*] fût aussi puissant en Angleterre qu'il l'était en France, et pour cela, sous prétexte de religion, rendre le roi Jacques aussi absolu que Louis XIV' (*Mémoires*, f.4r).

De même, Challe attribue aux jésuites la révocation de l'édit de Nantes, et, plus spécialement, les difficultés qui sont faites aux religionnaires désirant rentrer en France. Ce n'est pas au fanatisme religieux qu'il impute cette attitude, mais à la recherche de l'intérêt (*Mémoires*, §8):

Le confesseur, s'il avait été homme de probité et vraiment chrétien, aurait fait entendre au roi ce que dit saint Bernard, *Religio suaditur* [*sic*], *non imponitur:* mais, bien loin de le faire, il poussait le premier à la roue et mettait les machines en branle, non seulement pour leur expulsion, mais pour leur boucher la rentrée. Ce n'était pourtant pas le zèle de la religion qui le faisait agir, ni lui ni les autres, ce n'était que le seul intérêt temporel, parce que lui, ses parents, son indigne société, et la Maintenon, ministre publique des voluptés du prince, et la plus hypocrite créature qui fut jamais, et d'autres de leur faciende, jouissaient des biens de ces fugitifs, et qu'ils auraient été obligés à les restituer si ces malhureux [*sic*] étaient rentrés en grâce.

On touche ici au point essentiel pour Challe. Lorsqu'il reproche aux jésuites leur 'mauvaise foi', il ne se place pas du point de vue de ce que nous appellerions 'l'honnêteté intellectuelle'. Ce qu'il entend, c'est qu'ils

14. *Mémoires*, f.45v. L'histoire de la 'fourberie de Douai' est attestée par diverses brochures parues en 1691, 1692 et dans les années suivantes; voir par exemple Pierre Leroy, 'La fourberie de Douai', in *Les Amis de Douai* (1964), no. 12.

15. Par le pillage du fort de Chedabouctou, où était entreposées toutes les peaux de castor qu'il comptait vendre en France.

ont ruiné la 'bonne foi' qui est, aux yeux de ce bourgeois parisien et de ce colbertiste, l'âme du négoce indispensable à la France du temps. De cette ruine de la bonne foi, ils sont responsables et par leur conduite, exemple pour 'les peuples', et par les mauvaises leçons qu'ils donnaient au roi, lequel servait à son tour de mauvais exemple pour les Français (f.21):

Je n'aurais jamais fait si j'entreprenais de dire toutes les causes de l'extinction de la bonne foi. Il suffira de dire que le règne de Louis XIV l'a tout à fait bannie de France et que tous les Français, se conformant sur l'exemple que le Roi et son conseil lui [sic, pour leur] donnaient de prendre à toutes mains, tant sur le sacré que sur le profane, se sont figurés que le vol n'était point un crime, et que la seule manière de voler était punissable; ils étaient autorisés par l'exemple de Louis XIV, et lui l'était par celui des gens auxquels il confiait sa conscience, je veux dire les jésuites et l'archevêque de Paris.

Si on en croit Challe, les jésuites usent de deux moyens pour dominer l'âme du roi, la crainte et la flatterie. Ils flattent son goût pour le pouvoir absolu (f.5v):

Son amour propre et sa vanité lui faisaient croire, par leurs suggestions, que le pouvoir sans borne était le plus parfait de tous les gouvernements. Il était ravi de se voir flatté par des gens d'Eglise dans ce qui flattait son amour propre et son ambition; ce pouvoir immense qu'il s'est attribué à leur persuasion et à leur exemple l'a jeté dans une espèce de nécessité de violer les privilèges les plus sacrés tant de ses propres sujets que des gens d'Eglise de l'un et l'autre sexe qui ont souffert sous son règne tout ce qu'on peut souffrir sous celui d'un prince ignorant.

Mais aussi le roi lui-même redoute cette 'société formidable même aux têtes couronnées',[16] comme tend à le prouver une anecdote promise dans les *Mémoires* (f.6r) et contée dans le *Journal de voyage* (ii.171). Challe ayant dit à Seignelay que l'argent du roi était bien mal employé pour envoyer aux Indes des jésuites, gens 'plutôt capables de perdre la France de réputation chez les étrangers que de l'y mettre en bonne odeur', le ministre lui répond: 'Nous les haïssons plus que le diable: trouve le moyen de mettre la vie du roi en sûreté contre le poison et le poignard, et je te jure, sur ma damnation, qu'avant deux mois il n'y en aura pas un en France.' Et comme Challe s'étonne que le roi semble les craindre, il ajoute: 'Oui, il les craint; il n'a que cette seule faiblesse. Il les hait du fond du cœur et ne les estime point: cependant, lui qui fait trembler

16. Lettre au *Journal littéraire* du 22 janvier 1714 dans, 'Une correspondance littéraire', p.160.

tout le monde, tremble sous cette misérable société, toujours fertile en Cléments, en Châtels et en Ravaillac. Il tremble aux morts d'Henri III et d'Henri IV, et n'en veut point courir les risques.'

Quant aux manifestations de la 'mauvaise foi' des jésuites, les *Mémoires* et le *Journal de voyage* en multiplient les exemples. Pour la France, plusieurs sont annoncés, relatifs à Paris notamment,[17] quoiqu'un seul soit effectivement produit, aux folios *21v-23r*. C'est celui d'un marché passé entre les jésuites de la rue Saint-Antoine et un menuisier nommé Marteau relatif à des aménagements au couvent de la rue Saint-Antoine et à la maison de campagne du père La Chaise; les jésuites sont astreints à la restitution de 4 000 livres lorsque le magistrat établit qu'ils ont commis un faux en écritures majorant d'autant la somme qu'ils prétendent avoir déjà payée. Si Challe renvoie à une suite qui ne viendra jamais l'histoire des autres fourberies parisiennes et provinciales des jésuites, il profite au moins de l'occasion pour dégager quelques-unes des maximes des jésuites pour 'économiser et augmenter' leur bien, comme, pour une maison riche, telle que celle de Paris, de ne point assister une maison pauvre, telle que celle d'Arras, et de choisir toujours pour père procureur 'un homme adroit dont le cœur est à l'épreuve de tout, la conscience facile, et le front incapable de rougir' (*Mémoires*, f.23v); pour rappeler à cette occasion le mot de Pascal, à savoir que les jésuites ne devraient pas souffrir 'que les juges fissent pendre en pratique ceux que la société absolvait par théorie'; et pour démentir 'à propos de Mr. Pascal', qu'il se soit 'rétracté de ses lettres au Provincial' (f.22v).

C'est surtout à propos de l'évangélisation pratiquée par les jésuites au Canada et en Asie que Robert Challe se déchaîne. Il en condamne les motifs, le caractère idolâtre ou du moins superficiel, les fâcheuses conséquences pour le commerce et le nom français.

Ainsi, chaque fois qu'il évoque la présence des jésuites c'est pour dénoncer leur 'esprit de primatie et de commandement, et surtout d'avarice et de luxure' (*Journal de voyage*, ii.117), tantôt, dans les *Difficultés sur la religion*, en évoquant le faste des jésuites de Montréal, contrastant avec

17. Après avoir évoqué la conduite des jésuites au Canada, Challe continue dans ses *Mémoires*, f.45: 'Je laisse là ces bons et chastes pères; j'espère les retrouver encore à Paris, dans un vaisseau, dans S. Yago aux isles de Feu, au Cap de bonne espérance, à Pontichery [*sic*], à Goa, à Siam, encore à Paris, et puis après en Flandre à Courtrai et à Douai.' L'épisode de 'Courtrai' (au f.23 Challe parle de 'Tournai et Douai') n'a pu être identifié. Les autres le seront dans l'édition des *Mémoires* que nous préparons.

la simplicité des logis du gouverneur et de l'intendant à Québec;[18] tantôt, dans les *Mémoires*, en rapportant l'histoire – d'ailleurs totalement controuvée – d'un siège mis devant Québec par les Iroquois et levé par eux en échange de la livraison d'une pseudo-religieuse (une fille de petite vertu vêtue en ursuline), le tout à l'instigation des jésuites las du jeûne forcé qu'ils enduraient (ff.42-43); tantôt encore, à la fois dans les *Mémoires* et le *Journal de voyage*, pour tenter de 'prouver' que 'ce n'est pas la gloire de Jésus Christ qui les conduit dans le Canada' (*Mémoires*, f.41v) et qu'on ne les y verrait pas 'si on n'y trouvait ni femmes ni castors'.[19] Cette dernière démonstration est menée avec un tel luxe de détails et d'une façon apparemment si convaincante qu'il est intéressant de l'exposer pour en faire une critique précise. En voici la teneur d'après la version la plus brève, celle du *Journal de voyage* (ii.169-70):

J'étais à Montréal en Canada en 1682 lorsque M. de La Barre, vice-roi, fit la paix avec les Iroquois. Le père Bêchefer, supérieur des jésuites, y était aussi. Un sauvage que les Français à cause de la longueur de sa bouche avaient surnommé Gran-Gula, et dont le nom sauvage était Arouim-Tesche, portait la parole pour toutes les nations iroquoises. J'appris, ce jour-là, quantité de choses qui regardaient la société de Jésus, qui faisaient enrager le père Bêchefer, et rire tous les auditeurs; car le sauvage y parla en sauvage, c'est-à-dire sans flatterie ni déguisement. Les jésuites étaient démontés de l'effronterie de sa harangue, et perdirent tout à fait patience à la conclusion de leur article, qui fut que tous les sauvages ne voulaient plus de jésuites chez eux. On lui en demanda la raison; et il répondit, aussi brutalement qu'il avait commencé, que ces jaquettes noires n'iraient pas, s'ils n'y trouvaient ni femmes ni castors.

Pour preuve de ses dires, Challe 'prend à témoins' tous les Français présents, notamment l'interprète de La Barre, 'qui se nomme Denizy, à présent médecin à Compiègne': 'Il avait été douze ans entiers avec les sauvages quand nous revînmes ensemble du Canada; et en 1713, je le trouvai à Compiègne, où j'étais allé voir une sœur religieuse, et lui parlai de cette aventure, qu'il répéta en présence de quantité de monde à moi inconnu, excepté un M. Auvray, directeur des Aides' (*Journal de voyage*, ii.170).

La version des *Mémoires*, rédigée sans doute avant celle-ci, en 1716, comporte le discours *in extenso* de Gran Gula, lequel comporte aussi la requête des Indiens qu'on leur envoie les 'jaquettes grises' (les récollets)

18. p.94. Le passage pourrait avoir été corrompu. La fin du paragraphe parle du séminaire des sulpiciens, ce qui est exact.

19. Respectivement, *Mémoires*, f.44v; *Journal de voyage*, ii.170.

et non les jésuites. Challe place aussi la scène en 1682 – alors qu'elle a eu lieu effectivement en 1684 – et ajoute que 'comme il était allé à Québec l'année suivante 1683, des coureurs de bois [lui] répétèrent cette harangue'. Il cite aussi Denisy comme témoin et raconte que, l'ayant recontré à Compiègne en 1713, 'quoiqu' [il sût] déjà l'affaire comme témoin quasi oculaire et par lui-même dans notre traversée de Canada en France, [il se fit] un plaisir de la lui faire confirmer en si bonne compagnie' (f.44v).

On aperçoit déjà que l'auteur du *Journal* ajoute un mensonge à son récit en disant qu'il a été témoin de la scène qu'il donnait dans la version initiale comme lui ayant été seulement rapportée. Il a dû en commettre un autre à l'appui de celui-là en disant qu'il était allé à Montréal, alors que, quittant Québec le 7 août 1683 pour aller trouver à Montréal le gouverneur La Barre et l'intendant il n'avait pu, malade de pleurésie, dépasser Sillery. Il dit encore, tant dans les *Mémoires* que dans le *Journal*, qu'il a fait le voyage de retour du Canada avec Denisy: nous savons que le retour de Challe eut lieu en octobre 1683. Mais alors, comment Denisy aurait-il pu lui raconter une aventure qui n'avait pas eu lieu, ou même simplement s'y trouver!

Même si on porte au crédit de Challe que certaines de ses inexactitudes résultent peut-être de confusions (par exemple, il est allé en Acadie en 1685: n'est-ce pas alors qu'il a pu entendre parler de la conférence de La Barre et d'Otréouti, dit Gran Gula?), il n'en est pas moins certain qu'il déforme la vérité. Du reste, il existe sur l'entrevue de La Barre et d'Otréouti un témoignage beaucoup plus exact, car il est d'un témoin. Or celui-ci, La Hontan, ne dit rien d'une exclusion des jésuites par les Iroquois, ni non plus des thèses déistes que Challe prête au chef des Indiens.[20] Or La Hontan, dont on connaît les sentiments peu orthodoxes, n'aurait aucune raison d'omettre un trait allant si bien dans le sens de son anticléricalisme. Il nous paraît, en conclusion, probable que toute la documentation de Challe consiste seulement dans les propos plus ou moins bienveillants et de toute façon tardifs de Denisy, qui a peut-être été employé comme interprète au Canada dans certaines occasions, mais

20. Voir Frédéric Deloffre, 'Du vrai sauvage au bon sauvage: La Hontan, Robert Challe et "la Grand Gueule"', à paraître dans *L'Ailleurs au XVIIIème siècle*, Publications de l'université d'Ottawa, sous la direction de Pierre Berthiaume et M. Vaillancourt.

qui, d'après les documents qui nous sont parvenus, ne l'a pas été dans la conférence avec Gran Gula.[21]

Le témoignage de Challe sur la conduite des jésuites aux Indes est apparemment plus circonstancié. Certes, lorsqu'il dit dans les *Difficultés sur la religion* 'J'ai vu les jésuites à Goa. Quelle opulence! qu'ils jouissent bien du travail de leurs missionnaires' (p.94), la première phrase – si elle n'est pas interpolée – contient un mensonge; de même que, dans les *Mémoires*,[22] il ne faut pas prendre au pied de la lettre, à propos des mêmes jésuites, la mention de 'Goa' parmi les lieux où Challe promet de retrouver les bons pères. Le *Journal de voyage* plus véridique, se contente de rapporter, de seconde main, une anecdote de source portugaîse relative à des talons de souliers évidés que les jésuites utiliseraient pour transporter clandestinement des diamants (ii.149-51), ou d'indulgences établies à Goa enjoignant à saint Pierre, au nom de la Vierge, de leur ouvrir le paradis (ii.151-52).

C'est sur l'action des jésuites dans les territoires où s'exerce l'influence française et que Challe a visités (Pondichéry, Balassor au Bengale) ou sur lesquels il est informé de bonne source (Siam) que l'auteur du *Journal de voyage aux Indes* se fait le mieux écouter.

A propos du Siam, dont il parle à plusieurs reprises et sur les événements duquel il dit avoir 'plusieurs mémoires et journaux dont [il fera] peut-être un corps assez curieux pour attirer l'attention du public',[23] Challe fait état d'informations parvenues à Pondichéry pendant son séjour et dont il aurait eu connaissance par François Martin. Dans la 'révolution' qui a abouti en 1688 au détrônement de l'empereur et de son ministre Constance Phaulkon au profit de 'l'usurpateur Pitrachard', autant, selon ses dires, les missionnaires français, le clergé et les fidèles siamois ont 'souffert avec une constance égale à celle des saints martyrs de la primitive église', autant les jésuites ont été bien traités par l'usurpateur, sans qu'ils en aient profité pour aider les officiers et soldats français 'réduits à la dernière misère', et tandis que leurs nouveaux convertis, 'sans en excepter un seul', abandonnaient 'la religion de Jésus Christ' (*Journal de voyage*, ii.156). Il est du reste dit ailleurs que si les conversions opérées par les missionnaires sont bien moins nombreuses que celles

21. L'interprète de La Barre était un officier, Le Moine, surnommé Akouessan ('la Perdrix') par les Indiens.
22. Dans le passage cité à la note 17.
23. *Journal de voyage*, ii.156; cf. *Mémoires*, f.121.

dont se flattent les jésuites, elles sont incomparablement plus sincères et plus solides.[24]

Le reproche le plus important, aux yeux de Robert Challe, qu'il fait contre les jésuites est sans doute celui de cet 'esprit de commerce' qu'on a vu qu'il leur attribuait (*Mémoires*, f.121v). Il est développé dans un discours prononcé, significativement, par François Martin, directeur de la Compagnie des Indes, qui aurait même écrit sur ce sujet plusieurs mémoires envoyés à Paris.[25]

A une époque où l'on ne conçoit guère le trafic lointain qu'à l'abri de monopoles, Martin insiste sur le tort que le commerce caché des jésuites ferait aux intérêts de la Compagnie et du royaume, 'qui sont ici confondus ensemble' (*Journal de voyage*, ii.144), tort au moins égal à celui que leur feraient 'toutes les nations européennes ensemble' (ii.146). Il égalerait à peu près en valeur celui des Portugais, lequel n'est dépassé, de loin il est vrai, que par celui des Hollandais. Il serait pratiqué par des jésuites déguisés, en banians notamment, grâce aux marchandises transportées par les navires de la Compagnie sous prétexte des nécessités de la mission. Ainsi, des 58 ballots apportés par l'escadre pour le compte des jésuites, une trentaine aurait été déjà acheminés sur Madras, ville occupée par les Anglo-Hollandais, et ces ballots ne seraient pas remplis 'de reliquaires, de chapelets, d'*agnus Dei*' (ii.147). Alors que la Société devrait déjà à la Compagnie 150 000 piastres, soit 450 000 livres, la dernière ne pourrait espérer aucun 'retour', celui-ci se faisant par les bâtiments appartenant aux hollandais ou anglais (ii.148).

Telles sont les accusations portées. Il ne nous appartient pas d'en juger. Seule une étude approfondie de ce qui reste des archives de la Compagnie des Indes permettrait peut-être de déterminer quelle part de vérité et quelle part d'exagération elles peuvent comporter. Il est du reste clair que le trafic des jésuites était mis par eux au service de leur politique d'évangélisation, mais la discussion sur ce point reste forcément très subjective. Ce qui reste en tout cas, c'est que Challe a vu, beaucoup plus clairement que ses contemporains, ou même, plus tard, que Voltaire, que

24. 'Les missionnaires, bien moins faciles et plus attachés à l'Evangile, ne font pas à beaucoup près tant de prosélytes, parce que leur morale est bien plus chrétienne, et ainsi plus resserrée, qu'ils prêchent un Dieu mort en croix avec ignominie, et non un Jésus Christ sur le Tabor, rayonnant de gloire et de splendeur' (*Journal de voyage*, ii.155).

25. Cf. une note du *Journal de voyage*, ii.147: 'C'est encore à la Compagnie à savoir si tout ceci est une imposture. Le fait est grave, mérite l'attention du lecteur, et d'être approfondi.'

ces activités commerciales recélaient pour la Société un péril mortel. C'est, on le sait, la faillite du père Valette, en 1761, qui a largement justifié, aux yeux du public, le processus qui devait aboutir quelque temps après à l'expulsion des jésuites de France.

Cet examen, incomplet, de l'attitude de Challe vis à vis des jésuites permet pourtant de dégager quelques points intéressants et quelquefois inattendus.

Le premier est que, pour un bourgeois parisien gallican, mais non janséniste, la morale des jésuites est plus choquante que leur théologie. Si on ajoute que Challe, comme Voltaire, est déiste, le molinisme des jésuites n'a rien pour le gêner: il ne va pas même assez loin.

Le second est l'importance qu'il accorde à la 'bonne foi', indispensable condition du commerce: en se mêlant de commerce, en y introduisant des pratiques inspirées d'une 'morale relâchée', les jésuites se condamnent aux yeux d'un 'colbertiste'.

Le troisième, propre à Challe, consiste dans le rapprochement qu'il établit entre la forme et le fond. Le style, pourrait-il dire, c'est le jésuite même. Les ornements de la rhétorique sont la marque de la fausseté.

Le quatrième et dernier sur lequel nous conclurons est qu'à certains moments de sa vie Robert Challe a vu dans l'esprit des jésuites l'essence même du christianisme. Alors, il évite d'en faire une exception dans l'Eglise; il les cite même le moins possible. C'est lorsqu'il reviendra, à la fin de sa vie, à une sorte de christianisme épuré, celui du Christ mort en croix et non du Christ triomphant dans le monde, qu'il se retournera avec le plus de furie contre ses vieux adversaires.

Buffier and the impossibility of science

SHEILA MASON

IT has become a commonplace of the intellectual history of the Enlightenment that the introduction of John Locke's ideas into France, particularly those of the *Essay concerning human understanding*, contributed in no small measure to the elaboration of sensationalist epistemologies and the general spread of empiricism.[1] Locke, one of the immortals of Voltaire's *Lettres philosophiques*, is a founding father of the philosophic movement. Yet certain, immediate and decisive as his influence was on such an early and authoritative transitional figure as the Jesuit educationist and philosopher Claude Buffier,[2] or on the consciously 'engaged' propagandists and vulgarisers who followed after, like the marquis d'Argens, or, indeed, Voltaire, it is a paradox, and one not without relevance to the clarification and, perhaps, correction of our generalised historical notions, that some early offshoots of Lockian thought fail to promote empiricism in anything other than a narrowly technical epistemological sphere. To the extent that Locke's impact could be adequately condensed in d'Argens dictum, 'je sens, donc je suis',[3] these annexations did no service to the cause of non-linguistic science, and less than justice to their source; but now, in contrast, throw into relief the fertility of indigenous currents of thought, and indicate, in particular, the probable epistemological autonomy of the natural sciences.

Writing recently on 'The sources of modern methodology', a philosopher of science (in the modern sense) makes the point forcibly that no single methodological concept or school as yet boasts a satisfactorily established history, and divines the reason for this failure of scholarly enquiry in the fallacy of assuming the exclusivity and primacy of the

1. Locke's *Essay* was published in 1690; its fourth edition was translated by Pierre Coste, *Essai philosophique concernant l'entendement humain* (Amsterdam 1700).
2. 1661-1737. The most comprehensive introduction to his life and works is K. Wilkins, *A study of the works of Claude Buffier*, Studies on Voltaire 66 (Geneva 1969), which reviews previous criticism (pp.28-29), and presents a full bibliography of his works. Referred to in the notes following as Wilkins.
3. J.-B. Boyer, marquis d'Argens (1704-1771), *La Philosophie du bon-sens, ou réflexions philosophiques sur l'incertitude des connaissances humaines* (London 1737), ii.III.

philosophical roots of methodology.[4] Laudan's remedy would lie in promoting and applying the contrary thesis that, 'the historically original and influential contributions to methodology have come *primarily* from working scientists and only secondarily from philosophers' (p.8). This sanely pragmatic response to the historical impasse is complemented by two potentially much more sweeping and contentious propositions relating to philosophy proper, namely that 'the epistemological theories of an epoch have generally been parasitic upon the philosophies of science of that epoch rather than vice-versa', and that 'the waxing and waning of methodological doctrines cannot be related neatly to their epistemic credentials'. The avenues of research suggested here are extensive and exacting, and fall well outside the competence and scope of a non-specialised article. Yet even a limited examination of areas of Buffier's writings and of some sources and parallels, would seem to lend direct support to Laudan's general thesis, and to furnish some evidence for his further contentions.

Buffier's work offers itself as a significant 'test case' for several reasons. There is general consensus among his scholarly critics that his thought, besides original elements, in particular those which anticipate the 'common-sense' school of the Scottish philosopher Thomas Reid, owes much to both Descartes and Locke. In relation to the latter, he is one of the earliest French Catholic thinkers to draw extensively upon the *Essay concerning human understanding*. His major work, the *Traité des premières vérités*, dates from 1724, and his study of the use and limitations of logic, which anticipates some of its salient ideas, *Des vérités de conséquence ou principes du raisonnement*, in its first edition from 1714.[5] In her study, K. Wilkins quotes a letter of 1713 to the Oratorian priest, Pierre Desmaiseaux, where Buffier expresses his intention of composing a metaphysic whose elements 's'accorderont beaucoup plus avec les principes de M. Locke (ou d'ailleurs il y a quelque mécompte) qu'avec ceux de Malebranche et de Descartes' (p.69). Buffier, in fact, as a *scriptor* at the Collège Louis-le-Grand, and a member of the editorial team of the *Mémoires de Trévoux* (p.19) had a professional interest in digesting and evaluating new work, and, where appropriate, adapting it for the use of Jesuit pupils. In relation to Locke, he appears to reflect the prompt and, at least in the

4. L. Laudan, in *Historical and philosophical dimensions of logic, methodology and philosophy of science*, ed. R. E. Butts and J. Hintikka (Dordrecht, Boston 1977), pp.3-19.

5. See Wilkins, pp.185-215.

fields of epistemology and education, where the Peripatetic tradition might be assumed to generate a certain predisposition, friendly reception accorded by his Society to the English theoretician.[6] From a rather different angle of our enquiry, Buffier as pedagogue and pedagogic theorist, and it is in the area of composer of grammatical, historical and geographical textbooks that his other claim to innovative activity lies, can be reasonably expected both to have entertained a certain breadth of curiosity in relation to curricular developments, and to have been particularly involved on a practical and educationally propaedeutic level with the field of methodology.[7] The author of the article 'Logique' in the *Encyclopédie* thought fit, after all, to bestow the accolade of consanguinity upon the collected edition of his works, the *Cours de sciences*.[8] This latter compilation does indeed contain a *Discours sur l'étude et la méthode des sciences*, to which we must shortly turn our attention, where, in parallel with a decided subjectivism and individualism, he reiterates the claim to general validity, already made in the folio's 'Avertissement', for the methods embodied in his manuals, establishing their credentials through his practical pedagogic concern and experience.[9]

While, however, the genuineness of Buffier's empirical stance in such a context cannot be doubted; and, indeed, there are also good grounds, as we shall see, for concluding with Wilkins, in relation to the core of his metaphysics, that he is primarily concerned with the functioning of the mind as a practical agent (pp.82-83), examination of his account of the composition and scope of human knowledge, and, more technically, of its nature, certainty, and the methods of its acquisition, reveals greater affinities of attitude with the sceptical humanism of his Order and of the preceding century, and with aspects of Cartesianism's legacy, than with the thrust, if not the detail, of Locke's thought.

The *Cours de sciences* provides a full account of his view of the branches

6. See P. C. Sommervogel, *Table méthodique des Mémoires de Trévoux (1701-1775)* (Paris 1864); and, for an analysis of the journal's reception of Locke, A. Desautels, *Les Mémoires de Trévoux et le mouvement des idées au XVIIIe siècle. 1701-1734* (Rome 1956), ch.3.

7. For an evaluation of Buffier as educationist, see Wilkins, pp.31-63.

8. Wilkins, p.104. Wilkins studies in some detail Buffier's influence on the *Encyclopédie*, and its literal borrowings from his texts.

9. See *Cours de sciences sur des principes nouveaux et simples pour former le langage, l'esprit et le cœur, dans l'usage ordinaire de la vie* (Paris 1732), col.1481. This edition will be referred to as *Cours*.

of human learning.[10] Even before surveying its scope, the motto of this enterprise (and equally of the *Traité des premières vérités*) speaks for the Cartesian tinged, aristocratic traditionalism of his curricular stance: 'La véritable science consiste, non à savoir beaucoup; mais à savoir ce que l'on doit, et à le bien savoir.'[11] The *Cours* duly comprises, in order of priority, treatises on grammar, eloquence, poetry, metaphysics, logic and its applied uses, morals, religion, and finally, method.[12] It is superfluous here, since we are essentially concerned with his omissions, to investigate for their particularities the methodologies embedded in his presentation of these disciplines. The hallmark of his programme, and the key to his whole educational philosophy and system is the emphasis placed on grammar. Its fundamental importance he explains as follows: 'Quoiqu'elle soit répandue, on ne la connoît peut-être pas encore, comme la base de toutes les sciences [...]. Celle-ci a pour fondement de représenter le langage comme l'image de nos pensées. Elle apprend à les connoître et à les discerner; à les arranger et à les unir' (*Cours*, cols. ix-x). Thus, the paradigm of all knowledge is linguistic: language also provides its medium, and the means whereby it may be extended. Logically, in his scheme, linguistic skills take precedence, grammar being followed by 'l'éloquence' and 'la poésie'.

Now, on the one hand, given Buffier's Jesuit vocation, and his explicit objective of shaping 'un homme sensé et un homme de bien',[13] it is possible to regard the primacy accorded to communicative skills as socially and culturally conditioned, unexceptional, perhaps, in pedagogic terms. On the other hand, references to Buffier's metaphysics, where one finds an unmitigated nominalism, reveals that, at least in its human connection, the essence of truth is for him, in a sense, inescapably linguistic. This added dimension indicates both his distance from the rational idealism characteristic of much contemporary thought, and suggests a debt to Locke, so projecting the novelty of his posture in a French

10. 'Plan général du cours de sciences', cols.ix-xvi.
11. *Discours sur l'étude et la méthode des sciences*, *Cours*, col.1473. This becomes in the *Traité*: 'La vraie science consiste moins à savoir beaucoup qu'à savoir avec précision et netteté'; see *Œuvres du père Buffier*, ed. F. Bouillier (Paris 1843), p.2, the edition cited throughout for the *Traité* and for the *Examen des préjugés vulgaires*, and referred to hereafter as Bouillier.
12. Omitted are the specialist textbooks Buffier compiled on history and geography, disciplines with a factual basis, but which he regarded, traditionally, as a school of morals, and where his chief methodological preoccupation was the development of mnemotechny.
13. *Discours sur l'étude et la méthode des sciences*, *Cours*, col.1477.

context. It also identifies his significance for Condillac, and consequently the seminal impact of his adaptation of the English source.[14]

The extended discussion of *essence* in Part Two of the *Traité des premières vérités* is central to an understanding of how Buffier comes to his view of the possibility of science, its level and limitations. His nominalism, for being gradually unveiled, loses nothing of its reductionist force in relation to idealist metaphysics. Starting from the customary philosophical distinction between metaphysical and physical essence, he poses as his principle that the former can be no more than nominal essence: 'Tous doivent se souvenir que l'essence métaphysique n'est qu'une pensée qu'ils se forment à eux-mêmes, souvent l'un d'une façon et l'autre de l'autre, comme on le voit par les définitions toutes différentes d'une même chose, formées selon les idées particulières qu'ils ont conçues chacun de leur côté' (para. 202; Bouillier, p.83). Metaphysical essence he prefers to designate as 'essence représentée', and must be clearly distinguished from *real* essence, or physical essence, which is invariably elusive as far as human perception is concerned: 'car celle-ci consiste dans un amas intime de qualités, qui ne pouvant pas toujours être aperçues, démêlées ou exprimées, n'est pas précisément ni ce qui s'exprime par la définition, ni cette essence représentée par la définition'. Put more directly, 'l'essence métaphysique est, ordinairement parlant, beaucoup moins la nature de la chose que l'idée que chacun s'en forme' (Bouillier, p.84).

There follows a rebuttal of Platonic idealism in the cause of vindicating God's creative omnipotence, which issues in the proposition that the nature or essence of things, their real and physical essence that is, consists in that constitution, divinely ordained, which is 'd'ordinaire impénétrable à nos sens et à notre esprit, au moins dans toute son étendue' (para. 213; Bouillier, p.89). Here one encounters the main theological ground of the scientific scepticism which is as characteristic a feature of Buffier's thought as his espousal of Lockian sensationalism, and which indeed, paradoxically, seems reinforced by the peculiar way in which he vulgarises, simplifies, and yet, in some instances, deepens Locke's tenets.

14. Wilkins gives a cautious account of Buffier's probable influence on Condillac (strictly impossible to prove from extant sources, it seems); and a more tentative appreciation of Buffier's conception of language: 'both stress the importance of language as an instrument of thought and misuse of language as a principal cause of error. Condillac, however, goes further in seeing language as the essence of thought' (pp.110-11).

In the matter of essence, one might suppose from the text so far examined, that he maintains Locke's distinction between words and ideas, verbal propositions and mental propositions,[15] in that he alludes both to definitions and to the essence represented by definition. However, his subsequent observations on definitions seem to imply a reversal of Locke's persuasion that the meaningfulness of words is explicable only in terms of the ideas that they signify,[16] a reversal which, though never crystallised in a conscious rebuttal of the notion of pre-verbal thought, or in a formal discussion of the relationship of ideas and verbalisation, would accord with the priority over logic accorded to language in his educational programme, and can be seen to correspond also to his eventually explicit rejection of what he took to be Locke's reification of ideas. It is arguably implicit in his simple introduction to the educational trinity of language, rhetoric and poetry, that words provide the impulsion to think, even the stuff of thought: 'Comme la grammaire enseigne à parler, pour nous bien faire entendre; l'éloquence et la poésie enseignent à faire une impression sensible sur l'esprit de ceux à qui nous nous faisons entendre [...] L'éloquence est le talent de faire dans l'âme des autres, par le moyen du langage les impressions que nous prétendons' (*Cours*, col.ix).

Buffier, in his metaphysical treatise, suggests even more clearly that understanding, active or passive, is intimately and indissolubly linked with linguistic conventions. For example, the relationship between the perceived qualities in an external object, that is to say between their 'represented' essence or our idea of them, and the name which usage attaches to these qualities, is so close, that when the name of a thing changes, so our conception of them follows suit. A peeled orange is in its real nature no different from a crushed orange, yet one is called 'orange', and the other 'juice', and our idea of them differs accordingly.[17] In fact, the definition of things can and should be reduced to the science of verbal meanings, consecrated, as it is, by common choice and custom:

La définition explique au fond beaucoup moins la nature de la chose que la signification du mot qui indique la chose. *Or, la signification d'un mot qui indique une chose, n'est rien moins que la nature totale et complète de cette chose même.* Pour en être

15. *Essay on human understanding*, IV, v, 2.

16. IV, v, 4, where Locke, as a specific against confusion of words, urges closer attention to thought.

17. *Traité*, paras.213, 214; Bouillier, pp.89-90.

convaincu d'une manière sensible, il suffit de considérer que le nom de chaque chose a été établi par le commun des peuples, qui ne sont rien moins que philosophes, et qui n'ont prétendu, en établissant un mot, que faire distinguer parmi eux ce qu'actuellement ils ont dans l'esprit quand ils prononcent un certain mot.[18]

Once it is understood that the referent in question ('la nature totale et complète de cette chose même') is not the external object itself, but those elements of it which we perceive, a point which Buffier repeatedly stresses and to which we shall return, then the fineness of the line dividing sense of word from sense of thing is demonstrated. Though the question of priority must be shelved, ideation and language are for Buffier correlated and intercommunicating processes. The dominance of the word in his conception of ideas is further confirmed, when he does, in fact, take issue with Locke over the question of simple ideas,[19] claiming that the English thinker wrongly presents 'pleasure', 'pain', 'desire' etc., as devoid of composition. Their composite nature is proven for him by their susceptibility to verbal definition, this susceptibility extending so far that he will admit only two simple ideas himself: those of being and of modification. Similarly, though he must perforce treat them as objects of the mind, Buffier disposes trenchantly of the fallacy that ideas possess any sort of reality independent of it. They are pure modifications of the understanding, just as motion may be a modification of matter and is inseparable from it.[20]

It so seems that viewed from one angle, Buffier begins to shape a simplified doctrine of ideas, where one might discover an emergent grasp of the sufficiency of the mind and its sensory equipment to create of its own resources a human science, adequate to its physical environment and self-validating. Without resorting to a full description of his meta-physics, it is easy enough to marshal those articles which testify to his espousal of sensationalism, and to indicate the general ways in which, even in relation to establishing and validating the mind's purely intellec-tual furniture, the 'premières vérités', he attempts to apply what can be construed as empirical yardsticks. Certain knowledge of both the inner and of the outer world is possible; and in relation to the latter it is

18. *Traité*, para.217; Bouillier, p.92. My italics.
19. *Traité*, 'Eclaircissement D'; Bouillier, pp.242-43.
20. *Traité*, III, 8, 'Ce qu'on peut dire d'intelligible sur les idées'. Bouillier presents this as a notable advance upon Locke (p.187, n.1), though some modern Lockian criticism would be inclined to disagree.

direct, unobstructed, it appears, by intervening *ideas*, which mediate in Berkeleyan fashion with an inaccessible, even conjecturally non-existent original. Chapters 14 to 18 of the *Premières vérités* are devoted to the witness of the senses, and to establishing their competence and reliability. The senses report faithfully on what they perceive; it is the job of active reason, instructed by knowledge and experience to collate and interpret the data transmitted: 'Les sens rapportent toujours fidèlement ce qui leur paraît: la chose est manifeste, puisque ce sont des facultés nécessaires qui agissent par l'impression nécessaire des objets, à laquelle est toujours conforme le rapport de nos sens [...] Leur fidélité ne consiste pas à avertir l'âme de ce qui est, mais de ce qui leur paraît: c'est à elle de démêler ce qui en est.'[21] Similarly, the sense impressions of the individual, which may be faulty or misconstrued, are controlled by the common experience of mankind: 'Autrement ce serait la nature qui mènerait au faux le plus grand nombre des hommes; ce qu'on ne peut juger raisonnablement' (para. 127; Bouillier, p.57).

However, throughout this discussion of sense data, one is struck by the definition of it which Buffier imposes: 'ce qui leur paraît'. This is not an inadvertent lapse into Lockian representationalism, but an indication of strict limitations which Buffier imposes on the senses' perceptive competence, superseded as they are, in any case, metaphysically by the operation of reason. The harbingers of what one might have taken to be a 'new realism' (as opposed to idealism) in Buffier, do not herald a grand unveiling of nature at all. Metaphysically, their combined witness serves by the vivacity of its impression, to assure us of the existence of the external world. Their existential testimony – sane men are convinced by what they perceive – participating in 'ce que l'esprit humain a de plus intime et immédiat à lui-même', though it may not contribute to the fundamental 'sentiment intime' by which we know we exist, is accessory to it, and obviously annexed to the function of the 'sens commun' or 'sentiment commun de la nature', in overcoming the Berkeleyan impasse:[22] 'L'existence d'un objet hors de nous ne se prouve pas simple-

21. *Traité*, para.121; Bouillier, p.55. See also paras.124-26.
22. See *Traité*, i, 5 for the senses' role in furnishing the content of common sense. The work's opening sections are largely devoted to the issue of sensationalist solipsism, which opens like a chasm once Buffier has established his first axiom, 'Je pense, je sens, j'existe' (para.11). As Wilkins has noted (p.67), he is certainly one of the earliest French thinkers to confront Berkeley, though her location of this encounter in the later *Eléments de métaphysique* needs revision. The *Traité* in fact reads initially as a response to Descartes and Berkeley,

ment par une convenance d'idées qui sont uniquement au-dedans de nous; elle ne se peut prouver que par le sentiment que la nature a mis dans les hommes pour porter un tel jugement sur l'existence des objets qui sont également à la portée de tous' (*Traité*, para.88; Bouillier, p.40). Physically, while the senses do connect us with external objects, they only instruct us of the possession of certain *qualities*: 'Ils peuvent bien nous assurer qu'il se trouve, dans les choses corporelles, des dispositions propres à faire telle impression sur nous, et c'est ce qu'on appelle *telle qualité*. Ainsi, ils sont infaillibles [...] mais cette connaissance, bien que certaine, est quelque chose de fort vague et d'assez imparfait' (para.112; Bouillier, p.51). The reason for the paucity and imprecision of the information yielded is that the cause of qualities in objects, that is to say, their *real* nature remains inaccessible both to the senses and to the rational understanding. Our only recourse is conjecture, even though the competence of our faculties may be extended by modern inventions. Moreover, sense-data, for constitutional reasons, are infinitely variable between individuals, and the problem of certain knowledge is further compounded by the continual flux engulfing all matter. Thus, despite an acceptance that machines may extend information beyond present imagination, the bases of Buffier's sensationalism and empiricism lead him to a profound scientific scepticism:

Je pourrai bien m'apercevoir du changement d'impression; mais de savoir à quoi il faut l'attribuer, si c'est ou à l'objet ou à moi, c'est ce que je ne puis faire par le seul témoignage de l'organe de mes sens; sur quoi on doit observer que c'est un des points qui rendent très incertaines les règles de la médecine. Elles se fondent sur l'expérience; mais l'expérience n'est jamais bien précisément la même à l'égard des différentes personnes, ni de la même personne en différents temps.[23]

His conclusion is pragmatic: the senses are sufficient only to the function for which they were given us, namely satisfying the ordinary needs of life. It is superfluous to know through the application of microscopic ingenuity, that vinegar and cheese swarm with invisible life, for, 'les sens nous ont été donnés principalement pour nous conduire dans l'usage de

rather than as a dialogue with Locke. Also, since, as we show, much of the primary text *is* concerned with testing our perception of reality, Wilkins's assertion (p.82) that he differs from Berkeley and Hume in neglecting the question of the truth of external manifestations of reality needs qualification.

23. Para.116; Bouillier, p.53. For the full statement of Buffier's scepticism, see *Traité*, II, 15.

la vie, et non pour nous procurer une science de pure curiosité' (paras. 123, 119; Bouillier, p.54).

Returning now to Buffier's discussion of essence, it becomes clear that the avoidance of epistemological dualism by his doctrine of ideas and of the mind, is as illusory as his realism is tenuous and deceptive. Knowledge of real essence is the exclusive privilege of angels and God.[24] Knowledge of 'represented' essence, which the sensory perception of miscellaneous qualities in things allows us, is the closest approximation to truth to which mere humans may aspire, and it is in its form inescapably linguistic.[25] To an extent it is ironical and futile that Buffier turns his nominalism against the modish idealism of contemporaries who mistake the abstractions of geometry for real essences (Traité, paras. 48, 49, 216). For the 'representations' to which he reduces these abstractions are no less divorced from nature, and in refusing mathematics any epistemic validity in relation to external reality, he incidentally, and, no doubt, inadvertently, closes the door on a world, whose nature, in his presentation of it, could be construed as elusively and exclusively material as anything imagined by Diderot: 'L'essence d'un cercle réelle et existante hors de nous, n'est donc que le fer ou le bois ou l'encre qui existe en figure de cercle, laquelle n'est jamais parfaitement ronde, et qui fait un cercle existant en particulier, différent de tout autre cercle particulier existant' (para.216; Bouillier, p.90). Within the inner sanctum of the mind, however, there open up endless scientific vistas based on the use of definitions. No doubt, in evoking their infinite potential, Buffier had in mind, having already denounced the scientific bankruptcy of axioms, and the pure 'liaisons d'idées' that they engender, to heap opprobrium upon the abuse of deductive logic; yet his assimilation of geometry and linguistic representation is as tacitly symptomatic of his own proclivities, as it is indicative

24. Para.218. Buffier's doctrine of perception is not dissimilar to Leibniz's in the matter of knowledge. But for Leibniz, the rectified perspective of angels, involving direct vision of causal sequences, is the means whereby we may move closer to the perfection of divine perception. See R. E. Butts, 'Leibnitz on empirical methodology', Abstracts of the Seventh International Congress of Logic, Methodology and Philosophy of Science, 1983: Salzburg, vol.vi, ed. G. Dorn (Salzburg 1983), pp.44-46.

25. Condillac was to propose subsequently an analytical scientific method utilising linguistic algebra, a logical outgrowth of the view that the system of nature corresponds to the order of ideas. See W. R. Albury, 'The methodology of Condillac's Logic and the natural sciences in France during the Revolutionary period', Abstracts, pp.10-12; and A. M. Rieu, 'Le complexe nature-science-langage chez Condillac', in Condillac et les problèmes du langage, ed. J. Sgard (Genève 1982), pp.27-46.

of the futility of speculative reasoning, or indeed, on the evidence of his own epistemological premisses, of most generalised perceptions (para.225; Bouillier, p.95):

Cette nature (exprimée par la définition d'un mot, quel qu'il soit) étant supposée une fois on en tire des conséquences dont le tissu forme une science aussi véritable que la géométrie, qui a uniquement pour base la définition de mots. Tout géomètre commence par dire: j'entends par le mot *point*, telle chose [...] et de cette définition de mots, on parvient aux connaissances les plus profondes [...] Mais il faut toujours se souvenir que ce sont là des vérités qui n'ont pour fondement que des natures idéales de ce qu'on s'est mis arbitrairement dans l'esprit, sans que cela montre ou enseigne rien de la nature existante et réelle des choses.

The main body of the *Traité des premières vérités* offers little reassurance on the possibility of natural science, and only the most oblique indications of a methodology appropriate to its establishment. On various occasions Buffier ridicules the principles of Cartesian physics by bringing out their logical contradiction with central tenets of common belief and experience; but he has almost nothing to offer in its place, beyond a science of pure denominations.[26] While he discusses probability at some length, and admits as tests, alongside his own neo-Cartesian yardstick of 'évidence',[27] such quasi-empirical checks as repetition of similar experience, enhanced practical familiarity, and analogy of cases, it is quite clear, first, that he finds the cognitive status of the concept itself questionable, that which is probable, being for all the contingencies which matter, as good as true; secondly, that only when construed as moral certainty in such fields where the source of information is *human authority* does it hold the slightest relevance for him (*Traité*, I, 19; 21-24). As far as his own method is concerned, at least as applied in the field of metaphysics, his critics are in agreement that its obvious parentage is Cartesian,[28] and so the task delineated in the 'dessein et division de l'ouvrage' introducing the *Traité* registers it to be: 'Connaître les vérités dans leur source, faire une analyse

26. See *Traité*, IV, 1; 'Remarques sur Descartes'; 'Eclaircissement A'; and cf. for his view of physics, *Traité*, para.496.

27. This must be construed as that quality in non-derived propositions which excites the consent of common judgement; see *Traité*, I, 12.

28. Wilkins (p.75) follows F. Bouillier here (p.xi). Buffier's most recent commentator, L. Marcil-Lacoste, *Claude Buffier and Thomas Reid: two common-sense philosophers* (Kingston, Montreal 1982), goes even further; in a convincing demonstration of the possibility of re-integrating Buffier's epistemology into the tradition of the *cogito*, she reduces his method to the formulation of a double logic: of identity and of differences.

de celles où il faut remonter pour établir tout ce qui a besoin d'être prouvé, et au-delà desquelles on ne remonte point [...] en effet, le discernement des premières vérités est comme la clef de toutes les sciences' (Bouillier, p.3).

The science of physics, both as a topic of theory and in its contemporary substance, commands, surprisingly, some direct attention in Buffier's writings, although his treatment of it proves exactly correspondent to the ambivalence of his attitude to sensory perception. As a discipline involving theoretical principles, he appears to have come to grips with it when considering the use and limitations of logic in the earlier treatise, *Les Principes du raisonnement*, possibly with a view to revising its first edition, for the material found in the text of this work published in the *Cours* duplicates exactly 'Eclaircissement B' of the *Premières vérités*, and could provide the groundwork for specific comments made in the body of the treatise, which are predictably by and large dismissive. In addition, the *Discours sur l'étude et la méthode des sciences*, contains an interesting, and, in some ways more positive reappraisal of the subject.

The negative content of Buffier's treatment, easily guessed from the consideration of essence which we have already examined, is summarised in the first chapter of Part Five of the *Premières vérités*. Here one finds the prototype of subsequent eighteenth-century denunciations of the use of hypothesis, already sporting as weapons of derision the defamatory labels 'système' and 'roman'.[29] In short, theoretical physics comprise an assemblage of imaginary explanations of various facets of nature, each internally logical in itself; all, as a result of their abstract contexture, totally divorced from reality. Buffier adduces as proof, the equal failure of mechanical and chemical theory to account for the simple transformation in the human body of food into blood. The proper object of physics, he concludes, is the gathering of facts, 'les effets de la nature qui tombent sous nos sens', not the investigation of causes (*Traité*, para.506). These judgements complement the material of the *Principes du raisonnement*, where the opposition of internal truths (logical truths, abstractions, ideas of the mind) and external truths (facts of nature, largely inaccessible to the mind), together with the assimilation of mathematics, geometry and all other sciences commanding a theoretical infrastructure, are set out at

29. He has his Cartesian precursors; see Lamy, below, p.221.

length.[30] In stressing the absence of any necessary correlation between theory and fact, Buffier deploys a range of absurdities susceptible of logical demonstration: geometry can prove that a globe a thousand times bigger than the earth can be supported on an axis infinitely more slender than a pin; physics that man is immortal; ethical science that perpetual peace is attainable;[31] the abbé Dangeau that rational orthography is possible.[32] All such conjectures he derides as 'le globe de la terre, sur une éguille'; but, significantly, here impelled it seems, by some awareness of the practical potential of theoretical knowledge, he adds an outline of what might pass as valid inductive hypothesis: 'Si donc l'expérience s'accorde avec nos idées, et la vérité externe avec la vérité interne; les démonstrations nous guideront aussi surement dans toutes les sciences, par raport à leur objet particulier, que les démonstrations de géométrie, par raport aux démonstrations sur l'étendue' (para.343; *Cours*, col.861). Furthermore, he can also conceive that the purely ideal model of the human mind may facilitate the creative applications of human industry. Although no perfect globe exists in nature, the precision of the intellect teaches that the more closely it approximates to a true sphere, the smaller its axis can be, and the better it will pivot.

Such concessions are important, but they are presented, in Buffier's typical style, as pragmatic observations fortuitously arising. That he is unperturbed by the breach that he opens in his own argument can only arise from the tenacity of his pyrrhonism, from the dualism of his conception of substance, and from the linguistic bias of his own intelligence. He can offer no account of a method which would facilitate the coincidence of internal and external truth, because of his profound reservations with regard to human perceptive faculties. Thus, his imagination can furnish no clue of the means of overcoming the partiality and arbitrariness of sense data; for therein lies the root, according to his

30. 'Que toutes les sciences sont susceptibles de démonstrations aussi évidentes, que celles de la géométrie', paras.339-44.

31. This would appear to be a comment on the abbé de Saint-Pierre's *Projet de paix perpétuelle*, published in 1717. Buffier may well have encountered the abbé through their common association with Mme de Lambert's salon.

32. The abbé de Dangeau participated in the Académie's abortive projects to compose a French grammar, and published, again in 1717, *Opuscules* including papers on orthography and phonetics, and *Réflexions sur la grammaire française*. Sommervogel (n.10) lists three articles by Buffier in the *Mémoires de Trévoux* dealing with works on orthography, from 1707, 1719 and 1724 (table reproduced in Wilkins, pp.215-16). For Louis de Dangeau's works, see A. François, *La Grammaire du purisme et l'Académie française au XVIIIe siècle* (Paris 1905).

analysis of the genesis of ideas, of the fallaciousness of represented essences, which are the coinage in which the mind conducts its business. The empiricism of sensory operations is not to be generalised, even though the specific functions of the mind itself are, as he describes them, to collect and compare information. Similarly, proper humility prevents him from jettisoning the qualitative distinction sustaining his scepticism, between represented and real essence, even though the supreme import-ance of common sense, the collective judgement of mature rational beings, to validating his whole metaphysics, suggests that, for the purposes of constructing human science, the perceptions vouchsafed to human beings, once presumed adequate (or rendered adequate by ingenuity), should suffice. And finally, for all that his ideas are of the substance of the mind itself, and not uncomfortably lodged in an epistemological limbo, and that he allows himself a glimpse of the possibility that mind may be the product of body, he maintains a formal dualism between the spiritual and the corporal.[33] Indeed, his ontology is implicitly ternary, so acutely does he differentiate divine intelligence from the spiritual world of the human mind, and that again from corporal being. Far from eroding the division between man and nature, as his sensory empiricism might lead one to expect, Buffier appears, no doubt as a reflection of his nominalism, to introduce an intermediate order of the artificial (paras.329-30; Bouillier, pp.142-43):

L'artificiel n'est donc que ce qui part du principe ordinaire des choses, mais auquel est survenu le soin et l'industrie de l'esprit humain, pour atteindre à quelque fin particulière que l'homme se propose [...] En ce sens-là, il n'est presque rien dans l'usage des choses qui soit totalement naturel, que ce qui n'a point été à la disposition des hommes.

Thus, although human creativity is not in doubt, there is no sense in Buffier of its being conditioned by, or conditional upon the participation of man in nature.

The *Discours sur l'étude et la méthode des sciences* confirms the paralysing methodological vacuum characteristic of Buffier's attitude to knowledge in general. The relativism and scepticism investing his view of our perceptive capacities lead him to declare method infinitely variable according to individual talent and temperament, particular discipline, and different conditions and vocations. Physics, if it is to be considered at

33. See *Traité des premières vérités*, III, 1.

all – and for familiar reasons he has excluded it from the *Cours de sciences*, being 'moins une science qu'une sorte de vraisemblance; pour ne pas dire de pirrhonisme'[34] – is only accessible to methodological control in its purely factual aspect: he aligns it with history and jurisprudence as a science of memory. Those natural phenomena and their immediate causes, to which our senses bear witness, are worthy of attention and description; and Buffier pays tribute to the efforts of the preceding century in this field. But to the science of first principles, knowledge of 'la vertu et l'étendue des forces naturelles',[35] he remains obdurately dismissive. Nevertheless, here, the Panglossian dimension of this obduracy is revealed, for, despite himself, he shows, even in demolishing the pretensions of the 'scientists', a sound grasp of the sort of questions to which physics should address itself. What explains the phenomenon of balance, or the variations in the behaviour of columns of different liquids given a constant air pressure, for instance? Conventional answers – proportion, or 'que les liquides pésent selon leur hauteur et non pas selon leur largeur' – he understandably rejects as verbal evasions (*Cours*, col.1481). Moreover, he introduces into this reductionist scrutiny of science's credentials two remarkable concessions, which he allows to pass without comment. The first of these appears to represent the sort of simple extension of his principle of 'common-sense' to the field of natural science, that one might have anticipated in the section on physics in the *Premières vérités*. With time, he avers, it should be possible to show by comparison the element of common ground in the work of physicists, so taking a first step towards the discovery of truth. Such common ground would include not simply readily accessible empirical knowledge of immediate causation, but also those theories on hidden forces, which are integrally confirmed by a range of observed phenomena: 'Les causes qui ne sont point aperçues par nos sens, mais qui sont indiquées par un sistême si heureux, que tout ce qui se rencontre d'effets ou de phenoménes qui y ont raport, sont par-là expliquez d'une manière sensée et plausible' (*Cours*, col.1478). The conception of scientific law as a theoretical proposition of limited scope, empirically verifiable, seems thus to be glimpsed, and behind it the notion of the application of inductive procedures. Certainly, as he expresses himself here, Buffier's 'sistême heureux' derives credibility from its experiential framework, rather than from its logically

34. 'Avertissement'; *Cours*, cols. xv-xvi.
35. *Discours sur l'étude et la méthode des sciences*; *Cours*, col. 1478.

elaborated dependence on a nucleus of universal principles.

Small breaches do then develop in Buffier's defensive pyrrhonism, and it seems likely that these changes reflect something of the shifts in the Society's attitude in general to the subject of natural science.[36]

But, for us, another paradoxical feature, unrelated to the date of Buffier's work, is equally significant. Many passages of the *Traité des premières vérités* testify to his bold use of scientific 'fact' in demonstrating points of argument, especially points made against scientific theorising. Clearly, Buffier was not unfamiliar with the substance of contemporary enquiry, and, indeed, perfectly consistent with his own priorities in amassing such useful data. The slogan he invented and deployed so effectively, as we have seen, in disparaging the ideal models of the geometrician, 'c'est le globe de la terre, sur une éguille', arose, it seems, out of his monitoring of the proceedings of the Académie des Sciences concerning the shape of the earth:

Cette essence du globe [...] n'est donc pas un objet qui soit, hors de ma pensée, précisément tel qu'il est dans ma pensée [...] puisqu'il s'est trouvé, selon les observations de l'Académie des sciences de Paris (année 1713), que la terre que nous habitons n'était point un *globe*, mais un ovale. (On la croit maintenant un sphéroïde aplati vers les pôles.)[37]

Similarly, his treatment of the senses, where, above all, such data should find a natural place, yields up fascinating documentation. For, contrary to what might be anticipated given Buffier's espousal of Lockian principles, the crucial section of the *Premières vérités* devoted to sensory range and competence reveals clear divergences from his ostensible source. For example, while firmly projecting the notion that the senses, in their

---

36. See A. Desautels (n.10), where the split in relation to Newtonianism, during Castel's incumbency at the *Mémoires*, between condemnation of the 'archaism' of its content, and by the late 1720s, oblique recognition of methodological worth is established. Lallemant's original review of Locke's *Essay* (1701) showed no appreciation of empiricism and sensualism as systematic alternatives to reason (p.35); and in 1721, Castel, very much in harmony with Buffier's pragmatic spirit, reproaches Newton for accumulating 'ces expériences rares, curieuses, ingénieuses, sans presque aucune des observations simples, naïves, faciles que la nature fournit abondamment dans tous les pays' (p.53).

37. *Traité*, para. 199; Bouillier, p.82. For the involved debate on this question, see R. Mousnier, *Progrès scientifique et technique au XVIIIe siècle* (Paris 1958), pp.49-58. Since the observations of Cassini, sustaining the theory of an oval, were not discredited until Maupertuis's work on the polar meridian was completed in 1737, it seems that Buffier's parenthesis here was inspired by some preference for the astronomical theory of either Huyghens or Newton.

operations, combine and complement each other, Buffier insists that registering size is *not* the specific function of sight, whereas detecting colour is. Touch, for him, is the faculty that measures, both size and distance. Impressions of distance, involuntarily gathered by the eye or the ear, are a function of the angle of incidence of light rays on the retina, or of the force of sound waves.[38] Terse as Buffier's account of the senses is, and its very brevity may indicate recognition of his incompetence to add significantly to existing work, its salient features point to Descartes's *Dioptrique* as its most likely source. There one finds, fully and methodically recorded, and also translated into diagrammatic form, all the *experimental* data necessary to substantiate Buffier's rapid analysis. Descartes had already, in anticipation of Diderot, used the sensory skills of the blind man as a means of establishing the functional range of normal capacities; just as, using his collation of experimental data from a camera obscura with observations on the dissected organs of cadavers, he had composed an impressive account of the mechanics and physics of vision.[39] Buffier offers no more than a dim echo of Cartesian conclusions, since the *Dioptrique* could inform him that 'La lumière et la couleur [...] seules appartiennent proprement au sens de la vue [...] La force des mouvements [...] lui fait avoir le sentiment de la lumière; et la façon des mouvements, celui de la couleur; ainsi que les mouvements des nerfs qui répondent aux oreilles, lui font ouïr les sons;'[40] also that: 'pour la situation [...] nous ne l'apercevons pas autrement par l'entremise de nos yeux que par celle de nos mains' (Bridoux, p.220), and: 'la vision de la distance ne dépend, non plus que celle de la situation, d'aucunes images envoyées des objets, mais, premièrement de la figure du corps de l'oeil' (Bridoux, p.221). Indeed, without attempting to particularise the importance of the *Dioptrique* to the fortunes of sensationalism, one should bear the potential resonances of its opening words in mind: 'Toute la conduite de notre vie dépend de nos sens'.

Thus, while Buffier made his admiration for Locke quite explicit,[41] the

38. *Traité*, paras. 128-31. In the *Essay*, Locke is as perfunctory as Buffier on the ideas received directly from sensation; see Bk.II, chs.3-5. For him, in furnishing ideas of space, extension, figure, rest and motion, sight and touch combine.

39. *Dioptrique*, 'De la lumière', 'Des images qui se forment sur le fond de l'œil', and 'De la vision'.

40. *Dioptrique*, VI *Œuvres et lettres*, ed. A. Bridoux (Paris 1953), p.217.

41. See *Traité*, 'Remarques sur Locke': 'Sa philosophie semble être en ce point (démêler les opérations de l'esprit humain) par rapport à celle de Descartes et de Malebranche, ce

nature and extent of his material indebtedness needs careful examination, particularly with regard to the parentage of such empiricism as informs his work. On the one hand, in that he is ready to approach metaphysics as no more than 'l'histoire de l'âme humaine', the dissection of the content and apparatus of mind, his inspiration is true to Locke. Moreover, the opening chapters of the *Premières vérités* make clear that in elaborating the substance of his analysis, he sets out, in some senses, to provide Cartesian conceptualism with an experiential basis. Thus, the clear idea, as ultimate principle and source of truth, is replaced by intuitive certainty, 'sentiment intime'. Similarly, logical inference no longer constitutes the paradigm of true thought, nor provides, further than its formal aspect may be objectivised and applied as a negative test, a universal tool of validation. In order to move from knowing, to knowing something, Buffier seems to have sought out the means of empirical verification at the mind's disposal: sensory information; the rule of non-derivation; mature common sense. His tests apply the basic mental processes of experience and reflection, in their individual and collective aspects. Thus, although his procedure and method of exposition still bear the Cartesian stamp, in that he presupposes the necessity of establishing first truths, this necessity derives from the *existential* vacuum of doubt (*Traité*, para. 6; Bouillier, p.5):

Il faut rencontrer enfin des propositions qui n'aient plus besoin [de preuve]; autrement toute la vie se passe à prouver [...] sans jamais savoir à quoi s'en tenir. Il s'ensuit donc manifestement qu'il y a des propositions qu'il ne faut point entreprendre et qu'il n'est nullement nécessaire de prouver, mais qu'il est de la dernière importance de discerner: et ce sont celles que j'appelle des *premières vérités*.

Similarly, the certainty of such propositions rests on the congruence of individual and collective judgement, when informed by mature experience. They do not possess supreme 'évidence', but merely logical priority (para.40). They reside, in fact, in the common sense, that faculty (para.33; Bouillier, p.15):

que la nature a mise dans tous les hommes ou manifestement dans la plupart d'entre eux, pour leur faire porter, quand ils ont atteint l'usage de la raison, un jugement commun et uniforme sur les objets différents du sentiment intime de leur propre perception; jugement qui n'est point la conséquence d'aucun principe antérieur.

On the other hand, without embarking on an exhaustive comparison

qu'est l'histoire par rapport à un roman' (Bouillier, p.225).

between their respective treatments of the certainty and extent of knowledge, it is clear from a fairly rapid perusal of Book Four of Locke's *Essay*,[42] that the latter's valuation both of abstract knowledge, as exemplified in mathematics, and of the means, tentative as they may be, at our disposal in seeking knowledge of substances, is far more positive than Buffier's. Certain basic postures they do, indeed, share. Buffier was, no doubt, most persuasively impressed by Locke's eloquent commentary on the severe limitations of our sensory faculties as gatherers of knowledge, and the 'abyss of our ignorance' viewed against the vastness of the universe, whence the general verdict, 'no science of bodies' (IV, 3, paras.23-26). Similarly, he absorbed Locke's corollary, that the scope of our faculties serving 'convenience, not science', we are primarily fitted for moral knowledge (IV, 12, paras.10-11). But he overlooked the absence in the *Essay* of an impenetrable barrier between nominal and real essence, just as he muffled Locke's endorsement of the certainty of ratiocination, and narrowed the discussion of probability to a consideration of human testimony. No less than for Descartes, real (as opposed to verbal) truth lies for Locke in the intuitive perception of congruence or incongruence in clear ideas; and, of ideas, those that Locke defines as simple, including mathematical abstractions, but not exhausted by them, comprehend both nominal and real essence.[43] Thus he was able to concede the possibility of the expansion of human knowledge following a mathematical paradigm:

General and certain truths are only founded in the habitudes and relations of abstract ideas [...] whether something like this, in respect of other ideas, as well as those of magnitude, may not in time be found out, I will not determine. This, I think, I may say, that if other ideas that are the real as well as the nominal essences of their species were pursued in the way familiar to mathematicians, they would carry our

---

42. 'Of knowledge and opinion'. The edition quoted is J. Yolton (London 1961), reproducing the complete text of the definitive Fifth Edition of 1706. Although this does not correspond in all particulars with the First Edition of Coste's translation, those passages involved here show no divergences from the text which Buffier used, *Essai philosophique concernant l'entendement humain* (Amsterdam 1700), to which parallel references are given.

43. See IV, 2: 'Thus the mind perceives that white is not black, that a circle is not a triangle, that three are more than two and equal to one and two. Such kind of truths the mind perceives at the first sight of the ideas together by bare intuition, without the intervention of any other idea [...] It is on this intuition that depends all the certainty and evidence of all our knowledge' (Yolton, ii.138; Coste, pp.673-74); and, on essence: III, 3, para.18; IV, 4, paras. 4-6.

thoughts further, and with greater evidence and clearness than possibly we are apt to imagine.[44]

By extension, the almost insuperable, but not inherent inadequacy of our complex ideas of substance, may be mitigated by the cautious application of experimental methods:

Here [...] the want of ideas of their real essences sends us from our own thoughts to the things themselves as they exist. *Experience here must teach me* what reason cannot: and it is by trying alone, that I can certainly know what other qualities co-exist with those of my complex idea. Here, [...] for assurance I must apply myself to *experience*; as far as that reaches, I may have certain knowledge, but no further.[45]

Locke wishes neither 'to disesteem or dissuade the study of *nature*', and to this end, he prescribes and carefully describes the correct empirical application of hypotheses. Also, with regard to those natural operations surpassing our sensory capacities, he introduces analogy as an essential tool of judgement, linking it with the 'best conduct of rational experiments' (IV, 12, para.13; IV, 16, para.12).

Two brief paragraphs from Locke's chapter 'Of the reality of knowledge' will serve to crystallise the distance that separates him from the enclosed mental world of Buffier's nominalism:

Herein, therefore, is founded the *reality* of our knowledge concerning *substances*: that all our complex ideas of them must be such, and such only, as are made up of such simple ones as have been discovered to co-exist in nature. And our ideas, being thus true though not perhaps very exact copies, are yet the subjects of *real* (as far as we have any) *knowledge* of them [...] Whatever ideas we have, the agreement we find they have with others will still be knowledge. If those ideas be abstract, it will be general knowledge. But to make it *real* concerning substances, the ideas must be taken from the real existence of things. Whatever simple ideas have been found to co-exist in any substance, these we may with confidence join together again and so make abstract ideas of substances. For whatever have once had an union in nature may be united again. (*In our enquiries about Substances, we must consider Ideas, and not confine our Thoughts to Names, or Species supposed set out by Names.*) This if we rightly consider, and confine not our thoughts and abstract ideas to names, as if there were, or could be no other *sorts* of things than what known names had already determined, [...] we should think of things with greater freedom and less confusion than perhaps we do.[46]

44. IV, 12, para.7; Yolton, ii.239-40, Coste, p.829. Significantly, Newton is presented in the *Essay* as a discoverer of mathematical truths (IV, 7, para.3).

45. IV, 12, para.9; Yolton, ii.240-41, Coste, pp.830-32.

46. IV, 4, paras. 12-13; Yolton, ii.172, Coste, pp.724-25. Cf.Buffier's reversal of this recommendation, above, p.206.

Indeed, the same passage might be used as a warning at the other extreme, against too facile an association between Locke and the proposition that truth resides primarily in the evidence of empirical observation. It thus seems reasonable to conclude that while Buffier's sensationalism might well have been reinforced by tendencies already visible in Cartesianism itself, it was his pyrrhonism that derived, by direct inspiration as also by direct disagreement, greatest reinforcement from the encounter with Locke. Empiricism hardly figures in the intercultural balance sheet, and its promotion in relation to the increase of our knowledge was of marginal and belated concern to Buffier.[47]

Certainly, appreciation of the rôle of experiment in methodology is more evident in the writings of practising scientists, be they Cartesians or no. One of them, a physician, provides, a quarter of a century before Buffier took up his pen, a precise account of reason and experiment productively combined in inductive methodology: 'Les véritables Philosophes assemblent des expériences diverses, et en tirent des inductions qui s'écartent du sujet le moins qu'il est possible; ils les vérifient par d'autres expériences.'[48] Similarly, in considering the tradition of pedagogic writing, to which Buffier made so substantial a contribution, one discovers in Bernard Lamy's classic Cartesian manual, *Entretiens sur les sciences* (1694 ed.), not only a more comprehensive and historically sensitive introduction to natural science, but one where sympathetic promotion of intelligent curiosity already goes hand in hand with sober recognition of the pitfalls of system building, and of the immense obstacles to a genuine science of causation. Moreover, Lamy repeatedly emphasises the conclusive importance of experimentation. Although he values Cartesian method as an intellectual hygiene, rather than regurgitating its precepts, he endorses direct observation as a route to limited, but certain knowledge:

Si nos Phisiciens pouvoient executer leurs Sistemes ils apercevroient bien-tôt leur impossibilité. Dans la plus part des choses les éfets ne sont pas assez connus pour deduire consequemment leurs causes [...] Le véritable Phisicien ne doit rien oublier pour remarquer les effets naturels. Son Etude est toujours utile; car au moins on

47. The consistency of Buffier's attitude is demonstrated by reference to his early *Examen des préjugés vulgaires* (1704), where he sets Aristotle not Locke against Descartes and Malebranche, in a sceptical reduction of the 'new philosophy', a subject in general which he already perceives as belonging properly to 'de simples grammairiens' (VIe proposition).

48. Abbé Pierre Bourdelot, in F. Bayle, *Discours sur l'expérience et la raison* (Paris 1675), p.87; quoted by J. Roger, *Les Sciences de la vie dans la pensée française du 18e siècle* (Paris 1963), p.197.

aprend des faits constans dont il est plus utile de s'instruire que de faire des Sistemes en l'air. Rechercher les faits de la Nature, c'est faire des expériences.[49]

At the end of his survey of physical science, he even reminds his reader, in a way which anticipates only too well the distribution of Buffier's attention, that 'il est plus important de connoître les Esprits que le Corps' (p.262).

Lamy's methodological persuasions arise out of scientific intelligence derived from his attempts to verify some of Descartes's theories. Buffier's practical and intellectual, as opposed to merely journalistic, involvement in science was, one suspects, minimal; and it certainly derived no stimulation or nourishment from the doctrines received from Locke. His influence upon the successive climate of opinion in which scientific investigation was pursued can be seen to lie above all in nourishing the pervasive scepticism towards the systematic uses of reason which both Mornet, and more recently, Jacques Roger have isolated as the characteristic accompaniment, during the first half of the eighteenth century, of scientific vocation, confined in Baconian manner, to the accummulation of observational data.[50] Roger notes the natural alliance of anti-rationalism and sensationalism;[51] and the nature of Buffier's legacy is most tellingly encapsulated by pronouncing Condillac, in the *Traité des systèmes*, his direct spiritual heir.

More generally, the juxtaposition of Cartesian precursors with Buffier, and even Locke, tends to confirm the main historical contentions made at the beginning of this essay: scientific methodology emerges pragmatically from scientific experience, and its disseminated influence creates appropriate conditions for the germination or accreditation of epistemological theory, not vice-versa. Similarly, the discrediting of particular methodologies – here hypothesis or systematic abstraction – may ensue

49. *Entretiens sur les sciences*, ed. F. Girbal and P. Clair (Paris 1966), pp.259-60. The work was published in 1683, but the 'Discours sur la philosophie', treating of physics appeared in the second edition, 1694.

50. See D. Mornet, *Les Sciences de la nature en France au XVIIIe siècle* (Paris 1911), ii.1; J. Roger, *Les Sciences de la vie*, ii.1.

51. p.205: 'A partir de 1720, toute tentative de construction intellectuelle relève de 'l'esprit de système'. Il n'est plus question de chercher les lois de la Nature, il s'agit d'en recueillir les 'Anecdotes' [...] Les lois existent, mais nous ne pouvons les atteindre. La seule activité possible du savant est un travail de dénombrement. Il n'est pas besoin de dire combien cette attitude s'accorde avec la conception sensualiste de l'esprit: ce n'est pas par hasard que Condillac a écrit un *Traité des systèmes*.'

as much in consequence of coincidental preconceptions or prejudices, like Buffier's commitment to the theological premiss of divine omnipotence, as from inherent inefficacy. The fortunes of methodological doctrines may not then relate neatly to their epistemic credentials; true in Buffier's case, not only as concerns his critique of rationalism, but also his positive recommendations, so secondary is his formal attention either to empiricism, or, indeed, to its sensationalist adjuncts.

Nor, moreover, can Buffier's example be readily dismissed as a limited instance, without consequence for the claims traditionally associated with the dissemination of Lockian theories.[52] For the pattern that he sets up reproduces itself faithfully in the work of the later, free-thinking, and more blatantly eclectic vulgariser, the marquis d'Argens, who, while assertively promoting sensationalist fundamentals,[53] dismisses physics as a harmless but frivolous intellectual amusement – 'des songes agréables et amusants' – and, steadfast under the banner of *L'Art de penser*, unconcernedly reproduces the essentials of Cartesian analysis in his deliberations on method, these being firmly annexed, for good measure, to the subject of logic.[54] Though d'Argens allows rival cosmologies, Newtonianism pre-eminent among them, substantial attention in his work, his final evaluation of natural science simply mimics Buffier's pragmatic pyrrhonism (III, para.23; ii.71):

Mais qu'importe de savoir précisément comment les premiers principes agissent? [...] Dieu en nous cachant les premières opérations de la nature, qui sont des secrets connus à lui seul, nous a donné le pouvoir de les occasionner par des moyens dont il nous a accordé la connaissance. En se réservant les premiers principes de la Physique, il nous a laissé une science expérimentale qui suffit à nos besoins.

Locke is exalted as a model of philosophical excellence ('Discours préliminaire', para.5), but, as with Buffier, it is the critical dimension of

52. Classically embodied in D. Mornet's introductory survey, *La Pensée française au XVIIIe siècle* (Paris 1926): 'En un mot, la philosophie consiste moins à raisonner qu'à observer les faits et les enchaînements des faits. Cette philosophie des faits, *sensualiste* (parce qu'elle s'appuie sur les faits des sensations), a eu au XVIIIe siècle l'influence la plus profonde [...] Voltaire à vingt reprises a fait de Locke un éloge enthousiaste. Tous les philosophes l'admirent comme lui: d'Argens [...], et ceux mêmes qui ne sont pas 'philosophes', comme le père Buffier' (1969 ed., p.102).

53. See *La Philosophie du bon-sens* (La Haye 1768), II, paras.3-5: 'Il faut supposer qu'au commencement l'âme est comme une *table unie*, vuide de tous caractères, et sur laquelle il n'y a encore rien de tracé; ainsi, elle n'a aucune idée quelle qu'elle soit' (i.181).

54. III, para.1; and on method, II, paras.16, 17.

his epistemology which leaves its strongest imprint.[55] For his authority is directly solicited, not on the subject of the senses, but on that of our ignorance: 'Qu'on demande à Locke, jusqu'où s'étendent nos connaissances: il répondra de bonne foi que *notre connaissance est non seulement au-dessous de la réalité des choses, mais encore qu'elle ne répond pas à l'étendue de nos propres idées.*'[56] While in d'Argens one can discern significant mutations of the notion of *évidence*, the 'table vuide', if it may be filled at all, remains for him, like Buffier, in great and irreducible measure, a screen for shadow play.[57]

55. II, para.9, 'Des causes de notre ignorance', enumerated as lack of ideas, failure to relate them, inadequate reflexion, and, preliminary to all of these, the insuperable divide between our faculties and the nature of things: 'Il nous est impossible de déduire en aucune manière *les idées, les qualités sensibles que nous avons de l'esprit, d'aucune cause corporelle, ni de trouver aucune correspondance ou liaison entre ces idées et les premières qualités qui les produisent en nous.* L'expérience nous démontre cette vérité' (i.213).

56. III, para.1; i.248. On the priority of sensory experience, d'Argens in fact cites Gassendi rather than Locke (II, para.3).

57. The co-existence in d'Argens of 'évidence' construed as axiomatic truth and as conformity with available sense data is well demonstrated in *Bon sens*, II, para.1: 'La certitude de nos jugements dépend aussi de l'évidence qui les fait paroître nécessaires [...] Il faut que nos sens agissent et nous la démontrent évidemment'; but also, 'Pour s'accoutumer à former des jugements justes et évidents, il faut munir son entendement d'une quantité de propositions évidentes et générales, telles que sont celles qu'on appelle *maximes* ou *axiomes*. Ce sont des sources [...] d'un nombre d'autres idées qui se ressentent de la pureté de leur origine' (i.218-19).

'Ces esclaves sont des hommes': Prévost's account of the negroes of Senegal in his *Histoire générale des voyages*

SHIRLEY JONES

THE scholarly study which has been made of the *Histoire générale des voyages* during the last decade or so has helped us to see that Prévost was not only a novelist of great imaginative powers, but also that he played an important role in the evolution of Enlightenment thought.[1] As we know, Prévost was proud of the fact that it was d'Aguesseau who commissioned him to undertake the French translation of Astley's *New general collection of voyages and travels*, which had begun to appear in England in 1745.[2]

That Prévost conceived of his task as being an attempt to write a kind of modern world history is explicit in his translation of the English editors' preface to the work: 'Ainsi cette collection devient un systeme de Géographie Moderne, & d'Histoire, autant qu'un corps de Voyages; & représente, avec autant d'ordre que de plénitude, l'état présent de toutes les Nations' (i.v). In this attempt to transcend the bounds of a collection of travel accounts, to impose an order on the presentation of the material so that the whole work can be regarded as an exercise in modern history, Prévost claimed to have been hampered by the arbitrary layout of the English original, where the accounts of the journeys were separated from the observations. Clearly, from the point of view of his concern for the systematic presentation of knowledge, Prévost is very

1. See, among others, Michèle Duchet, *Anthropologie et histoire au siècle des lumières* (Paris 1971), esp. pp.81-95; Michèle Duchet, 'L'*Histoire des voyages*: originalité et influence', in *L'Abbé Prévost: Actes du Colloque d'Aix-en-Provence* (Aix-en-Provence 1965), pp.147-54; Jean Sgard, *Prévost romancier* (Paris 1968); Jean Sgard, 'Prévost: de l'ombre aux lumières (1736-1746), in *Studies on Voltaire* 27 (1963), pp.1479-87; Carminella Biondi, *'Ces esclaves sont des hommes'*: *lotta abolizionista e letteratura negrofila nella Francia del Settecento* (Pisa 1979), pp.62-85.

2. *A new general collection of voyages and travels: consisting of the most esteemed relations, which have been hitherto published in any language: [...] so as to form a compleat system of modern geography and history exhibiting the present state of all nations* (London 1745). The full title of Prévost's work reproduces the essential elements of this English rubric. All quotations from Prévost's work in this text are made from the Paris edition begun in 1746.

SHIRLEY JONES

much a man of the Enlightenment. Mme Duchet has already studied the question of the inhibiting effect which the English model had on Prévost. This effect she sees as persisting even after volume viii of the *Histoire des voyages*, when, after the collapse of the English enterprise, Prévost was, so to speak, able to fly with his own wings.[3]

Bearing in mind the question of the influence which Prévost's sources had on him, I would like to examine that part of the second volume of the *Histoire des voyages* which deals with the region of West Africa centering on Senegal. Three main reasons prompt this choice. First, looking more generally at the question of the negro in Enlightenment polemical writing, one of the most harrowing episodes in Voltaire's dark masterpiece, *Candide*, deals with the negro slave in Surinam, the maroon whose frightful mutilations stand as a symbol of the cruelty of 'civilised' man, as well as symbolising, by extension, the mutilating and therefore mutilated nature of civilised man himself. Although Voltaire's interest in 'primitive' societies was overshadowed by his interest in ancient civilisations, still this haunting image of man's inhumanity to man has its origins in the attitudes which underlie the *Histoire des voyages*.

Moreover, as far as Prévost himself is concerned, the work which has been considered as one of his finest novels, also a work of his maturity, the *Voyages de Robert Lade*, published in 1743, is set largely on the West Coast of Africa.[4] Admittedly this is because the narrator is an adventurer who seeks to re-establish his fortunes by means not practicable in the Old World – a fact which in itself is not without significance. The sources for some of the most memorable, as well as the most terrible, episodes of the *Voyages de Robert Lade* are to be found in the *Histoire des voyages*.

In the third place, the section dealing with Senegal in the *Histoire des voyages* provides interesting material for studying Prévost's methods as a translator and editor as well as giving evidence on which to base cautious conclusions about his own attitudes to the nascent problems of colonial adventurism and slavery. The material on which this section of Prévost's work was primarily based was that of detailed reports compiled by André Brue, Director General of the French Royal West African Company from 1697 to 1702 and from 1714 to 1719,[5] which form the

3. See Michèle Duchet, 'L'*Histoire des voyages*', p.150.
4. *Voyages de Robert Lade*, in *Œuvres choisies* (Amsterdam, Paris 1783-1785), vol.xiv.
5. For an assessment of André Brue's life and work see E.-F. Berlioux, *André Brue ou l'origine de la colonie française du Sénégal* (Paris 1874); Roger Mercier, *L'Afrique noire dans la*

226

basis of Labat's *Nouvelle relation de l'Afrique occidentale*.[6] During his period of directorship Brue travelled widely in the region between Cape Verde in the North and the River Gambia in the South, compiling detailed accounts of the many journeys he made into territories which were almost totally unknown as far as Europeans were concerned, with the aim of establishing trade between his company and the inhabitants. The energetic père Labat, in many ways a man after Prévost's own heart, and one who might easily have stepped out of the pages of a Prévost novel, mixes up the chronological order of Brue's travels in his full and yet at the same time unfocused account of the fauna and flora of these regions, together with even more incomplete essays on the human geography of the area. It is an account in which the engaging lack of order serves occasionally to throw into relief the sometimes cold and clinical precision of Brue's comments.

In its turn Labat's work formed the basis of the section on Senegal and Sierra Leone in Astley's *New general collection of voyages and travels*; and it was this work which Prévost chose to re-translate into French rather than returning to the original French text for his *Histoire des voyages*. That he chose to do so might be imputed not so much to lack of conscientiousness on his part as to a preference for the more systematic approach of the English work.

There are fundamental differences between the two texts, La Brue/Labat on the one hand and Astley/Prévost on the other. At the same time there are also fundamental similarities which the elegant order of the latter, as opposed to the idiosyncratic chaos of the former serves to obscure. The vital key to understanding the philosophy which underlay Brue's account is to see that the writer is in all important respects a product of late seventeenth-century French culture. So it is that in his political observations he seeks analogies with political structures he is familiar with, seeing Senegal as being divided into a series of states, either monarchies or republics, while in his moral judgements he betrays a mentality where total acceptance of Christian values is blended with

littérature française: les premières images (XVII-XVIIIe siècles) (Dakar 1962), pp.53-88.

6. *Nouvelle relation de l'Afrique occidentale contenant une description exacte du Sénégal & des païs situés entre le Cap Blanc & la rivière de Sierrelionne*, [...] *L'Histoire naturelle de ces païs, les différentes nations qui y sont répanduës, leurs religions & leurs mœurs*, [...] par le père Jean-Baptiste Labat de l'Ordre des Frères-Prêcheurs (Paris 1728). All quotations in this text are made from this edition, with the appropriate volume and page number.

the late seventeenth-century French belief in the superiority of their own civilisation. Thus, the comments of this shrewd and sharp-eyed observer, subsequently repeated in the *Histoire des voyages*, are valuable in helping us to comprehend the image of the negro as it was evolving during the first part of the eighteenth century.

Brue, no mean observer, is careful to adopt a systematic formula in his observations of the peoples he encountered, giving a brief physical and moral portrait of them, describing their government, their religion and their economy. He has left important accounts of the five main tribal groups he encountered: the Wolofs, the Mandingos, the Fulani, the Papels and the Floups, as well as giving sometimes intriguing, sometimes vivid pen portraits of other groups whose presence impinged on his work: Serer, Balantes, Bissagots, Biafaras.[7] In order to see how Brue perceived these peoples, in the sense of what it was he saw in them and what judgements are implied in his descriptions and then to see how these initial perceptions are transmuted into the images which, through Prévost, became common currency in Enlightenment thought, I should like briefly to compare the originals of some of these images with their later renderings.

First presented, and summarily dismissed, by Prévost are the Wolofs: 'Les Négres du canton sont d'assez belle taille, & la plûpart n'ont pas le nez écrasé. Ce sont les meilleurs Esclaves de l'Afrique' (ii.467). An immediate question of the effects of editing is raised here, since there is no parallel in Labat for the lapidary final sentence of the Astley/Prévost versions. Of the reasons that prompted the English editor summarily to describe the Wolofs in these terms all that one can safely say is that all editors by definition choose to present what they regard as true and important, while bearing in mind what they believe will be of interest to their readers. Thus the Astley vignette implies cultural assumptions affecting the negro, mutually held by editor and reader – assumptions which are then handed on to the eighteenth-century French readers through Prévost.

Between the summary reference to the Wolofs and the next tribe to be described, the Fulani, Prévost intercalates a passage on the Serer, a group outside the conventional tribal patterns of this area and described

---

7. For convenience, I have used the modern English spelling of the names of these tribes rather than the versions found in Brue/Labat and Prévost, hence the two forms Wolofs/Jalofs which appear in the text and quotations.

in these terms in the *Histoire des voyages* (ii.468, 469):

Ces Sereres [...] sont une Nation libre et indépendante, qui n'a jamais reconnu de Souverain. Ils forment, dans les lieux de leur retraite, plusieurs petites Républiques, où ils n'ont d'autres loix que celles de la nature. [...] L'Auteur prétend que la plûpart n'ayant aucune Idée d'un Etre suprême, croyent que l'ame périt avec le corps. Ils sont entiérement nuds. Ils n'ont aucune correspondance de Commerce avec les autres Négres. [...] Leurs voisins les traitent de Sauvages & de Barbares. C'est outrager un Négre que de lui donner le nom de *Serere*. Cette Nation d'ailleurs est simple, honnête, douce, généreuse, & très-charitable pour les Etrangers. Elle ignore l'usage des liqueurs fortes. Un si bon caractere, sans aucunes lumieres de Religion, les rendroit peut-être plus capables de celles du Christianisme, que les Négres Mahométans, [...]

Il n'y a pas de Négres qui cultivent leurs terres avec autant d'art que les Sereres. Si leurs voisins les traitent de Sauvages, ils sont bien mieux fondés à regarder les autres Négres comme des Insensés qui aiment mieux vivre dans la misere & souffrir la faim, que de s'accoutumer au travail pour assurer leur subsistance.

The original French account in Labat reads as follows (iv.156-57):

Les Cereres sont des Negres qui n'ont jamais voulu reconnoître de Souverain; ils forment des Republiques dans les endroits où ils sont retirez, élevent quantité de bestiaux, vont nuds, n'ont point d'autres loix que celle de la nature, la plûpart ne reconnoissent point de Dieu, ils n'en ont pas même la moindre idée, croient que l'ame périt avec le corps, n'ont de commerce avec personne; [...] Ils ne s'allient point avec les Negres leurs voisins, qui les regardent comme des Sauvages, de sorte qu'on ne peut gueres dire une plus grande injure à un Negre que de l'appeller Cerere. Hors ce que je viens de dire, ce sont de bonnes gens, simples dans leurs manieres, recevant bien les Blancs qui passent chez eux, officieux & même assez liberaux. L'usage de l'eau-de-vie n'est point passé jusqu'à eux, & ne les a pas encore gâtez, cela ne manquera pas d'arriver si les Blancs passent souvent par leur païs: leur naturel doux, & leur manque de religion les rendroit infiniment plus susceptibles des verites de la foi que ceux qui ont embrassé le Mahométisme [...]

Il n'y a point de Nation Negre qui cultive leurs terres avec plus de soin & de propreté que les Cereres: Ils marquent en cela qu'ils ne sont point paresseux, qui est le vice dominant de tout la Nation Noire; & si les autres les regardent comme des Sauvages, ils peuvent à leur tour les regarder comme des insensez qui souffrent les plus cruelles extremités de la famine, [...]

As one compares these two passages, one is quickly aware of the different angles from which these tribesmen are viewed. In the original text Brue briefly comments on the general character of the people, their government, their religion and finally their economy. In spite of the generally approbatory tone, however, it would be wrong to see in this description an incipient image of the Noble Savage: the Serer are deemed to be good because they make the stranger welcome, thus facilitating his task of trading, we presume. In addition, they distinguish themselves from their fellow negroes by their industry, thus winning further approbation. Last but not least important, however, is that the reference to the corrupting influence of the European has been suppressed in the Prévost version.

The next area dealt with in Prévost, inhabited by the Fulani, is described in the following terms in Labat: 'Ce pays est très peuplé, la terre y est bonne, & si les peuples qui l'habitent étoient plus laborieux & plus industrieux, ils retireroient de leurs terres dequoy faire un commerce avantageux aves les Etrangers, & à peu de choses dequoy se passer d'eux. On espere que les Européens seront assez sages pour ne leur pas donner des lumieres là-dessus' (ii.154). This last sentence, revealing in its most crude light a prime motive for European penetration into this part of Africa, is duly translated by Astley with a censorious footnote ('Can they blame these People then for concealing the Mysteries of their Trade from the *Europeans*', ii.62), while Prévost, for his part resorts here to the elegant prevarication: 'si les Habitans avoient plus d'industrie, ils pourroient tirer, des productions de leurs propres terres, le fond d'un commerce fort avantageux avec les Etrangers' (ii.514)

The Labat account continues as follows (iii.169-71):

Generalement parlant les Foulis ne sont pas si noirs que les Jaloffes, il s'en faut beaucoup; la plupart sont de couleur de bistre. Ils ne sont ni si grands ni si forts; leur taille est mediocre, dégagée & bien prise. Quoiqu'ils paroissent delicats, ils ne laissent pas d'être forts & laborieux; ils cultivent leurs terres avec soin, [...] & ils élevent une quantité prodigieuse de bestiaux de toutes les especes [...] leurs boeufs sont gras & bien nourris; c'est de leur païs que la Compagnie tire les plus beaux cuirs & à meilleur marché.

Ils aiment la chasse, & ils y sont fort adroits; [...] Outre les sabres & les saguayes qui sont leurs armes ordinaires, ils ont des arcs & des fleches dont ils se servent avec beaucoup d'adresse, & ceux à qui les François ont appris à manier les armes à feu, le font avec une justesse surprenante. Ils ont plus d'esprit que les Jaloffes, & plus de politesse; ils aiment les marchandises d'Europe, & ceux qui leur en apportent, ils leur font caresse, les reçoivent parfaitement bien chez eux; mais il ne faut pas oublier qu'ils sont fripons, cela est attaché à la couleur noire, ils le sont tous, & ne different entre eux que du plus au moins. Ils aiment les instrumens, & au lieu que les Rois & les Princes Jaloffes se croiroient deshonorez s'ils avoient touché quelqu'un, ceux des Foules se font un merite d'en sçavoir toucher plusieurs, [...] Ils ont une passion extrême pour la danse, cela leur est commun avec tous les Negres; rien n'est plus de leur goût que cet exercice, & quand ils ont travaillé ou chassé toute la journée, trois ou quatre heures de danse avant de s'aller coucher les délasse à merveille. Ils s'habillent à peu près comme les Jaloffes, mais ils sont plus délicats qu'eux sur le choix des étoffes, et au lieu que leurs voisins aiment la couleur rouge, la jaune est leur couleur favorite.

In the Prévost text we read (ii.514):

La plûpart sont d'une couleur fort bazanée; mais on n'en voit pas qui soient d'un beau noir, tel que celui des Jalofs au Sud de la riviere. On prétend que leurs alliances avec les Mores ont imbu leur esprit d'une teinture de Mahométisme, & leur peau de cette couleur imparfaite. Ils ne sont pas non plus si hauts & si robustes que les Jalofs. Leur taille est médiocre, quoique fort bien prise & fort aisée. Avec un air assez délicat, ils ne laissent pas d'être propres au travail, bons Fermiers, & capables de se procurer d'abondantes moissons de millet, [...] & d'entretenir un grande nombre de bestiaux, dont la plus grande partie sert à leurs propres besoins. Aussi vivent-ils beaucoup mieux que les Jalofs. [...] & la Compagnie n'a pas de meilleurs cuirs ni & meilleur marché que ceux qu'elle tire de cette Contrée.

Les Foulis aiment la chasse, & l'exercent avec beaucoup d'habileté. [...] Outre le Sabre & la zagaye, ils se servent fort adroitement de l'arc & des fléches. Ceux qui ont appris des François l'usage des armes à feu, s'en servent avec une adresse surprenante [...]

The judgement on the Mandingos is also on the whole favourable. Prévost, following the Labat original quite closely on this occasion, says of them (ii.528-29):

La Nation qu'on appelle les *Mandingos* est originaire de Jaga; mais elle s'est établie dans le Pays de Galam, où elle est devenue fort nombreuse, avec assez d'union pour former une espece de République, [...] Tout le commerce du Pays est entre les mains des Mandingos. Ils l'étendent dans les Royaumes voisins, & n'étant pas moins ardents pour la Religion de Mahomet que pour les richesses, ils font gloire d'être tout à la fois Marchands & Missionnaires. [...] Si l'on excepte les vices propres aux Negres, il y a peu de reproches à faire à leur Nation. Elle est douce, civile, amie des Etrangers, fidelle à ses promesses, laborieuse, industrieuse, capables de tous les Arts & de toutes les Sciences. Cependant tout leur sçavoir consiste à lire & à écrire l'Arabe. On a peine à juger si c'est par inclination qu'elles aiment les Etrangers, ou pour le profit qu'ils tirent d'eux par leur Commerce.

If these tribal groups meet with at least qualified approval, there are, on the other hand, those who met with qualified, if not outright, condemnation. First, the Floups, of whom Prévost writes (ii.546-47):

Les Habitans de cette Contrée sont distingués par le nom de *Flups* ou *Floups*. Ils ont une Langue, ou plutôt un dialecte qui leur est propre. Leur Religion n'a pas d'objet fixe; ou s'ils ont quelques divinités, ils ne leur rendent que des adorations arbitraires. Ceux qui habitent l'intérieur des terres sont farouches, & souvent cruels pour les autres Negres qui passent dans leur Pays, à moins qu'ils ne soient à la suite de quelque Européen. A Bintam, & dans les lieux voisins, ils ont un naturel plus doux. Ils aiment les Etrangers, ils sont de bonne foi dans le commerce; mais comme ils ne sont pas capables de tromper, ils n'aiment pas non plus qu'on abuse de leur simplicité.

Finally, the Papels, inhabitants of the Islands of Bissao and the surrounding coast of Kachao: their dress, or lack of it and their skill as oarsmen are commented on. Of their character and beliefs, Prévost informs his readers (ii.565):

Ils ont un langage qui est propre aux Papels, comme ils ont des usages qui leur sont particuliers. Le Commerce n'a pas servi peu à les civiliser. Ils sont Idolâtres; mais leurs idées de religion sont si confuses, qu'il n'est pas aisé de les démêler. Leur principale Idole est une petite figure qu'ils appellent *China*, dont ils ne peuvent expliquer la nature ni l'origine. Chacun d'ailleurs se fait une Divinité suivant son caprice. Ils regardent certains arbres consacrés, sinon comme des Dieux, du moins comme l'habitation de quelque Dieu. Ils leur sacrifient des Chiens, des Coqs & des Boeufs, qu'ils engraissent & qu'ils lavent avec beaucoup de soin avant que de les faire servir de victimes. Après les avoir égorgés, ils arrosent de leur sang les branches & le pied de l'arbre. Ensuite on les coupe en pieces, dont l'Empereur, les Grands & le Peuple ont chacun leur partie. Il n'en reste à la Divinité que les cornes, qu'on attache au tronc de l'arbre jusqu'à ce qu'elles tombent d'elles-mêmes.

Il ne paroît pas que l'Isle de Bissao ait jamais été troublée par des guerres civiles; preuve assez honorable de l'humanité des Habitans & de leur soumission pour leur Prince, [...]

A reading of these texts, Labat's and Prévost's, thus reveals both the general nature of the approach and at times the subtle changes that have taken place from the first (Labat's) to the final (Prévost's) version. From the outset we see how, inevitably, things are perceived through European eyes, with, implicit in every judgement, a belief in European superiority – hence for instance the naïve surprise that the Fulani should prove skilful marksmen when taught how to use European weapons. A more important consequence of this attitude is that the 'good' tribes are those who welcome white visitors and who have been 'civilisés' by contact with European traders. Those who, as far as possible, given their 'black' nature, conform to European values: industry, honesty. On the other hand, the bad tribes are those who prove recalcitrant to European influence and attempts at infiltration into their territory.

However, within this framework of interesting information on the variations in the way of life and character among these peoples, there remains the overriding judgement on characteristics deemed to be inalienably attached to their negritude: laziness and dishonesty. The words *paresse, paresseux, indolence* invariably accompany comments on the natural resources of the country, as opposed to the methods of their exploitation,[8] while the term *fripons* invariably accompanies accounts of the relations between European and negro, to describe the conduct of the latter.[9]

A further important aspect of these accounts of the West Coast of Africa, certainly as far as the late seventeenth- and early eighteenth-century reader was concerned, was that of the government which each of these people enjoyed. By virtue of his mission as representative of French interests, Brue was bound to examine carefully the social structure of the peoples he dealt with and to have first-hand dealing with the respective rulers of each state or region where he was trying to establish trading. Some of his most memorable accounts, visually speaking, are of the tribal chiefs ceremonially arrayed to meet him, together with their wives and attendants of different sorts.[10] He records, on occasion, the laws or customs relating to the succession to the throne as well as royal burial customs involving the sacrifice of wives and attendants (a custom which Brue thought had been practically discontinued).[11] In general, he clearly viewed the societies into which he penetrated in terms analogous with European forms of government familiar to him, as monarchies or republics; and the image he presents is that of a society which it would be tempting but inaccurate to view as feudal, in the sense that the ruler is portrayed as exercising unlimited power over his subjects, including that of life and liberty.

Here we encounter the question of the role of slavery in this society. The Labat account abounds with references to *captifs*, a term which has disappeared in the *Histoire des voyages*. Slaves, it would seem, were of two kinds: on the one hand the king could take away a subject's liberty as punishment for a crime (and this, we are told, was much more frequent than capital punishment – for obvious reasons)[12] or on the other, the aim of the more or less constant tribal wars was to take the enemy, men,

8. See for instance Labat, ii.154, 176-77, 188, 303, iii.118, 203, 317, iv.49, 50; Prévost, ii.514, 578, 606.

9. See for instance Labat, iii.199, iv.17, 29, 45, v.187, 189; Prévost, ii.583.

10. See for instance Labat, iii.6-9, 131ss., iv.101, 163, v.174-77.

11. See for instance Labat, iii.72, iv.178; Prévost, ii.567, 595, 600.

12. See Prévost, ii.509.

women and children, captive, and use them either as a source of labour or as a source of income in trade with European and Moor.[13] In addition, we are told that in return for 'feudal' services, 'vassals' had the right to enslave anyone they encountered on their lord's lands whilst serving him in tribal wars.[14] Furthermore, a sad consequence of European penetration into West African life is the apparent fact that some natives, addicted to alcohol, were prepared to sell their families into slavery in return for brandy.[15]

Sadly indeed, to twentieth-century eyes, the overall impression of these societies of West Africa is one of a state of warfare, the cruel use of power; the powerful preying on the weak with the example being set by those who wielded untrammelled power.[16] Probably one of the most poignant examples of this state of affairs is the story, which lingers in the memory like a bad dream, of native slave-traders carrying off their prey by night: men and women bound and gagged and their children tied up in sacks.[17] How accurate these stories of monstrous abuse of power on the part of the rulers were we cannot now begin to know. Given that the confessed aim of French penetration into Africa was to trade in slaves, it is natural to assume that their accounts of native customs in this respect would be biased. The effect of Brue's descriptions of feasting with local potentates prior to buying as many of their subjects as possible makes rather chilling reading to the twentieth-century reader. That it did not affect the eighteenth-century reader in this way is almost certainly the case. For him the African negro, set apart from recognised and recognisable norms of humanity by virtue of his very negritude, by this same token forfeited the right to human pity.

The third topic which Brue, as a late seventeenth-century Frenchman, would feel bound to provide information on was that of religion. And here the African revealed himself in an even more unfavourable light,

13. See Labat, iv.133-35; Prévost, ii.565: 'Loin de leur offrir leur médiation, les Européens trouvent leur intérêt à les voir souvent aux mains, parce que la guerre augmente le nombre des Esclaves.'

14. See Prévost, ii.515.

15. See Prévost, ii.575.

16. References to native rulers selling their subjects as slaves to the European traders abound in the texts under discussion. See for instance Labat, iii.159, 232, 262, iv.83-84, 85, 148, v.180, 204; Prévost, ii.464, 470-71, 481, 509, 512, 524, 525, 527, 529, 557, 567, 586, 587, 591, 601, 602, 603, 604, 605.

17. See Labat, iv.351.

since, if social structures might be interpreted an accordance with systems known to French observers, such evidence of religious beliefs and practices as Brue encountered excited either his restrained hostility or his total contempt. If for instance the Mahometanism of the Wolofs, described in some detail, is viewed with a qualified approbation in so far as it represented a recognisable, if debased, form of religious belief, the 'idolatrous' Papels, for instance, seem to have been received with a mixture of scorn and blank incomprehension. Brue's description of the 'King' of Bissago taking the auguries before deciding whether or not to trade with the French, is a delightful example of the ironical tone which betokens the scepticism, not of the unbeliever, but of the Christian in face of other religions: 'M. Brue étoit bien sûr que la réponse des Divinités seroit favorable; car en ce payïs-là comme dans l'ancienne Grece, il y a des moiens sûrs de faire parler les oracles selon les besoins que l'on a, & M. Brue ne les avoit pas negligez' (Labat iv.107-108; see also Prévost, ii.561).

The ironical tone which is the distinguishing feature of the Brue account, whether describing the young Wolof scholars bawling out passages from the Koran so that the French visitors were deafened, the prowess of the tribal warriors whose victories consisted of carrying off a handful of unarmed victims, or, one suspects, the tongue-in-cheek descriptions of the ceremonial finery of tribal rulers, is the irony of the superior, which Montesquieu was to make such devastating use of when he reversed its aim and criticised his own country. Here it is merely the indication of a condescension which is in the last analysis naïve. Brue was clearly a man of action, clear-headed, a cool administrator, a skilful negotiator, at bottom little concerned with religious beliefs of any kind. His brief was to open up West Africa to French trade, not Christianity. Apart from passing comment that the 'idolatrous' tribes would be more ripe for conversion to Christianity than the Muslim negroes of the North, and a fairly laconic account of certain Portuguese missionaries who had made themselves *personae non gratae* with their home government by declaring it a sin for Christians to enslave their fellow men, Brue has little to say on the matter.[18]

The implications of his remarkable character and official status are far-reaching, however, both for the history of this particular encounter

18. See Labat, v.218-19; Prévost, ii.554, 581.

between European civilisation and African barbarism and, what concerns us most here, the impact which his account would be bound to have on the audience it eventually reached through the intermediary of Prévost. We do not know the exact nature of the role of slavery in West African society before any encounter with traders from elsewhere, that is to say, with the Arab traders who had preceded the Europeans, but we are fully aware of the motives for Europeans pressing open the gates of trade with a people they clearly despised. The means by which they achieved their ends were ruthless. An essential implement of trade was the supplying of brandy to which, like the use of firearms, the African was entirely unaccustomed until the advent of European merchant adventurers. Brue's account is punctuated with references to the use of *eau de vie* as a bargaining weapon: the native rulers had to be softened up with gifts and especially with brandy before trading deals were concluded.[19] It would be both arrogant and anachronistic for us to adopt a censorious attitude to methods of trading which seem with hindsight to depend for their success on the corruption of one's trading partners. Certainly Brue's contemporaries did not see it as such, since the negro was already regarded as an inferior being and his corruption would not be regarded as a matter of any moral weight.

Labat's *Nouvelle relation de l'Afrique occidentale*, based on Brue's memoirs, is a kind of official history that all modern – and indeed ancient – colonising ventures have produced. A history written by the conquering power describing the means, military, diplomatic and commercial, by which they achieved power, and viewing the conquered people with a detached and at the same time suspicious eye. This latter element, inevitably enhanced in an encounter between peoples as different as those of West Africa and Western Europe, is an essential part of the subtext of Brue's account. As we have seen, the African is condemned as dishonest, dangerous and is labelled 'barbare', 'sauvage', culturally loaded terms which in themselves reveal some of the nature of the fear and greed which were fundamental, although completely unacknowledged, motives for European behaviour.[20] The reasoning is easy enough to follow: the

19. See for instance Labat, iii.187-88, 190, iv.179, v.169; Prévost, ii.503.
20. See for instance Labat, iv.83-84: 'ce commerce ne peut qu'être très avantageux à la Compagnie & à l'Etat; puisqu'il donnera un nouveau débouchement aux marchandises de nos manufactures, & qu'il fera entrer chez nous une quantité très considérable d'or, & plus de quinze cent à deux mille captifs tous les ans pour nos colonies de l'Amérique'.

African is alien from the cultural point of view, he is thus both contempt-ible and potentially dangerous, since only by force or by skilful manipu-lation can he be made to comply with European demands – and laws.[21] Vastly outnumbered, armed only with assumptions of spiritual superior-ity and the technological advantage of the firearm, the Europeans pressed home their advantage. Careful to build forts to protect their goods and the merchandise, animate and inanimate, they had acquired, their determination being occasionally put to the test, when, under attack from the 'savage' tribes they were trading with, they were obliged to run down the native canoes with their long boats and shoot at the natives at point blank range.[22]

It would be very much a *nez de Cléopâtre* kind of speculation to conjecture what this first seminal source of information on West Africa would have been like if, instead of being written by the prototype of the early colonial administrator, it had been written by a Christian mission-ary. The *Lettres édifiantes* of this period were concerned with Jesuit activities in China, the Carnatic and South America. Père Margat's letter from St Domingo, published in 1728, and père Fauque's letter from Cayenne published thirty years later, make sorry reading.[23] For them, the negro's intrinsic inferiority can only be compensated for by baptism and a grounding in the Christian Truths. In the first letter, the author has to summon his Christian love of his fellow men to his aid to quell the repugnance which the ignorance and the evil smell of the negro slave inspired in him (xviii.362); while in the second, the author's role in returning to captivity a band of maroons reveals the limitations of those like Fauque (xxviii.121-48), who elsewhere expressed their distress to witness their fellow men being sold like cattle (p.121: 'Qu'il est triste pour un homme raisonnable & susceptible de réflexions de voir ainsi vendre son semblable comme une bête de charge'). Doubtless whatever the calling of the European observer visiting Africa at that time, the general tenor of his account would have been the same. To men of this

21. An example of European attitudes to the enforcement of the 'laws' laid down by them for trading with the negroes is to be found in Labat, iii.198: '& quand on ne peut obliger ces Princes à satisfaire à ces prêts forcez, on pille quelque Village, on enleve les Habitans que l'on fait Esclaves, & ensuite on compte avec le Roy, & si on a enlevé plus d'Esclaves qu'il n'en devoit, on luy en tient compte'. See also Labat, iv.81.

22. See for instance Labat, v.53, 180, 190; Prévost, ii.584.

23. *Lettres édifiantes et curieuses* vol.xviii (Paris 1728), pp.331-63; vol.xxviii (1758), pp.119-48.

time the very colour of his skin seemed to raise doubts about the common humanity of the negro.[24] What then are the general conclusions to be drawn about the influence of the Brue mémoires, through Labat and Astley, on Prévost? And in turn what may we conclude about Prévost's version in relation to the original? Manifestly, the Astley/Prévost account is much easier to read and comprehend. Gone is the disorderly presentation of events, the riotous assembly of details, the repetitions. The anecdotal element has been whittled down, the forcefully expressed judgements toned down. By virtue of his post, Brue was bound to have close dealings with local potentates and his colourful accounts help to create an air of unreal exoticism which is one of the features of Labat's work. In Prévost, the idiosyncratic element is attenuated so that the whole has acquired an air of objectivity which serves to conceal the nature of the source. The *Histoire générale des voyages*, as its author hoped, can lay claim to being a work of modern history and geography. It is also in some essential respects a work of modern colonial history.[25]

To say this is to attack neither Brue nor Prévost. Both were men of their time as we all are. Both men of high intelligence, they were also shaped by their own culture, a culture to which the negritude of Western Africa was alien. In a recent discussion of the question of the changing attitude to colonial slavery in the *Encyclopédie*, the lack of concern for the question of the negro slave trade in the early volumes of the *Encyclopédie* has been examined.[26] Not until volume v, published in 1755, did the burning humanitarian issue come to the fore, following the death of Montesquieu. A final point relating to Prévost as a source of information and as a spokesman for his time may be made here. First, as scholars have already demonstrated, Prévost's work remained a primary source of information on Africa, so that the prejudices it contained died hard.[27] For instance, the article on 'Sénégal', published as late as volume xv of the *Encyclopédie*, contains the following judgement, clearly inspired by the *Histoire des voyages*: 'les Negres sont sédentaires, & ont des rois qui

24. For a contemporaneous discussion of this question see Labat, ii.256-70. For a recent study of this question see P. J. Marshall and Glyndwr Williams, *The Great map of mankind* (London 1982), pp.227-55.

25. See Michèle Duchet, 'L'*Histoire des voyages*, p.153.

26. See Barbara M. Saunderson, 'The *Encyclopédie* and colonial slavery', *British journal for eighteenth-century studies* 7 (1984), pp.15-37.

27. See Michèle Duchet, 'L'*Histoire des voyages'*, p.153.

les font esclaves. Les Maures sont petits, maigres, d'un esprit fin & délié: les Negres sont grands, gras, sans génie.'[28]

The question of European attitudes to the negro, together with what seems to be its corollary, European attitudes to the negro slave trade, are obviously too vast even to be attempted in this present study. Much has already been written on these topics.[29] However, a study of Prévost's account of West Africa in the *Histoire générale des voyages* is highly relevant to the related topic of the diffusion of knowledge or information about the negro during the Enlightenment since it illustrates precisely how knowledge and cultural prejudice inevitably intermingle to produce phenomena of incalculable importance. The 'knowledge' in the sense of information purveyed by Prévost, initially provided by Brue, left the European reader with a view of the West African as being not only different from but actually inferior to himself. The negro, with his lazy and lascivious ways, his dishonesty, the apparent unconcern of the ruler for the welfare of his own people, was morally set apart from the white man, so it seemed. In his native environment he could inspire neither liking nor respect. Thus it was that articles referring to Africa in the early volumes of the *Encyclopédie* are generally unfavourable in tone. Thus it was too that only when he ceased to be perceived as a black man, an idolator, and became a negro slave stripped of his original identity and assimilated into the ambit of European culture and sensibilities, could he become an object of interest, a cause for concern and indignation.

Thus it was that the negro, stripped of the cultural stigma attached to his African inheritance and transformed into a slave, a concept culturally intelligible to men of the Enlightenment who could perceive him as an example of a social evil representing an impediment to human progress, could in this guise become integrated into European consciousness. The *Histoire générale des voyages* clearly indicates the distance European consciousness had to travel before such a position could be reached.

28. The origins of such sentiments may be found for instance in Labat, p.12. iii.118: '[les Maures] ont [...] de l'esprit autant qu'on en peut avoir [...] au lieu que les Negres leurs voisins sont grands, gros, gras, charnus, peu spirituels, paresseux, yvrognes, grands mangeurs quand ils ont de quoy'.

29. See for instance D. B. Davis, *The Problem of slavery in Western culture* (Ithaca, New York 1966), pp.392-421; A. J. Barker, *The African link* (London 1978); P. J. Marshall and Glyndwr Williams, *The Great map of mankind*.

Philosophical speculation and literary technique: the systematic context of Du Marsais's *Des tropes*

J. S. SPINK

... Cette faucille d'or dans le champ des étoiles.

IDEOLOGICAL delving prepares the ground for literary fruition. Du Marsais's acumen and *esprit de suite* succeeded in establishing an intellectual *continuum* all the way from Locke's theory of knowledge (and even further afield)[1] to what was to be the practice of metaphor, as distinct from synecdoche, or any other metonymy, in Hugolian poetics, profoundly modifying Port-Royal grammar in the process. Hugo's metaphors are immediate in their effect, appealing directly to remembered impressions, predominantly visual. Synecdoche, whether on the model of the part for the whole, or any other, requires a mental step. This is true of metonymy in general, to the exclusion of metaphor, so that we may speak of metaphor on the one hand, and metonymy on the other. The distinction made by some modern linguists, notably Roman Yakobson, between the simultaneous and the successive linguistic operations, relating the ones to metaphor and the others to metonymy, is more than implicit in Du Marsais's *Des tropes*, it is manifest there, as it is elsewhere in his writings on the theory of knowledge, grammar and the use of words.[2]

Du Marsais's *Des tropes* was entirely neglected when it appeared in

---

1. Towards physiology, in that he identifies the internal sense with the brain; towards anthropology in that he looks upon a language as the product of, and evolving in, a given community. Though only in outline, Du Marsais's humanistic science covers the ground that Charles Morris, in his *Foundations of the theory of signs* (Chicago 1938) allots to *Semiotic*, except for the formalistic parts thereof (symbolic logic, for example) for which Morris names Leibniz, and not Locke, as the forerunner.

2. Yakobson (Jacobson) makes this distinction in his *Foundations of language* (with M. Halle), *Janua linguarum* (The Hague 1956). He held that the distinction is borne out by the experimental study of linguistic aphasia, and that it throws light on certain cerebral locations. He was supported by medical evidence in *Pathologie du langage: l'aphasie*, by H. Hécaeb and R. Angelergues (Paris 1965).

1730.[3] No new edition was published before he died in 1756.[4] A year after his death, a second edition appeared and was copied in Leipzig by S. Formey, but no more until 1775. It was not until the end of the century and the beginning of the next that the book became famous. At that time a spate of editions, reprints and abbreviations followed one upon the other, and the book became popular in the schools.[5] It had been possible, since 1797, to form a complete idea of Du Marsais's writing on the theory of knowledge and general grammar, up to that time scattered and fragmentary, thanks to an edition of his collected works published in that year. It appeared too late to influence the programme of the Ecoles Centrales, in which theory of knowledge led to general grammar; this part of the programme was inspired by Condillac and supervised by the *Idéologue* Destutt de Tracy. Accounts of Du Marsais's life and works were available, thanks to the *idéologue* L.-J.-J. Daube and to Naigeon,[6] but it was not until 1797 that the scope of his enquiries became apparent.[7]

3. *Des tropes, ou des différens sens lesquels peut prendre un même mot dans une même langue* (Paris 1730), in-8°, x + 292 pp. In some editions the work is called *Traité des tropes*. The edition published in 1818, with a commentary by the rhetorician Fontanier, has been photographically reproduced, with an introduction by G. Genette (Geneva 1967). Genette calls it 'le monument sans doute le plus important de toute la rhétorique française'.

4. César Chesneau Du Marsais was born on 17 July 1676, and died on 11 June 1756.

5. The preface of the 1797 edition of Du Marsais's works recalls that Desfontaines had been condescending towards *Des tropes* in his *Nouvelles du Parnasse*, i.144, but adds that this work 'jouit maintenant de la célébrité qu'il mérite' (p.xiv), and F. Tamisier, writing in 1862, in his *Dumarsais, sa vie et ses écrits*, notes that it 'devait populariser plus tard, dans nos écoles, le nom de Dumarsais'.

6. L.-J.-J. Daube published a short account of Du Marsais's work in 1792 with his *De l'influence de l'imprimerie sur la Révolution*, and Naigeon in the *Encyclopédie méthodique* (*Philosophie ancienne et moderne*, t.iii, 1794, pp.171-208, following the account given by d'Alembert in the *Encyclopédie* vii.2ss.), with a few additions.

7. With two exceptions, the texts contained in this edition (Paris, 7 vols) are authentic. The two exceptions are the *Analyse de la religion chrétienne* and the *Essai sur les préjugés*. The *Analyse* is an estimable piece of scholarship, sometimes at second hand. The *Essai* is an earnest and well-informed piece of radical moralising, and gave rise to one of Frederick the Great's literary competitions (see W. Krauss's *Est-il utile de tromper le peuple?* (Berlin 1966). But neither is by Du Marsais. The *Analyse* contains the words, 'On n'a qu'à parcourir les traités des cérémonies superstitieuses des Juifs' (*Œuvres*, 1797, vii.11); the *Recueil nécessaire*, usually thought to have been published by Voltaire in 1765, gives the same text (p.11). This reference to one of the titles of Saint-Glain's very rare translation of Spinoza's *Tractatus theologico-politicus*, and also a reference to Fabricius's Hamburg edition of the *Apocrypha* cannot reasonably be associated with Du Marsais. The *Essai* contains references to English literature and life (Wollaston, S. Butler the poet, teaching at Oxford and Cambridge) which take us a long way from Du Marsais. The words taken from *Hudibras* must have been translated from the English original, seeing that the only French version avoids these words ('pulpit', 'drum

The apogee of his reputation as a grammarian was reached in 1805, when Gérando's still useful discourse in his honour[8] won an *Institut* prize, but Gérando looked upon his philosophical ideas merely as derived from Locke. In any case, the counter-revolution in the philosophical domain to be carried out by Victor Cousin and his pupils was already beginning, and Du Marsais was pushed aside by it. By the middle of the century, Cousin's pupil Damiron was in a position to pour unopposed scorn on Du Marsais's work, in a series of memoirs presented to the *Académie des sciences morales et politiques*.[9]

Damiron made no attempt to co-ordinate Du Marsais's ideas. He was content to summarise the various works, authentic and inauthentic, in a tedious manner, and held them to be without value or distasteful. A perfect conformist himself, and the type of the career academic, he did not hesitate to accuse Du Marsais of having had a low and unheroic conception of the philosopher's role (*Séances et travaux*, xxix.26). A nineteenth-century père Garasse, he made it clear that he himself would have fixed the price of decent burial higher than did the priest who attended Du Marsais at his death.

Damiron's onslaught appeared in 1859. Three years later, a biographer attempted to show that Du Marsais had been a believer.[10] But this author was prepared to take the distinction made by Du Marsais, in his *Logique*, between angelic intellection and human understanding as a proof of his belief in angels, whereas Damiron, on the contrary, had observed with acerbity that this in no way committed him, any more than another of Du Marsais's distinctions, this time between body and soul, based on

---

ecclesiastic') at the beginning of the poem. Moreover, the constant presentation of the Stoics as model philosophers is out of keeping with Du Marsais's thinking. The *Analyse* probably originated in the Netherlands, early in the century. The *Essai* must be much later, judging by its predilection for the Stoics and for the idea of citizenship. These features point to the youthful d'Holbach, as do also the English references. Neither work is ascribed to Du Marsais by Naigeon.

8. *Eloge de Dumarsais, discours qui a remporté le prix proposé par la seconde classe de l'Institut national le 15 nivôse an xii*, Paris an XIII. In this work Gérando made a serious attempt to co-ordinate Du Marsais's thinking, but in his *Histoire comparée des systèmes de philosophie* (Paris 1894), t.i, ch.11, p.337, he made a passing reference only to Du Marsais as a disciple of Locke.

9. *Séances et travaux de l'Académie des sciences morales et politiques ... sous la direction de M. Mignet* (t.xlviii and t.xlix), 3e série, xxviii.94-113; xxix.5-33; and 161-89 (Paris 1859).

10. F. Tamisier, *Dumarsais, sa vie et ses écrits*.

our always thinking of them as different.[11] He was right, in an inquisitorial sense, not because he wished to understand Du Marsais, but because he wished to destroy him.

In the early years of the Third Republic was published, at the Librairie de la Bibliothèque Nationale, with Daube's account of his life, an edition of the *Essai sur les préjugés*, attributed, though mistakenly, to Du Marsais, and this attempt to defend him was a straw in the wind. In our own times, two substantial theses have secured his reputation as a great and original grammarian.[12] However, the philosophical aspect of the work of the *grammairien philosophe* he wished to be[13] has been overshadowed by erudite curiosity concerning his irreligion. Irreligion is an intriguing feature of eighteenth-century French life in its own right, fraught as it was with the perils of the galleys and death for the poor, the unprotected and the ingenuous, compelling and daunting as it was for the scholar. This necessarily hidden and anecdotic aspect of Du Marsais's biography is doubtless secondary when his contribution to the two main developments of intellectual method characteristic of the *Philosophes*, namely common-sense rationalism and empiricism, is being considered. However, such biographical information as is available on this topic is an aid to understanding why his systematic thinking, as regards theory of knowledge and language, admits of no metaphysical context.

Du Marsais broke away from the Oratorians in a very final manner at the age of 25, the age of majority. He had been educated at the Oratorian college in Marseilles and had stayed on to teach, but in 1700 left for Paris and followed the law for three years before becoming a private tutor. As his paedagogical talent must have been in no doubt, in view of his later career, he cannot have been dismissed for incompetence. According to Daube,[14] a story went the rounds in the Oratorian college of Vendôme to the effect that an aged teacher named Norjeu had known Du Marsais at Juilly and had disapproved of him because of an impious catechism he had taught his pupils, and for having made fun of popular

11. *Séances et travaux*, xxix.43. He adopts the same attitude towards Du Marsais's statement (in his *Logique*) that the idea of God comes from experiences.

12. G. Sahlin, *César Chesneau Du Marsais et son rôle dans l'évolution de la grammaire générale* (Upsala 1928); J.-C. Chevalier, *Naissance de la notion de complément dans la grammaire française (1530-1750)* (Genève 1968).

13. In the article on 'Construction' in the *Encyclopédie*.

14. In a footnote to his biographical sketch (1792) reproduced in editions of the *Essai sur les préjugés*, 1822 (p.59) and 1886.

belief in miracles. The story is doubtless apocryphal, seeing that Du Marsais was not at Juilly, and it may well come from two passages of Du Marsais's *Logique* in which he describes the *a posteriori* source of the idea of God, and excludes all confusion between biblical stories of miracles and the methods of modern physics. In point of fact, neither of these matters would, by itself alone, have caused a scandal in an Oratorian college in the 1690s, and the story represents the exacerbated sentiments of a century later, but these sentiments do reflect Du Marsais's reputation in an Oratorian college.[15] He was a renegade. He had indeed broken completely with his old teachers and colleagues, and our assumption must be that he had lost his faith on attaining manhood and found his position in an Oratorian college uncongenial.

Du Marsais's first attempts to participate in intellectual exchanges in Paris were a defence of Fontenelle on the question of the cessation of oracles, against the Jesuit Balthus, and a defence of the rights of the Gallican Church, commissioned by the *président* Des Maisons. Des Maisons died in 1715 and this date is therefore the last possible for the composition of the second of these two works, but neither was published at the time. The first was never published and we know only the summary of it made by d'Alembert from the manuscript and included in his *Eloge* (*Encyclopédie*, t.vii). The second was published in Geneva in 1757, also from a manuscript found after its author's death. A short dissertation entitled *De la raison*, published by Naigeon in his *Recueil philosophique* (1770) as being by Du Marsais, must date from the earliest period of his intellectual development, and certainly from before the writing of his Latin method (1723).[16] It makes use of Cartesian and Malebranchist expressions and is theistic, but critical, in the manner of Fontenelle, of stories of miracles and the like, and already open to the influence of Locke with regard to the origin of our ideas. Des Maisons evidently

---

15. Saint-Simon, writing before 1743, claimed to know that both Du Marsais and his employer Des Maisons were secretly without religion (see W. Krauss, 'L'énigme de Du Marsais', *Revue d'histoire littéraire de la France* 62 (1962), p.515. The Jesuit *Mémoires de Trévoux* noted Du Marsais's reputation as an unbeliever (1760, p.2485).

16. The way the author uses the terms *immédiat* and *médiat* (*Œuvres*, 1797, vi.5) is as good as a signature. They are used to distinguish between perceptions which do not involve mental operations and those which do. In Du Marsais's *Logique*, their use is similar, although not identical. In *De la raison*, some abstract ideas are included as objects of immediate perceptions. In the *Logique* 'immediate' perceptions correspond to Locke's 'ideas of sensation' and 'mediate' ones to Locke's 'ideas of reflection'. *De la raison* goes half way towards Locke. Littré gives only one example of this special use of *médiat* and it is from Du Marsais's *Logique*.

thought there was still enough of an Oratorian in his son's tutor to make of him a suitable defender of the rights of the Gallican Church, and indeed there were always to remain at Du Marsais's command sufficient traces of Augustinian,[17] Cartesian and Malebranchist themes for the erudite Boindin's reference to him as a 'Jansenist' to have some meaning. According to Duclos, the Maréchal de Noailles called him 'mon philosophe', and he was known generally as 'le Philosophe'.[18] To use the word thus was to use it in the new, eighteenth-century manner, and not according to the current usage, which made of the *philosophe* a severe critic of his fellow-men, like the ancient Cynics, a supercilious, misanthropic or melancholy figure, as did Marivaux, jocularly, in his *Cabinet du philosophe*, or, seriously, Prévost in his *Cleveland ou le philosophe anglais*. Duclos and Boindin were both regulars at the Café Procope. A story told by d'Alembert in his *Eloge* may well have been located there, seeing that Du Marsais's interlocutors also claim to be philosophers. The subject was Descartes's refusal to allow the brutes any feeling. Du Marsais took the opposite view (as he does in his *Logique*, unpublished at the time when d'Alembert told the story). His interlocutors tried to force him into a corner, arguing that he was weakening the case for the human soul's immateriality. Du Marsais escaped by alleging (as he does in his *Logique*) that, before Descartes, the brutes had always been allowed feeling. But he was disturbed by the encounter and complained of it in a statement which d'Alembert says was found amongst his papers. This incident gives colour to the oft-told story of Boindin's remark to Du Marsais, 'On vous tourmente, vous, parce que vous êtes un athée janséniste; moi, on me laisse en paix, parce que je suis un athée moliniste'.[19] Had Du Marsais's anti-Cartesian sentiment surprised, coming from a 'Jansenist'?

17. In the article on 'Construction' in the *Encyclopédie*, Du Marsais quotes st Augustin's *Confessions* (XI, 3) to the effect that thought is internal and precedes its expression in any given language, but he does not develop this in the direction of dualism; he must be understood as saying that man, had he not lived in society, would not have gone beyond the stage of perception, remembered perceptions, associations and comparisons of perceptions, without ever analysing them to produce successions of signs.

18. *Mémoires sur la vie de Duclos écrits par lui-même* in Lescure's *Bibliothèque des mémoires*, nouvelle série (Paris 1881), xxxvii.29.

19. This is the wording given by La Place in his *Recueil d'épitaphes* (Bruxelles 1782), ii.181. La Place does not give Du Marsais's name, but his identity is not in doubt. The story was current as early as 1764, seeing that Grimm gives a shorter version of it in his *Correspondance littéraire* (1 Oct.; Paris 1829, iv.86): 'Du Marsais est athée janséniste et moi, je suis athée moliniste.'

Is the word 'tourmente' to be understood in this limited sense? At any rate, arguments of this kind were often engaged in at the Procope.

In 1743 there appeared at Amsterdam a collection of essays under the title *Nouvelles Libertés de penser*, reminiscent, doubtless intentionally, of Collins's *Discourse on free-thinking*. It contained a dissertation entitled *Le Philosophe*, which Naigeon attributes to Du Marsais in his *Recueil philosophique* of 1770, and again in his *Philosophie ancienne et moderne*, mentioning that Du Marsais had confided his manuscript to a bookseller named Prigent.[20] Internal evidence confirms Naigeon's attribution. Not only is the theory of knowledge contained in *Le Philosophe* that of Du Marsais, but also the phraseology at one point is that of Du Marsais's *Fragments sur les causes de la parole*, unpublished at the time.

In *Le Philosophe* one reads: 'Que si les hommes ont tant de peine à unir l'idée de la pensée avec l'idée de l'étendue, c'est qu'ils n'ont jamais vu d'étendue penser. Ils sont à cet égard ce qu'un aveugle-né est à l'égard des couleurs, un sourd de naissance à l'égard des sons; ceux-ci ne sauraient unir ces idées avec l'étendue qu'ils tâtent, parce qu'ils n'ont jamais vu cette union' (*Œuvres*, 1797, vi.29). In the *Fragments* is a passage in which the brain is called 'le sens intérieur',[21] and it is declared that we cannot understand the relationship between the brain and mental operations, because this is 'le secret du créateur', with the same reference to the man born blind and the man born deaf:

Comment tout cela se fait-il? C'est le secret du créateur. Nos connaissances ne peuvent aller que jusqu'à un certain point, après lequel il vaut mieux reconnaître simplement les bornes de notre esprit que de nous laisser séduire par de frivoles imaginations. Si la nature a des procédés au-dessus de nos lumières, c'est savoir beaucoup que de reconnaître que nous ne pouvons les pénétrer, et que nous sommes à cet égard ce qu'est un aveugle-né par rapport aux couleurs et un sourd de naissance par rapport aux sons.[22]

The difference between these two texts must be viewed in the light of Du Marsais's hopes of being able to publish the second openly as part

20. Vol.iii, p.202. The Prigent in question is doubtless Jacques-François.

21. The *Fragments sur les causes de la parole* appeared in *Logique et principes de grammaire par M. Du Marsais, ouvrage posthume en partie et en partie extrait de plusieurs traités qui ont déjà paru de cet auteur* (Paris 1769). The expression *sentiment intérieur* appears on p.171 (*Œuvres*, 1797, iii.380). The 'internal sense' (*sensus internus, sensus communis*) was recognised by all except the Cartesians. It combined the impressions of the 'external' senses. Locke made of it a synonym of 'reflection'.

22. *Logique*, 1769, pp.171-72; *Œuvres*, 1797, iii.380.

of an introduction to his linguistic work. He completed the final version of the *Fragments* between 1747 and 1750, and in 1750 sent it, along with his *Logique*, of which the final version is posterior to 1744, to Rochebrune, a magistrate connected with the book-trade, with the request that he should deal with these manuscripts as he thought fit. Rochebrune did nothing, other than ask for certain changes, and neither manuscript was published until 1769.[23]

Du Marsais could not, of course, hope to publish *Le Philosophe* openly, as it stood, in France, although it did actually appear there, in the unprivileged *Encyclopédie* volumes in 1765, with modifications.[24] It cannot have been written with Diderot and d'Alembert in mind, given its date, but it is composed like an encyclopedia article on the word *philosophe*. It consists of an extended definition of the philosopher which fits its author very well. The philosophical cast of mind is rational, not passionate. The philosopher seeks to understand the workings of his own thought and actions. He is socially inclined, and the common good of his fellow-men being his supreme value, he needs no divine sanction for his morality, no god other than human society itself.

After the failure of *Des tropes* in 1730, Du Marsais himself published nothing further of his work, apart from articles which carried his symbol in the *Encyclopédie*. These were articles on language, except the article on 'Education'. Du Marsais had established a private school where he eked out a meagre living, and had come to the notice of d'Alembert. The article on education is full of good sense on the eighteenth-century theme of 'l'esprit et le cœur', and includes a section on child-care which refers specifically to Brouzet's book on the subject. This reference may well have led Rousseau to Brouzet, whom Rousseau certainly drew upon without acknowledgement.

Du Marsais died in 1756, and d'Alembert, who had known him well, wrote his eulogy, making use of the papers which he had left in several cardboard boxes.[25] D'Alembert says that on his death-bed he showed

---

23. *Logique*, 1769, p.ix. The editors say they obtained the manuscripts from Rochebrune. There is a reference in the *Logique* to d'Argens's *Histoire de l'esprit humain* (1769, p.142; *Œuvres*, 1797, v.371). W. Krauss, who noted this reference (p.517 n.) infers from it that the *Logique* was anterior to 1744, but this is doubtless a slip. There is a reference towards the end of the *Fragments* (1769, p.219) to the abbé Girard's *Vrais principes* (1747).

24. They have been studied by H. Dieckmann in *Le Philosophe, text and interpretation*, Washington University Studies (Saint Louis 1948).

25. According to the editors of Du Marsais's *Exposition de la doctrine de l'Eglise gallicane par*

great 'présence d'esprit' and 'tranquillité'. To Voltaire he explained later (15 Jan. 1764, Best.D11644) that after listening to the priest's exhortation, Du Marsais had said, 'Monsieur, je vous remercie; cela est fort bien; il n'y a point là-dedans d'alibiforain'. This is a *mot de caractère*. *Alibiforain* is a debating term, the equivalent of *mauvaise défaite*, red herring, avoidance. So Du Marsais, the teacher of logic, was paying a compliment. A severe interrogator might have insisted, but d'Alembert does not add anything, so we must conclude that Du Marsais's neat and non-committal remark, proof of 'présence d'esprit', ended the exchange.[26]

Du Marsais's systematic thinking needs no metaphysical context of any kind. He is more explicit than Locke himself in refusing to hypostatise (he says 'réaliser')[27] abstract terms. Like Locke, he gives no previous structure to the human understanding before the first impressions.[28] He looks for the simplest operations of the understanding in the perception of things and the perception of such perceptions ('un sentiment de sentiment'), a two-stage operation which he calls 'immediate' and 'mediate' *sentiment* (sensation-impression-perception). Independently of Locke, he allows for the expression of feelings (*passions*) by gestures which are responses to needs.[29] He mentions different temperaments of the brain as corresponding to different degrees of wit, following an age-old tradition, but he takes from Descartes and Malebranche his physiology of the sense-organs, the nerves and impulses to the brain.[30] One may indeed say that he retains of Malebranche's teaching concerning sense-impressions such elements as do not conflict with that of Locke and rejects the rest, notably Malebranche's theory of ideas. He rejects the 'roman' and the 'folles imaginations', and replaces them by what Voltaire called 'l'histoire de l'âme'. However, this 'histoire', in Du

rapport aux prétentions de la cour de Rome (Genève 1757), several 'cartons' of manuscripts were found and were being worked on.

26. Tamisier, who did not know the text of d'Alembert's letter, refused to believe that d'Alembert had told this story. One must infer that he looked upon it as not supporting the thesis that Du Marsais was a believer.

27. *Logique*, 1769, p.38. See below (pp.254-55) for the quotation.

28. He does not, however, look to cerebral structures for any predisposition of the understanding: the understanding begins with the first perceptions. Nor does he use any expression corresponding to *tabula rasa*, presumably because such expressions posit the pre-existence of a something, even though empty or blank. He opens no avenues towards dualism.

29. *Fragments* (in *Logique*, 1769), p.183; *Œuvres*, 1797, iii.385.

30. *Logique*, iii (1769), p.15; *Fragments* (in *Logique*, 1769), p.171; *Œuvres*, 1797, iii.380.

Marsais's case, goes beyond the Lockean meaning Voltaire gave to it, thanks to that 'histoire de l'esprit humain' which his contemporaries were undertaking,[31] and from his own experience as a comparative linguist. Du Marsais is not merely a Lockean. His systematic thinking is independent.

Du Marsais was systematising his thinking on language by 1729 at the latest, and probably by 1723.[32] D'Alembert gives a plan of a general grammar which he dates from 1729 and which resembles the plan which had appeared in the preface of *Des tropes* in 1730. *Des tropes*, the study of modifications of meaning, was to be the final section of the work. By hindsight, one can see that Du Marsais's method for teaching Latin, published in 1723, already presupposes the system. The pupil is to learn by heart as many words as possible before any attempt is made to relate the words to each other. A sentence is a series of inter-related signs. In this respect, Du Marsais recognises Lefebvre of the Oratorian college of Saumur as a predecessor, and this implies a continuation of the Port-Royal tradition, although Du Marsais's most original contribution to grammar was to change the Port-Royal conception of what constitutes a sentence considerably. While using the Port-Royal terms *sujet* and *attribut* (meaning the whole predicate, including the verb), he affirms that some sentences are not 'jugements', but simply 'énonciations'. For the Port-Royal grammarians all positive and negative sentences had been judgements, acts of the mind.[33] The more descriptive role ascribed by Du Marsais to those sentences which he calls 'enunciations' is in keeping with the theory of knowledge outlined in his *Fragments sur les causes de la parole*, and the beginnings of language as described in that work and in the article on 'Construction' contributed to the *Encyclopédie*. These discussions lead on to the study of the successive ordering of signs in the sentence.

These discussions embrace both the individual and the communal aspects of the question. Du Marsais begins with the individual, in the usual eighteenth-century manner, where the theory of knowledge is

31. See J. Dagen, *L'Histoire de l'esprit humain dans la pensée française de Fontenelle à Condorcet* (Paris 1977).

32. There are, in his Latin method of 1723, significant statements to the effect that 'particular' ideas come before 'general' and 'abstract' ideas. Similarly it is stated that the words *partie* and *tout* must be known by experience before the proposition 'le tout est plus grand que la partie' can be formulated or understood (*Œuvres*, 1797, i.185).

33. An interrogation would therefore be a request for a judgement.

concerned, but in dealing with these overlapping texts we shall invert this order with a view to emphasising the originality of his synthesis.

Languages are man's creation. Different peoples, in different parts of the world, have created different forms of language, just as they have adopted different manners, although the basic structure of language is universal, the same theory of knowledge applying universally. Different climates and other factors have had a moulding influence on particular languages, and explain, for instance, why some languages have a richer vocabulary than others.[34] Nature, that is to say men's needs, has provided physical responses to situations, and these have become signs,[35] but language, the *instrument*, as well as the signs of our analysis of sense-impressions,[36] is communal, being handed on from generation to generation.[37] A language analyses the flow of sense-impressions as a communal experience, and as an individual experience for each member of the community. The existing language is already an analysis, but each individual also makes analyses for himself. A child cannot do this at first. A child receives a sweet as an unanalysed experience, not as 'sugar' plus 'sweetness'.[38] We say therefore that our thought is at first undivided, a simple operation of the internal sense. We know no more about the working of the internal sense than a man born blind knows of colour or a man born deaf of sounds. We know that 'en conséquence de notre état naturel et des différentes impressions des objets, nous comparons, nous connaissons, nous jugeons, etc. Ces différentes pensées et ces divers jugements se font en nous par un point de vue de l'esprit'.[39] The expression 'point de vue de l'esprit' is used by Du Marsais in order to introduce the subjective approach. In his *Logique* he suggests that we believe other people perceive on account of the look in their eyes, and that this is true also of the brutes. In the *Fragments*, he places himself at

34. Not only is language 'd'institution humaine' (*Fragments*, (*Logique*, 1769), p.186), but without social relations man would have stayed in a pre-linguistic mental state, limited to impressions of objects and comparisons thereof. Like Fontenelle and Condillac, Du Marsais requires 'le commerce des hommes', for mental development (*Fragments*, 1769, p.185; Condillac, who refers to Fontenelle, *Essai sur l'origine des connaissances humaines*, I, IV, ii, 20).

35. *Fragments* (in *Logique*, 1769), p.171, pp.183-88; *Œuvres*, 1797, iii.380-86. In his *Logique*, he uses the expression 'un sentiment de sentiment' (art. IV, *Œuvres*, v.317).

36. *Fragments* (in *Logique*, 1769), p.183; *Œuvres*, 1797, iii.385; cf. 'Construction', *Œuvres*, 1797, v.5.

37. 'Construction', *Œuvres*, v.6-7.

38. *Fragments* (in *Logique*, 1769), p.181; *Œuvres*, 1797, iii.384-85.

39. *Fragments* (in *Logique*, 1769), p.172; *Œuvres*, 1797, iii.380.

the subjective standpoint, his intention being to follow the development of imaginative consciousness and then verbal consciousness from the first appearance of consciousness. The first mental operation the child performs is to recall a past impression and make a comparison with a present one. We may therefore say that Du Marsais recognises a pre-linguistic mental state which begins to exist when the internal sense first receives impressions from the sense-organs, retains them, recollects them and makes a comparison.[40]

The theory of *liaison des idées* (association), for such this is, was familiar to Malebranche on the one hand (who explains the process physiologically) and to Locke and all the empiricists, on the other. Condillac makes of it his basic principle. But, as the following passage from *Des tropes* of 1730 shows, Du Marsais combined it with a notion which was characteristic of his grammar, namely that of subject and 'attribute', implying a central impression and accompanying circumstances. In *Des tropes*, the expression *liaison des idées* is used and the modified notion is expressed thus: 'Les objets qui font sur nous des impressions sont toujours accompagnés de différentes circonstances qui nous frappent, et par lesquelles nous désignons souvent tous les objets, même qu'elles n'ont fait qu'accompagner ceux dont elles nous réveillent le souvenir.'[41] The separation of the central impression from its qualities and the accompanying circumstances is the second mental operation Du Marsais distinguishes, and it is made by means of language. The first phase of this second operation is naming. Men have named the 'affections intérieures' which are perceptions of things, and 'things' are what they must be in order to produce in us the impressions they do produce.[42]

40. 'D'abord il n'a que le sentiment, et lorsque, dans la suite, il se rappelle ce sentiment par la réflexion, ou qu'il le compare avec quelque autre sensation, tout cela se fait par autant de points de vue de l'esprit qui sont la suite ou le résultat de différentes impressions qu'il a reçues, sans qu'il se fasse encore aucune de ces considérations particulières qui divisent la pensée' (*Fragments*, in *Logique*, 1769, pp.181-82).
41. *Des tropes*, Genette edition (Genève 1967, i.50; see also p.31).
42. 'Il est nécessaire de la part des objets qu'ils soient tels qu'ils doivent être, afin que tel sentiment résulte de telle impression' (*Fragments*, in *Logique*, 1769, p.170); (*Œuvres*, 1797, iii.379); cf. *Logique*, 1769, p.12; 'Construction' (in *Logique*, 1769), p.295. Sahlin (p.168) is tempted to refer to Du Marsais's notion of substantives to Leibniz's theory of individual substances, but adds that there were other sources near at hand. Du Marsais's discussion does actually remain quite close to Locke's, which begins 'All things that exist being particulars' (*Essay*, III, iii, 1; cf. *Fragments*, in *Logique*, 1769, p.172). It is a non-metaphysical conception of things, which does not make of them modes or appearances of some substance other than themselves, but merely what they are, so that our knowledge of them cannot be

By imitation of the naming of particular things, men have also given names to classes of things, and thirdly, also by imitation they have invented abstract nouns such as *idée, concept, jugement, doute, imagination*, which are 'vues de l'esprit', and do not refer to any objects.[43]

This introduction to general grammar is also an introduction to logic, and indeed Du Marsais sent it along with the manuscript of his *Logique* to Rochebrune in 1750. In the *Fragments* he writes concerning what Locke called 'general terms', 'nous avons réduit à des classes particulières certaines sortes de points de vue de l'esprit'. These are the second kind of names mentioned above; and one recognises in the names of these 'classes particulières' those which figure in the major propositions from which logical inference begins in the syllogism.

Du Marsais's *Logique* is a teaching manual. At Marseilles he must have taught Latin in the humanities class, but, in Paris, as a private tutor and then as the keeper of a school, he doubtless took his students through the whole curriculum of the colleges. His *Logique* is in many ways conventional, its innovations being made obliquely. The beginning strikes one as being more than usually metaphysical, seeing that it makes a distinction between angelic intellection and human understanding. However, nothing remotely resembling even such pure intellection as a Cartesian might wish to endow the human mind with is left to the human understanding at the end of this introduction. On the contrary, Du Marsais associates the human understanding very closely with the human body. The names which logic begins from, that is to say those used in the major propositions of syllogisms, are those general names which the *Fragments* describe as being given, by imitation, to groups or classes of perceptions of particular things.

This beginning places Du Marsais, as it had done Locke, in opposition, not only to the Cartesian defenders of innate ideas, but also to the old school of logicians, for whom the definition or predication of general terms such as 'man', in 'man is a rational animal', for instance, expressed the real essence of the subject so defined. Such methods of definition

other than a relationship with them.

43. Du Marsais remains close to Locke, but makes a sharper distinction than does Locke when dealing with 'general terms', which Du Marsais calls 'noms appelatifs' (cf. the article on this word in the *Encyclopédie*), between those which he refers to as 'physical' and those which he refers to as 'metaphysical'. The ones refer to groups of objects; the others (abstractions) have no objects, only uses.

make use of the words *genus* ('animal') and *specific difference* ('rational'), in the Aristotelian tradition of the schools, and were held to contain knowledge not derived from the observation of individuals or particular objects. Many attacks had been made on this claim[44] and, if Du Marsais handles the matter prudently, it is not because his intention is not clear, but because he is covering the ground of logic academically. His examples are traditional, as far as their technical formulation is concerned, but the approach is empirical, as in the following example. I see various beings which enable me to form the general idea 'animal'. The sight of Pierre gives me this idea. So I conclude that Pierre is an animal. Then comes the synthetic formulation: 'Tout être qui a du sentiment et du mouvement est un animal; Pierre a du sentiment et du mouvement: donc, Pierre est un animal.' This is followed by Du Marsais's rule for inference: 'Le sujet de la conclusion est compris dans l'extension[45] de l'idée générale à laquelle on a recours pour tirer la conclusion.'

Much of the work is devoted to examples of correct and incorrect inference, in the traditional manner, but towards the end there is a discussion on method in general which combines elements of the 'new' philosophy of the previous century with empiricism and preference for induction which were gaining ground in the eighteenth. The rationalism of the 'new philosophy' was in keeping with the work of some Oratorians such as Bernard Lamy, and there are still traces of Malebranchist terminology, but Du Marsais makes a very explicit declaration of preference for Locke as far as the theory of ideas is concerned:

L'expérience, c'est-à-dire les impressions extérieures que nous recevons des objets

44. Locke engaged in a controversy with Stillingfleet, bishop of Worcester on this topic (see *Essay*, III, iii, 10 and note). In France, Boulainvilliers (or Boulinviller), a reader of Locke, wrote, about 1700: 'Si la définition donnait véritablement à connaître l'essence des choses, comme les logiciens le prétendent, avec plus de faste que de réalité, sans doute elle perfectionnerait l'intelligence en lui fournissant des connaissances qu'elle n'a pas, mais il est sensible que nos définitions sont pleines de faiblesse et qu'elles n'expliquent rien moins que l'essence des choses' (*Œuvres*, ed. Simon, ii.220). Condillac, in his *Essai* of 1746, reproached Descartes with looking upon definitions as 'principes propres à faire découvrir les propriétés'. In the article on 'Définition' in the *Encyclopédie*, Marmontel continued the attack, but gave some attention to mathematical definitions, with references to Wolff, the disciple of Leibniz. Du Marsais stops at what he calls 'idées exemplaires', of the circle, for instance, formed from the sight of round objects, but made 'exemplaires' by the imposition of the rule that all the radii are equal.

45. *Extension* is used in the sense of *étendue*. B. Russell used it, in English, in his controversy with G. Frege, who questioned it (see A. Schaff, *Introduction à la sémantique*, translated (from Polish) by G. Listowski, Paris 1960, p.24).

par l'usage de la vie, et les réflexions que nous faisons ensuite sur ces impressions, sont les deux seules causes de nos idées; tout autre opinion n'est qu'un roman. Il faut prendre l'homme tel qu'il est, et ne pas faire de suppositions qui ne sont qu'imaginées. La principale cause de ces sortes d'erreurs vient de ce qu'on réalise de simples abstractions, ou des êtres de raison. C'est ainsi que le père Malebranche regarde les idées comme des réalités distinctes et séparées de l'entendement qui les reçoit.

Between 1751 and 1756 appeared the articles on language contributed by Du Marsais to the *Encyclopédie*, including those on the letters of the alphabet, 'Abstraction', 'Appelatif', 'Construction', 'Datif', 'Déclinaison' and 'Diphtongue'. The article on 'Construction', in volume iv (1754) develops Du Marsais's theory of word order, or the successive ordering of signs in discourse. It may well have been drafted several years previously, seeing that a section on the 'proposition' precedes the section on tropes in the plan of 1729-1730, and the article on 'Construction' gives much attention to 'figurative' constructions, the discussion of which might well have led on to the discussion of the figurative use of words.

The basic structure distinguished by Du Marsais is that of 'sujet' and 'attribut'. He uses the Port-Royal terms, but his 'attribut' may be compared with our 'complement', as in 'complement of a noun, or of a verb', except that his 'attribut' includes the verb and refers to all that 'completes' the subject.[46] It includes the whole area of signification as drawn out by analysis from a global impression, and expressed successively as signs. The following passage distinguishes between the 'sujet' and the 'attribut', and also makes a distinction between a 'proposition' and a simple 'énonciation', introducing by this second term his new conception of the sentence:

La proposition a deux parties essentielles: 1° le sujet, 2° l'attribut. Il en est de même de l'énonciation. 1° *Le sujet*: c'est le mot qui marque la personne ou la chose dont on juge, ou qu'on regarde avec telle ou telle qualité ou modification. 2° L'attribut: ce sont les mots qui marquent ce que l'on juge du sujet, ou ce que l'on regarde comme mode du sujet. L'attribut contient essentiellement le verbe, parce que le verbe est dit du sujet, et marque l'action de l'esprit[47] qui considère le sujet comme étant de telle ou telle façon, comme ayant ou faisant telle ou telle chose. Donc voilà une différence essentielle entre les propositions; les unes sont directement

46. There is no grammatical article on 'Complément' in the *Encyclopédie*, a fact which Beauzé, Du Marsais's successor, noted in 'Gouverner'. The term was still very new.

47. This expression recalls the 'actes de l'esprit' which the Port-Royal grammarians and logicians saw in every proposition, but 'considère' refers here to the analysis of a global perception, not to a 'judgement'.

affirmatives ou négatives et énoncent des jugements, les autres n'entrent dans le discours que pour y énoncer certaines vues de l'esprit [perceptions]. Ainsi elle peuvent être appelées simplement *énonciations*.[48]

The novelty of this distinction was not brought out by M. Foucault, in *Les Mots et les choses* (Paris 1966, pp.97), nor by N. Chomsky in *Cartesian linguistics* (New York 1966). Both take a panoramic view of General Grammar and see it as an unbroken tradition from the Port-Royal grammar to the end of the eighteenth century. It has been emphasised, on the other hand, by J. C. Chevalier in his *Naissance de la notion de complément* (Genève 1968).

It is true that in the eighteenth century the distinction between *judgement* and *perception* was not easy to make, seeing that Malebranche, the representative of Cartesianism, accepted, like any empiricist, that the simple juxtaposition of impressions constituted implicit judgements, which he called 'natural judgements'. It was those who preferred a simpler dualism of body and soul who stressed the distinction between sense-impression and judgement.

Rousseau's *Vicaire savoyard* is an interesting example in that he attempts to use the Port-Royal conception of the proposition in order to refute sensationalism. The Port-Royal grammarians and logicians reduced sentences, even those containing finite verbs, to a model containing the copula *est* (*la pomme est verte*, *Pierre est chantant*), claiming them to be judgements, acts of the mind. This *est*, says the Vicaire, but without quoting his source, proves that sensation and judgement are entirely different (*Œuvres complètes*, Paris 1959- , iv.571). Like Rousseau himself, who read them at Les Charmettes, long before he became acquainted with Condillac, the Vicaire owes much to the Port-Royal writers.

Du Marsais's theory has the merit of disentangling the grammatical sentence from the logical proposition. Some sentences are logical propositions; others are not. These are 'enunciations'; their function is to

48. We must infer that in the sentence 'Pierre court', the verb completes the impression I have of Pierre, just as in 'Night falls and all is still', I analyse my impression and enunciate its elements successively. The importance of this way of looking at sentences is evident, in view of the fact that descriptive style developed strongly towards the end of the century and the beginning of the next. The abbé Girard actually used the word *peindre*, speaking of the present participle, in his *Vrais principes* (1747), but Girard usually follows the Port-Royal grammarians, and looks upon words as given to us to express our thoughts which are spiritual (p.5); it is Du Marsais who proved that systematic thinking is applicable to descriptive writing.

represent, as a series of signs, immediate and mediate perceptions, analysed thanks to language.

Using the basic structure of subject and 'attribut', Du Marsais attempts to define a sentence-structure that is 'simple, natural and necessary', and which he distinguishes from a second which he calls 'figurative' (elliptical, for example), and a third which he calls 'usual', as used in polite conversation, and which he looks upon as a mixture of the other two. This third type entails an incursion of descriptive grammar into Du Marsais's theory, and he refers his reader to Vaugelas, Bouhours, and others, without developing the theme extensively. Sahlin justifiably criticises the scheme as incoherent, but it is not negligible. On the fundamental level, Du Marsais's 'natural' construction, derived from the separation and successive ordering of the elements of global impressions, may be admitted to be universal on the ground that the discovery in any language of a subject and predicate structure would be no cause for surprise. On the higher level of linguistic performance which is that of the art of writing, the development of this structure may be recognised as the 'direct order' (subject and complements, verb and complements, with syntactical modifications) which is observed in the vast majority of sentences constructed in French. His figurative construction is to be found in fine writing, and his 'usual' construction in the 'style coupé' prose used by Fontenelle and Voltaire, which is commonly held to be derived from polite conversation.

The art of writing is indeed the branch of linguistics into which Du Marsais's grammar merges imperceptibly. The object of *Des tropes*, the final section in the plan of 1729-1730, is the whole lexis, and not merely the words and expressions used figuratively by orators, for whom the rhetoric course in the schools was originally planned. It is true that *Des tropes* does actually deal in an academic way with all the various types of figures of speech. But, as G. Genette points out, in his reprint of the 1818 edition of the book, the old rhetoric, or art of persuasion, was being replaced by a new rhetoric, which was an art of writing and study of style. Du Marsais was one of the operators of the change. *Des tropes* thus becomes a branch of linguistic study devoted to the figurative use of words.[49] The first part of the book relates this subject to Du Marsais's

49. Du Marsais chose the word *trope* deliberately. It best suits his intention. It was an unusual word and was not accepted by the Academy dictionary until 1740. In the preface he prepared for a possible second edition, he told the story of a 'rich man' who congratulated

theory of knowledge and theory of the simplest use of signs. It rejects the claim made by Rollin, following Quintillian, that figurative language is mainly a device for increasing the vocabulary of a language.[50] It maintains that figurative uses of words are to be explained by reference to 'les mouvements de l'imagination',[51] by which is meant not only the process of association, but also the first operation of analysis described by Du Marsais, which separates a global impression into main and accessory elements. A reference here to 'accompanying circumstances' is a clear indication of this. The use of the name of one thing for the name of another, or the use of the name of an accessory feature for the name of a thing, are not unnatural devices, even when they require a mental operation on the part of the interpreter of the signs (p.31):

Comme l'une de ces idées [impressions] ne saurait être réveillée sans exciter l'autre, il arrive que l'expression figurée est aussi facilement entendue que si l'on se servait du mot propre; elle est même ordinairement plus vive et plus agréable quand elle est employée à propos, parce qu'elle réveille plus d'une image; elle attache ou amorce l'imagination et donne aisément à deviner à l'esprit.

The second part of *Des tropes* deals with metonymy. This word, says Du Marsais, may be used for all tropes, but it is usually reserved for certain kinds. These kinds are listed as follows: the cause for the effect, the effect for the cause, the container for the contents, the contents for the container, the place-name for the product (*une marseille* for *une toile de Marseille*), the symbol for the thing, an abstract noun for a concrete one, the bodily organ for the passion, the householder for the house. Dealing specifically with synecdoche, he lists the container for the contents, the part for the whole, the species for the genus, the plural for the singular, a definite number for an indefinite one. Under the heading *Métalepse*, he mentions what precedes for what follows, and what follows for what precedes. The use of *sort* for *partage* is an example of metalepsis.

Du Marsais does not say explicitly, at this point in *Des tropes*, that all these figures require a mental step corresponding to the analysis which he describes elsewhere, and which, in his theory of knowledge, is the second mental operation, the first being the simple juxtaposition of

him on his book about a people called Tropes (and not 'the tropical regions', as H. Aarsleff says in his *From Locke to Saussure*, Minnesota, London 1982, p.167).

50. He qualifies this later and quotes *rayon (de miel)* used without figurative intent.
51. Genette edition, i.38.

impressions by memory and sense-impression.[52] But the fact that he now devotes a long separate discussion to metaphor is sufficient to establish a specific difference between metaphor and all the other figures listed as metonymy. His first example, 'un lion', for 'un homme en colère', is clearly an example of the juxtaposition of two independent global impressions by the association of ideas; one is not subordinated to the other.[53] The metaphor is an implicit comparison. But he also recognises that a great many words in the ordinary language are used in a manner which was originally metaphorical and is so no longer. It is when a metaphor is used intentionally that the implied comparison ought to be valid. This rule is, on the one hand, strict,[54] but, on the other, by according metaphor the full scope of the comparison, it gives a loose rein to the simple poetic imagination nourished by recollected sense-impressions. Victor Hugo in particular was to expand the scope of metaphor to the extreme limits that resemblance of outline and colour would permit.

The relationship between Du Marsais's theory of 1730 and Hugo's practice bestrides a whole school of adepts of poetic diction usually referred to as the 'descriptive' poets, who made great use of metonymy, and practically none of metaphor. One of the most widely read, the abbé Delille, even defined poetry as 'une métonymie continuelle'. These poets referred constantly to things of the real world, in gardens and elsewhere, but they used imagery to stimulate, not immediate impressions, but very mediate ones. Fontanes mentions hands 'de vin et de meurtre rougies', avoiding 'sang'. To say, as does Le Brun, 'un liège' for 'un volant' (shuttlecock), which is 'ce frêle émule de Dédale', is to appeal to his

52. To say, for instance, as does André Chénier, in *La Jeune Tarentine*, 'un cèdre', for 'un coffre' is to make a mental step and invite the reader to make one corresponding to Du Marsais's second mental operation (analysis into subject plus 'attribute': 'un coffre est fait de bois de cèdre'). The synecdoche replaces 'coffre' by 'cèdre'.

53. 'La métaphore est une figure par laquelle on transporte, pour ainsi dire, la signification propre d'un nom à une autre signification qui ne lui convient qu'en vertu d'une comparaison qui est dans l'esprit. Un mot pris dans un sens métaphorique perd sa signification propre, et en prend une nouvelle qui ne se présente à l'esprit que par la comparaison que l'on fait entre le sens propre de ce mot, et ce qu'on lui compare [...] De plus, il y a une sorte de comparaison ou quelque rapport équivalent entre le mot auquel on donne un sens métaphorique et l'objet à quoi on veut l'appliquer; par exemple, quand on dit d'un homme en colère: "c'est un lion", *lion* est pris alors dans un sens métaphorique; on compare l'homme en colère au lion, et voilà ce qui distingue la métaphore des autres figures' (ch.10).

54. He criticises Malherbe's 'Prends ta foudre, Louis, et va comme un lion', because 'comme Jupiter' is necessary for a coherent image!

reader's knowledge and literary experience. Metonymy used in this way may be referred ultimately to the second mental operation described by Du Marsais, which requires analysis, but certainly not to the first, which requires perception and remembered perception only. The practice of abstruse metonymies dates from antiquity. In any case, the lack of success of Du Marsais's *Des tropes* until the last years of the century would exonerate him from having encouraged the use of such *précieux* literary techniques and such 'Cartesian' over-intellectualisation. On the other hand, the revolt that took place against poetic diction may well have found increased consciousness of itself in the reading of *Des tropes*, by that time a recognised authority, seeing that *Des tropes* gives particular attention to metaphor as a natural means of expression. Metaphor was to become the dominant mode of nineteenth-century poetic imagery. Exactly a century after the publication and failure of *Des tropes*, but thirty years only after its triumph, appeared Victor Hugo's first imaginative poetry, *Les Orientales*, referred to at first as 'poésie matérielle'. Hugo had, before this, been capable of writing, in his *Odes*, such lines as these:

> Leur sacrilège main demandait à l'argile
> L'empreinte de son front glacé.

From *Les Orientales* onwards, his use of immediate imagery (directly rendered sense-impressions and metaphor) came to identify itself with his visual shaping of the world and his verbal fecundity.*

* It is with the greatest regret that the editors have to report Professor Spink's death, in June 1985.

Diderot, the *Encyclopédie* and Islam

AHMAD GUNNY

EUROPEAN knowledge of Islam in the seventeenth and eighteenth centuries owes much to the efforts of travellers, diplomats and Arabic scholars such as Edward Pococke the elder, Antoine Galland, Barthélemy d'Herbelot, Adrian Reland and Simon Ockley. The latter read their texts in Arabic and thus through access to original sources gained a better comprehension of the religion they wrote about. However, the learning of the scholars did not automatically ensure sympathy for Islam. There was, for example, nothing wrong with the scholarship of the Professor of Arabic at Oxford, Jean Gagnier, who edited Abul Fida's *Life of Mohammed* in Arabic with a Latin translation in 1723. What was questionable was Gagnier's attitude. A sounder view of Islam was probably offered by Henri Boulainvilliers despite his loudly proclaimed ignorance of Arabic.[1] Voltaire too knew no Arabic, yet maintained a lively interest in Islam from the 1730s to almost the end of his career, at times appearing fairly balanced.[2]

Diderot, who had little or no knowledge of Middle Eastern languages[3] and whose interest in Islam was over a shorter period than Voltaire's, nevertheless devoted serious attention to it from the late 1750s. The *Encyclopédie* naturally provided him with one of the most important vehicles for the dissemination of information about Islam in the eighteenth century. However, the reader who in trying to discover something about Diderot's own knowledge of his subject has the misfortune to start with the article 'Arabes' of the *Encyclopédie* is in for a shock. For at first sight it would appear that Diderot is utterly confused about the most elementary matters.[4] Three times he takes Islam, which he calls 'Isla-

1. 'Je ne sais point l'Arabe; et par conséquent je suis fort éloigné de pouvoir puiser dans les sources faute d'une telle connaissance', H. de Boulainvilliers, *La Vie de Mahomed* (London 1730), p.7.
2. The best study so far on this subject is by Djavad Hadidi, *Voltaire et l'Islam* (Paris 1974).
3. In 'Diderot savait-il aussi le persan?', *RLC* 32 (1958), pp.94-96, J. Proust suggests that Diderot knew no Persian.
4. In the article 'Sarrasins', in *Œuvres complètes*, ed. H. Dieckmann, J. Proust and J. Varloot (Paris 1975-), viii.272, Diderot at least seems to know the five pillars of Islam, although with

mime', to be a man, misunderstanding a sentence from Jacob Brucker's *Historia critica philosophiae* (1742-1744), his acknowledged source for the articles on Islam in the *Encyclopédie*.[5] Yet, despite his slip, Diderot's grasp was not superficial and one should note carefully his remark to Sophie Volland in his letter of 1 November 1759: 'Je sors des Arabes et des Sarrasins, où j'ai trouvé plus de choses intéressantes que je n'en espérois.'[6]

What can the reader with a theological interest in Islam hope to gain from the articles 'Arabes' and 'Sarrasins' in the *Encyclopédie*? As its subtitle indicates, the first article deals with the question of philosophy among the ancient Arabs. Diderot concedes that before the arrival of Muhammad the Arabs may have been good poets, excellent orators and clever astronomers, but in his opinion this hardly entitles them to be called philosophers. The second article has more to offer from a philosophical and theological point of view. Following Voltaire, Diderot was attracted by the controversy on free will in ninth-century Islam and by the fact that Islam had a great number of religious sects like Christianity. In his opinion, the application of philosophy to Revelation produced among Muslims 'une espèce de théosophisme le plus détestable de tous les systèmes', a number of fanatics, sectarians and impostors (*Œuvres complètes*, viii.248, 249). His account of Muslim sects, based on Brucker, is fairly accurate, though by no means exhaustive. According to him, the Mutazilites insist that God is not the author of evil, the Jabarians believe in rigid determinism while the Najarians stick to a limited determinism in the sense that God does good and bad, but man who has free will appropriates what is convenient. However, he oversimplifies in stating that the Asharians made everything depend on universal harmony.

Worse still, in 'Sarrasins' Diderot propagates Western views of Islam which are still current, namely that fatalism is the prevailing opinion of Muslims who ascribe everything to the power of God and nothing to man's free will (p.252). Later in the article he insists that Muhammad himself preached fatalism, a doctrine responsible for great courage and contempt for death and which teaches that prudence is useless 'devant celui qui a enchaîné les choses de toute éternité, d'un lien que sa volonté

regard to one of them, he simply says: 'Vous prierez', without saying how many times a day.

5. *Œuvres complètes*, v.422, 423, 424. In his notes on 'Arabes' and 'Sarrasins' for the *Œuvres complètes*, Jean-Claude Vadet gives a detailed account of Diderot's borrowing from Brucker.

6. *Correspondance*, ed. G. Roth and J. Varloot (Paris 1955-1970), ii.309.

même ne peut relâcher' (pp.272-73). The fact is that the Koran is firmly set against fatalism, with its excuses for evading duties imposed by divine law. Though the Koran vigorously opposes fatalism, it gives frequent expression to the truly religious sense of dependence on God for the power to act and for protection from evil. Determinism is mostly to be found in the *Traditions* which contain a certain amount of pre-Islamic material.[7]

The problem of free will is, of course, inextricably linked with the question of evil and optimism. There is an echo of the debate on optimism in early Islam in Diderot's letter of 30 October 1759 to Sophie Volland, which, in many ways, represents a first draft of the article 'Sarrasins'. Writing for a closed circle, Diderot tries to find equivalents in European thought for the main parties to the debate in Islam. This leads him to assimilate the latter with the manicheans and the optimists. Thus, in his version of the story of the three brothers,[8] the Asharians, that is, the followers of Al-Ashari (873-935), the Sunnite theologian who believes that God determines everything and that he acts through general laws and does not intervene directly in the way things happen, have become manicheans. The Mutazilites, who believe that God is bound to do what is best for each man, have become the optimists. Needless to say, the Asharians were never manicheans, nor were the Mutazilites simply optimists. According to the former, God is the creator and author of all man's acts. The latter insist on man's free will and rationalism.

In his article 'Sarrasins', Diderot refers to Ashari's new theology which he describes as a 'syncrétisme théosophique' and explains how Ashari had been a Mutazilite. In the first version[9] of the *Encyclopédie* (before the censorship of Le Breton), such as the edition of Douglas Gordon and Norman Torrey provides, Diderot, more in keeping with Islamic tradition, uses the story of the three brothers to justify Ashari's abandonment

7. See W. Montgomery Watt, *Free will and predestination in early Islam* (London 1948).
8. The story is used to refute the Mutazilite belief that Paradise was the reward for obedience and Hell the punishment for disobedience, and that God was bound to give reward and punishment in this way. Of the three brothers, one is good, one wicked and one died as a child. The first is in Paradise, the second in Hell and the third in Limbo. The third complains that by being made to die early, he has not been given the chance to deserve Paradise for obedience. He was told that God made him die young because he foresaw that if he grew up he would be very wicked. Thereupon the second brother asked why he too had not been made to die young before he committed the sins leading to Hell. To this there was no answer.
9. *Œuvres complètes*, viii.236 D.

of the Mutazilites. He now wisely discards the term 'manicheans' and correctly places the debate between Al-Ashari and Al-Jubbai (850-915), the leader of the Mutazilites and former master of Al-Ashari. Diderot's image of Islam appears authentic here and his original version offers the best way of discussing the problem of evil. He admires the subtle way in which Al-Ashari destroys the philosophy of Al-Jubbai, which he finds worth recording. In the end, he argues that one has to agree that the three brothers are an embarrassment to an optimist philosopher or to God. He also adds that Al-Jubbai in exasperation concluded that Ashari had a bit of the devil in him.

The problem of innocent suffering highlighted by the story of the three brothers was an embarrassment not simply to the optimists, but to all types of Muslim thinkers and was deemed to be insoluble as long ago as the twelfth century! It was admirably set out in his *Summa philosophiæ* by Al-Shahrastānī (1086-1153), who is mentioned in 'Sarrasins'. It is a pity that Diderot knows the followers of Shahrastānī (whom he associates with those of Ashari) merely as those who doubt the immortality of the soul. Shahrastānī is often mentioned in Pococke's *Specimen historiæ Arabum* (1650), one of the sources of Brucker. He was an independent thinker who gave a general but not blind allegiance to Asharite philosophy. He wrote in the *Summa*: 'To say that the salutary and the best must be done [by God] would necessitate the death of the infants that God knows will grow into infidels, so that there would not be an infidel in the world; and conversely it would necessitate the preservation of those whom God knows will become believers, so that the world would contain nothing but believers!' What is under attack here is a philosophy requiring a new world order. It is very much like Zadig asking: 'what if there was only good and no evil' and being told by Jesrad that this would be a different world! Al-Shahrastānī failed to justify the ways of God when he admitted that: 'Nothing happens that is not decreed by God. If miseries befall men they are to be judged good, whether they happen spontaneously or by divine compulsion without the assumption of antecedent deserts [...]. God does as He pleases whether the sufferer is innocent or not [...]. The problem of innocent suffering is one that we all desire to have solved [...]. We often see children and lunatics suffering, and to suppose that the principle of retribution applies to them is to make matters worse.'[10]

10. The *Summa philosophiæ* of Al-Shahrastānī, edited with a translation by A. Guillaume (Oxford 1934), p.131.

Unaware of the importance of Shahrastānī's contribution to the debate on free will, Diderot nevertheless had a better grasp of the impact of the philosophy of Al-Ashari among Muslims. In the article 'Sarrasins', he sketches its progress in Asia, Africa and Spain. To Diderot, Al-Ashari is the 'docteur orthodoxe par excellence'; all other theologians are described as 'heresiarchs'. After a period of decline, Asharism became the dominant religion: 'On l'explique dans les écoles, on l'enseigne aux enfants, on l'a mise en vers' (p.237). These verses were apparently learnt by heart by Leo the African, the Arab geographer of the fifteenth and sixteenth century. Diderot claims that Al-Ashari maintained that the existence of God differed from his attributes. In fact what Al-Ashari taught was that the Koran was uncreated and was the very speech of God and that it, like his other attributes, was eternal and, in a way, distinct from his essence.

In the article 'Aschariouns' or 'Aschariens', Diderot had a further opportunity of discussing the theology of Al-Ashari. The text owes a considerable debt to d'Herbelot's article on the same subject in the *Bibliothèque orientale*. To some extent, it may be considered simply as a shortened version of it. The unfortunate result is that the gain in concision is at the expense of clarity. Thus Diderot's quotation from the Koran: 'Dieu vous fera rendre compte de tout ce que vous manifesterez en dehors et de tout ce que vous retiendrez en vous-même'[11] is not as clear as d'Herbelot's: 'et de tout ce que vous tiendrez caché en vous-mêmes'.[12] D'Herbelot and Diderot claimed that Muslims were frightened by this line, and a deputation headed by Abu Bakr and Omar, destined to be the first two Caliphs of Islam, asked the Prophet for an explanation. Diderot makes the Caliphs ask: 'Si Dieu nous demande compte des pensées mêmes, dont nous ne sommes pas maîtres, comment nous sauverons-nous?' (*Œuvres complètes*, v.512). At this point, d'Herbelot adds: 'Tout ce que nous pouvons faire est de ne point mettre en pratique le mal qu'elles nous suggèrent' (*Bibliothèque orientale*, i.259).

If we are to believe Diderot, the Prophet shirked the issue by giving one of those answers which all leaders of religious sects are well provided with. From d'Herbelot's account, on the other hand, we learn that Muhammad gave his followers the example of the Jews who refused to

11. *Sura* ii, l.284 reads: 'Whether you publish what is in your hearts / or hide it, God shall make reckoning with you / for it.'
12. *Bibliothèque orientale* (The Hague 1777), i.258.

follow the lead of Moses in obeying God. Muhammad referred to the punishment of the Jews, and urged Muslims to conform to God's will. Both Diderot and d'Herbelot state that to satisfy people's consciences, Muhammad published another verse. In Diderot's rendering it is: 'Dieu ne charge l'homme que de ce qu'il peut, et ne lui impute que ce qu'il mérite par obéissance ou par rébellion.'[13] D'Herbelot, who understands better than Diderot the Muslim doctrine of 'acquisition', puts it like this: 'Dieu ne charge point l'homme, sinon de ce qu'il peut faire, et ne lui impute que ce qu'il a acquis par son obéissance, ou par sa rebellion.'[14] Diderot stresses the fact that the Asharians are acutely embarrassed by the knowledge that there is nothing in good or evil acts which belongs to man, as everything is determined by God. There is a finer nuance in d'Herbelot as he explains that in Ashari's philosophy man's acts are produced by God, but that man is entirely responsible for the use of them by obeying or not obeying the law.

As Abraham Chaumeix[15] pointed out, Diderot under the guise of attacking the Koran and the Asharians in 'Aschariens' is really attacking Catholic teaching on Providence and predestination. Diderot says all these matters cause controversy and heresies everywhere, and he attributes to d'Herbelot the suggestion that Christians might as well seek to tolerate one another when they differ. This suggestion is certainly not to be found in any edition of d'Herbelot's article. Diderot systematically uses Muslims to attack Catholic thinking in 'Sarrasins'. When he describes the dervish who dances until he reaches a state of death-like trance, he doubts whether anyone would believe that the dervish had been led to this extravagant practice by sublime truths. He also insinuates that the Muslim recluse waiting in the recesses of a cave for a beatific vision is as great a philosopher as he who considers him to be mad and who wanders around proudly believing that 'he sees everything in God'. It

13. Cf. The Koran, *Sura* ii, l.286 which reads: 'God charges no soul save to its capacity; / standing to its account is what it has earned, / and against its account what it has merited.'

14. *Bibliothèque orientale*, i.259. In the doctrine of 'acquisition', God creates a man's act, and the man 'appropriates' it. The term 'appropriation' is used to suggest that there is a sufficient relation between the man and the act for it to be called 'his' act; he is thus responsible for it and may properly be rewarded or punished. Everything else is ascribed to the continuing physical forces which are considered by Muslims as coming from God. The formula is an attempt to maintain divine omnipotence without making man a mere automaton. See W. Montgomery Watt, *What is Islam?* (London 1968), p.159.

15. In *Préjugés légitimes contre l'Encyclopédie et essai de réfutation de ce dictionnaire* (1758-1759), i.79. See also J. Proust, *Diderot et l'Encyclopédie* (Paris 1962), pp.260-61.

would appear that Diderot is hitting at Malebranche to whose teaching he refers in the article 'Malebranchisme' where he writes: 'Selon Malebranche, Dieu est le seul agent; toute action est de lui' (*Œuvres complètes*, viii.17).

Although we still do not know exactly who the philosopher is, we at least know that he is European from Diderot's letter of the 1 November 1759 to Sophie Volland. Diderot laughs at him while pouring scorn at the alleged Muslim veneration for fools who are considered privileged beings 'en qui la nature a opéré la bienheureuse imbécillité que les autres n'acquièrent que par le saint vertige' (*Correspondance*, ii.310). Claiming a pseudo-mathematical accuracy, Diderot uses virtually the same technique in his letter of 30 October 1759 to Sophie Volland. Islam becomes the springboard for the attack on Christianity. Diderot starts by suggesting that the more there are thinkers in Constantinople, the fewer the pilgrimages to Mecca. He then goes on to say that a common annual religious act performed in a capital is the yardstick by which one can judge the progress of incredulity and the decline of national superstition. Thus, if there were thirty thousand pilgrimages to Mecca or thirty thousand acts of communion in a parish in 1700, and if these numbers were reduced to ten thousand respectively in 1750, it is certain that faiths would be weakened by two thirds.

The similarity between Islam and Christianity is established even more clearly in 'Sarrasins'. Diderot further states that 'mahométisme' is divided into more than seventy sects, that opinion is divided particularly on the unity of God and his attributes, his decrees and judgement, his promises and punishments. Hence the various schools of thought in Islam and all those extravagant distinctions 'qui sont nées, qui naissent et qui naîtront dans tous les temps et chez tous les peuples où l'on appliquera les notions de la philosophie aux dogmes de la théologie' (*Œuvres complètes*, viii.234). Diderot insists that the keenness to conciliate Aristotle with Muhammad produced among Muslims the same follies that the same enthusiasm to conciliate Aristotle with Christ had produced among Christians. Although he deplores the existence of so many sects in Islam, Diderot chooses to mention only the four great rites of the Sunni creed, namely the Hanafite, the Malikite, the Shafite and the Hanbalite. He can easily confuse the reader by his linking the unorthodox Mutazilite sect with Muslim orthodoxy. Yet this grouping of sects is understandable in view of Diderot's interest in the Mutazilites. In the article 'Asiatiques', on the other hand, where a problem of space arises since he is dealing with the varied peoples of Asia, he narrows down the division in Islam to the followers of Abu Bakr and those of Ali, that is, the Sunnites and Shiites. Such a division is the one that the eighteenth and subsequent centuries have retained of Islam. Diderot mentions the mutual hatred, but points out that the difference between Sunnis and Shiites lies in ritual and secondary dogmas rather than in essential doctrine (*Œuvres complètes*, v.514).

What did Diderot think of the Prophet of Islam himself? In the article 'Théosophes', he places Muhammad alongside Aeschylus, Shakespeare and Roger Bacon (*Œuvres complètes*, viii.390). This does not necessarily mean that he is well disposed towards him: Diderot's attitude is rather ambivalent. For, as in the case of the above quoted figures, he finds that with Muhammad the demarcation line between genius and madness is very thin. He attributes to some periodic disorder the extraordinary and almost divine intuition that Muhammad is credited with. However, he cannot accept the idea that such insight as possessed by Muhammad is really supernatural.[16] Like others, Muhammad falls into a kind of lethargy, but roused from that state, he imagines that he is animated by a divine spirit. What is interesting in this article is that there is no reference, as in Bayle and many other writers, to Muhammad's so-called epileptic fit, his 'mal caduc'. Diderot's simple explanation is that an extraordinary imagination is at the basis of Muhammad's thoughts and deeds. Although he writes about a group of people, Diderot pinpoints circumstances which traditionally have been associated with Muhammad, for example, the retreat from the company of men. He also argues that times of ignorance and great calamities give rise to such geniuses.

The same ambivalence is to be found in the letters to Sophie Volland and in the article 'Sarrasins'. At times Diderot's hostility to Muhammad is most pronounced. In the letter of 30 October 1759 Muhammad is ironically described as the best friend of women as well as being the greatest enemy of reason. In both texts we are told that the 'holy Prophet' could not read or write and that this fact encouraged the first Muslims to hate all knowledge. It also encouraged their successors' contempt for knowledge and ensured long life to the 'mensonge religieux dont ils sont entêtés' (*Œuvres complètes*, viii.230). Muhammad was apparently so

16. See J. Proust, *Diderot et l'Encyclopédie*, p.271.

convinced by the incompatibility of philosophy and religion that he condemned to death anyone who might engage in the liberal arts. Reflecting a traditional Western view of Muhammad, Diderot depicts him as a skilful opportunist who knew how to exploit the division between peoples. Muhammad was surrounded by idol worshippers, Sabians, Jews and Christians. The latter were divided into monophysites or jacobites and orthodox. However, Diderot tries to be original in the way in which he presents Muhammad's success in making converts. Muhammad brought all these people to a faith which left them one of two choices: beautiful women or extermination! He caused enlightenment to disappear in the din of battle and in the midst of pleasure. Except for the Koran, all books were burnt, either because they were superfluous if they contained only what was in it, or they were pernicious if they contained anything that was omitted from it. The same reasoning led a Muslim general to use the precious manuscripts of the Library at Alexandria as fuel to warm the public baths![17] Moreover, a century after the death of the 'furious impostor', people animated with the same spirit were heard shouting that God would punish the Caliph Al-Mamoun (who reigned from 813 to 833) for having fostered the sciences in his empire at the expense of the 'holy ignorance' of the faithful believers.

There is no doubt that in this section, as in other sections of 'Sarrasins', Diderot is simply vulgarising popular anti-Islamic myths. Nothing in the teachings of Islam militates against learning, science and technology. The Koran contains numerous references to learning, education, observation and the use of reason. The first five verses of *Sura* 96, which Muslims believe was the first to be revealed to the Prophet, include references to God teaching the use of the pen and teaching man what he does not know. Moreover, the fact that Muhammad had little or no culture is put forward by Diderot as an argument to explain the contempt of learning among the first Muslims. There is absolutely no foundation for this suggestion. The opposite view is held by Muslims: Muhammad's lack of learning is considered to be a proof of his divine inspiration.

17. *Œuvres complètes*, viii.231. The legend that the library of Alexandria was destroyed because the Koran made other books superfluous became part of the Western image of Islam. Gibbon was tempted to deny both the fact and the consequences: 'the solitary report of a stranger who wrote at the end of six hundred years on the confines of Media [was] overbalanced by the silence of two annalists of a more early date, both Christians, both natives of Egypt and the most ancient of whom, the patriarch Eutychius, amply described the conquest of Alexandria', *The History of the decline and fall of the Roman Empire*, ch.51.

In his dislike of Muhammad, Diderot is led to castigate the Ummayad dynasty (632-750) which he portrays as the vigorous defender of the law of ignorance and of the 'politique du saint Prophète'. It is entirely to his credit, therefore, that he should give a thorough and painstaking account of the achievements of the Abbasid dynasty (750-1258) in philosophy, science and medicine.[18] This, however, leads him to conclude, as he did in the article 'Arabes', that the Arabs had no philosophical system before Islam. In 'Sarrasins' he adds that that fanatical enemy of reason, Muhammad, 'ajusta comme il put ses sublimes rêveries à quelques lambeaux arrachés des livres des Juifs et des Chrétiens, et mit le couteau sur la gorge de ceux qui balancèrent à regarder ses chapitres comme des ouvrages inspirés'.[19] Diderot even accuses Muhammad of having anthropomorphic notions about God. On the other hand, before talking of Saadi at the end of 'Sarrasins', Diderot does acknowledge Muhammad's success in bringing the idol worshippers to the knowledge of the unity of God and in securing the foundation of moral laws, the distinction of the just from the unjust.

It is obvious that many of Diderot's pronouncements on Islam and its Prophet are lacking in originality: they seem to perpetuate medieval myths. At times, Diderot even appears to contradict himself in 'Sarrasins'. How could Muhammad be preaching anthropomorphism when Islam had for so long been acknowledged as the most disembodied of religions, when the Koran takes so much pain to combat the idea of a Trinity? However, Diderot attempts to modify his stance when he discusses the nature of God in Islam (pp.250-55). He admits that Muslims are neither anthropomorphists nor materialists: he now claims that some Muslim sects – which ones he does not say – by sticking literally to the Koran attribute human characteristics to God. It is in this section of the article, where he is relying on his own resources and not vulgarising myths, that Diderot is true to the spirit of Islam. He may even surprise the reader with his intimate knowledge of the Koran when he says that God

18. Although he used an understatement to begin his account: 'L'aversion pour les sciences et pour les arts se ralentit un peu sous les Abbasides' (viii.231), Diderot struck a better balance than the modern editors of *The Cambridge history of Islam* (1970) who are silent about the achievements of the Abbasid dynasty, the highest point of Islamic civilisation. Edward Said has some harsh things to say about this *History*. See *Orientalism* (London 1978, 1980), pp.302-305.

19. *Œuvres complètes*, viii.248. Diderot is again reflecting a very traditional view of Islam.

is nearer to man than his jugular veins.[20] By recognising the Abbasid achievement, by drawing attention to the part played by Muslim theologians in the debate on free will, Diderot shows why serious eighteenth-century thinkers were interested in Islam. By acknowledging that Muslims have a lofty conception of the nature of God, and approving of Leibniz when he said that Christianity had not risen to anything more sublime, Diderot makes up for the prejudices and the gaps in his knowledge.

20. viii.251; *Sura* 1, l.16. Part of the research for this paper was undertaken with financial support from the British Academy.

Diderot, the *Voyage en Hollande* ... and Diderot

L. L. BONGIE

APART from many of his hastily compiled contributions to the *Encyclopédie*, perhaps no work by Diderot shows the great *philosophe* in a more vulnerable light than the *Voyage en Hollande*. Composed, at least in part, during his two visits to the Low Countries in 1773 and 1774,[1] the *Voyage* first came to light in the *Correspondance littéraire* between September 1780 and April 1782, where it alternated with *La Religieuse*.[2] Long neglected after its first publication by Belin in 1818, Diderot's travel account did not attract much attention until 1947 when Gustave Charlier[3] revealed the extent to which large portions of it were copied, slavishly and without acknowledgement, from the fourth edition of François-Michel Janiçon's *Etat présent de la République des Provinces-Unies et des Païs qui en dépendent*.[4] As Charlier was able to demonstrate, entire sections of such early chapters as 'Le médecin ou du pays' and 'L'homme d'état ou du gouvernement' are lifted holus-bolus from Janiçon and reproduced with only minimal changes as primary text.

Of course, as with similar examples of his plagiarisms in the *Encyclopédie*, it has generally been conceded that Diderot could not have been expected to come up with entirely first-hand data and observations in his

---

1. Time references within the text illustrate some of the difficulties involved in its dating. We read, for example, the following: 'L'année passée [1772] le secrétariat de Rotterdam'. But only a dozen lines further on, in a more historical perspective: 'Cela s'est passé en 1773 au mois d'août'. Later still: 'Mylord Gramby, qui existait encore en 1773' (*Voyage en Hollande et dans les Pays-Bas autrichiens, Œuvres complètes*, ed. Lewinter, Paris 1971, xi.358, 420). Most scholars have thought of the *Voyage* as unfinished. Stating the extreme case, Leon Schwartz recently described it as 'a set of notes for a projected work', adding that 'it is not possible to speculate on what its final form might have been' (*Diderot and the Jews*, London 1981, p.139). See, however, Herbert Dieckmann's discussion of the various manuscripts (*Inventaire du Fonds Vandeul*, Genève 1951, pp.70-71). Deciding which of Diderot's posthumously published works are 'finished' as opposed to 'unfinished' presents a thorny problem. To give us pause in the matter, we have only to recall how Naigeon would have preferred to 'finish' *Jacques le fataliste*!

2. See Jean de Booy, 'Inventaire provisoire des contributions de Diderot à la *Correspondance littéraire*', *Dix-huitième siècle* 1 (1969), p.390.

3. 'Diderot et la Hollande', *Revue de littérature comparée* 21 (1947), pp.190-229.

4. Published in 1755 by Jean Van Duren at The Hague.

technical descriptions of Holland and its institutions. Indeed, Diderot scholars for the most part seem nowadays to take for granted all such 'inadequately assimilated' borrowings, viewing them as rather forgivable venial sins. In the writings of eighteenth-century France's most original author, they remain troubling nevertheless.

Unfortunately, Diderot's borrowings in the *Voyage* were not restricted by any means to the areas of data gathering and technical description. We cannot help feeling some dismay, for example, on discovering that one of his best lines, describing religious toleration in the land of liberty, is copied directly from Janiçon: 'Il se peut que la religion fasse plus de bien dans les autres contrées, mais c'est dans celle-ci qu'elle fait le moins de mal.'[5] Other, similarly 'non-technical' or 'personal' statements in the *Voyage*, relating, for example, to political liberty and individual freedom, display the same apparent lack of originality and candour.[6] Worse still, as Charlier's article proves convincingly, Diderot even copied out so-called *choses vues* – 'personal' observations on Dutch manners and customs – from at least one additional source, the *Lettres hollandoises ou les mœurs, les usages et les coutumes des Hollandois, comparés avec ceux de leurs voisins*, by Aubert de La Chesnaye Des Bois (Amsterdam 1750). Diderot does not hesitate, for instance, to start off a paragraph with the words 'on m'a assuré [...]' and to follow up, not as we are led to expect, with a colourful observation recalled from an after-dinner conversation at prince Galitzin's, but rather with words taken almost verbatim from La Chesnaye's *Lettres hollandoises*.[7] Janiçon notes at one point that the Dutch custom of drinking strong beer contributes to a general state of drunkenness, 'd'autant plus dangereuse, qu'elle dure long-tems, & rend les gens brutaux & meme furieux'. The word-artist of the *Salons* was not at great pains to find his own adjectives when he in turn refers to the drinking habits of *le peuple hollandais* and writes: 'Son ivresse qui dure longtemps [...] le rend brutal et furieux.'[8] Careless errors in the transcrip-

5. Janiçon had himself dutifully acknowledged le Chevalier Temple as his source: the only variants in wording are (Janiçon's): *en d'autres Païs* and *en celui-ci où* ... Although this particular comment was very much *en l'air* at the time, (e.g. Voltaire uses it in a letter to Helvétius, 26 June 1765, Best.D12660) Diderot here clearly borrows it, in context with other passages, from Janiçon.

6. Not all of them specifically dealt with by Charlier; see, for example, Diderot, *Voyage* (ed. Lewinter, xi.377-78) and Janiçon, pp.38-39.

7. See, for example, Lewinter, xi.389 and Charlier, p.210.

8. Janiçon, p.11; Lewinter, xi.344.

tion of borrowed passages are not uncommon: Janiçon states that 'les Diacres sont élus, installez & relevez tous les deux ans, de la même manière que les Anciens' (pp.30-31); this becomes, in Diderot's version: 'Les diacres sont élus, installés et relevés *tous les ans* comme les anciens' (Lewinter, xi.411, my italics). Other such lapses could be added to Charlier's ample list that includes, for example, the howler of misconstruing La Chesnaye's reference to the painter Troost ('le premier peintre en Pastel qu'il y ait peut-être en Europe') as 'Troost, qui inventa le pastel'! The detail, the frequency and the extent of Diderot's borrowings make it clear, moreover, that he is working with his sources open in front of him and is not simply recollecting earlier readings, although such might well be the case in some other passages, as when he describes The Hague as 'peut-être le plus beau village qu'il y ait au monde' – an unconscious echo, possibly, of madame Du Boccage's earlier characterisation of that city as the 'plus beau village de l'Europe'.⁹ But whatever the case may be, Charlier's principal conclusions seem to stand and are difficult to ignore: 'Sur la centaine de pages que comporte le *Voyage de Hollande*, une bonne vingtaine au moins se trouvent empruntées, plus ou moins textuellement, aux deux ouvrages antérieurs de Janiçon et de La Chesnaye des Bois.'¹⁰ Nor can all of these plagiarised pages be entirely explained away by Diderot's own comment to Catherine II at around this time in the fragment 'Sur ma manière de travailler': 'Je ne lis ce que les autres ont pensé sur l'objet dont je m'occupe que quand mon ouvrage est fait. [...] Si je trouve dans les auteurs quelque chose qui me convienne, je m'en sers.'¹¹ As Charlier points out, a fair number of pages from at least the two works cited seem to have 'suited' Diderot rather too well.

9. *Lettres sur l'Angleterre, la Hollande et l'Italie*, in *Recueil des Œuvres de madame Du Boccage* (Lyon 1770), iii.86. R. Murris (*La Hollande et les Hollandais au XVIIe et au XVIIIe siècles, vus par les Français*, Paris 1925, p.47), though he does not mention Mme Du Boccage in this respect, cites an older source for the same cliché, Henri duc de Rohan's *Voyage [...] faict en l'an 1600 en Italie, Allemagne, Pays-Bas uni, Angleterre et Ecosse* (Amsterdam 1646), p.167 – warning enough, no doubt, to all overzealous source hunters!

10. Charlier, p.227. Equally difficult to ignore is the similar misuse Diderot, in the *Pensées détachées sur la peinture, la sculpture, l'architecture et la poésie*, made of Huber's translation (*Réflexions sur la peinture*, Leipzig 1775) of C.L. de Hagedorn's *Betrachtungen über die Malerei*. See Jacques Koscziusko, 'Diderot et Hagedorn', *Revue de littérature comparée* 16 (1936), pp.635-69; Paul Vernière, 'Diderot et C. L. de Hagedorn; une étude d'influence', *Revue de littérature comparée* 30 (1956) pp.239-54; Michael T. Cartwright, *Diderot critique d'art et le problème de l'expression, Diderot studies* 13 (1969), pp.209-18.

11. *Mémoires pour Catherine II* (Lewinter, x.773).

Equally unconvincing is the *encyclopédiste*'s attempt in the same fragment to blame the fickleness of public taste (Lewinter, x.774):

Nous faisons bien plus de cas de la couleur que du dessin. Point de salut pour celui qui ne sait pas écrire. Cet auteur travaille pour le premier écrivain qui saura se parer de ses dépouilles et joindre l'agréable à l'utile. Tout le monde crie au plagiat, mais tout le monde laisse le premier dans la poussière et lit le dernier. Les plumes du paon s'attachent si bien, à la longue, sur les ailes de la corneille, qu'elles lui restent en propre.

Do we hear the authentic voice of *Lui*, the reprobate Jean-François Rameau, in that passage? What *Moi* – or, better still, 'Diderot' himself – might have replied presents an interesting hypothetical question. Would his response have gone somewhat as follows: *Non. Il vaudrait mieux se renfermer dans son grenier, boire de l'eau, manger du pain sec, et se chercher soi-même?*

At the end of his study, Gustave Charlier offers as an explanation for Diderot's little sins the suggestion that bad habits acquired during the early days of the *Encyclopédie* carried over into his later work – a tendency that was aggravated too by the inevitable drying up of the philosopher's verve and inspiration as he approached his final years. One has only to look at Diderot's other productions during this same period, however, including the *Réfutation* of *De l'homme*, the *Commentaire* on Hemsterhuis's *Lettre sur l'homme et ses rapports*, the *Paradoxe sur le comédien*, the *Entretien d'un philosophe avec Mme la maréchale de ***, the *Principes de la politique des souverains*, at least some portions of the *Neveu de Rameau* – not to mention the various works for Catherine II – to find the last half of Charlier's explanation wanting. Moreover, if his powers were waning during this period, Diderot himself seems not to have noticed the fact and there is no hint of such fears, for example, in the letter he wrote to his wife and daughter from St Petersburg on 30 December 1773: 'Laissez-moi aller, et ne craignez pas qu'à mon retour, il ne me reste plus rien à dire. Je travaille prodigieusement, et avec une facilité qui m'étonne' (Lewinter, x.1119). Others, including Catherine II, agreed: 'Je trouve à Diderot une imagination intarissable; et le range parmi les hommes les plus extraordinaires qui aient existé.'[12]

Even so, it could perhaps be argued that the *Voyage*, as it has come down to us, was mainly researched and composed, not during this

12. To Voltaire, 'Le 7/18 janvier 1774', Lewinter, x.1123.

specifically productive period, but five or six years later, during Diderot's more obviously failing years and around the time the work appeared in the *Correspondance littéraire*. But that suggestion is also not without certain difficulties since, apart from the explicit time references within the text, it is clear from Diderot's correspondence that he was actively working on the *Voyage* before he left for Russia, near the end of August 1773: 'Je n'ai pas tout à fait perdu mon temps dans ce pays-ci,' he informed Mme d'Epinay several days before his departure; 'J'ai des notes assez intéressantes sur les habitants.' He then cites other current projects, presumably of equivalent scope or significance: 'J'ai barbouillé toutes les marges du dernier ouvrage d'Helvétius. Un certain pamphlet sur l'art de l'acteur est presque devenu un ouvrage. Je me suis amusé à écrire une petite satire dont j'avais le projet lorsque je quittai Paris.'[13] There are also numerous passages in the correspondence that closely parallel what he wrote in the *Voyage*,[14] and some evidence exists to suggest that Diderot began his research preparations and note-taking for the Dutch trip at least three years before the actual visit took place. In 1770 he assured the abbé Coyer that he would visit Holland 'après que j'aurai lû'.[15] References to Holland and the precise level of the sea held back by the dykes can also be found in the *Pensées détachées ou Fragments politiques échappés du portefeuille d'un philosophe* which circulated in the *Correspondance littéraire* in 1772.[16] It thus seems unlikely that a convincing plea in extenuation of Diderot's wholesale borrowings in the *Voyage* could be made on the grounds that he was both mentally drained at the time and hard pressed to meet a September 1780 deadline for the *Correspondance littéraire*.

Would an attempt to throw light on the question by pointing to Diderot's distaste for travel and his deep distrust of the travelogue genre seem equally unconvincing? It will be recalled that the celebrated *encyclopédiste* finally managed to make up his mind on the Russian trip

13. The Hague, 18 August 1773, Lewinter, x.1068-69.
14. See, for example, Diderot's comments on the two Bentincks in his letter of 22 July 1773 to Mme d'Epinay (Lewinter, x.1061 and xi.356) and on the absence of primogeniture to Mme Necker, 6 September 1774 (Lewinter, xi.1044 and 385-86).
15. See letter from R.-M. Van Goens to Pierre-Jean Grosley, 20 February 1772, quoted by Henri L. Brugmans 'Autour de Diderot en Hollande', *Diderot studies* 3 (Geneva 1961), pp.59-60. Coyer had visited Holland the year before, in 1769, but published his account six years later (*Voyages d'Italie et de Hollande*, Paris 1775).
16. Lewinter, x.72; cf. *Voyage*, Lewinter, xi.337.

and the stopover in Holland only after long hesitation. Perhaps without
the loneliness that followed Angélique's marriage and her departure from
the parental nest (where Mme Diderot's chronic bad temper was now
all too evident) the trip might not have taken place at all. 'Partons,
partons vite, mon ami', he wrote to Grimm: 'La vie me pèse.'[17] As for
travel accounts themselves, they represented in the main a fashionable
variety of scribbling regularly sniffed at in his own literary circle. The
seductive dangers of the genre were all too familiar. Not long after
reaching The Hague, Diderot wrote to Mme d'Epinay, promising to
avoid such temptations: 'Vous me défendez de vous parler de ce pays;
je m'en garderai bien; je sais à présent à peu près la confiance qu'il faut
avoir dans les récits de voyageurs. Combien je dirais aussi de sottises,
si je voulais!'[18] To Mme Necker, more than a year later, he expressed
similar sentiments:

J'ai fait bien du chemin, j'ai vu beaucoup de villes; voilà ce que j'ai de commun avec
Ulysse et tous les courriers. Pour les mœurs des hommes, c'est une étude dont je
n'ai pas tardé de me dégoûter. Il faut un long séjour pour connaître avec un peu
d'exactitude les phénomènes les plus communs; et le voyageur qui, à chaque tour
de roue, jette une note sur ses tablettes, ne se doute pas qu'il écrit un mensonge;
c'est pourtant ce qu'il fait.[19]

If Diderot's mistrust of the *récit de voyage* cannot in itself explain the
mixed performance he gives in the *Voyage en Hollande*, it does at least
help to clarify his reasons for drawing up a rather solemn introduction
to the work which he entitled 'Préliminaire: Des moyens de voyager
utilement'. Here are stated the basic qualifications (mature judgement,
wide knowledge) that are indispensable to the traveller. Above all, much
research must be carried out in advance: 'Ayez lu tout ce qu'on aura
publié d'intéressant sur le peuple que vous visiterez. Plus vous saurez,
plus vous aurez à vérifier, plus vos résultats seront justes' (Lewinter,
xi.332). Once arrived, it is equally important for the traveller to consult
with the best experts on the spot: 'Vous abrégerez votre séjour et vous
vous épargnerez bien des erreurs, si vous consultez l'homme instruit et

17. Paris, 9 December 1772, Lewinter, x.995; also, his letter to Grimm, 7 October 1772,
p.970.
18. The Hague, 22 July 1773, Lewinter x.1059-60.
19. The Hague, 6 September 1774, Lewinter, xi.1043-44. See also Diderot's scathing
comments on prince Orlof, written probably a year later: 'Il a vu Rome en cinq jours; il aura
vu Paris en quinze; et il en parlera, comme s'il y avait passé toute sa vie. Il y a des hommes
bien heureusement nés' (Lewinter xi.1110-11).

expérimenté du pays sur la chose que vous désirez savoir. L'entretien avec des hommes choisis dans les diverses conditions vous instruira plus en deux matinées que vous ne recueilleriez de dix ans d'observations et de séjour.' Other rules follow: the traveller is warned to observe carefully, to refrain from making hasty judgements, and to avoid mistaking particular cases for the general rule ...

Sensible as it was, it would not be difficult to show, using almost any page from the *Voyage* as evidence, how Diderot failed in nearly every respect to live up to his own sage advice. Much of what he found in Janiçon, for instance, could have been usefully supplemented by direct inquiries among such specified local experts as his *médecin*, his *homme d'Etat* or his *magistrat*. But Diderot almost entirely ignored his own precepts: 'Sortez de la capitale [...]', he had warned; 'parcourez les campagnes'; 'écoutez beaucoup et parlez peu'; 'et surtout, méfiez-vous de votre imagination [...]. L'imagination dénature, soit qu'elle embellisse, soit qu'elle enlaidisse' (Lewinter, xi.332-34). One can scarcely imagine, I think, a set of recipes less suited to the genius of Diderot!

Which brings us finally to our main point.

There is little doubt that a good travel account in Diderot's eyes, or rather in the view of the Diderot who wrote the 'Préliminaire', would end up as a kind of regional *Encyclopédie*: 'Je voudrais au voyageur une bonne teinture de mathématiques, des éléments de calcul, de géométrie, de mécanique, d'hydraulique, de physique expérimentale, d'histoire naturelle, de chimie, du dessin, de la géographie, et même un peu d'astronomie' (Lewinter, xi.331-32). Who, theoretically, was better suited to such a task than the man who had devoted so many thankless years to being a professional encyclopedist? Moreover, no country more than Holland symbolised so well the major aspirations of the *Encyclopédie*. Holland was a prosperous, democratic nation, a land of liberty, religious toleration and a free press; it was a modern state where commerce, the sciences and the mechanical arts flourished as nowhere else; where there was little poverty and therefore little crime – 'Le pays encyclopédique par excellence', as Roger Lewinter has described it in his introduction to Diderot's work (xi.328). But it can be argued, I think, that the essential Diderot – Diderot the *creator* as opposed to the *compiler* – was as much *dégoûté* with such *encyclopédisme* for most of his life as he was with the inevitable superficialities of travel and travel literature. His tastes, his truths and his particular genius (though he would perhaps never have admitted it, and as a blunt assertion it may sound too much like facile heresy even today) lay elsewhere than in the spirit of this land where there was so much neatness and so little nature, where avaricious, ignorant and loutish booksellers, sitting in their *boutiques* that resembled 'des nids à rats' (Lewinter, xi.1038), published anything, but regularly refused to pay their authors. It was a country where there was no religious persecution but where philosophy was seen as the enemy and where 'la liberté de penser en matière de religion' was opposed: 'Le matérialiste y est en horreur, mais y vit en paix' (*Voyage*, Lewinter, xi.403). What a paradox it was too that the distribution of *livres impies* was more difficult in Holland than in France 'et les incrédules plus rares et plus haïs' (p.403)! While it was true that the spirit of democracy prevailed there, that spirit had probably degraded the theatre: 'Les pièces faites pour le peuple, qu'il faut amuser, sont ordurières. Attendez-vous à ce vice dans toutes les démocraties; vous y trouverez Aristophane avec sa grossièreté, mais sans son génie' (p.404). The spirit of commerce, on the other hand, had trivialised painting: 'On connaît suffisamment les grands maîtres de l'école hollandaise. Ne serait-ce pas l'esprit de commerce qui a rétréci la tête de ces hommes merveilleux? Quelque habiles qu'aient été les peintres hollandais, ils se sont rarement élevés à la pureté du goût et à la grandeur des idées et du caractère' (p.405). Sculpture had fared no better, simply because good taste and *magots* are incongruent. Great painters were no more, 'parce que la peinture n'y est ni protégée ni cultivée, et que les beaux-arts qui mènent si rarement à la fortune n'y sont pas considérés' (p.405). We can almost hear ambivalent echoes of Voltaire's praise for the triumphs of Louis XIV's *grand siècle*, its aristocratic, militaristic and intolerant glories notwithstanding!

But even if Holland was a country, as it has been suggested, more after his head than his heart, Diderot did nevertheless set out to compose his *Voyage* conscientiously in the spirit of the *Encyclopédie*. And so we find the author of *Le Neveu* dutifully cribbing long passages from Janiçon, following on with page after arid page detailing the price of fish and cabbages, of chicken (both *gras* and *maigre*), of coffee, tea, flour, soap, tobacco, wool, wine, straw and a hundred other items. He outlines the various costs in a private householder's budget: it amounts to so much per month; it is distributed thus and so: butter, 15 florins; spices, 6 florins; soap, 2 florins; and so on. A comment follows which today we are perhaps allowed to decode as more wistful than defensively scolding or didactic: 'Il ne manque à ce minutieux détail que d'avoir été fait à Rome il y a deux mille ans pour être lu avec intérêt' (Lewinter, xi.396). We sense, nevertheless, that the price of cabbage, even in Seneca's day, does not weigh heavily in Diderot's ultimate scheme of things, any more perhaps than much of the *Encyclopédie*, or all the busy questions and observations generated by the Dutch trip and the Russian trip, so representative of the utilitarian spirit of the times. That spirit had provided the editor of the *Encyclopédie* with an almost regular income for years, and had given him as well a civic-minded sense of worth and usefulness: 'Je vais questionnant tant que je peux', he told Catherine II; 'Je voudrais bien être utile.'[20]

In fact, as travel literature, as a trustworthy source of technical or encyclopedic data, some of Diderot's *Voyage* is not really very useful at all and some of it is not very interesting either. We gain the impression that his research efforts are not so much incomplete as they are terminally slap-dash and offhand – hurriedly scribbled notes that the author himself deemed unworthy of verification and review. There is, of course, a good deal that is authentically alive and personal in the *Voyage en Hollande*, but we do not find it on this purely informational level, even though Diderot does count and measure and does try to be precise. Curiously enough, we find him even more convincing, more interesting, when his measurements come out rather approximately, as when he reports his tour of a 90-cannon Dutch warship: 'Quelle machine!' he exclaims. 'Je l'ai mesuré: il m'a paru avoir de longueur soixante de mes pas sur vingt-cinq de largeur, un peu plus ou un peu moins' (Lewinter, xi.369). On another occasion, he comes across some of his own contradictory data: 'Je lis ici sur mes notes que les honnêtes femmes sont malheureuses et qu'elles sont durement et grossièrement traitées par des maris sordides qui regardent à tout. Il me semble avoir dit le contraire ailleurs. Ai-je pris un fait particulier pour les mœurs générales, ou ai-je jugé des mœurs générales par quelques faits particuliers? Je l'ignore' (p.389). Here Diderot's puzzlement is extremely puzzling indeed! The vaguely recalled contradiction is only two pages back where he affirms quite the opposite: 'Elles aiment leurs maris brutaux, en sont aimées, les dominent dans le domestique et règnent chez elles' (p.387). Confronted in the same paragraph by a note stating that Dutch fathers are 'idolâtres de leurs

---

20. *Mémoires pour Catherine II*, Lewinter, x.781.

enfants ingrats', no matter how basely they are treated by their offspring, he asks the question: 'Cela est-il vrai? cela est-il faux? Je n'en sais rien [...].' Sometimes Diderot simply forgets, as when he singles out for mention Holland's three most distinguished contemporary scholars: Allamand ('son physicien'), Runkenius ('excellent littérateur'), and, finally, 'un célèbre professeur en droit public dont le nom ne me revient pas' (p.403). As for his own advice to the traveller to leave the capital and visit the cities and the country, Diderot seems to have forgotten it, for the most part. Under the heading *Delft*, he writes only two lines: 'Je ne dirai rien de Delft, sinon que Delft est la sépulture des princes d'Orange' (p.432). Rotterdam fares scarcely better, though it is granted a total of ten lines, the first two of which merely state that it is 'une grande et belle ville sur laquelle il y aurait beaucoup à dire' (p.436).

For a model encyclopedic traveller, Diderot indulges in rather frequent hit-or-miss generalisations. We learn, for example, that from time immemorial, no fisherman from Scheveling has put to sea without taking along a pitcher of oil to calm the ocean in case of storms, although use of this procedure increases the danger to other vessels in the vicinity. A detail is then added for the scientific minded ('L'huile animale a moins d'efficacité que l'huile végétale') and Hemsterhuis's wave-action experiment using beer and mercury instead of water is recounted.[21] As it turned out, Hemsterhuis, given a copy of the *Correspondance littéraire* by prince Galitzin in 1784, was dismayed to read Diderot's report concerning his supposedly scientific conclusions. Diderot had got it all wrong, he informed princess Galitzin, and had attributed to him 'une sottise physique qui prouve bien que la Géométrie et Notre Cher Diderot n'avaient rien de commun ensemble'.[22] In the same letter, Hemsterhuis also points

21. See Lewinter, xi.421 and 427, note 1 (which indicates the different location of the Hemsterhuis passage in a revised BN manuscript (n.a.fr.13759).

22. Hemsterhuis to princess Galitzin, published by Henri L. Brugmans, 'Diderot, le *Voyage de Hollande*', in *Connaissance de l'étranger, Mélanges offerts à la mémoire de Jean-Marie Carré* (Paris 1964), p.152.

In this important and well-documented study, Brugmans makes a 'best-case' attempt to rehabilitate the *Voyage* and defend it from some of Gustave Charlier's charges: 'On ne pourra mesurer l'étendue des emprunts faits par Diderot tant qu'une étude exhaustive de toutes les sources possibles n'aura pas été faite. Diderot, apparemment, a fait siennes les idées de Janiçon et de La Chesnaye-Desbois, comme il a adopté celles de Hagedorn dans ses *Pensées détachées*. Mais tout n'est pas emprunt dans le *Voyage de Hollande*. Il serait aisé d'y relever de nombreux passages dont la substance aussi bien que la forme sont indubitablement de lui et qui témoignent d'une observation personnelle' (p.152). With that conclusion, no one could

to another of Diderot's disturbingly uncritical observations, in which the philosopher affirms that in Harlem, for some time after a child is born, 'aucun Bailiff ou Fiscal aurait le courage d'intenter un procès quelconque contre quelqu'un qui appartiendrait à cette maison, qui vient de donner un citoyen à l'Etat'.[23] Hemsterhuis concluded with a general criticism – probably the earliest recorded concerning Diderot's *Voyage*: 'Enfin j'ai été affligé de voir du nyctologue dans un homme comme lui! Je crois que ce sont toutes des lettres à M. Grimm. [...] Ce que je souhaite c'est que ce ne soit jamais publié' (Brugmans, p.152).

It is not difficult to find other evidence of 'nyctology' at work in Diderot's *Voyage*. Patently suspect assertions abound: 'L'enfant qui frappe son père est puni, mais celui qui frappe sa mère est puni de mort' (Lewinter, xi.374). 'Les juifs rasés sont riches et passent pour d'honnêtes gens; il faut se tenir sur ses gardes avec les barbus, qui ne sont pas infiniment scrupuleux' (p.407). 'Les habitants de Scheveling ne se marient guère qu'il n'y ait un enfant de fait' (p.427). Routinely anti-semitic (along with most of his Enlightenment contemporaries), Diderot seems to go even further than the usual clichés when it comes to describing the physical charms of Dutch women: 'Les visages souvent laids des femmes n'inspirent guère le désir de vérifier la réputation des gorges et de connaître les autres appas' (p.345). A second note on the subject is more nuanced: 'Elles sont belles, si l'on peut l'être avec des gorges et des fesses énormes. Elles ont beaucoup d'embonpoint, de vilaines dents et des chairs molles: telles on les voit dans les tableaux de Rubens, telles elles sont dans les maisons' (pp.386-87). And two pages further on, another famous painter is cited: 'Les kermesses sont telles aujourd'hui qu'on les voit dans les tableaux de Teniers. Je jure sur mon âme de n'y avoir pas vu une femme qui ne fût à peu près hideuse. Le peintre a fait choix des plus belles ou des moins laides; qu'on juge des autres' (p.389).

disagree. Less convincingly, perhaps, Brugmans also makes the claim that Diderot for the most part respected his own formal precepts as set out in the 'Préliminaire': 'Il semble bien que, dans l'ensemble, Diderot se soit conformé à ces principes. La dernière partie du *Voyage* surtout ne laisse aucun doute à ce sujet' (p.154). His final assessment, gamely setting out Diderot's work in the best possible light, nevertheless remains inconclusive and is stated in the form of a rhetorical question: 'Ne pouvons-nous pas conclure que le *Voyage de Hollande* est, en partie du moins, un texte entièrement original? Il présente en tout cas un intérêt certain en ce qui concerne Diderot, sa philosophie, le mouvement des idées, et les relations entre deux pays' (p.163).

23. Cited in Brugmans, p.152. For Diderot's more felicitous version, see Lewinter, xi.428.

The situation, we see, was grim. We wonder that in another of his overstated observations Diderot did not attempt to establish a relationship of cause and effect: 'Quelquefois la pédérastie se décèle ici avec une fureur inconcevable. Alors la police s'empare du pédéraste notoire pendant la nuit et le jette dans les canaux' (p.346).

We may well ask who the particular experts were that Diderot consulted – following on his own precepts – in such matters! But the plain fact is that the author of *Le Neveu* and *Jacques* had no need of experts to help him caricature, dramatise and magically transform (often quite beyond recognition) the tiny fragments of everyday reality that fed his imagination. A casual word, a fleeting image, was usually enough to set it aflame. The end result is almost never reliable technical information, accurate history, biography or sociology but, rather, something aesthetically and morally much more powerful: reality invented, larger than life – in a word, true fiction.[24] Unfair as it may seem, those literary trifles, turned out by Diderot in a matter of days or weeks, today far outweigh the crumbling monument produced after so many years of drudgery in the vineyards of Briasson, David, Le Breton and Durand – with or without the *approbation et privilège du Roy*!

But to return now to Diderot and Holland, it is true that he did speak to a few 'experts', especially at the beginning of his stay – men like Allamand and Hemsterhuis, Dr Robert, Van Goens and 'le bon et célèbre Camper' (Lewinter, xi.424). His host, prince Galitzin, was even convinced for a time that Diderot delighted in such encounters and he informed Mme Geoffrin that the *encyclopédiste* loved 'tous ces docteurs hollandais à la folie'. There was even talk of his not continuing on to Russia but of spending the rest of his days instead in the land of liberty,[25] and it was felt too that he would probably make short work of electrifying all those sluggish 'tortues hollandaises'![26]

Diderot soon tired, however, of such time-consuming excursions, preferring, I think, to explore, in the quiet of his study, the labyrinth of his own 'monstrous' imagination (as it was soon to be labelled by his friend Hemsterhuis) (see Brugmans p.157). After a trip to Leyden, he wrote to Sophie and her sister on the subject: 'J'ai vu des tableaux, des

24. For a detailed defence of this general view, see my *Diderot's femme savante*, Studies on Voltaire 166 (Oxford 1977).

25. Mme d'Epinay to the abbé Galiani, Paris, 26 June 1773, Lewinter x.1050.

26. Abbé Galiani to Mme d'Epinay, Naples, 17 July 1773, Lewinter, x.1056.

estampes, des princes et des savants. Nous avons des projets de toute couleur. Si nous les remplissons, je verrai beaucoup, je ne manquerai pas d'amusement. Je résiderai peu et je ne travaillerai guère. *Je voudrais pourtant bien travailler.*'[27] Other references in the correspondence attest to his need to be away from the crowd and to have time to work. Life at Galitzin's was *tranquille, sobre et très retirée*: 'C'est ici qu'on emploie bien son temps. Point d'importuns qui viennent vous prendre toutes vos matinées.' Scarcely a month after his arrival, Diderot was able to report that he had already completed *deux ou trois petits ouvrages assez gais*: 'Je ne sors guère; et quand je sors, je vais toujours sur le bord de la mer. […] C'est là que je rêve bien.'[28] The sea, which Diderot came to know for the first time during this trip in 1773, now held a special fascination for him; its alien vastness had taken on a portentous meaning, just as it would for his young Mexican in the *Entretien d'un philosophe avec Mme la maréchale de* *** which he was busy writing at the time. What hidden mysteries lay beyond? 'Hélas! c'est bien là notre image: nous sommes chacun sur notre planche, le vent souffle, et le flot nous emporte.'[29] There are indeed many signs of such authentically personal literary activity simmering in the background of the *Voyage* – from word paintings of the fishermen of Scheveling returning to their terrified wives on shore, to unforgettable anecdotes and quick sketches (for example, the eternally pipe-smoking Dutchman: 'On le prendra pour un alambic vivant qui se distille lui-même' (p.345); they help us to forget the plagiarisms, the tedious lists, the inaccuracies, omissions, incoherencies and sheer unadulterated flimflam of the work. Clearly, other travellers were temperamentally (and even intellectually) more suited to following the ponderous directives that preface the *Voyage en Hollande*. One thinks, for example, of the astronomer Joseph-Jérôme de Lalande, cataloguer of 50,000 stars, measurer, bibliographer, list-maker and encyclopedist *par excellence* (*d'Yverdon, Supplément, Méthodique*) who visited Diderot at The Hague during the last week of May 1774. A seasoned tourist and much given to jotting down precise notes with almost every turn of the coach's wheels,[30]

27. My italics; The Hague, 18 June 1773, Lewinter, x.1047.
28. To Sophie Volland, The Hague, 22 July 1773, Lewinter, x.1058-59.
29. *Entretien*, Lewinter, xi.142.
30. See my 'J.-J. Lalande, standard clichés and the private man', forthcoming in *Studies on Voltaire*. I am currently preparing an edition of Lalande's unpublished 'Voyage de Hollande, 1774' (Ms 2195, Bibliothèque de l'Institut de France).

Lalande routinely sought out every occasion to do what Diderot seemed determined to avoid: the neglected *tableaux, estampes, princes* and *savants* of the one became the everyday stock-in-trade of the other. The astronomer, who not many years before had urged pope Clement XIII to remove the names of Copernicus and Galileo from the *Index*, was in Holland on a triumphant scientific mission. Local gazettes announced his comings and goings with flattering regularity, learned academies held special sessions in his honour, great windmills were started up to satisfy his scientific curiosity and everyone, from the Stadtholder on down, seemed anxious to meet with France's leading Freemason and noisiest stargazer whose idle speculations on comets colliding with the earth had, only the year before, caused widespread panic and what he himself proudly described as a 'fermentation prodigieuse' in Amsterdam, where at least one baker had given away his bread in anticipation of the end of the world.[31]

Information gathering was the essential purpose of Lalande's tour. During his ten-week stay, he visited and spoke with perhaps two hundred 'experts' – distinguished academics, scientists, diplomats, administrators, journalists, leading French exiles and publishers. He saw – I think without exception – every one of Diderot's friends and certainly all of his enemies, men like the ex-Jesuit chargé d'affaires, the abbé Desnoyers, who kept a close watch for the French Ministry on the Dutch 'clandestine' press as well as on the activities of one Denis Diderot, lately returned from Russia.[32] What is more, with every such encounter, Lalande gathered a note for his journal, sometimes maddeningly brief: the celebrated publisher M.-M. Rey has five children; one son lives in America and is 'deranged'; a daughter is married to Rey's business associate, the Bouillon publisher Veissenbruch. *Lalande visits her too*! She, it seems, misses her father terribly but she hates her mother. She has a charming two-year-old son whom she breast-fed. Thomas Hope, whose fine Rembrandts Diderot had admired, had made and lost a fortune three times over. He had had a choice of receiving either 150,000 florins or his magnificent art collection and, happily, had chosen the latter. The young genius Van

31. Lalande, 'Voyage', f.184. Contemporary references to such public alarm are frequent: see, for example, Condorcet to Voltaire, 16 May, and Voltaire to Sir William Hamilton, 17 June 1773 (Best.D18372 and D18429).

32. See Jacques Donvez, 'Diderot, Aiguillon et Vergennes', *Revue des sciences humaines* no. 87 (1957), p.291.

Goens has a huge library but he also has debts (as has Diderot's host, prince Galitzin) and his 19,000 volumes belong to Dufour of Maastricht and other booksellers. Hemsterhuis has a 12-foot telescope. Allemand, who earns the equivalent of 6000 livres annually, has a remarkable natural history collection that contains, along with an elastic rubber boot, a whale's penis 8 feet long and a spider 8 inches wide.

Clearly, many of Lalande's Dutch contacts were Masonic in origin and probably arranged well before his departure from Paris. Distinguished brother Masons, including nearly all of Diderot's Dutch acquaintances, wined and dined the astronomer, took him for festive excursions on their yachts and even to naughty all-night *musicos* where Diderot's own sense of the fitness of things had forbidden him to go. In the end, however, nothing of great significance was harvested from so much social activity – no *Entretien d'un philosophe avec la maréchale*, no fragments of *Le Neveu*, nor even a *Principes de la politique des souverains*. We recall the Neveu's despairing comment: 'Et vous croyez que cela dit, redit et entendu tous les jours, échauffe et conduit aux grandes choses?' We now know how right Diderot was to reserve something of his essential self for his *petits ouvrages assez gais*. Lalande's voyage of 1774 gave birth to only a 199-page notebook, crammed with thousands of bits of miscellaneous and entirely unprocessed (but no doubt precise and reliable) data, based for the most part on direct observation. While Diderot, borrowing verbatim from Janiçon, states, for example, that the salaries of Dutch pastors in the larger cities is 2000 florins (Janiçon, pp.26-27; Lewinter, xi.408), Lalande (who has also read Janiçon but regularly verifies all statistics) notes that the ministers of Rotterdam earn 1700 florins and those at The Hague are paid 100 more. He tells us also that there are two Roman churches in the city of Bayle and Erasmus, both with poor door locks; that Varmoes, Yonker and Ridder *straats* in Amsterdam are filled with *filles effrontées* but that there are quieter 'houses' nearby. Exquisitely precise time and distance notations are routine. We can have few doubts, in short, that this little *carnet* could one day have served as the nucleus of a workmanlike *Voyage d'un François en Hollande*, not unlike the astronomer's dull but reliable 8-volume *Voyage d'un François en Italie*[33] that stands even today, in the view of at least one expert, as the 'fullest, clearest, and most intelligent of the accounts of travels in Italy, and the

33. *Voyage d'un François en Italie fait dans les années 1765-1766* ... (Venise, Paris 1769).

best for the historically minded traveller of the twentieth century to rely on'.[34] That is the kind of endorsement that few of Diderot's informational pages in the *Voyage* could receive. The merit of his work lies elsewhere.

Lalande, of course, made it a point to see Diderot – indeed, he visited him no less than three times at The Hague. The famous *encyclopédiste*, he reports, was under a great cloud and socially ostracised because of his all too obvious materialism and atheism. Thirty years later, as France's self-proclaimed *doyen des athées*, Lalande would himself take fanatical pride in baiting the defenders of religion, from the emperor Napoleon down. But it was a very different world in 1774 and his own free-thinking had not yet evolved beyond the modish deism of Voltaire, whom he was soon to initiate into the Loge des Neuf Sœurs in Paris. As for Diderot, though nearly all of his contacts in Holland were Freemasons, it is unlikely that he was one himself and Lalande seems to have approached him only as a curious celebrity. He notes that Diderot praised Catherine II to the skies, that she had paid only for his travel expenses, Diderot having refused all other advantages. She had given him a fine portrait ring and had answered 132 detailed questions about her empire (not all of them traceable today).[35] But even more fascinating than these first-hand notes is the gratifying evidence in Lalande's journal which shows that Diderot was probably much less occupied at the time with the price of Dutch cabbages than he was with works like *Le Neveu* or the *Entretien avec la maréchale* (the latter not yet submitted to the treacherous Dutch publisher who subsequently denounced Diderot to the French Ministry).[36] At the height of his powers as a *conteur*, Diderot entertained Lalande with several after-dinner tales, probably from his latest pieces. Some we recognise as familiar, while others are obviously worth pursuing further: 'Diderot m'a raconté Sa fable du lezard, son Conte du Mexicain, le chien de la Berton,[37] les cochons de l'incendie, la p. sincère.'[38] As the evening wore on – and no doubt in answer to the astronomer's inquisitive probings – Diderot laid down his usual precautionary smokescreen concerning the identity of the author of *Système de la nature* and its related

34. Robert Shackleton, 'The Grand Tour in the eighteenth century', *Studies in eighteenth-century culture*, ed. Louis T. Milic (Cleveland 1971), p.132.

35. See above, note 30.

36. See Donvez, p.291; also, Jean de Booy, 'Note sur la publication de l'*Entretien avec la maréchale* (1777): Diderot et Laurent Van Santen', *Studi francesi* 22 (1964), pp.280-84.

37. Probable spelling. Is it a garbled recollection of Bouret?

38. Entry for 29 May 1774, Lalande, 'Voyage', f.48.

stream of scandalously impious works: 'Il croit que l'antiq. devoilée, le bon sens, le Syst. de la nature, la polit. naturelle, le Systeme Social, l'examen des apologistes, sont du meme auteur, qui n'a jamais écrit sous son nom, et que Rey même ne le conoit pas. il reçoit tout cela sans adresse' (f.48). M.-M. Rey, Lalande's fellow Mason, later confirmed this last assertion, adding that his situation of ignorance in the matter suited him (that is, his conscience and his pocketbook) perfectly.

Lalande, we see, was fortunate enough, as he toured Holland and busily gathered his miscellaneous notes, to have encountered the Diderot who interests us most today. But Diderot's *Voyage* itself provides other evidence of his indomitable fabulating spirit: for instance, the (perhaps largely fictional?) Vanderveld episode which, combined with various spicy hints concerning the activities of Isaac de Pinto, ends up as the *Neveu*'s misnamed 'Jew of Utrecht' anecdote.[39] Such characteristic transformation of incidental 'fact' into 'true' fiction leads us to speculate about other possibilities. We know, for example, that Diderot was already carrying out his early reading preparations for the *Voyage* around the time that *Ceci n'est pas un conte* was composed. Is it possible that he derived some inspiration for his learned heroine, the unfortunate Mlle de La Chaux, from accounts of the famous Dutch savante, Anne-Marie Van Schurman who, Diderot tells us (following closely on La Chesnaye Des Bois), knew so many languages, both ancient and modern, as well as philosophy and mathematics?[40] Does Van Schurman's undying attachment to the mystical seducer, Jean Labadie, remind us ever so slightly of another ex-ecclesiastic with Oratorian and Toulouse connections, the villainous Jean-Baptiste Gardeil? Such tenuously grounded speculations are perhaps scarcely worth mentioning but we are beginning to understand more and more nowadays how Diderot's wildly inventive genius worked, and without wishing to make much of the fact, it is interesting to note that only one page before the Schurman reference in the *Voyage* we find a line that echoes another from *Ceci n'est pas un conte*:

39. Cf. Lewinter, x.402 and xi.376-77. See Leon Schwartz, *Diderot and the Jews* (London 1981), p.148; Stephen J. Gendizier, 'Diderot and the Jews', *Diderot studies* 16 (1973), pp.46-48; Paul H. Meyer, 'The attitude of the Enlightenment towards the Jew', *Studies on Voltaire* 26 (1963), p.1178.
40. See Charlier, p.223; Lewinter, xi.402.

'Le libraire de Hollande imprime tout ce qu'on lui présente, mais ne donne point d'argent.'[41]

Perhaps we can, after all, conclude with the thought that Diderot's many surreptitious borrowings – as much in the *Encyclopédie* as in the *Voyage* – should really be a matter for rejoicing. He wasted, as a result, less time in plodding research on subjects that were sometimes of no great interest either to him or to us, managing in that way to protect something of his creative genius for better things. His circumstances were always such that the decision to stint may even have come rather easily. The *Encyclopédie*, defective as it was, regularly put bread on the Diderot table, over a long period. That need for 'bread', if anything, grew in later years and we sense that it was not really very difficult for him to set aside the preparation of his collected works, postponing arrangements for their publication, when the opportunity to redo the *Encyclopédie* for Catherine II presented itself. How grateful we must be that the Russian scheme fell through, that Diderot did not spend the last ten years of his life in even more futile compilation! We should not be taken in by his ecstatic rhapsodising to Dr Clerc and General Betski on the subject: 'Je ne mourrai pas sans avoir imprimé sur la terre quelques traces que le temps n'effacera pas! J'y mettrai les quinze dernières années de ma vie; mais, à votre avis, qu'ai-je à faire de mieux? [...] Faisons l'*Encyclopédie*, et laissons à quelque bonne âme le soin de rassembler mes guenilles, quand je serai mort.'[42] It is highly unlikely that Diderot, in good faith, ever thought of the *Encyclopédie* as a glorious monument that would forever withstand the test of time, or that he saw his own personal writings as amounting to no more that literary rags and tatters. What he had written earlier to madame Diderot about the handsome financial benefits to be gained from the Russian enterprise (and here, it is that future income and not the *Encyclopédie* which is labelled 'un dépôt sacré'!) has a much more authentic ring to it: 'Ainsi, bonne amie, prépare-toi incessamment à déménager. [...] Cette fois-ci, cette *Encyclopédie* me

41. Lewinter, xi.401. Cf. *Ceci n'est pas un conte*: 'Les Hollandais impriment tant qu'on veut pourvu qu'ils ne payent rien' (Lewinter, x.168). Perhaps with more justification we can ask the question whether Lalande, who also refers to Anne-Marie Van Schurman, was inspired by popular accounts of her spider-eating eccentricities (see *Nouvelle biographie générale*, xliii.603) to indulge his own digestive tract similarly in later years?

42. To Dr Clerc, The Hague, 15 June 1774 (Lewinter, xi.1022); see also Diderot's letter to General Betski, the same day (xi.1027-28).

vaudra quelque chose et ne me causera aucun chagrin.'[43]

Does that last sentence help us to place Diderot's many compilations and borrowings into perspective? Whether or not it does, we must be grateful, I think, that he did not turn out eight solid volumes, *à la Lalande*, on Holland and we cannot be surprised that he so brazenly ignored nearly all of the too sensible precepts in his 'Préliminaire'. His genius had little use for such methodological pieties and very little that he did well was done according to the rules. Borrowing by someone so rich in his own right was not, moreover, a true necessity. It was an expedient, a shortcut, outrageous in the absolute but really made no worse by our frankly acknowledging today that such short cuts would normally get even the most resourceful and amiable of *cancres* into trouble with the teacher. We recall again his words to Catherine II in those days when he showered her with queries about tar and pitch, tobacco and wax, and perhaps even the price of Russian cabbages: 'Je vais questionnant tant que je peux. Je voudrais bien être utile.' We have long revered that useful Diderot, the editor of the *Encyclopédie*; but, in truth, how much better was Diderot, the author of *Le Neveu*, of *Jacques* and so many other inconsequential rags and tatters, at simply being Diderot!

43. From The Hague, 9 April 1774, Lewinter, xi.989-90.

Saint-Lambert's articles in the *Encyclopédie*

RONALD GRIMSLEY

AMONG the many *Encyclopédie* articles for a long time attributed to Diderot but now restored to their rightful authors is an interesting group of ten apparently written by the marquis de Saint-Lambert (1716-1803): 'Fantaisie', 'Faste', 'Fragilité', 'Frivolité', 'Génie', 'Honneur', 'Intérêt (*Morale*)', 'Législateur', 'Luxe' and 'Manières'.[1] Soldier, poet and philosopher, Saint-Lambert is remembered today chiefly because of his love-affairs with Mme Du Châtelet and Mme d'Houdetot (and so makes his regular appearance in biographies of Voltaire and Rousseau) as well as for his poem *Les Saisons* (1769) on which he is said to have worked for fifteen years. Although his work no longer justifies the high reputation it enjoyed among some of his contemporaries, his *Encyclopédie* articles, which cover psychology, ethics and social and political philosophy, can still interest students of the French Enlightenment, for in them Saint-Lambert shows himself to have been a keen and intelligent observer both of human nature and of the social and political situation of his time. Four of the articles ('Fantaisie', 'Faste', 'Fragilité' and 'Frivolité') are quite short, consisting of no more than a few paragraphs, but the rest ('Génie', 'Honneur', 'Intérêt', 'Législateur', 'Luxe' and 'Manières') are much more substantial. Of these longer articles 'Génie' has often been discussed, usually on the assumption that it was by Diderot, and it is likely that he was interested in it, for it was subjected to considerable editorial revision. Three of the other articles ('Intérêt', 'Législateur' and 'Luxe') have been briefly analysed by John Lough in his introduction to the *Encyclopédie* (pp.193-95, 304-309, 351-54). The purpose of this essay is to take a closer look at 'Législateur' and relate it to other articles which throw further light on its essential ideas.

After indicating that the legislator's principal aim should be to promote

1. See John Lough, *The Encyclopédie* (London 1971), p.49, and the same author's 'The problem of the unsigned articles in the *Encyclopédie*', *Studies on Voltaire* 32 (1965), pp.327-90. In 1798 Saint-Lambert published his *Principes des mœurs chez toutes les nations ou Catéchisme universel*. Most of the *Encyclopédie* articles were reproduced in his *Œuvres philosophiques* (1801). Because of its length and important subject, 'Luxe' deserves a separate analysis and is not discussed in this essay.

the security of the State and the happiness of its citizens, the article immediately mentions the traditional contrast between 'the state of nature' and political society, indicating the advantages and disadvantages of each: whereas 'the state of nature' gives men equality and freedom, it offers them no protection against violence and insecurity, and it is in order to avert these dangers that they have agreed to live in a society that involves some reduction of their natural equality and freedom. The sucessful legislator, therefore, will be the one who provides them with the maximum security and happiness while taking away as little as possible of their freedom and equality.

Recognising that the precise form of government in any country will be determined by the constitutional laws established by the legislator, Saint-Lambert points out that these laws, in their turn, will have to reckon with the many precise factors which affect their original formulation – the size of the territory, the nature of the soil, the power and character of the neighbouring states and the character of his own nation. In this respect Saint-Lambert follows the example of political thinkers who, from the time of Plato and Aristotle, have sought to classify the different types of government. Small states, according to Saint-Lambert, are predominantly republican because they contain enlightened citizens who, being capable of managing their own affairs, would be irked by obedience to a king; large states, in which security is more important than freedom, will accept the authority of a monarch, for he will be an efficient ruler, achieve greater national unity than the republics and provide more effective protection against foreign aggression.

As these brief indications will already have shown, Saint-Lambert does not wish to keep his analysis at a purely abstract level, and this becomes still more apparent when he goes on to deal with a practical issue discussed at length by Montesquieu, whose influence is revealed throughout the article: the role of climate in shaping government and legislation. On the other hand, Saint-Lambert does not accept Montesquieu's ideas uncritically; he asks whether climate is as important as this thinker had supposed. His doubts seem to have been prompted by his reading of David Hume, the only other political thinker specifically mentioned in the article. In his essay 'On national characters',[2] Hume had explicitly rejected climate as a decisive influence on national character, except in

2. Cf. *Essays moral, political and literary* (7141-1742), Part I, p.21.

savage territories exposed to extreme temperatures. Saint-Lambert admits that the problem is complex, but tries to solve it by pointing out that, although human passions are everywhere the same, as Hume had maintained, physical sensitivity varies a great deal from one region to another: the inhabitants of cold northern climates require immense determination and effort in order to survive, while those of warmer, softer climates tend to think only of enjoying the passing moment. Saint-Lambert agrees with Hume that the legislator may have to offset the effects of a harsh climate by paying close attention to habits and customs as well as to the problem of physical subsistence. He concludes, however, that in temperate regions climate may not be as important as elsewhere.

One of the most decisive issues which the legislator has to face is that of self-interest. According to Saint-Lambert this psychological factor has been frequently misunderstood and he himself, in his article 'Intérêt', had tried to correct earlier errors on the subject. Like Rousseau and other political thinkers, he grants that no effective legislation can afford to ignore a man's justifiable concern with his own 'interest'. This means, however, that legitimate self-preservation must not be confused with 'ce vice qui nous fait chercher nos avantages au mépris de la justice et de la vertu' – for example, in the form of greed and avarice. The true interest of an individual, group or nation is 'ce qui importe ou ce qui convient à l'Etat, à la personne, à moi etc.' Properly understood, self-interest does not mean a narrowly selfish concern with 'pride' and 'vanity', for 'le désir continu du bien-être, l'attachement à notre être, est un effet nécessaire de notre constitution, de notre instinct, de nos sensations, de nos réflexions, un principe qui, tendant à notre conservation, et répondant aux vues de la nature, serait plutôt vertueux que vicieux dans l'état de nature'. In society, however, the situation is complicated by the need to reconcile a concern for our own interest with our obligation to other people; *amour-propre* becomes virtuous or vicious according to its particular mode of expression – selfish pride and vanity when the individual seeks an uncontrolled satisfaction of his own desires in defiance of the principle of order, and a beneficial impulse when it 'inspires passions and seeks pleasures which are useful to order and society'.

This does not mean that socially useful forms of *amour-propre* require men to suppress the self-interest which is at its source. Paternal love, patriotism and friendship are mentioned as examples of sentiments which combine self-interest with the desire to look beyond oneself. 'La passion de l'ordre, de la justice, sera la première vertu, le véritable héroïsme, quoiqu'elle ait sa source dans l'amour de nous-mêmes.' Saint-Lambert criticises that 'class of men of the previous age' who saw fit to pour scorn on all forms of *amour-propre*: Jansenists such as Pascal and Nicole and the moralist La Rochefoucauld whom he considers to have been influenced by them. Shaftesbury, on the other hand, with his exclusive emphasis on man's innate love of benevolence, order and moral beauty, required an unselfishness which is beyond the capacity of human beings living in corrupt societies. In a different way, Helvétius, 'the author of the book *De l'esprit*', has been wrongly blamed for maintaining that 'virtue is merely the effect of human conventions', whereas his real mistake was to have constantly used the term *intérêt* in place of *amour-propre* – which means that it is incorrectly associated with avarice and baseness instead of 'ce qui nous importe, ce qui nous convient'. This bold reference to the notorious Helvétius did not pass unnoticed by at least one contemporary critic.[3]

The legislator's principal task, then, is to ensure that self-interest is given a socially acceptable form of expression, so that the spirit of 'property' and 'ownership', 'the sources of every vice', is transformed into a 'spirit of community'. Only in this way can society be provided with the unifying force necessary for its survival. This is particularly true of large states where more legislative skill is needed than in small democratic societies containing citizens who willingly accept responsibility for their own destiny.

A true *esprit de communauté* requires every citizen to be imbued with a strong feeling of patriotism. This part of Saint-Lambert's article can be compared with Rousseau's enthusiastic eulogy of patriotism in his *Encyclopédie* article 'Economie politique'. Rousseau would certainly have approved of the comment: 'Tous marchent ensemble et contents vers le bien commun; l'amour de la patrie donne le plus noble de tous les courages: on se sacrifie à ce qu'on aime.' A people inspired by 'a love of peace, liberty and the fatherland' will show how the 'spirit of community' subordinates particular wills to 'the general will'. Gladly accepting their obligations to society and the general good, such citizens will be noteworthy for their happiness and joy and this will be proved by the rapidly expanding population. In the *Contrat social* Rousseau was also to treat an

3. See J. Lough. pp.194-95 for an interesting extract from Pierre Rousseau's *Journal encyclopédique*.

increased population as a sure sign of a nation's contentment and prosperity. Moreover, a nation like this – and the Swiss are given as a typical example – will command the respect of neighbouring states, however powerful, and so be left in peace.

Throughout his article Saint-Lambert stresses the legislator's need to promote the communal spirit by all the means in his power. Since men are led more by passions than by principles, it is necessary to reduce those passions which oppose us to our fellowmen and encourage the 'social' ones which bind us to them. It is especially important to generate a 'habit of humanity' by nurturing 'benevolence' – a point to which Saint-Lambert frequently returns. In certain countries – Peru, for example – much can be achieved by formal legislation, but this is not likely to unite the citizens of European states who need to feel a 'relation of benevolence' between their rulers and themselves; they will love a prince who is actively concerned with their happiness and he, in turn, must love those who entrust themselves to his care. True benevolence will thus transform the State into a 'family which obeys paternal authority alone'. Friendship, beneficence, generosity and gratitude will be characteristic of a government animated by such a spirit.

Patriotism and the *esprit de communauté* can be greatly strengthened by the principle of honour – a subject already discussed by Saint-Lambert in the article devoted to that subject. There he points out that the self-esteem which is the source of honour has to be compatible with 'the duties of man and citizen'. Montesquieu is criticised for having failed to see the close connection between honour and the 'love of order'. Admittedly, honour is a 'mobile' sentiment that sometimes assumes bizarre forms and imposes duties condemned by 'nature, reason and virtue', but these aberrations can be explained by the influence of the particular factors affecting its formation. To understand the meaning of 'honour' we have to study the birth and development of society and all the changes thus involved. Whereas the honour of primitive societies will be associated with the glorification of physical strength, enlightened societies will relate it to 'la force de l'âme'. Even in highly developed communities 'la masse des lumières est peu répandue' and *le peuple* simply follow 'des idées reçues'. The true character of honour – and its changing forms – can be grasped when it is related to 'David Hume's great principle of utility', for utility is inseparable from self-esteem. The truly enlightened man will learn that 'l'honneur sera bientôt dans chaque citoyen, la conscience de son amour pour ses devoirs, pour les principes de la vertu, et le témoignage qu'il se rend à lui-même, et qu'il attend des autres'. In spite of this an enlightened nation can be easily corrupted by 'luxury' and 'softness', but it is always possible to bring it back to a respect for honour and order, so that the State will not only be like a large family (as Saint-Lambert is so fond of affirming), but will reflect 'cet ordre utile, simple et grand qui fixe nos idées, élève notre âme, nous éclaire, nous protège et décide de notre destinée'. This should provide grounds for optimism since there is 'rien de si difficile à gouverner mal, rien de si facile à gouverner bien, qu'un peuple qui pense'. When honour is joined to patriotism, it will unite the citizens in their common zeal for the maintenance of the laws and the promotion of the general good.

Saint-Lambert does not hesitate to tackle the controversial subject of religion and its rôle in society, but his language is cautious and moderate. While clearly aligning himself with the anti-clericalism of the *philosophes*, he tries to distinguish between the effects of true and false religion. If a religion is false, enlightened citizens will finally see it for what it is, but if, in the meantime, their virtue has depended on such beliefs, they may be tempted to abandon all morality when they throw off the religious yoke. If, on the other hand, a religion is accepted as true, it may contain 'new dogmas and opinions' which will bring it into conflict with the government and so lead to violent revolution, as happened in the case of the Anabaptists of Westphalia. Saint-Lambert considers that it is always hazardous for a legislator to have recourse to religion in order to achieve his purpose, not only because of the well-known dangers of clerical despotism, but also because he is dealing with attitudes that are unpredictable in their consequences and liable to take the situation beyond his control. For this reason, although he must 'respect and love' religion and 'have it respected and loved', the wise legislator will ensure the complete separation of laws and religious dogmas.

In spite of all this, we have to remember man's constant tendency to fall into superstition, for this is a universal feature of human nature and will always form part of 'true religion'. Fortunately the progress of reason provides one of the most effective weapons against this evil, but since it is incurable, the legislator will have to treat superstition with a certain indulgence. Saint-Lambert considers the Chinese method of slowly eradicating superstition to be 'excellent'. In China, where 'philosophers are the prince's ministers', there are provinces still covered with 'gods and pagodas'. The worshippers are never treated harshly, but when a god does not grant a particular prayer or request, the mandarins take the opportunity of abolishing the superstition by breaking the god and overthrowing his temple.

Again like Rousseau in his article 'Economie politique', Saint-Lambert stresses the role of education as a means of encouraging patriotism and the communal spirit. Education is an indispensable way of forming and sustaining 'the kind of character and genius that are suitable to a nation'. He cites the Lacedaemonians and Chinese as examples of societies capable of preserving manners and customs for hundreds of years. Yet the legislator has to realise that since every country contains different orders and classes, it will be necessary to cultivate the particular forms of knowledge and virtue appropriate to each class as well as the knowledge and virtue common to all members of the community. Kings, for example, must be brought up with a consciousness of their special responsibility for the welfare of the peoples they rule; their function will not be to satisfy their own whims and desires but to respond to the needs of their subjects.

When all the factors so far considered – the nature of the civil and constitutional laws, the development of patriotism and a genuine *esprit de communauté* based on benevolence, and the cultivation of honour – have been made part of the national character by means of effective education, it is still necessary for the legislator to recognise that the most durable and powerful qualities sustaining the State are not always easy to define; these consist of 'une manière de penser qui se perpétue dans la nation', and yet in such a way as to make the citizens treat everything appertaining to the national constitution and *mœurs* as 'sacred'; they will not be continually examining the usefulness of particular laws and customs or analysing their specific duties, for their attitude and conduct will be based on a widely accepted 'opinion' of which they will not always be explicitly aware, for it has become an integral part of their lives, permeating every aspect of society and providing a stable basis for sound government by lending powerful support to formal legislation. Through this widely diffused outlook the large majority of subjects will obey without complaint the small minority of those wielding power. It is doubtful, however, whether any government can endure for long without the help of effective 'opinion'. Even despotic states like Turkey and the Roman Empire, though ruled by fear, made sure that the Janissaries and praetors were imbued with the right 'opinions'. Ultimately, however, the only worth-while 'opinion' is the one which is directed upon 'the happiness and approbation of the citizens'.

The influence of this all-pervasive opinion should not be allowed to obscure the importance of efficient administration, for this alone will enable the legislator to protect 'the power, happiness and genius of his people'. Moreover, it is not simply a question of making the citizens accept lawful authority; they must also participate as much as possible in the administration and government of the State. This is all the more essential when we recall that their involvement in society has led to a considerable diminution of their original equality and freedom, the 'two great advantages of the state of nature', so that they can find compensation for this loss by taking an active part in the life of the community.

In his ever-present concern with the need to spread sentiments of 'humanity' and 'benevolence' and to encourage respect for 'tout ce qui est homme, soit citoyen, soit étranger', the legislator must not forget to set a personal example of the qualities he is seeking; he must show that he is ready to sacrifice his personal interests to those of the community. A king should reveal himself as the father of his people – like the Persian ruler who admitted ploughmen to his table with the words 'I am one of you; you need me, I need you; let us live like brothers.' When the legislator 'neither respects nor consults the general will', the exercise of his power will have an insidiously corrupting effect upon society. As soon as regard for the law is replaced by gross partiality and injustice, the selfish pursuit of personal gain and the granting of favours to sycophants rather than to persons of merit, the citizens' loyalty will be rapidly undermined as they are brought to the point of 'looking for the State and seeing nothing but the master's prey'.

There is no greater test of a legislator's skill and wisdom than his handling of rewards and punishments – 'the reins with which he can control passions as he wishes'. Punishments must always be impersonal and carried out in the name of the law; but rewards can be distributed in a less rigid manner. In a nation based on 'patriotic principles and feelings of honour' a guilty man may be treated leniently, because he will be punished morally as well as legally by 'the looks of his fellow-citizens'. Here again, it is important to respect the character of each nation, for the great diversity of attitudes and customs means that there is no single code of behaviour appropriate to every nation. Above all else, rewards and punishments should require the subordination of personal interest to the general good. Although it is impossible to avoid a sharp division between rich and poor, extreme wealth should always come from work which benefits the State and never be acquired merely at the expense of the citizens. This involves a system of taxation that encourages the right kind of commercial activity and makes use of proper talents and virtues.

All this does not mean that rulers will have to rely on a continual appeal to general principles and sentiments. Apart from the important part played by 'opinion', etiquette, ceremonies and manners will often be very effective means of stimulating the subjects' senses and imagination. A wise legislator will pay as much attention to the sensuous and physical as to the moral and pyschological aspects of human nature, for the former can often give very useful support to the latter, as Saint-Lambert makes clear in his article 'Manières': 'L'habitude de certaines actions, de certains gestes, de certains mouvements, de certains signes extérieurs, maintient plus en nous les mêmes sentiments que tous les dogmes et toute la métaphysique du monde.' Since all our feelings have some physical effect, our bodies, as well as our minds, can contribute to the maintenance of certain emotions. The physical expression of manners helps to ensure their survival. 'Les manières sont corporelles, parlent aux sens, à l'imagination, enfin sont sensibles; et voilà pourquoi elles survivent aux mœurs, voila pourquoi elles les conservent plus que les préceptes et les lois; c'est par la même raison que chez tous les peuples il reste d'anciens usages, quoique les motifs qui les ont établis ne se conservent plus.' Public ceremonies can also play an important part in promoting the well-being of the community, especially if they recall the country's noble and heroic past. It is a pity, declares Saint-Lambert, that many of the ceremonies used by European rulers have become so completely separated from their historical origins that they are more suited to oriental despotisms than to moderate governments. Such activities as public games and entertainments in which the whole population can participate are other effective means of strengthening unity among citizens. Here again one is reminded of Rousseau's advocacy of similar public activities at the end of his *Lettre à d'Alembert sur les spectacles*. By such means citizens will become accustomed to respect the 'looks and judgements' of their fellow-citizens by increasing their 'love of glory and fear of shame'.

The successful legislator thus needs to have a sound grasp of general principles and at the same time an ability to understand all the practical complications of his task. It is quite pointless – and even dangerous – for him to pursue objectives which, though worthy in themselves, are irrelevant to the needs of his own nation. The Chinese, for example, sought 'tranquillity through the exercise of gentle virtues' when they should have been developing 'strong virtues' capable of making them withstand the assaults of the Tartar hordes. Likewise, the Roman policy of constant aggrandisement made the empire unfit for survival in times of peace. It is necessary, therefore, for the legislator to keep before his mind the country's needs as a whole, so that he does not concentrate exclusively on one particular aspect of the national life to the neglect of the rest. Trade, war, law, the arts all require his attention. 'Il n'y a point de nation, du moins de grande nation, qui ne puisse être à la fois, sous un bon gouvernement, guerrière, commerçante, savante et polie.'

Saint-Lambert ends his article 'Législateur' on an optimistic note. The rapid progress of enlightenment throughout Europe during the preceding fifty years has made it impossible, he declares, for any would-be despot to plunge his nation into darkness, 'for he will find free nations who will bring him back into the light'. Similarly, the destructive fanaticism of Mahomet could not flourish on a continent that firmly rejects 'prejudices contrary to the law of nations and of nature'. This may require the citizens to diminish some of their patriotic enthusiasm since 'there is scarcely any enthusiasm when there is a great deal of enlightenment'. It should now be recognised that there is no valid reason why one people is preferable to another, so that 's'ils conservent pour la patrie cet amour qui est le fruit de l'intérêt personnel, ils n'auraient plus du moins cet enthousiasme qui est le fruit d'une estime exclusive'. So widespread is this opinion that it is no longer possible today to stir up those national hatreds which formerly divided one nation from another.

One of the decisive reasons for this change of national outlook is the development of more enlightened religious attitudes, so that men now agree that 'we must not hate those who do not think like us'. The 'sublime spirit of religion' is to be distinguished from 'the suggestions of its ministers'. In spite of the wars between Roman Catholics and Protestants, no modern power has succeeded in producing 'this brutal, ferocious zeal' which was characteristic of religious sects, even in times of peace.

One of the most remarkable and beneficial results of this change of attitude is the general acceptance of the fact that men are dependent on one another. Economic and financial developments have been mainly responsible for this change. The new bond rapidly being created by the expansion of trade and commerce has led men to acknowledge that genuine self-interest requires the help of other people. A bankruptcy in Lima, Leipzig and Lisbon affects the whole of Europe. Enlightened self-interest, therefore, will produce harmony rather than hostility among men.

In spite of this optimistic view of the future of a Europe engaged in promoting economic prosperity rather than ruinous wars, Saint-Lambert finishes his article on a note of caution and with a point that is not unlike the one made by Rousseau in his *Discours sur les sciences et les arts*. If enlightenment has led to a diminution of ferocity and barbarism, it has also weakened the enthusiasm for virtue by extinguishing the spirit of selfishness in favour of a justice which gives every man his right. The enfeebling effect of commercial and artistic success also tends to make people ignore the need for 'war-like virtues'. The habit of turning men's minds to 'utility rather than to beauty, to prudence rather than to greatness' could reduce 'the force, generosity and nobility of their *mœurs*'. One political consideration which makes this warning necessary, according to Saint-Lambert, is the fact that European governments still have very different characters, being divided into republics and monarchies. Normally peace-loving, republics may be led into wars of conquest by rulers who pay no heed to the 'interest of their nation'; the active love of freedom and a 'superstitious fear' of losing it may induce them 'to lower or suppress' the power of monarchical states. The possible threat of war, therefore, will probably keep alive the 'emulation of the strong war-like virtues' which are being slowly undermined by the progress of 'this softness, this excessive gentleness of *mœurs*, which are the effects of commerce, luxury and long periods of peace'.

The principles inspiring the article 'Législateur' are in many ways typical of the French Enlightenment in their advocacy of rational values and their devotion to the cause of human dignity; legislation and government should be entrusted to those who recognise the importance of 'reason, nature and humanity'. In the article 'Génie' Saint-Lambert, while admiring the original creative power of genius, insists that it would be a disastrous quality in a ruler who has to be guided by *le sang-froid* rather than by passion. Whereas men of genius pay little heed to 'the requirements of circumstances, laws and usages', states have to be governed by reason and prudence – and not by feeling and imagination – if they are to have stability and permanence. Other articles such as 'Fragilité' and 'Frivolité' also call attention to the transitory and erratic character of feelings which are not based on fundamental human qualities. In a slightly different way the article 'Faste' criticises rulers who, being more concerned with their own reputation than with the true needs of their nation, indulge in extravagant expenditure in order to satisfy their vanity. 'Des provinces peuplées, des armées disciplinées, des finances en bon ordre imposeraient plus aux étrangers et aux citoyens que la magnificence de la cour.' The splendour worthy of enlightened nations consists of 'monuments, great works and the wonders of art which make us admire genius as much as they add to the idea of power'.

One of the most important qualities which the legislator should be constantly trying to develop among the citizens is virtue. No state can survive if its members are not prepared to subordinate their own pleasures and interests to the demands of duty and the 'general will'. In this respect Saint-Lambert, like Rousseau, establishes a firm link between politics and morality. Both thinkers also realise that this moral commitment must be allied to an intelligent regard for the many diverse factors which help to give each nation its own character and genius.

Saint-Lambert's eminently reasonable and moderate ideas on the subject of government and legislation do not have the boldness of Rousseau's principles or offer the same radical challenge to traditional political philosophy as the notions of sovereignty, government and the general will developed in the *Contrat social*; nor does Saint-Lambert's *législateur* have the mysterious power and genius of the one who plays such a vital part in Rousseau's treatise. Nevertheless, as a wide-ranging discussion of the problem of legislation in a characteristically 'philosophical' spirit which tries to relate the essential aspects of human nature to the relativities of men's situation in the real world, Saint-Lambert's article deserves a place – albeit a minor one – in any survey of the political and social ideas of the French Enlightenment.

In his *Confessions* Rousseau tells us how at one stage of his life he hoped to form an idyllic friendship with Sophie d'Houdetot and her lover Saint-Lambert; the three of them were to be a striking example of 'intimate companionship'. Although we do not know what the marquis thought of this idea (if, indeed, he was ever told of it!), Rousseau says that Saint-Lambert fell asleep during a reading of the letter to Voltaire on Providence (Leigh 424) and that he himself did not dare to wake him up. Posterity is prepared to admit that metaphysical speculation of this kind is not one of the more rewarding aspects of Rousseau's genius. Had he chosen on that particular occasion to talk about the ideas of his projected *Institutions politiques*, he might have found in Saint-Lambert an alert listener whose contributions to the *Encylopédie* showed him to be keenly interested in some of the issues which impelled Rousseau himself to deliver his political message to the world.

Chaudon's *Dictionnaire anti-philosophique*

JOHN LOUGH

IN studying the clash of ideas in France in the decades before 1789 it is not sufficient to confine one's attention to the works of the *philosophes* and other unorthodox writers. Though the writings of their critics undoubtedly make less absorbing reading, an examination of them brings out more clearly what was at stake in these often violent controversies. One of the most widely read of these works (it went through at least seven editions between its publication at Avignon in 1767 and 1785)[1] was the *Dictionnaire anti-philosophique* of the Benedictine, Louis Mayeul Chaudon (1737-1817). Passages from it were even reprinted in far-off Canada in the *Gazette littéraire de Montréal*.[2]

Although the title of this work was taken from Voltaire's *Dictionnaire philosophique*, published three years earlier, and although criticisms of the man and his writings crop up all over the place in it, decidedly less than half of the articles are a direct retort to the corresponding articles of the earlier work. As was the fashion of the time, Chaudon's work has a fairly long subtitle which it is worth reproducing as it describes its contents accurately: 'Pour servir de Commentaire & de Correctif au *Dictionnaire Philosophique*, & aux autres Livres qui ont paru de nos jours contre le Christianisme: Ouvrage dans lequel on donne en abrégé les preuves de la Religion, & la Réponse aux objections de ses Adversaires; avec la notice des principaux Auteurs qui l'ont attaquée, & l'apologie des Grands Hommes qui l'ont défendue.'

Thus other writings of Voltaire, from *Candide* ('ce Roman obscene, sans intrigue & sans caracteres') to his tragedies or the *Philosophie de l'histoire*, are sharply criticised along with those of a large number of other authors. Chaudon has also the positive aim of providing the antidote to such poison; hence the amount of space given to the defenders of religious orthodoxy and to their writings. How effective such a work

1. R. E. A. Waller, 'Louis-Mayeul Chaudon against the *philosophes*', *Studies on Voltaire* 228 (1984), pp.257-63.
2. G. Rouben, 'Propagande anti-philosophique dans les gazettes de Montréal et de Québec après la fin du régime français', *Studies on Voltaire* 216 (1983), pp.30-32.

can have been in its defence of orthodox religion a modern reader cannot easily judge. One wonders whether expounding, often in their own words, the scandalous ideas of 'les Incrédules' was not simply putting dangerous thoughts into the minds of readers to whom they might never have occurred, or making known to them authors and works of which they had never heard. Curiously enough, this point is made in one of the dialogues of which Chaudon's articles occasionally consist: 'Si le Livre que vous attaquez n'est pas connu, vous le faites connoître; & s'il est connu, on n'en a que plus d'empressement à se le procurer' (ii.198).

The work's success led to its enlargement. In the second edition (Avignon 1769), on which this article is based,[3] many of the articles were revised and another twenty-four were added. Few of these were a direct answer to articles in the *Dictionnaire philosophique*. The work had grown from a single volume of 471 pages to two with a total of 576. The eighteenth-century French writers subjected to criticism of varying degrees of severity are d'Argens, Boulanger, Diderot, Fréret, Helvétius, La Beaumelle, La Mettrie, Meslier, Montesquieu, de Prades, Rousseau, Toussaint and, of course, Voltaire who is chastised both in a separate article and in those which reply to selected articles from the *Dictionnaire philosophique*. Writers from an earlier age such as Bossuet and Pascal are eulogised, while Bayle is repeatedly attacked, and the bogeyman Spinoza and his 'monstrueux système' are dealt with in one page in which it is claimed, somewhat surprisingly, that 'le *Spinosisme* ne survécut guere à son Auteur' (ii.162). Quite why Chaudon should have chosen to lambast in separate articles the English deists, Tindal, Toland and Woolston, and to drag in Dodwell in 'Martyrs', it is difficult to see as there cannot have been many people in France who were aware of their existence. Servet and Vanini are figures out of the past who also merit an article. It is more understandable that Chaudon should devote several pages to an unfavourable account of the emperor Julian whom the *philosophes* praised as an enlightened ruler and an apostle of religious toleration.

In addition to articles such as 'Christianisme', 'Enfer', 'Foi', 'Jésus-Christ', 'Immortalité de l'âme', 'Messie', 'Miracles', 'Moyse', 'Pentateuque', 'Prophéties', 'Résurrection' and 'Révélation' in which orthodox doctrines are set forth, there are others in which 'les Incrédules' or 'les modernes Philosophes' are directly attacked: 'Athées', 'Déistes', 'Esprits-

---

3. The British Library does not possess a copy of any edition.

forts', Incrédules', 'Incrédulité', 'Injures', 'Plagiaires', 'Querelles philosophiques' and 'Travers'.

Chaudon is fairly frank about the fact that not all of the work is of his
own composition. 'MM. Bertier, Joannet, Gauchat, le François, Trublet',
he writes (i.xv), 'nous ont fourni plusieurs articles [...] Nous avons surtout profité du *Traité abrégé de la Religion*, qu'on trouve dispersé dans
différens volumes du *Journal Chrétien*.' All manner of other debts are
acknowledged in the text or even in the title of an article, as with one
added in the second edition, 'Mysteres, *Raisons que le p.* Bourdaloue *donne
pour les croire*'. On the other hand another addition, 'Cacouacs, *De la
maniere de les connoître*', is printed without the slightest acknowledgement
to the abbé Giry de Saint-Cyr who had published it in the *Mercure de
France* of October 1757.

In the preface (i.xvii-xviii) the author claims with some justification
that he has exercised restraint in his attacks on 'les Incrédules': 'La
plupart sont hommes,[4] ils méritent par conséquent de la charité, &
quelques-uns d'entr'eux sont des grands hommes; on leur doit des
ménagemens & de la modération.' Yet he makes the most of the fact
that the judicial authorities had linked the fate of the chevalier de La
Barre with the *Dictionnaire philosophique*. He reproduces at the end of the
work the complete text of the sentence passed by the Paris Parlement,
and he keeps on referring to the fate of the chevalier without showing
excessive compassion. In the *avertissement* (i.vi) he writes of 'les Incrédules': 'Leurs écrits impies & satyriques sont à présent la seule bibliothéque
des jeunes gens. Ils s'en nourrissent & leur imagination impétueuse,
s'allumant à ce funeste flambeau, éclate par des actions qui peuvent les
conduire au dernier supplice. C'est ce qu'on a vu il y a deux ans à
Abbeville.' In a footnote to the preface (i.vii-viii), after speaking of the
condemnation of the *Dictionnaire philosophique* by the Paris Parlement, he
goes on: 'Ces illustres Magistrats firent plus encore en 1766, lors de
l'exécution du Chevalier de la Barre à Abbeville. Ils ordonnerent que
cette production sacrilege seroit brûlée sur le corps du jeune criminel
qu'elle avoit séduit.' There are further references to the chevalier, and
the article on Vanini ends with this breathtaking comment on his fate of
being burnt at the stake: 'La crainte que la témérité atroce de ce Professeur
d'Irréligion n'eût des imitateurs, obligea sans doute le Parlement de

---

4. A curious statement.

Toulouse à s'armer de toute sa sévérité, & à le condamner avec la derniere rigueur. Il est des cas, où il ne suffit pas d'anathématiser l'impiété. Il faut encore proscrire la personne de l'Impie; & c'est ainsi sans doute que jugea le Sénat de Toulouse' (ii.214).

Yet despite his sharp attacks on the writers of his age he seldom fails to recognise that they had great gifts. If only they had abstained in their writings from dealing with matters of religion, most of them would have been fine fellows and a credit to their country. Exceptions are, of course, made. Perhaps understandably, Meslier is treated in a manner very different from that followed by Voltaire when he published extracts from the *Testament*. Chaudon gives the article on the curé of Etrepigny the subtitle, *Son impie testament; travers de son esprit*. The article has a curiously snobbish tone. It begins: 'Jean Meslier, fils d'un ouvrier en serge de Mazerai' and ends: 'En faut-il d'avantage pour prouver que la révolte de cet infidele contre le Christianisme, n'étoit que le fruit d'un cerveau ardent, troublé par la vie solitaire & par l'étude, & animé par le vain espoir d'illustrer après sa mort la navette de son pere?' (i.276-77). Nor has Chaudon anything good to say about La Mettrie whose writings are denounced in the strongest terms: 'Il pose pour base du bonheur, qu'il faut étouffer les remords, & se livrer à tous ses penchans. Il conseille au Brigand de voler; au Tyran, de se baigner dans le sang de ses Sujets; au Débauché, de se vautrer pour être heureux, à la maniere des animaux les plus immondes. Telle est la morale de ce Matérialiste & de ses disciples' (ii.4). Chaudon had to recognise that the leading *philosophes* took care to distance themselves from so compromising a writer, but he does so with a sneer: 'Les sages du jour n'ont pas voulu l'inscrire sur leur liste; cependant son nom ne pouvoit que leur faire honneur.' Yet he does attempt to insinuate that La Mettrie was one of their group: 'La Mettrie étoit un fou qui se paroit du titre de Philosophe, & qui méritoit bien ce titre aujourd'hui si avili. Il séduisit une foule de sots, qui se rangeoient autour de son théatre. Quoique son orvietan ne se soit pas soutenu, il eut une certaine vogue parmi la Populace Philosophique.'

Boulanger, to whom Chaudon attributes not only *Le Despotisme oriental* and *L'Antiquité dévoilée*, but also *Le Christianisme dévoilé*, is denounced as 'un enthousiaste sombre & mélancolique' (i.183), but on the opposite page Fréret is treated very differently for the recently printed *Examen critique des apologistes de la religion chrétienne* for which Chaudon holds him responsible. Of this work Chaudon writes, copying from Bergier's refutation: 'M. Fréret l'a écrit du même style de[5] ses dissertations acadé-miques; il y a répandu la même érudition; il semble avoir tout lu & tout approfondi. Il affecte une apparence de droiture & de sincérité qui ne peut manquer d'imposer, à moins que l'on ne soit très-instruit.' Although he refers the reader to Bergier's and Yvon's refutations of this work, one cannot feel that it was sensible to devote a long paragraph to summaris-ing, chapter by chapter, the contents of 'cet Ouvrage dangereux' and thus putting before the reader almost all the objections that could conceivably be made to orthodox Christianity.

Some writers could be treated relatively gently and welcomed back into the fold. The article on Saint-Foix begins: 'On a accusé cet Auteur d'incrédulité, & nous ne l'ignorons point. Les *Lettres Turques*[6] qu'on lui attribue, ont donné des soupçons sur sa Religion' (ii.127). However, Saint-Foix had redeemed himself by an attack on 'la nouvelle Philosophie' which Chaudon quotes from his *Lettres historiques sur Paris*, and he can thus conclude: 'On voit par ce morceau que si M. de Saint-Foix a été infecté des principes de la nouvelle Philosophie, il s'en est sagement repenti.'

Glossing over the absurd position in which the Sorbonne had landed itself by first approving and then condemning the thesis of the abbé de Prades, Chaudon condemns both thesis and *Apologie*; but then, two years after the condemnation, the abbé had signed a humiliating retractation 'telle qu'elle lui fut envoyée de Rome': 'Il s'y avoue coupable envers Dieu, envers l'Eglise Romaine, envers la Faculté, envers le Public, dont il a été le scandale; envers lui-même, puisqu'il s'égaroit, & qu'il n'a pas assez d'une vie pour pleurer sa conduite passée, & remercier Jésus-Christ de la grace que lui accorde son Vicaire en terre' (ii.79-80).

Toussaint receives a moderately severe rebuke for the unorthodox ideas contained in *Les Mœurs*. The work, Chaudon admits, 'est écrit purement & avec esprit, & il y paroît d'abord un air de vérité & de sagesse; mais sous ces beaux dehors, il enseigne l'erreur & le vice'. While conceding that it contained some quite orthodox ideas, he lists nine different topics on which Toussaint goes astray. He testifies, however, to the book's success, adding: 'L'Ouvrage d'ailleurs se fait lire avec plaisir, par un mélange heureux de raisonnemens, de tableaux & de

---

5. A misprint for 'que'.

6. *Lettres d'une Turque à Paris, écrites à sa soeur au serrail* (1731), an imitation of the *Lettres persanes*.

conseils, qui se donnent mutuellement de force.' This mild attitude on Chaudon's part was induced by the retractation which, he claims, Toussaint published in 1764 (ii.195-96):

C'est à la vérité se raviser un peu tard, mais une rétractation est toujours bonne à prendre, pourvu qu'elle soit sincere. Nous avons lieu de croire que celle de M. Toussaint est de ce genre. Il regne dans son Livre, à travers les sophismes & les erreurs que nous avons relevé, un caractere de galant homme qui intéresse. C'est sans doute celui de l'Auteur; & nous nous en félicitons avec lui, s'il continue de perfectionner un si heureux naturel par les sublimes vertus de la Religion.

And yet, as Chaudon had pointed out at the beginning of the article, this was a work which had been 'condamné au feu par le premier Tribunal du Royaume' to whose judgements he attached so much importance. Indeed after the preface he reprints the text of the *Arrêt du Parlement* of 19 March 1765 which, somewhat ironically, united in a common reprobation the *Dictionnaire philosophique* and Rousseau's *Lettres écrites de la Montagne*.

Because of his Protestant origins La Beaumelle could scarcely expect to be treated tenderly by Chaudon though the article does begin with a large concession: 'Cet Auteur est Calviniste, mais on peut être Protestant sans être impie.' La Beaumelle's early work, *Mes pensées*, is roundly condemned (i.50):

M. de la Baum** vouloit en faire le Breviaire des Politiques, & c'est souvent celui des Incrédules. Il s'abandonne au feu de son imagination & aux écarts de son esprit. Sans décence dans le style, sans respect pour les puissances, il affiche une indépendance téméraire, capable de tout bouleverser. Le fiel & l'amertume découlent de sa plume, & les éloges ne se trouvent dans son Livre qu'autant qu'ils accompagnent un nom célebre par l'irréligion.

Chaudon was even more scandalised by the *Mémoires pour servir à l'histoire de Madame de Maintenon*. 'L'Auteur', he asks indignantly, 'pouvoit-il se flatter que son Livre fût un Ouvrage d'instructions pour les Demoiselles de S. Cyr à qui une histoire de Madame de Maintenon devroit naturellement être si chere? [...] Madame de Maintenon si religieuse, si pleine de vertu & de piété, se seroit-elle jamais imaginé que le récit de sa vie deviendroit un sujet de scandale pour les simples & affoibliroit ou ébranleroit leur foi?' (i.50-51). When he mentions the quarrel between Voltaire and La Beaumelle, it was inevitable that, while blaming both, Chaudon should tilt the balance slightly in favour of the younger man.

This scandalous quarrel, he declares, arose out of 'l'orgueil du Vieillard qui n'étoit pas assez loué, & la sensibilité du jeune Auteur qui ne vouloit pas être critiqué. En cela il avoit quelque raison; car on ne peut lui refuser un esprit réfléchi & une imagination vive & pétillante.' After the sharp attacks earlier in the article its mild conclusion comes as rather a surprise: 'Nous apprenons avec plaisir qu'il travaille à des Ouvrages plus utiles; il est très capable d'en donner d'excellens, pourvu qu'il se borne à la littérature.'

The article on the marquis d'Argens contains one conciliatory remark – 'Il servit pendant quelque-tems avec distinction & se trouva au siege de Philisbourg où il signala son courage' (i.39) – and it has a fairly mild conclusion. However, some pretty severe criticisms are packed into these pages, from the very opening sentence: 'Voici une des plus fermes colonnes de l'impiété.' The *Lettres juives, chinoises* and *cabalistiques*, Chaudon declares, 'détruisent tous les dogmes du Christianisme, & s'ils laissent subsister l'existence de Dieu, c'est à condition qu'on pourra se conduire comme s'il n'y en avoit point; ce qui revient au même pour les libertins.' While he admits that these works had at the time a considerable success, he maintains, no doubt correctly, that they were now less popular, adding: 'Le fastueux étalage d'une vaine érudition, plusieurs plaisanteries de bas aloi, un acharnement ridicule contre les Moines, un style vif à la vérité, mais trop diffus, trop incorrect, trop ignoble ont dégouté les Lecteurs délicats.'

Naturally *De l'esprit* is bitterly denounced as 'un recueil de systêmes aussi anciens que l'impiété, de faux principes mille fois détruits, de paradoxes & d'inepties puérilement hazardés, de faits démentis, de citations altérées, d'anecdotes scandaleuses' (i.194). The humiliating *requêtes* which Helvétius and his censor addressed to the Parlement are reproduced, and five pages are devoted to reprinting abbé Gauchat's 'Catéchisme du livre *de l'Esprit*' which brought out the materialist implications of the work. Yet once he had retracted, Helvétius became quite a different man for Chaudon. The Parlement's indulgence, he declares, 'parut d'autant mieux placée, que cet Auteur étoit connu par des vertus & des actes de générosité, autant que par la douceur & la facilité de son caractere'. He had simply been led astray: 'On l'avoit séduit & on l'avoit inspiré.' The publication of the posthumous *De l'homme* in 1773 must have shattered this illusion.

Montesquieu, a writer who in the 1760s enjoyed a much greater prestige than any of those so far mentioned, is treated in a singularly mixed fashion, as can be seen from the opening words of the article on him: 'Ce célebre Ecrivain s'annonça en 1721, par ses *Lettres Persanes*. Cet Ouvrage, en faisant honneur au génie, à l'esprit & au style de Montesquieu, fit naître des soupçons très-graves sur sa Religion' (ii.26). A whole page is devoted to listing the ways in which this work offends against religion and morality, with the conclusion that, thanks to printing, Montesquieu's errors 'subsisteront éternellement pour faire gémir le Christianisme & la vertu'.

Chaudon then lists seven serious charges brought against the *Esprit des lois* by 'les gens de bien', and while he admits that certain important religious truths are set forth in it, he concludes: 'Tout tend à faire penser que l'Auteur n'étoit qu'un Déiste déguisé; & les accusations intentées contre lui ne peuvent être regardées comme téméraires.' The *Défense de l'Esprit des lois* is described as 'un modele de bonne plaisanterie, autant que de mauvaise foi'.

Chaudon reproduces the account given by the Irish Jesuit confessor, Routh, of Montesquieu's admission that what had persuaded him to cast doubt on the faith was 'le goût du neuf, le désir de passer pour un génie supérieur aux préjugés, l'envie de plaire aux personnes qui donnent le ton à l'estime publique'. He acknowledges that Montesquieu's friends 'se sont inscrits en faux contre cet aveu, mais s'il ne l'a pas fait, il devoit le faire'.

There follows a somewhat surprising eulogy of the man, no doubt partly inspired by a desire to separate him off from the *philosophes* and especially Voltaire (the latter's contradictions on the subject are listed in three paragraphs at the end of the article) (ii.29):

Toutefois en détestant les principes du Président de Montesquieu, nous rendons justice aux qualités qui le distinguoient dans la société. Sa façon de vivre & de penser dans le monde étoit digne de sa naissance. Il plaisoit aux Grands, & il ne dédaignoit pas les petits. Son commerce étoit enchanteur, & ce qui vaut encore mieux, il étoit très-sûr. Les malheureux pouvoient compter sur son crédit & les indigens sur sa bourse. Il ne se déshonora ni par des querelles scandaleuses ni par les travers de cette Philosophie altiere & dédaigneuse qui ramene tout à soi. Il sut être homme, Magistrat & citoyen.

When Chaudon came to compose the article 'Religion', he was able to draw on Montesquieu's writings for three pages of suitable extracts (ii.121-24).

In the eyes of his contemporaries in the 1760s Diderot was far from enjoying the same acclaim as two hundred years later, and the space given to him by Chaudon, even if one counts in the article on the *Encyclopédie*, is nothing like that given to Montesquieu or Rousseau or, of course, Voltaire. The article on him opens with the damning sentence: 'Parmi les Héros du parti, les Chefs de l'Incrédulité, aucun n'a montré autant d'enthousiasme que celui-ci.' The beginnings of his career are described sarcastically and inaccurately: 'Cet ennemi du Christianisme préluda dans de petites brochures & dans des Romans obscenes; car c'est dans ces Livres, que les Philosophes modernes apprennent & débitent leur Catéchisme; mais il porta les grands coups dans ses *Pensées Philosophiques* (1748. petit in-12, qui lui procura le malheureux avantage de philosopher à la Bastille)' (i.131). Like many other contemporaries, Chaudon was much impressed by this work. As often in the *Dictionnaire anti-philosophique*, he seizes the opportunity to have a side swipe at Voltaire by declaring that the *Lettres philosophiques* is inferior in style to this early work of Diderot. After offering a convenient summary of the unorthodox ideas contained in it, Chaudon declares that the *Lettre sur les aveugles* and the *Lettre sur les sourds et muets* were inferior in style to 'la netteté & la noblesse' of the earlier work. Yet in the midst of a further attack on the 'acharnement bien horrible' shown by Diderot's attacks on religion and his aim of replacing it by 'la chimere monstrueuse du Matérialisme, chimere qui ouvre la porte à tous les vices & à tous les crimes', one suddenly lights upon this unexpected tribute: 'Prions le Pere des lumieres d'y ramener M. Did*** qui a d'ailleurs des vertus, une ame forte & élevée, un génie étendu & une imagination brillante.'

Diderot reappears in the article on the *Encyclopédie*. The first sentence offers a fairly balanced judgement – 'cet Ouvrage dont on a dit trop be bien & trop de mal'. Yet the emphasis is definitely on the work's shortcomings in the eyes of the orthodox. The article summarises the criticisms made by Father Berthier in the *Mémoires de Trévoux* and gives extracts from the *réquisitoire* delivered before the Paris Parlement by Omer Joly de Fleury in 1759. In a brief conclusion Chaudon does not deny that the contributors to the work had much to offer the public; but, he repeats, if only they had kept off subjects which were above their understanding: 'Ils s'appellent les précepteurs du genre humain; qu'ils ne le corrompent donc point. Capables de nous donner de l'excellent dans plusieurs genres, qu'ils ne touchent plus aux objets qui sont au-dessus de leur portée &

qui méritent le silence du Philosophe qui veut être tranquille & le profond respect du Chrétien éclairé, qui aime sa Religion' (i.147).

Of the outstanding unorthodox writers in France in the 1760s only d'Alembert receives virtually no attention. Presumably he was numbered among 'quelques Philosophes célebres de ce siecle, qui sont accusés de mal penser sur la Religion; mais l'erreur étant enveloppée avec finesse dans leurs écrits & ces écrits n'ayant pas été condamnés, nous n'avons pas dû leur donner une place dans ce Dictionnaire' (ii.239). He has no article to himself, and in the article on the *Encyclopédie*, although we are told that it was edited by 'deux Auteurs célebres', only Diderot is named. D'Alembert was notorious for the outspoken way in which he aired his views on religion in private, but in his published works, though his views are clear enough to anyone who reads between the lines, he expressed himself with such skill that the orthodox had little to get hold of when they came to criticise such passages. In the article 'Religion' Chaudon manages to tear from their context and to use against 'les Incrédules' three passages from *De l'abus de la critique en matière de religion*, a work which d'Alembert had directed against just such critics as Chaudon himself (ii.114-15).

Rousseau, on the other hand, is given considerable prominence. Chaudon's treatment of Jean-Jacques throws some light on the thorny problem of producing a correct definition of the special sense which the word *philosophe* had recently acquired. Like most writers of the time, Chaudon often leaves the modern reader uncertain as to whether he is using the word in a broad sense or in its new special meaning. That the group or party and this new meaning of the word had emerged only round about 1750 is made clear by Chaudon when he writes rather rudely in 'Querelles philosophiques': 'Vers le milieu du siècle, on vit éclorre des Philosophes, c'est-à-dire, une société d'Ecrivains qui avoient coutume de s'appeller ainsi. Les sots les admirerent, parce qu'ils s'admiroient réciproquement' (ii.101). Equally impolite and implying that this special sense of the word would be short-lived is the comment in 'Christianisme': 'Déja on commence à rougir de l'épithete de Philosophe. Cette qualification est devenue une injure, & dès qu'on a honte du mot, on en aura bientôt de la chose' (i.97).

A sarcastic definition of a *philosophe* is furnished by Chaudon in the last paragraph of the article in which he examines what Voltaire has to say on this subject (ii.68):

Que faut-il aujourd'hui pour avoir le nom de Philosophe? l'impiété de Diagoras & l'effronterie de Diogene. Quiconque se croit sage & le dit est sûr de le persuader. Il faut seulement qu'il trouve mauvais ce qu'on avoit cru bon jusqu'à présent; qu'il fronde les vérités anciennes pour y substituer des paradoxes nouveaux ou rajeunis; qu'il annonce comme des découvertes des idées triviales parées du vernis Philosophique &c. A coup sûr un tel homme, avec quelques femmes & quelques sots, auroit bientôt autant de réputation que les *** ou les ***, &c.

The article on Woolston contains another diatribe against the *philosophes* and their nefarious influence, only to reach a rather surprising conclusion (ii.230)

Au milieu de cette corruption générale, tout n'est pas désespéré. Si la pureté des mœurs a été altérée, la foi a moins souffert. Car malgré le ton victorieux que prennent les Sophistes à la mode, qu'ont produit jusqu'ici leurs efforts multipliés contre l'édifice sacré du Christianisme? En a-t-il été ébranlé? non. On croit ce qu'on a cru. Il y a quelques infideles sur-tout dans les grandes Villes; mais la foi est toujours la même dans les petites, & les mécréans, qu'un vertige[7] passager avoit enlevés à la saine Doctrine, se rangent tôt ou tard sous les drapeaux de la Religion.

If that were the case, one wonders what need there was for these two volumes.

Chaudon's comments on Jean-Jacques make a further contribution to our understanding of the meaning of the word *philosophe*. In 'Rousseau' he writes of the *Discours sur l'inégalité*: 'Cet Ouvrage célebre est plus capable qu'aucun autre d'humilier la nouvelle Philosophie. Elle prétend seule instruire l'Univers, dissiper les ténebres, chasser les préjugés & la superstition, réformer, épurer la religion, faire briller par-tout un nouveau jour, en un mot, apprendre à penser; & voilà qu'elle finit par mettre l'homme à niveau de la bête.' Like all his contemporaries, including Voltaire, Chaudon takes it for granted that the message of the *Discours sur l'inégalité* was that Man could be happy, virtuous and free only in the primitive state; he was not farsighted enough to imagine that it would one day be argued that this was not at all what Rousseau meant. He continues: 'On ne peut disputer à M. Rousseau tous les avantages & les talens de cette Philosophie, le raisonnement, le calcul, l'érudition, l'éloquence, le feu, la modération même, & un desir d'annoncer le vrai. Mais qu'est-ce que ces avantages, lorsqu'on ne s'en sert que pour attaquer la religion?' (ii.131).

At first sight this somewhat confused passage would seem to support

7. The text has *vestige*.

the view of those who hold that the attention given to Rousseau in works like Chaudon's which attack the *philosophes* shows that their authors continued to regard him as one of the group. Yet the article 'Querelles philosophiques' shows that Chaudon was fully aware that Rousseau had developed his own ideas on religion, ethics and politics and that he had clearly signalled his departure from the group by sharp attacks on its members. After giving, as might be expected, a hostile account of the *philosophes*, Chaudon goes on:

Rousseau parut; nourri dans cette Secte qui s'en faisoit honneur, son esprit trop ardent en avoit reçu l'amour des paradoxes, & un orgueil effréné; mais il avoit du sentiment, du génie, une ame élevée, une éloquence vive & sublime. Il vit que le moment lui étoit favorable; il osa mettre au jour ses propres pensées ...

Pour mieux réussir dans le projet qu'il avoit de mener à la vertu par la Philosophie, il décria les autres Philosophes comme des empoisonneurs. Il s'éleva contre les plaisirs du théatre, que les prétendus Prédicateurs de la sagesse fréquentoient ou cultivoient. Dès lors les Philosophes lui jurerent une haine éternelle. Jean-Jacques donna son *Emile*, compilation monstrueuse de tout ce qu'on a dit contre notre Religion. Ce Livre devoit donner, ce semble, des Protecteurs à Jean-Jacques, parmi les Philosophes; mais le malheureux ayant été proscrit par des Magistrats respectables qui le poursuivoient en gémissant, les Philosophes ses ennemis découvrirent alors toute leur aversion pour lui.

After claiming that Voltaire had done his best to ensure that Rousseau was persecuted in Geneva, Chaudon refers to Rousseau's attempts to embroil Voltaire with the authorities there: 'En écrivant ses *Lettres de la Montagne*, il donna honnêtement quelques coups d'épingle à M. de V. Il se plaignoit de ce que ses Compatriotes, ayant permis l'impression de la *Pucelle* & de plusieurs autres rapsodies infames, n'avoient pas eu la même indulgence pour l'Auteur d'*Emile*, beaucoup moins coupable' (ii.102-103).

In the article 'Rousseau' *Emile* is denounced as 'la consommation de l'impiété de M. Rousseau', and Chaudon declares that in the *Lettres écrites de la Montagne* 'toutes ses erreurs sont reproduites'. Yet, not only does he fully recognise Rousseau's powers as a writer; he praises the man in the most flattering terms (ii.133):

Il est charitable, généreux, bienfaisant. Sa main a plusieurs fois séché les pleurs des malheureux; sa bourse s'est ouverte à leurs besoins, son cœur à leurs chagrins [...] Ses Ouvrages auroient pu l'enrichir; ses protecteurs lui auroient procuré des places considérables; & il a voulu demeurer dans sa médiocrité, se contentant du pur nécessaire, sobre, tempérant, juste, couchant sur la dure, remplissant tous les devoirs d'un Philosophe, autant qu'on peut les remplir, quand on n'est pas Chrétien.

In fact, despite this obvious drawback Rousseau is quite a pet of Chaudon's, especially as in many respects he could be contrasted with the *philosophes* and especially Voltaire.

It was not only that this heterodox writer was enlisted to furnish part of the article 'Dieu' (i.134-35); or that two pages of the article 'Religion' came from his pen (ii.119-21); or that in 'Théatre' with the *Lettre à d'Alembert* he is said to have written 'pour la défense de la vérité un ouvrage digne de la plume la plus éloquente' (ii.170). His writings are constantly drawn upon for weapons with which to attack Voltaire and the other *philosophes*. As early as the preface (i.xvi), in denouncing Voltaire's denials of his authorship of the *Dictionnaire philosophique*, Chaudon quotes one of the pinpricks administered by Rousseau in the *Lettres écrites de la Montagne*: 'Le même homme sera l'Auteur ou ne le sera pas devant le même homme, selon qu'ils seront à l'Audience ou dans un souper. C'est alternativement oui & non, sans difficulté, sans scrupule. De cette façon la sûreté ne coute rien à la vanité.'[8] In 'Persécution' he extracts from the same work another indirect attack on Voltaire, an argument somewhat strangely introduced by Rousseau in attempting to justify his *Emile* which had given such offence to the orthodox, Protestant and Catholic alike (ii.62):

Il faut honorer la Divinité & ne la venger jamais, dit Montesquieu; il a raison. Cependant les ridicules outrageants, les impiétés grossieres, les blasphêmes contre la Religion sont punissables; pourquoi? Parce qu'alors on n'attaque pas seulement la Religion, mais ceux qui la professent; on les insulte, on les outrage dans leur culte, on marque un mépris révoltant pour ce qu'ils respectent, & par conséquent pour eux. De tels outrages doivent être punis par les Loix, parce qu'ils retombent sur les hommes, & que les hommes ont droit de s'en ressentir.[9]

Two substantial passages from the *Profession de foi du vicaire savoyard*[10] are reproduced in the article 'Ame' (i.13-15) in order to refute Voltaire. More significant still is the way in which Rousseau is brought in to provide the whole of the article 'Fanatisme' (i.168) with an extract from the note at the end of the *Profession de foi* in which he denounces the whole outlook of the *philosophes* in the strongest terms.[11] It surely cannot

8. *Œuvres complètes*, éd. B. Gagnebin and others (Paris 1959-), iii.792.

9. *Œuvres complètes*, iii.798.

10. *Œuvres complètes*, iv.584-85, 589-90.

11. *Œuvres complètes*, pp.632-33 (from 'mais ce qu'il n'a eu garde de dire, et qui n'est pas

be suggested that orthodox writers such as Chaudon remained ignorant of the complete breach between Rousseau and the *philosophes*.

Perhaps partly to bring out how important was the task he had undertaken, Chaudon stresses how successful the *Dictionnaire philosophique* had been: 'Tout le monde le lit, tout le monde le cite; Militaires, Magistrats, Femmes, Abbés, c'est une coupe, dans laquelle tous les états & tous les âges s'abreuvent du poison de l'impiété' (i.VIII). A substantial volume would be required if one were to deal with all the criticisms of its author spread through the two volumes of the counterblast. Most of Chaudon's reactions are predictable except at the two extremes. Although his wrath is understandable, he does at times allow himself to be carried away by it, as in the opening sentence of 'Matérialisme': 'Cette doctrine abominable reparoît sous plusieurs faces différentes dans les Articles *Ame, Bêtes, Matiere, Sensation, Sens commun, Songes,* du *Dictionnaire philosophique*' (i.272). Yet of its author who, surely quite wrongly is here accused of preaching materialism, it is conceded in 'Ciel' that 'il parle souvent & très-bien de l'existence de Dieu' (i.98). Indeed every word of the article 'Dieu' is by two unorthodox thinkers, Rousseau and Voltaire, and the lion's share is given to Voltaire (i.135-37). Again and again in the midst of the most virulent attacks on Voltaire Chaudon makes clear his admiration for his literary gifts. 'Ce Poëte', the article 'Volt***' begins, 'est l'esprit le plus universel & l'Ecrivain le plus élégant de la Nation' (ii.217). If only these talents had not been used against the Catholic Church ...

A relatively small amount of space is given up to political questions, and here Chaudon is at his least convincing. Not only does he try to make out, by printing long quotations from *La Mort de César* and *Brutus*, that Voltaire advocated tyrannicide (ii.203-207), but in 'Christianisme' he produces an extraordinary travesty of his political ideas (i.83):

'Que les Souverains sont incapables d'aimer, de connoître le mérite, la vertu, & de les récompenser; que leur science est d'être injustes à la faveur des loix; que leur art consiste à opprimer la Terre; que ce sont des barbares sédentaires, des animaux pour lesquels ceux qui défendent la Patrie ont la folie de se faire égorger; que c'est eux qu'il faut punir personnellement & non pas les troupes qui dévastent les campagnes; enfin, que tel homme qu'il plaira au Peuple de mettre sur le Trône, en jouira à plus juste titre que celui qui l'occupoit par le droit de sa naissance.' Telles sont les gentillesses que M. de V. débite sur les Souverains dans tous ses Ouvrages;

moins vrai' to 'c'est la tranquillité de la mort; elle est plus destructive que la guerre même').

320

& on n'a pas rapporté les endroits les plus audacieux.

In 'Etats' he rejects in more temperate language the political outlook of the *philosophes* in favour of the *status quo* (i.156):

Les Philosophes voudroient de la liberté; mais c'est se tromper que de croire qu'on n'en jouit pas sous un Gouvernement où il y a de la raison & de l'ordre. Qui pourroit être appellé libre, si l'on cessoit de l'être pour être soumis à l'ordre? Les Rois eux-mêmes ne le seroient point. Les bons Rois ne reconnoissent-ils pas l'autorité des Loix? Les Rois politiques ne sont-ils pas assujettis à l'intérêt de leurs Etats? Les Rois les plus absolus ne sont-ils pas assujettis à l'ordre du Gouvernement?

These are certainly among Chaudon's feebler articles.

A gulf separated Chaudon and the *philosophes* on such matters as toleration and freedom of thought and of the press. In 'Liberté de penser', *Quelles bornes doit-on lui donner?*, while allowing that if a man has the wrong ideas on religion, that is a matter between him and God, he goes on: 'Mais si non content de mal penser, un génie hardi veut insinuer ses erreurs aux autres, l'autorité légitime a droit de le punir [...] Funeste liberté! On ne peut faire des Loix trop séveres pour la réprimer' (i.255). He rejects the argument that the English, thanks to the freedom of thought which they enjoy, have surpassed all other nations. He denies in particular that scientific progress has been held back in France by religious barriers: 'Newton auroit pu enfanter ses sublimes systêmes à Paris comme à Londres.' However, he continues: 'On ne veut donc pas gêner les Sciences, mais on veut que la Religion soit respectée. L'abandonnera-t-on à la langue des Impies?' If a writer were to carry freedom of thought so far as to preach atheism, 'il faudroit réprimer son audace, & lui arracher la plume, comme on arrache l'épée de la main d'un furieux' (i.257).

In 'Persécution' Chaudon declares that capital punishment is too severe a penalty for the authors of antireligious works, but such a crime merits in his eyes imprisonment, presumably for life: 'Si le glaive, le feu, & le gibet paroissent une punition très-violente, qu'on prenne des moyens aussi efficaces, quoique moins effrayans, pour les empêcher de dogmatiser. Qu'on les enferme & qu'on les dérobe aux yeux de ce monde, qu'ils voudroient bouleverser par leurs écrits' (ii.61). The same solution is offered in 'Presse'; for those who express the wrong ideas on government and religion there can be only one punishment: 'Qu'on n'attente pas à leur vie, qu'on n'ait point une intolérance sanguinaire; mais qu'on se laisse conduire par cette tolérance sage qui enferme le Corrupteur, pour diminuer la Corruption' (ii.83).

Such were the fetters in which Chaudon and others of their critics would have liked to see the unorthodox writers of their age confined. With the support of the temporal power in the shape of government and Parlement these men could have been silenced. That by the 1760s they had succeeded, despite all manner of obstacles, in loosening the bonds in which they were held and in securing for themselves some degree of freedom of expression was indeed galling for Chaudon and other orthodox writers.

The loss of Gibbon's literary maidenhead*

R. A. LEIGH

I

THE traditional iconography of great writers has perhaps a greater influence on the reader's imagination than is commonly realised. Some authors, of course, are hardly affected at all by their images. Shakespeare, to take an obvious example, dwells in a region where our conceptions of him are influenced neither by the Folio engraving, so like a figure from a gigantic pack of cards, nor by the fine Chandos portrait. But others are not, like him, *hors concours*; and our ideas even of the mighty Beethoven are perhaps directed into narrower channels than they ought to be by dim recollections of that demoniacal bust.

Gibbon, at all events, now seems almost inseparable from his image – the one created by Reynolds in 1779, engraved by James Hall in 1780, and often found inserted as a frontispiece to the *Decline and fall*. Perhaps it seems particularly appropriate, in its association of maturity with corpulence, to the style of the work, which is expansive, ripe and rotund, and in its way not lacking in fat. At any rate, we know that already in his own lifetime Gibbon seems to have become a by-word in both French and English society for conspicuous, almost legendary obesity. Boswell's dislike of him was partly based on his personal appearance. 'Gibbon is an ugly, affected, disgusting fellow and poisons our literary club to me,' he complained petulantly to Temple, in a letter of 8 May 1779 (he also feared and distrusted him, of course, as a dangerous 'infidel' or freethinker). Horace Walpole strikes a less brutal but more astringent note: 'I well know his vanity, even about his ridiculous face and person,' he once declared. But the most striking allusions to Gibbon's obesity come from the Continent. In her *Souvenirs de Félicie*, Mme de Genlis tells two stories of Gibbon. The first takes place in Lausanne:

Avec cette figure et ce visage étrange qu'on lui connaît, M. Gibbon est infiniment

* This article is a slightly revised version of a paper given to the Johnson Club.

galant, & il est devenu amoureux de […] Madame de Crousaz.[1] Un jour, se trouvant tête à tête avec elle, pour la première fois, il voulut saisir un moment si favorable, et tout à coup il se jeta à ses genoux en lui déclarant son amour dans les termes les plus passionnés. Madame de Crousaz lui répondit de manière à lui ôter la tentation de renouveler cette jolie scène. M. Gibbon prit un air consterné, et cependant il restait à genoux, malgré l'invitation réitérée de se remettre sur sa chaise; il était immobile et gardait le silence. 'Monsieur', répéta Madame de Crousaz, 'relevez-vous donc'. – 'Hélas, Madame, répondit enfin ce malheureux amant, *je ne peux pas*. … En effet, la grosseur de sa taille ne lui permettait pas de se relever sans aide. Madame de Crousaz sonna, et dit au domestique qui survint: *Relevez Monsieur Gibbon*.[2]

The second anecdote is set in Paris, and is even more malicious:

M. de Lauzun, très lié avec M. Gibbon, l'a mené chez Madame du Deffand. Cette dernière qui est aveugle, a l'habitude de tâter les visages des personnages célèbres qu'on lui présente […] M. Gibbon s'est empressé de la satisfaire en lui tendant son visage […] voilà Madame du Deffand promenant doucement ses mains sur ce large visage; la voilà cherchant vainement quelque trait, et ne rencontrant que ces deux joues si surprenantes. Durant cet examen, on voyait se peindre successivement, sur la physionomie de Madame du Deffand, l'étonnement, l'incertitude, et en fin tout à coup la plus violente indignation. … 'Voilà', s'écria-t-elle, 'une infâme plaisanterie!'[3]

Both stories are probably apocryphal. The second certainly is, as can be seen from a letter of Mme Du Deffand's to Horace Walpole of 18 May 1777 (*Correspondence*, ed. Lewis, iv.442). Indeed, Mme de Genlis probably realised she had gone too far, for this story, given in the 1813 edition, is omitted in subsequent ones. In any case, she was an inveterate liar, and nothing she says can be believed without independent evidence. However, her two anecdotes seem to show that by the 1780s Gibbon's obesity had become something of a legend. In fact, we may adapt to him something which he himself wrote about Galerius: 'His body, swelled by an intemperate course of life to an unwieldy corpulence' – though fortunately the rest of the passage is inapplicable (*Decline and fall*, 1776, i.417).

1. Née Elisabeth-Jeanne-Pauline Polier de Bottens. She later married a M. de Montolieu, and achieved celebrity, under this name, with the publication in 1786 of her novel *Caroline de Litchfield*.

2. *Souvenirs de Félicie* (Paris 1857), p.176: see also *Mémoires inédits* (Paris 1825), ii.256, note 1.

3. *Souvenirs de Félicie* (Paris 1811-1813), i.314-15, quoted in Horace Walpole, *Correspondence with Madame Du Deffand* […], ed. W. S. Lewis and Warren Hunting-Smith (New Haven 1939), iv.442, n.3.

II

However, we must try on this occasion to dismiss from our minds all such thoughts, for my subject is not the man of forty made famous by the publication of the first volume of the *Decline and fall*, but the slim and graceful youth of twenty who, as he himself puts it, lost his literary maidenhead (*Memoirs*, ed. G. A. Bonnard, London 1966, p.103)[4] with an *Essai* in French *sur l'étude de la littérature*.

The circumstances of the composition of this long little book[5] are somewhat odd, and help to explain why it is not at all what the title might lead a twentieth-century reader to expect. I shall not dwell unduly on the fact that this future master of English prose chose to write his first published book in French, since the reasons are so well known. Whilst an undergraduate at Magdalen College, Oxford, Gibbon became converted, at the tender age of sixteen, to the Church which he was later to describe as 'defending nonsense by violence'; that is to say, to Roman Catholicism. In retrospect, he seems to have blamed Oxford itself, at least by implication, for this youthful lapse. I pass by what he says in general about the University, which he goes out of his way to disclaim as an *alma mater*: 'To the University of Oxford I acknowledge no obligation, and she will as cheerfully renounce me for a son, as I am willing to disclaim her for a mother' (*Memoirs*, p.48). The fourteen months he spent at Magdalen he regarded as 'the most idle and unprofitable of my whole life' (*Memoirs*, p.48). His second tutor 'remembered well that he had a salary to receive, and only forgot that he had a duty to perform' (*Memoirs*, pp.56-57), but he was no worse than the professors: 'In the University of Oxford, the greater part of the public professors have for these many years given up altogether even the pretence of teaching' (*Memoirs*, p.50).

What was more immediately relevant to his conversion is that from a religious point of view, Oxford was worse than a complete write-off: it was a positive incitement to seek religious satisfaction elsewhere: 'Our venerable mother had contrived to unite the opposite extremes of bigotry and indifference' (*Memoirs*, p.57).

Anyway, whatever the causes of, or the reasons for, Gibbon's adolescent conversion, his Anglican father would brook no nonsense and

---

4. The quotations from the *Memoirs* which follow are all from this edition.
5. 159 pp. in-16, without counting the prefatory matter (32 pp.).

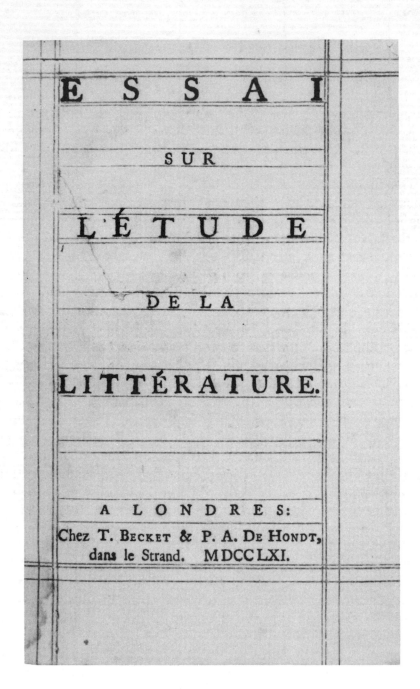

Gibbon's first book: titlepage (border in red)

packed him off to Lausanne for a course of systematic brain-washing by a protestant pastor named Pavillard. Gibbon's love of reading, 'chilled' at Oxford, soon revived, and by the end of his stay, he had almost completed a systematic course of study, designed by himself, of all the Latin authors, major and minor, arranged in four classes: historians, poets, orators and philosophers. He also tried, with less success, to learn Greek, and he seems also to have read some French authors, both classic and contemporary: Pascal, La Bruyère, Racine, Boileau, Montesquieu and, of course, Voltaire, whom he got to know personally, and whom he saw on at least half a dozen occasions, performing in his own plays at Lausanne in 1757 and 1758.

But Pavillard's family spoke no English, and, after some months, as Gibbon says, 'French, in which I spontaneously thought, was more familiar than English to my ear, my tongue and pen' (*Memoirs*, p.71). And so it came about that his first published work was written in French. In fact, the first chapter was actually composed at Lausanne, probably in the winter of 1757-1758, and the work was finished in his father's library at Buriton in Hampshire in the summer of 1758. The manuscript was then transcribed by one of the French prisoners of war at Petersfield. (This was, of course, the time of the Seven Years' War). It was then sent to Maty at the British Museum for comment, extensively recast in the light of his criticisms, and assumed its final form at the end of January 1759. It was not, however, sent to the press until early in the summer of 1761.[6] Towards the end of June in that year, Gibbon, then on active service with the Hampshire Militia, received his author's copies, some of which he proceeded to distribute to his bewildered fellow officers.

III

For the modern reader, the title of the work raises high hopes. The study of literature! Will Gibbon be speaking to us of the great educative value of the discipline in which so many readers of this book are actively engaged? Will he dwell on the incomparable stimulus produced by the meeting of the student's mind with the great minds of the past? Will he stress the expansion of the personality made possible by access to the great and varied storehouse of wisdom and experience contained in the

6. Maty supplied a long preface (pp.xv-xxxiii), dated 16 June 1761.

masterpieces of world literature? Of course, we should be foolish to expect from a youth of twenty any profound or original insights into these same masterpieces: but considering that a marginal heading on p.1 introduces the phrase 'histoire littéraire', we may well look forward with anticipatory pleasure to following the thoughts of this future great historian on 'literary history'. We may legitimately wonder how he conceives the subject, so new in the eighteenth century. Will he spring like a chamois from peak to peak of past literary achievement? Or will he aim at a more continuous texture, anticipating, however remotely, the theories of Taine or Lanson? Will he even discuss the intriguing question of whether literature *has* a history? Again, the term 'littérateurs' recurs quite frequently in his text. These 'littérateurs' are not the authors themselves: so who are they?

If the answers to these questions are surprising and more than a little disappointing, that is to some extent our fault. It is not so much that we should have forgotten that it is a youth of twenty or twenty-one who is wielding the pen. No doubt some of the shortcomings of the *Essai* are due to that cause, including its disconcerting lack of any kind of coherent argument. It seems to have been composed in independent fragments, without any general plan. In his *Memoirs*, where he writes about himself and his achievements with a complacency which is not invariably free from self-satisfaction, Gibbon admits quite freely that his *Essai* lacks order and organisation: 'A number of remarks and examples, historical, critical and philosophical, are heaped on each other without method or connection, and if we except some introductory pages, all the remaining chapters might indifferently be reversed or transposed' (*Memoirs*, p.103). At the same time, he blamed the influence of Montesquieu, who is often mentioned and always with admiration in the *Essai* itself, for the 'obscurity of many passages', ascribed to 'the desire of expressing, perhaps a common idea, with sententious and oracular brevity': 'Alas, how fatal has been the imitation of Montesquieu!' He nonetheless concludes that the '*Essai* does credit to a young writer of two and twenty years of age, who had read with taste, who thinks with freedom, and who writes in a foreign language with spirit and elegance' (p.104). That may well be so: but it does not help us to discover what the *Essai* is really about: nor, if (as Gibbon asserts) in a first work an author 'ventures to reveal the measure of his mind' (p.105), are we led to think very highly of this one.

However, to be absolutely fair, only part of our disappointment arises from the confusion and indistinct focus of the *Essai*. Another obstacle is the semantic complexity of the words 'littérature' and 'littérateur' in eighteenth-century French. Let us leave aside the fact that Gibbon used the word 'littérature' in different senses, as he himself concedes in his *Memoirs*: 'Instead of a precise and proper definition, the title itself, the sense of the word *Littérature* is loosely & variously applied' (p.103). That is no doubt true: but a greater obstacle to the modern reader is that since the eighteenth century the word itself has undergone a significant shift in meaning. If we open the Academy dictionary of 1762, which, though a little later than the *Essai*, records the usage of the 1750s, we discover that 'littérature' is defined as: 'Erudition, doctrine. Ce mot regarde proprement les Belles-Lettres'. As for 'littérateur', that is defined as 'celui qui est versé dans la littérature'. Slightly put out, we then consult 'Lettres' in the plural, which, we learn, 'se dit [...] de toute sorte de Science & de doctrine. *Les Belles-Lettres. Les lettres humaines. Un homme de Lettres. La République des Lettres.* [...] *Cet homme* a beaucoup d'esprit, mais il n'a point de Lettres.' Finally, on looking up 'Belles-Lettres', we discover that 'on entend par Belles-Lettres, La Grammaire, l'Eloquence, la Poesie'. Here then is at least a clue to what the *Essai* is mostly about: not about literature, but about literary scholarship. It is Gibbon's intention to defend traditional literary scholarship, that is to say, scholarship connected with the literature of the Ancient world, against the aspersions of d'Alembert, both in the *Discours préliminaire* to the Encyclopédie (1751), and in the article 'Erudition'. In fact, Gibbon very much objects to the words 'érudition' and 'érudit', which he regards as pejorative neologisms not in common use before 1720 or thereabouts, and deliberately and slightingly substituted for the terms 'littérature' and 'littérateur'. But 'érudition' and 'érudit' are in fact what he means in terms of today's usage. It is this apologia which is the principal aim of Gibbon's first book. In the *Essai* itself, it has been slipped unobtrusively into a longish footnote, and the barb somewhat blunted (p.12). The *Memoirs*, however, make the intention quite explicit (p.99):

In France, to which my ideas were confined, the learning and language of Greece and Rome were neglected by a philosophic age. The guardian of these studies, the Academy of Inscriptions, was degraded to the lowest rank among the three Royal societies of Paris: the new appellation of *Erudits* was contemptuously applied to the successors of Lipsius and Casaubon; and I was provoked to hear (see Mr d'Alembert's Discours préliminaire a l'Encyclopédie) that the exercise of the memory, the sole merit, had been superseded by the nobler faculties of the imagination and the judgment. I was ambitious of proving by my own example as well as by my precepts that all the faculties of the mind may be exercised and displayed by the study of ancient literature.

So the *Essai* is basically a sort of 'défense et illustration' of the work of the Académie des inscriptions. And as if to rub the point in, Gibbon tells us that one of his first acts on returning to England, was to blue twenty pounds of his first quarter's allowance on acquiring the proceedings of the Academy: 'I cannot forget the joy with which I exchanged a bank-note of twenty pounds for the twenty volumes of the Memoirs of the Academy of Inscriptions' (*Memoirs*, p.97).

As we turn over the pages of the *Essai*, the names we meet with in the main are those of a whole series of illustrious unknowns, whose lives and learning were devoted to clarifying the language and elucidating the allusions and chronology of Latin and Greek texts: Fréret, Brumoy, Sellier, La Bleterie, Banier, Le Clerc, Le Bossu, Rapin, Terrasson, Lefebure, besides earlier scholars like Isaac Vossius, Justus Lipsius, Casaubon and Erasmus.

It is true that when at last Gibbon actually defines what he means by criticism, he appears to give it a much broader scope (pp.44-45):

La critique est, selon moi, l'art de juger des écrits et des écrivains; ce qu'ils ont dit, s'ils l'ont bien dit, s'ils ont dit vrai. De la première de ces branches découle la grammaire, la connoissance des langues, et des manuscrits, le discernement des ouvrages supposés, le rétablissement des endroits corrompus. Toute la théorie de la Poësie et de l'éloquence se tire de la seconde. La troisième ouvre un champ immense, l'examen et la critique des faits. On pourroit donc distinguer la nation des critiques en critiques Grammairiens, en critiques Rhéteurs, et en critiques Historiens. Les prétensions exclusives des premiers ont nui non-seulement à leur travail, mais à celui de leurs confrères.

There is a kind of concertina effect here, in which the perspective is at first enlarged and then narrowed, with an emphasis on purely historical research. Occasionally, it is true, Gibbon whets our appetite, for instance by declaring: 'Tout ce qu'ont été les hommes; tout ce que le génie a créé; tout ce que la raison a pesé; tout ce que le travail a recueilli, voilà le département de la critique' (p.45).

But he soon shies away from these limitless perspectives (which in any case apply in his mind only to classical literature), and confines himself in the main to questions of historical detail. For that, we discover, is what he really means by 'histoire littéraire': not the history of literature at all, but the historical context of Latin and Greek masterpieces, the historical allusions they contain, and in one or two instances their historical origins. We hear little of the theory of poetry and eloquence. Gibbon informs us that the object of poetry is to charm, move and elevate the mind, but obviously feels happier with more pedestrian topics, such as the writer's duty to respect both history and mythology in dealing with traditional material, an idea which comes straight out of Horace and Boileau. 'Les anachronismes d'Ovide nous deplaisent,' says Gibbon gravely (p.63), rather in the manner of Queen Victoria not being amused.

What we read elsewhere in the *Essai* about poetry is curious rather than illuminating. He has, for instance, discovered a hidden political and patriotic purpose in the *Georgics*. Virgil is alleged to have written this work at the behest of Augustus who, fearing the restlessness and boredom of demobilised soldiers on the land with which they had been rewarded, resorted to this method of reconciling them to their lot. The glorification of rural pursuits would make contented farmers out of disaffected soldiers (pp.39ff.). This idea is unlikely to be widely held today, nor do demobilised soldiers spring to mind as an obvious public for the *Georgics*.

Of greater interest, in his general attempt to establish the superiority of Ancient over modern literature, is the remark that 'Les Mœurs des Anciens étoient plus favorables à la Poësie que les nôtres' (p.19). I suspect Gibbon of having borrowed this idea, without acknowledgement, from Diderot, who had said exactly the same thing in his *Essai sur la poésie dramatique*, published in 1758: 'Plus un peuple est civilisé, poli, moins ses mœurs sont poétiques,' and had added: 'la poésie veut quelque chose d'énorme, de barbare et de sauvage'. Gibbon illustrates this view by comparing Homer's battle scenes with Voltaire's in his *Poème sur la bataille de Fontenoy*: and again in explaining why *Paradise lost* must necessarily be a failure compared with Homer's accounts of the doings of the gods of Olympus. Eighteenth-century conceptions of God lie far beyond the scope of poetry, and details which would have been sublime in Homer are simply puerile in Milton (p.23).

Both examples illustrate the thesis of this confirmed champion of the *Anciens* against the *Modernes* that the manners of the *Anciens* being more favourable than our own to poetry, this itself is 'une forte présomption qu'ils nous y ont surpassés' (p.19). Indeed, the work as a whole may be regarded as a belated or lingering echo of the famous *Querelle*.

This explains a conspicuous lacuna in the *Essai* – the absence of any reference to Italian literature. Gibbon mentions only the historian Giannoni. At this time, it is true, Dante's star appears to have suffered some sort of general eclipse. But what of Petrarch, Ariosto and Tasso, to say nothing of Boiardo, whose works in the mid-eighteenth century seem to have formed part of the cultural equipment of most educated gentlemen, and indeed of many ladies? A similar lacuna is, of course, English literature. Few English names occur in the *Essai*: Bentley, the Cambridge classical scholar, and Milton, compared unfavourably with Homer. The fact is that the *Essai* is concerned mainly with the historians and poets of ancient Rome, and with the French scholars who had edited or commented on them. Even the references to Greek literature, as Gibbon later admitted, were something in the nature of window-dressing.

In his attempt to refute d'Alembert by both precept and practice, Gibbon inserts a number of mini-essays into the framework of the larger one. There is, for instance, a five-page disquisition on a treaty between Rome and Carthage (pp.50ff.), offered as an example of critical investigation of the facts. Of greater interest is the oblique attack on the contemporary French *philosophes*, to whom he would deny the title (p.84):

Je mets sans balancer l'esprit philosophique avant celui de discernement. C'est la chose du monde la plus pronée, la plus ignorée et la plus rare. Il n'y a point d'écrivain qui n'y aspire. Il sacrifie de bonne grace la science. Pour peu que vous le pressiez, il conviendra que le jugement sévère embarasse les opérations du génie: mais il vous assurera toujours que cet esprit philosophique, qui brille dans ses écrits, fait le caractère du siècle où nous vivons. L'esprit philosophique d'un petit nombre de grands hommes a formé, selon lui, celui du siècle. Celui-ci s'est répandu dans tous les ordres de l'état, et leur a préparé, à-son-tour, de dignes successeurs.

Then after a page or two of general remarks directed against the *esprit frondeur* and the pretensions of mathematics, Gibbon tells us that the true philosophical spirit is to be found in the works of Cicero, Tacitus, Bacon, Leibnitz, Bayle, Fontenelle and Montesquieu (p.86).

Montesquieu in fact is the only modern French writer whom Gibbon whole-heartedly admires in the *Essai*. It is indeed surprising how few are mentioned, much less quoted: Montaigne, Racine, Boileau, La Bruyère, Voltaire, and of course the scholars to whom I have already referred. At this time, Montesquieu is clearly Gibbon's hero. The *Esprit des lois* is not actually mentioned, but there is a quotation from the *Considérations*, one of the numerous pointers in this *Essai* to Gibbon's future vocation. (The preference expressed for the patient study of the facts, as against the fashion for brilliant or flashy generalisations, is another.)

This admiration for Montesquieu may be partly explained, as Gibbon indeed does, by the fascination of his style (his 'sententious and oracular brevity'). It was fortified by his respect for the *Considérations*, perhaps unjustly eclipsed today by the twin suns of the *Lettres persanes* and the *Esprit des lois*. But there was also perhaps something of a temperamental affinity between Montesquieu and Gibbon. The great French writer felt able to refer to himself one day as 'n'ayant jamais eu de chagrin qu'un quart d'heure de lecture n'ait dissipé'. Such serenity could in the nature of things be the birthright only of a favoured few. We think of Gibbon, perhaps unfairly, as having passed most of his life in a state of feline contentment. Reynolds did not paint him poring over an immense folio, pen in hand: but that is how we picture him. At all events, he seems to have had little in common with a French-speaking writer, of whom predictably he disapproved, and whose name he conceals behind an anonymous 'on' (p.158):

Les sciences, dit-on, naissent du luxe: un peuple éclairé sera toujours vicieux. Je ne le crois pas. Les sciences ne sont point les filles du luxe: mais l'une et l'autre naissent de l'industrie. Les arts ébauchés satisfont aux premiers besoins de l'homme. Perfectionnés ils lui en trouvent de nouveaux. [...] Mais à mesure que le luxe corrompt les mœurs, les sciences les adoucissent, semblables aux prières dans Homere, qui parcourent toujours la terre à la suite de l'injustice, pour adoucir les fureurs de cette cruelle Divinité.

Gibbon's attitude to Rousseau was not destined to become more favourable as the years went by, partly because, though doubting in the *Essai* the pretensions of his age to philosophy, he never seriously questioned its fundamental optimism. One day, in fact, he was to write: 'We may readily acquiesce in the pleasing conclusion, that every age of the world has increased and still increases, the happiness, the knowledge and perhaps the virtue of the human race.' None the less, other things being equal, which they were not, it would not have been impossible for a certain amount of Rousseau to have leaked into Gibbon's mind through the crack opened up by that inconspicuous 'perhaps'.

However that may be, the author of the *Essai* does not yet attempt to view humanity from those panoramic heights: and read as a defence of scholarship, the *Essai* is perhaps not very effective or impressive. What is impressive, however, is the extent of Gibbon's reading and his attention to detail. Never, it may be confidently asserted, was a literary maidenhead lost with so much learning.

'De l'horrible danger de la lecture': la bibliothèque de Monsieur Parangon

JEAN EHRARD

Dis moi qui tu lis, je te dirai qui tu es: cette variante d'une maxime populaire est la devise des historiens qui de nos jours s'attachent à l'analyse des catalogues de bibliothèques privées d'autrefois. On sait par exemple ce que notre connaissance actuelle du dix-huitième siècle français doit à ce type de recherches dont Daniel Mornet avait le premier compris l'intérêt: non seulement pour une familiarité intellectuelle plus intime avec des personnalités de premier plan – un Montesquieu, un Massillon, un Dortous de Mairan – mais aussi dans la perspective plus large de l'étude socio-culturelle des milieux.[1] Or les bibliothèques qui apparaissent dans les catalogues d'usage ou de vente ainsi que dans les inventaires après décès, prestigieuses ou modestes, ne sont peut-être pas les seules à mériter attention: pourquoi ne pas s'arrêter aussi sur les bibliothèques imaginaires? Pourquoi ne pas poser à celles-ci également les questions précises que nous savons adresser aujourd'hui à leurs homologues de la réalité? Sur la formation de la bibliothèque – patrimoniale ou personnelle – sur sa richesse, sur sa composition et la part relative des différentes catégories d'ouvrages, sur sa destination – professionnelle, de recherche ou de loisirs – sur l'origine géographique et l'âge de ses livres, etc., que d'interrogations possibles et, à partir de là, quelle ample matière à réflexion! A condition, bien sûr, de ne pas oublier qu'un texte littéraire n'est pas un document brut et que le témoignage d'une bibliothèque imaginaire, dévié par la fiction et les choix narratifs d'un roman, doit être interprété au second degré, selon les exigences de la logique romanesque.[2]

De tous les romanciers du dix-huitième siècle Rétif est probablement le plus enclin à prêter à ses héros sa propre boulimie de lecture. Leur

1. Voir en particulier M. Marion, *Recherches sur les bibliothèques privées à Paris au milieu du XVIIIe siècle (1750-1754)* (Paris 1978).

2. Sur l'intérêt que présentent pour l'historien les bibliothèques imaginaires, et pas seulement les bibliothèques romanesques, voir l'article stimulant de G. Benrekassa, 'Bibliothèques imaginaires: honnêteté et culture, des lumières à leur postérité', *Romantisme* (1984), no 2, pp.3-18.

protecteur et mauvais génie, Gaudet, dans *Le Paysan perverti* puis dans *La Paysanne pervertie*, est un véritable érudit. Aussi apporte-t-il grand soin à composer la bibliothèque d'Edmond. La bibliographie qu'il adresse à Ursule est relativement succincte: opéras comiques et comédies à ariette, romans ('tous les romans qui sont bien écrits'), chansons et contes suffiront à son sexe.[3] Le catalogue des livres d'Edmond est au contraire étonnamment riche, en particulier pour l'histoire ancienne. Un jeune peintre mondain a-t-il vraiment besoin de lire *Arpien*, 'pourtant peu sûr',[4] Vopisque ou Eutrope? De ce catalogue dont l'érudition traduit l'une des manies de Rétif, sinon l'un de ses phantasmes, trois sortes de textes sont toutefois absents: absence de fait de la littérature sacrée, absence, soulignée par Gaudet, des journaux et des livres licencieux.[5] On comprend qu'Edmond, fût-ce à ses dépens, comme le précise aussi son mentor, se soit quelquefois écarté des conseils de celui-ci: mais nous ignorons en quel sens, de même que nous ne savons pas quel usage il a réellement fait de l'impressionnante collection ainsi réunie. Pas plus dans les bibliothèques imaginaires que dans celles de la réalité la possession d'un livre n'est signe assuré de lecture ... Aussi est-il plus intéressant de suivre Edmond dans sa première initiation au monde des livres: à Sacy, puis et surtout à Auxerre où la bibliothèque du ménage Parangon a peut-être beaucoup à nous apprendre.

Le jeune paysan au 'cœur innocent et droit' qui découvre avec émerveillement en octobre 1748 l'animation et les beautés d'Auxerre,[6] s'il a la naïveté de ses seize ans et de ses origines rurales, n'est ni un sot ni un ignorant. Son père en a témoigné auprès de Mme Parangon: 'il aime la lecture, et il sait la sainte Bible par cœur et quant au latin, il l'entend fort bien, et même un peu le grec; M. le curé dit que c'en est assez pour ce que doit savoir un peintre'.[7] Tout ce savoir n'est pas purement imaginaire: la même année 1748 le jeune Nicolas étudiait le latin sous la férule de son frère, le curé de Courgis. Il est vrai qu'à la différence du héros du

3. *La Paysanne pervertie*, éd. B. Didier (Paris 1972), lettre CVII, pp.353-54.
4. Entendons *Appien*: c'est Gaudet qui est 'peu sûr'!
5. *La Paysanne pervertie*, pp.352-53. Sur ce passage et, de façon plus générale, sur l'importance éducative que Rétif accorde aux livres, voir P. Testud, *Rétif de La Bretonne et la création littéraire* (Genève, Paris 1977), pp.47-52.
6. Trois ans avant Nicolas Rétif dont le brevet d'apprentissage sera signé le 24 septembre 1751. Né en octobre 1734, Rétif atteindra alors ses dix-sept ans.
7. *Le Paysan perverti*, éd. D. Baruch (Paris 1978), i.27.

Paysan perverti on le destinait alors à l'état ecclésiastique. L'autobiographie romancée qu'est *Monsieur Nicolas* nous apporte toutefois une indication complémentaire qui rejoint celles du roman. Le narrateur dit en effet avoir appris à lire dans un syllabaire latin. Cela ne signifie pas qu'il comprenait déjà la langue: 'je lisais du latin que je n'entendais pas'.[8] De même l'éducation latine d'Edmond s'est faite en deux temps: d'abord par le simple apprentissage de la lecture et de l'écriture – sous la férule d'un 'Maître Jacques' qui nous rappelle le Jacques Berault de *Monsieur Nicolas*, instituteur ignorant et brutal – apprentissage complété hors de l'école par la passion de la copie ('j'avais toujours la plume à la main, je copiais les hymnes et les antiennes qu'on chante à l'église'); plus tard par l'étude de la langue elle-même, auprès du prêtre du village ('nos pauvres pères et mères [...] me crurent fait pour devenir un docteur; ils me mirent chez M. le curé pour apprendre le latin'). A son arrivée à Auxerre Edmond est donc en état de lire 'couramment un livre latin en français'.[9] *Lire*, mais non *rédiger*. La distinction a son importance, et le héros ne tarde pas à en prendre conscience. Glorieux à Sacy, il se découvre bien gauche à Auxerre au moment d'écrire à son frère ses premières impressions. Comme on ne lui a jamais appris à s'exprimer, et pas plus en français qu'en latin, le voici en butte aux railleries de la malicieuse Manon: 'je sens bien que j'écris mal, n'ayant jamais écrit de moi même, car quand j'écrivais mes versions de latin, M. le curé me dictait et ne me laissait rien faire de mon estoc' (p.30).

Assurément ces nuances et ces précisions sonnent juste. En va-t-il de même de la mention du grec? *Monsieur Nicolas* affirme avoir appris cette langue tout seul, dans un recueil de *Racines grecques* emprunté à la bibliothèque de son 'frère-parrain', le curé de Courgis.[10] S'il faut prendre le propos pour argent comptant – et pourquoi pas? – nous devons en conclure qu'Edmond n'a été ni plus ni moins précoce que son modèle: à seize ans il a déjà acquis les quelques notions que le jeune Rétif avait découvertes à quinze.[11] Accordons au romancier que l'écart entre les deux

---

8. *Monsieur Nicolas ou le cœur humain dévoilé* (Paris 1959), t.i, Première époque, pp.23-24 (le syllabaire latin) et p.61: 'Fatigué, je lisais du latin, que je n'entendais pas, mais que j'aimais chanter à l'église'. Rappelons que l'ouvrage n'a été publié qu'en 1796-1797. S'il nous arrive de dire que *Le Paysan perverti* (1775) 'rappelle' *Monsieur Nicolas*, ce n'est évidemment valable que pour le lecteur d'aujourd'hui.

9. *Le Paysan perverti*, Première lettre, p.32.

10. *Monsieur Nicolas*, t.i, Troisième époque, pp.240 et 345.

11. Monsieur Nicolas date en effet cette découverte de 1749 (p.345).

textes, et sans doute entre le roman et l'expérience personnelle, est à peu près nul. Quant à la Bible, on sait la place qu'elle occupe dans les veillées familiales de *La Vie de mon père* où le petit Edme affirme au père Brasdargent la savoir 'quasi par cœur':[12] cette Bible paternelle, 'complète, un peu gauloise' – c'est à dire ancienne – n'est pas le simple 'abrégé' que le maître d'école de Nitry, 'le vénérable Berthier', recommande à ses élèves comme pieuse distraction quand ils vont paître leurs bestiaux (pp.29, 10). Sans entrer ici dans un débat problématique sur la lecture populaire des saintes Ecritures dans la France rurale de l'Ancien Régime, et en nous gardant de prendre *La Vie de mon père* pour un témoignage à recevoir sans critique,[13] nous pouvons du moins souligner la forte cohérence de l'univers rétivien: de la fiction romanesque à la geste paternelle, comme du roman à l'autobiographie la continuité est évidente. Quelques exceptions pourtant: au même âge qu'Edmond Nicolas avait déjà des rudiments de culture littéraire profane dont le roman ne fait pas mention. Edmond n'a jamais entendu parler du *Polexandre* de Gomberville, sujet de 'ravissement', à Joux, pour le petit Nicolas auquel la douce et sensible Julie en faisait lecture 'des heures entières'.[14] Rien n'indique non plus qu'il connaisse ces 'histoires, soit anciennes, soit modernes' dont Edme Rétif divertissait les siens dans les longues soirées d'hiver:[15] des histoires que le père de famille pouvait tenir de la tradition orale, mais qui lui venaient aussi des livres que ce 'passionné de lecture' achetait dès l'enfance aux 'merciers-colporteurs' de passage à Nitry (p.27, note a). Entendons des brochures de la *Bibliothèque bleue*, comme le *Fortunatus* dont nous parle, entre autres contes, Monsieur Nicolas: le héros au petit chapeau magique et à la bourse inépuisable.[16] Manifestement le romancier

12. *La Vie de mon père*, éd. Gilbert Rouger (Paris 1970), Livre premier, p.24. Voir aussi *Monsieur Nicolas*, t.i, Première époque, pp.91-92.

13. Sur l'utilisation naïve de *La Vie de mon père* comme document historique au premier degré, voir G. Benrekassa, 'Le typique et le fabuleux: histoire et roman dans *La Vie de mon père*', *Revue des sciences humaines* 43 (1978), pp.31-56. La lecture populaire de la Bible au dix-huitième siècle est un champ de recherches encore à peu près inculte. J'ai moi-même effleuré le sujet dans une communication présentée au colloque *Diderot et Greuze* de Clermont-Ferrand (16 novembre 1984): 'Tableaux de famille: la lecture de la Bible' (à paraître dans les Actes du colloque).

14. *Monsieur Nicolas*, t.i, Première époque, p.105.

15. *La Vie de mon père*, Livre quatrième, p.132.

16. *Monsieur Nicolas*, t.i, Première époque, pp.93-94. Sur Fortunatus voir R. Mandrou, *De la culture populaire aux 17e et 18e siècles* (Paris 1964), pp.50-51 et G. Bollème, *La Bible bleue: anthologie d'une littérature 'populaire'* (Paris 1975), p.429.

choisit de simplifier pour mieux opposer: les lectures rurales sont marquées du double sceau de la gravité et du sacré; les lectures urbaines, orientées vers les plaisirs du sentiment ou par les curiosités d'une intelligence vite dévoyée, auront un tout autre caractère.

Peu de semaines après son entrée en apprentissage, Edmond a pris ses habitudes chez M. Parangon. Rebuté par son initiation laborieuse à un 'art difficile', et surtout par les tracas et les petites humiliations inséparables de son nouvel état, en proie pendant ses loisirs au désœuvrement et à l'ennui, il fréquente assidûment la bibliothèque de son patron.[17] L'existence de celle-ci, chez un maître-artisan, est un indice social qui confirme ce que nous devinons par ailleurs de la maison Parangon: un immeuble assez vaste sur trois niveaux, avec des dépendances – cave, jardin et atelier.[18] Nous ignorons s'il s'agit d'un local spécialement affecté aux livres ou simplement de rayonnages ou d'armoires installés dans le *salon* ou dans la *salle* … Toujours est-il qu'avec sa collection de livres M. Parangon, par ailleurs propriétaire foncier,[19] portraitiste en vogue (p.35),

17. *Le Paysan perverti*, lettre II, pp.31-32.
18. Au rez-de-chaussée, la cuisine (p.32); la *salle* ('je suis descendu dans la salle', p.54) où l'on dîne (p.102) et où Edmond dessine (p.54); le *salon* ('étant descendu sur les 11 heures […] j'ai trouvé Mme Parangon dans le salon', p.99) où la maîtresse de maison reçoit Ursule et Bertrand (p.96), où l'on lit (p.92), et qui est aussi un lieu de passage, comme dans les anciens appartements aux pièces en enfilade ('je restai dans le salon où tout le monde passe', dit Tiennette, p.122).
Au premier étage, l'*appartement* de Mme Parangon ('il vint me trouver dans l'appartement de sa femme', p.122), sans doute aussi celui de son mari – les deux époux, comme des gens distingués, font chambre à part – la *chambre* où Ursule est accueillie (pp.96, 100, 172), et le *cabinet à coucher* de Manon (p.65).
Au second étage le *réduit* situé au-dessus de la chambre de Mme Parangon et d'où Edmond surprend indiscrètement une conversation entre celle-ci et Ursule (p.172), sans doute attenant à la *chambre* inoccupée ('jamais ouverte') dont il a été question précédemment (p.53).
Mentionnons encore la *chambre* d'Edmond, dont nous ne savons pas la situation exacte (sous les combles, comme la 'guérite' de Monsieur Nicolas – ii.109 – qui existe encore aujourd'hui?), mais qui est en étage ('je suis descendu sans qu'on me vît', p.142), la *chambrette* de Laure (p.164), sans oublier les lieux incertains où doivent nécessairement être logés Tiennette, la cuisinière, les deux autres apprentis … Rappelons enfin que la maison Fournier – toujours visible à Auxerre et que l'auteur de cet article a pu visiter, sous la conduite de l'éminent *rétiviste* qu'est M. Charleux – comportait deux corps de bâtiments séparés par une cour intérieure: le bâtiment principal, avec l'imprimerie, donnant sur la cour des Cordeliers, l'autre avec la librairie – sur la rue de l'Horloge, selon le plan restitué par G. Rouger. *Monsieur Nicolas* évoque souvent la *salle*, contiguë à la boutique (t.i, Quatrième époque, p.488), mais il n'y est pas question de *salon* …
19. Est-ce pour un motif professionnel ou pour visiter un domaine qu'il part 'à la campagne'

époux d'une riche héritière (p.123), riche lui-même (p.35), doit être placé, fût-ce à un rang modeste, au nombre des notables auxerrois. En transformant en peintre le libraire-imprimeur Fournier, Rétif fait plus que conserver à son personnage la dignité sociale que l'*Almanach d'Auxerre* attribuera encore, à la fin de l'Ancien Régime, aux deux imprimeurs de la ville, à côté des professionnels de la santé – médecins, chirurgiens, apothicaires – et des professeurs du collège.[20] Non seulement Parangon est l'ami du médecin Tiennot,[21] mais la nature particulière de son métier, qui fait de lui plus un artiste qu'un artisan, son succès et ses revenus l'élèvent nettement au-dessus du commun des corporations pour l'assimiler aux membres des professions libérales. Dans la société du roman M. Parangon est de ceux qui tiennent le haut du pavé: personnage d'autant plus important qu'à l'exception du conseiller au présidial qui va s'éprendre d'Ursule la haute bourgeoisie et la noblesse en sont absentes. La possession d'une bibliothèque est donc bien, dans ce contexte, un élément supplémentaire de prestige social. Car à la différence de celle de maître Fournier – connue par l'inventaire après décès de sa première femme, morte en 1745[22] – elle n'est pas à usage professionnel, mais purement privé.

La différence des fonctions entraîne celle des contenus. Si l'on en croit *Monsieur Nicolas* la librairie de M. Fournier tenait aussi le rôle de cabinet de lecture.[23] La bibliothèque de M.Parangon ne compte peut-être pas 4,000 volumes, mais elle est fortement personnalisée. Les trois quarts des volumes de la librairie Fournier se répartissaient entre ouvrages de piété et de morale d'un côté, manuels scolaires de l'autre; pour le reste, les grands auteurs du dix-septième siècle, des livres d'histoire et de chirurgie, des dictionnaires, mais aucun roman, sauf douze volumes de Mme de Villedieu. On la fréquentait pour s'instruire ou s'édifier, non pour se divertir. Avec quelques éléments communs, la bibliothèque de

(p.99)? N'est-ce pas de ses terres que doivent provenir les fruits et le gibier réclamés de Paris par sa femme (p.128)? Ce domaine ne serait-il pas à Seignelay où séjournent Mme Parangon, Ursule et Tiennette (p.115).?

20. Cf. Daniel Roche, *Le Siècle des lumières en province: académies et académiciens provinciaux (1680-1789)* (Paris, La Haye 1978), ii.347-54.

21. *Le Paysan perverti*, pp.66 et 176. Le nom de Thienot apparaît, avec celui de trois autres médecins, dans l'*Almanach* de 1756. Aucune mention du collège, en revanche, dans le roman.

22. Voir H. Forestier et G. Rouger, 'En marge de Monsieur Nicolas', *Annales de Bourgogne* (1938), pp.198-213, ainsi que P. Testud, p.29, n.86.

23. Le narrateur distingue parmi ses livres 'ceux qu'on donnait à lire' (t.i, Quatrième époque, p.477).

M. Parangon offre un tout autre visage, du moins à la juger – mais comment faire autrement? – aux seuls ouvrages qui sortent de ses rayons. Les goûts d'Edmond, comme ceux de Mme Parangon, sont exclusivement littéraires: point de morale ni de dévotion! Edmond découvre d'abord les grands classiques – Boileau, Molière, Corneille, Racine – et ces lectures, la dernière surtout, le consolent si bien de ses maux qu'il fait partager son plaisir à la cuisinière en lui lisant à haute voix la tragédie: que de pleurs mêlés sur *Bérénice*![24] Un peu plus tard c'est la servante Tiennette – jeune fille d'une condition supérieure à son état du moment – qu'il fait pleurer à une autre lecture émouvante: 'un livre où se trouve l'épître d'une certaine *Arianne* à un traître nommé *Thésée*, qui l'avait abandonnée dans une île déserte' (p.41). Ainsi le jeune Nicolas attendrissait-il autrefois l'aimable Aimée d'une héroïde d'Ovide (i, Quatrième époque, p.420). Ce goût des larmes, où la sensualité s'éveille dans la sentimentalité, le héros ne tardera pas à le cultiver en compagnie de Colette. En pleine communion avec elle il se laisse toucher par une œuvre pourtant médiocre, de son propre aveu: 'les *Lettres d'Héloïse à Abailard*, en vers français assez méchants, ou plutôt mauvais'. Entendons sous ce titre non la première héroïde de Colardeau, publiée en 1758, mais plutôt la traduction par l'obscur Feutry, en 1751, de l'*Epître d'Héloïse à Abélard* de Pope (1717); et ne chicanons pas l'auteur sur la chronologie: quand celle du roman situe l'événement en février 1750 elle n'anticipe que d'un an sur la sortie du livre ... Il est plus important de noter que cette traduction est une *nouveauté*: l'élégante Colette, qui revient de Paris, se tient informée – parfois par anticipation! – de l'actualité littéraire. Le trait était encore plus marqué précédemment quand Edmond, aux côtés de Mme Parangon et de Tiennette, reconnaissait son propre cœur dans les *Lettres du marquis de Roselle*: la première édition du roman de Mme Elie de Beaumont date en effet de 1764.[25]

A l'occasion de cette dernière lecture Mme Parangon avait exprimé 'les sentiments les plus tendres et les plus honnêtes'. Rien de tel à attendre de son mari dont la culture et les goûts sont tout opposés, soit qu'il cite

---

24. *Le Paysan perverti*, p.31 – A rapprocher de *Monsieur Nicolas*, i.471-73. C'est *Zaïre* et non *Bérénice* que Nicolas lit à Mme Parangon (p.479).

25. *Le Paysan perverti*, p.79. C'est la même lecture qui aurait valu au narrateur de *Monsieur Nicolas* (t.ii, Quatrième époque, pp.50-51), pour la première fois, le contact ineffable du pied de Colette. Pierre Testud souligne justement à ce propos 'combien l'œuvre romanesque a influé sur la rédaction de l'autobiographie' (p.32).

JEAN EHRARD

Boccace et les *Contes* de La Fontaine, soit qu'il s'égaie d'une réminiscence de *La Métromanie* (pp.110, 200). En fait Rétif répartit entre les deux personnages ses propres lectures d'autrefois: Nicolas évoque le temps où il passait de Corneille à Boileau, à Chaulieu, La Fontaine, Grécourt, Vergier, pour revenir à la *Phèdre* de Racine.[26] Parangon, quant à lui, ne manifeste pas une telle dualité de goûts. Esprit caustique par nihilisme moral, franc épicurien, il a du reste une réputation bien établie de libertinage (p.64). On sait comment il a séduit et engrossé sa cousine avant de la faire épouser à son apprenti. Or c'est à l'aide de livres qu'il l'a corrompue, mettant en œuvre à cette fin les plus secrètes ressources de sa bibliothèque, selon une progression très étudiée. D'abord des 'lectures voluptueuses': *Tombeau philosophique* – un roman de Jean-François de Bastide: *Le Tombeau philosophique, ou histoire du Marquis de * à Mme d'***, par le chevalier de la B*** (Amsterdam 1751); *Le Sopha* de Crébillon (1745) et 'quelques romans de Mme de Villedieu où l'on voit des femmes mariées écouter et favoriser des amants' (p.150). Mais ce n'était là que prélude. Une fois les sens de la jeune fille mis en émoi par l'intermédiaire de 'l'esprit' et du 'cœur',[27] il fallait préparer plus directement la victoire en levant l'obstacle des principes moraux et religieux. Un livre, 'chef d'œuvre en son genre', *agréable poison*, était en mesure de transformer un simple *égarement* (Rétif n'emploie pas le mot, mais il est appelé par la situation et la référence à Crébillon) en corruption irrémédiable, '*la P. de M. de V....*, qui ne faisait que de paraître pour lors'. Là encore la liberté du romancier lui autorise un manifeste anachronisme, qui ne sera du reste pas le dernier: *La Pucelle* n'a été éditée qu'en 1762. Le fait importe moins que sa raison d'être: comprenons que le goût des nouveautés est aussi vif chez Monsieur que chez Madame. Mais le premier fait servir à ses mauvais desseins une curiosité qu'il a, comme sa femme, les moyens de satisfaire. Pour triompher de Manon, ébranlée dans sa dévotion par les alertes décasyllabes de *La Pucelle*, poussée par leur ironie corrosive à éprouver 'du mépris pour les saintes vérités de la religion', il restait à porter à ces dernières le coup décisif. M. Parangon y avait pourvu par une double démarche qui combinait argumentation rationnelle et appel à la sensibilité. Retournant Pascal contre lui-même, ce libertin sait en effet qu'une vérité abstraite est sans conséquence pratique si elle n'est

26. *Monsieur Nicolas*, t.i, Quatrième époque, p.471.
27. 'il tâcha d'exciter le feu qui couvait dans mon sein [...]; enfin, il séduisit à la fois mon esprit et mon cœur'.

pas vivifiée de l'évidence du cœur. C'est pourquoi les lectures théoriques qu'il imposait à Manon s'accompagnaient de livres d'une autre sorte: 'en même temps que M. Parangon m'éclairait, selon lui, il songeait à porter dans mon cœur une corruption qui me fît désirer que ce que je trouvais dans ces livres fût la vérité. En conséquence, il me donnait à lire tout ce que la lubricité a dicté de plus infâme' (pp.150-51).

Restons sur notre curiosité malsaine. Nous ne saurons rien d'autre de ces lectures lubriques qui appartiennent à l'enfer des bibliothèques et relèvent de l'innommable. La confession de Manon nous donne en revanche les titres de plusieurs des 'livres damnables' qui ont intellectuellement contribué à sa perte. Il est assez facile de les compléter et d'identifier, au moins de façon plausible, les ouvrages auxquels ils correspondent. Dans l'ordre où elle les cite ce sont: *Le Christianisme dévoilé* du baron d'Holbach (1762), *Le Dîner du comte de Boulainvilliers* de Voltaire (1767), *La Contagion sacrée, ou histoire naturelle de la superstition* (1768) et l'*Essai sur les Préjugés, ou de l'influence des opinions sur les mœurs et sur le bonheur des hommes* (1770) du même d'Holbach. On peut hésiter sur le titre suivant: '*Bolinbrocke*' [*sic*]. S'agit-il de la *Défense de Milord Bolingbrocke*, de Voltaire (1752) ou des six volumes d'*Œuvres posthumes* du philosophe anglais (1754-1755)? Beaucoup plus vraisemblablement de l'*Examen important de Milord Bolingbroke ou le tombeau du fanatisme*, publié par Voltaire en 1767. Dans ce contexte les *Lettres sur les miracles* mentionnées ensuite sont peut-être bien les *Discours sur les miracles de Jésus-Christ* de Thomas Woolston, ouvrage relativement ancien (1727-1729) dans sa version anglaise, mais dont la traduction française, probablement rédigée par d'Holbach, date seulement de 1769. Nous restons dans la même période, et nous retrouvons Voltaire, avec la *Confession de foi des Théistes*: c'est en effet sous ce titre qu'en 1769 l'*Evangile du jour* reproduit une brochure de l'année précédente intitulée *Profession de foi des théistes par le comte D...*, *traduite de l'allemand*. Au total la foi vacillante de Manon doit donc affronter la grosse artillerie antichrétienne de la fin des années 1760: un ensemble de publications militantes unies dans une même dénonciation de 'l'infâme', mais idéologiquement dissemblables. Bientôt le *Système de la nature* va consacrer la scission entre le déisme voltairien et l'athéisme à la d'Holbach. On notera qu'entre celui-ci et celui-là Parangon ne fait pas de distinction. L'amalgame n'est pourtant pas sans fondement: il traduit bien le jugement dont les deux partis 'philosophes' devaient être l'objet, au plus fort de la lutte, de la part non de leurs adeptes, mais de leurs adversaires. En aucun temps la polémique ne s'est accommodée de nuances. Vers 1770 les croyants heurtés dans leur foi et, de façon générale, les esprits traditionalistes bousculés dans leurs habitudes mentales n'analysaient pas les forces perturbatrices avec les scrupules d'un historien des idées: ils réagissaient violemment et indistinctement à tout ce qui les choquait ou les dérangeait. C'est leur point de vue que le romancier adopte en 1775, de même qu'il leur emprunte l'assimilation éculée de la libre-pensée au libertinage de mœurs.

La pédagogie libertine prêtée à M. Parangon est donc très pesamment chargée d'intentions idéologiques qui font ici du rousseauiste Rétif l'allié de fait des pires conservateurs. Aussi est-elle très éloignée de celle que pratiqueront bientôt Valmont et la marquise de Merteuil. Le premier n'aura pas besoin de livres pour séduire ses victimes, sauf à composer lui-même le 'catéchisme de débauche' destiné à son 'écolière'.[28] Quant à la marquise, s'il lui arrivera de relire quelques pages de La Fontaine, de Crébillon et de Jean-Jacques, ce sera 'pour recorder les différents tons' qui lui seront nécessaires à l'adresse du chevalier: travail d'actrice, et non d'institutrice (lettre x, p.37). Par contraste la lourde machine de guerre de M. Parangon apparaît bien pédante et l'on s'étonne un peu qu'il ait trouvé en Manon une 'écolière' aussi studieuse: à moins de conclure à la naïveté de ce redoutable séducteur!

Assurément, Rétif ne le voit pas ainsi. Il tient à faire de son professeur de libertinage un esprit fort, un Philosophe dont la mauvaise conduite discrédite le rationalisme des Lumières. On est loin de François Fournier, vendeur au grand jour de livres de piété anodins et imprimeur clandestin, non de libelles voltairiens, mais des *Nouvelles ecclésiastiques*, le périodique janséniste.[29] Plus loin encore lorsque le romancier, pour compléter le portrait de son personnage, en fait un franc-maçon. Sans doute la chronologie aurait-elle permis à Fournier de se faire initier: la loge d'Auxerre – le *Vrai Zèle* – de création tardive, existait à coup sûr en 1778 et lui-même devait vivre jusqu'en 1782.[30] Mais à supposer que ses orientations personnelles aient été autres que ce que nous pouvons supposer et qu'il ait souhaité cette affiliation, rien ne prouve qu'il l'aurait

---

28. *Les Liaisons dangereuses*, lettre cx (Paris 1964), p.254.

29. La fabrication du périodique interdit faillit l'envoyer en prison. Voir la plaquette de R. Fauchereau, *L'Histoire du 'Perroquet' de Michel-François Fournier, imprimeur à Auxerre de 1742 à 1782* (Auxerre s.d.).

30. D. Roche, i.257, 259 et n.17 (ii.99).

obtenue. Dominée par le clergé, la noblesse et les gens de robe, la loge d'Auxerre ne compte que trois artisans et marchands.[31] Ce qui est sûr, malgré le 'témoignage' de *Monsieur Nicolas* (t.ii, Quatrième époque, p.26), c'est qu'il était impossible, et pour cause, d'être maçon à Auxerre vers 1750. Mais là aussi l'anachronisme mériterait à peine d'être relevé s'il ne se doublait d'une invraisemblance morale tellement grosse qu'elle ne peut être sans signification. Quand on sait la religiosité de la franc-maçonnerie, l'idée d'un maçon athée – ou au déisme particulièrement agressif – et, qui plus est, non à Paris, mais dans une petite ville de province, est aussi étonnante que celle d'un maçon libertin et bambocheur. Or M. Parangon a aussi cette dernière réputation. Son ami, le médecin Tiennot, lui-même maçon, est 'l'un des meilleurs biberons de la ville', et l'on imagine les motifs des visites que lui rend Parangon. C'est du moins Edmond qui l'écrit (p.66), de même qu'antérieurement il lui prêtait, comme à ses pareils, des messes sulfureuses: 'il est franc-maçon, de ces gens qui voient le Diable dans leurs assemblées, sous la forme d'un gros taureau noir' (p.41). Une note de l'auteur nous avertit que l'accusation résulte d'un 'préjugé populaire dans les campagnes'. Des préjugés analogues, plus ou moins rationalisés, n'existaient-ils pas à la ville, et en particulier dans les petites villes aussi rurales que l'Auxerre du dix-huitième siècle? Le narrateur n'en serait-il pas l'interprète? Souvent tenus dans des tavernes, faute d'autres lieux, les banquets fraternels des maçons faisaient jaser.[32] Ici comme dans le cas de la littérature philosophique d'avant-garde le jugement porté a moins valeur individuelle qu'il n'est l'écho de la rumeur publique: la fiction devient réalité dans la mesure où elle traduit un fait d'opinion, et c'est de cette manière indirecte qu'elle présente pour l'historien un intérêt documentaire.

Bien involontairement représentatif, le personnage de M. Parangon doit en fin de compte beaucoup plus à l'idéologie qu'à l'expérience et au souvenir: à l'image de sa bibliothèque telle que le romancier l'a constituée, bien différente de celle de maître Fournier et néanmoins historiquement intéressante, au second degré. Bien que la commodité du coche d'eau mît Auxerre à quatre jours seulement de Paris, rien n'est moins assuré que

31. 'Dans les villes qui se sont dotées d'un seul atelier, Auxerre, Béziers, Chalons-sur-Marne, Cherbourg, Pau, Valence et Villefranche, la méfiance vis-à-vis d'une bourgeoisie médiocre est évidente' (D. Roche, i.269, et ii.103, note 56).

32. D. Roche, i.276.

l'arrivée rapide et massive au petit chef-lieu bourguignon, siège d'un évêché très marqué de jansénisme jusqu'à la mort de Mgr de Caylus en 1754, des productions nouvelles, et surtout des productions clandestines, de la librairie parisienne.[33] C'est le romancier Rétif qui choisit d'ouvrir sur Paris le vie culturelle et les lectures du ménage Parangon. Pour son héros Auxerre n'est qu'une étape, une première initiation à la vie urbaine, un prélude à la découverte de la capitale. Alors que *La Vie de mon père* affectera le goût des livres d'un signe positif – 'j'ose ici défier qu'on me cite un sot qui ait aimé la lecture' (p.27 note a) – les lectures d'Edmond doivent être comptées parmi les 'dangers de la ville' que dénonce le sous-titre du roman. Certes, il y a livres et livres. Ceux que le jeune homme connaissait avant sa venue à Auxerre ne présentaient aucun risque, et dans la bibliothèque des Parangon ceux de Madame ne sont pas ceux de Monsieur. On ne peut réduire les clivages culturels de l'univers rétivien à une opposition sommaire entre la campagne et la ville. Dans le même milieu urbain, sous un même toit, les lectures féminines se différencient nettement des lectures masculines. Reste à savoir si la sentimentalité des premières n'était pas aussi 'dangereuse' que l'idéologie agressive des secondes. Une certaine culture poétique et romanesque ne présentait-elle pas pour la sensualité naissante d'un tout jeune homme autant d'inconvénients que les multiples tentations de la vie urbaine? 'La ville', commente l'auteur (p.176), est un dangereux séjour pour quiconque a le cœur fait comme Edmond.' Sur ce cœur trop 'sensible' l'élégance parisienne et les charmes capiteux de la vertueuse Colette devaient avoir des effets aussi funestes que les discours cyniques de Gaudet. Comment l'émotion partagée, les larmes versées à l'unisson sur le malheur d'Héloïse ne les auraient-elles pas accentués? C'est toute l'ambiguïté du 'rousseau-isme' de Rétif, toute l'équivoque morale de la 'sensibilité'. Lui-même n'en était qu'à demi dupe, même s'il lui plaisait de s'y être laissé prendre. A quelques pages d'intervalle Monsieur Nicolas témoigne de la double impression ressentie dans son adolescence à la lecture des romans de Mme de Villedieu: 'je lisais alors les romans de Villedieu [...] je me persuadai que j'étais aimé' (t.i, Quatrième époque, p.449). 'En lisant les romans de Villedieu je puis protester, d'après ma conscience, qu'ils me

---

33. Avant la loge du *Vrai Zèle* Auxerre a pourtant compté une Académie (1749-1772). Cf. D. Roche, i.32, et les *Mémoires concernant l'histoire civile et ecclésiastique d'Auxerre et de son ancien diocèse* de l'abbé Lebeuf, continués [...] par M. Challe et M. Quantin (Auxerre 1848), t.ii.

portèrent à là vertu'.[34] Ne soyons donc pas surpris de voir se rejoindre, autour de Mme de Villedieu, la réalité et la fiction: est-il indifférent de se rappeler que ses œuvres sont un des rares éléments communs au fonds de librairie passablement austère de maître Fournier et à la bibliothèque si dangereusement engagée dans le siècle de Monsieur Parangon?

34. t.i, Quatrième époque, p.471. Sur cette ambiguïté morale du romanesque à la Villedieu, voir P. Testud, pp.30-31.

Montfaucon's antiquarian shopping-list: d'Antraigues's delayed deliveries

COLIN DUCKWORTH

WHEN Dom Bernard de Montfaucon died at Saint-Germain-des-Prés in 1741 at the age of eighty-seven, he had laid the foundations of the sciences of archaeology and palaeography.[1] His contribution to knowledge about the writings and monuments of the ancient world, both sacred and profane, great as it was, has been so thoroughly superseded since then that it can now hold interest only for the historian of eighteenth-century ideas, not for the modern archaeologist or historian. However, where information that forms part of the eighteenth-century corpus of knowledge about the ancient world has remained in manuscript form, unpublished, or largely unknown; or where its repercussions may have escaped notice because they are recorded in unpublished documents, then it may be of more general interest.

Montfaucon, as a Benedictine monk, would not have approved of Louis de Launay, comte d'Antraigues, despite the elements of their lives they shared, albeit a generation and more apart: sons of provincial nobility of the *midi*, they were both to transcend the genteel and pious mediocrity of their privileged but unremarkable background; both spent short periods in the army, and followed this experience of military life with intense intellectual discovery – Montfaucon as a Benedictine, d'Antraigues as an apparently feckless, impious and rebellious young man who might be cured, so his family thought, of his radical ideas by a journey to the Near East, where he would find out what real tyranny was. He returned even more revolutionary and anti-Church – but certainly not frivolous; his contemporaries would have been very surprised by the amount of homework he did beforehand in preparation for the journey, which is recorded in minute detail in all its meanderings from Cairo to

---

1. E. de Broglie, *Bernard de Montfaucon et les Bernardins* (Paris 1891); J. E. Sandys, *A history of classical scholarship* (Cambridge 1908), ii.385-89; L. D. Reynolds and N. G. Wilson, *Scribes and scholars* (Oxford 1976), pp.131-33.

Warsaw, in his eight hundred and fifty-five pages of 'Mémoires sur la Turquie', which remain unpublished.[2]

D'Antraigues spent several months of 1778 in Constantinople (where he purchased the curved dagger with which he would eventually be assassinated in Surrey), and then took to the sea again away from the plague-ridden city and headed for Alexandria in the company of his multi-lingual dragoman. There, he exchanged the comforts of the captain's cabin (and the voyeuristic pleasures of the harem of the powerful and fortunate Pacha Ismael of Cairo) for the agonies of the camel's back. On a day in early Spring 1779 he gained admission to the ancient monastery of Deir Anba Makar (Sainte-Macaire), thanks to a letter of introduction from the Pacha, and was even allowed to look more closely than most travellers were at the contents of the library. He was astounded at the richness and variety of the collection of ancient manuscripts he found there. Here is his account of what he discovered, as he gives it in his 'Mémoires sur la Turquie':

Aujourd'hui je vais passer ma journée à la bibliothèque qui consiste en une mauvaise chambre remplie de vieux parchemins.

[...] Il est six heures et demie du soir. A peine ai-je resté un quart d'heure pour dîner et depuis six heures du matin je ne suis pas sorti de la bibliothèque. Ainsi j'ai cherché, secoué de vieux papiers pendant huit heures. J'ai eu le chagrin d'être forcé de convenir après avoir vu des écritures de tous les siècles qu'il n'a pas existé un seul homme qui peigne aussi mal que moi. Voilà, mon aimable amie, la découverte la plus sûre que j'aie faite et ce n'en sera pas une nouvelle pour vous.

Avant de vous rien dire de nos recherches il faut vous mettre un peu au fait de l'art nécessaire pour reconnaître un manuscrit, en fixer la date, il faut vous dire quelle écriture est la plus estimée, et enfin quelles sont d'ordinaire les vues qu'on se propose en recherchant de vieux manuscrits.

For the next two pages d'Antraigues goes on to give a potted history of ancient tablets and manuscripts, and of the development of orthography, paying particular tribute to pope Nicholas V, who devoted his life to gathering together ancient manuscripts that had been dispersed and mutilated during the long years of barbarian domination throughout Europe.

Après avoir déplié plusieurs rouleaux et feuilleté plusieurs manuscrits peu import-ants, Adanson, mon drogman, en remarqua un que j'ai jugé très précieux. C'étaient les Hypotiposes de Clément d'Alexandrie écrites en lettres capitales dans le VIIme

2. The 'Mémoires sur la Turquie' are kept in the Bibliothèque de Dijon.

siècle avec des notes à la marge d'un autre caractère. Ce Clément d'Alexandrie vécut dans le second siècle de l'église et fut catéchiste et prêtre d'Alexandrie. Il écrivit plusieurs ouvrages, quelques-uns se sont conservés mais celui qu'on nomme Hypotiposes était perdu. On nomme Hypotiposes les descriptions d'objets quelconques peintes avec tant de chaleur, peintes avec une si vive énergie qu'il semble au lecteur que les scènes qu'on lui trace se passent sous ses yeux au moment qu'il en lit le récit. Je ne sais si Clément avait atteint le but qu'il se proposait sans doute en donnant ce titre à son ouvrage. Les Hypotiposes de St. Clément sont rassemblées dans un grand volume in folio de parchemin couvert en bois et garni de plaques de losanges. Il contient 208 feuilles.

Nous retrouvâmes un Polybe du 3me siècle mais il n'était point entier et vous savez que cet auteur célèbre ami de Scipion et de Laelius écrivit la guerre de Carthage jusques à la fin de celle de Macédoine. Le vertueux Brutus qui assassina César l'aimait et l'admirait. [...]

Mais une découverte infiniment précieuse, c'est un Diodore de Sicile entier que nous trouvâmes écrit dans le milieu du même siècle. Cet écrivain écrivait du temps d'Auguste. Il écrivit après avoir beaucoup voyagé ce qui le distingue de nos savants modernes. Son histoire universelle était contenue dans quarante livres. L'illustre Pline disait qu'il était le premier qui n'eut pas écrit des bagatelles. Il ne nous restait que quinze de ces livres mais St. Macaire en possède une copie entière, au moins je le crois: ne sachant pas le grec je n'ai pu que compter les livres avec Adanson qui l'entend parfaitement. L'écriture en est assez belle et les premiers feuillets de chaque livre sont en lettres [*illegible*].

Nous trouvâmes un Herodas du VIII siècle et un Pausanius du VII assez beau.

Voilà quels ont été nos succès et la découverte du seul Diodore récompenserait les fatigues d'un long voyage. Ce serait un présent inestimable qu'on ferait à la république des lettres, celui de qui elle le tiendrait aurait des droits éternels à sa reconnaissance. D'après cela vous allez croire que j'en suis possesseur. Non, ma princesse, il restera à St. Macaire jusques à ce que les moines soient plus complaisants ou le hasard amène quelque fripon chez eux. Je leur ai proposé deux cents sequins pour ce livre. Le chef m'a refusé en disant que leur loi leur prohibait de rien vendre de ce qui était dans leur maison, que sa conscience lui permettait encore moins de se défaire de ce livre, qu'il savait que nous autres francs étions adonnés à la magie, que ces livres étaient les vraies grammaires de cet art diabolique, qu'il aimerait mieux embraser la bibliothèque entière que de céder à mes désirs. Il ne se démentit jamais de cette résolution, enfin il me pria à genoux de sortir de la bibliothèque en me disant qu'il était cruel de l'affliger, lui qui nous avait reçu le mieux qu'il avait pu, que je cédai à l'instant. [...] D'autres, je le sçais, auraient dérobé cet ouvrage, et je conviens que rien ne nous eut été plus facile, mais les tours d'un vil escroc ne peuvent me convenir. Les hommes de lettres se permettent en ce genre des bassesses indignes et je ne manquerais pas de défenseurs et de panégiristes si je m'étais permis de ravir l'ouvrage que j'ai tant convoité, mais le cri de ma conscience me punirait cruellement de ce lâche abus de l'hospitalité.

This passage is remarkable in two respects: in the first place, his enthusiasm is that of a genuine scholar, and the historical and technical information he has at his disposal, even though it is derivative, is of no mean order and is quite adequate for the task of recognising the value of ancient manuscripts. None of this is characteristic of the rather giddy, if intense, young aristocrat of twenty-six, with only the vestiges of the solid education which had been made available to him by the good offices of the abbé Maydieu and the Collège d'Harcourt but which he had largely resisted.

In the second place, the sightings of particular manuscripts are of considerable, and in one case, extraordinary, interest, even today. He states he saw a *complete* Diodorus Siculus, whereas out of the forty books of his *World history* only fifteen are fully known to scholars, twenty-five being fragmentary. The Herodas *mimiambi* (literary mimes), dating from the third century B.C., were almost unknown (apart from fragments) until 1891. Most important, the *Hypotyposeis* of Clement of Alexandria are still known only by fragments quoted by Eusebius. The significance of d'Antraigues's discovery is being discussed in detail elsewhere.[3]

The purpose of this present article (which, surprising though it might appear, is consistent with its title) is to provide an answer to the question, 'How did d'Antraigues obtain the inspiration and the information he needed, to deal with such ancient manuscripts?' The explanation is not to be found in the several volumes listed in the inventory of books rescued from pillaging when his châteaux were sacked in 1792: several tomes on ancient history and on the Levant are mentioned, but nothing as precisely bibliographical or palaeographic as would be necessary for this task.[4]

There is, however, buried in the middle of the manuscript of d'Antraigues's 'Mémoires sur la Turquie' a set of six pages, written neither by d'Antraigues nor by the amanuensis responsible for the copy of the

3. Colin Duckworth and Eric Osborn, 'Clement of Alexandria's *Hypotyposeis*: a French eighteenth-century sighting', *Journal of theological studies* (May 1985). In this, d'Antraigues's discovery is placed in relation to the history of the monastery and of the reports made on its library by other visiting bibliophiles, such as Gilles de Loches, Robert Huntingdon and others in the seventeenth century, Tischendorf and Greville Chester in the nineteenth century, and Evelyn White in the 1920s. Professor Osborn, of Queen's College, Melbourne, a world authority on Clement, also reports on the visit he undertook to St Macarius in 1983 in search of d'Antraigues's *trouvaille*, and the repercussions thereof.

4. '20 et 21 juillet 1793: Inventaire des livres [...] provenant du château de Laulagnet ayant appartenu à l'émigré Louis Launet jadis appelé comte d'Antraigues', *Revue du Vivarais* 81 (1977), Nos. 3 and 4, pp.168-72, 180-90.

'Mémoires' accompanying his own holograph. These pages, written recto and verso, are headed: 'Recherches à faire dans le voyage de Constantinople', and they are anonymous. Among the occasional marginal notes in d'Antraigues's own hand (which prove that he did, in fact, read the document) is one that states: 'Ière observation la paléographie grecque et la couleur des Encres.' The text, at this point, provides us with a clue as to the authorship of the manuscript, with the words: 'Il faut d'abord s'exercer à connoître l'âge des manuscrits en Lisant attentivement la Paléographie Greque que j'imprimai in fol. en 1708.'

This establishes the author as Montfaucon, who published his *Palaeographia graeca* in 1708.[5] One will look in vain for the 'Recherches à faire' in bibliographies of Montfaucon's works, but it was published, in 1742; at least, a version of it appeared then, in the *Mercure de France* of January of the year following Montfaucon's death (pp.60-73). The editor of the *Mercure* states that it did not come direct from Montfaucon's literary testators, but 'par un pur hazard, de Constantinople, il y a environ deux ans' (p.73), from M. Desroches, First Secretary to two French Ambassadors to the Sublime Porte.

This link with Constantinople would make it very likely that d'Antraigues obtained his copy, his version, through his uncle, François-Emmanuel Guignard, comte de Saint-Priest, who was Ambassador to the Porte from 1768 until 1785 – a period which includes the time when d'Antraigues made his protracted visit to the Levant, travelling in his uncle's company to Constantinople.

Montfaucon had written these 'Recherches à faire' to assist the Benedictines with their projected *expédition littéraire* to the Levant and to Greece, which was to be pre-empted in 1728 by Maurepas's decision to send the abbés Sevin and Fourmont out in search of manuscripts to grace the Bibliothèque du Roi.[6] The Benedictines having lost their chance, Montfaucon's shopping list, or guide to best buys in monuments, apparently remained in the Embassy in Constantinople. One version of it was published, as stated, in 1742; but the one d'Antraigues used for his journey was not the same: a comparison of the two versions reveals ninety-nine variants: d'Antraigues's version contains twenty-five additions, thirty omissions, and forty-four other changes of text. None of

---

5. *Palaeographia graeca, sive de ortu et progressu literarum graecarum* [...], Parisiis M.DCC.VIII.
6. See Henri Omont, *Missions archéologiques françaises en Orient aux XVIIe et XVIIIe siècles* (Paris 1902), pp.412-32.

them are significant, but are of sufficient note, stylistically and numerically, to make the d'Antraigues manuscript worth reproducing in its own
right. In one case, the *Mercure de France* version is incomprehensible
through misreading of punctuation; the passage concerned refers precisely to Clement of Alexandria, and reads, in the *Mercure* version: 'Un
Manuscrit des Œuvres de Saint Justin seroit très-bon à acheter, de
Clement-Alexandrin; le Protreptique & le Pédagogue se trouvent assés-
souvent dans nos Bibliothèques des Stromates du même, il n'y en a qu'un
Manu[s]crit qui est à Florence' (etc.) (p.67). The correct reading, from
the d'Antraigues manuscript, offers no difficulties, as will be seen from
p.359 below.

Omont (p.415) dates Montfaucon's 'Recherches à faire'[7] 'sans doute
vers l'année 1720' (p.414); but internal evidence permits one to suggest
a slightly later date – namely, the reference to Sherard. The botanist and
antiquarian William Sherard (1659-1728) is correctly referred to by
Montfaucon as 'Consul de la Nation angloise dans les Echelles du Levant'
(he was appointed Consul for the Turkey Company at Smyrna in 1702),
and he remarks that he returned 'il y a cinq ou six ans de ce pays-là avec
un gros recueil d'inscriptions grecques tirées de différens endroits de
l'Asie Mineure' (see below, p.357). Sherard did indeed leave Smyrna late
in 1716, and returned to London at Christmas, 1717.[8] Thus, this establishes the date of the Montfaucon manuscript as 1722 or 1723, that is to
say, contemporaneously with his *Supplément* to *L'Antiquité expliquée*.[9]

Although the style of the *Antiquité expliquée* and that of the 'Recherches
à faire' are very similar – one recognises the same rather inflated but direct
and magisterial clarity – the emphasis and purpose are quite different.
L'Antiquité expliquée deals with what has been discovered and considered

7. Omont includes yet another version (under the title *Mémoire pour servir d'instruction à
ceux qui cherchent d'anciens monumens dans la Grèce et dans le Levant* (pp.414-20). However, its
contents are sometimes very different, as is their organisation (Inscriptions. – Manuscrits. –
Les Poètes. – Les Historiens. – Geographes. – Autres auteurs. – L'Ecriture sainte, les Pères et
autres ecclésiastiques Grecs.). These differences, and above all the fact that Montfaucon is
referred to therein in the third person ('Dom Bernard de Montfaucon publia, en 1708, sa
Paléographie grecque...', cf. p.358 below), seem to indicate that the Omont version is a gloss
based on Montfaucon's original.
   I am most grateful to Professor Louis Robert, of the Académie des inscriptions, for his
assistance in tracking down the other versions of the 'Recherches à faire'.
   8. On Sherard: see the *Dictionary of national biography*, ed. Sidney Lee (London 1897), lii.67-
68.
   9. *L'Antiquité expliquée, et représentée en figures* (Paris 1719); *Supplément* (Paris 1724).

worthy of Montfaucon's verbal and above all pictorial description, so that repetitions may be avoided by collectors; the 'Recherches à faire' tackle the same problem in a more speculative and open-ended way, in terms of what still needs to be discovered, recorded, and if possible brought back. In short, it offered exactly the sort of guidance needed by an intelligent but fairly ignorant acquisitive traveller such as d'Antraigues.

A reading of the Montfaucon manuscript immediately explains how d'Antraigues was so alert to the rarity of the manuscripts he mentions having seen in the library of St Macarius monastery. The Clement of Alexandria *Hypotyposeis* are specifically mentioned and classed as 'un trésor'. Diodore de Sicile's historical works are referred to as one of those items which would be sufficient to pay for a voyage to the Levant, if a manuscript of it were found. And he notes that 'les manuscrits de Pausanias sont aussy fort rares'.

One phrase which d'Antraigues applies to Diodorus – 'Ce serait un présent inestimable qu'on ferait à la république des lettres' – is used by Montfaucon with reference to Polybius: 'ce seroit un beau présent qu'on feroit à la République des Lettres'. The Polybius manuscript which d'Antraigues claims to have seen was incomplete, but his admiration for this author was to reveal itself many years later, when he would make him the vehicle for a polemical work against Napoleon's Empire: his *Traduction d'un fragment du XVIIIe livre de Polybe, trouvé dans le monastère Sainte-Laure au Mont Athos*, published in Berlin in 1805.[10] By thus adapting Polybius to his purposes, and providing a key (the Romans were the French, the Macedonians the Austrians, the Syrians the Prussians, the Parthians the Russians, Antiochus was Friedrich-Wilhelm, Arsaces was tsar Alexander, and so on) d'Antraigues utilised a formula, the *histoire à clefs*, that was popular at a time when the educated reading public still knew its classics; but it demanded considerable erudition, which

10. First edition printed in Berlin 1805, by Decker (printer to the king), 80 pp. Second edition, 'London 1806', 108 pp. A third edition was rapidly printed in London, with keys to the *figurants*. D'Antraigues also mentions a sequel, *Le XXIVe livre de Polybe*, in a letter to Budberg of 30 December 1806 (quoted by Pingaud, *Un agent secret: le comte d'Antraigues*, Paris 1894, p.407), but it has not been found. As for the original 'fragment' of Polybius, Pingaud states that d'Antraigues probably went to Mount Athos 'avec deux voyageurs célèbres, d'Ansse de Villoison et Savary' and 'y eût découvert et acheté à grand'peine un fragment du XVIIIe livre perdu de Polybe' (p.312). There is no mention of this in the 'Mémoires sur la Turquie', however, and his itinerary did not include Mount Athos (see note 12 to the 'Recherches à faire', p.358, below).

COLIN DUCKWORTH

d'Antraigues may well not have acquired but for the sensible guidance provided by Montfaucon's 'Recherches à faire', and which was a very creative way of making Polybius part of the *république des lettres*.

Thus, although Montfaucon's shopping-list of objects and manuscripts that were still 'bons à prendre' in 1723 is not the most riveting of texts for the literary scholar, either for its content or its style, the transmission of its information inspired a polemical work of some interest and – at the present time – may lead to a discovery of the extremely important work of Clement.

In presenting this text of Montfaucon, I have provided a note only where a reference or spelling could be confusing. The non-classical scholar will find all the information he needs in *The Oxford classical dictionary*, the *Encyclopaedia britannica*, *Larousse*, and *The New Bible dictionary*. Neither have I encumbered the text with variants, which would have been rather trivial and pedantic. The antiquarian can compare this with the *Mercure de France* 1742 version if he wishes. It is the fact there are so many variants that seems to justify the reproduction of the full text here.

Recherches à faire dans le voyage de Constantinople

Quoyqu'on ait déjà fait bien des recherches dans le Levant, et qu'on en ait apporté beaucoup de monuments antiques, marbres, médailles, manuscrits; il y reste encore une ample moisson à faire. Plusieurs voyageurs qui n'y alloient que par pure curiosité, ne se sont point mis en peine de chercher des monuments; les autres manquoient des moyens nécessaires pour en acquérir; d'autres enfin n'avoient pas les connoissances requises pour réussir dans ces recherches. Il seroit à propos que ceux qui entreprennent ces voyages pour l'utilité publique fussent instruits sur bien des choses. Faute de bien connoître on laisse quelque fois échapper des monuments qu'on pourroit avoir à bon marché, et si l'on achète au hazard on risque de dépenser son argent inutilement.

Marbres, Bronzes et médailles antiques

Les marbres qu'on doit chercher consistent en inscriptions, bas reliefs, statues ou bustes, tombeaux et urnes. Il y en a un très grand nombre de toute espèce dans les Etats de l'Empire Ottoman; mais surtout dans la Grèce. Athènes en peut plus fournir et de plus curieux qu'aucune autre ville. Il y en a beaucoup à Corinthe et dans tout le Péloponnèse; mais surtout dans la partie occidentale, qui répond à l'Isle de Zanthe: c'étoit l'ancienne Elide où se célébroient les Jeux Olympiques auxquels toute l'ancienne Grèce concourut et où étoit ce fameux temple de Jupiter, renommé par

356

la statue de ce Dieu fait par Phidias, qui passoit pour une des sept merveilles du monde. Généralement parlant tous ces pays sont pleins d'inscriptions et de marbres précieux par les images qu'ils représentent et par les histoires que les inscriptions aprennent. Ceux qu'on a déjà apportés de ces pays-là en Italie, en France, en Angleterre et dans d'autres parties de l'Europe et qui ont été publiés, font juger qu'on peut tirer de ces monuments beaucoup d'éclaircissements pour l'histoire et pour l'antiquité. Les Isles de l'archipel en peuvent encore fournir beaucoup. Je voudrois qu'on fît des recherches principalement dans l'Isle de Samos fameuse par le temple de Junon tout plein de statues: et dans celle de Delos, qui est aujourd'huy un monceau de marbres et de ruines de temples et d'autres bâtiments détruits. Il est à croire qu'on trouveroit dans ces mazures bien des choses non moins curieuses qu'instructives. Toute la côte de l'Asie Mineure est aussi semée de ces sortes de marbres, inscriptions, bas reliefs &ᵃ. On en trouve beaucoup non seulement dans toute la côte; mais aussi bien avant dans les terres, surtout dans les villes, comme Ancyre [Ankara], Cogni, et jusqu'à Trébizonde.

Comme il n'est pas toujours aisé d'acquérir les marbres, et qu'il s'en trouve quelque fois de si grands, que le transport en seroit très difficile, il faut du moins en faire copier exactement les inscriptions et dessiner les bas reliefs. M. Sherard Consul de la Nation angloise dans les Echelles du Levant, revint il y a cinq ou six ans de ce pays-là avec un gros recueil d'inscriptions grecques tirées de différens endroits de l'Asie Mineure.[11] Il avoit dessein, disoit-il, de les faire imprimer; mais il ne l'a pas encore fait, et je ne sai s'il le fera. Si l'on veut donc rendre service à la république des Lettres, il faut avoir un dessinateur, et outre cela un homme qui sache bien le Grec, tant pour copier exactement les inscriptions, que pour connoître le mérite des manuscrits et indiquer ceux qu'il sera bon d'acheter, ou en copier les pièces, si l'on ne peut les avoir autrement.

Pour ce qui est des bronzes et surtout des médailles, on y en pourroit trouver une grande quantité et de fort curieuses. Mais il faut être connoisseur, ou ne pas s'en mesler. Les Juifs en font beaucoup de fausses, qu'ils vendent aux Européens. Il faut d'ailleurs savoir distinguer les rares d'avec les communes: autrement on court risque de faire de la dépense inutilement.

Manuscrits Grecs tant Ecclésiastiques que prophanes

On peut faire une grande récolte de manuscrits, dans toute la Grèce, à Constantinople et dans l'Asie Mineure. Il y a peu de Monastères qui n'en ayent quelques uns, qui plus, qui moins. On en trouve aussi dans les Villes de Grèce. Mais le Mont Athos en a plus que tous les autres lieux de l'Empire Ottoman. Voici comme en parle Jean Commene dans sa description de Mont Athos, imprimée en Grec vulgaire en Valachie l'an 1701, que j'ay depuis rimprimer en Grec et en Latin à la fin de la Paléographie Gre[c]que. *On voit là*, dit-il, *beaucoup de manuscrits anciens, tant de ceux qui concernent toute autre sorte de science, dont plusieurs ne sont pas encore imprimez.* Il parle

11. William Sherard (1659-1728); botanist and antiquarian. He did not, in fact, publish the many inscriptions he transcribed in Asia Minor. See comments above on dating.

plus en détail des principales Bibliothèques qui se voient en différents monastères.

Au Monastère de St. Athanase, dit-il, il y a sur le Narthex, qui est le bas de l'Eglise une bibliothèque admirable, où l'on voit beaucoup de manuscrits anciens et fort précieux. En parlant d'un autre Monastère appellé Vatopedi, il dit qu'il y a sur le Narthex une grande Bibliothèque et une autre dans le trésor, qui est aussi bien fournie de manuscrits. Il dit du grand Monastère des Ibériens, qu'il a en trois endroits différents trois belles Bibliothèques, et un grand nombre de Bulles d'or de divers Empereurs. Il assure encore que le Monastère appellé *Dionysi* a une riche Bibliothèque. Ces moines du mont Athos vivent dans une profonde ignorance.[12]

Il y a apparence qu'on trouveroit là des ouvrages précieux tant Ecclésiastiques que prophanes qui ont échappé aux naufrages des tems, mais qui n'on[t] pas encore été mis au jour. C'est une grande moisson à faire mais il faut pour cela se prémunir de certaines connoissances nécessaires.

Il faut d'abord s'exercer à connoître l'âge des manuscrits en Lisant attentivement la Paléographie Gre[c]que que j'imprimai in fol. en 1708 où l'on voit successivement des Exemples des escritures de tous les siècles à commencer 450 ans avant Jésus Christ.[13] Il est vrai que je n'ay pas pu y représenter une chose qui aide beaucoup à connoître l'antiquité de l'écriture, qui est une certaine couleur plus ou moins rousse, que l'encre contracte ordinairement dans la suite des siècles: mais lorsqu'on connoîtra bien la forme du caractère de tous les âges, l'expérience apprendra bientôt le reste.

Ce qui est encore plus nécessaire est de savoir de quels ouvrages les manuscrits sont ou rares ou communs. Faute de cette connoissance bien des gens achètent des manuscrits qui à la vérité sont beaux et anciens; mais qui ne sont presque de nul usage parceque nous en avons déjà des centaines dans nos Bibliothèques. Je tiens fort peu de compte par exemple des manuscrits quelques beaux qu'ils puissent être des oraisons de S: Grégoire de Nazianze, des Homélies de S: Jean Chrysostome sur la Genèse, sur S: Mathieu, sur S: Jean, sur les Statües, et du Sacerdoce.[14] Toute l'Europe en est pleine, et l'on en a de si beaux manuscrits, que tous les nouveaux qu'on apportera, n'enrichiront nos bibliothèques que pour le nombre. Cependant j'ay vû des gens qui croioient avoir parfaitement bien négotié dans le Levant, en nous apportant ces sortes de marchandises. Pour bien réussir dans ces recherches, il faut savoir quels traitez sont rares, quels communs, et quels sont ceux qui ont

12. It is useful to place this unflattering comment on the monks of Mount Athos, coming as it does from such an impeccably Christian Benedictine, in the context of the comte d'Antraigues's own statement in the 'Mémoires sur la Turquie', which would otherwise appear to be simply an example of the extreme hostility to the Church and priesthood characteristic of d'Antraigues up to the time of his emigration in 1790: 'le mont Athos dans le Golfe de Salonique [...] cette montagne est le siège de la sottise et de la superstition, elle est peuplée de moines grecs'. Since d'Antraigues got no closer to Mount Athos than the Dardanelles, whence he looked across to the Gulf of Salonika, his view may well be coloured by that of Montfaucon, who did not visit Mount Athos either, according to L. D. Reynolds and N. G. Wilson, *Scribes and scholars* p.172.

13. D'Antraigues's marginal note: 'Ière observation la paléographie grecque et la couleur des Encres.'

14. D'Antraigues's marginal note: 'Noms des ouvrages.'

autrefois existé[s]; mais qu'on na pu encore trouver. Je vais tâcher d'en donner icy quelque connoissance: car traiter la chose à fond, c'est ce qu'on ne peut faire que dans un gros ouvrage. J'avertiray seulement qu'il sera bon d'avoir dans le voyage le livre de Cave in fol.[15] sur les auteurs Ecclésiastiques, et la Bibliothèque des auteurs Grecs de Fabricius en neuf volumes in 4°. Mais quoyqu'ils ayent traité la matière à fond j'espère de donner icy quelques notices, qui leur ont échappé.

Manuscrits de L'Ecriture Sainte

On trouve assez de manuscrits du vieux Testament dans nos Bibliothèques: il ne faut pas se mettre en peine d'en ramasser à moins qu'ils ne fussent écrits en Lettre onciale ou capitale, ou qu'ils n'eussent en marge des notes des Hexaples reconnoissables par ces Lettres α, c, θ, qui signifient Aquila, Symmaque, et Theodotion.

Les Livres Deutérocanoniques, comme la Sagesse, Syracides ou l'Ecclésiastiques[16] [sic], Judith, Tobie, les Maccabées, et quelques livres d'Esdras, ne sont pas si communs que les autres.

Les Manuscrits du nouveau Testament sont encore plus communs que ceux du vieux, nos Bibliothèques en ont un grand nombre. Je ne conseillerois pas d'en acheter de nouveaux, à moins qu'on n'en trouvât de très anciens écrits en Lettres onciales.

Le Livre du Pasteur ou Hermas n'a pas encore paru en Grec hors quelques longs fragmens qu'on a déterrés. Si on le trouvoit entier, ce seroit une bonne découverte.

Les Lettres de S! Ignace, surtout celles qui ne sont pas interpolées, sont très bonnes à prendre, de même que les deux lettres de S! Clément Romain.

On a peu de manuscrits de Théophile d'Antioche, d'Athénagore, ou de Tatien. Je crois que le premier est plus rare que les deux autres.

Les ouvrages de S! Justin se trouvent assez rarement dans les manuscrits. Il y a des traitez qu'on trouve plus aisément que d'autres. Un manuscrit des oeuvres de S! Justin seroit toujours bon à acheter.

De Clément Alexandrin Le Protreptique et le Pédagogue se trouvent assez souvent dans nos Bibliothèques. Des Stromates il n'y a qu'un manuscrit, qui est à Florence dans la Bibliothèque de S! Laurent. Le premier feuillet y manque et de là vient que ce même défaut se trouve dans toutes les éditions. Un manuscrit bien entier de cet ouvrage seroit fort précieux.

On a perdu de Clément Alexandrin ses Hypotyposes. Si l'on en trouvoit quelque manuscrit dans le Levant ce ceroit un trésor.

Tous les manuscrits des ouvrages d'Origène sont fort rares. On a perdu un grand nombre de ces ouvrages, et de ceux qui nous restent la pluspart ne sont qu'en Latin: ainsy ce qu'on pourra trouver sur cet auteur sera toujours bien venu. Il faut se donner garde de prendre pour manuscrits d'Origène certaines chaînes [catenae] sur

---

15. William Cave's *Scriptorum ecclesiasticorum historia litteraria a Christo nato usque ad saeculum XIV* [...] was published in London in 1688-1698.

16. 'Ecclesiasticus' or 'The Wisdom of Jesus the Son of Sirach' – one of the Apocrypha.

l'Ecriture, où Origène se voit cité et ses passages rapportez avec ceux des autres Pères. Ces chaînes se voient en assez grand nombre dans nos bibliothèques.

L'Histoire Ecclésiastique d'Eusèbe n'est pas rare en manuscrit. On en a de fort beaux dans nos bibliothèques. Mais l'ouvrage est si important, quand on en apporteroit encore du Levant, ils ne laisseroient pas de servir à rectifier plusieurs passages. Sa démonstration Evangélique est imparfaite en certains endroits. Il n'y en a promprement [sic] qu'un manuscrit qui puisse servir: s'il s'en trouve d'autres, ils sont tous modernes et copiez sur celuy-là, comme il paroît évidemment en ce qu'ils ont tous les mêmes défauts et les mêmes *hiatus*. Les manuscrits de la Préparation Evangélique sont aussy fort rares: il sera bon d'acquérir tous ceux qu'on trouvera.

Les Manuscrits de S.ᵗ Athanase, qui contiennent un recueil de ses ouvrages, sont rares: ce Père est si important qu'il ne faut pas les manquer s'il s'en rencontre. Nous avons perdu ses épîtres Pascales ou festales, qui avoient été recueillies au nombre de quarante-sept. Si l'on pouvoit les déterrer dans le Levant, ce seroit une heureuse trouvaille.

Les Epîtres de S.ᵗ Basile sont si importantes pour l'histoire de l'Eglise de son tems, que tous les manuscrits qu'on en trouvera seront bons à prendre. Peut-être pourrat-on découvrir quelques-unes de ses épîtres, qui n'auront pas encore vu le jour.

Les oraisons de S.ᵗ Grégoire de Nazianze se trouvent en Europe dans plus de soixante beaux manuscrits. Il n'en faut plus acheter à moins qu'il n'y en eût quelques-unes qui n'eussent pas encore vu le jour. Ses épîtres sont beaucoup plus rares: ses vers encore davantage: on en découvre de tems en tems, qui navoient pas encore paru.

Le Panarion de S.ᵗ Epiphane est un des plus rares ouvrages. Je ne sai s'il y en a deux manuscrits entiers en Europe. Il ne faudra pas laisser échapper ceux qui se présenteront.

Nous avons une infinité de manuscrits de ces ouvrages de S.ᵗ Jean Chrysostome: des Homélies sur la Genèse, sur S.ᵗ Mathieu, sur S.ᵗ Jean, sur les Actes, des Homélies sur les Statües, du Sacerdoce, de ses deux épîtres à Théodore et d'autres ouvrages ascétiques. Les suivants sont beaucoup plus rares: ses Homélies sur toutes les épîtres de S.ᵗ Paul, celles sur la pénitence, contre les Juifs. Les Homélies sur le commencem.ᵗ des Actes des Apôtres, le corps de ses Epîtres, et peut-être d'autres ouvrages qui n'ont point encore paru et qui sont cachez dans les Bibliothèques du Levant.

Les manuscrits de l'histoire Ecclésiastique de Socrate, Sozomène et Théodoret ne sont point à négliger. Ceux d'Evagre [Evagrius Pontus] et de Théodore Lecteur sont encore plus rares: ce dernier historien n'a point été imprimé.

Si l'on trouve quelque ancien manuscrit de la Bibliothèque de Photius il ne faudrait pas les manquer. Il n'y en a dans nos Bibliothèques que du plus bas tems.

Historiens Prophanes

Les Manuscrits d'Hérodote, de Thucydide et de Xénophon sont bons à prendre. Il y en a quelques-uns en Europe; mais peu d'anciens.

Rien de plus rare que les manuscrits anciens de Polybe: si l'on en rapportoit quelqu'un bien ancien, ce seroit un beau présent qu'on feroit à la République des

Lettres, surtout s'il y avoit un ou plusieurs des Livres perdus. De Vingt livres que cet auteur a écrits il n'en reste plus que cinq entiers. Les manuscrits de Diodore de Sicile, de Dion Cassius [Dio Cassius Cocceianus] et de Denys [Dionysius] d'Halycarnasse ne sont pas moins rares: nous avons aussy perdu une bonne partie de leurs livres historiques. Un seul de ces Livres perdus recouvré payeroit plus que suffisamment un voyage du Levant.

Les manuscrits de Plutarque sont très bons à prendre. Nous avons perdu de cet excellent auteur un grand nombre de bons ouvrages.

Ceux d'Hérodien, de Zosime [Zosimus], d'Elien [Aelian Tacticus] et de Polyen [Trebellius Pollio?] ont des lacunes qu'on pourroit remplir sur de bons manuscrits.

Géographes

Rien de plus rare que les manuscrits de Strabon, ils seroient fort nécessaires pour remplir un grand nombre de lacunes, et corriger des mauvaises leçons qu'on trouve dans cet excellent auteur. Ceux d'Etienne de Byzance [Stephanus Byzantinus] sont aussy très rares. Il est à remarquer que j'apelle rares ceux-là même dont il se trouve plusieurs copies manuscrites; mais toutes faites dans les plus bas siècles sur l'autorité d'un seul manuscrit ancien.

L'Etienne de Byzance d'aujourd'huy n'est qu'un abrégé d'un plus grand ouvrage, dont il ne nous reste qu'un fragment, qui nous fait regreter la perte de cet ancien Etienne, qui dans sa Géographie donnoit mille belles connoissances sur les anciens auteurs.

Les manuscrits de Pausanias sont aussy fort rares, ils nous seroient très nécessaires pour corriger bien des passages obscurs de cet auteur. Nous n'avons guère de manuscrits anciens de la Géographie de Ptolémée. Denys Periegete et tous les petits auteurs de Périples sont aussy rares dans nos Bibliothèques.

Athénée.[17] Lucien

Il ne s'est jamais trouvé qu'un manuscrit ancien d'Athénée. De là vient qu'il y a un grand nombre de Lacunes et de passages qui auroient besoin d'être confrontez sur d'anciens manuscrits. Tous ceux qu'on pourra trouver dans le Levant seront bons à acheter aussi bien que ceux de Lucien.

Auteurs de Lexicons

On ne connoît aucun manuscrit d'Hélychius, et l'on ne sait même qu'est devenu celuy sur lequel il a esté imprimé pour la première fois. Ceux de Suidas sont aussy fort rares et presque tous modernes. Il en est de même de Julius Pollux et d'Harpocration [Valerius] Tous ces auteurs sont bons à prendre.

17. Presumably the reference is to Athenaeus, author of *Le Banquet des Sophistes* (*The Learned Banquet*), his only extant work.

Condorcet and the art of eulogy

DAVID WILLIAMS

So far the recent revival of interest in Condorcet has not extended to his work as a biographer. Scholarly reference continues to be made of course to his substantial studies of Voltaire, Turgot, Pascal and Michel de L'Hôpital,[1] though very little has been said about them as biography.[2] Even less has been said about the seventy-seven portraits cast in the set of convention of academic *éloges*[3] that Condorcet delivered to the Académie royale des sciences over two critical decades in France's history between 1772 and 1791.[4] These *éloges*, ostensibly memorial panegyrics praising a selection of the dead luminaries of the Academy from the time of its foundation by Colbert in 1666 until well after the Revolution, have a literary polish, an elegance of argument and a polemical bite that go well beyond the solemn requirements of the genre. The innovations that

---

1. The *Vie de Voltaire* was published in 1789 in volume lxx of the Kehl edition of Voltaire's collected works which Condorcet edited in collaboration with Beaumarchais, Decroix and Letellier between 1784 and 1789; the *Vie de M. Turgot*, 'ce tendre hommage à la mémoire d'un grand homme que j'ai tendrement chéri' ('Avertissement'), was published in 1786; the *Eloge de Blaise Pascal* prefaced a selection of the *Pensées* published in 1778; see R. Brooks, 'Condorcet and Pascal', *Studies on Voltaire* 55 (1967), pp.297-307; the *Eloge de Michel de l'Hôpital, chancelier de France* was presented as a competitive *discours* to the Académie française in 1777, and published in the same year. The Academy awarded the prize to Joseph Honoré Remy, see Voltaire, *Correspondence and related documents*, definitive ed. Theodore Besterman, *The Complete works of Voltaire* 85-135 (Genève, Banbury, Oxford 1968-1977), Best.D20789, cf.D20803, D20808, D20854. It was reviewed by La Harpe in the *Journal de politique et de littérature* (25 September 1777), iii.118-22.

2. Of the four, only the *Vie de Voltaire* has survived for its *biographical* interest in a formal, rather lifeless way, largely as a consequence of its position in Kehl, and subsequently Beuchot and Moland.

3. K. M. Baker comments on the history of the *Eloges* in his authoritative *Condorcet: from natural philosophy to social mathematics* (Chicago, London 1975), pp.36-40, and makes brief passing reference to individual *éloges*. See also by the same author, 'Un éloge officieux de Condorcet: sa notice historique et critique sur Condillac', *Revue de synthèse* 88 (1967), pp.227-51; 'Les débuts de Condorcet au secrétariat de l'Académie royale des sciences', *Revue d'histoire des sciences* 20 (1967), pp.229-80; J. F. E. Robinet, *Condorcet: sa vie, son œuvre 1743-1794* (Paris 1893 [Genève 1968]), pp.13-16.

4. Robinet suggests that composition ended in 1790 (p.16), but the *Eloge de M. de Fourcroy* postdates January 1791, the date of Fourcroy's death on 12 January being recorded in the text (iii.451).

Condorcet brought to this highly stylised branch of the biographer's art, and the relationship of his use of the panegyric format of his day to his aims and methods as a committed *philosophe*, deserve closer scrutiny.

Sixty-one of these *éloges* were assembled in the first collective edition of Condorcet's works[5] and published under the title *Eloges des académiciens de l'Académie royale des sciences*. The first eleven had been written in somewhat unseemly haste during the last two months of 1772, and issued for publication in time to bolster Condorcet's candidacy for the secretaryship of the Academy in succession to the elderly Grandjean de Fouchy, a post that d'Alembert hoped to see filled as soon as possible,[6] 'car il nous en faudra bientôt un autre que le pauvre viédase que nous avons' (Best.D18179). Quite simply then, Condorcet entered the field in order to provide evidence of his talents outside mathematics as a potential *secrétaire perpétuel*, and was pushed into action in particular by Julie de Lespinasse who advised him to publish a few pieces before Saint Martin's Day 1772 to counter any objections to his candidacy.[7]

The first trial *éloge*, that of the mathematician Alexis Fontaine, who had died on 21 August 1771, was completed in mid-July 1772, and used by d'Alembert to persuade Grandjean de Fouchy of Condorcet's natural inclination for this peculiar aspect of secretarial responsibility. The *Eloge de m. de Fontaine*, printed in the following year (ii.139-56), became the opening public shot in Condorcet's campaign for the Academy post – in competition with another of d'Alembert's *protégés*, the young mathematician-astronomer Jean-Sylvain Bailly, whom d'Alembert was also encouraging as a panegyrist.[8] Suitably impressed, Grandjean de Fouchy entrusted Condorcet with the task of helping to compose a history of the Academy for the year 1771. Condorcet reported this development to Turgot on 1 December 1772: 'Mon ouvrage avance: il y aura treize éloges

5. *Œuvres complètes de Condorcet*, edited by Mme de Condorcet, A. A. Barbier, P.-J.-G. Cabanis and D. J. Garat (Paris 1804). A second enlarged edition of Condorcet's works, edited by A. Condorcet-O'Connor (Condorcet's son-in-law) and F. Arago, was published as the *Œuvres de Condorcet* (Paris 1847-1849). Of the sixteen very brief *éloges* not included in the first edition, but printed in the second, fourteen are those of the Academy's foreign corresponding members (ii.94-129). The other two are those of Le Cat and père Le Seur (ii.130-33; see D20417). This is still the standard edition despite its many faults and omissions. Unless otherwise stated, references are to the Arago edition.

6. D'Alembert would have to wait until 24 July 1776 before Condorcet finally assumed the secretaryship, although he was elected to the post on 6 March 1773.

7. *Lettres inédites de mlle de Lespinasse*, ed. C. Henry (Paris 1887), pp.79-80.

8. See F. Arago, *Biographie de Bailly* (Paris 1852), pp.20-21.

[...]. Mon affaire traînera parce que beaucoup de gens se sont, disent-ils, engagés avec Bailli et qu'il faut leur donner des raisons de se dégager. Or m. de Fouchy m'a chargé de l'aider dans son histoire et ce sera là d'ici à quelques mois une très bonne raison.'[9] Condorcet modified this project, producing instead a volume of *éloges* devoted to academicians who had died before 1699, the year when Fontenelle had been charged first with the task of celebrating academicians' lives. By the end of 1772 the *Eloges des académiciens de l'Académie royale des sciences, morts depuis 1666, jusqu'en 1699* were ready for the press, and the volume was published in Paris with the *privilège* in 1773 by Thou (reprinted in facsimile by A. Lahure in July 1968).

This first group of eleven *éloges* (not thirteen as promised) was in most cases little more than 'une courte notice de ce qu'ils ont fait dans les sciences' (i.12), but contains interesting pointers to Condorcet's future use of the form with the pro-Newtonian attack on systems and metaphysical speculation in the *Eloge de Frenicle*, and the substantial extra-biographical commentary in the cases of Mariotte, Perrault and Huyghens. In this volume Condorcet also lists alphabetically thirty-one members of 'l'ancienne académie' (ii.82-91) who were not, he had informed Turgot, worth praising.[10] A second group of *éloges* soon followed, the first of these being the key strategic *éloge* of Fontaine, supplemented by seven important pieces on La Condamine, Trudaine de Montigny, Bernard de Jussieu, Bourdelin, Haller, Malouin and Linné. Carl von Linné (Linnæus) died on 10 January 1778, and Condorcet pronounced the *éloge* on 14 April 1779. Interestingly, Condorcet wrote to Voltaire on 25 October 1776: 'Je fais l'éloge de Linnæus' (Best.D20368), indicating that some of the *éloges* at least were often prepared in draft form well in advance of the occasion for their delivery. A third group, entitled *Suite des éloges des académiciens* [...], *morts depuis l'an 1771*, contains seventeen *éloges*, some, such as those of Maurepas, Duhamel and Bernoulli, being very long studies indeed. The *Eloge de M. Bernoulli* (ii.545-80) is probably the most scientifically rigorous of the *éloges*, Bernoullian science being of course central to the development of probability theory and seminal to Condor-

9. *Correspondance inédite de Condorcet et de Turgot, 1770-1779*, ed. C. Henry (Paris 1883), p.116. On 14 July Turgot had already told Condorcet that he had heard from Mlle de Lespinasse that Condorcet was working 'sur quelque objet de littérature' (*Correspondance inédite*, p.93).

10. *Correspondance inédite*, p.116.

cet's visualisation of social science, and his interests in the mathematics of the probable. A fourth group of academicians, who had died after 1783, contains eighteen *éloges*, and is dominated by d'Alembert, but includes also interesting studies of Euler, Tressan, Praslin and Bergman. The fifth and final group of seven *éloges* of academicians who had died after 1787 includes major pieces on Buffon (iii.327-71) and Franklin (iii.372-421), and completes the collection. The *éloges* range from brief, slightly laconic, thumbnail sketches to fully rounded, information-packed, polemically vigorous essays.

Reception was generally favourable, though Grimm had reservations.[11] Contemporaries were struck by Condorcet's considerable expository skills in the elucidation of abstruse scientific material, and a comparison with Condorcet's illustrious predecessor, Fontenelle, came naturally to mind. Lagrange wrote from Berlin on 19 october 1773: 'ils m'ont plu pour le fond et pour la matière. Le style simple, noble et vrai dont ils sont écrits me paraît le seul propre à ces sortes de matière et les rend infiniment supérieurs à beaucoup d'autres qui ne brillent que par un style précieux ou guindé.'[12] Comment was still favourable on this point among Condorcet's readers two decades later.[13]

Enthusiasm for the early *éloges* was naturally inseparable from the electioneering politics of the Academy, though private correspondence even at the time of the election reflects perceptive evaluations of Condor-

11. In the February 1773 issue of the *Correspondance littéraire*, Grimm referred to the first volume of the *Éloges* as 'une brochure', and rejected favourable comparisons with Fontenelle: 'Il règne dans ses *Éloges* en général un très bon esprit avec beaucoup de simplicité. On a dit, à cette occasion, que m. de Condorcet avait autant d'esprit et un goût plus sûr que Fontenelle: les amis, en outrant et exagérant, font tort et gâtent tout. Je désirerais en général à m. de Condorcet un style un peu plus intéressant: chose essentielle au métier auquel il se destine. La lecture de ses *Éloges* n'attache pas assez: il faut savoir répandre la vie et la lumière sur les objets les plus arides, sur les matières les plus sèches. La tâche d'un secrétaire de l'Académie des sciences, c'est de mettre à la portée de tout le monde les systèmes les plus compliqués, les vues les plus profondes, les matières les plus abstraites. Fontenelle, esprit clair, précis et lumineux, avait supérieurement ce talent. M. de Condorcet apprendra sans doute, par l'exercice de sa place, à répandre un peu plus d'intérêt sur ses extraits et ses *Éloges*' (*Correspondance littéraire, philosophique et critique 1753-93*, ed. M. Tourneux, Paris 1877-1882, x.197-98).

12. Joseph-Louis Lagrange, *Œuvres*, vols i-xii, ed. J. A. Serret and G. Darboux; vols xiii, xiv, ed. L. Lalanne (Paris 1867-1892), xiv.12.

13. See, for example, Joseph-Jérôme Le Français de Lalande, 'Notice sur la vie et les ouvrages de Condorcet', *Mercure de France* (20 January 1796), pp.141-62. Lalande liked particularly the *éloges* of La Condamine and Etienne-François Turgot (the minister's brother).

cet's skill. On 1 February 1773 d'Alembert, who, with the abbé Bossut, had been charged by the Academy with the official examination of the pre-1699 *éloges*, advised Voltaire of the forthcoming arrival of 'un ouvrage [...] qui je crois ne vous déplaira pas. Ce sont les éloges des académiciens des sciences morts avant le commencement du siècle, et que Fontenelle avoit laissés à faire. Vous y trouverez, si je ne me trompe, beaucoup de savoir, de Philosophie, et de goût' (Best.D18179).[14] Again, in a letter to Voltaire, d'Alembert itemised the qualities that he had detected in the biographical work of the youngest *philosophe*: 'Quelqu'un me demandoit l'autre jour ce que je pensois de cet ouvrage; je répondis en écrivant sur le frontispice, *justice, justesse, savoir, clarté, précision, goût, élégance et noblesse*' (Best.D18222). When the *éloges* duly arrived at Ferney[15] Voltaire thanked Condorcet for the 'petit ouvrage d'or' and added: 'Cet ouvrage est un monument bien précieux. Vous paraissez par tout le maître de ceux dont vous parlez, mais un maître doux et modeste; c'est un Roi qui fait l'histoire de ses sujets' (Best.D18232, cf.D18496). Replying to d'Alembert, he commented: 'J'ai lu en mourant le petit livre de m^r de Condorcet. Cela est aussi bien en son genre que les éloges de Fontenelle. Il y a une philosophie plus noble, et plus hardie, quoique modeste' (Best.D18231).

Condorcet sent Voltaire the printed version of the Fontaine *éloge*[16] on 22 July 1774 (Best.D19043), and Voltaire, recognising in Condorcet the new public voice of science, assured him that he was Fontenelle's master, and that the Fontaine *éloge* was a masterpiece: 'J'aime mieux voir Alexis Fontaine dans vôtre ouvrage qu'en original [...]. Vous tirer *aurum ex stercore Ennii*. Bernard De Fontenelle en tiroit quelquefois du clinquant' (Best.D18705, cf.D18664, D18683, D19196); he rechristened him 'm. Plusquefontenelle' (Best.D20377). The enthusiasm of d'Alembert and Voltaire for Condorcet's *éloges* continued undiminished. In November 1776, over three years after Condorcet's nomination to the secretaryship, d'Alembert reported to Voltaire the successful reading in the Academy of 'un Eloge charmant' of Tommaso Leseur (Best.D20417), which Condorcet subsequently sent to Voltaire on 16 February 1777 (Best.D20569).

14. See J. Bertrand, *L'Académie des sciences et les académiciens de 1666 à 1793* (Paris 1869), pp.219-20. The 1968 Lahure facsimile reprint of the first volume of *Eloges* reproduces the relevant parts of the *Extraits des registres* (10 February 1773) in which Grandjean de Fouchy approved the volume for publication on the advice of d'Alembert and Bossut.
15. Ferney catalogue, B710; BV839.
16. Ferney catalogue, B709; BV838.

On 9 April 1777 Voltaire told Condorcet that he had read the *éloge* of Leseur and also that of Cassini, and that the bust of their author should be commissioned for the Academy immediately 'sans attendre la triste coutume de ne paier à un grand homme ce qu'on lui doit que quand il n'est plus' (Best.D20632).

Condorcet was attempting to make his name in a widely practised medium whose rules and requirements had been formally defined in a three-column entry in the *Encyclopédie* in which the pre-eminence of Fontenelle as an exponent of the art was declared to be unassailable.[17] Several of the subjects of his own *éloges* were themselves official panegyrists – Wargentin, Bergman, Tressan, d'Alembert and of course Grandjean de Fouchy himself in whose *éloge* Condorcet speculates on the delicacy of the secretary's position as the recipient of the confidences and gossip of the academicians, 'ces secrètes faiblesses d'amour-propre [...] dont les lumières ne guérissent pas toujours' (iii.320), whose praises he would eventually have to sing. While the models of the genre were familiar to him, Condorcet did not feel inhibited by them, and he appears to have been unaffected by Grimm's strictures on the first volume. Neutrality and impartiality did not imply self-abnegation, as he noted in his observations on Grandjean de Fouchy: 'Obligé à l'impartialité, sans l'être cependant à dissimuler ses opinions de tenir une balance égale sans abjurer ses affections personnelles' (iii.320-21).

In the *avertissement* to that first volume Condorcet opens up some of the fundamental themes with which he would concern himself in the *éloges* themselves, and which would give shape to the portraits and cohesion to the whole collection. An examination of the role of government in the foundation of the Academy, and the whole question of governmental self-interest in the protection and encouragement of the sciences, provides a natural link with Condorcet's intention to use the *éloges* as a propagandist instrument for the exploration of that dynamic interaction between the pursuit of knowledge and the improvement of society so characteristic of his thinking as a moral scientist in the *Esquisse* itself.[18] When Colbert founded the Academy he provided the first

17. *Encyclopédie ou Dictionnaire raisonné des sciences, des arts et des métiers* (Paris 1751-1780; repr. Stuttgart 1966), v.527-28. The author was d'Alembert.

18. See particularly the *Eloge de M. le comte de Maurepas* (ii.492) for an example of the way in which the question of state patronage is broadened into a far more inflammatory discussion of tolerance. On the general question of the relationship between the moral and physical sciences in Condorcet's thought, see K. M. Baker, 'Scientism, elitism and liberalism: the case

European example of 'cette protection éclairée' (ii.II), a statement of historical fact that allows Condorcet to raise the whole question of the philosophic mission, to extol academies in general,[19] and to defend the Académie royale des sciences in particular. 'On a donc besoin d'une société d'hommes instruits, qui jugeant sans prévention et loin de tout intérêt particulier, éclaire le gouvernement sur les moyens qu'on lui propose' (ii.II-III). A number of key points are now raised in rapid succession in the *avertissement* which encourage the reader to situate the *éloges* that follow in the context in which Condorcet wishes them to be read and understood. The reader is alerted to the need to look beyond the immediate biographical horizons of a particular *éloge* to a consideration of the implications for contemporary France of Colbert's enlightened action.

Only through the political enlightenment of state patronage can the benefits of science be released for the public good. The precept is implanted in the reader's mind with Condorcet's praise of Philippe d'Orléans, who had given the Academy its first *secrétaire perpétuel*, Fontenelle: 'On sait avec combien de clarté, et même d'agrément, il parlait la langue des sciences les plus abstraites: il connaissait et leur utilité directe, et cette autre utilité cachée aux yeux du vulgaire, qui consiste à produire dans les opinions une révolution insensible' (ii.v).[20] Almost every *éloge* illustrates in different scientific contexts the practical advantages derived from the state's original investment in the Academy: 'L'utilité réelle ou supposée, éloignée ou prochaine, est la mesure des encouragements que le gouvernement donne aux sciences' (ii.38). In the *éloge* of Montigni, for example, Condorcet reformulates the relationship between *lumières*, government policies and the public good, pointing to concrete evidence of the benefits enjoyed by the carpet and fabric manufacturing industries of Beauvais, agriculture in Franche-Comté, the Montmorot salt business: 'En exposant avec simplicité ce qui était vrai, en inspirant la confiance par ses lumières, comme par sa franchise, il réussit sans peine [...] par les hommes de génie qu'il a produits, et par

of Condorcet', *Studies on Voltaire* 55 (1967), pp.129-65.

19. On this important issue, see J. McClellan, 'Un ms inédit de Condorcet: "Sur l'utilité des académies"', *Revue d'histoire des sciences* 30 (1977), pp.241-53.

20. See also Condorcet's comments on Frederick the Great's treatment of Euler (iii.29-30).

le prix qu'il attache aux lumières' (ii.591).[21] In other *éloges* the issue is considered from a different angle when Condorcet considers not the contribution made by government to science, but rather the contribution of science to government.

Most important of all, Condorcet introduces in the *avertissement* the five key terms whose implications will infiltrate each *éloge*, and illuminate the contemporary meaning and purpose of the lives treated: *vérité, utilité, bienfaisance, liberté, progrès*. These constitute the essential ideals of the scientific mission, and of the role of the academicians to guard truth for posterity against the encroachment of error, prejudice, superstition and charlatanism.[22] Not every academician in Condorcet's judgement lived up to these ideals, and he does not hesitate to cast critical shadows over his portraits if he feels that his subject has fallen down on the moral or scientific terms of his mission. The works of Cureau de La Chambre are forgotten 'comme tous ceux qui ne contiennent ni faits nouveaux, ni découvertes, et qui, ne représantant la nature qu'à travers les opinions du moment, périssent avec elles' (ii.2); Roberval sacrificed his brilliance, and the interests of science, 'à une petitesse d'amour-propre' (ii.11); Blondel's mathematical skills benefited only 'deux arts bien chers à l'orgueil des grands, l'art d'élever des masses éternelles, et surtout celui de détruire les hommes' (ii.42). At the end of a long, rather evasive introduction in the *Eloge de M. Bouvart* Condorcet finally refuses to offer any evaluation of his subject's scientific work, and instead comments ambiguously: 'nous nous bornerons à donner le précis très court de la vie, et à tracer les principaux traits du caractère d'un homme qu'une longue célébrité et des services multipliés ont rendu digne d'exciter à la fois l'intérêt et la curiosité' (iii.274). The 'précis' then highlights Bouvart's unenlightened opposition to inoculation,[23] his injudicious views on the calculation of pregnancy dates, which were to have unfortunate legal implications, his caustic manner of censuring fellow scientists and his

21. Cf. the *éloges* of Maurepas (ii.471-89), Vaucanson (ii.652-55), Macquer (iii.134-36), and Etienne-François Turgot (iii.453-54).

22. See the *Eloge de M. le comte de Milly* (iii.184-85).

23. The inoculation controversy is a highly charged subject in the *éloges*, the attitudes of the academicians towards it often being treated as a test of their commitment to progress. In the *éloge* of La Condamine, Condorcet develops a small essay on the troubled history of the introduction of inoculation practices into France (ii.190-99), cf. *éloges* of Lieutaud (ii.407) and Tronchin (ii.503). See also P. M. Conlon, 'La Condamine the inquisitive', *Studies on Voltaire* 55 (1967), pp.383-93.

dogmatic officiousness towards his patients, whose painful lives he so often prolonged for no good reason (iii.284-90). In a genre that necessarily imposed constraints of diplomacy and tact upon official exponents, the Bouvart *éloge* is a daringly unsympathetic memorial.

Condorcet defends his right to criticise in the *avertissement* by asserting the pre-eminent claims of truth and justice over the need to avoid embarrassment: 'Je dis leur histoire plutôt que leur éloge; car on ne doit aux morts que ce qui peut être utile aux vivants, la vérité et la justice' (ii.vii). In the *Eloge de M. le duc de Praslin* (ii.219-20) Condorcet observes that truth and justice are the fruits of praising the dead, not the living, giving further critical authority to the academic panegyrist to expose blemishes as well as beauties: Gua's misplaced enthusiasm for lotteries, 'un de ces impôts pour lesquels la nation paye beaucoup' (iii.254), and his inclination to indulge in fanciful scientific conjecture (iii.255); Huyghens's attachment to 'préjugés antiques' in the matter of his failure to discover all of Saturn's satellites (ii.62-63); Haller's exotic domestic life (ii.309-10); d'Arcy's dissipations (ii.386-87); Bertin's piety (ii.455); Guettard's quarrelsome nature (iii.234, 240); Bernoulli's meanness (ii.576); Euler's spitefulness towards König (iii.31); Milly's lack of originality and suspect masonic affiliations (iii.182, 185-86); Fougeroux's lack of enthusiasm for the Revolution (ii.439) and even d'Alembert's occasionally 'maligne' turn of mind[24] (iii.105-107). Buffon's towering status, despite his allegiance to the pre-scientific method of classification, meant of course that any reservations in his *éloge* had to be carefully modulated, but the shadows are nevertheless clearly indicated with references to Buffon's 'goût des systèmes vagues et des vaines déclamations' (iii.352), his ignorance of modern chemistry (iii.345), and his apparent indifference to the cause of enlightenment (iii.362).[25] Condorcet

24. It will be remembered that d'Alembert had been one of the few top-ranking mathematicians in France to have doubts about the validity of the calculus of probabilities, and this possibly had an inhibiting effect on Condorcet's own reception of Laplace's work in this area; see Baker, *Condorcet*, p.171. The *éloge* certainly reflects Condorcet's regrets at the memory of his friend and mentor's mathematical Achilles heel.

25. Buffon had been the patron of Condorcet's rival Bailly, and had played a mischievous part in the politics of the election to the secretaryship. He was also leader of the anti-*philosophe* faction opposing d'Alembert on a number of other issues, see Baker, *Condorcet*, p.38. Condorcet had been himself at loggerheads with Buffon over a number of scientific matters, not the least of which was the method of evaluating probability, see Buffon, *Œuvres philosophiques*, ed. J. Piveteau (Paris 1954), p.459; Condorcet, *Essai sur l'application de l'analyse à la probabilité des décisions rendues à la pluralité des voix* (Paris 1785), p.cvii; Baker, *Condorcet*,

DAVID WILLIAMS

had already intimated to Voltaire that he was crossing swords with
Buffon in the matter of classification in the *Eloge de M. de Linné*: 'M. le
comte n'en sera pas content, il n'a jamais pardonné à Linnæus de s'être
moqué de ses phrases' (Best.D20368). However, unlike the case of
Bouvart, in all of these *éloges* the academicians' personal flaws are used
to humanise rather than to denigrate the subject, and Diderot noted
correctly that vice and virtue in most of Condorcet's *éloges* are held in a
discreet equilibrium.[26]

The professional lives of a number of academicians presented Condorcet with potentially more awkward dilemmas. Several *éloges*, for example,
deal with professional soldiers, or academicians with war-related careers,
such as military surgery, behind them. In a note appended to the early
éloge of Blondel, Condorcet had warned categorically against the dire
consequences of progress made in the technology of warfare: 'Les progrès
qu'a faits l'art militaire ont été funestes à l'humanité' (ii.42 n.2). The
issue re-surfaces with the *Eloge de M. le comte d'Arcy*, but Condorcet is
clearly reluctant to allow it to cloud an otherwise positively presented
portrait. Patrick d'Arcy had come to Paris in 1739 as a jacobite refugee,
and had ended up as *maréchal des camps et armées du roi*. He was also a
mathematician whose work on projectile velocities and other aspects of
artillery science had been distinguished, and he had entered the Academy
in 1749 as *pensionnaire-géomètre*.[27] Having praised d'Arcy's obviously
lethal line of research, Condorcet retreats from his position in the Blondel
éloge, and separates the science of war from its application: 'La guerre
est un fléau, mais c'est la guerre elle-même, et non l'art de la guerre, qui
est funeste; à mesure même que l'art se perfectionne, les maux qu'elle
enfante deviennent moins cruels; car, plus les succès dépendent de la
science et du talent, moins les passions et la fureur multiplient les
massacres et la dévastation. Ainsi en même temps que les progrès des

p.241, 'Scientism, elitism and liberalism', pp.145-151.

26. 'M. de Condorcet se fait distinguer par la force et l'art dont il présente les vertus et les
défauts; il rassemble les uns et les autres dans ses portraits, mais les vertus sont exposées à
la grande lumière, et les défauts sont cachés dans la demi-teinte' (*Essai sur les règnes de Claude
et de Néron et sur les mœurs et les écrits de Senèque*, Londres 1782; *Œuvres complètes*, ed. R.
Lewinter, Paris 1969-1973, xiii.412n).

27. D'Arcy was the author of the *Réflexions sur la théorie de la lune donnée par m. Clairaut, et
sur les recherches de D. C. Walmesley concernant la même matière* (s.l.1749), the *Mémoire sur la
théorie de l'artillerie ou sur les effets de la poudre*, published as part of the *Mémoires de l'Académie
des sciences* in 1751 (repr. Paris 1846). This formed the basis of the *Essai d'une théorie de
l'artillerie* (Paris 1760; second edition 1766).

lumières en morale rendront les guerres plus rares et moins acharnées, les progrès des lumières en physique les rendront moins sanglantes et moins destructives. Il est donc permis, sans blesser l'humanité, de louer des travaux qui ont pour objet la perfection d'un art destructeur' (ii.378-79).

The problem of progress in the field of military science is treated more indirectly, though with an equally loud Panglossian echo, in the *éloge* of one of the Academy's foreign correspondents,[28] Dr John Pringle. With his famous hospital and prison reforms, his sanitation and other public health schemes, Pringle was for Condorcet the incarnation of humanitarian *bienfaisance* (ii.518-22) and his 'fanaticism' as a Quaker could not be faulted: 'Depuis environ un siècle et demi, il n'y a pas eu, dans l'histoire d'Angleterre, un événement important où ces hommes pacifiques n'aient donné quelque exemple éclatant de bienfaisance et de générosité; et, parmi tant de sectes qui ont desolé la terre en déshonorant la raison humaine, celle des quakers a été la seule jusqu'ici où le fanatisme ait rendu les hommes meilleurs, et surtout plus humains' (ii.516). As Head of the army's medical corps during the '45 rebellion, however, Pringle had worked at the point of collision between the *bienfaisance* of medicine and the hideous destructiveness of military science. As with d'Arcy, Condorcet carefully separates science from society's use of science, leaving Pringle, and indeed science itself, morally intact: 'Au milieu de la dévastation et du carnage, lui seul exerce un ministère consolateur; citoyens, ennemis, tous également confiés à ses soins, ne sont pour lui que des frères' (ii.516-17). From evil springs a greater good in the form of improved treatment of the injured, the establishment of neutral hospital zones on battlefields, even a kind of advancement in human sensibilities: 'On doit compter parmi les progrès que le genre humain a faits dans notre siècle, ces actions de bienfaisance ou de justice exercées au milieu des horreurs de la guerre, avec une simplicité et une noblesse inconnues dans les siècles précédents' (ii.515).[29]

Religion and the religious affiliations of certain academicians raised

28. Eight seats were reserved for foreigners in the Académie royale des sciences. On the Academy's foreign corresponding members, see Condorcet's *Essai d'une histoire des correspondants de l'Académie royale des sciences*, ii.93-94.

29. See also the *éloges* of the duc de Praslin, *lieutenant-général* of the armies of France (iii.209-11), and Charles-René de Fourcroy, director of the Royal Corps of Engineering (iii.440-53).

further problematic issues for a *philosophe* author of *éloges*, one of whose main objectives was to illustrate in biographical terms the inexorable victory of enlightenment over obscurantism. Here, in sharp contrast to his direct approach to the war-science problem, Condorcet chooses reticence and a muted indirectness, and promulgation of the values of enlightenment at the expense of those of the Church is achieved obliquely for the most part. The only jesuit among the dead academicians, père Gouye, is omitted (see *avertissement*, ii.VIII). In the case of the two abbés who are admitted to Condorcet's pantheon, Picard and Gua, no reference is made to religion. That leaves the cardinal de Luynes as the only other major clerical figure to be given an *éloge*, and in Luynes's case Condorcet was able to portray an ally of the Enlightenment rather than an opponent. Fortunately, Luynes had not seen any conflict between his scientific interests in astronomy and gnomonics and his role as a churchman. Indeed, his pastoral career provided Condorcet only with positive evidence of Luynes's *philosophe* mentality, and an opportunity to attack superstition with an anecdote relating to Luynes's early career in Bayeux and his policy on the problem of demonic possession (iii.308). In other *éloges* direct references either to the Church as an institution or to the personal beliefs of the subject of the portrait are succinct, and not pursued in any explicitly controversial way, as in the *éloges* of Duhamel (ii.638) and Bernard de Jussieu (ii.269-70), although much is made of William Hunter's refusal to take holy orders (ii.661-62). With regard to père Leseur, who had produced a commentary, with Jaquier, on Newton's *Principia*, and was responsible for major contributions to integral calculus, Condorcet offers only the dry comment: 'La dévotion, qu'il tenait de sa première éducation, avait été remplacée par une piété plus digne d'un sage' (ii.136).

However, if overt allusion to the injurious effects of religious values and their byproducts, superstition and fanaticism, is minimised in the *éloges*, the covert inference of Condorcet's implacable hostility towards the ecclesiastical enemy is inescapable, and it deeply influences his use of biographical detail. Nowhere is this inferential technique more effectively deployed than in Condorcet's accounts of the terminal illnesses and deaths of his subjects. Condorcet's death-scenes, in particular, are models of propagandist narrative, illuminating both his aims and his originality as a panegyrist. In many *éloges* they play a dominant part structurally and thematically, often embodying the dramatic and ideological high points of the *éloge* towards which the philosophical undercurrents of Condorcet's commentary have been moving from the outset.

Death in Condorcet's *éloges* is without exception, an heroic, stoic and above all, emphatically secular event, a final, starkly poignant challenge to the irrational and the mystical. The majority of his death-scenes depict scientists casually struck down in their laboratories or at their desks, 'les victimes de leur zèle', like Perrault fatally infected by a corpse that he had just dissected (ii.54), or La Condamine sacrificing himself on the operating table in the cause of experimental surgery (ii.201), or Bucquet pursuing his researches on marsh-gas, and keeping his agony at bay with gigantic doses of opium (ii.430-32). Death in the *éloges* is an arbitrary interruption, devoid of transcendental meaning, a final illustration that human life, like everything else, is subject to the operation of natural effects emanating from natural causes. Courage, calmness and the absence of clerical assistance are the hallmarks of these dying academicians. Death is final, but it is also defeated, for hope is sustained, not by promises from beyond the grave, but by what the dead hand on to the living and to posterity. The mission of science is not snuffed out with the individual scientist, but is preserved intact, a process symbolised in the account of William Hunter who died in the classroom in the very act of teaching his surgical skills, and who bequeathed his precious library, and the means to maintain it, to the nation (ii.667-68; cf. the *éloge* of Montigni, ii.597-98).

Condorcet's treatment of La Condamine's death offers a particularly striking illustration of his biographical polemics. At the time of composing this *éloge* the matter of La Condamine's death had been the occasion for an amusing exchange of views with Voltaire. Voltaire had queried the circumstances:[30] 'On dit qu'il est mort d'une manière très antiphilosophique en se mettant entre les mains d'un charlatan qui l'a tué' (Best. D18822). Condorcet's reply had been firmly reassuring: 'La Condamine est mort en héros d'une opération à laquelle il s'est soumis par zèle pour l'humanité. Elle était nouvelle et il a voulu qu'on en fît l'épreuve sur lui. S'il en était revenu il aurait été le plus beau soprano du monde. Trente-quatre jours après il fit venir m^r de Buffon chez lui et lui fit confidence de son aventure en vers gaillards, sur le peu de regret qu'il devait avoir

30. Despite the hints of sexual mutilation in the Condorcet-Voltaire letters, according to Grimm La Condamine's operation was for a hernia; see *Correspondance littéraire* (February 1774), x.369. See Best.D18837, n.2.

de ce qu'il avait perdu' (Best.D18837). La Condamine's illness, his submission to the 'épreuve utile' of his operation, and his long drawn-out death are accordingly allotted a major position in the *éloge*, and narrated with considerable literary power to maximum *sensible* effect: 'Il se soumit à de longues expériences d'éléctricité [...]. Enfin, lorsqu'il n'eut plus rien à donner à l'humanité, il lui fit le sacrifice de sa vie' (ii.201). For Condorcet La Condamine's death, even more than his life, confirmed him as one of the great heroes of the Enlightenment, to the last a man of action and the epitome of both *bienfaisance* and *utilité*.

The academicians' lives and deaths are dramatic enactments of the dynamics of progress, and the techniques of inference at work in these portraits combine to persuade the reader of a view of progress as an essentially moral phenomenon. In the *Eloge de M. Bucquet* Condorcet refers explicitly to *sciences morales* 'qui ont pour sujet de leurs recherches, ou l'esprit humain en lui-même, ou les rapports des hommes entre eux, et qui, par la liaison plus intime de leur objet avec notre bonheur et avec nous-mêmes, paraîtraient devoir exciter un intérêt plus vif, et inspirer plus d'ardeur' (ii.410-11). In the *éloges*, particularly those dealing with the scientists who had died after 1771, it is a moral and social, rather than a scientific, pageant that unfolds, more relevant to human happiness than to the growth of technology. Even in the midst of a highly technical exposition Condorcet always manages to insinuate an essentially moral formulation of the scientist's role, responsibilities and achievements. At Tronchin's funeral, 'on apprit alors combien il avait été bienfaisant; une foule de pauvres entourèrent son cercueil. Il avait regardé son état comme un ministère d'humanité' (ii.511-12). The justification for science is the public good, and Condorcet's evaluation of the scientists' lives in each *éloge* is firmly anchored to that premise. *Bienfaisance* links the moral and scientific worlds, giving humanitarian purpose and direction to the quest for new knowledge. Accordingly, the lives and personal characteristics of the academicians are made into reflections of the moral grandeur of the scientific enterprise itself; the academicians share a common blue-print of *philosophe* virtues: they are selfless, courageous, singleminded, tolerant, indifferent to personal glory, attuned only to the needs of suffering humanity. *Bienfaisance* and *utilité*, key factors in Condorcet's equation for human happiness, are the real subjects of the *éloges* of Bourdelin, Lieutaud, Maurepas, and d'Alembert, for example.

Such an approach to biography means that in varying degrees, Condorcet uses historical material emblematically to construct heroic archetypes, epic exemplars of Enlightenment idealism. In the *Vie de Voltaire*, Condorcet occasionally loses contact with the humanity of his subject, producing in the end a schematic rather than individualised portrait of Voltaire, but in the *éloges*, possibly because of the compactness of the format, the academicians are never totally eclipsed as recognisable human beings. Even in the longest and most discursive *éloges*, such as those of Trudaine,[31] La Condamine, and d'Alembert (but not Franklin), Condorcet demonstrates his ability to use the genre emblematically without fracturing the human identity of his subject. Nevertheless, biography was for Condorcet ultimately about emblems, though the balance of emphasis varies considerably from *éloge* to *éloge*.

The *éloge* of La Condamine was delivered on 13 April 1774. It has an easy, smooth narrative flow, variability of pace, and the passages dealing with La Condamine's voyage to Martinique, the crossing of the isthmus of the Panama, and of course the descent of the Amazon, have considerable descriptive appeal and literary power. Anecdotal material is intercalated with hard information, and La Condamine himself is brought to life for the reader more vividly than any other academician in Condorcet's gallery.[32] Even here, however, biography defers to biographical symbols, and Condorcet gradually superimposes upon La Condamine the universalised traits of the explorer-*philosophe*, pushing forward the frontiers of enlightenment, 'chargé des intérêts de l'humanité entière' (ii.169). This process of magnification is particularly evident in the description of 'l'époque la plus glorieuse' in La Condamine's life, namely his contri-

31. Baker correctly observes that Trudaine's *éloge* 'celebrated more than a man; it glorified an administrative ethic – a conception of the relationship between power and enlightenment that lay at the heart of Turgot's reforms – and it bore witness to the shattering of a brief moment in which everything had seemed possible' (*Condorcet*, p.47).

32. Voltaire wrote to Condorcet on 25 February 1774: 'Il me semble que La Condamine vous a laissé un beau canevas à remplir. Son histoire philosophique sera curieuse' (Best. D18822), and he was duly impressed with the result: 'Vous avés sçu tirer *aurum ex stercore Condamini*. Votre ministère de Secrétaire fera une grande époque dans la nation. Je vois dans tout ce que vous faites toutes les fleurs de l'esprit & tous les fruits de la philosophie: c'est la corne d'abondance. On courra à vos Eloges comme aux Opera de Rameau & de Gluck. La réputation que vous vous faites est bien au dessus des honneurs obscurs de quelque Légion. Tout le monde convient qu'une Compagnie de cavalerie n'immortalise personne: & je puis vous assurer que vos Eloges de l'Académie des sciences éterniseront l'Académie & le Sécrétaire. Il n'y a qu'une chose de fâcheuse, c'est que le Public souhaittera qu'il meurre un académicien chaque semaine, pour vous en entendre parler' (Best.D18923, cf.D19916).

bution to the cause of inoculation (ii.190-99). Surprisingly, it is not so evident in the treatment of La Condamine's other claims to scientific fame, such as his 1735 mission to measure a degree of the meridian in Ecuador, and his proposals relating to the establishment of a universally recognised standard measure[33] to benefit the international scientific community as a whole.

In the *Eloge de M. d'Alembert* Condorcet reviews the achievement of the *encyclopédistes*, and takes the opportunity to rehearse again his defence of science as an instrument for progress and the public good, 'l'entreprise la plus grande et la plus utile que l'esprit humain ait jamais formée' (iii.67). At the same time, this *éloge* contains one of the most warmly intimate portraits in the collection, and the feel of a literary monument is entirely absent. D'Alembert was still co-editor of the *Encyclopédie*, however, and has a natural role to play in the polemics of the piece.[34] Again, human individuality is not entirely sacrificed in the cause of emblems, and the reader can still see in the description of the 'hasard heureux' of the abandonment of an infant bastard on the steps of the Church of Saint-Jean-le-Rond both the child and the symbolism with which the event is imbued (iii.52).[35]

The *éloge* of Benjamin Franklin is the exception. Franklin is the only academician whom Condorcet compares in stature and historical significance to Voltaire in the battle against fanaticism (iii.379-81), and as with Voltaire, the giant shadow that Franklin casts over his times overwhelms the figure of the private individual with which the *éloge* starts. The essentially political use to which the art of eulogy is to be put in the Franklin *éloge* is apparent even at the start, moreover, as Condorcet links the circumstances of the Franklin family's emigration from England to America to the broader themes of liberty (iii.372-73) and the abandonment of the values of the old world for those of the new: 'Ce sont les atteintes portées à l'indépendance des opinions religieuses qui, en Europe, ont réveillé l'esprit de liberté et peuplé l'Amérique. C'est

33. It was to be based on the length of a pendulum beating seconds at the Equator. Condorcet and Turgot did not accept the proposals, and located the pendulum at the forty-fifth parallel near Bordeaux instead. Condorcet took an active part in that project, and this might have affected what he had to say in the *éloge*, see Baker, *Condorcet*, p.65.

34. The commentary in this *éloge* on d'Alembert's *Discours préliminaire* (iii.67-69) raises the question of the status of d'Alembert's *discours* as an inspirational source for the *Esquisse*.

35. Baker sees in this episode, as it is presented in the *éloge*, a reflection of the 'primacy of the professional claims of science over the social claims of family' (*Condorcet*, p.5).

la persécution qui a forcé les hommes à s'apercevoir enfin de leurs véritables droits méconnus même dans les républiques anciennes, et le genre humain a dû son affranchissement et ses lumières à ce qui n'avait été inventé que pour achever de l'enchaîner et de l'abrutir' (iii.372).

The *éloges* of the academicians who had died after 1787 were to be *éloges* for their times. Earlier eulogies, especially those of public office holders such as Trudaine, Maurepas, Praslin and others, had been used as devices for sporadic political commentary on specific, topical issues close to Condorcet's heart – slavery, colonial trading abuses, the liberalisation of the grain trade, the constitution, taxation reform. With the Franklin *éloge*, however, Condorcet sets out a sustained political statement. Franklin's career as a scientist at the centre of revolutionary events, creator of an Academy and of a country, provided a challenging illustration of the confrontation of the past with the future, and lent itself admirably to an unveiling of Condorcet's liberating vision of a new world, a new society and a new man. The details of Franklin's life are depicted with a ringing triumphalism matched only by that of the *Vie de Voltaire* and the *Esquisse* itself. The genre of the academic *éloge* now assumes the trappings of radical political discourse[36] as Condorcet surveys the turbulence of recent historical events from the Seven Years War through to Franklin's defiance of the English Parliament, and the outbreak and conduct of the War of Independence.

In the end, Franklin functions simply as a mechanism for expressing Condorcet's views on France's own nascent turmoil on the eve of Revolution (iii.409-10):

La France durant cette guerre, lui avait offert un spectacle bien digne d'intéresser son génie observateur. Il avait vu les opinions que l'on condamnait dans les ouvrages des philosophes, établies dans les manifestes, un peuple tranquille dans ses chaînes antiques s'enivrer du bonheur de briser celles d'un autre hémisphère, les principes républicains ouvertement professés sous un gouvernement arbitraire, les droits des hommes violés par les lois et par l'autorité, mais établis et approfondis dans les livres, des lumières en politique dignes du siècle le plus éclairé, et du peuple le plus sage briller au milieu d'une foule d'institutions absurdes et barbares, la nation applaudissant aux maximes de la liberté sur ses théâtres, mais obéissant dans sa conduite aux maximes de la servitude; libre dans ses sentiments, dans ses opinions, dans ses discours même, et paraissant voir avec indifférence que ses actions restassent soumises à des lois qu'elle méprisait. Il lui était aisé de prévoir qu'un peuple déjà

---

36. Cf. Condorcet's comments on the democratic spirit in the *Eloge de M. le marquis de Paulmy* (iii.262), and the attack on claustration in the *Eloge de M. de Lassone* (iii.299-300).

si digne de la liberté, devait bientôt la reconquérir, et que la révolution de la France, comme celle de l'Amérique, était un de ces événements que la raison humaine peut soustraire à l'empire du hasard et des passions.

With the *Eloge de Franklin*, not the last of Condorcet's academic panegyrics, but certainly the most powerfully written, praise for the dead is transformed into an explosive exhortation to the living. Condorcet's archetypal *philosophe*, his evolution complete, now personifies not only Condorcet's essentially Manichean perception of the historic encounter between progress and error in the post-Cartesian age, but speaks ultimately the language of political revolution.

Les voies obliques de la propagande 'philosophique'

ROLAND MORTIER

LA 'philosophie' du dix-huitième siècle n'a pas toujours cheminé sur les grandes avenues, celles de l'essai, du discours, du traité ou de l'exposé systématique. Elle a emprunté, on le sait, des voies moins nobles, et parfois moins avouables, afin d'étendre son audience à un public resté fermé à une littérature de haut niveau ou indifférent à toute forme d'idéologie. Les plus grands ont dû composer avec ce lecteur rétif; ils lui ont fait des concessions qui leur ont parfois coûté, même si elles nous ravissent aujourd'hui. Voltaire n'était pas particulièrement fier d'avoir écrit *Candide* et la prudence à elle seule n'explique pas son peu d'empressement à avouer ce qu'il appelait une 'coïonnerie'. Diderot, dans sa vieillesse, affirmait être prêt à sacrifier un doigt pour n'avoir pas écrit *Les Bijoux indiscrets*, mais outre le caractère douteux de l'anecdote, on peut s'interroger sur la sincérité du propos. Les chapitres résolument 'philosophiques' des *Bijoux* ne pouvaient passer qu'à la faveur des récits piquants, salaces et grivois qui les encadraient.

Les traités attribués à Dumarsais, à Fréret, à Boulanger, le *Système de la Nature* du baron d'Holbach, le *Militaire philosophe*, les nombreux *Examens de la religion* étaient, dans leur conception même, réservés à un public restreint et choisi. La philosophie nouvelle devait se trouver d'autres modes d'expression, d'un accès moins ardu, d'une finalité moins nettement affichée. Les formes littéraires tenues pour basses s'y prêtent à merveille: l'érotisme, le libertinage, voire même la pornographie littéraire, touchent un public rebelle en principe à la réflexion philosophique, mais disposé parfois à l'entendre sous une forme habilement calculée, dans la mesure où ce public potentiel est, lui aussi, en rupture avec le système des valeurs régnantes et où il éprouve, peut-être inconsciemment, le besoin de justifier la subversion morale à laquelle il se livre. Cette alliance momentanée n'offre pas que des avantages. Elle peut discréditer la 'philosophie' et servir d'argument à ses ennemis. Elle peut créer l'impression d'une liaison nécessaire, qui rendrait vaine, dérisoire ou hypocrite, la prétention des 'philosophes' à fonder une nouvelle morale en parlant au nom de la Vertu. Peut-être est-ce ainsi qu'il faudrait expliquer l'embarras tardif de Diderot à propos de son premier roman? Le fait est que l'alliance de la littérature d'idées et du roman leste s'est limitée le plus souvent à des 'minores', si ce n'est à cette bohème misérable et vénale que Robert Darnton a fort bien étudiée.

Quel que soit le jugement qu'on porte sur cette production, il est incontestable que son rôle historique, sa diffusion, ses nombreuses rééditions et sa survie même justifient l'intérêt qu'on peut lui porter. La littérature triviale et la 'sous-littérature' sont des forces sociales non négligeables: Paul De Kock et Eugène Sue, Maurice Leblanc et Gaston Leroux, Jean Ray et Hergé ont été, et sont parfois encore, plus connus et plus lus que bien des auteurs dont le nom figure dans les anthologies. Le dix-huitième siècle n'a pas échappé à cette règle. Notre objet n'est pas, dans le cadre limité de cet article, de défricher la totalité d'un terrain encore peu exploré, mais de poser quelques jalons et d'étudier quelques cas révélateurs, pris en dehors de la littérature aujourd'hui tenue pour 'canonique' (comme par exemple *Zadig* ou *La Religieuse*).

Le premier cas que nous étudierons est celui d'un roman pornographique à grand succès, qui a circulé abondamment sous le manteau depuis sa publication clandestine tout au début de 1741. Il s'agit de l'*Histoire de Dom B..., portier des Chartreux*, que l'on attribue, sans preuves convaincantes, à l'avocat Jean-Charles Gervaise de Latouche.

A côté des prouesses érotiques aussi grossières que répétitives (et qui s'achèvent symboliquement par la castration du héros), le roman contient un certain nombre d'ingrédients 'philosophiques' qui ne semblent pas servir uniquement d'alibi à l'écrivain anonyme.

Dans le droit fil de l'œuvre, plusieurs passages dépoétisent brutalement l'amour en le ramenant au pur désir physique. L'instinct de génération nous est naturel, et – la Bible à l'appui – l'auteur nous montre qu'il balaie tous les interdits (les enfants d'Adam et d'Eve, ceux de Noé, les filles de Loth). 'Voilà la nature dans sa première simplicité.' Malheureusement, 'ils oublièrent cette tendre mère [...] ils se forgèrent des chimères qu'ils qualifièrent de vertus et de vices, ils inventèrent des lois qui, bien loin d'augmenter le nombre de leurs prétendues vertus, n'ont fait qu'augmenter celui de leurs prétendus vices; ces lois ont fait les préjugés, et ces préjugés, adoptés par les sots et sifflés par les sages, se sont fortifiés d'âge en âge' (p.245). Ce matérialisme assez primaire se double d'un anticléricalisme virulent, qui culmine dans la haine des moines, 'ces pourceaux sacrés que la piété des fidèles nourrit dans l'abondance', 'moines scélérats, débauchés, corrompus [...] qui rient de la crédulité des peuples, et, sous le masque de la religion, dont ils se jouent, ministres infidèles, font tout ce qu'elle condamne l'objet de leurs plus chères occupations'.[1]

Ils ont été conduits au cloître par les pires mobiles, 'la paresse, la paillardise, la lâcheté, l'ivrognerie, le mensonge, la perte des biens et de l'honneur', et ils y commettent 'des mystères d'iniquité'.

L'auteur se laisse emporter par la passion lorsqu'il parle d'eux: 'il faut les regarder comme autant d'ennemis de la société. Inhabiles aux devoirs que la qualité d'honnête homme exigeait d'eux, ils se sont soustraits à sa tyrannie et n'ont trouvé que le cloître qui pût servir d'asile à leurs inclinations vicieuses.' Il les compare aux nuées de sauterelles ou aux invasions barbares. Déchirés par les factions, les complots et la brigue, ils se réconcilient pour endoctriner la masse et la maintenir dans la superstition: 'dociles aux ordres de leurs supérieurs, ils se rangent sous leurs drapeaux, montent en chaire, prient, exhortent, persuadent, entraînent des peuples imbéciles qui suivent aveuglément leurs caprices' (p.207).

La pratique de la confession, inventée par les moines, leur a valu richesse, prestige et puissance. Quant au poste de confesseur, il attire 'les bénédictions du peuple, les éloges, les caresses des femmes', il fait la fortune de celui qui l'exerce et facilite la réalisation de ses désirs les moins avouables (pp.264-65).

Ailleurs, il s'en prend ouvertement à l'abbé Desfontaines et à ses goûts 'antiphysiques'. Il trace de lui un portrait au vitriol, dénonce la malignité de ses *Observations sur les écrits modernes* et stigmatise ses mœurs scandaleuses en des termes qui rendent les récriminations de Voltaire passablement modérées (pp.217-18).

Les 'sœurs' qui vivent dans ce qu'elles appellent 'la piscine' de ce singulier monastère se vouent entièrement au plaisir et refusent de retourner au monde et à sa prétendue liberté. Elles s'en expliquent devant le pauvre Saturnin dans un passage très 'féministe', qui est sans doute un des plus étonnants du livre:

est-ce vivre que d'être continuellement exposées à tous les caprices des hommes, est-ce vivre qu'être continuellement dans les tourments d'une chasteté involontaire; une fille brûle d'amour, et un préjugé fatal la note d'infamie quand elle fait les

1. Cité d'après la réimpression parue à L'Or du Temps (Paris 1969), pp.201-202. Nous avons, ici comme ailleurs, modernisé la graphie.

premières avances [...] si elle se livre à l'amour, une indiscrétion peut la perdre, ses plaisirs sont toujours empoisonnés par la crainte du *qu'en dira-t-on*; si elle reste dans les bornes de la sagesse, il faut que son bonheur lui amène un mari: s'il ne vient pas, le temps fuit, les années se passent, ses charmes se flétrissent, elle meurt vierge et martyre [...] Ici, avons-nous quelque chose de semblable à craindre? [...] le couvent est pour nous un sérail qui se peuple tous les jours de nouveaux objets [...] désabuse-toi si tu nous crois malheureuses!

Et pour bien souligner la portée qu'il donne à son texte, l'auteur fait dire à Saturnin: 'Je ne m'attendais pas à trouver tant de raisonnements, des pensées aussi justes, une résolution fondée sur des motifs aussi sensibles, dans une fille que je ne croyais que capable de sentir le plaisir' (p.256). Philosophie eudémoniste et antimonachisme frénétique se conjuguent ainsi pour donner au *Portier des Chartreux*, livre souvent cité et sans doute fort lu, sa physionomie très particulière.

Avec *Vénus dans le cloître* (1719?), c'est – bien avant *La Religieuse* de Diderot – le saphisme qui est au cœur de l'œuvre. L'auteur inconnu s'efforce, dès le premier *Entretien*, de le légitimer en nature et en morale. Sœur Angélique rapporte à la jeune Sœur Agnès les propos que lui a tenus un R. P. Jésuite 'dans le temps qu'il tâchait à [lui] ouvrir l'esprit et à le rendre capable des spéculations présentes'.[2] La religion se scinde en deux corps, 'dont l'un est purement céleste et surnaturel, et l'autre terrestre et corruptible, qui n'est que de l'invention des hommes; l'un est politique, et l'autre mystique par rapport à Jésus-Christ, qui est l'unique chef de la véritable Eglise'. Les deux corps se sont confondus, 'et la voix des hommes confuse avec celle de Dieu'.

De ce désordre sont nés 'les illusions, les scrupules, les gênes, et ces bourrèlements de conscience qui mettent souvent une pauvre âme au désespoir'. Nous ne devons obéir qu'à Dieu seul et il est donc licite à une nonne de 'se dispenser, autant que prudemment elle pourra faire, de tout *ce fatras de vœux et promesses* qu'elle a faits, indiscrètement, entre les mains des hommes, et rentrer dans les mêmes droits où elle était avant son engagement, ne suivant que ses premières obligations' (p.20). La prudence l'incitera cependant à respecter les formes extérieures de son état et à en faire, au besoin, un 'dévot étalage'.

Les vœux monastiques sont une invention de la politique humaine, inspirée au départ par une intention pure et sainte, mais qui a progressivement transformé le cloître en réceptacle du trop-plein de la population,

---

2. Rééd. (Paris 1962), p.18.

isolé ainsi du corps social.[3] Jeûnes, pénitences, macérations sont d'habiles prétextes à réduire le nombre croissant de ces misérables. L'argent joue un rôle important dans les prétendues vocations: ainsi, Sœur Angélique n'est entrée au couvent que pour faire bénéficier son frère aîné de son 'droit de noblesse'; elle-même n'a reçu pour dot que quatorze mille livres en faisant profession. La vie au couvent n'est supportable que lorsqu'on a déchiré le voile des superstitions: Sœur Angélique accède à la sagesse en démystifiant les vérités humaines ('hors les choses de la religion, il n'y a rien de certain, ni d'assuré dans ce monde'). L'essentiel est de 'se conserver toujours l'esprit libre et dégagé des sottes pensées et des niaises maximes dont le vulgaire est infatué' (pp.116-17). La bonne philosophie consiste à se garder à la fois de la corruption ou des vices vulgaires[4] et d'un excès de rigueur qui voudrait ignorer les passions. Elle est faite d'équilibre et de quiétude, elle établit 'cette tranquillité spirituelle qui est le principe de la joie et le commencement du bonheur que nous pouvons raisonnablement désirer' (p.126).

On croit entendre encore ici l'écho du libertinage du dix-septième siècle, entre son mépris du vulgaire et son goût d'une volupté discrète.

C'est dans *Thérèse philosophe* – dont le titre militant a valeur programmatique – que la part faite à l'élément idéologique atteint la plus haute proportion, au point d'annoncer parfois le ton et l'étendue des dissertations dont nous gratifieront les personnages de Sade (et tout particulièrement Dolmancé).

D'auteur inconnu, publié vraisemblablement en 1748, *Thérèse philosophe* a été attribué par Sade au marquis d'Argens, ce que le témoignage de Casanova ne semble pas corroborer. En juillet 1749, l'avocat Barbier croit savoir que l'auteur pourrait bien être celui des *Pensées philosophiques*, c'est-à-dire Diderot. La rumeur n'a qu'une valeur indicative, mais le commentaire de Barbier a de quoi nous surprendre. Ce bourgeois rangé, vite scandalisé, appelle *Thérèse philosophe* un livre 'charmant et très bien écrit'. Il a remarqué judicieusement qu'il contient 'des conversations sur la religion naturelle qui sont de la dernière force, et très dangereuses'. Le fait est que les digressions philosophiques de ce roman se situent à

---

3. Sœur Agnès résume brutalement cette analyse en disant 'Que les cloîtres sont les lieux communs où la politique se décharge de ses ordures' (p.26). Sœur Angélique trouve l'expression 'un peu forte'.

4. Ce qui conduit à la critique de quelques classiques de l'érotisme littéraire (entre autres *Aloysia Sigeia*).

un niveau très supérieur à tout ce que l'on avait vu auparavant, et c'est sans doute pourquoi on en a crédité l'auteur des *Pensées philosophiques*. Il semble, au demeurant, que les années 1750 aient vu l'apogée du mouvement d'intérêt pour la religion naturelle, de même que les classiques du matérialisme se succéderont autour de 1770.

Indépendamment des amours du Père Girard et de Mlle de La Cadière (ici le Père Dirrag et Mlle Eradice), qui avaient fait les gorges chaudes des esprits forts et la délectation cruelle du parti janséniste, indépendamment aussi d'une deuxième partie qui tourne au catalogue des perversions et change d'ailleurs d'héroïne, *Thérèse philosophe* peut être lu, jusqu'à un certain point, comme une initiation progressive à la sagesse à travers l'acquisition d'une nouvelle morale. Naïve et tendre, mais pénétrée dès son enfance de tous les préjugés de la morale traditionnelle, Thérèse va découvrir la volupté en même temps qu'elle accédera, grâce aux leçons de l'abbé T..., aux lumières de la philosophie.

Ce cheminement sera l'aboutissement logique de la réhabilitation des passions, et de son corollaire la condamnation de l'ascétisme, qui constituent aussi les thèmes conducteurs des *Pensées philosophiques*.

D'emblée, Thérèse se justifie au nom d'un argument presque leibnitzien, l'excellence d'une création où tout est venu de Dieu:

Imbéciles mortels! vous croyez être maîtres d'éteindre les passions que la nature a mises dans vous, elles sont l'ouvrage de Dieu. Vous voulez les détruire, ces passions, les restreindre à de certaines bornes. Hommes insensés! Vous prétendez donc être de seconds Créateurs plus puissants que le premier? Ne verrez-vous jamais que tout est ce qu'il doit être, et que tout est bien; que tout est de Dieu, rien de vous, et qu'il est aussi difficile de créer une pensée que de créer un bras, un œil?[5]

Sa vie sera l'illustration de ce principe et le renversement d'une morale religieuse qui conduit à l'hypocrisie et aux perversions incarnées dans le Père Dirrag:

Le cours de ma vie est une preuve incontestable de ces vérités. Dès ma plus tendre enfance, on ne m'a parlé que d'amour pour la vertu et d'horreur pour le vice. 'Vous ne serez heureuse', me disait-on, 'qu'autant que vous pratiquerez les vertus chrétiennes et morales; tout ce qui s'en éloigne est le vice; le vice nous attire le mépris, et le mépris engendre la honte et les remords qui en sont une suite'. Persuadée de la solidité de ces leçons, j'ai cherché de bonne foi, jusqu'à l'âge de vingt-cinq ans, à me conduire d'après ces principes: nous allons voir comment j'ai réussi.

5. Nos citations de *Thérèse philosophe* sont empruntées à la réédition Slatkine (Genève 1980) de l'édition de Paris 1780.

C'est avec les mêmes prémisses, mais dans un autre esprit, que Sade concevra le personnage et le destin de Justine.

Thérèse, mise au courant, constate assez vite qu'elle est habitée par deux passions, 'l'amour de Dieu, et celui du plaisir de la chair', sans pouvoir opter résolument pour l'un et renoncer à l'autre. D'où découle un long débat sur la fausse notion de liberté, qui aboutit à la conclusion que 'Pour admettre que l'homme fût libre, il faudrait supposer qu'il se déterminât par lui-même: mais s'il est déterminé par les degrés de passion, dont la nature et les sensations l'affectent, il n'est pas libre; un degré de désir plus ou moins vif le décide aussi invinciblement qu'un poids de quatre livres en entraîne un de trois' (p.25). Dès lors, 'supposer que l'homme est libre et qu'il se détermine par lui-même, c'est le faire égal à Dieu' (p.29). Tout comme le discours amoureux du P. Dirrag est imprégné de souvenirs du quiétisme, celui de Thérèse philosophe rappelle parfois étrangement les thèses jansénistes (morale et puritanisme en moins). Il s'efforce en tout cas de réconcilier Dieu et le déterminisme le plus rigoureux.

Cette sagesse tirée de l'acceptation de notre nature, Thérèse la doit aux leçons de son directeur de conscience, l'abbé T..., esprit indépendant, détaché de toute orthodoxie, qui cumule auprès de la sage Madame C... les fonctions de l'amant discret et celles de l'audacieux maître à penser. Il semble même qu'il ne soit jamais aussi éloquent que lorsque l'amour l'inspire. Ce qui nous vaudra de longs exposés théoriques, qui constituent en fait le centre du roman (pp.118-26, 136-58). L'importance de ces discours et la place privilégiée qu'ils occupent dans l'œuvre suscitent l'impression que la narration érotique n'était qu'un prétexte, ou un moyen détourné, pour y amener le lecteur non préparé.[6] Les propos de l'abbé T... illustrent et nuancent, sur plusieurs points déterminants, la position des 'lumières' au milieu du dix-huitième siècle.

D'emblée, il dissocie sexualité et procréation et, pour ce faire, il s'appuie sur le célibat des moines et des religieuses, tout aussi contraire à la multiplication du genre humain. Interrogé sur l'idée de Nature, il rétorque que 'c'est un être imaginaire [...] un mot vide de sens'. Les créateurs de religions, esprits politiques, ont imaginé cet être intermédiaire entre Dieu et l'homme pour lui attribuer nos passions, nos maladies,

---

6. L'auteur signale au passage (p.130) la parenté de son livre avec *Le Portier des Chartreux*, mais il en note la différence de ton: 'S'il était moins ordurier, ce serait un livre inimitable dans son genre.'

nos crimes et préserver ainsi l'idée de la bonté infinie de Dieu. En réalité, estime l'abbé T…, tout vient de Dieu, et à son égard tout est bien: 'il n'y a rien de mal dans le monde eu égard à la Divinité'. Bien que l'abbé évite de citer Spinoza, le caractère néo-spinoziste de son raisonnement ne peut manquer de nous frapper.

Les notions de bien et de mal moral ne sont pas des absolus; elles n'existent qu'en relation avec l'intérêt des sociétés établies: le voleur doit être puni parce qu'il trouble l'ordre établi et en proportion du désordre qu'il a causé, bien que son crime soit la conséquence nécessaire de sa conformation personnelle. Le criminel agit nécessairement; il n'est pas libre de commettre ou de ne pas commettre son crime, mais cette irresponsabilité ne l'excuse pas. Elle ne peut justifier le tort qu'il inflige aux autres. Le seul correctif véritable au déterminisme est dans l'éducation, l'exemple, le discours, donc dans la pression du groupe social en vue de bonheur général.

On retrouvera ces thèses sur la pure 'socialité' du droit pénal chez Diderot, et Beccaria – bien éloigné cependant du déterminisme matérialiste – consacrera dans *Des délits et des peines* la dissociation du droit et du péché, du social et du sacré.

Thérèse est fortement impressionnée par cet exposé et elle commence dès lors son cheminement vers la philosophie: 'je voyais clairement que Dieu et la Nature n'étaient qu'une même chose,[7] ou du moins que la Nature n'agissait que par la volonté immédiate de Dieu. De là je tirai mes petites conséquences, et *je commençai peut-être à penser pour la première fois de ma vie*' (p.127).

Le côté rhétorique de la démonstration et son caractère très étudié sont soulignés au passage par le romancier-philosophe (pp.100-101, 125):

Je vous promets, dans notre promenade, demain matin, de vous expliquer *l'idée que l'on doit avoir* de cette mère commune du genre humain [la Nature].

Je crois que vous sentez présentement ce que l'on doit entendre par le mot de *Nature*. Je me propose de vous entretenir demain matin de *l'idée qu'on doit avoir des Religions*.

Le propos, comme on le voit, se veut ouvertement, et assez lourdement, didactique et directif. L'interlocuteur y sert de faire-valoir et de disciple

---

7. Diderot dira le contraire, en 1753, au début des pensées *De l'interprétation de la Nature*: 'Aie toujours présent à l'esprit que la *nature* n'est pas *Dieu*.' Paul Vernière a noté l'ambiguïté de cette recommandation (dont l'ordre est d'ailleurs inversé).

consciencieux, ce qui n'a rien de surprenant si on veut bien prendre en considération le caractère *initiatique* de ces longs monologues.

Le sage, identifié ici avec un prêtre détaché de toute orthodoxie, a pour devoir de soumettre sa religion à un examen, s'il veut avoir le droit d'examiner celle des autres. On sait le grand nombre de ces *Examens de la religion* composés pendant la première moitié du dix-huitième siècle, et conservés en manuscrits dans divers fonds d'archives et de bibliothèques.[8]

Dans le cas présent, cet examen aboutit très vite à relativiser la valeur du catholicisme: ses adeptes représentent la vingtième partie d'un des continents, les Pères de l'Eglise se contredisent dans leurs écrits, la Genèse montre Dieu sujet à des passions, faible, inefficace dans ses moyens. La grâce, la prescience de Dieu, sa relation avec le Diable, 'quelles pitoyables absurdités!' (p.142). Le péché originel, les interdits alimentaires, l'exaltation de la virginité, l'importance donnée à la prière: autant d'idées attentatoires à la dignité du vrai Dieu, 'créateur et maître de toutes choses' (p.148). Le vice majeur du christianisme est dans sa condamnation de la nature humaine, laquelle 'n'opère sûrement que par la volonté de Dieu'.

Le vrai devoir de l'homme est de contribuer, par son travail et par son action, au bonheur général, tout en préservant l'ordre de la société établie. 'Le reste n'est que chimère, qu'illusion, que préjugés' (pp.149-50).

Les religions sont les ouvrages des hommes (le Militaire philosophe les appelait 'factices'). Elles ont été établies par la crainte ressentie devant les phénomènes naturels destructeurs: c'est aussi, on le sait, la thèse développée dans les ouvrages attribués à l'ingénieur Boulanger. Plus tard, des ambitieux ont tiré parti de la crédulité des peuples pour annoncer des dieux tyranniques et pour former des sociétés dont ils seraient les chefs ou les législateurs. Ils sont donc les inventeurs des grandes religions modernes et des valeurs qui s'y associent.

Le porte-parole du romancier ne conçoit qu'un Dieu 'créateur et moteur de tout ce qui existe', principe de tout ce qui s'est combiné ensuite. Il n'y a donc pas de hasard, mais un déterminisme sans la moindre faille. Nous devons aimer Dieu parce qu'il est souverainement bon, et respecter les lois parce qu'elles sont nécessaires au bien public.

---

8. Il en a été beaucoup question au colloque de 1980 sur *Le Matérialisme du XVIIIe siècle et la littérature clandestine* (Paris 1982), principalement dans les exposés de Miguel Benítez, d'Ann Thomson et de Françoise Weil.

Tout ce qui ne blesse ni Dieu, ni les hommes, tout ce qui évite le scandale, est innocent.

Reste la question posée à ce moment par Madame C…: pourquoi ne pas répandre le fruit de ces 'méditations métaphysiques' pour le plus grand bonheur des hommes?

La réponse de l'abbé est celle des partisans de l'ésotérisme, ou du moins de la vérité réservée aux élites. Ce long débat entre ésotérisme et exotérisme se prolongera jusqu'à la fin du siècle, et au-delà:

Gardons-nous bien de révéler aux sots des vérités qu'ils ne sentiraient pas, ou desquelles ils abuseraient. Elles ne doivent être connues que par les gens qui savent penser, et dont les passions sont tellement en équilibre entre elles qu'ils ne sont subjugués par aucune. Cette espèce d'hommes et de femmes est très rare: de cent mille personnes, il n'y en a pas vingt qui s'accoutument à penser; et de ces vingt, à peine en trouverez-vous quatre qui pensent en effet par elles-mêmes, ou qui ne soient pas emportées par quelque passion dominante. De là il faut être extrêmement circonspect sur le genre des vérités que nous avons examiné aujourd'hui.

L'auteur ne semble nullement sensible à la contradiction qu'il y a d'inclure de tels propos dans un ouvrage destiné au public. L'ésotérisme pessimiste du prêtre, parfaitement cohérent dans le cadre du trio où il est supposé s'exprimer, devient paradoxal dès l'instant où il tourne au discours ouvert. Ou bien faudrait-il croire que le roman lui-même n'était destiné qu'à un public sélectionné, jugé apte à l'entendre sans dommage? C'est ce que semble suggérer la suite de ce petit traité, dépourvu d'illusions sur la majorité des hommes. Ceux-ci n'ont guère le souci du bien commun, et les règles religieuses les maintiennent dans le devoir par l'espérance des récompenses éternelles. Elles sont, à leur égard, le voile de l'intérêt général. Que le grand nombre s'en accommode, et qu'il laisse l'honneur, les lois humaines, l'intérêt public guider 'les gens qui pensent', leur nombre est 'en vérité bien petit' (p.158).

Le long exposé de l'abbé T… a pour effet d'infléchir le roman dans un autre sens et d'en modifier la structure. La narration érotique ne peut plus concerner une adepte de la philosophie telle qu'est devenue Thérèse. Elle bifurque vers le personnage de Madame Bois-Laurier et vers le récit de ses expériences sexuelles. Nous ne retrouverons Thérèse que dans les pages finales, où elle rencontre le Comte à qui elle destine son histoire. Cet homme sensé, d'apparence un peu froide, lui proposera de l'accompagner dans ses terres, à quarante lieues de Paris et d'y être son amie, avant d'y devenir sa maîtresse, si elle le souhaite et le juge propice à sa félicité (2e partie, p.62).

Le sage, dans ce nouvel avatar, a changé de figure, et c'est le Comte (sans précision) qui va esquisser, en finale, le programme de vie le plus apte à créer les conditions du bonheur. Il consiste, pour l'essentiel, à aimer Dieu et à 'contribuer au bonheur public par la régularité de ses mœurs', ce qui ne manque pas de piquant par rapport à la matière du roman, mais s'inscrit parfaitement dans la philosophie déterministe qui le sous-tend. Celle-ci, à son tour, est récupérée par l'ordre social, si bien que *Thérèse philosophe* s'achève sur cette recommandation toute conservatrice: 'Les Rois, les Princes, les Magistrats, *tous les divers Supérieurs*, par gradations, qui remplissent les devoirs de leur état, *doivent être aimés et respectés*, parce que chacun d'eux agit pour contribuer au bien de tous.'

Les textes osés ne sont pas nécessairement les plus révolutionnaires. On trouve des accents ouvertement matérialistes cette fois dans un roman de politique-fiction[9] qui eut son heure de gloire, l'*Histoire d'un pou français* (1779). La biographie mouvementée de ce pauvre pou était prétexte à des variations sur la politique étrangère de Vergennes et à une série de portraits-charges (Linguet, Sartine, Beaumarchais, Franklin). Au beau milieu de ce pamphlet d'une ironie corrosive, le récit s'arrête soudain pour faire place à des considérations nettement philosophiques. Le pou, entraîné par les flots d'une averse soudaine, a perdu presque toute sa famille et il a pu croire un instant sa mort venue. Il interrompt alors son histoire pour méditer sur la mort, sur l'âme et sur son éventuelle survie:

Je revins enfin de ma profonde léthargie; c'était comme une nouvelle existence pour moi [...] Mais dans cet assoupissement universel de mes sens et de toutes mes facultés, où était alors mon âme, cette substance céleste sans laquelle mon corps ne serait qu'une matière insensible, et telle que la pierre sur laquelle j'étais par hasard tombé? Partageait-elle l'engourdissement de la machine qui la tenait renfermée? Etait-elle tellement inhérente à mon corps, que, lors de l'anéantissement de celui-ci, elle en dût suivre le triste sort? Pourquoi ne pouvait-elle plus sentir? Pourquoi n'avait-elle plus la liberté de penser? Qu'était-elle alors? Où était-elle? Les hommes, d'après les réflexions que je leur ai entendu faire plusieurs fois, prétendent que l'âme est une substance spirituelle, distincte du corps, et immortelle. Si elle l'est, comme ils le disent, et si la preuve de son existence réside dans la faculté de penser, il

9. Nous lui avons consacré une analyse plus détaillée dans le tome x des *Etudes sur le XVIIIe siècle* (Bruxelles 1983).

s'ensuivrait que, quoique mon corps fût comme anéanti, mon âme aurait toujours dû dans ce moment jouir de sa raison, de son entendement, et ne pas cesser d'exister, indépendamment de l'autre substance. Toutes ces idées, que je me forme actuellement, me font croire que *cette âme n'est qu'une chimère, qu'elle ne consiste que dans l'organisation de nos corps*, et que cette organisation une fois dérangée, tout est dissipé et rentre dans le néant d'où il a été tiré.

Notre pou-philosophe en tire la conclusion que rien de fondamental ne sépare l'homme de ceux qu'il appelle 'les bêtes'. La hauteur de ton de ce passage, perdu au milieu d'aventures cocasses et de portraits satiriques, illustre la diffusion de la pensée matérialiste, après 1770 surtout, et la qualité de ses analyses. Une fois de plus se pose la question de savoir quel mobile a pu déterminer l'auteur à se servir du roman pour mettre en forme sa réflexion sur l'âme, dont l'argument découle visiblement des traités sur l'âme matérielle qui ont circulé en manuscrit quelques décennies plus tôt.

L'enquête pourrait, et devrait, être poursuivie. On pourrait y adjoindre *Le Compère Mathieu* à côté d'œuvres moins connues. Dès à présent on peut cependant considérer comme établi le rôle important joué par la littérature narrative, et aussi par la littérature dite triviale, dans la circulation des idées philosophiques. Dans ce domaine aussi, les héros discoureurs et sentencieux de Sade se situent au terme d'une longue et constante tradition au sein de la veine romanesque.

Resterait à établir quelle audience réelle ces 'excursus' ont eue dans le public: n'ont-ils touché que des adeptes? ont-ils entraîné des 'conversions'? n'ont-ils suscité que l'indifférence ennuyée? ou les a-t-on tout simplement sautés à la lecture? Nous pouvons d'autant moins répondre à ces questions que nous connaissons très mal les acheteurs et les lecteurs des genres littéraires mineurs et que d'énormes obstacles moraux et sociaux ont limité les échos et les allusions qui auraient pu nous éclairer.

The catalogue of the library of the Collège de l'Oratoire de Riom: preliminary remarks

JOHN RENWICK

IN August 1792, when the destruction of the religious congregations signified the equally rapid demise of the teaching orders in France, the Collège de l'Oratoire had been serving the city of Riom, with undoubted success, for over 170 years. It was on 8 January 1618, following more than a decade of parental dissatisfaction with the existing educational services that the Oratoire, in the person of the père François Bourgoing, negotiated a contract with the city fathers and became the successor to a long line of educators, in this the judicial capital of the Auvergne, which stretched back to Gallo-Roman times.[1] Riom was not the oldest of the Oratorian establishments (for example, Dieppe and La Rochelle had been founded in 1614, Orléans and Tours in 1615, Lyon in 1616), nor was it to become one of the jewels in the Oratorian diadem (Saint-Magloire, Juilly and Le Mans were to establish a firmer claim to that honour). Regularly, however, it was to produce pupils whose contributions to the judicial, religious, cultural or political life of the nation were to be famous, even – depending on point of view – infamous: Pierre Faydit, Jean Soanen, Antoine Danchet, Dom Touttée, Marivaux (?), Pierre-Victor Malouet, Gilbert Romme.

The general solidity of its reputation was thus well-known and appreciated. Even in the nearby city of Clermont, which was so jealous of its own prerogatives and generally adamant in its own claims to pre-eminence, those who felt obliged to stress the marked superiority of the RR.PP. de la Société de Jésus de Clermont-le-Riche over the PP. de l'Oratoire de Riom-le-Beau gave indirect confirmation to the fact that

---

1. For the early history of the establishment, see the chanoine Régis Crégut, *Histoire du Collège de Riom* (Riom 1903), pp.7-24; see also the *Journal historique pour la maison et le collège de l'Oratoire de Riom* (manuscript history containing the most salient events in the history of the College), published by Marc de Vissac (Riom 1885) [hereafter: *Journal*]. A dense article on Riom is to be found in Marie-Madeleine Compère et Dominique Julia, *Les Collèges français 16-18e siècles* 1 (Répertoire, France du Midi) (1984), pp.559-63.

the rivals in Riom were a threat not to be taken lightly.[2]

Pride in its achievements and contributions, regret at its demise (particularly in the light of what was to follow in the course of the nineteenth century) were to prompt nostalgic local historians – best among whom was the chanoine Régis Crégut – to keep its memory alive in a series of monographs and articles, the most recent of which appeared in 1966.[3] In the main these publications may be consulted with profit, though judged by today's standards of historical scholarship most fall short – and some by far – of giving total satisfaction: the chief weakness, shared even by the best, is the almost exclusive reliance on documentary sources limited to Riom alone ... and alas! to the same tired, old sources. In more recent times it has even seemed to some (cf. P.-F. Aleil, p.63) that these sources have for so long been exploited that all has been found and that all, therefore, has been said.

One piece of original material – among hosts of others – did however consistently escape; a piece of material by its very nature so essential that any neutral observer, particularly in recent decades, would have remarked that its unavailability deprived any study devoted to an educational institution in seventeenth- and eighteenth-century France of one vital dimension: I mean the complete catalogue of its library holdings. When, in 1903, the chanoine Crégut (p.99 n.1) noted its disappearance, one can indeed detect in his comment an expression of regret ... not, however, for the straightforward scholarly opportunities denied the researcher, but for the occasion denied himself to judge thereby the rapacity of his fellow Riomois, tempted beyond endurance in the period 1792-1842 by the valuable incunabula once owned by the Oratoire before they passed into the safe-keeping of the Bibliothèque municipale de

2. Was not Jean-François Marmontel strongly and amusingly advised, in 1738, to throw in his lot with the Oratorians of Riom? Marmontel's account of his education in Mauriac, Clermont and Toulouse – though he was a pupil of the Jesuits – is most helpful since a clear parallel exists between the practices of the two Orders. For details of his own education in Clermont (a mere 15 kilometres distant from Riom) and, more importantly, of the way in which the rival Oratorians were viewed, see his *Mémoires* (my edition, Clermont-Ferrand 1972), i.22-31 and specially 26-27.

3. P.-F. Aleil, 'L'enseignement des pères de l'Oratoire au Collège de Riom', in *Gilbert Romme (1750-1795) et son temps*, Actes du Colloque tenu à Riom et Clermont les 10 et 11 juin 1965, Faculté des Lettres et Sciences Humaines, Université de Clermont-Ferrand, Publications de l'Institut d'Etudes du Massif Central 1 (1966), pp.63-68. I quote the article because it testifies to a continuing (if not overwhelming) interest in the Collège de l'Oratoire.

Riom (1842).[4] The regret of the modern-day scholar (though somewhat different in quality) has been equally great; or, at least, it was so until Antoinette Ehrard, within weeks of the election of our colleague Jean Ehrard as mayor of Riom and of his assuming responsibility for the city, made a number of priceless discoveries in the (largely uncatalogued) municipal archives. Not the least of these discoveries was the manuscript 'Catalogue des Livres Composant La Bibliothèque du Collège de La Ville de Riom' which had lain undetected since its completion on 4 November 1822.[5]

Given our joint interest in the libraries of eighteenth-century France and the problems associated with the exploitation of the varied information which they can, or can be made to, provide, it is hardly surprising – faced with a document of such interest – if Jean Ehrard and I should intend to handle it in the same way as, some ten years ago, we handled the manuscript catalogue of Massillon's private library.[6] The problems to be solved, though similar to those that we faced a decade ago, are nevertheless more numerous and have meant (as they will continue to mean) that the project is by nature long-term. Judge from the following: necessarily we shall have to retrace once more, from archival sources (both exploited and hitherto untapped) the various periods in the college's existence, its academic policies, its fluctuating size, its financial situation and, hence, its (perhaps changing) financial priorities, its doctrinal difficulties, its curriculum and its *exercices publics*. For all these fundamental

4. Crégut is interested more by the value and fineness of the library than by the type and quality of the knowledge which composed it. He wrote (pp.98-99): 'La bibliothèque de l'Oratoire avait une réelle valeur pour le temps. S'il fallait la considérer au point de vue du nombre des volumes, elle ferait modeste figure [...] les Oratoriens grevaient lourdement leur maigre budget en faveur des livres. On s'en fait une idée à l'examen des débris échappés à tous les pillages. Ils s'attachaient de préférence aux belles éditions. Aussi avaient-ils acquis une bonne série d'incunables et d'éditions princeps. [...]. La bibliothèque de la ville de Riom a recueilli ces richesses précieuses [...]. La collection des classiques, exécution elzévir ou aldemanuce, a spécialement souffert d'un long pillage; la Patrologie a souffert moins d'avaries; néanmoins les vides y sont nombreux' [n.1, p.99: 'Le catalogue de la bibliothèque oratorienne a disparu; on ne peut donc mesurer l'étendue des pertes'].

5. As will become evident, the catalogue (93 large foolscap sides – 38 × 24 cm – of coarse and much dog-eared paper), drawn up in response to a ministerial *arrêté* of 8 prairial an XI (27 May 1803), is the catalogue of the Bibliothèque du Collège *de l'Oratoire* which had been sequestrated under the Revolution.

6. *Catalogue de la Bibliothèque de Jean-Baptiste Massillon*, édité et présenté par J. Ehrard et J. Renwick, Faculté des Lettres et Sciences Humaines, Université de Clermont-Ferrand II, Publications de l'Institut d'Etudes du Massif Central 15 (1977), pp.7-127.

problems are inevitably reflected in some manner by its library which, without perhaps invariably being the central preoccupation of the College officers, was hardly ever – in contradistinction – one of their more peripheral concerns. Conversely, the state of that library, the presence of certain authors and authorities, certain texts and editions, the material condition of the books themselves (mentioned by the catalogue), the presence of multiple copies, etc. will start to find the semblance of an explanation only by reference to all or some of those same fundamental problems.

Such research, broad in span of years (1618-1792) and equally arduous because of the multiplicity of issues involved, will be greedy of time. The central item itself will be greediest of all: before it can be used effectively in response to the simplest of queries, it will require the same type of patient attention that had to be expended on the ms. catalogue of Massillon's private library. It presents – and for broadly similar reasons – identical weaknesses and shortcomings[7] ... but in exacerbated form. Drawn up in response to a ministerial *arrêté*, and almost certainly seen by the Principal of the new Collège de Riom (which did not even have the use of the books) as a *corvée*, the catalogue looks to have suffered in its confection from a certain lack of commitment.[8] Rarely, in a word, do the entries satisfy the norms expected for the satisfactory transmission of bibliographical information, whereas (with a regularity that is daunting) the majority of them pose more or less serious problems as to the true identity of the texts whose existence they are supposed to chronicle: abbreviated entries of an idiosyncratic nature; truncated entries due to the omission either of the author's or of the textual editor's name, to the omission of dates of editions, even to all three at one and the same time. How often, moreover, given that secondary titles, without supporting author's names, can be recognised spontaneously in this catalogue (and therefore be rectified with the minimum of toil), will equally fatherless secondary titles, but of a *more recondite* nature, prove to be serious tests

7. See *Catalogue Massillon*, pp.25-28; see also my article 'Peut-on reconstituer la bibliothèque de Massillon?', in *Etudes sur Massillon*, réunies par J. Ehrard et A. Poitrineau, Faculté des Lettres et Sciences Humaines, Université de Clermont-Ferrand, Publications de l'Institut d'Etudes du Massif Central 13 (1975), pp.13-20.

8. It is a little early to be categorical, but it would seem that this lengthy catalogue – all in the same handwriting – was in fact the work of the Principal himself, Gabriel Dumontel. It was Dumontel (who, in 1790, had been an *élève de Théologie* in the College) who, in 1800, obtained permission from the municipality of Riom to open a new school in the buildings of the former Collège de l'Oratoire.

of ingenuity? This general difficulty, if not testing enough already, will be given an added dimension by the fact that duplicates are (or seem to be) liberally sprinkled throughout the catalogue, occasionally under different rubrics and slightly different titles. All this is to say that the task of bringing an exact image of the original library into sharp focus promises to be a particularly delicate enterprise.[9]

Transcription of the catalogue, preliminary rectifications to it, supplemented by fairly elementary calculations and questions, do nevertheless begin to reveal already certain contours, indicate specific lines of enquiry, invite broad statements of intention. The operative word must necessarily be *broad*, because a library catalogue, whether private or public, cannot be studied properly if it is divorced from the rich context which saw it as a living, growing entity. This is a glaring truism. But sometimes – quite demonstrably in this field of scholarship – glaring truisms need frequent repetition. Unless the present catalogue is seen as an expression of historical, financial, educational, ideological, religious and even local political considerations in a very precise period (1618-1792), it will remain so much dead matter. Let us attempt therefore – even in these preliminary stages – to characterise that context and to identify thereby those problems which will require close attention.

The Collège de Riom, which was to prove so successful for over 170 years, found its way into Oratorian hands in January 1618, almost by chance (or so it would seem if we are to take contemporary accounts quite literally). In the opening years of the seventeenth century it is clear that educational provision in Riom had been unsatisfactory. Parental complaints about the schooling available had become so commonplace and vociferous that c.1612 the *édiles de Riom* had felt obliged to seek help and advice from the Jesuit College in Billom which was widely considered in Auvergne to be an *établissement modèle*. No help or advice are definitely chronicled as having been forthcoming and Riom had to endure a further six years of uncertainty until 5 January 1618, when the père François Bourgoing, one of the six original members of the recently-founded Oratoire, 'passant par ceste ville pour voir s'il y auroit moyen d'y établir des pères de leur congrégation', was also persuaded to take control of

9. It remains to be seen exactly how many of the volumes of the original collection are still to be found in the possession of the municipalité de Riom, but a comparison between them and the catalogue will, of course, permit useful rectifications to rapid or careless entries.

the College ... in perpetuity.[10] The contract to that effect was signed by the pères de l'Oratoire de Lyon, three days later, on 8 January 1618.[11]

By any standards, the Collège de Riom was a significant prize: it served a city of great importance (seat of the Présidial, the Bureau des Finances, the Election, the Monnaie, the Maîtrise des Eaux et Fôrets), while its broader catchment area was considerable. For the vast majority of its recorded existence, its roll does not seem – except in inexplicably lean years – to have dropped below 210/230,[12] but never to have risen beyond 300.[13] The numbers of pupils present in any given period is, of course, significant since there is little doubt that they had, in several respects, to influence policy, for example regarding the quantities of texts, as well as works of scholarship or exegesis to be made available. As will be seen, we also have equally precious information about the curriculum, the set texts and the specific type of academic activity which characterised this Oratorian school, not unfortunately for every moment

10. Although extant documentary evidence is scarce, I would surmise that the *édiles de Riom* and the père Bourgoing had, in fact, prepared a somewhat elaborate scenario which would allow the Oratoire to assume responsibility for education in the city without the Jesuits' being able to claim that their up-and-coming rivals had actively sought it. The fact that the Jesuits, who were already established in the region, did not extend (or did not manage to extend) their influence into Riom will certainly need examination.

11. When it opened on 1 January 1619, the College had only three classes: 6e, 5e and 4e. Three years later (22 December 1622), when the original cohorts were progressing through the school, a second contract with the city of Riom allowed classes of 3e, 2e and *Rhétorique* to be added, while – on 8 October 1638 – a third contract allowed the creation of a *classe de Philosophie*. On 13 June 1660, despite external opposition (which will continue for the next hundred years in alternately muted and acute forms), the Oratoire in Riom was allowed a *classe de Théologie*. For these contracts, see AD Puy-de-Dôme, 4D Oratoriens de Riom: Baux et Rentes divers: unnumbered dossier containing unnumbered documents entitled 'Oratoriens de Riom. Titres relatifs à l'établissement du Collège et des Classes d'enseignement. 1618 à 1661 à 1689, à 1699'.

12. The *exact* numbers are known only for the period 1736-1792, during which time they are never higher (not counting Theology) than 299, never lower in general than 210/230, but with some bad years (1748-1749: 192 pupils; 1749-1750: 181 pupils); between 1775-1781 figures range between 169 and 197 with an ever-rising intake between 1782 and 1788 (respectively 207, 220, 243, 247, 275, 290, 300). But, thereafter, the College, for unknown reasons, regresses quite dramatically: 227 in 1789-1790; 162 in 1790-1791; 120 in 1791-1792.

13. We must be wary of the enormous totals quoted for 1583, i.e. the pre-Oratorian establishment (600-700 pupils), for 1661 (800 pupils) and for 1685 (600 pupils) because – given the circumstances under which these claims were made – I would suggest that they are deliberately inflated: in those precise years the Consuls de Riom or the Regents of the College are either replying to enquiries from central government or are presenting requests to it.

of its existence, but certainly for one well-defined period: topics for the *exercices publics* (1728-1781) and a list of set texts for the year 1788. Hence we can ascertain what – in the sixty years preceding the Revolution – was being taught in this *collège de plein exercice* from the 6e up to and including *Rhétorique* and *Philosophie*,[14] and understand perhaps more clearly why certain types of scholarly material were available to the pupils (whose use of the library, as we shall understand, was no doubt intensive) as opposed to certain others.

The acquisition of those books and our finding an adequate explanation for their presence will necessarily take us into the domain of specific educational philosophies and strategies. Incidentally, a more problematical series of considerations will be ideological and political in nature: the Collège de Riom, throughout the period when the question was a living issue, was a more or less Jansenist institution. From 1660 onwards hostility to its *classe de Théologie* (which inevitably extended to the *classe de Philosophie*) was without a doubt fired by *anti*-Jansenist sentiment. The questions which the library will raise in this domain will therefore be manifold. Chiefly, but not exclusively, I can detect the following: to what extent are the theological (and political) sympathies of the establishment reflected in its holdings and do those sympathies fluctuate; to what extent do the holdings allow us to suspect that account (if any at all) was taken of hostile opinion and, above all, hostile ecclesiastical authorities; are the periods of crisis and scandal, the rarer moments of self-confidence (for example, during Massillon's episcopacy in Clermont, 1718-1742) in any way reflected in the patterns of acquisition?[15]

Let us return, however, to the broad educational philosophy of the Oratorian Order and to the specific curriculum/*exercices publics* of its establishment in Riom. For the patterns and lines of force which we thereby discern will greatly facilitate the interpretations to be placed on the library catalogue.

Throughout the history of its educational ministry, the Oratory (much like the Society of Jesus) placed its emphasis squarely on the value of a

14. Since we have the *Ratio studiorum collegiorum Oratorii* of 1745, which details authors and texts (6e – *Rhétorique*), we shall also be able, one day, to hasard an opinion about the degree of local autonomy which was exercised with regard to the curriculum.

15. For basic material on the problem of Jansenism in Riom, see *Journal*, pp.30-50, 57, 95-98, 100-101, 109-10, 115, 117-19, 120-21, 132, 134, 135-39, 141. See also P.-F. Aleil, 'Le Jansénisme à Riom, 1742-1790', *Revue d'Auvergne* 65 (1951), pp.3-74; also 'Massillon, évêque de Clermont, et le Jansénisme', in *Etudes sur Massillon*, pp.71-78.

humane culture. Pre-eminence was hence accorded exclusively to the arts in the belief that they alone – unlike the sciences which were supposed to appeal uniquely (or perhaps rather too narrowly) to pure reason – brought the whole man into play: intelligence, imagination, sensitivity. At the base of such a curriculum were Classical letters. Indeed, the *Ratio studiorum*, the topics for the *exercices publics*[16] and the list of set texts for 1788 all indicate that the core of the cursus, from the 6e to the *Rhétorique*, was a solid, ever richer diet of Phaedra, Cicero, Cato, Ovid, Tibullus, Terence, Martial, Sallust, Livy, Virgil, Tacitus, Suetonius, Horace, all of whom were evidently multi-purpose vehicles to be used (in conjunction with certain French authors) in the gradated study of language and grammar; literary forms; stylistics and poetics. These were also the authors – in particular Caesar (*Commentaries*) as we shall see later – who were used as an introduction to the study of that national and international history which seems to have played a considerable role throughout the school.[17] (The catalogue itself does not, of course, point to such a highly *detailed* interpretation, but conversely we might well assume from the substantial holdings in Ancient and Modern History that the discipline as such was particularly important ... in what probably had to be the upper half of the school.)[18]

The formal teaching was intimately linked at all levels to the *exercices publics*, of which there were several each year for each class. These were, on the one hand, a pedagogical instrument of encouragement (for I

16. Whereas Elie Jaloustre ('Les anciennes écoles d'Auvergne', in volume 83 (1881) of the *Mémoires de l'Académie des sciences, belles-lettres et arts de Clermont-Ferrand*, pp.35-557) and Edouard Everat (*Le Collège et l'Oratoire de Riom. Des études et des exercices scolaires (1728-1781)*), in *Auvergne historique, littéraire et artistique*, 1896, pp.237-52) had access to great numbers of the complete (*printed*) programmes for the *exercices publics* (part of the collections, respectively, of François Boyer and of the comte de Chabrol-Tournoëlle), I unfortunately have, as yet, found only one complete example in public ownership: the *Exercice littéraire sur l'Histoire des Gaules pour servir à l'intelligence des Commentaires de César*, to which I shall return later (BMU Clermont-Ferrand, A70209).

17. In 1780, for example, one of the topics for the *exercices publics* in the *classe de 2e* was the history and geography of the United States of America (cf. Everat, p.16).

18. At the end of this quite linear progression, there came however a sudden break: in the *classe de Philosophie* (for which I can hitherto glean little precise information) emphasis was placed upon the *soutenance de thèses* within the general framework of a philosophy which was essentially spiritualist and Cartesian (Descartes and his disciples are – given the bleak welcome afforded modern philosophers on these library shelves – particularly well-represented). It was also in this class that specific attention was paid to geometry, algebra, trigonometry and arithmetic.

would presume that only the best pupils were ever selected to uphold the honour of the class) while, on the other, they must also have been seen – not without some understandable self-interest – as the occasion to demonstrate *coram populo* how sound and successful pupils and teachers alike were. Here, however schematically, is the sequence of events: the teacher would explain to his pupils the subject matter for the forthcoming *exercice*. Depending upon the class and its curriculum that subject matter could be Biblical, Roman, national or local history; geography; mythology; the theory of poetics with precise reference to Horace and Boileau; a detailed commentary on a specific Classical text; a mathematical problem. Having thoroughly prepared themselves in and out of class (and having, in the main, I would strongly presume, had recourse to the College library), the pupils held themselves in readiness to take on all-comers who, by printed programme, had been invited to attend the College at a given time, not only to listen but also to participate in the proceedings should they so wish: any person present was at liberty to question or cross-examine the 'performers'.[19]

Here, for instance, in revealing detail are the questions for a *séance publique* held on 26 July 1779:[20]

Les élèves de sixième du Collège de Riom auront à répondre aux questions suivantes:

Divisions de l'Auvergne, sa situation, son étendue. Description de la Limagne. La Haute-Auvergne est-elle aussi fertile? Le climat est-il le même partout? Quelles sont les rivières qui prennent leur source ou qui passent en Auvergne? Y a-t-il des mines en Auvergne? Quelles sont les fontaines minérales qu'on trouve dans cette province? Quelles sont les montagnes les plus hautes?

Quel a été autrefois le gouvernement de l'Auvergne? Le royaume est-il héréditaire? Comment fut gouvernée l'Auvergne sous les rois de France? Quelle était l'étendue du Comté d'Auvergne? Qui possède la petite portion du comté d'Auvergne?

Combien y a-t-il d'évêchés? Quand fut créé l'évêché de Clermont? Combien y a-t-il de paroisses, de chapitres et d'abbayes dans le diocèse?

Comment se gouverne l'Auvergne? Quels sont les tribunaux qu'il y a dans cette province? Par qui sont administrées les finances? Combien y a-t-il d'élections dans la Généralité de Riom?

En quoi consiste le commerce de cette province? Quelles sont les manufactures les plus considérables? Combien y a-t-il de collèges? Quelles sont les terres titrées de cette province? Nommer les principales villes de la Basse-Auvergne et de la

19. Though it concerns the *classe de Philosophie*, in the Jesuit college in Toulouse, Marmontel's own lively description, in this instance, of a *soutenance de thèse* makes valuable reading (cf. *Mémoires*, i.51-52).

20. Published by Jaloustre, pp.461-62 and also by Everat, p.5.

Haute-Auvergne et les hommes célèbres qu'elles ont produits [etc.]²¹

While here, in greater detail, is the programme concerning Caesar's *Commentaries*, referred to earlier, which had exercised the *élèves de 3e* ten years before (29 August 1769):

C'est parce qu'elle offre aux hommes le tableau fidelle de ce qui peut le plus les intéresser et les instruire, que l'Histoire mérite d'être préférée à toutes les autres sciences. Elle orne l'esprit en même-temps qu'elle forme les mœurs; quelle utilité n'en retirera donc pas l'homme qui sçait penser? A son école les Rois apprennent à faire le bonheur des peuples; les Législateurs quelles sont les plus sages Loix; les Magistrats la manière la plus sûre de les faire observer; le Guerrier, comment il peut perfectionner son art destructeur mais nécessaire; le Particulier, les Hommes de tous les états y trouvent des maximes et des exemples capables de régler leur conduite dans toute sorte de circonstances. A de si précieux avantages que procure la connoissance de l'Histoire en général, quelle source d'agréments n'ajoute pas pour un cœur citoyen l'histoire du Pays où il est né! invités par des attraits si puissants, nous nous sommes livrés avec ardeur à l'étude pénible de l'Histoire des Gaules. [...] Le but de cet Exercice étant de faire connoître les Gaulois en détail, autant que le peuvent permettre les bornes que nous nous sommes vus obligés de nous prescrire, nous avons pensé que l'étude réfléchie de leur Religion, de leurs Loix, de leurs Mœurs, pourroit seule nous mettre en état d'y parvenir. Persuadés avec le célèbre Rollin, que dans l'étude de l'Histoire les faits ne sont pas ce qu'il y a de plus essentiel à apprendre, nous ne nous sommes attachés qu'à ne rien omettre de ce qui pouvoit caractériser ces Peuples, et peindre l'esprit de la Nation. Nos études, pour être dans l'ordre, devant toujours avoir un rapport aux Auteurs que nous expliquons, nous commencerons par donner l'idée la plus générale et la plus juste qu'il nous sera possible de l'illustre Auteur des Commentaires auxquels nous sommes redevables de ce que nous avons de plus assuré sur l'Histoire des Gaules; et nous ferons quelques réflexions sur le genre dans lequel ces Commentaires sont écrits.

Quel a été l'état des Gaules depuis le moment où les Historiens Grecs et Latins commencent à parler de ses Habitans, (600 ans avant J.C.) jusqu'à la conquête des Romains; et depuis la conquête jusqu'à l'invasion des Francs (420 ans après J.C.) c'est-à-dire pendant un espace de plus de mille ans?²² Nous avons traité les deux parties en forme de questions.

21. A 'puff' in another programme devoted, in August 1779, to Geography (made on behalf of the teachers by themselves) is not without interest in turn: 'Nous nous sommes appliqués avec ardeur à l'étude de la géographie. Elle aplanit le chemin de l'Histoire et porte devant elle le flambeau qui l'éclaire [...]. Elle tire l'homme de la sphère étroite qui l'environne pour le placer sur la cime du monde entier dont elle le constitue citoyen' (quoted by Jaloustre, p.462 and also by Crégut, p.90).
22. The programme tells us that the sources used in the preparation of the exercise were the following: 'Polybe, César, Saluste, Diodore de Sicile, Strabon, Tite-Live, Lucain, Pline l'Ancien, Plutarque, Athénée, Tacite, Suétone, Justin, Florus, Orose, Mérula, le P. Berthault

L'article de la Religion sera l'objet d'un premier Dialogue, où le principal Interlocuteur est un des anciens Ministres de la Religion gauloise [...].

Un second Dialogue comprendra les Loix et les Mœurs. [...] [on a double page, the *Plan de l'Exercice* with detailed information concerning all the preparation devoted to the *Vie de César*, the *Religion, Loix, Mœurs, Coutumes et Usages des Gaulois*, and the questions to be treated]. *Première Partie. Questions*: 1° Situation, Etendue, Climat des Gaules, Qualité du Terroir, ses Productions. 2° Portrait, Emigrations, Conquêtes des Gaulois, Prise et Incendie de Rome. 3° Leur Réputation chez les Asiatiques et les Romains. 4° Leur Caractère comparé à celui des François. 5° Division des Gaules sous César, rapprochée de la division qu'en donnent les Géographes Modernes. 6° Etat des Gaules lorsque César entreprit de les subjuguer. Politique des Romains [...]. *Seconde Partie. Systêmes sur la situation de la célèbre Gergovia. Questions*: 1° Eclaircissemens sur quelques anciennes Villes, et sur le rang que les Auvergnats ont occupé dans les Gaules. 2° Division et état des Gaules sous Auguste et les Empereurs des trois premiers siècles. 3° Changement arrivé dans la Religion des Druides. Etablissement des Académies. Révoltes. 4° Nouvelles divisions des Gaules par Constantin, suivie dans l'établissement du Gouvernement de l'Eglise. 5° Irruption des Peuples Barbares. Etat des Gaules au tems de l'invasion des Francs; introduction de deux Langues nouvelles.

In fine, the central concerns of the curriculum are reasonably clear from the official documentation which has survived in a variety of forms, as conversely these central concerns can be discerned in the presence and sheer numbers of certain authors/critical studies in the College library ... which thereby in turn become more readily explicable. In this respect the catalogue plays a secondary, supportive role in any quest to understand the inner workings of the Oratoire de Riom. But, on the other hand, the catalogue becomes pre-eminently important when it can help to demonstrate that certain inferences concerning that curriculum, made by earlier scholars who based themselves on the official documentation alone, are in fact incorrect. P.-F. Aleil, for example (p.65), casts doubt on the teaching of modern foreign languages, while the chanoine Crégut (p.247) – without specifying, however, whether he had a particular period in mind – claims that the physical and natural sciences were neglected. Had these scholars been able to consult the manuscript catalogue, it is doubtful whether they would have made such contentions.

A curriculum and a teaching style which seem to point to the necessity for a solid, well-chosen library raise, however, problems of a financial

de l'Oratoire, Dom Pezron, D. Montfaucon, &c. Mais nous ne pourrions oublier sans ingratitude ni le Dictionnaire Encyclopédique, ni les Mémoires de l'Académie des Inscriptions et Belles-lettres'.

nature. Not only will we have to identify and quantify the different types of books and authors which were being acquired at given periods, but such acquisitions will also have to be understood – if possible – in the light of the crude question: how much money was available, from what sources, for the purchase of stock in those given periods?[23] Establishing the nature and the importance of the College's income will be an essential element in understanding, however obliquely, its policy with regard to replenishing, renewing and extending its library holdings. Specific information on this subject is, for the moment, lacking. Notwithstanding, certain things are plain. For example, the beginnings of the College are manifestly mediocre: in 1618, the municipality made over to the Oratory the extant school buildings and guaranteed an annual revenue of 1000 livres. Some forty years later, on 27 November 1658, an *Arrêt du Conseil d'Etat* (quoted by Grégut, p.55) ordered that 'il sera imposé pour chacune année, sur les contribuables aux tailles de l'élection de Riom, la somme de 2000 livres pour être employée à la dotation et entretien du Collège' (a decision incidentally which may help to explain how, in 1660 – cf. *Journal*, p.101 – the authorities could order from various dealers in Lyon books to the total value of 1368 livres). Official munificence was, however, supplemented in these and the years to come by gifts and bequests from private individuals,[24] and also by the astute placement or loaning of capital on the part of the College officers (*Journal*, pp.29-30, 74-79, 85, 87, 88, 90-91, 92-93, 98-100, 105, 106-107, 112 etc.).

To all appearances the authorities also, both within the city and at the level of the Intendant,[25] took a discreet interest in the financial affairs of

23. It is again a truism to say that the date of an edition is not inevitably the date of its purchase; but it will be necessary – once all the relevant bibliographical details have been added to the catalogue – to examine the corpus (against the unfolding background of the college's successes and difficulties, its general and particular pedagogical / ideological orientation) in a rigorously chronological fashion, year by year, in order to determine whether rhythms and patterns can be discerned and, if so, what deductions can be made from them. The difficulty (not to be underestimated) resides, however, in the fact that 980 of the 2403 separate titles (2522 entries) are entered *without date of publication*.

24. It is interesting (but in no way surprising) to note that the library must periodically have received bequests of books ... in particular from past teaching members of the Oratoire de Riom (cf. *Journal*, p.133).

25. It was, for example, Bouchet, the Intendant de l'Auvergne, who in 1718 directed that annual prizes should be awarded to the best pupils and who 'ordonna pour cela une imposition de cinquante écus sur les deniers communs de la ville. Cette somme est payée d'avance par les Consuls' (*Journal*, p.122).

the establishment: on 7 October 1766, for example, a further *Arrêt du Conseil d'Etat* (AD Puy-de-Dôme, C7015) channelled an extra 2400 livres from the 'tailles de la Généralité' into the annual allocations destined for the College, while the municipality – even from the very earliest times, and despite the fact that the 'gratuité de l'enseignement' had been part of the original understanding between the contracting parties – had nevertheless allowed the Oratoire to charge each pupil *un sou marqué* per month (*Journal*, p.112), that is, 10 *sous* per pupil each academic year. This charge continued unaltered until 1760 when the municipality authorised the raising of that fee to 14 *sous* per year for the established pupils and 20 *sous* for the newcomers (*Journal*, p.142). In 1782, in order to facilitate the creation and equipping of a 'cabinet de physique', those fees were once again raised, to 24 and 30 *sous* respectively (*Journal*, p.150).[26] For the moment it is not possible to explain how the funds generated by these (and other) multiple sources were ventilated *within the College* (as strictly opposed to the *Congrégation*).[27] What is clear, however, is the modest financial success that the institution had managed to achieve over the years, which stands nakedly revealed in the final itemised statement of income and expenditure drawn up for the scrutiny of the Conseil général de la Commune on 19 October 1792: from 27 specified sources, the Oratoire de Riom had an income of 12524 livres and fixed outgoings in *Cens* or *Rentes* of 744 livres 10 sous.[28]

26. We know precisely how many pupils there were in the College between 1782 and 1792; we know exactly how much the authorities could raise from them in the form of fees; it is therefore interesting to be able to consult the lengthy *Inventaire des pièces et machines qui composent le cabinet de physique du Collège national de Riom*, AD Puy-de-Dôme L5327, unnumbered piece dated 28 pluviôse an III (16 February 1795).

27. Various (though alas! fragmentary) archival sources would lead me to suggest that the vast majority of these funds – some of which were, in fact, specifically earmarked for the maintenance of the teachers – were channelled into the *Congrégation*. I have been able to examine the *Comptes des Revenus de l'Oratoire de Riom* for the period 1783-1792 (AD Puy-de-Dôme 4D, unnumbered dossier) and can find no evidence that, in that period at least, any of the money found its way into the College library, which was nevertheless still being added to. Conversely, the pupils' fees are nowhere itemised … and I suspect that these constituted part of the library funds.

28. AD Puy-de-Dôme, 4D fol.159. The same account – certified 'sincère et véritable' by the Conseil général de la Commune on 26 October 1792 – is to be found in AD Puy-de-Dôme L2185, unnumbered piece. These documents are unquestionably authentic and the reader is therefore advised to pay no attention to the 'document' produced by Marc de Vissac (*Journal*, pp.58-59, no indication of source) which, whatever it stands for, emphatically does *not* stand – as we are led to believe – for an annual statement of revenue for 1792: according to this 'document' the Oratoire de Riom was in receipt of an income of 45670 livres!

The chanoine Crégut (p.98), who was not in possession of the catalogue, who appears moreover to have had little interest in the capital
problem of solvency and who was not prompted therefore to ask how
much income in different periods must, or could, have been devoted to
the maintenance and enrichment of the library (even less to ask what
precise source generated the library income) claimed – though his claim
rings suspiciously like a surmise – that it was *significant*: 'les Oratoriens
grevaient lourdement leur maigre budget en faveur des livres. On s'en
fait une idée à l'examen des débris échappés à tous les pillages. Ils
s'attachaient de préférence aux belles éditions. Aussi avaient-ils acquis
une bonne série d'incunables et d'éditions princeps […]. La bibliothèque
de la ville de Riom a recueilli ces richesses précieuses'.[29]

In reality, however, we know even less about the financing of the
library than we do about its more material history. But the latter is, in
turn, cause for equal regret, particularly if we refer to its destiny from
1792 onwards, when the Assembly in Paris, having voted the destruction
of the religious congregations (26 August), set the seal on the Collège
de l'Oratoire and all its possessions: within a year the College ceased to
exist, its buildings were offered for sale, its chapel was turned into a
grain-store and its library sequestrated … for the next fifty years. Those
who are familiar with the conditions endured by Massillon's library (its
torments were, however, to be, by comparison, a mere passing dis-
comfort) and with its ultimate salvation will not be surprised to read the
chanoine Crégut's description of what was to transpire (pp.199-200):

En 1842, une demande, exposée par le maire, attire l'attention sur la bibliothèque,
dont les volumes, encore superbes sous la couche de poussière et de moisissure qui
les ronge, traînent dans un complet désordre au fond d'une série de galetas. Ils sont
là ces remarquables in-folio, ces rarissimes incunables enlevés aux Oratoriens et
leur nombre s'amincit de jour en jour, parce que, insouciants et espiègles, les élèves
les poussent du pied, ou les utilisent pour leurs jeux en guise d'armes offensives et
défensives. Les gravures font la joie des fureteurs. On se prend à penser que, sous
ces vieilles reliures, il pourrait y avoir des richesses. On établit une sorte de

29. On p.99 n.1, the chanoine Crégut produces a list of 22 incunabula (4 from the *première
série*, that is, pre-1500; 18 from the *seconde série*) which he presents as having survived from
the Bibliothèque de l'Oratoire. This list does not correspond to what the catalogue leads us
to expect. Without yet having been able to examine the *fonds ancien* of the BMV Riom, I
would not wish to hasard a premature explanation, but it is most likely that the texts seen
by the chanoine Crégut came, in the main, from other libraries in Riom likewise *mises sous
séquestre* in 1792. They might, in short, have come from any one of three *Chapitres*: Saint-
Amable, Le Marturet, La Sainte-Chapelle.

classement, et la municipalité, mue par un sentiment bizarre d'économie, propose de mettre en vente les volumes dépareillés.[30] Le Conseil s'y opposa et prit tous les volumes sous sa protection officielle. Il fut même question de leur offrir, au sein du Collège, une salle spéciale où le public serait admis sinon à les lire, du moins à les contempler. Ce fut l'origine de la Bibliothèque de la ville.

As we have now seen, the catalogue raises a variety of problems which cannot be ignored. Naturally enough, little will be deduced from the document itself until the natural framework for any investigation into it and its various meanings has been delineated. Many of the problems identified will require considerable labour in their elucidation. It would be better therefore to limit (however artificially) the final series of comments to the purely academic, intellectual and ideological configurations that the catalogue either betrays or suggests. For even in these preliminary stages of the enquiry certain lines of force, certain possible interpretations are apparent.

Let us examine the fundamental data: the catalogue which is – in strict bibliographical terms – an inadequate document was drawn up in 1822, and reflects, no doubt faithfully, the library holdings of the College such as they were to be found 'au fond d'une série de galetas' thirty years after the demise of the Oratoire de Riom. It details, under eighteen different rubrics, (at least) the crude identity of 2403 separate titles – the earliest dating from 1480, the latest from 1792 – making a bulk of 9137 volumes.[31] The breadth of the library and its relative strengths can be

30. Crégut notes also the following piece of information (not in the least unexpected) and which might represent merely the tip of the proverbial iceberg: 'Il y eut même des poursuites dirigées contre un élève qui avait dérobé un des volumes de la magnifique Bible polyglotte et qui l'avait vendu pour un prix dérisoire à un brocanteur. Ce dernier se hâta de rendre le livre.' We shall probably never know the full extent of such indelicacy during the period 1792-1842, but a thorough comparison between the catalogue – once reconstituted – and the *fonds ancien* of the BMV Riom may one day provide a rough answer to this question.

31. The various figures are computed from the catalogue *as it stands*; unfortunately, part of the catalogue (and not the least important in my opinion: the rubric primarily concerned is *Histoire*) is missing (ff.54v-58v). Bearing in mind the average number of entries per page, we are probably dealing with between 240-280 missing titles, with the result that all the rubrics as they stand – except *Vies des saints* and particularly *Histoire* (where the opposite will happen) – are somewhat inflated.

By the most curious but happy of coincidences, however, a second manuscript catalogue emerged from the Archives Municipales de Riom in the very days preceding the submission of the present article (but far too late for me to be able to incorporate any interpretations arising from it into the text). It would seem that this newly-discovered manuscript (dating, from simple internal evidence, from the 1850s), which was shown to me by Mme Francine

gauged from the following tabulation. *Première Division*: *Ecriture sainte*, number of separate titles: 108 (% of total: 4.49), number of volumes: 261 (% of total: 2.85); *Conciles* 28 (1.16%), 65 (0.71%); *Pères de l'Eglise* 102 (4.24%), 247 (2.7%); *Commentaires sur l'écriture sainte* 111 (4.61%), 201 (2.19%); *Théologie scolastique* 246 (10.23%), 545 (5.96%); *Ouvrages polémiques en matière de religion* 195 (8.11%), 288 (3.15%); *Liturgie* 72 (2.99%), 173 (1.89%); *Sermons et autres ouvrages de piété* 468 (19.47%), 1003 (10.97%); *Histoire ecclésiastique* 59 (2.45%), 309 (3.38%); *Vies des saints et des personnages illustres par leur piété* 24 (0.99%), 47 (0.51%); *Histoire ancienne (?) | Histoire profane ancienne et moderne*[32] 52/163 (2.16%/6.78%), 292/692 (3.19%/7.57%). It is with these two rubrics that the *Première Division* of the catalogue, clearly presented as such, is complete.

The composition of the *Seconde Division* is as follows: *Grammaire; Dictionnaire; Pédagogie* [sic] 80 (3.32%), 207 (2.26%); *Art oratoire, épistolaire; poésie; théâtre* 256 (10.65%), 474 (5.18%); *Philosophie; Logique; Morale; Métaphysique* 145 (6.03%), 291 (3.18%); *Mathématiques; architecture; astronomie; marine; art militaire; mécanique; histoire naturelle; physique; chimie; médecine &c* 98 (4.07%), 190 (2.07%); *Droit canon; droit civil; politique; économie* 135 (5.61%), 196 (2.14%); *Article supplémentaire contenant quelques ouvrages anglois et des collections d'ouvrages classiques français, latins, allemands, ainsi que des Arithmétiques, Géométrie et Algèbre* 61 (2.53%), 3656 (40%).

The two divisions – such as they are made within the catalogue – must correspond to a system of classification, the exact logic of which is, however, not totally evident. In a word, I can find no ready explanation (and even less so when I make reference to normal library practice of

Mallot, Archiviste Municipale, almost by chance and merely as an example of another library catalogue, is almost *totally identical to the one drawn up by Dumontel*. However, only a close and careful comparison will allow me to say whether it will allow us to reconstitute, with total confidence, the missing ff.54v-58v. But in the time available, it seemed to me that we are dealing with a catalogue describing the same basic collection (plus other texts and new acquisitions for the young BMV Riom) and that the rubric *Histoire profane* – as I suggest later in the article – is indeed much larger than presently appears. Needless to say, this second catalogue, which also generally seems to transmit fuller bibliographical information, will (if it is what it appears to be) permit useful additions and corrections to its predecessor.

32. We know that the catalogue differentiates between these two rubrics, respectively the *onzième* and the *douzième articles* (though since ff.54v-58v are missing, we have little way of knowing either how the *onzième article* was titled or how the division between the two rubrics was understood). However, since – on the evidence available – there appears to be an extensive overlap between the two rubrics, they could arguably be counted as one.

the seventeenth and eighteenth centuries) as to why the two historical rubrics are kept distinct from all those disciplines which compose the *Seconde Division*.[33] For it is possible to argue that the natural break in the catalogue occurs rather earlier with the completion of the *Vies des saints et des personnages illustres par leur piété*, seeing that the *Seconde Division*, and its rubric headings, encompass all those categories of books which are not directly religious and/or spiritual, but which are (though not, of course, to the total exclusion of these latter) more directly concerned with the pedagogy and the curriculum of the College (*6e – Philosophie/Physique*).

There is a clear division within the library holdings, and, following the normal practice of 200-300 years ago, it would make better sense if, in making our calculations, we were to include Canon Law within the *Première Division* (50 separate titles: 2.08% of the total; 67 volumes: 0.73% of the total) and the two historical rubrics in the *Seconde* under the usual single heading: *Histoire profane* (215 separate titles: 8.94% of the total; 984 volumes: 10.76% of the total). This rearrangement gives the following result: the *Première Division*, which encompasses exclusively religious and spiritual subject matter, accounts for 60.82% of all the separate titles composing the library, while the broadly secular *Seconde Division* amounts to 39.07%. Given that the Collège de l'Oratoire de Riom embraced two distinct, but mutually dependent entities – the educational establishment and the religious congregation (itself composed of priests-teachers along with a *classe de Théologie*) – the ratio appears in no way unnatural or illogical (though this reaction on my part might be linked more securely to the modern academic way of deciding how things should be apportioned rather than to a sure historical sensitivity to the internal workings and priorities of the establishment in Riom).

The individual elements embraced by the *Première Division* do not call, here, for any special elucidation, though it is interesting to note in passing that the three best-represented areas (significantly stronger than any other) are respectively *Sermons et autres ouvrages de piété* (19.47%), *Théologie scolastique* (10.23%), and *Ouvrages polémiques en matière de religion* (8.11%). Not surprisingly, Jansenism, Port Royal, the *Unigenitus* controversy, the *Convulsionnaires*, the *Formulaire* and the anti-Jesuit campaigns are all well in evidence in the *Ouvrages polémiques* (mostly in works of undoubted acerbity), each one showing how closely the Oratoire had

33. Incidentally, nor can I fathom the reason why Canon Law should figure here rather than among all those earlier rubrics of the *Première Division* with which it has natural affinities.

chosen to keep abreast of current religious events and controversies and which of these latter interested it the most.

The *Seconde Division*, in its broad outlines, does nothing to upset the patterns of interest, emphasis and need which one would expect to find within such an educational institution. We should remember, however, in establishing which areas are best covered and in which order, to make due allowance for the impact which the loss of ff.54v-58v has upon the rubric *Histoire profane* (215: 8.94%) because a mere 41 extra titles would put it on a par with *Art oratoire, épistolaire; poésie; théâtre* (256: 10.65%). But since the general configurations of the catalogue put it beyond reasonable doubt that the missing pages contained many more historical titles than that, it would not be unwise to consider *Histoire profane* as the best-represented rubric, followed respectively by *Art oratoire* etc.; *Philosophie, Logique, Morale, Métaphysique* (145: 6.03%); *Mathématiques, architecture*, etc. (98: 4.07%); *Droit civil; politique; économie* (85: 3.53%); *Grammaire; Dictionnaire; Pédagogie* (80: 3.32%). Given the various strands of the curriculum (*6e – Rhétorique*), the constant insistence on History, the training in literature, rhetoric and poetics in all six classes, followed by one year of *Logique* and one (even two) of *Philosophie/Physique*, the emphasis is unexceptional.

Beyond these broad masses, which serve to delineate (and more or less faithfully reflect) what we know to have been the day-to-day teaching concerns of the College, can the catalogue – even in its present unsatisfactory form – tell us any more about those concerns? Fortunately it can, because unsatisfactory though it often is, the catalogue nevertheless identifies items which are in poor condition or which are incomplete, as it will implicitly identify multiple copies. Used with some circumspection, such information will one day tell us something about primary and secondary reading matter within the curriculum and, perhaps, a little about the preferences or the habits of both teacher and taught.

The section which proves to be particularly helpful, however, with reference to those texts which were being used in the classroom in the years leading up to the Revolution, is the final one entitled *Article supplémentaire*. Here we find, in multiple copies, certain of those titles which figure on the list of set texts for 1788; and the fact that the College kept large numbers of these specific texts (which the pupils were supposed to purchase from Martin Dégoutte, imprimeur-libraire of Riom) suggests that not all could or did do so. For example, the following texts (part of the course in the *classe de 6e* in 1788) figure in the catalogue: *Rudiment de L'Homond*, 1 vol. in-12, 16 exemplaires en mauvais état, 16 vol. in-12; *Selectae e Novo Testamento*, Parisiis, Barbou, 1786, 1 vol. petit in-18, 38 ex., 38 vol. in-18; *Appendix de diis* avec une traduction suivant les principes de M. de Wandelaincourt, 1 vol. in-12, 44 ex., 44 vol. in-12; *Fables* de Phèdre traduites en français par Wandelaincourt, 1 petit v. in-12, 12 ex., 12 vol. in-12; Phaedri *Fabulae* […], 1 vol. in-12, 12 ex., 12 vol. in-12. Much more revealingly, however, the following texts – not known from any other source to have been in use – have clearly seen solid service: *Apparat royal* dictionnaire français et latin, Paris, Barbou, 1783, 1 vol. in-8, 42 ex. en mauvais état, 42 vol. in-8; *Dictionnaire* latin français, par Beridot, Paris 1773, 1 vol. in-8, 86 ex. en mauvais état, 86 vol. in-8; *Gradus ad Parnassum*, Parisiis 1758, 1 vol. in-8, 17 ex. en mauvais état, 17 vol. in-8; *Rudiment de la langue latine à l'usage du Collège de Clermont*, 1 vol. in-12, Paris 1778, 66 ex. mauvais, 66 vol. in-12. These and other titles (Erasmus, Epictetes, Cicero, Virgil) distinctly supplement or confirm the information available in the *Ratio*, the topics for the *exercices publics* or the list of set authors for 1788.

In another equally precise respect the catalogue serves, however, a much more useful purpose. *Here alone* can be found an indication that, certainly in the years prior to the Revolution, two modern foreign languages were in fact being taught in Riom. But if the ratio of texts, grammars and dictionaries is to be taken as a sign – and no doubt it must – that one language was more studied than the other, that is, by greater numbers of pupils, we must conclude that German, and not English, was the first language. Numerically far superior, the holdings in the former comprise: *Nouvelle méthode allemande pour l'usage de l'école militaire d'Effiat* par M. Géraud de Palmfeld en 2 vol. in-8, Paris 1777, 93 tomes premiers, 21 tomes seconds, 114 vol. in-8; *Grammaire allemande* de Gottsched, 1 vol. in-12, en mauvais état, 10 ex., 10 vol. in-12; *Grammaire* [allemande], 20 ex., 20 vol. in-12; *Déclinaisons et conjugaisons françaises, latines et allemandes*, Strasbourg 1772, 5 paquets de 25 ex. chaque in-12 très mince, 125 ex., 125 brochures in-12; 53 paquets à 25 chaque de la petite pièce allemande intitulée *der edel Knabe*, Clermont 1782, 1325 brochures in-12; Le *Robinson* de Campe, Munich 1781, 2 vol. in-12, 24 ex. (allemand), 48 vol. in-12; *La Mort d'Abel* par Gesner en allemand, Zurich 1782, 1 vol. in-12, 18 ex., 18 vol. in-12; *La vie et les fables* d'Esope en français et en allemand, Strasbourg 1758, 1 vol. in-12, 16 ex., 16 vol. in-12.

The attention paid to English seems to have been less well developed and somewhat less mindful of (what we may surmise to have been at that time) reasonably interesting and stimulating subject matter: formal grammars are represented by Berry (no date, 1 vol. in-8), Peyton (*Les Eléments de la langue anglaise développés d'une manière nouvelle*), Londres 1783, 1 vol. in-12, 36 ex., 36 vol. in-12) and an unidentified *Meilleur instructeur de l'enfance pour la manière d'épeller et de lire l'anglais* (en anglais), (1 vol in-12), while reading and comprehension practice are provided by a curious combination of bi-lingual editions of Sallust (Londres 1774, 1 vol. in-8, 6 ex., 6 vol. in-8) and Justin (Londres 1780, 9 ex. à 1 v. in-8, 9 vol. in-8), by the *New Testament* (Oxford 1786, 1 vol. in-12, 20 ex., 20 vol. in-12) and *The Adventures of Robinson Crusoe* (Paris 1783, 1 vol. in-12, 20 vol. in-12). A small and rather forlorn body of texts – a mere 8 titles – comprising both British authors and French authors in English translation – can only be considered as private extra-curricular reading matter (there is no such section for German or German-language culture) since they are available in single copies only. Here we find a fourth volume of the *Spectator*; Dryden's verse translation of the *Fables ancient and modern* [...] *from Homer, Ovid, Boccace* (1 vol. in-12); the *Voyages de Cyrus* (Londres 1745, 1 vol. in-12); *Clarissa Harlowe* (Londres 1768, 8 vol. in-12); *Tom Jones* (Edimbourg 1767, 3 vol. in-12); Bacon's *Essays* (1 vol. in-12); a second volume of *The Vicar of Wakefield* and, finally, Marmontel's *Contes moraux* (Edimbourg 1768, 3 vol. in-12).[34]

The final question must be: what type of knowledge was in favour at the Collège de Riom and, consequently, what view of the world was it expected to foster? An answer can already be glimpsed in the catalogue. Since, however, an authentic voice can be heard talking *about Riom*, it would be better to give priority in the preliminary formulation of the answer to the Visitor of the Congregation who, in 1786, after an inspection of the College, wrote:

Il paraît par le grand nombre d'écoliers qui fréquentent le collège qu'il continue à jouir de la même réputation qu'il a eue autrefois [...]. Ce ne sera jamais dans la

---

34. Marmontel himself was not a little flattered by the fact that the *Contes moraux* were widely used in European schools for the teaching of French. In a letter to Beaumarchais of July 1781 (*Correspondance*, Faculté des Lettres et Sciences Humaines, Université de Clermont-Ferrand 1974, ii.9), he wrote: 'les contes moraux, en trois volumes sont traduits dans toutes les langues et sont du nombre des livres dans les quels toute la jeunesse de l'europe apprend notre langue'. He might have been somewhat surprised, however, to learn that, in Riom, he was also a vehicle for the learning of English.

lecture des écrits du jour et celle des brochures que les jeunes gens parmi nous réussiront à se former un goût sûr. Ce ne peut être que dans la lecture assidue, méditée, réfléchie, des meilleurs auteurs de la littérature, tant ancienne que moderne.[35]

Such a clear (and, in reality, uncompromising statement) can only find total confirmation in the catalogue. The core of the curriculum, which aimed to instil an understanding of the unvarying rules and values of literature, was Classical letters. It is moreover hardly surprising that – by a simple extension of those principles – the classical authors to be studied in the vernacular seem to have been Racine, Molière, La Fontaine, Boileau and – in later years – Jean-Baptiste Rousseau. History and Geography, though studied fairly intensively, were not studied for their own sakes: they were rather a necessary (but imaginative) adjunct to the teaching of classical culture.[36]

The peremptory dismissal of any 'lecture des écrits du jour et celle des brochures' – by which, for a variety of reasons, we have to understand any piece of writing which was (even vaguely) inimical to the maintenance of the religious, moral and social *status quo* – again finds striking confirmation in the catalogue in the most purely negative fashion: the Collège de l'Oratoire de Riom made not the slightest concession to what is described (rather one-sidedly) as the 'esprit du siècle'. The library chooses to go in ignorance of the Enlightenment and all its works ... to such an extent that a specialist of the period can only wonder what chance or what culpable accident, what misguided pedagogical initiative, should have brought an (unidentified) edition of the abbé Raynal's *Histoire philosophique et politique des établissements et du commerce des Européens dans les deux Indes* into this totally conservative environment whereby its presence becomes excruciatingly conspicuous? For otherwise the only indication that the Oratoire de Riom did acknowledge the existence of the Enlightenment comes in the shape of a one-volumed, incomplete copy of [l'abbé Chaudon's] *Dictionnaire antiphilosophique*. In fine, the outside and evolving world is, in its more 'scandalous' manifestations, quite simply held at bay.[37]

35. Archives Nationales S6792. Quoted by Compère et Julia, p.562.

36. See once more the *Exercice littéraire sur l'histoire des Gaules pour servir à l'intelligence des Commentaires de César* (BMU Clermont-Ferrand, A70209).

37. Current events and problems, which specialists of the Enlightenment look upon as being significant, are likewise paid little attention. I note therefore, as being doubly conspicuous, the third volume of Necker's *De l'administration des finances* (1784), the *Réponse de M. de Calonne*

There is already ample proof, in a word, that the 'Catalogue des Livres Composant La Bibliothèque du Collège de la Ville de Riom' shows us an institution which, in the 170 years of its existence, remained wedded, by its scholarship and the values that it consistently sought to inculcate, to the staid and unchanging world of authority and tradition, and which – in the eighteenth century – also clearly became, by its general complexion, anti-modernist.[38] Perhaps we could hardly have expected otherwise.

à l'écrit de M. Necker publiée en 1787, Necker's *Nouveaux éclaircissements sur le compte rendu au roi en 1781* (1788, 2 copies); and Linguet's *La France plus qu'anglaise* (1789).

38. Though physics was taught in Riom, it was clearly Cartesian in nature. Moreover, it was only in 1782 that the 'cabinet de physique' was equipped ... no doubt as a (very belated) move towards, or sanction of, the teaching of *experimental* physics. However, if I am not mistaken, this movement is fairly typical of French education in the later decades of the eighteenth century.

Etait-ce 'la faute à Voltaire, la faute à Rousseau'?

RENÉ POMEAU

LE calendrier nous a remis en mémoire, il y a quelques années, la disparition quasi-simultanée en 1778 de Voltaire et de Rousseau.[1] Devant nous se rapproche le deuxième centenaire de ces mois où en 1788 s'enclencha le processus révolutionnaire. Entre ces deux anniversaires, l'occasion s'offre de s'interroger sur une relation: celle qui peut exister entre les phénomènes Voltaire et Rousseau et l'explosion qui s'amorça dix ans après leur mort.

Vieille question, agitée par les polémistes bien avant que les historiens ne la posent. Pour y répondre l'opinion publique, grâce à Victor Hugo, est en possession d'une formule aussi frappante que simpliste: 'C'est la faute à Voltaire, c'est la faute à Rousseau.' Tel est, on le sait, dans les *Misérables* – épisode de l'émeute parisienne du 5 juin 1832 – le refrain que chante Gavroche, lorsque devant la barricade il se glisse pour ramasser les cartouches sous le feu des forces de l'ordre.[2] Hugo n'a pas inventé le refrain. Un poète suisse, Jean-François Chaponnière, l'avait imaginé, pour des couplets qu'il avait rimés en 1817. Cet honnête Suisse avait alors respecté la langue française: 'C'est la faute *de* Voltaire, c'est la faute *de* Rousseau.'[3] Ce qui était une faute, non contre la correction, mais contre l'efficacité verbale. Hugo a popularisé la formule dans sa version du français parlé dans la rue, le seul que connaissait l'enfant Gavroche. Et au vingtième siècle 'la faute à Voltaire, la faute à Rousseau' ont bénéficié de la seconde existence que le cinéma a donnée, dans de multiples adaptations, au roman de Victor Hugo.

---

1. Parmi les manifestations du double bicentenaire, on se rappelle l'inauguration, présidée par William H. Barber, d'une plaque apposée sur l'un des domiciles londoniens de Voltaire, dans Maiden Lane.

2. Voir *Les Misérables* (Paris 1951), pp.1264-65, 1766.

3. De même Béranger avait respecté la correction grammaticale dans une chanson comportant ce refrain: voir J. Vercruysse, 'C'est la faute à Rousseau, c'est la faute à Voltaire', *Studies on Voltaire* 23 (1963), pp.61-76, et R. Trousson, 'Jean-Jacques et les évêques: de Mgr Lamourette à Mgr Dupanloup', *Bulletin de l'Académie royale de langue et de littérature françaises* 61 (Bruxelles 1984), p.289.

Pour dépister l'origine de l'idée, il faudrait remonter bien au-delà de Chaponnière. Il faut même aller si haut et si loin que l'historien en vient à une constatation surprenante. Le premier qui a dit: 'C'est la faute à Voltaire', ce fut Rousseau. Et le premier qui a dit 'C'est la faute à Rousseau', ce fut Voltaire. L'accusation n'était pas exprimée dans les termes de Gavroche. Mais la pensée était bien celle-là. A vrai dire, il ne s'agissait encore que des affaires de Genève.

Le 17 juin 1760, Rousseau rédige la dernière lettre qu'il adressera à Voltaire, mettant un terme à une correspondance jusqu'alors espacée mais courtoise. C'est la lettre stupéfiante où il fait à Voltaire une déclaration de haine: 'Je ne vous aime point, Monsieur [...]. Je vous hais enfin, vous l'avez voulu.' Pourquoi cette haine? Il le lui dit: 'Vous avez perdu Genève, pour le prix de l'asile que vous y avez reçu.' Des lettres de Jean-Jacques à d'autres correspondants expliquent en quoi, selon lui, Voltaire a 'perdu' Genève: il a diffusé dans cette république calviniste les mœurs françaises. Si aujourd'hui les Genevois sont tous 'si brillants, si élégants, si agréables' (à Vernes, 14 juin 1759), c'est par la faute de Voltaire, ce 'baladin' (à Moultou, 29 janvier 1760), qui reçoit la bonne société de la ville dans son salon des Délices, qui donne chez lui des spectacles et favorise l'entreprise d'établir un théâtre dans la cité de Calvin. Mais Voltaire va lui rendre la pareille, cinq ans plus tard. Des troubles politiques et sociaux ont éclaté dans la république, opposant à l'oligarchie du Petit Conseil les citoyens 'représentants' et le prolétariat des 'natifs'. Le responsable de ces bagarres et émeutes? A en croire Voltaire, c'est Rousseau. 'Jean-Jacques voulait tout brouiller', écrit-il (à Florian, 16 novembre 1765). Voltaire s'évertuerait, quant à lui, à 'éteindre le feu que [Rousseau] a soufflé de toutes les forces de ses petits poumons' (à d'Argental, 28 novembre 1765); il passerait son temps à 'jeter de l'eau sur les charbons ardents allumés par Jean-Jacques' (au même, 29 novembre 1765).

Dans cet échange d'accusations, on voit comment chacun se laisse emporter à prêter à l'autre une influence démesurée, hors de toute proportion avec ses moyens réels. L'évolution des mœurs à Genève ne fut pas l'œuvre de Voltaire. Elle résultait des changements intervenus dans la cité depuis des décennies. Rousseau vivait sur un mythe, nourri par les souvenirs de son enfance: la Sparte calviniste qu'il imagine n'était plus depuis longtemps, si elle a jamais existé. Rousseau le reconnaît quand il est de sang-froid.[4] Et dans les troubles de 1765, Jean-Jacques était bien loin de jouer les boutefeux, comme l'en accuse Voltaire: il est alors en fuite, chassé de Môtiers, puis de l'île Saint-Pierre. Errant, pour aller trouver enfin un refuge en Angleterre, il n'était pas en mesure d'intervenir dans la politique genevoise. Voltaire le savait bien, mais les griefs lancés contre l'exilé s'inscrivent dans sa campagne anti-Jean-Jacques.

Au cours de ces deux épisodes, nous apercevons que chacun d'eux, sans en avoir bien conscience, accorde à l'autre le statut privilégié de ce que nous appelons une vedette. Une optique déformante le fait apparaître comme la cause principale d'événements ou de situations amenés en réalité par une évolution en profondeur.

Cette même optique de la vedette va se retrouver lorsque l'opinion va attribuer à Voltaire et à Rousseau un rôle sur un théâtre infiniment plus vaste que la scène genevoise, celui de la Révolution à partir de 1789.

Cet événement majeur qui allait éclater onze ans après leur mort, il est bien évident qu'aucun des deux n'eut l'idée d'en accuser l'autre par avance, pour la raison que ni l'un ni l'autre ne l'avait prévu. On doit résister à la tentation de prêter une valeur prémonitoire à des déclarations qui avec le recul nous paraissent prophétiques.

On cite souvent une lettre de Voltaire du 2 avril 1764: 'Tout ce que je vois jette les semences d'une révolution qui arrivera immanquablement, et dont je n'aurai pas le plaisir d'être témoin. [...] La lumière s'est tellement répandue de proche en proche qu'on éclatera à la première occasion et alors ce sera un beau tapage; les jeunes gens sont bien heureux, ils verront de belles choses.'

Sur ces phrases, deux remarques. Voltaire s'adresse à Chauvelin, un courtisan exerçant les fonctions de 'maître de la garde-robe' de Louis XV. S'il avait voulu prophétiser 93, il aurait choisi sans doute un autre correspondant. En second lieu, ces réflexions viennent à propos des 'mandements d'évêques qu'on brûle tous les jours'. Ce qui est annoncé, c'est un changement fondamental de la religion, la révolution étant une 'révolution dans les esprits': autrement dit cette diffusion de la 'lumière' qui selon Voltaire gagne de proche en proche depuis le milieu du siècle

4. Ainsi que l'a montré Henri Gouhier, *Rousseau et Voltaire, portraits dans deux miroirs* (Paris 1983), p.146, la polémique sur le théâtre et contre Voltaire lui fit prendre conscience de ce qu'était la vie genevoise dans sa réalité.

précédent. Il ne conçoit pas la rénovation de la France autrement que dans le cadre de la monarchie et même de la société alors existante: une société qu'il croit évolutive.

Rousseau, quant à lui, en vient à expliquer dans l'*Emile* pourquoi il veut enseigner à son élève un métier manuel: 'Nous approchons de l'état de crise et du siècle des révolutions.' Il inscrit en bas de page une note: 'Je tiens pour impossible que les grandes monarchies de l'Europe aient encore longtemps à durer: toutes ont brillé, et tout état qui brille est sur son déclin.'[5]

Intuition remarquable, certes, en 1762, de la fragilité des monarchies européennes. Mais notons qu'il dit 'les révolutions', ce qui au dix-huitième siècle n'est pas un synonyme de la Révolution. On parle par exemple des 'révolutions de Suède'. Le pluriel désigne des bouleverse-ments tels que le passage d'un régime autoritaire à un régime libéral, ou l'inverse, ou un changement de dynastie. Et Rousseau se réclame d'une sorte de biologie politique qui veut qu'un Etat, comme un organisme vivant, vieillisse et meure. Au reste, il a lui-même mis en garde contre les conclusions révolutionnaires, au sens moderne, qu'on pourrait tirer de ses idées. Dans une 'observation' sur le *Discours sur les sciences et les arts* il écrit ceci: 'Il n'y a plus de remède, à moins de quelque grande révolution, presque aussi à craindre que le mal qu'elle pourrait guérir, et qu'il est blâmable de désirer et impossible de prévoir' (*Œuvres complètes*, iii.56).

En fait, ni Voltaire ni Rousseau, ni à peu près personne parmi leurs contemporains n'a prévu les bouleversements de la fin du siècle. Ils les ont encore moins voulus. Ils sont l'un et l'autre, selon l'expression de Jean Starobinski, des 'malgré eux' de la Révolution. Mais il faut tenir compte aussi de l'action qu'ils ont exercée sans le vouloir.

François Furet a remis en valeur récemment une idée de Tocqueville.[6] L'une des faiblesses de la monarchie française au dix-huitième siècle, c'est que dans le régime d'opinion qui s'est désormais instauré le public ne dispose pas auprès du pouvoir de mandataires institutionnels. Les parlements tentent d'usurper la fonction, sans vraiment y parvenir. Tocqueville pense qu'en cette situation de vacance l'opinion suit les écrivains. D'où l'autorité qu'ils acquièrent, notamment dans la seconde moitié du siècle. L'idée paraît juste, surtout si l'on y ajoute ce qu'implique

5. Rousseau, *Œuvres complètes* (Paris 1959-) iv.468.
6. François Furet, *Penser la Révolution* (Paris 1978).

l'expression appliquée, par Paul Bénichou, à ces mêmes gens de plume: 'le sacre de l'écrivain'; l'écrivain supplantant les gens d'Eglise défaillants dans la mission de direction morale que ceux-ci assumaient jusque là.

Or nul dans les décennies précédant la Révolution n'avait plus de prise sur l'opinion que Voltaire et que Rousseau. Chacun d'eux est une vedette à sa manière: ses faits et gestes, ses écrits suscitent une attente qui leur assure d'avance le retentissement maximal. Et l'on assiste bientôt au phénomène bien connu des gens du spectacle: le double vedettariat. Sans l'avoir voulu ni l'un ni l'autre, ils forment couple devant le public. Le contraste des personnalités, l'incompatibilité des œuvres, leurs querelles sanglantes les font valoir l'un par l'autre, les rendant inséparables devant les contemporains comme devant la postérité. Aujourd'hui même, on ne peut parler de l'un sans se référer peu ou prou à l'autre.

En 1978 nous avons reproduit une estampe révolutionnaire[7] qui les réconciliait sur le mode idyllique. Dans un Paris orné de bocages, ressemblant aux Champs-Elysées, ils cheminent côte à côte, d'un même pas, vers le sommet où s'élève le Panthéon. Disons que depuis lors ils y sont parvenus, et qu'ils continuent à accueillir le visiteur à l'entrée de la crypte, symétriquement disposés. Que les ossements des deux cercueils soient ou non ceux des deux grands hommes, peu importe. Ce qui compte ici, c'est le symbole.

Voltaire et Rousseau réconciliés relèvent du mythe révolutionnaire. Dans la réalité, au moment du double transfert, les choses se passèrent moins sereinement. L'abbaye de Scellières, où se trouvait la tombe de Voltaire, allait être vendue comme bien national. Il n'était décemment pas possible de vendre dans le même lot les restes du grand homme. Le marquis de Villette obtint donc de l'Assemblée Constituante le transfert. Mais les partisans de Rousseau protestèrent, tant les deux philosophes paraissent indissociables. On vote alors l'érection d'une statue de Rousseau par souscription. L'affaire ayant traîné, Rousseau finit par obtenir aussi son transfert au Panthéon, avec le même défilé dans Paris, et le même cérémonial de la fête révolutionnaire. Or dans les deux cas les circonstances allaient les associer l'un et l'autre à de graves épisodes de la Révolution.

Quelques jours avant le transfert de Voltaire, Louis XVI captif était revenu piteusement de son évasion manquée de Varennes: il avait traversé

7. Sur la couverture du programme du colloque international de Paris, juillet 1978.

Paris entre deux rangées de la population, gardant sur son passage un silence hostile. Ce fut ce qu'on a appelé le 'sacre à l'envers'. Peu après, par une coïncidence combien significative, devait avoir lieu, le 11 juillet 1791, le 'sacre' de Voltaire au Panthéon: apothéose contrastant avec l'abaissement du roi légitime.

Quant à Rousseau, il fut 'panthéonisé' par la Convention thermidorienne, les 9, 10 et 11 octobre 1794, le discours d'usage étant prononcé par Cambacérès. Mais le décret de translation avait été pris le 14 avril, au pire moment de la Convention robespierriste. Rousseau apparaissait comme en collusion, pour ne pas dire en complicité, avec les terroristes les plus sanguinaires.

A partir de là, le culte révolutionnaire de Voltaire et de Rousseau se prêtait, par la plus élémentaire des dialectiques, à une inversion. Roland Mortier a écrit l'histoire d'un épisode majeur de la vie intellectuelle sous l'Empire: le concours sur 'le tableau littéraire de la France au XVIIIe siècle', institué par l'Académie française en 1804, et renouvelé d'année en année.[8] Dans la plupart des dissertations, Voltaire et Rousseau demeurent associés. Tel concurrent abhorre Voltaire pour son impiété et Rousseau pour sa rhétorique 'au service de l'erreur'. Tel autre les réunit au contraire dans l'éloge, pour avoir éclairé en commun les bases de l'ordre social. Mais déjà l'heure n'était plus à l'équanimité académique. La mentalité révolutionnaire s'était approprié l'idée du complot et en avait fait comme une catégorie intellectuelle. En 1798, l'abbé Barruel, comme on sait, retourne contre les révolutionnaires le mythe du complot. Selon ses *Mémoires pour servir à l'histoire du jacobinisme*, la Révolution résultait des sombres machinations tramées dans les loges maçonniques et les sociétés de pensée. Après 1815, l'idée tourne au délire. Assoiffés de revanche, les tenants de la contre-Révolution se déchaînent contre la 'philosophie' en général, et plus particulièrement contre les deux têtes du mouvement. C'est à cette époque que Chaponnière (sans se laisser aller lui-même aux emportements de ses contemporains) lance: 'c'est la faute de Voltaire, c'est la faute de Rousseau'. A travers le dix-neuvième siècle, la polémique contre-révolutionnaire ne va cesser d'accuser la 'philosophie'. Avec la suite des événements, la responsabilité des philosophes et spécialement de Voltaire et de Rousseau est étendue bien au-delà de 1789 et 1793.

Dans une immense littérature on remarquera un volume intitulé

8. Roland Mortier, Le *'Tableau littéraire de la France au XVIIIe siècle'*, un épisode de la *'guerre philosophique'* à l'Académie française sous l'Empire *(1804-1810)* (Bruxelles 1972).

Voltaire, ses hontes, ses crimes, ses œuvres et leurs conséquences sociales, paru en 1877 pour tenter de faire obstacle à la célébration du premier centenaire de sa mort. L'ouvrage est signé d'un nom breton, Armel de Kervan: manifestement un pseudonyme. Il était publié par un libraire-éditeur parisien spécialisé dans les romans édifiants et les vies de saints.[9] Mais c'est la vie d'un Voltaire diabolique que raconte Armel de Kervan. Qu'on en juge par ce portrait au vitriol (p.267):

Il promène à plaisir le brandon de l'incendie, se rue contre tout ce qui existe, brise pour briser, avec rage, avec délire, jusqu'à ce que la vieillesse l'étende sur les débris qu'il entasse, jusqu'à ce que son dernier soupir se confonde avec les derniers souffles de la royauté agonisante, avec les derniers craquements de la société qui s'effondre, avec le premier cri de guerre de 89.

A ce morceau d'anthologie ajoutons-en un autre, au dernier paragraphe du livre (p.274):

Le nuage de scandale, grossi de jour en jour par le souffle impur de la philosophie, se déversa tout à coup sur notre malheureuse France en un déluge de boue et de sang. On vit éclore des monstres au fond du nid de l'incrédulité. Les théories voltairiennes eurent, en 1793, pour conclusion finale la guillotine et le bourreau, et en 1871, la fusillade, le massacre des otages et le pétrole.

Ce 'pétrole' est le mot de la fin de notre incendiaire auteur, possédé lui-même par le délire qu'il attribue à l'objet de son exécration. Il va donc jusqu'à attribuer, contre toute raison, la responsabilité de la Commune de 1871 à celui qui écrivait dans le *Siècle de Louis XIV* que 'la populace est presque partout la même',[10] c'est-à-dire capable des pires atrocités. Mais Armel de Kervan ignore ce *Siècle de Louis XIV*, comme il ignore la *Henriade* et les autres textes qui contrediraient ses visions sectaires. Il s'est constitué un Voltaire fantasmatique. Il l'englobe dans la même haine que les hommes de gauche ses contemporains, ceux qu'il désigne par une gracieuse expression (p.61): 'notre infecte radicaille'.

Et Rousseau? Il n'était pas mieux traité, quoique peut-être avec moins de fureur. Un auteur d'une tout autre envergure qu'Armel de Kervan, Louis Veuillot, soupirait, en 1860: 'Les gens du XVIIIe siècle me font mal au cœur.' Et il enchaîne: 'Rousseau surtout m'est insupportable.

9. Bray et Retaux, 'libraires-éditeurs', 82 rue Bonaparte. Voir à la fin du volume l'ˣExtrait du catalogue'.

10. Voltaire, *Œuvres historiques* (Paris 1957), p.720, à propos du massacre par une 'populace effrénée' des deux frères de Witt, rapproché des assassinats du maréchal d'Ancre, de l'amiral de Coligny, etc.

C'est ma bête noire.' Suit une diatribe sur 'le vilain être, avec son habit arménien, sa sonde, sa Julie, sa Thérèse [...] sa noire et méchante folie'. En Rousseau Veuillot vitupère des contemporains qu'il déteste, en qui il croit reconnaître autant de disciples rousseauistes: 'Tous les professeurs, tous les révolutionnaires, toutes les femmes de lettres émancipées raffolent de Rousseau. Il est l'homme de Robespierre, de M. Jules Simon, de Mme Sand; l'homme de l'Ecole Normale et l'homme de Genève.'[11] Ahurissant amalgame!

A peine moins abominable, le Rousseau de Jules Lemaître. Lemaître hésite à affirmer que 'c'est la faute à Rousseau', mais finalement il le dit. Pourquoi la Terreur? 'parce qu'il avait plu à un demi-fou, trente ans auparavant, de rêver' le *Contrat social*, et que d'autres demi-fous entreprirent d'imposer ce *Contrat* à la France par la guillotine.[12]

L'opinion conservatrice dénonce alors en Rousseau un dangereux ennemi de la propriété et de l'ordre social. C'est la raison pour laquelle en 1912 Maurice Barrès, devant la Chambre des députés, refuse les crédits pour le deuxième centenaire de la naissance de Jean-Jacques. Après un hommage aux mérites littéraires de celui qu'il nomme un 'extravagant musicien', il s'insurge contre un Rousseau qu'il désigne comme 'l'apôtre éminent et le principe de toutes les anarchies', et Barrès cite nommément le théoricien russe de l'anarchie Kropotkine, ainsi que la bande à Bonnot.[13]

Ce fut le livre de Pierre-Maurice Masson sur *La Religion de Rousseau*, en 1916, qui entraîna une réévaluation fondamentale. Après ce livre Jacques Maritain en 1925, François Mauriac en 1930 manifestent quelque gêne. Ils concèdent que Rousseau a favorisé la religion, mais cette religion ne serait pas la bonne. Mauriac particulièrement se montre encore très marqué par les préjugés des milieux conservateurs français. Il ose écrire que Rousseau est l'homme-chien de Nietzsche, et il continue à le rendre responsable de la Terreur. 'Déjà, lisons-nous, [dans l'œuvre de Rousseau] la vertu devient le prête-nom du crime; déjà la conscience instinct divin est dressée à l'approbation de ces grandes tueries.'[14]

A lire ces textes, nous avons peine aujourd'hui à reconnaître notre

11. Cité par Raymond Trousson, *Rousseau et sa fortune littéraire* (Bordeaux 1971), p.186.
12. Cité par Trousson, p.190.
13. Cité par Trousson, pp.193-94.
14. François Mauriac, *Trois grands hommes devant Dieu* (Paris 1930): l'étude sur Rousseau fut reprise – bizarrement – comme préface de l'édition des *Confessions* du Livre de poche (Paris 1963). Nous renvoyons aux pages 9, 17 de cette édition.

Rousseau, notre Voltaire. Vers 1930 en effet les perspectives allaient changer. Le Rousseau apôtre de l'anarchie s'efface. Simultanément la religion prend un nouveau visage, fort différent de ce que furent en France le catholicisme d'Ancien Régime et celui du Concordat. Cela, sans que Voltaire y soit pour rien. Dès lors, un certain voltairianisme devient périmé. Ce qui permet en même temps une meilleure appréciation de l'anti-christianisme voltairien.

En définitive, de nos jours, qu'en est-il de 'la faute à Voltaire, la faute à Rousseau'? Il va sans dire qu'aucun historien sérieux n'accepte l'explication de l'histoire par les complots. Les accusateurs de Voltaire et Rousseau, pour véhéments qu'ils soient, ne s'en font pas moins une vue naïve du passé. On croirait, à les entendre, que l'ancienne société fut un meilleur des mondes, et que des gens de lettres, par pure méchanceté, s'évertuèrent à la détruire, à coups de propagande subversive. Comme si l'Ancien Régime n'avait pas été en proie à une crise profonde, aux aspects divers; comme si le pouvoir royal n'était pas mort de son impuissance à réaliser à temps les réformes nécessaires.

Imaginer des complots de la franc-maçonnerie, des sociétés de pensée, des philosophes, c'est la meilleure manière de ne pas 'comprendre la Révolution', en refusant de la penser.

Penser la Révolution française: sous ce titre François Furet a publié un livre où il est démontré, de façon convaincante, combien un tel phénomène est difficile à appréhender pour l'historien. On récusera toutes explications trop simples. François Furet propose, quant à lui, une interprétation qui conduit à réexaminer la relation entre révolution et lumières. On connaît la thèse qu'il soutient. Il s'interroge sur le formidable dynamisme de la Révolution entre 1788 et 1794. Pour expliquer un mouvement si puissant, localisé dans une période relativement brève, des causalités à moyen ou long terme, comme les conflits de classe, les facteurs démographiques, paraissent inadéquates. C'est dans les esprits qu'il faut chercher les moteurs de la poussée révolutionnaire. Un système de représentation et d'action s'était imposé, qui prétendait imposer une démocratie directe, et à cette fin pratiquait l'élimination de l'ennemi, selon les catégories manichéennes du Bien et du Mal. La Révolution serait l'œuvre d'un imaginaire révolutionnaire, instaurant un nouveau fanatisme, non plus religieux, mais idéologique. Dans cette perspective on peut concevoir que Voltaire et Rousseau ont apporté leur contribution, en fournissant

RENÉ POMEAU

certains des matériaux culturels avec lesquels s'est construite la conscience révolutionnaire. Voltaire, si on le suppose quasi centenaire et toujours lucide en 1793, aurait sans doute abhorré le fanatisme de la Terreur. Mais il faut reconnaître qu'il avait, avec d'autres et plus que d'autres, par sa campagne contre l'Infâme habitué les esprits à un manichéisme virulent: la différence sera dans le visage nouveau que la Terreur prête au monstre de l'Infâme. Quant à Rousseau, nous savons, grâce au grand travail de Roger Barny, à quel point son œuvre, et spécialement le *Contrat social*, obsède la classe politique de la Révolution. C'est à partir de lui que les révolutionnaires tentent l'entreprise para-doxale d'intégrer la société et l'Etat par la démocratie directe.

Cela dit, des objections se présentent. On ne peut pas croire que tout se soit passé dans l'imaginaire. Le regretté Albert Soboul avait raison lorsqu'en réponse aux critiques qui lui furent adressées il alléguait les facteurs socio-économiques. L'idéologie révolutionnaire ne fonctionne pas dans la pure sphère des spéculations. Elle prend appui sur de dures réalités: la crise des subsistances, les antagonismes de classes. Ainsi que le note d'ailleurs François Furet, 'il y a à l'œuvre une autre force que celle des livres ou des idées' (p.251). Ce qui relativise l'influence d'un Voltaire, d'un Rousseau, et en général de la philosophie.

Autre considération: celle que fait valoir Robert Darnton dans un livre récent, *Bohème littéraire et Révolution*.[15] En 1789, l'âge des 'hautes lumières' est révolu. Les Voltaire, Rousseau, Diderot, Condillac, d'Alembert ont disparu, depuis plusieurs années, et leur période la plus active remontait à vingt ou trente ans, ou davantage. Ils n'ont à la veille de la Révolution que d'assez médiocres successeurs. Mais des médiocres fort nombreux, constituant un prolétariat intellectuel, avide et envieux. Parmi eux, on remarque certains protagonistes de la future Révolution, notamment Marat. 1789 va donc éclater au moment où se dégradent les lumières philosophiques.

Concluons. Voltaire, Rousseau causes de la Révolution? Sans doute, mais à distance, et de façon diffuse, leur action interférant avec d'autres facteurs de nature non idéologique. Ils ont eu leur part indirecte dans les événements, ce qui ne veut pas dire qu'il faut les en accuser.

Quant à 'la faute à Voltaire, la faute à Rousseau', elle doit rester ce qu'elle est sur les lèvres de Gavroche, une variation humoristique,

15. Robert Darnton, *Bohème littéraire et Révolution, le monde des livres au XVIIIe siècle* (Paris 1983), pp.7-41 (réédition en traduction française d'un article paru en anglais en 1971).

424

éveillant des rimes cocasses, notaire et ruisseau, Nanterre et Palaiseau:[16] un pied-de-nez en direction des soldats de l'ordre et, derrière eux, des polémistes furibonds de l'anti-Révolution.

16. Voir dans l'édition citée des *Misérables*, pp.1765-66, les variations essayées par Hugo.